P9-EIF-121

Contents

PRINCIPAL SIGHTS

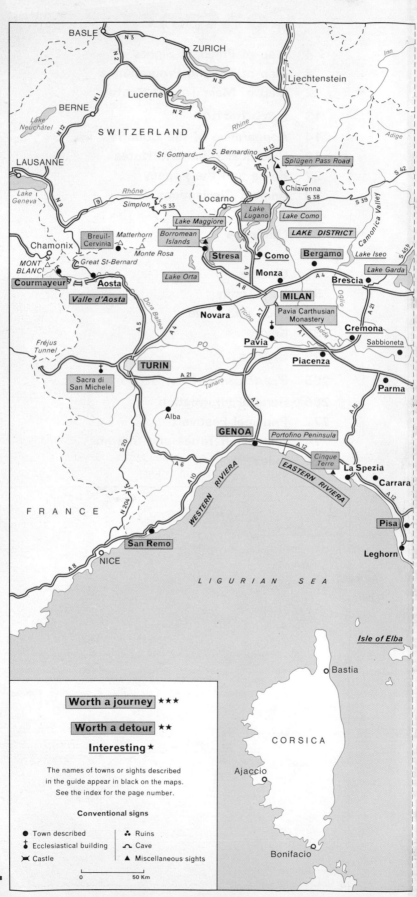

Worth a journey ★★★

Worth a detour ★★

Interesting ★

The names of towns or sights described
in the guide appear in black on the maps.
See the index for the page number.

Conventional signs

- ● Town described
- ✝ Ecclesiastical building
- ⤭ Castle
- ⁂ Ruins
- ⌒ Cave
- ▲ Miscellaneous sights

0   50 Km

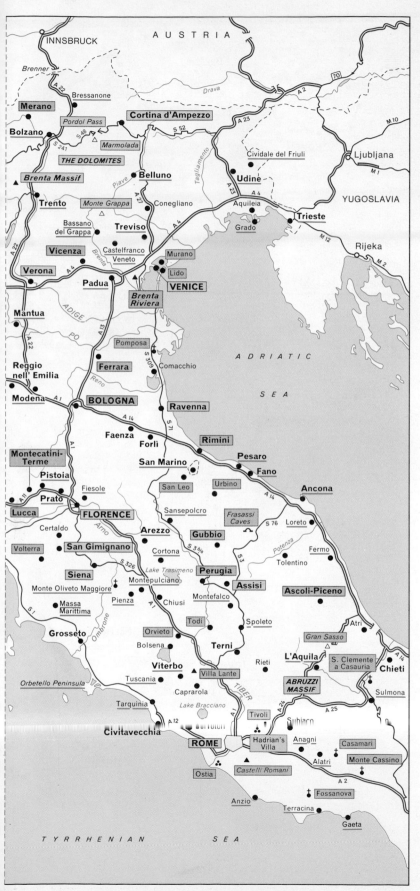

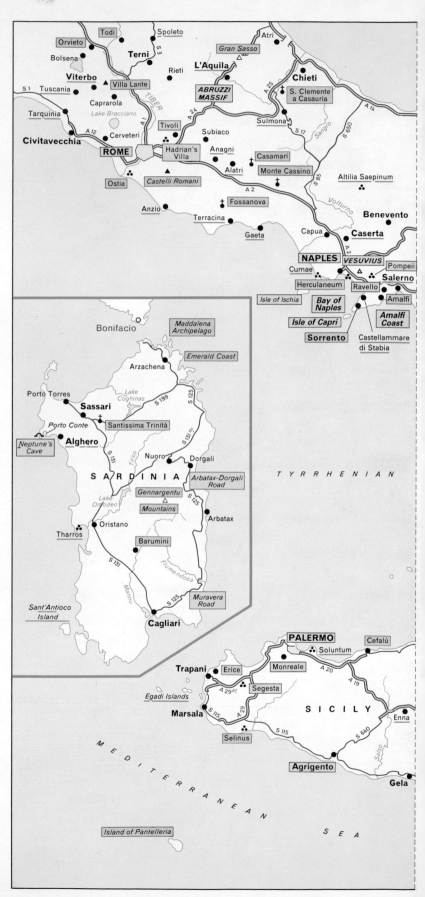

Todi
Spoleto
Orvieto
Atri
Bolsena
Terni
S 3
Gran Sasso
△ ▥▥▥
L'Aquila
Rieti
Chieti
Viterbo ▲ *Villa Lante*
A 25
S. Clemente
a Casauria
S 1 Tuscania
ABRUZZI
MASSIF
A 14
Caprarola
Lake Bracciano
A 24
Sulmona
S 650
A 12
Tivoli
Subiaco
S 17
Sangro
Cerveteri
TIBER
Civitavecchia
ROME
Hadrian's
Villa
Anagni
Casamari
Altilia Saepinum
Monte Cassino
S 85
Ostia
▲ *Castelli Romani*
Alatri
A 2
Volturno
Benevento
Fossanova
Capua
Caserta
Anzio
Terracina
A 2
Gaeta
NAPLES *VESUVIUS*
Cumae △
Pompeii
Salerno
Herculaneum
Ravello
Isle of Ischia
Bay of
Naples
Amalfi
Amalfi
Coast
Isle of Capri
Castellammare
di Stabia
Sorrento

Bonifacio
Maddalena
Archipelago
Emerald Coast
Arzachena
Lake
Coghinas
Porto Torres
S 199
S 125
Sassari
Porto Conte
Santissima Trinità
S 131 dir
Neptune's
Cave
Alghero
S 131
Nuoro
Dorgali
Tirso
S A R D I N I A
Arbatax-Dorgali
Road
Lake
Omodeo
Gennargentu
△
S 125
Mountains
Arbatax
Tharros
Oristano
Flumendosa
Barumini
S 131
Mannu
S 125
Muravera
Road
Sant'Antioco
Island
Cagliari

T Y R R H E N I A N

PALERMO
Cefalù
Soluntum
Trapani
Erice
Monreale
A 20
A 19
Egadi Islands
Segesta
A 29 dir
S I C I L Y
A 29
Marsala
S 115
Enna
Selinus
S 115
S 640
Salso
Agrigento
M E D I T E R R A N E A N
Gela
S E A
Island of Pantelleria

6

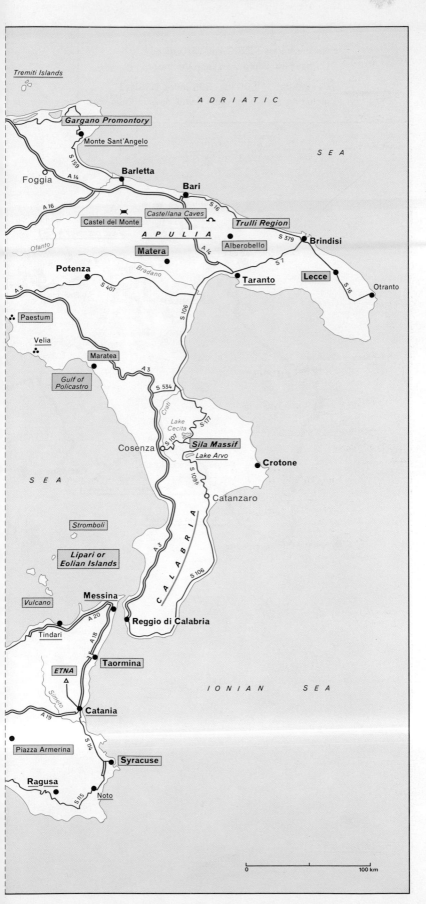

7

TOURING PROGRAMMES

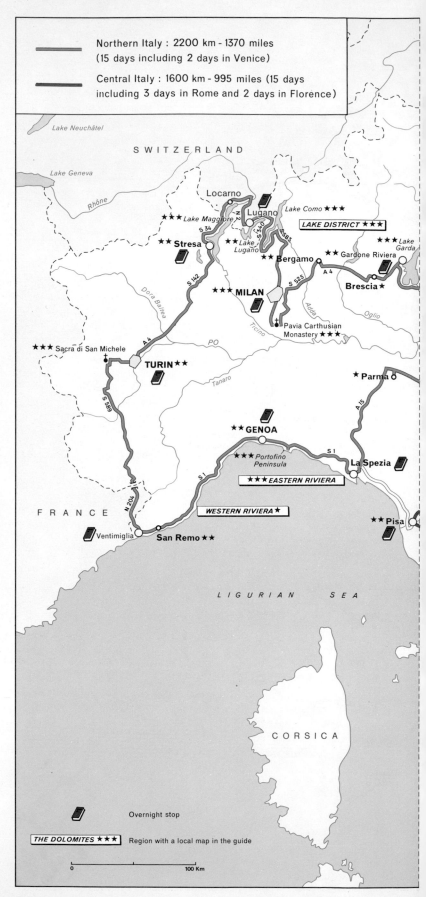

Northern Italy : 2200 km - 1370 miles
(15 days including 2 days in Venice)

Central Italy : 1600 km - 995 miles (15 days
including 3 days in Rome and 2 days in Florence)

Lake Neuchâtel

SWITZERLAND

Lake Geneva

Rhône

Locarno

★★★ Lake Maggiore
Lugano
Lake Como ★★★

LAKE DISTRICT ★★★

S 34

★★ Stresa

S 340
S 583

Lake Lugano

★★★ Lake Garda
★★ Gardone Riviera

★★ Bergamo

Brescia ★

S 142

A 4

★★★ MILAN

S 525

Adda

Oglio

Ticino

Pavia Carthusian
Monastery ★★★

Dora Baltea

A 4

PO

★★★ Sacra di San Michele

TURIN ★★

Tanaro

★ Parma

A 15

S 589

★★ GENOA

★★★ Portofino
Peninsula

S 1

La Spezia

S 1

★★★ EASTERN RIVIERA

N 204

WESTERN RIVIERA ★

★★ Pisa

Ventimiglia

San Remo ★★

LIGURIAN   SEA

CORSICA

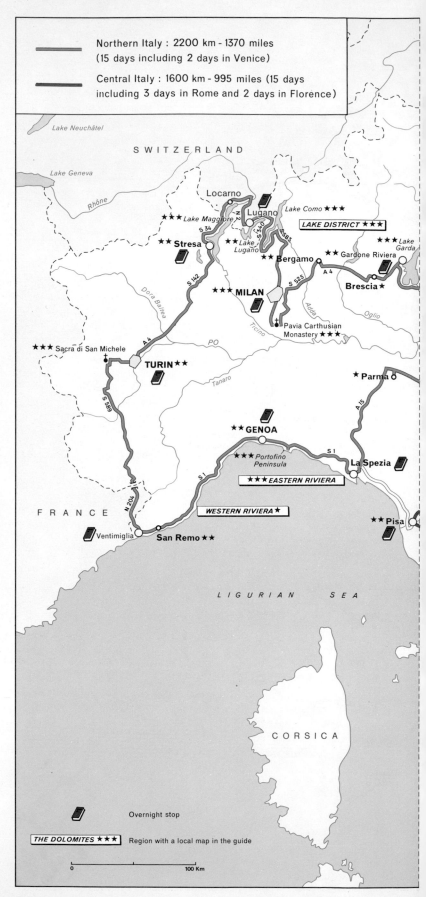 Overnight stop

THE DOLOMITES ★★★ Region with a local map in the guide

0   100 Km

8

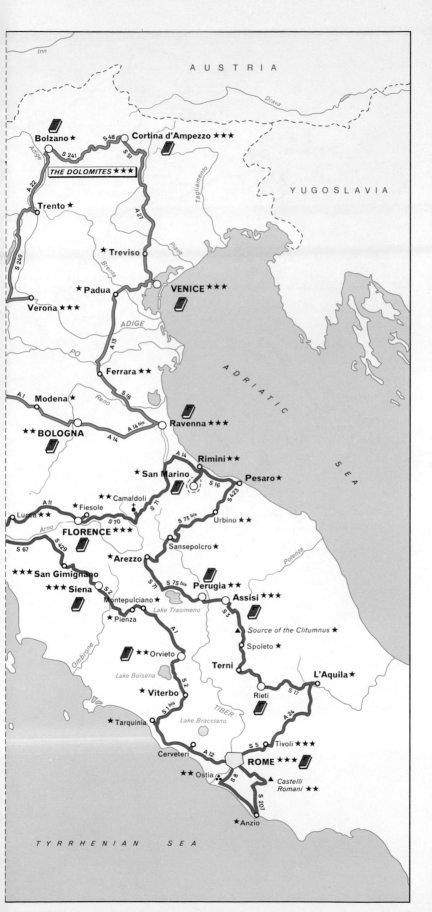

AUSTRIA

YUGOSLAVIA

Inn

Drava

Bolzano ★

S 48

Cortina d'Ampezzo ★★★

S 241

S 51

THE DOLOMITES ★★★

Adige

A 22

Trento ★

S 27

Tagliamento

Piave

★ Treviso

Brenta

★ Padua

VENICE ★★★

Verona ★★★

ADIGE

S 249

A 13

PO

A D R I A T I C

Ferrara ★★

S 16

A 1

Modena ★

Reno

A 14 bis

Ravenna ★★★

S E A

★★ BOLOGNA

A 14

A 14

Rimini ★★

★ San Marino

Pesaro ★

S 16

S 423

★★ Camaldoli †

S 71

Fiesole ★

Urbino ★★

S 70

S 73 bis

Lucca ★★

Arno

FLORENCE ★★★

Sansepolcro ★

S 67

S 429

Potenza

★ Arezzo

★★★ San Gimignano

S 71

S 75 bis

Perugia ★★

Assisi ★★★

★★★ Siena

S 2

Montepulciano ★

Lake Trasimeno

S 3

▲ Source of the Clitumnus ★

★ Pienza

A 1

Spoleto ★

Ombrone

★★ Orvieto

Terni

L'Aquila ★

Lake Bolsena

S 2

★ Viterbo

Rieti

S 17

S 1 bis

TIBER

A 24

★ Tarquinia

Lake Bracciano

S 5

Tivoli ★★★

Cerveteri

A 12

ROME ★★★

★★ Ostia

S 8

▲ Castelli Romani ★★

S 207

★ Anzio

T Y R R H E N I A N   S E A

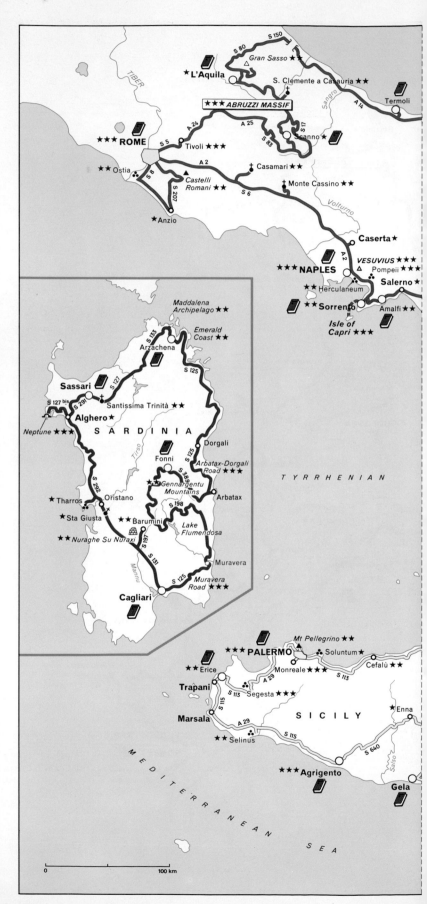

TIBER

★ L'Aquila

S 80
Gran Sasso ★★
△
S. Clemente a Casauria ★★

S 150
Termoli

★★★ ABRUZZI MASSIF

Sangro
A 14

A 24

A 25

S 83
Scanno ★

★★★ ROME
S 5
Tivoli ★★★
A 2
† Casamari ★★

★★ Ostia
S 8
▲ Castelli
Romani ★★
S 207
S 6
† Monte Cassino ★★
Volturno

★ Anzio

Caserta ★

A 2
VESUVIUS ★★★
△ Pompeii ★★★

★★★ NAPLES
Salerno ★
★★ Herculaneum
★★ Sorrento
Amalfi ★★

Isle of
Capri ★★★

Maddalena
Archipelago ★★

Emerald
Coast ★★

S 133
Arzachena

S 125

Sassari
S 127
S 127 bis
S 291
† Santissima Trinità ★★
Alghero ★

S A R D I N I A

Neptune ★★★

Tirso
Dorgali
Fonni
S 125
Arbatax-Dorgali
Road ★★★

★ Tharros
S 292
S 389
Gennargentu
Mountains ★★
Oristano
Arbatax

★ Sta Giusta
S 198
★★ Barumini
Lake
Flumendosa
S 197
S 181

★★ Nuraghe Su Nuraxi

Mannu

Muravera

S 125
Muravera
Road ★★★

Cagliari

T Y R R H E N I A N

Mt Pellegrino ★★
❖ Soluntum ★

★★★ PALERMO
Cefalù ★★
★★ Erice
Monreale ★★★
S 113

Trapani
S 113
A 29
Segesta ★★★

S 115
S I C I L Y
★ Enna

Marsala
A 29
S 115

★★ Selinus
S 115
S 640

Salso
★★★ Agrigento

Gela

M E D I T E R R A N E A N   S E A

0   100 km

ADRIATIC

SEA

Gargano Promontory ★★★

Manfredonia

S 159

Trani

Barletta

Bitonto

Bari

★★ Castel del Monte

S 98

S 96

★★★ Castellana

Trulli Region ★★★

Brindisi

APULIA

Altamura

S 71

★★★ Alberobello

S 379

Lecce ★★

★★ Matera

S 106

★ Taranto

Bradano

S 611

Otranto

Ofanto

Gallipoli

S 173

Paestum ★★★

★ Rocca Imperiale

Zinzulusa

S 18

Velia

Maratea ★★

★★ Gulf
of Policastro

Crati

S 18

Lake
Cecita

S 106

Sila Massif ★★

S 107

Crotone

SEA

S 179 d

Catanzaro

IONIAN

CALABRIA

★ Purple Coast

S 18

S 106

SEA

Messina

★ Tindari

S 113

Reggio di Calabria

S 114

Taormina ★★★

★★★ ETNA
△

Simeto

Catania ★

Piazza

S 117 bis

Syracuse ★★★

S 115

S 114

S 115

Ragusa

Noto ★

───── Southern Italy : 3500 km - 2175 miles
(19 days including 3 days in Rome
and 1 day in Naples)

───── Sicily : 1100 km - 685 miles (7 days)

───── Sardinia : 1100 km - 685 miles (4 days)

11

MAIN TOURIST ROUTES

This map gives the distances and journey times between some main towns in Italy.
It does not aim to show all the fast routes throughout the country but to give an
indication of the journey time to be allowed for on a trip.
The Italian road network ranks second in Europe; its bold design has produced some
remarkable feats of engineering and brings the landscape into play to spectacular
effect.

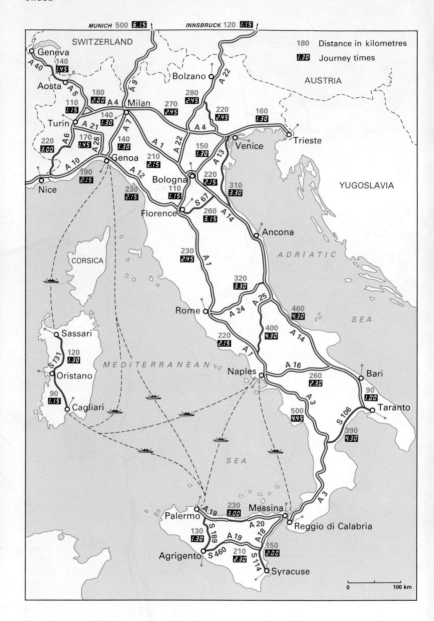

When planning a trip travellers should also consult:
● the map of Principal Sights *(pp 4-7)*
● the map of Touring Programmes *(pp 8-11)*
● the list of Principal Festivals *(p 272)*

Introduction

San Gimignano – Towers

APPEARANCE OF THE COUNTRY

Italy extends for 1 300km – 808 miles from north to south and juts like a pier into the Mediterranean between Greece and Spain. The peninsula has an extraordinary variety of climate and topography.

Italy's relief is rugged and contrasting and plains occupy barely one quarter of its total area of 301 262km² – 139 087sq miles. Its almost 7 500km – 4 660 mile long coastline is washed by the waters of four inner seas: the Ligurian, Tyrrhenian, Ionian and Adriatic.

The **Alps**, which arose from the folding of the earth's crust in the Tertiary Era, form a gigantic barrier and a reservoir of electrical power. Several transalpine passes and tunnels link Italy with France and northern Europe. On the southern side of the Alps between the fertile Po Plain and the foothills there are several lakes of glacial origin.

The **Apennines**, a limestone range formed by a more recent Tertiary folding movement, run from Genoa down into Sicily. They are the backbone of the Italian Peninsula and divide the country into two zones of quite different influences, which have for long remained independent of one another. The peaks of this limestone chain are generally lower than those of the Alps. The Corno Grande at 2 914m – 9 560ft is the main peak of the chain's highest massif, the Gran Sasso.

The earth's crust from Naples to Sicily is a zone of instability with much underground activity: volcanoes, changing land and sea levels, as well as earthquakes. These processes are all responsible for altering the relief of this southern part of the peninsula.

The distribution of vegetation and crops follows quite closely the subdivision of the peninsula into natural regions *(see map p 3)*.

By the end of 1987 the population of Italy had reached 57 339 108, making it the fifth most densely populated country in Europe after the Benelux countries and West Germany. Towns are more numerous in northern and central Italy and over 54% of the population is urban, residing in towns of 20 000 or more.

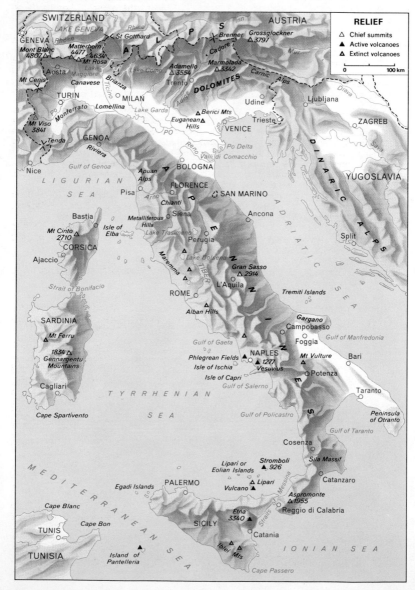

THE REGIONS

The Valle d'Aosta. – This great deep furrow between the highest mountains in Europe is watered by the Dora Baltea River, whose tributaries form picturesque lateral valleys: the Valtournenche, Val di Gressoney, Val d'Ayas, Val Grisenche...
Aosta, well situated in the centre of the valley, is the capital of this region which has enjoyed a certain degree of administrative authority since 1947. In addition to the pastoral activities of the mountain people and the iron mines at Cogne, the valley's economy depends primarily on tourism which has developed as a result of the Great St Bernard and Mont Blanc Tunnels.
From Pont-St-Martin to Courmayeur the local population – essentially mountain people and shepherds – remain attached to their traditions and have retained their French family names. Many still speak French and other varied dialects.

Piedmont. – Piedmont at the foot of the mountain range consists mainly of the extensive Po Plain. Between the Alps and the Apennines this fertile area is intersected by long rows of poplars where grassland alternates with cereals and rice growing. Three-fifths of the Italian rice production is concentrated in the districts of Vercelli and Novara. Southeast of Turin the gently-rolling chalk hills of the **Monferrato** bear the well-known Asti vines and produce the Gorgonzola cheese. Numerous hydro-electric power stations supply electricity for the textile factories of Biella and the metal, engineering and chemical works of Turin. **Turin,** on the Po, is a dynamic town which attracts followers of fashion and those with a passion for cars.

Lombardy. – This is the busiest region in Italy and it occupies the green Po Plain between the Ticino and the Mincio, which together with the Adda supply Lakes Maggiore, Como and Garda. To the north the great lake valleys give access to the Alpine passes. Lombardy, with the mulberry bushes of the **Brianza** district, takes first place in the production of silk. The permanent grazing and grasslands are used by a modern dairying industry. In the **Lomellina** district, extensive areas are given over to rice growing.
The many towns, scattered over the countryside, were important banking and trading centres in medieval and Renaissance times and spread the name of Lombards all over Europe. Today Como is the centre of the silk industry, Brescia steel, chemical and engineering industries, Bergamo textile and engineering works, Mantua petrochemicals and plastics, Cremona agriculture and Pavia the seat of an important university.
It is Milan, the economic capital of Italy, that has the highest density of population and businesses. This town with its modern architecture and numerous commercial enterprises and cultural institutions has an outer ring of industrial suburbs which are the home base of textile, oil, chemical, steel and food industries.

Venetia (Veneto). – This is essentially composed of the vast alluvial Po Plain and its tributaries which are overlooked in the north by the Venetian Pre-Alps, and further north again in the **Cadore** district by the western massifs of the Dolomites. It is an essentially agricultural region growing wheat, maize, mulberry bushes, olives, fruit trees and vines. The industrial sector includes oil refineries, smelting works and chemical plants which are concentrated in the vicinity of Venice at Mestre-Marghera, as well as a large production of hydro-electric energy in the valleys of the Pre-Alps. The latter supplies the textile industry.
The landscape is punctuated by two small volcanic groups, the Berici Mountains south of Vicenza and the **Euganean Hills** near Padua. The slopes of these blackish heights carry vines and peach orchards, and are the site of hot springs.
In the **Po delta** (Polesina) and that of the Adige lie improverished, grandiose and desolate areas, subject to river floods. Following reclamation certain areas are farmed on an industrial scale for wheat and sugar beet.
The coastline takes the form of lagoons *(lido)* separated from the sea by spits of sand pierced by gaps *(porti)*. **Venice,** whose industrial sector is continually growing, is built on piles in one of these lagoons.

Valle d'Aosta: Courmayeur

Trentino-Alto Adige. – This is one of five Italian regions to enjoy a special autonomous statute and the people are partly of Germanic culture and German-speaking. The area includes the Adige and Isarco valleys and the surrounding mountains. The Adige Valley, at the southern exit from the Brenner Pass, has always been easy of access and much used for traffic. Though deep, it opens out towards the sunny south and it is fertile. Cereals are grown on the flatter areas of the valley bottom, with vines and fruit trees on the lower slopes and pastures above. Avelengo in the vicinity of Merano is well known for its breed of horses. **Bolzano** and **Trento**, where there is some industrial development, are the regional markets.

The highly-eroded, limestone massif of the **Dolomites** extends across Venetia and Trentino-Alto Adige.

Friuli-Venezia Giulia. – This region prolongs Venetia to the east and it forms the Italian boundary with Austria and Yugoslavia. The area enjoys a large degree of autonomy in administrative and cultural affairs. In the north is the schistose massif of the **Carnic Alps** with its forests of conifers and alpine pastures. Friuli-Venezia Giulia is an important silkworm breeding and spinning area. Udine is one of the busiest towns. By way of the **Trieste** Riviera you will reach this town which was once the busy port of Austria and now trades with the Far East. Trieste is still subject to a special statute.

Emilia Romagna. – The plain skirting the Apennines derives its name from the Via Emilia, a straight Roman road that crosses it from Piacenza to Rimini. South and east of Bologna the district is known as **Romagna.** Its soil, which is intensively cultivated, is among the best in Italy for wheat and beet. The monotonous landscape consists of extensive fields intersected at regular intervals by rows of mulberries and vines clinging to tall poles, and of maples or elms. Other vines grow on the slopes of the Apennines.

The towns are strung out along the Via Emilia: the most important, **Bologna**, famous for its very old university, is today a communications and industrial (steel, engineering and food) centre and a market for wheat and pigs.

The region to the east of Ferrara through which runs the Po river is devoted to rice growing. To the south is an area of great lagoons, **Valli di Comacchio**, where fishermen catch eels. **Ravenna**, which has been somewhat revived by its port and its oil refinery, was once the capital of the Western Roman Empire, and the chief town of Romagna before the creation of Emilia-Romagna, with Bologna as the regional capital.

Liguria. – Liguria, furrowed by deep, narrow valleys at right angles to the coast, had a maritime civilisation before the Roman era. The steep slopes of the inner valleys are dotted with poor hilltop villages, watching over groves of chestnut or olive trees and cultivated terraces. The rocky, indented coastline has few fish to offer but has enjoyed heavy coastwise traffic since the time of the Ligurians, facilitated by many small deep-water ports. The Roman Empire gave its present appearance to the country, with olive groves and vineyards, to which have been added vegetables, fruit (melons and peaches) and flowers grown on an industrial scale.

The **Riviera di Ponente** (Western Riviera) west of Genoa, is sunnier and more sheltered than the **Riviera di Levante** (Eastern Riviera), but the latter has a more luxuriant vegetation. The chief towns are Imperia, Savona and **Genoa** (shipyards, oil terminal and thermal power station) and La Spezia (naval base, commercial port, thermal power station and the manufacturing of arms).

Tuscany. – Low-lying hills with clean, graceful curves under a limpid light, plains, forests and vineyards join with the serenity of cypress and pine to make this country a temple of beauty. By some mysterious influence, sometimes called "the Tuscan miracle", this harmony has gifted the Tuscan people with great artistic sense.

The region has a variety of soils. The Tuscan Archipelago, with the mountainous **Island of Elba** and its rich iron-bearing deposits, faces a shore which is sometimes rocky (south of Leghorn), sometimes flat and sandy as in the area around Viareggio, known as **Versilia**. To the north of the Arno the **Apuan Alps** are quarried for marble.

Portofino

In the heart of Tuscany the **Arno Basin** lies fertile and beautiful, an ideal setting for **Florence**. Festoons of vines and silvery olives come to meet fields of wheat, tobacco and maize. Peppers, pumpkins and the famous Lucca beans grow among the mulberries. The old farms, with their nobly designed buildings, often stand alone on hill tops.

Southern Tuscany is a land of hills, soft and vine-clad in the **Chianti** district south of Florence, quiet and pastoral near Siena, dry and desolate round Monte Oliveto Maggiore, and massive and mysterious in the **Colli Metalliferi** (metal-bearing hills) south of Volterra. On the borders of Latium, **Maremma**, with its melancholy beauty, was formerly a marshy district haunted by bandits and shepherds. Much of the area has now been reclaimed.

Umbria. – The gentle land where St Francis lived is a country of hills, valleys and river basins, where the poplars raise their rustling heads to limpid skies. This is the green Umbria of the **Clitumnus Valley** (Valle del Clitunno), whose pastures were already famous in ancient times. Umbria has two lakes, **Trasimeno** and Piediluco, and many rivers, including the Tiber. Medieval cities which succeeded Etruscan settlements overlook ravines and valleys: grim Gubbio, haughty **Perugia**, the capital of Umbria, Franciscan Assisi, Spoleto and Spello. Others stand in the centre of a plain, such as Foligno and Terni, the metallurgical centre.

The Marches. – So called because they were formerly frontier provinces of the Frankish Empire and the papal domains, the marches form a much sub-divided area between San Marino and Ascoli Piceno, where the parallel spurs of the Apennines run down into the Adriatic, forming a series of deep, narrow valleys. There is, however, a flat and rectangular coastal belt dotted with beaches and canal-ports. The inhabitants of the Marches have a reputation for friendliness, piety and diligence. Apart from the capital, Ancona, a busy port, most of the old towns are built on commanding sites: among them Urbino and Loreto should be noted, one as an art centre and the other for its venerated church.

Latium. – Lying between the Tyrrhenian Sea and the Apennines, from Tuscan Maremma to Gaeta, Latium, the cradle of Roman civilisation, borders a sandy coast whose ancient ports, such as Ostia at the mouth of the Tiber, have been silted up. Civitavecchia today is the only modern port on the coastline. In the centre of Latium, **Rome**, the Italian capital and seat of the Catholic Church, is mainly a residential city attracting civil servants, churchmen and tourists alike. To the east and north, volcanic hills, with lonely lakes in their craters, overlook the famous **Roman Campagna**, beloved by the writers and painters who have often described its great, desolate expanses, dotted with ancient ruins. Today these waste lands *(latifundia)*, formerly hotbeds of malaria, have regained a certain life: the drainage of the Pontine Marches, near Latina, was the most spectacular achievement of this project. Cassino is the most important industrial centre. A flourishing industrial zone has developed around the atomic centre at Latina.

To the south is the distinctive **Ciociaria**. This area takes its name from the shoes *(ciocie)*, which are part of the traditional costume. They have thick soles and thongs which are wound round the calf of the leg. It is a mainly agricultural area with strong folklore traditions.

The Abruzzi. – Under its harsh climate, this is the part of the Apennines which most suggests a country of high mountains, grand and wild, with its **Gran Sasso** and **Maiella Massifs**. The Upper Sangro Valley is now a nature reserve. In basins sheltered from the wind are vineyards, almond and olive groves, whose products are sent to the market town of Avezzano. Near the latter is the great drained marsh which is now given over to beet growing. The area is slowly acquiring an industrial sector with the development of the Chieti-Pescara zone and implantation of firms in other areas such as Vasto (glass making), Sulmona (car factories) and L'Aquila (steel works).

Molise. – Molise, with its capital, **Campobasso**, extends south of the Abruzzi, with which it has several common features: a mountainous relief, dark valleys and wild forests which are still haunted by wolves. The region is bordered to the west by the Maiella. Agriculture forms the basis of the local economy and the main crops are wheat, oats, maize, potatoes and vines (dried raisins).

Campania. – Campania forms a fertile crescent around the Bay of Naples. Hemp, tobacco and cereals alternate with olive groves and vineyards, **Naples** is the port for a region which is slowly developing its industrial sector (food industries, steel works, oil refineries and engineering works). As for the **Bay of Naples**, its charm and its mystery stirred the imagination of the ancients and it was here that they located the entrance to the Underworld. The characteristic silhouette of **Vesuvius** dominates the landscape at all times. Although the coast has lost much of its charm owing to building developments, the **Sorrento Peninsula** and the **Island of Capri** are two notable beauty spots.

Apulia, Basilicata and Calabria. – These three regions cover the foot of the Italian "boot". Apulia, on the east side, facing the Adriatic, is less poor than commonly supposed. Cereal growing flourishes in the plain between Foggia and Manfredonia but also in the plains of Bari, Taranto, Lecce and Brindisi. Vines grow almost everywhere and are associated with olives (the Apulian production of olive oil represents 10% of the world total) and almonds on the coast. The relief of the **Gargano Promontory**, otherwise known as the "boot's spur", is quite high, distinguishing it from the rest of the area. The country to the south of Bari has an almost Oriental aspect, with strange dwellings, known as *trulli*, and customs.

Bari, the capital of Apulia and a busy port, still enjoys numerous trading links with the Middle East. Along with Taranto and Brindisi it is one of the three main industrial centres in the region. Basilicata or **Lucania**, and Calabria, comprise very different types of country; the rocky corniche from the Gulf of Policastro to Reggio; the grim, grand mountains of the **Sila Massif** with its extensive mountain pastures and wide horizons; and at the southern extremity of the peninsula between two inner seas, lies the **Aspromonte Massif** clad with pine, beech and chestnut forests.

Sardinia and Sicily. – *Description p 239 and p 246.*

BC	**From the Origins to the Empire (753-27 BC)**
753	Foundation of Rome by Romulus according to legend. (In fact it was born of the union of Latin and Sabine villages in the 8C).
7C-6C	Royal Dynasty of the Tarquins. Power is divided between the king, the senate, representing the great patrician families, and the *comitia,* representing the rich families.
509	Establishment of the Republic: the king's powers are conferred on two consuls, elected for one year.
451-449	Law of the XII Tables, instituting equality between patricians and plebeians.
390	The Gauls invade Italy and take Rome but are expelled by Camillus.
281-272	War against Pyrrhus, King of Epirus; submission of the southern part of the peninsula to Rome.
264-241	First Punic War: Carthage abandons Sicily to the Romans.
218-201	Second Punic War. Hannibal crosses the Alps and defeats the Romans at Lake Trasimeno. Hannibal routs the Romans at Cannae and halts at Capua *(qv).* In 210 Scipio carries war into Spain, and in 204 he lands in Africa. Hannibal is recalled to Carthage. Scipio defeats Hannibal at Zama in 202.
146	Macedonia and Greece become Roman provinces. Capture and destruction of Carthage.
133	Occupation of all Spain and end of the Mediterranean campaigns.
133-121	Failure of the policy of the Gracchi, who promoted popular agrarian laws.
118	The Romans in Gaul.
112-105	War against Jugurtha, King of Numidia (now Algeria).
102-101	Marius, vanquisher of Jugurtha, stops invasions of Cimbri and Teutons.
88-79	Sulla, the rival of Marius, triumphs over Mithridates and establishes his dictatorship in Rome.
70	Pompey and Crassus, appointed Consuls, become masters of Rome.
63	Plot of Catiline against the Senate exposed by Cicero.
60	The first Triumvirate: Pompey, Crassus, Julius Caesar. Rivalry of the three rulers.
59	Julius Caesar as Consul.
58-51	The Gallic War (52: Surrender of Vercingetorix at Alesia).
49	Caesar crosses the Rubicon and drives Pompey out of Rome.
49-45	Caesar defeats Pompey and his partisans in Spain, Greece and Egypt. He writes his history of the Gallic War.
early 44	Caesar is appointed Dictator for life.
March 15	Caesar is assassinated by Brutus, his adopted son, among others.
43	The second Triumvirate: Octavius (nephew and heir of Caesar), Anthony, Lepidus.
41-30	Struggle between Octavius and Anthony. Defeat (at Actium) and death of Anthony.

The Early Empire (27 BC to AD 284)

Hadrian (Louvre Museum, Paris)

27	Octavius, sole master of the Empire, receives the title of Augustus Caesar and plenary powers.
AD	
14	Death of Augustus.
14-37	Reign of Tiberius.
54-68	Reign of Nero, who causes the death of Britannicus, his mother Agrippina and his wives Octavia and Poppaea, and initiates violent persecution of the Christians.
68	End of the Julio-Claudian dynasty: Augustus, Tiberius, Caligula, Claudius, Nero.
69-96	Flavian dynasty: Vespasian, Titus, Domitian.
96-192	The Century of the Antonines, marked by the successful reigns of Nerva, Trajan, Hadrian, Antoninus and Marcus Aurelius, who consolidated the Empire.
193-275	Severus dynasty: Septimius Severus, Caracalla, Heliogabalus, Alexander Severus, Decius, Valerian, Aurelian.
235-268	Military anarchy; a troubled period. The legions make and break emperors.
270-275	Aurelius re-establishes the unity of the Empire.

The Later Empire (AD 284-476)

284-305	Reign of Diocletian. Institution of Tetrarchy or 4-man government.
303	Persecution of the Christians: reign of Diocletian known as "the age of martyrs".
306-337	Reign of Constantine, who establishes Christianity as the state religion. By the Edict of Milan (313) Constantine decrees religious liberty. Constantinople becomes the new capital.
379-395	Reign of Theodosius the Great, the Christian Emperor. At his death the Empire is divided between his two sons, Arcadius (Eastern Empire) and Honorius (Western Empire) who settled at Ravenna.
5C	The Roman Empire is repeatedly attacked by the Barbarians: in 410, Alaric, King of the Visigoths, captures Rome. Capture and sack of Rome in 455 by the Vandals under Genseric.
476	Deposition by Odoacer of the Emperor Romulus Augustus ends the Western Empire.

From the Roman Empire to the Germanic Holy Roman Empire

493	Odoacer is driven out by the Ostrogoths under Theodoric.
535-553	Reconquest of Italy by the Eastern Roman Emperor Justinian (527-565).
568	Lombard invasion by King Alboin.
752	Threatened by the Lombards, the pope appeals to Pepin the Short, King of the Franks.
774	Pepin's son, Charlemagne (Charles the Great), becomes King of the Lombards.
800	Charlemagne is proclaimed Emperor by Pope Leo III.
9C	The break-up of the Carolingian Empire causes complete anarchy and the formation of many rival states in Italy.
951	Intervention in Italy of Otto I, king of Saxony, who becomes King of the Lombards.
962	Otto I, now crowned Emperor, founds the Holy Roman Empire.

The Quarrel of the Church and the Empire

11C	Progressive establishment of the Normans in Sicily and southern Italy.
1076	Quarrel between Pope Gregory VII and the Emperor Henry IV about Investitures.
1077	Humbling of the Emperor before the Pope at Canossa *(qv)*.
1155	Frederick Barbarossa crowned Emperor. Resumption of the struggle between the Empire and the Papacy, with the **Ghibellines** supporting the emperor and the **Guelphs** supporting the pope.
1167	Creation of the **Lombard League.** An association of Lombard cities with Guelph tendencies to counter the Emperor.
1176	Reconciliation between Frederick Barbarossa and Pope Alexander III.
1216	Triumph of the Papacy on the death of Pope Innocent III.
1227-1250	A new phase in the struggle between the Empire (Frederick II) and the Papacy (Gregory IX). New triumph of the Papacy.

French Influence and Decline of Imperial Power

13C	Peak of economic prosperity of the Communes.
1252	The Florentine florin, a silver coin from 1182, is minted in gold and is a popular currency in international trade.
1265	Charles of Anjou, brother of St Louis, crowned King of Sicily.
1282	Sicilian Vespers: massacre of French settlers in Sicily *(qv)*.
1302	The Anjou Dynasty establishes itself in Naples.
1303	Attack of Anagni, instigated by King Philip of France, on Pope Boniface VIII.

Florin

1309-1377	The popes established at Avignon, France. The Avignon popes included Clement V to Gregory XI who took the papacy back to Rome at the instigation of St Catherine of Siena.
1328	Failure of the intervention in Italy by the Emperor Ludwig of Bavaria. This is the first sign of the slow erosion of the German Emperors' will to exercise political and economic power over the territories of the old Roman empire.
1378-1418	The Great Schism of the West (anti-popes in Pisa and Avignon) is brought to an end by the Council of Constance (1414-18).
1402	Last German intervention in Italy (emperor defeated by Lombard militia).
1442	Alfonso V, King of Aragon, becomes King of the Two Sicilies.
1453	Constantinople, capital of the Christian Eastern territories, falls to the Turks.
1492	Death of Lorenzo de' Medici, the Magnificent. Christopher Columbus discovers America.
1494	Intervention of King Charles VIII of France at the behest of Ludovico II Moro.

Economic and Cultural Golden Age (15C, early 16C)

The centre and the north of the country were transformed by the dynamism of the bourgeois class, while the south kept its feudal structures based on land ownership. The economic importance of Italy at that time derived from the large-scale production of consumer goods (cloth, leather, glass, ceramics, arms etc) as well as from trade and wide-ranging banking activities. Merchants and bankers who had settled in countries throughout Europe spread the influence of the Italian civilisation, which flourished at the courts of the Italian rulers. There was great rivalry regarding the patronage of artists and the commissioning of splendid palaces among enlightened patrons of the arts such as the Medici of Florence, the Sforza of Milan, the Montefeltro of Urbino, the Este of Ferrara, the Gonzaga of Mantua and the Popes in Rome (Julius II, Leo X).

Decline set in as trade shifted towards the Atlantic with grave consequences for the maritime republics which had prospered during the Middle Ages. Genoa soon faced ruin, Pisa was taken over by its age-old rival Florence, and Venice was in serious trouble as the Turks advanced westwards. In addition, Italy which still had great economic potential fell once again under foreign domination because of the failure to achieve the unity of the country.

From the 16C to the Napoleonic era

16C **1515-1526**	France and Spain engage in a struggle for the supremacy of Europe. François I, victor at Marignano but vanquished at Pavia, is forced to give up the Italian heritage.
1527	Capture and sack of Rome by the troops of the Constable of Bourbon, in the service of Charles V.
1559	Treaty of Cateau-Cambrèsis: Spanish domination over Naples and the district of Milan, Sicily and Sardinia until the early 18C.
17C **1713**	Savoy becomes the most powerful state in northern Italy. Victor-Amadeus II of Savoy acquires Sicily and the title of King. The Duke of Savoy is compelled to exchange Sicily for Sardinia in 1720.
1796	Napoleon's campaign in Lombardy. Creation of the Cispadan Republic.
1797	Battle of Rivoli (p 119). Treaty of Campo-Formio. Creation of the Cisalpine and Ligurian Republics.
1798-1799 **1805**	Proclamation of the Roman and Parthenopaean (Naples) Republics. Napoleon transforms the Italian Republic into a Kingdom, assumes the iron crown of the Lombard Kings and confers the vice-royalty on his stepson, Eugène de Beauharnais.
1808	Rome is occupied by French troops. Murat becomes King of Naples.
1809	The Papal States are attached to the French Empire. Pius VII is taken to France as a prisoner (1812).
1814	Collapse of the Napoleonic regime. Pius VII returns to Rome.

Towards Italian Unity (1815-1870)

1815	Congress of Vienna. Hegemony of Austria.
1815-1832	The "Carbonari" patriots oppose the Austrian occupation but their revolts are crushed.
1831	Founding of the Young Italy movement by Mazzini. Growth of national feeling against Austria: the **Risorgimento.**
1834-1837	Revolts at Genoa and in the Kingdom of the Two Sicilies.
1848	First War of Independence against Austria, led by the King of Sardinia, ruler of Piedmont. Italian successes followed by a violent Austrian counter-attack.
1849-1852	Accession of Victor Emmanuel II. Cavour's government reorganises the State of Piedmont.
1854	Participation of Piedmont, with Britain and France, in the Crimean War.
1856	Paris Congress. Cavour officially raises the question of Italian unity.
1858	Meeting of Cavour and Napoleon III at Plombières. Alliance between France and Piedmont.
1859	Second War of Independence against Austria led by Piedmont with France as ally. Franco-Piedmontese victories of Magenta and Solferino (p 119) and Villafranca Armistice. Piedmont obtains Lombardy and France, Savoy and the County of Nice.
1860	Bologna, Parma, Modena and Tuscany unite with Piedmont. Expedition of Garibaldi and the Thousand to Sicily and Naples. Union of the South.
1861	Proclamation of the Kingdom of Italy with Turin as its capital. Death of Cavour.
1865-1870	Florence becomes the capital of the Kingdom of Italy.
1866	Austria at war with Prussia and Italy. Venetia united to Italy.
1867	Garibaldi, marching on Rome, is defeated at Mentana.
1870	Occupation of Rome by the Piedmontese. Rome becomes the capital of Italy. Italian unity is complete.

UNIFICATION OF ITALY

Although Machiavelli had already dreamed of a united Italy in the 16C, it was not until after the French Revolution that the question of uniting the various regions under the same political regime was seriously contemplated. The Risorgimento provided the initial impetus which resulted in the uprisings of 1848 against Austrian rule and their defeat at Novara (1849). The problem of Italian unity was brought to the forefront of European affairs with the accession of **Victor Emmanuel II** and the skilful campaigning of his minister **Camillo Cavour**, an ardent advocate of Italian liberty. Napoleon allied himself with the Piedmontese in order to oppose the Austrians. After the combined Franco-Piedmontese victories of 1859 and the disillusionment caused by the Treaty of Villafranca when Savoy was surrendered to France, several regions of central Italy planned a concerted revolt and united with Piedmont. **Garibaldi** liberated Sicily and southern Italy from the domination of the Bourbons. On 17 March 1861 the inauguration of the Kingdom of Italy was proclaimed with Turin as

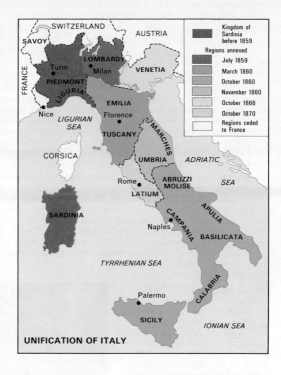

UNIFICATION OF ITALY

the capital and Victor Emmanuel as King. Five more years had to pass before the war of independence with the Prussians as allies led to the annexation of Venetia, and more than ten before Italian troops captured Rome in 1870, thus achieving the unification of Italy.

From 1870 to the Present Day

1882	Italy, Germany and Austria sign the Triple Alliance.
1885	The Italians gain a footing in Eritrea and on the Somali Coast.
1900	Assassination of King Umberto I by an anarchist. Accession of Victor Emmanuel III.
1904-1906	Rapprochement of Italy with Britain and France.
1915	Italy enters the First World War on the side of the Allies.
1919	Treaty of St Germain: Istria and the Trentino are attached to Italy.
1921	Social disturbances fomented by Mussolini's Fascist Party.
1922-1926	The March on Rome. Mussolini becomes Prime Minister, then *Duce* (Leader).
1929	Lateran Treaty concluded between the Italian Government and the Papacy *(p 22)*.
1936	Italian occupation of Ethiopia. Rapprochement with Germany. Rome-Berlin Axis formed.
1940	Italy enters the Second World War against Britain and France.
1943	Fall and arrest of Mussolini. Italy goes to war with Germany.
1945	Execution of Mussolini.
May 1946	Abdication of Victor Emmanuel III and accession of Umberto II.
June 1946	Proclamation of the Republic after a referendum.
1947	Treaty of Paris: Italy loses its colonies as well as Albania, Istria, Dalmatia and the Dodecanese. Frontier redefined to the benefit of France.
1954	Trieste is attached to Italy.
March 1957	Treaty of Rome instituting the European Economic Community (Common Market): Italy is one of the six founder-member states.

ROME AND THE PAPACY

Capital of Christendom. – Vatican City is a Free State ruled by the pope. Although in terms of the priesthood the pope has the same powers as a bishop, in the hierarchy he is the head of the Roman Catholic Church. The Vatican Council of 1870 laid down the principle of papal infallibility in matters of dogma. The pontiff is the symbol of the spiritual influence of the Roman Catholic Church throughout the world.

Papal Election and Influence. – The pope is elected by the cardinals, who form the Sacred College and meet in conclave in the Sistine Chapel. A majority of two-thirds plus one is required to make an election valid.
As the Christian community grew in numbers the pope began to assume a growing political role in parallel with his functions as Head of the Church. Thus the history of the papacy reflects the relationship between Church and State.

Birth of the Church and Origin of the Papacy. – Christianity was born in the Levant with the preaching of Jesus and reached the west through the proselytizing of the apostles and their disciples. By the end of the 1C the early Church was made up of small communities led by bishops who were Christ's representatives. From the end of the 2C the Bishop of Rome, the capital of the Empire, claimed primacy over the other bishops. Gradually the term Pope (Low Latin *Papa*: Father) ceased to be used in relation to all bishops but was reserved exclusively for the Bishop of Rome.

Growth of the Church. – At first regarded as a harmless cult, Christianity was soon subjected to persecution under Nero and Domitian as well as under Decius, Valerian, Diocletian and Maximian. However, these events failed to check the spread of the new religion, and the Church stood out as the only great moral force able to withstand the fall of the weakened and divided Empire. In 313, the Emperor Constantine granted religious freedom to Christians by the **Edict of Milan**. Pagan cults were tolerated and later banned. When Christianity was recognised as the state religion in 382 it became the surest prop of imperial power and when Rome reeled under the repeated assaults of the Barbarians, it remained the last bulwark of civilisation.

Papal Authority. – The authority of the pope and the ascendancy of the Church grew all the stronger over the next centuries, in particular owing to the strong personality of **Gregory the Great** (590-604). In the 8C, when faced with the occupation of the imperial territories by the Lombards, the then pope appealed to Pepin the Short, King of the Franks, thus initiating an era of alliances with the Carolingian dynasty culminating in two important events. By the Donation of **Quiersy-sur-Oise** (AD 756) the King of the Franks gave an undertaking to return all occupied territories to Pope Stephen II and not to the Byzantine emperor. This donation is the origin of the Papal States and of the pope's temporal power. The second event was the coronation of Charlemagne as Emperor of the West in the year AD 800. In the period of anarchy which

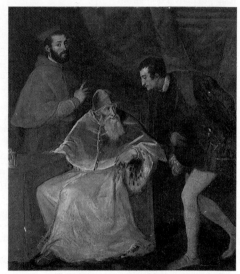

Pope Paul III (Alessandro Farnese) with his nephews by Titian (Capodimonte Palace, Naples)

followed the fall of the Carolingian Empire at the end of the 9C, the papacy lapsed into great laxity; its prestige was restored under the strong leadership of **Gregory VII** (1073-85). The decrees of this great reformer led to the Quarrel of the Investitures, a long-drawn out conflict between the pope and the emperor.
The papacy emerged weakened from the Captivity of Avignon (1309-77) but after its return to Rome it had to face a still more serious crisis with the **Great Schism of the West** (1378-1417), as a succession of antipopes elected by the Sacred College ruled in Avignon. In the 16C, from 1520 onwards, the Reformation started by Martin Luther posed a new threat to Church authority which was countered by the Council of Trent *(qv)*. The Church emerged stronger after each religious crisis. In the 18C it countered the challenge from the philosophical movement, and after the fall of Napoleon (1814) the pope returned to Rome.

The "Roman Question". – As the spiritual head of the Church and also as a temporal sovereign, the pope was involved in the 19C in the problem of Italian unity. Unity brought about by the House of Piedmont-Sardinia could be achieved only if the pope renounced all temporal power. When the troops of Victor Emmanuel II occupied Rome in 1870, the pope was a virtual prisoner in the Vatican.
The problem was solved by the **Lateran Treaty** of 1929 signed between the Holy See and Mussolini. From then on the people enjoyed sovereignty over the Papal State which comprises Vatican City, the four major basilicas, the catacombs, the Roman Curia, several colleges and Castel Gandolfo. The authority of the Church was also recognised in the fields of education and marriage. It was on this basis that in 1947 the Constitution defined the relations between the Church and the State. A further agreement modifying the 1929 Lateran Treaty was signed in 1984.

ANCIENT CIVILISATIONS

Since 2000 BC and throughout antiquity, Italy, the meeting-place of races, has seen the Etruscan, Greek and Latin civilisations flourish on her soil. Two thousand years later, western civilisation is still impregnated with them. Greeks, Etruscans and Romans were preceded by two peoples who came from the north: the Ligurians, who also occupied southern Gaul and the Iberian Peninsula, and the Italics or Italiots, who settled in Umbria and Latium and from whom the Latins sprang. The former transmitted their fair hair and blue eyes to some of the present inhabitants of Liguria. The latter built acropolises of which the gigantic foundations still exist in some places, as for instance at Alatri.

THE GREEKS

Cities and Men. – The shores of Sicily and southern Italy held a sort of fascination for the ancient Greeks, who regarded them as the limits of the inhabited earth. Many scenes of Greek mythology are set there: the Phlegrean Fields, near Naples, hid the entrance to the Kingdom of Hades; Zeus routed the Titans,

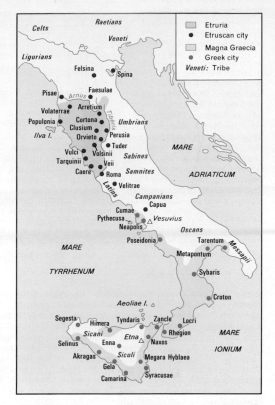

Akragas: Agrigento
Caere: Cerveteri
Clusium: Chiusi
Faesulae: Fiesole

Felsina: Bologna
Poseidonia: Paestum
Selinus: Selinunte
Tuder: Todi

Velitrae: Velletri
Veii: Veio
Volsinii: Bolsena
Zancle: Messina

with the help of Hercules, on the site of Etna, where the Cyclops lived and Hephaestus, the God of Fire, had his forges; Kore, the daughter of Demeter, was kidnapped by Hades, who had emerged from the Tartara River near Enna.

In the *Odyssey*, Homer (9C BC) relates the adventures of Ulysses (Odysseus) after the siege of Troy, sailing between Scylla and Charybdis in the Straits of Messina and resisting the temptations of the Sirens in the Gulf of Sorrento. Pindar (5C BC) describes these mysterious shores, to which Virgil (1C BC) also refers in the *Aeneid*. After the Phoenicians had settled at Carthage and their seamen had set up a few trading posts, the Greeks founded, as early as the 8C BC, a large number of colonies on the coasts of Sicily and southern Italy. The whole settlement took the name of **Magna Graecia**. In it were Ionian, Achaean and Dorian colonies, named after the Greek peoples who had colonised them. The social unit was the "city". One of them, Crotone, was governed by a school of philosophers, the Pythagoreans.

The 6C and 5C BC marked the zenith of Greek civilisation in Italy, corresponding to the period of Pericles in Athens. The Greek cities drew such profit from their seaborne trade that Syracuse soon rivalled Athens. Syracuse and Taranto were the two main centres of this refined civilisation.

Philosophers, scientists and writers settled in Sicily. Aeschylus lived at Gela, and Syracuse was where Theocritus defined the rules of bucolic poetry and the geometrican Archimedes was murdered by a Roman soldier.

The number and diversity of these cities led to rivalry and dissension. Warfare between the "tyrants" of neighbouring towns and Carthaginian raids' caused a decline, which ended in the Roman conquest at the end of the 3C BC.

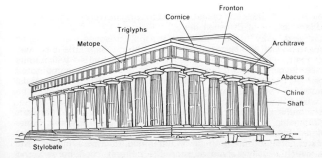

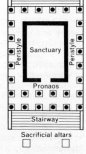

An ancient temple

Art in Magna Graecia. – The 6C and 5C BC saw the building of the temples of Paestum, Selinus and Agrigento, magnificent examples of Doric architecture whose vigorous design contrasts with the delicate grace of the Ionic order.

At the end of the 5C BC the Doric style was still used for the beautiful temple at Segesta, while in Greece itself the Ionic style was at its height and the Corinthian style was just making its appearance.

Doric Order   Ionic Order   Corinthian Order

Decline began in the 4C BC, after the Peloponnesian War between Sparta and Athens, which impoverished the Greek world. This was the beginning of the so-called **Hellenistic** period, marked by the neglect of architecture in favour of sculpture.

The museums of Naples, Paestum, Reggio di Calabria, Taranto, Palermo and Syracuse illustrate the development of sculpture, from the archaic low reliefs of the metopes of Paestum or Selinus and the monumental telamones (male figures used as pillars) of Agrigento to the delightful statuettes of the decadent period modelled at Taranto in the 3C BC. Innumerable youths, Apollos and Aphrodites also issued from the sculptors' studios. They were all more or less copied from Phidias, Praxiteles, Scopas or Lysippus, but their harmony of form and proportion remained admirable.

THE ETRUSCANS

While the Greeks were impregnating the south of the peninsula and Sicily with their civilisation, the Etruscans were building up in central Italy, from the 8C BC onwards, a powerful empire whose growth was checked only by that of Rome (3C BC). They are a little-known people whose alphabet along with certain tombstone inscriptions have now been deciphered. Some authorities think they were natives of these parts; others, following the example of Herodotus, say they came from Lydia in Asia Minor. The Etruscans at first occupied the area between the Arno and the Tiber *(map p 23)* but later spread into Campania and the Po Plain. They reached their zenith in the 6C BC. **Etruria** then comprised a federation of twelve city-states known as *lucumonies*, among which are named Veii, Bolsena, Tarquinia, Volterra, Perugia etc.

Having grown rich by working iron (Island of Elba), copper and silver mines and by trading in the western Mediterranean, the Etruscans, who were artisans and technicians, had a civilisation derived from a mixture of savagery and refinement. In religion their gods were the same as those of the Greeks. They believed in life after death and in divination, and they studied the entrails of animals (for haruspices) and the flight of birds (for auspices), a form of superstition which the Romans adopted and developed.

Their towns, built on elevated sites with walls of huge stones, show an advanced sense of town planning. Near them are vast burial grounds with underground chambers or hypogea filled with utensils and adorned with mural paintings. These reveal the customs of the Etruscans, which formed the basis of one branch of Latin civilisation.

Etruscan Art. – Etruscan art is primitive in character, though strongly influenced by the Orient and especially by Greece from the 5C BC onwards. It has a marked individuality sustained by realism and expressive movement. Etruscan art was discovered in the 18C, but was regarded as an offshoot of Greek art. The discovery in the 19C of masterpieces like the Apollo and Hermes of Veii and the systematic study of artefacts in the 20C have given this vigorous and refined art the place it deserved.

Sculpture. – Since architectural specimens are lacking, sculpture appears to us as the artists' favourite medium. The great period is the 6C BC, when large groups of statuary adorned the pediments of the temples: the famous Apollo of Veii (in the museum of the Villa Giulia in Rome) in which Greek influence is obvious, belongs to this period. Some portrait busts are more original in their striking realism, intensity of expression and stylised features: their large prominent eyes and enigmatic smiles are characteristic of the Etruscan style. The same remarks apply to the famous groups of semi-recumbent figures on the sarcophagi, many of which are portraits.

The sense of movement is shown mainly in sculptures of fantastic animals (such as the Chimera from Arezzo in the Archaeological Museum of Florence) and in figurines representing warriors fighting, women at their toilet etc.

Painting. – The only surviving specimens are in the burial chambers of the cemeteries (Cerveteri, Veii and especially Tarquinia), where they were supposed to remind the dead of the pleasures of life: banquets, games and plays, music and dancing, hunting etc. The delicate paintings, in colour laid on flat, show amazing powers of observation. They form an excellent record of Etruscan life.

Pottery and goldsmiths' work. – Even more than artists, the Etruscans were artisans of genius. In pottery they used the **bucchero** technique, about which little is known, producing black earthenware with figures in relief. Initially decorated with motifs in *pointillé*, the vases developed more elaborate shapes with a more complicated ornamentation. In the 5C BC they modelled beautiful burial urns, *canopae*, in animal or human shape adorned with geometric designs. Greek pottery continued to be popular in Etruria where it was faithfully copied.

In the domain of goldsmiths' work, both men and women wore heavy gold ornaments of remarkable workmanship : often of solid gold they were a good example of the oustanding skill of the Etruscan goldsmiths. They were particularly skilful in the filigrane technique and perfected the granulation technique. Engraved mirrors, cists (cylindrical vessels which usually served as marriage coffers), scent-burners and bronze candelabra of great decorative elegance also show the skill of the artisans.

THE ROMANS

For about twelve centuries, from the foundation of Rome in the 8C BC to the end of the Western Empire in AD 476, a civilisation, from which Western Europe emerged, reigned in Italy. Royal Rome (753-509 BC) was followed by the Republic (509-27 BC) and then the Empire (27 BC). The Roman eagle then spread its wings from Britain to the Persian Gulf and from Africa to Germany. Decline set in the Later Empire (AD 284-476) in civil wars and with Barbarian invasions.

Political and Social Life. – At the time of the kings, the political organisation of Rome comprised two bodies, the Senate and the *Comitia*, composed of patricians. These were a privileged class who kept idle but devoted hangers-on. The plebeians had no access to public affairs. The scale the slaves formed the under-privileged section of the population, but they could be freed by their masters.

Under the Republic, power was given to two consuls, elected for one year and assisted by quaestors in charge of public finance and the criminal police, together with censors of public morals, aediles in charge of the municipal police, and judicial praetors. The Senate had a consultative role and sanctioned laws. Ten Tribunes of the People watched over the rights of the masses. Consuls or praetors administered the provinces.

Generally speaking, the Empire kept the administrative structure of the Republic, but the powers of the consuls were taken by an emperor *(Imperator)* who was commander-in-chief of the army; he appointed the Senate, and had the right to make peace or war. Under the Later Empire the power of the emperors became absolute. Outside the State, society was divided into clans *(gentes)*, or groups of people descended from a common ancestor, and families, each under a *pater familias* who wielded absolute authority.

Religion. – Religion played a part in public or private life. As regards **domestic cults,** a small oratory called the *lararium* enshrined the household gods, Lares and Penates, before whom a sacred flame burned always. The souls of the dead were also venerated. **Public worship** took place in buildings copied from the Etruscan or Greek temples *(sketch p 23)*. Sometimes they were circular in form, as in the case of temples dedicated to Vesta.

With the exception of Janus, the chief gods were derived from the twelve (if Pluto god of the Underworld is omitted) Greek gods of Olympus.

A Roman Town

Planning. – Roman towns often have a military origin: when the land placed under their control was shared out, the legionaries and veterans who had stayed in the camps were joined by the civil population. Towns which had been surrounded with walls during troubled periods were divided, whenever possible, into four quarters by two main streets, the *decumanus* and the *cardo*, intersecting at right angles and ending in gateways. Other streets parallel to these two gave the town a chess-board plan.

Streets. – The streets were edged with footpaths, sometimes 50cm-18in high, and lined with porticoes to shelter pedestrians. The roadway, paved with large flagstones laid diagonally, was crossed at intervals by stepping-stones laid at the same level as the pavements but between which horses and cart-wheels could pass.

The Roman house. – Excavations at Herculaneum, Pompeii and especially Ostia have uncovered Roman houses of various types: the small bourgeois house, a dwelling of several storeys, shops open to the street and finally large, luxurious patrician mansions.

These last had a modest external appearance owing to their bare walls and few windows. But the interiors, adorned with mosaics, statues, paintings and marbles and sometimes including private baths and a fish pond, revealed the riches of their owners. A vestibule overlooked by the porter's lodge led to the *atrium*.

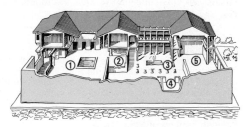

A Roman house

The **atrium (1)** was a large rectangular court open, in the middle, to the sky. A basin called the *impluvium*, under the open section, caught rainwater. The rooms *(cubiculae)* opened off the atrium, which was the only part of the house to which strangers were usually admitted. At the far end was the **tablinum (2)** or study and reception room of the head of the family. Money and books were kept there.

The atrium and the adjoining rooms constituted the primitive, simple house of the poorer citizen. High officials, rich colonials and prosperous tradesmen often added a second house, of the more refined Greek type, joined onto the *tablinum*.

The **peristyle (3)** was a court surrounded by a portico in the centre of the part of the house reserved for the family. Here the peristyle was generally made into a garden with basins lined with mosaics, fountains and statues. The living quarters opened on to it: bedrooms, dining-room or **triclinium (4)** and the saloon or **œcus (5)**. The bedrooms were simple sleeping-chambers. They contained a stone or marble dais built against the wall or a movable bed. There were mattresses, cushions and blankets but no sheets. In the dining-room, the guests reclined on couches placed on three sides of the table, the fourth being left open for service.

The servants' quarters included the kitchen with a sink and drain, a built-in stove and an oven for roasting and pastry; baths, which were like the public baths on a smaller scale, and the slaves' quarters, attics, stables etc. The latrines with drains were either in a corner of the kitchen or in some other recess.

The forum. – The forum was a large square, often surrounded by a portico. Originally it was a market, usually at the crossing of the two main streets, but it became the centre of the public and commercial life of Roman towns. Men came there to read public notices, listen to political speakers, stroll and talk. The women did their shopping, either in shops round the square or from hawkers and artisans who set up their stalls under the porticos. Slave markets were held on certain days.

Government offices were placed round the forum. These included the *curia* or headquarters of local government; the voting hall for elections; the public tribune from which candidates for office harangued the crowd; the Temple of Money or exchange; the municipal treasury; the public granaries; the Temple of Justice or law courts; the prison and one or more temples.

The tombs. – Roman cemeteries were placed along the roads, a little away from the towns. The most famous in Italy is that on the Via Appia Antica, south of Rome. Directly after death the body of the deceased was exposed on a funeral couch surrounded with candlesticks and wreaths of flowers. Then it was buried or burnt by the family. The deceased was provided with funeral furnishings for use in his second life: clothes, arms and tools for the men, toys for the children, as well as jewellery and toilet articles for the women.

Buildings

Great builders. – The art of building was highly developed by the Romans. The speed with which they erected their buildings was due less to the number of workmen employed than to the special training of workers, the methods of work and the use of lifting devices such as levers, winches and tackle to move heavy material into place. The Roman vault is semicircular in shape. At the end of the Empire, brick was used in preference to stone. The Roman architectural orders *(see sketch p 24)* were derived from the Greek orders, from which they are distinguished by certain details. Roman Doric, the simplest and strongest, is found in the ground floors of buildings. The Corinthian order was the most popular one with the Romans.

Temples. – Rome liberally adopted gods from all the mythologies. The emperors, when raised to divine status, were themselves objects of worship. The Roman temple *(see sketch p 23)* consists of a closed chamber, the *cella* (sanctuary) containing the image of the god, and an open vestibule *(pronaos)*. The building is surrounded, partly or completely, by a colonnade or peristyle.

Triumphal arches. – In Rome these commemorated the "triumphs" of generals or conquering emperors. The low reliefs on the arches recorded their feats of arms. In the provinces, such as Aosta, Benevento and Ancona, are municipal arches commemorating the founding of a city or erected in honour of some member of the imperial family.

The baths. – The Roman baths, which were public and free, were not only baths but centres of physical culture, casinos, clubs, recreation centres, libraries, lecture halls and meeting-places, which explains the amount of time people spent in them. Decoration in these great buildings was lavish: mosaic ornaments, coloured marble facings, columns and statues. The bather followed a medically approved circuit. From the gymnasium *(palestra)* he entered a lukewarm room *(tepidarium)* to prepare him for the high temperature of the hot room *(caldarium)* and the steam-room. Then came the hot cleaning-bath, the tepid transition-bath and the cold plunge *(frigidarium)* to tone up the skin.

To heat air and water a number of underground furnaces *(hypocausts)* were used. The hot air was circulated to heat the rooms from below and from the sides.

The amphitheatre. – This typically Roman structure, several storeys high, encircles the usually oval arena and was destined to seat the spectators. Posts were fixed to the upper part of the wall to carry a huge adjustable awning, the **velum**, to shelter the spectators from the sun and rain.

Inside, enclosing the arena, a wall protected the spectators in the front rows from the wild animals, released in the ring. Three circular galleries forming promenades, various staircases and corridors made it possible for all the spectators to reach their seats quickly without crowding and without any mingling of the classes.

Always very popular, the performances were announced in advance by painted posters, giving the names of the performers and details of the programme which included fighting of three kinds: between animals, between gladiators and animals, and between gladiators. In principle, a duel between gladiators had always to end in the death of one of the opponents. The public could ask for a gladiator's life to be spared and the President of the Games would indicate a reprieve by turning up his thumb. The victorious gladiator received a sum of money if he was a professional, or he was freed if he was a slave or a prisoner.

Other performances included chariot races, naval battles *(naumachia)*, Olympic games or impressive boxing contests, when the opponents wore copper gloves.

The theatre. – Theatres had rows of seats, usually ending in colonnades, a central area or **orchestra** occupied by distinguished spectators or used for acting, and a raised **stage**. The actors performed in front of a wall which was the finest part of the building: its decoration included several tiers of columns, niches containing statues, marble facings and mosaics. The perfect acoustics were generally due to a combination of subtle architectural features. The scenery was either fixed or mobile and there was an ingenious array of machinery either in the wings or below stage.

The chief function of the theatre was the performance of comedies and tragedies; however, Roman theatres were also used for competitions, lottery draws and the distribution of bread or money.

Until 100 BC all actors wore wigs of different shapes and colours according to the nature of the character they represented. After that date they adopted pasteboard masks and again each character had a distinctive mask. Tragic actors, to make themselves more impressive, wore buskins or sandals with thick cork soles.

ART

To appreciate fully Italian art in all its diversity and richness from the 12C to the late 18C, it is necessary to keep in mind the illustrious historical backdrop. The rightful heir of the Greek, Etruscan and Roman civilisations, Italian art has adopted from each period some of the most essential principles and characteristics. Italy, with its vast geographical extent from the Alps in the north down to Sicily, has always been open to diverse foreign influences. Following the fall of the Western Roman Empire, it was Byzantium that held sway and greatly influenced the southern Adriatic shores for several centuries. A succession of invading peoples followed, namely the Ostrogoths, Lombards, Franks, Arabs and Normans, and each left their imprint on the conquered territory.

The extraordinarily malleable Italian character absorbed the various foreign influences and one after another the cities of Florence, Siena, Verona, Ferrara, Milan, Rome, Venice, Naples and Genoa became the cradle of a flourishing artistic movement. As early as the 12C, in spite of the regional diversities, Italian artists were already beginning to show certain common characteristics. This phenomenon gathered momentum right up to the Renaissance. Initially it was a common taste for harmony and solidity of form as well as an innate sense of space. Both as an idealist and a mystic, the Italian has always worshipped beauty: the Italian landscapes were his source of inspiration where the clearly defined outlines are softened by the effect of the colours and the play of shimmering light.

The Italians rejected the importance accorded to realism which was so popular with northern schools, and diminished the excessive emphasis placed on decoration by Oriental artists. Slowly the Italian artist evolved a representational technique which contained his emotion. A preoccupation with idealisation is evident in the emphasis given to femininity whether it be profane or religious in inspiration.

In spite of this scholarly and well-mastered image, Italian art is not all exclusive. Take, for example, the medieval square, the famous **piazza**, which groups together on the site of the Roman forum the main public buildings: the church, baptistry, communal palace or the princely seat. To these were added at times the law courts, a hospital or a fountain. This was the venue for local markets and meetings.

Often designed like stage scenery and embellished with ornamentation, the piazza is also the place for business, political decision-making and other important events. History can be interpreted by studying how certain elements were reused, how ornamental motifs were copied and how styles were mingled or superimposed. This is where the artist who also aspires to be architect, sculptor and painter can best exercise his talents where it may be admired by all.

These excellent town planners, however, achieved a harmonious relationship with nature and the Italian countryside. Ever since Roman times they embellished the beautiful countryside with sumptuous **villas**, splendid terraced gardens cooled by basins, fountains and springs and landscaped with skill to create shade and please the eye. In addition all sorts of follies invited the passer-by to rest, meditate or simply enjoy the intimate or grandiose aspect of nature. Thus the Italian architects and landscape gardeners, often indifferent to the solemn grandeur of French classicism, have created an infinite number of places where man has established a harmonious relationship with nature: from Hadrian's Villa near Rome to the flower-decked terraces of the Borromean Islands, including the Oriental charm of the Villa Rufolo in Ravello, the elegant buildings of the Florentine countryside, the fantastic Mannerist creations of Rome, Tivoli or Bomarzo adorned with grottoes and statues, and finally the delightful mansions of the Brenta Riviera, all the work of Palladio.

BYZANTIUM

When Constantine transferred the seat of the Empire to Constantinople in the 4C AD, Rome began to decline and ancient Byzantium became the centre of a brilliant civilisation, while part of Italy was overrun by the Barbarians. After Honorious, who with his sister Galla Placidia fixed the capital of the Empire at Ravenna, and Theodoric, King of the Ostrogoths, who favoured the Greco-Latin civilisation and died there, this town came under Byzantine rule in the reign of Justinian (527-565 AD) and his wife Theodora. The Byzantine Emperors held the region of Ravenna and Venezia Giulia only until the 8C, but they kept a footing in Sicily and part of southern Italy until the 11C.

Byzantine art was born of the Christian art of the catacombs and early Christian basilicas and the Greek Oriental style, with its rich decoration. The capital of Byzantine art in Italy was Ravenna, whose tradition was carried on by Venice, Rome, Sicily and even Lombardy until the beginning of the 13C. The Byzantine artists had a sense of sanctity which appears in their works, with their air of grandeur and mystery.

Architecture and sculpture. – The palaces have vanished but religious buildings remain. They are built in brick, with domes, on the basilical plan inspired by the Roman basilica, or on a circular plan for mausoleums or baptistries. The sober exteriors of these buildings give no hint of the splendour of the mosaic-decorated interiors. The low reliefs on the sides of sarcophagi, chancel parcloses, ambos and pulpits, assume an essentially decorative character: symbolic and stylised figures, animals facing front to front etc.

Mosaics. – Byzantine artists showed their full powers in this sumptuous art form. Mosaics were composed of *tesserae*, or fragments of hard stone, glazed and irregularly cut to catch the light. They covered oven-vaults, walls and cupolas, their gold scintillating gently in mysterious semi-darkness. Enigmatic and grandiose figures stood out against midnight blue backgrounds and landscapes enlivened with trees, plants and animals, depicted with amazingly accurate observation.

The most famous mosaics are those of Ravenna, dating from the 5C and 6C; however, the Byzantine style still prevailed in the 11C-12C at St Mark's in Venice, in Sicily (Cefalù, Palermo, Monreale) and as late as the 13C in Rome.

MIDDLE AGES – ROMANESQUE AND GOTHIC (11C-14C)

As elsewhere in Europe, cathedrals were built all over Italy, but here the Italian predilection for harmony and the Roman tradition of monumental ensembles meant that architecture did not reach the sublime heights of the great achievements of religious art in France.

Romanesque Period. – Romanesque architecture in Italy received constant contributions from the Orient and, in the 12C especially, was influenced by France, notably by Normandy and Provence.

Lombard Style

Pisan Style

Florentine Style

Sicilan-Norman Style

The most flourishing school was that of Lombardy, whose master masons, the **maestri comacini**, created the **Lombard style** which spread all over north and central Italy. They built vaulted churches decorated with bands and arcades, detached campaniles, carved façades and porches supported by lions (Como, Milan, Pavia, Verona etc). In the **Pisan style**, architecture showed a strong Lombard influence, while the decorative work borrowed more from Oriental art. This style included tiers of arcades with a multitude of small columns on the façades, tall blind arcades on the side walls and east end, and decorative marble incrustations.

The highly original **Florentine-Romanesque style** did not spread beyond the city. It is characterised by simple lines inspired by antique art and by the decoration of façades with white and green marble used alternately.

In Latium and as far as Campania in the 12C-13C, the **Cosmati**, a Roman guild of mosaic and marble workers, held sway. They specialised in assembling fragments of multi-coloured marble (pavings, episcopal thrones, ambos or pulpits and candelabra) and the incrustation of columns and friezes in the cloisters with enamel mosaics.

Finally, in southern Italy and Sicily, Lombard, Saracen and Norman influences mingled, the first two exercising their effect chiefly on decoration and the last on the building plan. The combined result was the **Sicilian-Norman style** *(see p 248)*. **Sculpture** was closely linked with architecture, which was essentially religious and decorative.

Gothic Period. – As far as architecture was concerned it was the Cistercians who systematically introduced Gothic formulae into Italy in the 13C, starting at the Abbey of Fossanova *(p 104)*; the Franciscans (at Assisi) and the Dominicans (at Florence) soon followed their example. In the same period the Angevin architects imported by the Anjou Dynasty, which reigned at Naples, spread the use of arched vaulting and façades flanked by turrets in part of southern Italy.

Arnolfo di Cambio, the architect and sculptor, was influenced by both these traditions. He worked mainly in Florence and Rome.

In the 14C the Cathedral of Genoa and the huge unfinished Duomo at Siena were derived from Burgundian art, but in the 15C the great Church of St Petronius at Bologna and the gigantic and florid Milan Cathedral marked the end of a style for which the Italians never showed much enthusiasm.

There was more originality in civil architecture of the Gothic period. Numerous prosperous towns chose to show their civic pride by embellishing their city centres with municipal palaces and loggias. In Venice *(see p 29)* the ornate Gothic style relieved bare façades with window openings and loggias. Venetian Gothic was to persist until the late 15C.

Siena Cathedral

Romanesque

Gothic

Renaissance

Classical

Baroque

Venetian Palaces

The **Pisano** family from Pisa gave a decisive impetus to the art of **sculpture** by combining their continued use of ancient traditions (Nicola) and their vigorously expressive realism (Giovanni). These masters influenced the Sienese **Tino di Camaino** and the Florentines **Andrea Orcagna** and **Arnolfo di Cambio** with their new iconography and ambitious projects for pulpits and funerary monuments, all of which exhibited the new humanism.

The painted Crucifixes in relief which appeared in the 12C were the first specimens of Italian painting. Gradually the hieratic tradition inherited from Byzantine art lost its extreme rigidity. In the 13C a Roman, **Pietro Cavallini**, executed frescoes and mosaics with a greater breadth of style reminiscent of antique art. His Florentine contemporary, **Cimabue** (1240-1302) adorned the Upper Basilica of Assisi with frescoes displaying a new sense of pathos. This new approach influenced **Giotto** (1266-1337) who revolutionised painting by introducing naturalism into his works: movement, depth and atmosphere were indicated or suggested, and emotion came to light in the frescoes at Assisi, Padua and Florence.

In Siena at the same time **Duccio**'s (born c1260) work still showed a strong Byzantine influence. He founded the Siena school which continued to employ a graceful linear technique and show a pronounced taste for the decorative use of colour. Some of the most delicate exponents of this school were **Simone Martini** and the brothers, **Pietro** and **Ambrogio Lorenzetti**. A famous school of miniaturists was founded at Rimini. The leaders of the Florentine Trecento period (14C) were **Andrea Orcagna** and **Andrea di Bonaiuto**, known also as **Andrea da Firenze**. Their mystical and realistic style became known as **International Gothic**, which is characterised by harmonies of line and colour as well as a great refinement in the decorative elements. Several artists of the Marches, Umbria, Lombardy and Piedmont, such as **Allegretto Nuzi** and **Gentile da Fabriano**, worked in this style, as also did the Veronese, Stefano da Zevio and **Pisanello** (15C) a portraitist, animal painter and distinguished medallist *(p 231)*, as well as the Piedmontese Giacomo Jaquerio.

QUATTROCENTO (15C)

The early Renaissance was characterised by an abiding passion for antiquity and distant lands, the well-organised city-states governed by a noble or princely patron, a new vision of man's place at the centre of the universe, and a large number of artists, scholars and poets. The Medici city of Florence united all these conditions and it was an appropriate birthplace for this cultural movement, designated much later as the Renaissance.

Architecture. – Filippo Brunelleschi (1377-1446) revealed himself as a great innovator in the art of building. Drawing on antique sources he advocated a purity and elegance of line. Among his disciples were **Michelozzo** (1396-1472) **Leon Battista Alberti**, Antonio and Bernardo Rossellino, Giuliano and Benedetto da Maiano, as were Francesco di Giorgio Martini in Siena and Luciano Laurana at Urbino.

Sculpture. – In the design of the doorways of the Baptistry at Florence, **Lorenzo Ghiberti** (1378-1455) shook off the Gothic tradition, still followed by the Sienese **Jacopo della Quercia,** who like Brunelleschi was eliminated from the competition.
The most powerful sculptor of the period was undoubtedly **Donatello** (1386-1466) who, although a Florentine, worked throughout Italy. His contemporary **Luca della Robbia** (1400-82) specialised in coloured and glazed terracotta works, while Agostino di Duccio, Desiderio da Settignano and Mino da Fiesole continued in the Donatello tradition. At the end of the Quattrocento, **Verrocchio** (1435-88) showed remarkable power in the famous statue of Colleoni at Venice. The most remarkable sculptor outside Florence was the Dalmatian, **Francesco Laurana** a sculptural portraitist of the greatest sensibility.

Painting. – With **Masaccio** (1401-28), a new era opened for Italian art. He was the first to insist, in the Carmine frescoes in Florence *(p 102)*, on an illusion of perspective and the notion of space. **Paolo Uccello** (1397-1475) made clever use of foreshortening in his admirable battle scenes. At the same time the Dominican friar, **Fra Angelico** (1387-1435), who remained very attached to Gothic tradition, was attracted to the new theories of the Renaissance. His successors such as **Domenico Veneziano** and **Fra Filippo Lippi** (1406-69) developed his technique while retaining his delicacy of detail. **Benozzo Gozzoli** (1420-97) also recalls Angelico but adapts his style to the portrayal of brilliant festivities, always purely secular.

Florence – Annunciation
by Donatello

29

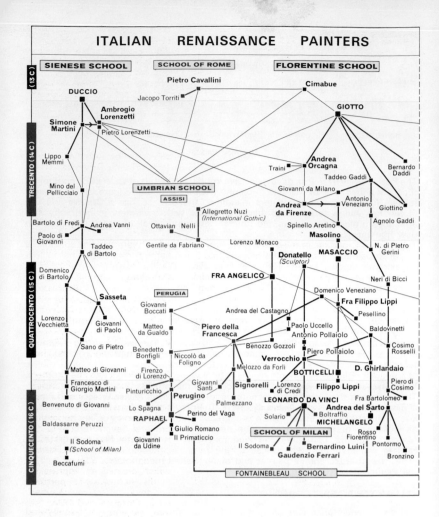

ITALIAN RENAISSANCE PAINTERS

No one has produced better than **Sandro Botticelli** (1444-1510), a pupil of Filippo Lippi, that miraculous purity of line which gives a graceful and almost unreal fragility to the figures and a deep sense of mystery to his allegorical scenes. Baldovinetti (1423-57) adopted Botticelli's manner while **Andrea del Castagno** (1423-57) emphasised modelling and monumental qualities *(p 103)*. **Domenico Ghirlandaio** (1449-94) on the other hand had a particularly good gift for narrative painting. The work of **Piero della Francesca** (c1415-92) from Sansepolcro is a supreme example of Tuscan Renaissance art displaying faultless harmony and sure draughtsmanship *(p 53)*. He influenced other artists such as Melozzo da Forlì.

At the Gonzaga court in Mantua, **Mantegna** (1431-1506) *(p 154)* painted scenes full of grandeur and rigour. In Ferrara **Cosimo Tura** with his realism inherited from northern painters created his troublingly strange but original compositions.

The first Venetian painters to emerge from the Byzantine style were the **Vivarini**. It was however the **Bellini** family *(p 223)* which gave Venetian painting its outstanding characteristic of luminosity. **Carpaccio** *(p 223)* and the elegant but somewhat precious artist, **Carlo Crivelli**, with his minutely detailed drawings and refined colours, are both chroniclers.

CINQUECENTO (16C)

The 16C saw the development of human sensibility which had already marked the previous century. Artists were attracted more and more by antiquity, mythology and the discovery of man.

The artistic centre of the Renaissance moved from Florence to Rome where the popes rivalled one another to embellish palaces and churches. The artist became more independent and acquired a certain prestige.

By the end of the century, the canons of Renaissance art were already being exported and put into practice elsewhere in Europe, notably at Fontainebleau and in the Low Countries.

Architecture. – It was in the course of this century that the style of the Florentine palace was formed. The imposing rustication and elaborate cornices were replaced by a less massive appearance with a strong classical influence.

Bramante (1444-1514) invented the "rhythmic bay" *(p 128)*. He worked at Milan then Urbino before conceiving the original central plan of St Peter's in Rome. **Vignola** (1507-73) also worked in Rome and **Palladio** (1508-80) did much in Vicenza *(qv)*. In his important works on architecture he advocated the Classicism of ancient art and was himself responsible for many churches, palaces and luxury villas in Venetia.

30

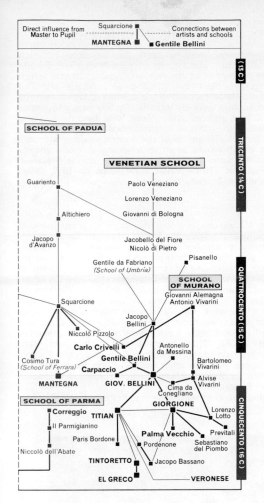

Direct influence from Master to Pupil Squarcione ■ **Connections between artists and schools**
MANTEGNA ■ ■ Gentile Bellini

(13 C)

TRECENTO (14 C)

SCHOOL OF PADUA

Guariento

Altichiero

Jacopo d'Avanzo

VENETIAN SCHOOL

Paolo Veneziano

Lorenzo Veneziano

Giovanni di Bologna

Jacobello del Fiore
Nicolò di Pietro

Pisanello

Gentile da Fabriano
(School of Umbria)

SCHOOL OF MURANO

Giovanni Alemagna
Antonio Vivarini

QUATTROCENTO (15 C)

Squarcione

Jacopo Bellini

Niccolò Pizzolo

Carlo Crivelli ■

Antonello da Messina

Cosimo Tura
(School of Ferrara)

Gentile Bellini

Carpaccio

Bartolomeo Vivarini

MANTEGNA

GIOV. BELLINI

Cima da Conegliano

Alvise Vivarini

CINQUECENTO (16 C)

SCHOOL OF PARMA

GIORGIONE

■ **Correggio**

TITIAN

Lorenzo Lotto

■ Il Parmigianino

Palma Vecchio ■

Previtali

Paris Bordone ■

Pordenone

Sebastiano del Piombo

Niccolò dell'Abate ■

TINTORETTO ■

Jacopo Bassano

EL GRECO ■

VERONESE

Sculpture. – **Michelangelo** (1475-1564) did most of his life's work in either Florence or Rome and was the most outstanding character of the century owing to his creative, idealist and even troubled genius which found its expression in such works as *David, Moses* or the groups of slaves for the tomb of Julius II.

His contemporaries paled beside him: neither the elegant and refined **Benvenuto Cellini** (1500-71), a skilled goldsmith and able sculptor known for his *Perseus* now in Florence, nor the powerful sculptor **Giambologna** or **Giovanni Bologna** (1529-1608) of Flemish origin and author of numerous group sculptures, bore comparison with the master Michelangelo.

Painting. – The 16C is an important period for painting with numerous outstanding artists producing works in the new humanist vein in several centres throughout Italy (Rome at first, then Venice, Mantua and finally Parma) and France.

The century began with exceptional but complementary masters. The fascinating **Leonardo da Vinci** (1452-1519) was the archetype of the enquiring mind of the new humanists. He is famous in painting for his *sfumato* (literally mist), a sort of impalpable, luminous veil which created an impression of distance between persons and things. After having worked in Florence and Milan he went to France at the behest of that Renaissance prince, François I. **Raphael** (1483-1520) was not only a prodigious portraitist and painter of gently drawn madonnas, but also a highly inventive decorator with an exceptional mastery of composition which was given free rein in the Stanze of the Vatican. **Michelangelo** (1475-1564), the last of the three great men, although he was really a sculptor, took on the formidable task of decorating the ceiling of the Sistine Chapel where his skill with relief and his power are triumphant. His powerful figures are the origins of Roman Mannerism.

In addition there was **Andrea del Sarto** and the portraitist **Bronzino** at Florence, **Sodoma** at Siena, **Correggio** at Parma *(qv)*, **Bernardino Luini** at Milan etc. The 16C Venetian school produced many great colourists. **Giorgione** *(p 76)* had a wonderful sense of landscape and atmosphere. **Titian** (c1490-1576), a disciple of Bellini, was as a youth influenced by Giorgione and imbued with his skill for both mythological and religious compositions. He was also a fine portraitist and was commissioned by numerous Italian princes and European sovereigns. His work represents the high point in Venetian painting. **Tintoretto** (1518-94) added a tormented violence to the luminosity of his predecessors, and ably exploited this in his dramatic religious compositions. He had a strong influence on his amiable pupil, the Cretan, Theotocopoulos, known as **El Greco**, who finally took refuge in Toledo. **Veronese** (1528-88) was first and foremost a decorator in love with luxury and sumptuous schemes who delighted in crowd scenes with grandiose architectural backgrounds. As for the very endearing **Jacopo Bassano** (1518-92), he handled rustic and nocturnal scenes with a freedom of touch and composition.

Lady with a Veil by Raphael
(Pitti Palace, Florence)

*The towns and sights described in this guide are shown in **black** on the maps.*

MANNERISM (16C-17C)

The art of the Counter-Reformation, with its continued use of Renaissance canon often in an exaggerated or mannered way, marked the transition between Renaissance and baroque. If Mannerism was widely adopted throughout Europe it was countered in Italy by the opposition of the Roman Catholic Church, which following the Council of Trent proposed the purging of religious art. The Counter-Reformation movement was characterised in the domain of architecture by the Church of Gesù in Rome, an austere work by Vignola. The numerous fountains and gardens where the natural and artificial were found side by side are also expressions of the Mannerist taste for festivities and frivolities.

The art of the period shows a certain elongation of the figures, unusual attitudes and rather violent light, factors which would seem to translate a certain anxiety and impatience in the artists of the time. The main exponents include **Beccafumi, Pontormo** (1494-1556), **Rosso Fiorentino** (1494-1540), **Parmigianino** *(p 157),* Giulio Romano, Niccolò dell'Abbate, and the Zuccaro brothers.

BAROQUE (17C-18C)

Painting. – In reaction against Mannerism, a group of Bolognese artists founded the Academy of the Eclectic (Incamminati), under the leadership of the **Carracci** family (Annibale, the most original, Lodovico and Agostino). They tried to codify beauty in large, careful but rather cold compositions which paved the way for baroque art. Their Bolognese followers, Guido, Albano and Guercino, continued in this manner with rather more vigour. However it was the work of **Caravaggio** (1573-1610) which revolutionised several centuries of Italian idealism. His intense and often cruel realism drew its inspiration from everyday life in Rome. His unusual use of contrasting light gave a dramatic visual impact to his work. He was widely imitated both in Italy and in France and was without doubt the most influential artist in 17C Europe. The characteristics of baroque art and architecture are effects of movement, inverted perspectives, *trompe-l'œil*, and scrolls. Often painting and architecture were associated, giving sumptuous interior decoration schemes such as Andrea Pozzo's work in Sant'Ignazio in Rome. Rome was the main centre of this movement but other exponents worked in Florence **(Luca Giordano)**, Venice **(Tiepolo)** and Naples (Giordano again, **Mattia Preti** and **Ribera)**.

During the 18C, Venetian painting became more serene with **Pietro Longhi, Canaletto** and **Francesco Guardi** *(p 223).*

Lecce – Fronton of the Basilica of the Holy Cross

Architecture and sculpture. – The Gesù Church built in 1568 in Rome became the prototype of baroque churches. Under the sway of the **Jesuits** architecture and sculpture gained an ornate and theatrical quality with architects such as **Carlo Maderno,** who designed the façade of St Peter's (1614) in Rome; **Borromini,** a tormented spirit, who built the elliptical Church of St Charles by the Four Fountains in Rome; and especially **Bernini** (1598-1680), the most creative of them all, who designed the colonnades of St Peter's Square, the unusual baldachin and the tombs inside the basilica as well as many sculptures and fountains.

In Piedmont baroque architecture evolved in an interesting way with Guarini and **Juvara.** This was also the case in Apulia (especially in Lecce) and in Sicily where buildings were decorated with great fantasy and ornateness under the influence of the Spanish Plataresque style.

Information in this guide is based on data provided at the time of going to press. Improved facilities and changes in the cost of living make alterations inevitable; we hope our readers will bear with us.

MODERN ART

In the late 18C and early 19C the vogue for all things Classical spread throughout Italy and all over Europe. The Italian neo-classical style is exemplified by the sculptor **Antonio Canova** (1757-1822) whose statue of Pauline Borghese, now in Rome, displays purity of line and rather cold elegance. The 19C makes a clean break with the creative richness of previous centuries.

In the field of architecture, Alessandro Antonelli (1798-1888) adopted the neo-classical idiom for the curious buildings which he designed for Milan and his native town, Novara.

The Citys rises by Boccioni (M.O.M.A., New York)

As regards painting, the **Macchiaioli** group, founded in 1855, started a revolt against academism, which was to last about twenty years. The group, who were also known as the "spotters" and were the precursors of the Impressionist school, often worked outdoors, used colour and simple lines and drew inspiration from nature. The main exponents of this movement were **Giovanni Fattori** (1825-1908), Silvestro Lega and Telemaco Signorini (1835-1901). The last named travelled widely in Britain and was known for his street scenes of Edinburgh and London. Three artists worked with the Impressionists in Paris: the society painters De Nittis and Boldoni, and Zandomenighi who benefited most from his stay in the French capital. At the end of the 19C **Segantini**, the leader of the divisionist school, ensured the transition into the 20C.

The 20C began in an explosive manner with the sensational and anti-aesthetic style of the Futurists, who under the leadership of the poet Marinetti, the movement's theorist, proclaimed their belief in the age of speed, crowds and machinery. They attempt to render the dynamism of the modern world often by fragmented forms similar to the cubist style but with a marked difference in the strong and vibrant colour combinations. The members of this avant-garde movement were: Boccioni, Balla, Severini, **Carrà** (who later joined the surrealists) and the architect Sant'Elia. **Giorgio de Chirico** created metaphysical painting, **Modigliani** outlined all his figures, while Giorgio Morandi painted still-lifes of everyday objects on a table which are conducive to meditation.

Contemporary sculptors include Arturo Martini who paved the way for dramatic simplicity and a return to archaic art; his followers were Marino Marini who adopted a less passionate but angular style and **Giacomo Manzù** who showed deeper feeling. There are many famous names in architecture: Pier Luigi Nervi, a pioneer in the use of reinforced concrete, and Gio Ponti who embraced rationalism. Finally the interior designers Carlo Scarpa and Gae Aulenti are renowned on the international scene.

LITERATURE

Birth and splendour of Italian literature. – The Italian language acquired a literary form at the same place and time as painting was breaking free from foreign influences and acquiring a character of its own. At Assisi St Francis (1182-1226) wrote his **Canticle of the Creatures** in the vernacular instead of the traditional Latin, so that the people could read the word of God. In Florence and in the other cities where he spent his exile **Dante Alighieri** (1265-1321) established the basis of a national language, the Tuscan or Florentine. As justification of his choice he invoked antiquity and the Christian religion and it was with this new tool that he wrote one of the most powerful masterpieces of Italian literature. The **Divine Comedy** (begun c1307) is the account of a lively, enquiring and impassioned visitor to *Inferno, Purgatorio* and *Paradiso*. It is also an epic account of the Christianised western world and the height of spiritual knowledge of the period.

During the 14C **Petrarch**, the precursor of humanism and the greatest Italian lyrical poet *(p 155)*, and his friend **Boccaccio**, the astonishing story-teller who seems almost modern at times *(p 77)*, continued in the tradition of Dante. Each enriched the Italian language in his own way.

Petrarch in his **Sonnets** brought a fluidity and depth of psychological interrogation, while Boccaccio in his **Decameron** added a liveliness of narration and accuracy of description.

Political and administrative organisation. – The referendum of June 1946 set up the Republic and the Constitution of 1 January 1948, a Parliamentary Republic headed by a President who holds office for seven years, with two Houses of Parliament – the Chamber of Deputies and the Senate. Members of both houses are elected by universal suffrage.

The Italian state is unusual in that it is neither unitary nor federal. Political power is shared by two autonomous tiers: the state or central government and the regional councils. The latter are also chosen by the people and enjoy some legislative, administrative and financial powers. Their authority must not exceed those prescribed by the laws passed or approved at national level. The 1948 constitution established 20 regions *(map p 3)*, although it was not enacted until 1970. Five of these (Sicily, Sardinia, Trentino-Alto Adige, Friuli-Venezia Giulia and Valle d'Aosta) have a special statute and enjoy greater administrative autonomy. The regions are subdivided into 95 provinces, which are themselves composed of districts, each headed by a *Sindaco.*

The socio-political patterns in Italy are dominated by its pronounced regionalism, which is part of its heritage from the time when Italy was composed of a multitude of independent states whose capitals were constantly at war with one another. Rome is essentially a residential city with a high percentage of civil servants, while Milan is the acknowledged economic capital, and Florence, Bologna and Padua the intellectual centres. The one-time state capitals of Turin, Genoa, Naples and Palermo are now important industrial centres. Venice retains its very own captivating character.

Economy. – Far from being hampered by its illustrious past, Italy has transformed its essentially agricultural economy into that of an industrial power which is today one of the most active in Europe and ranks sixth in the world.

In addition to the traditional crops and stock raising, Italy has specialised in rice growing (Po Plain) and the production of **silk** (Lombardy and Venetia). Lacking in raw materials such as coal and iron ore, the Italian industrial sector has been geared to manufacturing industries where cheap labour is more important than raw materials. Italy has always been an important manufacturer of **motor vehicles** and small machines such as sewing machines, typewriters and other domestic appliances. One of its more unusual industries is the making of **pasta**, the national dish, in all its forms to meet both the home market and export requirements.

The southern part of the peninsula is an exception in that it remains economically underdeveloped. The **Mezzogiorno** (impoverished south) as it is known, extends southwards from a line joining the Gulf of Gaeta to the southern edge of the Abruzzi. The economic backwardness of this area has increased ever since the unification of Italy. In 1950 a special organisation and a fund were created to develop both the agricultural (agrarian reform with the subdividing of large estates, soil improvement, land reclamation and reafforestation) and industrial (creation of gigantic complexes often badly integrated, building of dams...) sectors of this area which has a particularly small working population.

Press. – As a general rule the press is decentralised, at least as regards daily newspapers. The Rome *Repubblica,* the Turin *Stampa* and the Milan *Corriere della Sera* as well as the most important financial daily the Milan *Il Sole 24 ore* are the only papers distributed all over Italy.

The Italian love of sport means that there are three sports dailies: the Milan *La Gazzetta dello Sport* and the Turin *Tuttosport* in the north, and the Rome *Il Corriere dello Sport-Stadio* in the south. In addition the weekly *Guerin Sportivo* has a national circulation.

Fashion. – The Italians who are lively and passionate by nature show great fashion flair. Fashion shows are held at yearly intervals in Rome and Florence (Palazzo Pitti) but the fashion capital is undoubtedly Milan where every year the best ready-to-wear collection for women's fashion is awarded the Occhio d'Oro. Many great designers have salons in Milan: Armani, Versace, Gianfranco Ferré, Nicola Trussardi, Mila Schön, Laura Biagiotti, Romeo Gigli as well as the avant-garde stylists Krizia and Moschino. Valentino and the Fendi sisters have set up their operation in Rome.

Fashion-related professions and products are part of one of the most successful industrial sectors in Italy. The clothing industry is concentrated mainly in Lombardy, Venetia (Benetton and Stefanel for knitwear), Tuscany and Emilia-Romagna. Como is famous for silk wear, Prato and Biella for wool products, Florence for leather goods (Gucci) and Vicenza for jewellery.

The Italian way of life. – The lively and colourful open-air markets offer an abundance of local produce. Shops which are closed for the mid-day siesta usually remain open late in the evening, especially in the seaside resorts and the south of the country. Italian fashion wear (shoes, clothes and leather goods) and handicrafts (ceramics, glassware, wood and leather work, jewellery, embroidery, fabrics etc) are generally elegant and well designed.

Italian men like to gather on the café terraces in the evening to discuss politics or sport, while the women, children and young people go for the traditional evening stroll *(passeggiata)* and enjoy a chat and ice cream *(gelato).*

The various traditional festivals with numerous participants dressed in fine local costumes often attract large crowds *(see p. 272).*

Help us in our constant task of keeping up to date.
Send your comments and suggestions to

Michelin Tyre PLC
Tourism Department
Davy House
Lyon Road
HARROW Middlesex HA1 2DQ

FOOD AND WINE

Italy is rich in tasty products and its cooking is among the best known in the world. A traditional meal consists of an **antipasto** or hors d'œuvre (raw vegetable salads with a dressing, fine pork-butchers' meats, pickled vegetables), **primo** *(primo piatto:* first course) rice or *pasta* in its numerous forms, plain or combined with various sauces and trimmings; **secundo** (meat or fish course) often accompanied by a **contorno** (vegetable or green salad). After the cheese (**formaggio**) is served fruit (**frutta**) as well as a choice of numerous other desserts: cakes, pastries and sweets (**dolci**), ices (**gelati**) or frozen cakes (**semi-freddo**). A young wine is usually served in carafes *(sfuso)* of 1/4 *(quarto)*, half *(mezzo)* or litre *(litro)*. Ask for a wine list if you prefer better quality wines. There is a wide choice of mineral waters available. Traditionally the meal ends with a strong-black espresso coffee. The frothy **cappuccino** dusted with cocoa is also delectable.

SOME REGIONAL SPECIALITIES

Piedmont. – Cooking here is done with butter. A popular dish is **fonduta**, a melted cheese dip of milk, eggs and white truffles *(tartufi bianchi)*. *Cardi* (chards) are prepared *alla bagna cauda,* i.e. with a hot sauce containing oil or butter, anchovies, garlic and truffles. Monferrato produces the famous **Gorgonzola** cheese and delicious wines: Barolo, Barbaresco, Barbera, Grignolino, red Freisas, white **Asti**, still or sparkling *(spumante)*, with a strong flavour of grapes.

Lombardy. – Milan, where cooking is done with butter, gives its name to several dishes; *minestrone alla milanese,* a soup of green vegetables, rice and bacon; *risotto alla milanese,* rice cooked with saffron; **costoletta** *alla milanese,* a fillet of veal fried in egg and breadcrumbs with cheese; **osso buco,** a knuckle of veal with the marrow-bone; **panettone,** a large fruit cake containing raisins and candied lemon peel. Here the commonest cheese is again the excellent **Gorgonzola.** Few wines are produced, apart from those of Valtellina or the Pavia district.

Venetia. – As in the Po Plain, the people eat **polenta**, a form of semolina made from maize, sometimes accompanied by small birds, *risi e bisi* (rice and peas), and **fegato alla veneziana** (calf's liver fried with onions). The shell-fish, eels and dried cod *(baccalà)* are excellent. The best wines come from the district of Verona; **Valpolicella** and Bardolino, *rosé* or red, perfumed and slightly sparkling, and Soave, which is white and strong.

Liguria. – The chief speciality of Genoa is **lasagne al pesto**, flat leaves of *pasta* baked in the oven and seasoned with *pesto,* a sauce based on olive oil in which basil, pine-kernels, garlic and ewes' cheese have been steeped. Sea-food is famous, including **zuppa di datteri,** a shell-fish soup with which the Ligurians drink Cinqueterre or Coronata, strong, liqueur-like white wines.

Emilia-Romagna. – This is an eminently gastronomical region, whose pork-butchers' meat is the most famous in Italy: Bologna **salami** and **mortadella,** Modena *zamponi* (pigs' trotters), Parma **prosciutto** (ham). *Pasta* is varied and tasty when served *alla bolognese* – that is, with meat-gravy and tomato sauce. **Parmesan cheese** *(parmigiano),* hard and pale yellow, is strong yet delicate in flavour. Emilia produces **Lambrusco,** a fruity, sparkling red wine, and white Albano.

Tuscany. – This is where Italian cooking was born, at the court of the Medici. Florence offers its *alla fiorentina* specialities: dried cod *(baccalà)* with oil, garlic and pepper, *costata* grilled steak fillets with oil, salt and pepper, **fagioli** (beans with oil, onions and herbs); Leghorn produces **triglie** (red mullet) and **cacciucco** (fish soup) and Siena offers the **panforte,** a sugar cake containing almonds, honey and candied melon, orange or lemon. **Chianti** (both red and white) is drunk everywhere.

Umbria, Marches. – The regional dish is the **porchetta**, a whole sucking pig roasted on the spit. One of the Marches specialities is *vincigrassi*, pasta cooked in the oven with meat gravy and cream sauce. The wines are white, including the famous **Orvieto** of Umbria, the Verdicchio of the Marches and the delicious Moscato of San Marino.

Latium. – There are many Roman specialities: **fettucine** or strip macaroni, **gnocchi** alla Romana, **saltimbocca,** a fillet of veal rolled in ham, fried in butter and sprinkled with Marsala and flavoured with sage, and **abbacchio al forno** or roast lamb. Vegetables include *carciofi alla Giudia,* artichokes cooked in oil with garlic and parsley. **Pecorino,** ewes' milk cheese, and the famous white wines of Montefiascone *(see p 235)* and the **Castelli** (Frascati) will satisfy the most discerning gourmet.

Abruzzi, Molise. – Among the *pasta* note **maccheroni alla chitarra**, made by hand and cut into strips. **Latticini** (fresh mountain cheeses) are popular.

Campania. – Naples is the home of **spaghetti**, which is often prepared with shell-fish *(alle vongole). Trattorie* and *pizzerie* serve *costata alla pizzaiola,* a fillet steak with tomatoes, garlic and wild marjoram, **mozzarella** *in carrozza* (cheese savoury) and especially the **pizza,** a cheese *(mozzarella)* tart containing tomato and anchovy and flavoured with capers and wild marjoram. Wines from volcanic soil have a delicate, slightly sulphurous taste: red and white Capri, white Ischia, white **Lacryma Christi** and red Gragnano (Vesuvius wines).

Apulia, Basilicata, Calabria. – The oysters *(ostriche)* of Taranto are tasty. The most original dish is **capretto ripieno al forno,** a roast kid stuffed with herbs.

Sicily. – The island is rich in fruit (lemons, oranges, mandarins, olives, almonds), pastries and ices. The real Sicilian **cassata** is a partly-iced cream cake containing chocolate cream and candied fruits. Other specialities; **cuscusu** (couscous) and fish – tunny, sword-fish, anchovies. The best-known wine is **Marsala,** which is dark and strong, but **Malvasia** and the white wines of Etna and Lipari are also delicious.

Sardinia. – *See p 239.*

KEY

Sights

★★★ **Worth a journey**
★★ **Worth a detour**
★ **Interesting**

Sightseeing route with departure point indicated

on the road	in town

✕	⚭	Castle – Ruins	⬛	⬩	Ecclesiastical building
⟂	◎	Wayside cross or calvary – Fountain	⬛		Building with main entrance
☀	Ⱳ	Panorama – View	⬤─●		Ramparts – Tower
⟈	⚐	Lighthouse – Windmill	═══		Gateway
⌒	⌂	Cave – Nuraghe	▪		Statue or small building
☆		Fort	▨		Gardens, parks, woods
▲		Miscellaneous sights	**B**		Letter locating a sight

Other symbols

▬▬▬	Motorway (unclassified) (Autostrada)	⬓	Public building	
═══	Major through road	✚ ⬭	Hospital – Covered market	
═══	Dual carriageway	✝✝✝✝	Cemetery	
▭▭- - -	Stepped street – Footpath	▶₉	Golf course	
╞══╡	Pedestrian street	⚞	Racecourse	
ⲭ═ⲭ	Unsuitable for traffic	⚓ ⬙	Outdoor or indoor swimming pool	
→1429←	Pass – Altitude	⊤	Viewing table	
🚆 🚌	Station – Coach station	⚑	Pleasure boat harbour	
⊚	Underground station	**B**	Ferry (river and lake crossings)	
─•─•─	Tramway	⬯	Stadium	
⏖	Ferry services: Passengers and cars Passengers only	⛫	Water tower	
✈	Airport	☎	Telephone	
⊶++++++⊷	Rack-railway, funicular	✉	Main post office with poste restante (Fermo posta)	
⊶•••••⊷	Cable-car, chairlift	🛈	Tourist information centre	
		P	Car park	

MICHELIN maps and town plans are north orientated.

Main shopping streets are printed in a different colour in the list of streets.

Town plans: roads most used by traffic and those on which guide listed sights stand are fully drawn; the beginning only of lesser roads is indicated.

Local maps: only the primary and sightseeing routes are indicated.

Abbreviations

H	Town Hall (Municipio)	M	Museum (Museo)	POL.	Police station (in large towns: Questura)
J	Law Courts (Pal. di Giustizia)	P	Préfecture (Prefettura)	T	Theatre (Teatro)
				U	University (Università)

⊘ Times and charges for admission are listed at the end of the guide

38

Sights

Venice – Church of St Mary of Salvation

Michelin map ▨▨▨ folds 26 and 27 or ▨▨▨ folds 27, 28, 38 and 39.

The Abruzzi Massif, the highest of the Apennine range, is a harsh region which due to its isolation and climate has preserved its beautiful landscapes and noble traditions. Bordered to the north by the formidable limestone barrier, the Gran Sasso, the massif extends from L'Aquila to Sulmona and beyond to Alfedena and the Abruzzi National Park. The massif has a variety of landscapes composed of gorges, sheer gullies, lakes, forests, desolate high plateaus and green pastures. In recent years there has been a growth in winter sports facilities and many centres now cater for the ski enthusiasts from the capital. The massif is easily reached by motorway from Rome.

Sightseeing. – The adjoining map locates the towns and sites described in the guide and also indicates other beauty spots in small black type.

★★ GRAN SASSO

From L'Aquila to Castelli *159km – 99 miles – allow half a day*

This is the highest massif in the Abruzzi and its main peak is **Corno Grande** with an altitude of 2 914m – 9 560ft. On the northern side spines with many gullies slope away gently, while on the southern face, Gran Sasso drops abruptly to the great glacial plateaux edged by deep valleys. The massif provides contrasting aspects: to the north lush pastures and tree-covered slopes and to the south desolate and grandiose expanses.

★ **L'Aquila.** – *Description p 51.*

Beyond Paganica the road passes through the gorges and climbs to Fonte Cerreto.

★★ **Campo Imperatore** ⊙. – *Take the road from Fonte Cerreto.* It passes through splendid mountain country grazed by large flocks of sheep or hordes of wild horses. It was from here that Mussolini escaped on 12 September 1943, thanks to a daring raid by German airmen whose plane landed and took off near the hotel in which the Duce had been interned.

Return to Fonte Cerreto.

The road then skirts the lower slopes of the Gran Sasso, as it follows the long green **Vomano Valley**★★ before entering the magnificent gorges *(5km – 3 miles beyond Tintorale)* which have amazingly stratified rock walls.

On leaving Montorio, take the S491 to the right, the road to Isola del Gran Sasso.

★ **Castelli.** – This town, which stands on a wooded promontory at the foot of Monte Camicia, has been famous since the 13C for its highly colourful and richly decorated faïence (glazed pottery).

GREAT PLATEAUX

Round tour leaving from Sulmona

138km – 86 miles – allow 1 day

The Great Plateaux with their wide horizons stretch between Sulmona and Castel di Sangro, at a height of over 1 000m – 3 281ft. Cattle graze these expanses and their herdsmen make egg-shaped soft cheese *(scamorza)* which can be purchased at Rivisondoli.

★ **Sulmona.** – *Description p 204.*

Beyond, the road runs sometimes along a corniche, or in a tunnel or over a viaduct, and leads to the largest of the Great Plateaux, **Piano dei Cinquemiglia**, so-called because it was five Roman miles long (8km – 5 miles).

Near the old village of Rivisondoli, take the S84 to the left.

★ **Pescocostanzo.** – This attractive village with its paved streets and old houses is a flourishing craft centre specialising in wrought-iron work, copper, gold and wood work as well as lace-making. The **Collegiate Church of Santa Maria del Colle** although built to a Renaissance plan has several Romanesque features and baroque additions (organ loft, ceiling and grille of the north aisle).

Castel di Sangro. – The town dominates a mountain-rimmed basin. The cathedral, built to the plan of a Greek cross, is surrounded by a Renaissance portico.

★ **Alfedena.** – The houses of this small town are grouped about the ruined castle. Paths lead northwards to the ancient city of Alfedena with its cyclopean walls and necropolis.

★ **Scanno.** – From its high mountain site, Scanno overlooks the lovely **Lake Scanno**★ (Lago di Scanno) formed by a landslide which blocked the bed of the river Sagittario. This holiday resort is attractive with its steep and narrow streets bordered by houses and churches. Women still wear the dignified black local dress which is probably of Oriental origin. In the main street stands a curious 14C fountain decorated in the Byzantine manner.

Between Lake Scanno and Anversa degli Abruzzi, over a distance of 10km – 6 miles the Sagittario River has hollowed from the grey rock a series of **gorges**★★ (Gole del Sagittario) of impressive depth and wildness, which the road follows with many twists and turns.

Anversa degli Abruzzi. – The village church has a doorway (dated 1540) with a carved tympanum representing the Entombment and other sculptures of masks and Biblical personages.

★★★ ABRUZZI NATIONAL PARK (PARCO NAZIONALE D'ABRUZZO)

A nature reserve was founded in 1923, in the very heart of the massif, to protect the fauna, flora and outstanding landscapes of the region. It extends over an area of approximately 40 000ha – 155sq miles which is mostly forest with beech and maple predominating. The fauna includes the royal eagle, the Apennine wolf, the brown bear, the Abruzzi chamois and the wild cat and more recently roe deer and red deer.

Access and sightseeing ⊙. – Start either from Gioia Vecchio in the north, Forca d'Acero in the west or Villetta Barrea and Barrea in the east.

Within the park's limits there are four different protection zones according to the importance of the site to be protected and the type of activity permitted in each zone. The visitor is however free to visit a large part of the park using the well-surfaced roads or tracks. Facilities include observation posts, camping and picnic sites as well as visitors' centres. It is only possible to study either the fauna or the flora at close range on foot or on horseback in some cases. It is advisable to keep to the signposted footpaths and go along with an official guide if possible.

Pescasseroli. – This is the main centre in the valley and is the home of the park's administrative services. The village lies in a basin whose outer sides are covered with beech and pine forests. Tourism and timber-related activities are the village's main industries. Pescasseroli is the birthplace of the philosopher and politician, Benedetto Croce (1866-1952).

ADDITIONAL SIGHTS

★ **Bominaco.** – Two Romanesque churches stand about 500m – 1 640ft above the hamlet of Bominaco, and are all that remain of a Benedictine **monastery** which was destroyed in the 15C. The **Church of San Pellegrino** ⊙ is a 13C oratory with **frescoes**★ also of the 13C, which portray in a rather maladroit but detailed way the Life of Christ and a giant St Christopher. The **Church of Santa Maria**★ (11C and 12C) is more characteristic of the local style. This has an elegant chevet and on one of the outer walls an opening flanked by four projecting lions. The bare but well-lit interior has a beautiful 12C cubic **ambo**★ resting on four columns with palm leaf capitals adorned with foliated scrolls and finials.

Corfinio ⊙. – Away from the village stands the **Basilica of San Pelino** or **Basilica Valvense** in the Romanesque style, with the adjoining 12C Chapel of Sant'Alessandro. Walk round the church to admire the **east end**★. Inside there is a fine 12C pulpit.

Popoli. – The main square, Piazza Grande, of this busy market town, is overlooked by the Church of San Francesco, which has a Gothic façade with a baroque upper part. The **Taverna Ducale**★, near the Piazza Grande, is an elegant Gothic edifice formerly used for collecting tithes payable to the prince.

Alba Fucens ⊙. – These are the ruins of a Roman colony founded in 303BC. Amidst the ruins, mostly cyclopean in nature, are the remains of a basilica, the forum, baths, the covered market as well as of paved streets, wells and latrines.

★ ALATRI Latium

Michelin map ▓▓▓ fold 26 or ▓▓▓ fold 37

This important city, which was built in the 6C BC, retains a great part of its cyclopean walls (4C BC). The **acropolis★** can be reached on foot from the grandiose Porta di Cività. It is laid out on a trapezoidal plan and is one of the best preserved examples in Italy. It affords a very fine **view★★** of Alatri and the Frosinone Valley. The town has a maze of steep flights of stairways, and alleyways lined with Gothic houses. The **Palazzo Gottifredi** *(Largo Luigi di Persiis)* is 13C and the **Church of St Mary Major★** (Santa Maria Maggiore) in the transitional Romanesque-Gothic style has a façade with three porches. Inside there is interesting 12C-15C **carved woodwork★**. On the by-pass is the 13C **Church of St Sylvester** (San Silvestro) which is built using the dry-stone technique and contains frescoes dating from the 13C to the 16C.

ALBA Piedmont

Michelin map ▓▓▓ fold 12 or ▓▓▓ fold 23

Alba was the ancient Roman city of Alba Pompeia, which gave Rome the Emperor Pertinax (AD 126-193). It is a gourmets' resort made famous by its delicious **tartufi bianchi** or white truffles (annual truffle fair in autumn) and its wines (Barolo, Barbaresco and Barbera). The town boasts several **towers of nobility,** churches and medieval houses. Inside the Gothic Cathedral **(Duomo San Lorenzo)** are Renaissance stalls inlaid with intarsia work of very delicate craftsmanship.

To the south of Alba is the **Langhe** region, an area of limestone hills and clay soils planted with vineyards. Take the Alba-Ceva road, which follows the crests and affords **views★** of both slopes. The road passes through picturesque villages.

★ ALTILIA SAEPINUM Molise

Michelin map ▓▓▓ fold 27 or ▓▓▓ fold 40 – 25km – 16 miles to the south of Campobasso

The ruins of Roman **Saepinum** spread over 12ha – 30 acres of the fertile plain which lies at the foot of the Matese Mountains. The present-day village of Altilia, built with stone quarried from the ruins, stands nearby. This Samnite settlement was occupied by the Romans who made it a municipium and then fortified it in the 1C BC. Saepinum was at the height of its glory at the end of the 5C BC. The Saracens destroyed it in the 9C.

TOUR ⊙ *time: 1 1/2 hours (start in the southwest)*

Terravecchia Gate (Porta di Terravecchia). – This ruined gateway commands the southern end of the north-south Cardo Maximus, one of the city's two main streets.

★ **Basilica, forum and temple (Basilica, foro e tempio).** – These are to be found at the junction of the Cardo Maximus and the Decumanus Maximus, a paved street crossing the city from east to west. To the left are the 20 Ionic columns of the **basilica's** peristyle. To the right are the forum, a vast rectangular paved area and the Decumanus Maximus *(turn right into this street)* which is bordered by the ruined senate house *(curia)*; a temple dedicated to Jupiter, Juno and Minerva and a semicircular recess belonging to the "house of the oil presses" with four brick oil containers still visible. Beyond lie the remains of a fountain carrying the sculpture of a hippogriff and a Samnite house with an impluvium.

Benevento Gate (Porta di Benevento). – At the eastern end of the Decumanus Maximus. The outer face of this arch is decorated with a helmet-clad head. The adjoining **museum** ⊙ gives an account of the excavations and has displays on the first floor of sculpture, steles and fragments of mosaics.

Mausoleum of Ennius Marsus Volmarso (Mausoleo di Ennius Marsus Volmarso). – This beautiful crenellated semicircular building stands beyond the Benevento Gate. The square plinth is guarded by two very badly damaged lions.

Return to the main crossroads and continue up the Decumanus Maximus.

This is a residential area with the remains of shops on the right.

★ **Boiano Gate (Porta di Boiano).** – This gate with its semicircular main arch is flanked by two round towers. It was dedicated to the future Emperor Tiberius and his brother Drusus. From the top there is a good view of the western part of the fortifications and the ruins of the central part of the city.

Fortified ramparts. – The wall built of finely-worked stones in a diamond pattern, with its total length of 1 250m – 1 367yds, describes a rectangle. It is punctuated by 25 round towers, now reduced to the height of the wall, and four fortified gateways. The western part is the best-preserved section.

Mausoleum of Numisius Ligus (Mausoleo di Numisius Ligus). – *Once beyond the wall, turn right.* This tomb, crowned by four acroteria, has an elegant simplicity.

★ **Theatre (Teatro).** – The small, semicircular theatre standing against the wall has kept its monumental entrance of white stone.

Museum (Museo) ⊙. – *In front of the theatre.* On the ground floor, interesting sculptures decorate the sarcophagi and the sepulchral monuments *(cippi)*. Upstairs the excavation work is illustrated by photographs and documents.

From the far side of the theatre return to the Cardo Maximus and turn left.

Tammaro Gate (Porta Tammaro). – This simple archway leads to the village of Sepino.

Michelin map ▨▨▨ fold 27 or ▨▨▨ fold 13

Amalfi, which has given its name to the beautiful Amalfi Coast *(see below)*, is a rather Spanish-looking little town of tall white houses built on slopes facing the sea in a wonderful **setting**★★★. Amalfi enjoys a very mild climate, making it a popular holiday resort.

The Maritime Republic of Amalfi. – This is Italy's oldest republic. Founded in 840, by the end of the 9C it was under the rule of a doge. It enjoyed its greatest prosperity in the 11C, when shipping in the Mediterranean was regulated by the *Tavole Amalfitane* (Amalfi Navigation Tables), the oldest maritime code in the world. Amalfi traded regularly with the Orient, in particular Constantinople, and the Republic had an arsenal where many large galleys were built. This fleet of galleys played a large part in carrying Crusaders to the Levant.

SIGHTS

★ **St Andrew's Cathedral (Duomo Sant'Andrea).** – Founded in the 9C, enlarged in the 10C and 13C and subsequently altered numerous times, the cathedral is a good example of the Oriental splendour favoured by maritime cities. The crypt enshrines those relics of St Andrew which had been removed from Patras to Constantinople, from whence they were transferred in 1206 to Amalfi.
The façade, rebuilt in the 19C on the original model, has a great deal of character: it stands at the top of a stairway and its varied geometrical designs in multicoloured stone are striking. The campanile, on the left, is all that remains of the original church. A beautiful 11C bronze **door**★, cast in Constantinople, opens onto the vast atrium which precedes the church.
The interior of the cathedral is baroque. Two antique columns, two candelabra decorated with mosaics and two 12C ambos are of special interest.
The atrium leads into the **Cloisters of Paradise**★★ (Chiostro del Paradiso) ⊘ which date from 1268. The architecture combines Romanesque austerity and Arab fantasy. The arcades shelter some fine sarcophagi.

★ **Via Genova and Via Capuano.** – These two streets starting from the Piazza del Duomo are the main shopping arteries. With a succession of varied shop fronts, balconies and flower-bedecked niches they are most attractive. Many alleys, stairways and vaulted passageways lead off the main streets into little squares with fountains.

Piazza Flavio Gioia. – This street takes its name from the native of Amalfi who is said to have perfected the mariner's compass. The workshops of the **arsenal** stood to the left of the gateway, Porta della Marina.

★★★ **AMALFI COAST (COSTIERA AMALFITANA)** *79km – 49 miles – allow 1 day*

The corniche road follows the indentations of the rocky coast between Sorrento and Salerno which is Italy's finest coastline, namely the Amalfi Coast. For over 30km – 19 miles its innumerable bends afford constantly changing views of enchanting landscapes, wild, fantastically-shaped rocks plunging vertically into a crystal-clear sea, deep gorges spanned by dizzy bridges and Saracen towers perched on jagged rock stacks. The Amalfi Coast, with its wild and rugged landscape, is formed by the jagged fringe of the Lattari Mountains, a deeply-eroded limestone range. Contrasting with these scenes of sublime awe are the more charming views of fishing villages and the luxuriant vegetation, a mixture of orange trees, citron trees, olives, almonds, vines and all the Mediterranean flora. The region is very popular with foreigners and artists and the local cuisine is an important attraction. Seafood is the keyword and fish, crustaceans and shellfish are served regularly. The local cheese *mozzarella (p 37)* should be accompanied by the red Gragnano or white Ravello and Positano wines.

Sightseeing. – The map overleaf locates the towns and sites described in the guide, and also indicates other beauty spots in small black type.

The Amalfi Coast

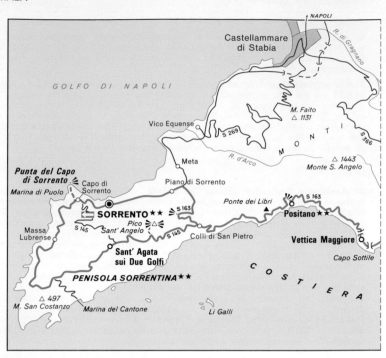

★★ **Sorrento and the Sorrento Peninsula.** – *Description p 203.*

★★ **Positano.** – This fishermen's village is one of the busiest resorts on the coast. The small white cubic houses with a strong Moorish influence are only just visible as they lie scattered on the slopes amid the greenery of their gardens.

Vettica Maggiore. – Its houses are scattered over the slopes. From the esplanade there is a fine **view**★★ of the coast and sea.

★★ **Furore Valley** (Vallone di Furore). – The Furore Valley, between two road tunnels, is the most impressive section of the coast owing to the dark depths of its steep, rocky walls and, in stormy weather, the thunder of wild, rough seas. A fishermen's village has, nevertheless, been built where a small torrent gushes into the sea. The houses clinging to the slopes and vividly-coloured boats drawn up on the shore are an unexpected feature in this bleak landscape.

Those who wish to discover the spot on foot should take the path that goes along one side of the gorge.

★★ **Emerald Cave** (Grotta dello Smeraldo) ⊘. – This marine cave at the end of a rocky creek washed by the sea is best visited by boat. The exceptionally clear water is illuminated indirectly by rays of light which give it a beautiful emerald colour. The bottom looks quite near, though the water is 10m – 33ft deep, but it was not always covered by the sea. Fine stalactites add to the interest of the trip. The cave became submerged as a result of variations in ground level under the influence of the volcanoes which affect the whole region.

★ **Atrani.** – This pleasant fishermen's village at the mouth of the Dragon Valley (Valle del Dragone) has two old churches: Santa Maria Maddalena and San Salvatore. The latter was founded in the 10C and has a fine bronze door which strongly resembles the one in Amalfi Cathedral. An excellent winding road leads to Ravello.

★★★ **Ravello.** – *Description p 175.*

★ **Cape Orso** (Capo d'Orso). – The cape, consisting of oddly-formed rocks, affords an interesting view of Maiori Bay.

Vietri sul Mare. – At the eastern end of this stretch of coastline, the houses of Vietri sul Mare, as elsewhere, are terraced up the slope. The town is known for its ceramic ware. It affords magnificent **views**★★ of the Amalfi Coast.

★ **Salerno.** – *Description p 195.*

To plan a special itinerary

– consult the map on pp 4-7 which shows the main towns, individual sights and recommended routes described in the guide;
– read the descriptions of the above which are described in the middle section of the guide in alphabetical order under their own name or are incorporated in the excursions radiating from a particular town or tourist centre;
– use the appropriate Michelin Maps which show places of interest, scenic routes, viewpoints and natural features...

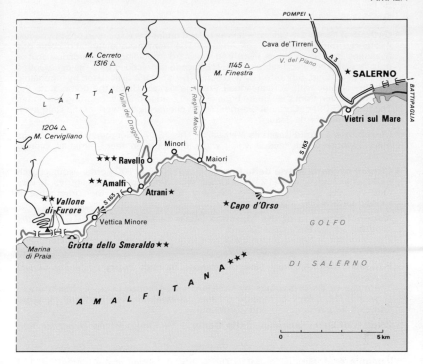

A number of Touring Programmes is given on pp 8-11.
Plan a trip with the help of the Principal Sights Map on pp 4-7.

★ ANAGNI Latium   Pop 19 388

Michelin map 988 fold 26 or 430 fold 37 – 65km – 40 miles southeast of Rome

Anagni is a small medieval town, built on a rocky spur, overlooking the Sacco Valley. This was the birthplace of several popes, including Boniface VIII who excommunicated Philip the Fair. Dante consigned Boniface to Hell for misusing his authority.

★★ **Cathedral (Cattedrale).** – The town's most important building stands on the site of the former acropolis. This Romanesque edifice was built in the 11C and 12C and remodelled in the 13C with Gothic additions. Go round the outside to admire the three Romanesque apses with Lombard mouldings and arcades, the 14C statue of Boniface VIII over the loggia on the north side and the detached massive Romanesque campanile. The interior contains three aisles; the 13C **paving★** was the work of the Cosmati *(qv)*. The high altar is surmounted by a Romanesque ciborium or canopy. The **paschal candelabrum** with a spiral column is adorned with multicoloured incrustations and rests on two sphinxes. The work like the nearby **episcopal throne** is by Pietro Vassaleto and has strong similarities with the work of the Cosmati. The **crypt★★★** ⊙ with its beautiful pavement by the Cosmati also has magnificent 13C **frescoes** depicting the story of the Old Testament, scenes from the lives of the saints and men of science such as Galen and Hippocrates. The **treasury** contains some fine liturgical items, notably Boniface VIII's cope of embroidered red silk.

★ **Medieval Quarter.** – This quarter consists almost entirely of 13C buildings and is particularly evocative. The façade of **Boniface VIII's Palace** has two pierced galleries one above the other. One has wide round-headed arches while the other consists of attractive twinned windows with small columns. In the Piazza Cavour is the 12C-13C **Palazzo Comunale** with a great **vault★** at ground level. The rear façade is in the Cistercian style.

★ ANCONA Marches   Pop 104 255

Michelin map 988 fold 16 or 429 fold 37
Town plan in the current Michelin Red Guide Italia

Ancona, the chief town in the Marches, an Adriatic region of Italy, is built in the form of an amphitheatre on the slopes of a rocky promontory, forming an acute angle from which the name of the town is derived (Greek *ankon* – elbow). Ancona was founded in the 4C BC and became an independent maritime republic in the Middle Ages. It is today a busy port and the main point of embarkation for Yugoslavia and Greece. The town specialises in the production of accordions, electronic organs and guitars.

SIGHTS

★ **Cathedral (Duomo San Ciriaco).** – It was placed under the invocation of St Cyriacus, 4C martyr and patron saint of Ancona. The Romanesque building combines Byzantine (the Greek cross plan) and Lombard (mouldings and arcades on the outside walls) architectural features. The façade is preceded by a majestic Gothic **porch** in pink stone, supported by two lions. The interior is articulated by monolithic marble columns with Romanesque-Byzantine **capitals**. Under the dome, note the clever transition from the square base to the 12-sided drum supporting the dome. The tomb (1509) of Cardinal Giannelli in the chancel is the work of the Dalmatian sculptor Giovanni da Traù.

★ **Merchants' Loggia (Loggia dei Mercanti).** – This 15C hall for merchants' meetings has a Venetian Gothic façade which was the work of another Dalmatian, Giorgio Orsini.

★ **Church of Santa Maria della Piazza** ⊘. – This small 10C Romanesque church has a charming façade (1210) adorned with amusing popular figures. It was built over the site of two earlier (5C and 6C) **churches** and their fragments of mosaic pavements.

National Museum of the Marches (Museo Nazionale delle Marche) ⊘. – *At the southern end of Piazza del Senato.*
The museum, installed in the Palazzo Ferretti, has interesting prehistoric and archaeological collections on view.

Podesti Public Gallery (Galleria Comunale Francesco Podesti) ⊘. – *Via Ciriaco Pizzecolli.*
The museum displays works by Crivelli, Titian, Lorenzo Lotto, C. Maratta and Guercino. The gallery of modern art has canvases by Luigi Bartolini, Massimo Campigli, Bruno Cassinari and Tamburini.

Church of San Francesco delle Scale. – *Via Ciriaco Pizzecolli, not far from the Podesti Public Gallery.*
This 15C church has a splendid Venetian Gothic doorway by Giorgio Orsini.

Trajan's Arch (Arco di Traiano). – The arch was erected at the northern end of Lungomare Vanvitelli in honour of the Emperor Trajan who built the port.

EXCURSIONS

★ **Portonovo.** – *12km – 8 miles to the southeast.*
Portonovo lies in the picturesque setting formed by the rocky coastline of the **Conero Massif.** A private path leads through woodland to the charming 11C **Church of Santa Maria★** ⊘, built on an almost square plan inspired by Norman churches.

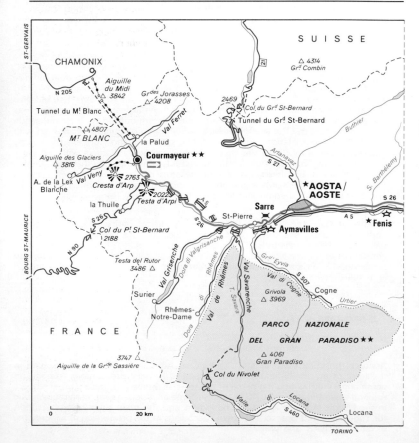

Jesi. – *32km – 20 miles to the southwest.*
Jesi with all its aspect of a medieval town, has a **picture gallery★** ⊘ with an important collection of works by Lorenzo Lotto, a Venetian artist of the early 16C, who was influenced by German art. **Palazzo della Signoria★** is an elegant Renaissance structure built by Francesco di Giorgio Martini, a pupil of Brunelleschi.

★ # ANZIO Latium   Pop 31 403

Michelin map 988 fold 26 or 430 fold 36

Anzio backs against a promontory facing out to sea and forms with **Nuttuno** a pleasant modern seaside resort. It has a popular yachting harbour.
Anzio is the Antium of antiquity, a Volscian city where Coriolanus took refuge, having abandoned his original intention of engaging in a fratricidal struggle with Rome. Antium was also the birthplace of Nero, in whose villa were found the statues of the Apollo Belvedere, the Fanciulla (young girl) of Anzio and the Borghese Gladiator, now respectively in the Vatican, the National Roman Museum in Rome and the Louvre in Paris.
The name of Anzio is also remembered for the Anglo-American landing of 22 January 1944, which, after a long struggle, ended in the taking of Rome on 4 June 1944. Several military cemeteries, monuments, memorials and museums recall those who gave their lives during this operation.

EXCURSION

★ **Island of Ponza.** – *Access: see the current Michelin Red Guide Italia.*
This volcanic island, lying beyond the Gulf of Gaeta, has a verdurous ridge and white or blue-grey cliffs, which either are bordered by narrow beaches or drop abruptly into the sea. At the southeast end of the island is the village of **Ponza★** with its serried ranks of cubic and gaily-painted houses in a semicircle around a small harbour. The latter is busy with fishing boats, coasting vessels, pleasure craft and the ferries which ply back and forth to the mainland. The island is popular with underwater fishermen.

★ # AOSTA Valle d'Aosta   Pop 36 716

Michelin map 988 fold 2, 219 fold 2 or 428 fold 12
Town plans in the current Michelin Red Guide Italia

Aosta stands in the valley of the same name and is the capital of the region. It has retained the geometric plan of a military camp *(castrum)* and some interesting monuments from the Roman period. Aosta, an active religious

centre in the Middle Ages, was the birthplace of the theologian St Anselm, who became Archbishop of Canterbury where he died in 1109. Today it is an active industrial town and, since the opening of the Mont Blanc Tunnel in 1965, an important tourist centre, at the junction of the transalpine routes to France and Switzerland via the St Bernard Tunnel.

★ **Roman buildings.** – These are grouped in the centre of Aosta and include the **Pretoria Gateway**, the majestic **Arch of Augustus** (Arco di Augusto), both dating from the 1C BC, the **Roman bridge**, the **theatre** and the ruins of the **amphitheatre**.

Collegiate Church of St Orso (Collegiata di Sant'Orso) ⊘. – The church has some lovely carved 15C **stalls** and a baroque rood screen. Beside the 11C **crypt** a doorway opens onto charming little Romanesque **cloisters★** with historiated **capitals★★** illustrating Biblical and secular scenes. The **Priory of St Orso** (Priorato di Sant'Orso) is a Renaissance-style building with elegant **windows★**.

Cathedral (Cattedrale) ⊘. – The cathedral was built in the 12C and has been remodelled several times; it now has a neo-classical façade (1848). The chancel has 12C mosaic paving, 15C Gothic stalls and the 14C tomb of Thomas II of Savoy. The sacristy contains a rich **treasure** ⊘. The cloisters are 15C.

★★ VALLE D'AOSTA

The Valle d'Aosta comprising the Dora Baltea and adjacent valleys is surrounded by high peaks of both the French and Swiss Alps: Mont Blanc, the Matterhorn (Cervino), Monte Rosa, Grand Combin, Dent d'Hérens, Gran Paradiso and Grande Sassière. With such a marvellous situation there are some splendid **viewpoints★★★**. Its secluded valleys, numerous castles, villages with balconied and stone-roofed houses, a traditional way of life, the numerous possibilities of excursions by cable-car, motor-car or on foot, scenic routes leading up to glaciers, all go to make the Valle d'Aosta a captivating place to discover.

The inhabitants of the high valleys are deeply religious and remain strongly attached to their customs and freedom as well as to the Provençal language. Since 1948 the Valle d'Aosta has been, for administrative purposes, an autonomous district. Living in houses roofed with flat stone slabs *(lauzes)*, the people raise cattle and prepare a cheese called *fontina* which is often used for a cheese fondue. During the long winter evenings many still carve wood as a pastime.

Sightseeing. – The map on pages 46-47 locates the towns and sites described in the guide, and also indicates other beauty spots in small black type.

★★ **Gran Paradiso National Park (Parco Nazionale del Gran Paradiso)** ⊙. – This park covering an area of almost 70 000ha – 270sq miles includes an area previously preserved as a royal hunting ground. It can be reached by the Rhêmes, Savarenche, Cogne and Locana valleys or the Nivolet Pass road. The park is rich in wildlife and is important as a reserve for endangered species, such as the ibex, and some of the rarest specimens of Alpine flora.

FROM COURMAYEUR TO IVREA
162km – 101 miles – allow 1 day

★★ **Courmayeur.** – *Town plans in the current Michelin Red Guide Italia.* This well-known mountaineering and winter sports resort is a good excursion centre. Take a cable-car to the Cresta d'Arp and to cross the Mont Blanc Massif and make a short detour into France *(for the area beyond La Palud see the Michelin Green Guide Alpes du Nord, in French only)*. By car explore one of the following valleys: Veny, Ferret or Testa d'Arpi and the road to the little St Bernard Pass, one of the most frequented transalpine routes which was used by the Romans in ancient times.

The itinerary follows the Dora Baltea Valley. Once through St-Pierre and past the road to the right going up the Cogne valley, there stands on the left **Sarre Castle**, the former summer residence of the Counts of Savoy. Further on, to the right, there is the 14C **Aymavilles Fortress**, impressively quartered with great round crenellated towers.

★ **Aosta.** – *Description p 47.*

★ **Fenis Castle** ⊙. – This imposing fortress contains fine carved furniture in the local Valle d'Aosta style. The inner courtyard has remarkable frescoes portraying the Golden Legend.

★★ **Breuil-Cervinia** ⊙. – This winter sports resort is admirably situated at 2 050m – 6 822ft. Cable-cars climb up to the Rosa Plateau (Plan Rosa) and the Furggen Pass at 3 491m – 11 453ft.

★ **St-Vincent.** – The Casino de la Vallée in its fine park is very popular.

The road passes Montjovet Castle and then the 14C **Verrès Castle** which curiously enough has no keep or corner towers.

★ **Issogne Castle** ⊙. – The castle was built at the end of the 15C by Georges de Challant. It has a fine courtyard with a fountain surmounted by the wrought-iron figure of a grenadier. The arcaded gallery is painted with 15C frescoes and inside the furniture is typical of the Valdotain area.

★ **Bard Fortress.** – The colossal fortress, dismantled on the orders of Napoleon in 1800 and rebuilt during the 19C, commands the upper Dora Baltea Valley.

Pont St-Martin. – This village is named after the Roman bridge which was guarded by a chapel dedicated to St John Nepomucene.

Ivrea. – This busy industrial town stands at the mouth of the Valle d'Aosta. To the east of Ivrea is the largest moraine in Europe, the Serra d'Ivrea.

*Some hotels have their own gardens, tennis courts,
swimming pool, beach facilities;
consult the current **Michelin Red Guide Italia.***

★ APULIA

Michelin map ▨▨▨ folds 28, 29 and 30

This region takes its name from the ancient Roman province of Apulia and extends from the spur to the heel of the "boot" along the Adriatic coast to the south. With the exception of the Gargano Promontory and the limestone Murge Hills which rise behind Bari, it is a flat plain planted with cereals, olive trees, vines or in pasture.

Away from the main tourist haunts, Apulia offers the visitor the rather severe beauty of its scenery, quiet beaches and some marvellous architectural gems, both religious and military.

HISTORICAL NOTES

As early as the late 8C BC Greeks from Laconia and Sparta founded the towns of Gallipoli, Otranto and especially Taranto on the Apulian coast. In the 5C and 4C BC Taranto was the most prosperous town in Magna Graecia. The local tribe, the Lapyges, tenaciously resisted Greek colonisation; in the 3C BC the Greek cities and the Italiots both came under Roman domination.

Taranto declined as Brindisi, a trading-post facing the eastern part of the Mediterranean, flourished. The latter was linked to Rome when Trajan prolonged the Appian Way. The Roman colonisation greatly benefited this area with improved communications and political organisation. Christianity was first introduced to the area in the 3C and was strengthened in the 5C with the appearances of the Archangel Michael at Monte Sant'Angelo *(qv)*.

The area was occupied successively by the Byzantines, Lombards and Arabs before Apulia sought help in the 11C from the Normans who then dominated the entire area. Apulia greatly increased its trade and its architectural heritage during both the early Crusades, most of which embarked from the Apulian ports, and the reign of Roger II of Sicily (1095-1154).

It was under the Emperor Frederick II of Hohenstaufen, an unusual, authoritarian and cruel character, an atheist but a cultured and highly intelligent person, that the region knew a period of splendour in the first half of the 13C. The king was captivated by the country and chose to reside here. This favoured trading, the unification of the country and the establishment of an efficient administration. His son Manfred continued his work but had to submit to Charles of Anjou in 1266. The French lost interest in the region and it began to lose its vitality and prestige. Apulia then passed to the Aragon dynasty who by isolating the region greatly contributed to its decline.

After a period of Austrian domination, the Bourbons of Naples improved to some small extent the misery and stagnation to which the country had been reduced by the Spanish. The brief Napoleonic period followed a similar policy. In 1860 Apulia was united with the rest of unified Italy.

During the 20C Apulia has progressively emerged from the difficult position of inferiority which was prevalent throughout the rest of the Italian south or Mezzogiorno. The region has achieved a certain independence and vigour and now claims two thriving industrial towns, Taranto and Lecce, a Trade Fair in Bari and several newly-founded universities.

TOWNS AND SIGHTS

★★★ **Castellana Caves (Grotte di Castellana)** ⊙. *– 40km – 25 miles to the southeast of Bari, at Castellana-Grotte.*
This network of caves was created by the underground rivers which filter down through the limestones of the Murge Hills. The vast chamber, now void of water, was discovered in 1938 and has an infinite variety of magnificent concretions: draperies, richly-coloured stalactites and stalagmites. The **White Cave,** 70m – 230ft underground, glistens with calcite crystals.

★★★ **Gargano Promontory.** *–ˌDescription p 105.*

★★★ **Trulli Region and Alberobello.** *– Description p 214.*

★★ **Castel del Monte** ⊙. *– 29km – 18 miles southeast of Barletta.*
The Emperor Frederick II of Hohenstaufen built this powerful castle *c*1240. It stands, proud and solitary, on the summit of one of the Murge Hills. With its octagonal plan the Castel del Monte is the sole exception in a series of 200 quadrilateral fortresses built by this sovereign on his return from the Crusades.

Apulia – Trulli in Alberobello

The octagonal plan of this fortress, built in a pale-coloured stone, is strengthened at each of its angles by a 24m – 79ft tall octagonal tower. The overall plan combines balance, logic and strict planning with delicate decoration.

The superb Gothic gateway takes the form of an ancient triumphal arch and opens into the inner courtyard. Arranged around this at ground-floor level are eight vast trapezoidal chambers with pointed vaulting. Above, the eight identical rooms are lit by delicately ornamented windows. The arrangement of the water conduits is quite ingenious: water runs from the rooftops into the cisterns of the towers and is then piped into the different rooms.

★ **Gallipoli.** – The old town with its attractive small port is set on an island and linked to the modern town by a bridge. Note the **Hellenistic fountain** *(to the left of the bridge)* with a baroque pediment, the Angevin castle, the cathedral with a baroque façade which recalls Lecce and, nearby, the baroque Church of Santa Teresa. The **interior★** of the **church (la Purissima)** is sumptuously decorated.

★★ **Lecce.** – *Description p 119.*

Locorotondo. – *36km – 22 miles north of Taranto.*
This town takes its name from the layout of its alleyways which wind in concentric circles *(loco rotondo:* round place) around the hill on which it is set. The road from Martina Franca offers an astonishing **view★** of a multitude of white houses with tall pointed gables.

The road from Martina Franca to Locorotondo follows the **Itria Valley★★**, a vast and fertile plain planted with vines and olive trees and dotted with *trulli (qv),* those peculiar beehive-shaped houses.

★ **Martina Franca.** – This white city rises on a hilltop in the Murge Hills. The architecture of the old town, girdled by its ramparts, is an attractive combination of the baroque and rococo styles. The pleasant **Piazza Roma** is bordered by the former ducal palace (1668). The **Collegiate Church of San Martino** with its lovely façade embellished with high reliefs is the principal monument in Piazza Plebiscito. Walk down the **Via Cavour★** which is lined by numerous baroque palaces.

★ **Monte Sant'Angelo.** – *Description p 137.*

★ **Ostuni.** – *35km – 22 miles west of Brindisi.*
This large market town now spreads over several hillsides. At the centre of the old town with its white alleyways and ramparts stands the late-15C **cathedral** built in the Gothic style. The **façade★** is crowned by an unusual curved gable which is a precursor of the baroque school.

★ **Taranto.** – *Description p 204.*

★ **Tremiti Islands.** – *Description p 209.*

Altamura. – This large market town in the Murge Hills also has its old quarter on a hilltop. The 13C **cathedral** in the transitional Romanesque-Gothic style forms the focal point at the upper end of the main street. The façade is crowned with two bulbous bell towers, 16C additions, and pierced by a delicately decorated 13C **rose window★** and a richly sculptured 14C-15C **doorway★**.

Bari. – *Description p 57.*

Barletta. – *Description p 58.*

Bitonto. – *17km – 11 miles to the southwest of Bari.*
Set amidst a sea of olive groves this small town has a fine **cathedral★** which strongly resembles those in Trani and Bari. The three-part façade is enlivened by large, richly sculptured openings. On the south side an elegant gallery with small columns surmounts the ground-floor arcade. Inside, columns with fine capitals support a gallery with triple openings. The fine pulpit dates from 1229.

Brindisi. – *Description p 69.*

Canosa di Puglia. – *23km – 14 miles southwest of Barletta.*
The inhabitants of this Greek, then Roman, city were known for their ceramic vases *(askoi).* The 11C Romanesque **cathedral** which shows a certain Byzantine influence, was remodelled in the 17C following an earthquake. The façade is 19C. Inside note the 11C episcopal throne and the **tomb★** of Bohemond, Prince of Antioch (d 1111), the son of Robert Guiscard (1015-85), a Norman adventurer who campaigned in southern Italy. This curious mausoleum is in the form of a domed cube. In the Via Cadorna there are three 4C BC **hypogea** (Ipogei Lagrasta) ⊙ and to the right of the Andria road stand the remains of a paleo-Christian basilica **(San Leucio)** which was itself built on the site of a Roman temple.

Foggia. – *Town plan in the current Michelin Red Guide Italia.*
Foggia is set in the heart of a vast cereal-growing plain, the Tavoliere. This trading and industrial centre was founded in c1050 by the Norman, Robert Guiscard. In 1223 the Emperor Frederick II of Hohenstaufen built a castle which has now disappeared. The present **cathedral** incorporates parts of an earlier building (1172), notably the lower walls with some blind arcading and a sculptured cornice above, and the crypt. This earlier building was destroyed by the 1731 earthquake.

Galatina. – This craft and wine-making centre stands on the flat and stony Salento Peninsula. The Cathedral with its baroque façade recalls the gracious style of Lecce. The 14C **Church of Santa Caterina di Alessandria★** is decorated with a marvellous cycle of **frescoes★** by several 15C artists. The frescoes in the cloisters are 18C.

Galatone. – *24km – 15 miles southwest of Lecce.*
The **Church of Crocifisso della Pietà** has a lovely **façade**★ embellished in the baroque style so typical of the Lecce area. The sumptuous interior decoration includes gilding and stucco ornamentation.

Lucera. – Already important in Roman times, Lucera was ceded by the Emperor Frederick II of Hohenstaufen to the Saracens of Sicily, who in turn were expelled by Charles II of Anjou, the grandson of Louis IX (St Louis). Lucera has an imposing 13C **castle**★ built by the Angevins, a **cathedral** (Duomo) dating from 1300 and a **Roman amphitheatre** built during Augustus' reign. The **museum** (Museo Civico) ⊙ has a marble **Venus**★, a Roman replica of a model by the school of Praxiteles.

Manfredonia. – Manfred, the son of the Emperor Frederick II of Hohenstaufen, founded the port in the 13C. It is guarded by a fine 13C **castle**. The **Church of Santa Maria di Siponto**★ *(3km – 2 miles to the south by the S 89)* is an elegant 11C building in the Romanesque style which shows influences both oriental (square plan and terraced roof hiding the dome), and Pisan (blind arcades with columns enclosing lozenges). The late-11C **Church of San Leonardo** *(beyond Santa Maria, take the Foggia road to the right)* has a fine delicately sculptured **doorway**★ dating from the early 13C.

Otranto. – *Description p 152.*

Ruvo di Puglia. – *34km – 21 miles to the west of Bari.*
On the edge of the Murge Hills Ruvo has an Apulian-style Romanesque **cathedral**★ with a sober façade embellished by a rose window, a twin opening, a sculptured doorway and at the very top a frieze of arches. Inside the lofty nave, tall arches carry a deep cornice supported by sculptured corbels. The **Jatta Archaeological Museum** ⊙ owns the superb **Crater of Talos**★★, a red-figured vase with a black background.

Trani. – This wine-growing town has an ancient port surrounded by old houses. The 11C-13C Romanesque **cathedral**★★ is one of the finest in Apulia and is dedicated to St Nicholas the pilgrim, a humble Greek shepherd who arrived in Trani on the back of a dolphin. Blind arcades encircle the building and there is a lovely **bronze door**★ which was cast in 1180. Beyond the very lofty transept the chancel has a delicately decorated window. Inside, one detects a strong Norman influence. The nave and aisles are slightly raised as they are built over two immense crypts, the lower of which is literally a forest of ancient columns. The upper church is well lit but severe with slender twin columns carrying the main arches and an elegant gallery with triple openings.
From the **public gardens**★ to the east of the port there is an attractive view of the old town and its tall cathedral. The **castle** on the seashore was built by Frederick II.

Troia. – *17km – 11 miles to the southwest of Foggia.*
This agricultural market town is well situated on a hilltop overlooking the Tavoliere plain. The Romanesque **cathedral** in the Apulian style was begun in the 11C and completed two centuries later. The façade is embellished with blind arcading and an asymmetrical **rose window**★. A lovely 12C **bronze door**★ in the Byzantine tradition opens into the nave and two aisles separated by columns with finely worked capitals. The north doorway has a sculptured **tympanum** depicting Christ flanked by two angels.

★ # L'AQUILA Abruzzi   Pop 66 722

Michelin map 🗆🗆🗆 fold 26 or 🗆🗆🗆 fold 27 – Local map p 40
Town plan in the current Michelin Red Guide Italia

L'Aquila was founded in the 13C on the initiative of the Emperor Frederick II of Hohenstaufen who gave it an imperial eagle as its emblem. Charles I of Anjou took control of the town in 1266 and was responsible for building part of the fortifications. The town has many Romanesque or Renaissance churches and palaces, often marked with the initials IHS (*Iesus Hominum Salvator* – Jesus Saviour of Mankind) after the preaching and motto of St Bernardino of Siena. The saint died here in 1444.

★★ **Basilica of St Bernardino (San Bernardino).** – This superb edifice, built between 1454 and 1472, was given a remarkable façade by Cola dell'Amatrice in 1527. The interior, in the form of a Latin cross, is spacious and well-lit and roofed with a lovely baroque wooden ceiling. The **mausoleum**★ of St Bernardino is adorned with figures by the local sculptor, Silvestro dell' Aquila, as is the elegant **sepulchre**★ of Maria Pereira.

★ **Castle (Castello)** ⊙. – This square castle, quartered with powerful bastions, is a good example of 16C military architecture. The great rooms now house the **National Museum of the Abruzzi**★★ with its archaeological, medieval (mainly interesting examples of local craftsmanship of the period) and modern sections.

★ **Basilica of Santa Maria di Collemaggio.** – This Romanesque building was begun in 1287 at the instance of Pietro da Morone, founder of the Celestine Order and future Pope Celestine V. The wonderful **façade**★★ of white and pink stone is pierced with rose windows and round-headed doorways, all added in the 14C.

★ **Fountain of the 99 Conduits (Fontana delle 99 cannelle).** – This imposing fountain was remodelled in the 15C. 99 masks spout water into its basins. This figure corresponds to the legend which relates that the town sprang up by a miracle with 99 quarters, 99 castles, 99 squares and 99 fountains. Even today a bell in the tower of the Law Courts tolls 99 times every evening.

AQUILEIA Friuli - Venezia Giulia

Pop 3 493

Michelin map 988 fold 6 or 429 fold 17

While the plan of the town was being outlined (181 BC) with the plough, according to Roman custom, an eagle *(aquila)* hovered overhead: hence its name. Aquileia was a flourishing market under the Roman Empire and was used as general headquarters by Augustus during his conquest of the Germanic tribes. The town then became one of Italy's most important patriarchates (554-1751) ruled by bishops.

★★ **Basilica.** – It was built in the 11C on the foundations of a 4C building and restored in the 14C. It is preceded by a porch and flanked by a campanile. The interior with its nave and two aisles is in the form of a Latin cross. The splendid 4C mosaic **paving**★★ is one of the largest and richest in western Christendom. Numerous religious scenes are depicted. The timber ceiling and the arcades are both 14C, the capitals are Romanesque and the decoration of the transept Renaissance. The 9C Carolingian **crypt** ⊘ is decorated with fine Romanesque **frescoes**★★.
The **Cripta degli Scavi** ⊘ is reached from the north aisle. Finds from the excavations are assembled here, notably admirable 4C mosaic **pavings**★★.

★ **Roman Ruins** ⊘. – Excavations have uncovered the remains of Roman Aquileia: behind the basilica, the Via Sacra leading to the river port, houses and the forum. The **Archaeological and Paleo-Christian Museums** ⊘ contain an important collection of finds from local excavations. Note in particular the remarkable series of portraits, including those of Tiberius and of Augustus as a youth, in the archaeological museum.

★ AREZZO Tuscany

Pop 91 899

Michelin map 988 fold 15 or 430 folds 14 and 15

After being first an important Etruscan city and then a rich Roman one, Arezzo was an independent commune before it was annexed by Florence in 1384, following a protracted struggle. The town has many reminders of its past and was the birthplace of several famous men: Guido d'Arezzo (c 990) the inventor of the musical scale, Petrarch the poet (1304-74), Aretino the author (1492-1566), Giorgio Vasari *(qv)* and probably Maecenas (69-68 BC), the legendary patron of art and letters.

Cavour (Via) .... **ABY** 2	Madonna del Prato (V.) . **AYZ** 13	Pescioni (Via) .... **BZ** 26
Grande (Piazza) .... **BY**	Maginardo (Viale) .... **AZ** 14	Pileati (Via del) .... **BY** 28
Italia (Corso) .... **ABYZ**	Mecenate (Viale) .... **AZ** 16	Ricasoli (Via) .... **BY** 30
	Mino da Poppi (Via) ..... **BZ** 17	S. Clemente (Via) .... **AY** 32
Cesalpino (Via) .... **BY** 3	Mochi (Via F.) .... **AY** 19	S. Domenico (Via) ...... **BY** 33
Chimera (Via della) ...... **AY** 5	Monaco (Via G.) .... **AYZ** 20	Saracino (Via del) ...... **AY** 35
Fontanella (Via) .... **BZ** 6	Murello (Piaggia del) .... **AY** 22	Sasso Verde (Via) ...... **BY** 36
Garibaldi (Via) .... **ABYZ** 8	Niccolò Aretino (Via) ... **AZ** 23	Vittorio Veneto (Via) .... **AZ** 38
Giotto (Viale) .... **BZ** 9	Pellicceria (Via) .... **BY** 25	20 Settembre (Via) ...... **AY** 40

52

SIGHTS

St Francis' Church (San Francesco) (ABY). – This aisleless church is large, being designed for preaching; it was built for the Franciscans in the 14C in the Gothic style and remodelled in the 17C and 18C.

★★★ **Frescoes of Piero della Francesca.** – The frescoes depicting the Legend of the Holy Cross were executed from 1452 to 1466 on the walls of the apse. This fresco cycle is undoubtedly a milestone in the history of art. Scenes include the death and burial of Adam, Solomon and the Queen of Sheba, the dream of Constantine, the victory of Constantine over Maxentius, the invention of the Cross, the victorious Heraclius overcoming Chosroes and the announcement of Christ's death to Mary. Piero della Francesca, a pupil of the Florentine school, wrote two treatises on perspective and geometry in later life, and the cycle is the result of his wide-ranging experimentation with two-dimensional space and volume; the poses and expressions of the figures are treated with great realism in a strict composition and reflect the Renaissance ideals of serenity and timelessness. The subtle light suffusing the scenes reveals the influence of Domenico Veneziano, who was the artist's master.

★ **Church of Santa Maria della Pieve (BY B).** – This lovely 12C Romanesque church is flanked by a powerful campanile. The Pisan Romanesque-style façade★★ is articulated by three tiers of small columns, adorned with various motifs, whose ranks become closer as the height increases. On the high altar is a 14C polyptych by the Sienese, Pietro Lorenzetti.

★ **Piazza Grande (BY).** – This square, behind the above church, is surrounded by medieval houses, Renaissance palaces and the Logge or galleries designed by Vasari (16C). The square is the setting for the **Saracen's Tournament**, when costumed horsemen attack a dummy figure with lances *(see the table of Principal Festivals at the end of the guide).*

Cathedral (Duomo) (BY). – This large church was built from the 13C onwards on the town's highest point. Inside are some fine **works of art★**: stained glass by the Frenchman Guillaume de Marcillat (1467-1529), a fresco by Piero della Francesca of Mary Magdalene and the tomb of St Donatus (14C).

St Dominic's Church (San Domenico) (BY). – This 13C church has frescoes by the Duccio school and an admirable painted **crucifix★★** (*c*1260) attributed to Cimabue.

Vasari Mansion (Casa del Vasari) ⊙ (AY A). – The house was sumptuously decorated by **Giorgio Vasari** (1511-74), painter, sculptor, architect and early art historian. Also exhibited are works by Tuscan Mannerists.

★ **Museum of Medieval and Modern Art ⊙ (AY M¹).** – The collections are housed in the Renaissance Bruni-Ciocchi Palace and include paintings from the 13C (works by Margherito d'Arezzo) to the 19C; **maiolica★** from Umbria; arms, coins and small bronzes.

Archaeological Museum (Museo Archeologico) ⊙ (AZ M²). – The museum overlooks the 1C-2C **Roman amphitheatre (ABZ)**. There is a remarkable collection of 6C-3C BC Etruscan and Roman bronzes as well as ceramics from the Hellenistic and Roman periods.

Church of St Mary of Grace (Santa Maria delle Grazie). – *1km – 1/2 mile to the south via Viale Mecenate* (AZ). In front of the church rises a graceful **portico★** by the Florentine, Benedetto da Maiano (15C). Inside is a marble **altarpiece★** by Andrea della Robbia.

★★ **ASCOLI PICENO** Marches   Pop 52 923

Michelin map 〔988〕 fold 16 or 〔430〕 fold 28
Town plan in the current Michelin Red Guide Italia

Ascoli, an austere but picturesque town lies in a narrow valley at the confluence of the Castellano and the Tronto. This walled town has a medieval quarter which is rich in churches, palaces, houses and picturesque streets.

★★ **Piazza del Popolo.** – The People's Square, elongated and well-proportioned and paved with large flagstones, is surrounded by Gothic and Renaissance buildings. It is a popular meeting-place and is the setting for the town's main festivities. The **People's Captains' Palace★** (Palazzo dei Capitani del Popolo) is an austere 13C building with an imposing Renaissance doorway, surmounted by a statue of Pope Paul III which was added in 1549 by Cola dell'Amatrice. At the far end of the square **St Francis' Church★** (San Francesco) was begun in 1262 and consecrated in 1371. The church has several Lombard features. Abutting the south front is the **Merchants' Loggia★** (Loggia dei Mercanti), a graceful early-16C building showing Tuscan influence, particularly in the capitals.

★ **Old Quarter (Vecchio Quartiere).** – The quarter lies between the Tronto River and the **Corso Mazzini★** lined with old mansions, in particular at no 224 the 16C Malaspina Palace. At the beginning of **Via delle Torri** is the Renaissance façade of **St Augustine's** (Sant'Agostino) which has a moving fresco of Christ bearing the Cross by Cola dell'Amatrice. The Via delle Torri ends at the 14C **Church of St Peter the Martyr** (San Pietro Martire). Behind is the Romanesque **Church of Sts Vincent and Anastasius★** (Santi Vincenzo ed Anastasio) with its curious compartmented façade dating from the 14C. The **Ercolani Tower** (Torre Ercolani) in Via Soderini, is the tallest of the feudal towers of Ascoli. Adjoining is the 12C Lombard Romanesque mansion, **Palazzo Longobardo**. Through the medieval gateway, a single-arched Roman bridge, the **Ponte di Solestà★**, spans the Tronto at a height of 25m – 82ft. From the far end there is an attractive view of the old quarters.

Cathedral (Duomo). – The grandiose façade of this 12C building was the work of Cola dell'Amatrice. Inside there is a superb **polyptych★** (1473) by **Carlo Crivelli**. This Venetian artist with a love for meticulous realism settled in Ascoli Piceno in 1470 and he was a motivating force in the development of a local art movement. The **baptistry★**, square at the base and octagonal above, standing to the left of the cathedral, is one of the finest in Italy.

Near the baptistry, in Via Buonaparte, is the **Palazzo Buonaparte**, a lovely example of 16C Renaissance architecture.

Picture Gallery (Pinacoteca) ⊘. – The collections are displayed in the Communal Palace in Piazza Arringo and include works by Crivelli and his pupils, Carlo Maratta, Titian, Van Dyck, Bellotto, Guardi and Callot. The precious and delicately worked 13C English relic, the cope of Nicholas IV, is a prized exhibit.

★★★ ASSISI Umbria   Pop 24 439

Michelin map **988** fold 16 or **430** fold 16 – Town plan below

The walled city of Assisi is prettily spread across the slopes of Monte Subasio and retains its medieval character. It is closely associated with **St Francis** as related in the numerous accounts of his life and work. Under the influence of the Franciscan Order of Minors founded by St Francis, a new, essentially religious, artistic movement developed which marked a turning-point in Italian art. Born in 1182 Francis was a rich and brilliant youth who dreamed of military glory; he was converted following an illness in 1201.

Several apparitions of the Virgin and of Christ were seen by Francis; the most famous is that of La Verna (qv) during which he received the stigmata. But this mystic also had a deeply poetic soul and was a lover of the beauties of nature, which he praised in texts written in the Umbrian language. In addition, he befriended a young woman of rare beauty, Clare, who founded the Order of Poor Clares. St Francis himself died in 1226 after having founded, in 1210, the Order of Minors, mendicant monks known thereafter as Franciscans.

The son of the rich Assisi draper preached poverty, obedience and chastity, a credence which gave rise to a new artistic vision which found its expression in the purity and elegance of Gothic art. During the 13C the churches were embellished with a new splendour. At the end of the 14C famous masters came from Rome and Venice to Assisi to work on the Basilica of St Francis. These artists abandoned for ever the rigid traditions of Byzantine art in favour of a more dramatic art imbued with a spiritual atmosphere. Cimabue and then Giotto were its most powerful exponents.

★★★ ST FRANCIS' BASILICA
(SAN FRANCESCO) (A) time: 1 1/2 hours

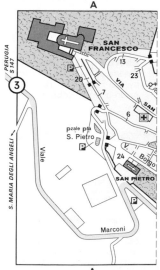

The basilica consists of two superimposed churches, resting on a series of immense arches. The whole building, built after the death of St Francis to the plans of Brother Elias, was consecrated in 1253. It was this monk who influenced the Franciscans to use more splendour and decoration.

Lower Basilica. – Beyond the long narthex, the walls of the dark and sombre four-bay nave are covered with 13C and 14C **frescoes★★★**.

From the narthex pass through the Chapel of St Anthony the Abbot into the 15C **Cloisters of the Dead★★★** with two storeys full of gentleness and peace. Return to the nave and the first chapel on the left with **frescoes★★** by Simone Martini illustrating the life of St Martin. These are remarkable for their delicate drawing and colour, graceful composition and beauty of expression. Further along, above the pulpit is a fresco of the Coronation of the Virgin attributed to Maso, a pupil of Giotto (14C).

The choir **vaulting★★** is painted with scenes symbolising the Triumph of St Francis and the virtues practised by him. They are the work of one of Giotto's pupils. In the south transept is the majestic work by Cimabue, a **Madonna with Four Angels and St Francis★★**. The north transept is decorated with **frescoes★★** of the Passion. Those on the ceiling, attributed to pupils of Pietro Lorenzetti, are valued for their narrative design and charm of detail; those on the walls, probably by Lorenzetti himself, are striking for their dramatic expression **(Descent from the Cross)**.

From the north transept make for the Renaissance main cloisters and the **treasury★★** ⊘ with its many valuable pieces and the Perkins collection of 14C and 15C paintings.

Upper Basilica. – This accomplished Gothic work with its tall and graceful nave, bathed in light, contrasts with the lower church. The apse and transept were decorated with frescoes (many have since been damaged) by Cimabue and his school. In the north transept Cimabue painted a **Crucifixion★★★** with an unforgettable sense of tragedy.

St Francis Preaching to the Birds
by an unknown 13C master, Maestro di San Francesco
(Lower Basilica)

Between 1296 and 1304 **Giotto** and his assistants depicted the life of St Francis in a now-famous cycle of **frescoes★★★**. There are twenty-eight clearly distinguished scenes, each showing a greater search for realism. They mark a new dawning in the figurative traditions of Italian art, which was to reach its apogee during the Renaissance.

Step out of the basilica onto the esplanade to admire the harmonious façade with its doorway and rose window in Cosmati work *(qv)*.

ADDITIONAL SIGHTS

★★ **Medieval Castle (Rocca Maggiore)** ⊘ (B). – This castle is a good example of 14C military architecture. From the top of the keep there is a splendid **view★★** of the town of Assisi and the surrounding countryside bathed in golden light.

★★ **St Clare's Church (Santa Chiara) (BC).** – From the terrace in front of the church there is a pretty view of the Umbrian countryside. The church was built between 1257 and 1265 and closely resembles the Gothic Upper Basilica of St Francis'. Inside there are numerous works of art including 14C frescoes depicting the life and history of St Clare. These were influenced by Giotto.

The Crucifix, which is said to have spoken to St Francis, can be seen in the small Church of St George, which adjoins the south aisle. The crypt enshrines the remains of St Clare.

ASSISI

Fontebella (Via)	**B**
Frate Elia (Via)	**A** 7
Mazzini (Corso)	**B** 12
Brizi (Via)	**B** 2
Comune (Piazza del)	**B** 3
Fosso Cupo (Via del)	**AB** 6
Galeazzo Alessi (V.) .	**C** 8
Garibaldi (Piazzetta)	**B** 9
Giotto (Via)	**B** 10

Merry del Val (Via) .	**A** 13
Porta Perlici (Via) ...	**C** 14
Portica (Via)	**B** 16
S. Apollinare (Via) .	**B** 17
S. Chiara (Piazza) .	**BC** 19
S. Francesco (Pza) .	**A** 20
S. Gabriele della Addolorata (Via) .	**BC** 21
S. Giacomo (Via) ...	**A** 23
S. Pietro (Piazza) ...	**A** 24
S. Ruffino (Via)	**B** 26
Seminario (Via del)	**B** 28
Torrione (Via del) ...	**C** 30
Villamena (Via)	**C** 31

* **Cathedral (Duomo San Rufino) (C)**. – The cathedral was built in the 12C. The Romanesque **façade**★★ is one on the finest in Umbria, with a harmonious arrangement of its openings and decorative ornamentation.
The interior, on a basilical plan, was rebuilt in 1571. To the right as one enters is the baptismal font used for the baptism of St Francis, St Clare and Frederick II.

* **Piazza del Comune (B 3)**. – This square with its attractive fountain occupies the site of the forum: the **Temple of Minerva**★ **(B A)**, converted into a church, with its portico of six Corinthian columns, is one of the best-preserved in Italy.

* **Via San Francesco** ⊙ **(AB)**. – This picturesque street is lined by medieval and Renaissance houses. At no 13A the **Pilgrims' Oratory (B B)** is decorated inside with 15C frescoes, notably by Matteo da Gualdo.

* **St Peter's Church (San Pietro) (A)**. – A Romanesque church built by the Benedictines. It contains a charming triptych by Matteo da Gualdo.

EXCURSIONS

★★ **Carceri Hermitage (Eremo delle Carceri)** ⊙. – *4km – 2 miles to the east.*
The road climbs through olive groves, oaks, cypresses and broom to reach this hermitage, a series of caves where St Francis came to meditate and pray, together with some disciples. The minute church, hollowed out of the rock, already existed when St Francis was wont to retreat to these cells *(carceri).*

* **Monastery of St Damian (Convento di San Damiano)** ⊙. – *2km – 1 mile to the south of the gateway, Porta Nuova.*
This convent and small adjoining church stand alone amidst olive and cypress trees and are closely associated with St Francis, who received his calling here, and also with St Clare who died here in 1253. The humble and austere interior is a moving example of a 13C Franciscan monastery.

* **St Mary of the Angels Basilica (Santa Maria degli Angeli)** ⊙. – *5km – 3 miles to the southwest.*
The basilica was built in the 16C on the site of the chapel, Porziuncola, in which St Francis consecrated St Clare as the Bride of Christ. Inside are two remarkable works of art: above the altar a dazzling **fresco**★ dating from 1393 and portraying the Pardon of Assisi and the Annunciation; and in the crypt a charming glazed terracotta **polyptych**★ by Andrea della Robbia representing the Coronation of the Virgin. Also accessible are the Transito chapel where St Francis died on 3 October 1226, and the little courtyard with the rose bush into which St Francis threw himself to overcome temptation. The plant lost its thorns from that moment. The cave to which the saint retired for prayer may also be visited.

* **Spello.** – *12km – 8 miles to the southeast.*
This picturesque little town preserves some traces of its rich Roman past (fortifications and gateways) and the Church of St Mary Major (Santa Maria Maggiore, the first church on the right as one goes up Via Consolare). Inside are a series of splendid **frescoes**★★ by Pinturicchio which display the realistic verve and freshness of his technique. The life of Christ decorates the walls and the Sibyls the vaulting.

Foligno. – *18km – 11 miles to the southeast.*
Piazza della Repubblica is overlooked by the 14C **Palazzo Trinci,** built by the local overlords, and the **cathedral** (Duomo) with its magnificent doorway decorated with Lombard-style geometric decoration.
Foligno is famous for the **Game of the Quintana** when horsemen in 17C costumes representing the ten different quarters of the town must carry away, with the points of their spears, a ring which is hung from the outstretched hand of the Quintana, an early-17C wooden statue. On the day before this tournament there is a procession with over one thousand people also in 17C costumes *(see the table of Principal Festivals at the end of the guide).*

*Each year the **Michelin Red Guide Italia**
revises its selection of stars for cuisine (good cooking)
mentioning the culinary specialities and local wines;
and proposes a choice of simpler restaurants offering
a well prepared meal often with regional specialities
at a moderate price.*

ATRI Abruzzi   Pop 11 466

Michelin map 🞄🞄🞄 fold 27 or 🞄🞄🞄 fold 28

The inland town of Atri has a beautiful situation looking out to sea. To the west lies the strange **landscape**★★ known as the **Bolge** of Atri, which resulted from the fluvial erosion of a Tertiary plateau. The flat-topped hills with steep sides and gullies are covered with vegetation.

* **Cathedral (Cattedrale)**. – Built in the 13C-14C on the foundations of a Roman edifice, this structure is in the transitional Romanesque-Gothic style. A Romanesque doorway with a rose window above adorns the otherwise sober and compartmented façade. The lower part of the campanile is square but becomes recessed and polygonal in its upper part. Inside, there are tall Gothic arches and, in the apse, **frescoes**★ by the Abruzzi artist, Andrea Delitio (1450-73), illustrating in a very realistic way and in detail the Lives of the Virgin and of Jesus.

BARI Apulia

Michelin map 988 fold 29 or 431 fold 11 – Town plan below
Plan of the built-up area in the current Michelin Red Guide Italia

Bari, the capital of Apulia and an agricultural and industrial centre, is first and
foremost a port with shipping connections with both Yugoslavia and Greece.
The Levantine Fair *(Fiera del Levante)*, held in September, is an important trade
fair which was inaugurated in 1930 to encourage trade with other Mediterranean
countries.

Bari comprises the old town, clustered on its promontory, and the modern town
with wide avenues, laid out on a grid plan in the 19C. Bari was the capital of
Byzantium's possessions in Italy and a very prosperous city in the Middle Ages
due partly to its role as a pilgrimage centre to St Nicholas' shrine and as a port
of embarkation for the Crusades. It declined under the Sforza of Milan and Spanish
rule in the 16C.

★ **OLD TOWN** (CITTÀ VECCHIA) (CDY) *time: 1 1/2 hours*

★★ **St Nicholas' Basilica (San Nicola) (DY A)**. – The basilica in the heart of the
old town was begun in 1087 and consecrated in 1197 to St Nicholas, Bishop
of Myra in Asia Minor, who achieved fame by resurrecting three children, whom
a butcher had cut up and put in brine. St Nicholas' relics were brought home
by sailors from Bari and it was decided to build a church to him. The building
is one of the most remarkable examples of Romanesque architecture and it was
the model for many churches built locally. The plain but powerful façade, flanked
by two towers, is relieved by several twinned openings and a sculptured doorway
with bulls supporting the flanking columns.
On the north side there is the richly decorated 12C Lions' Doorway.

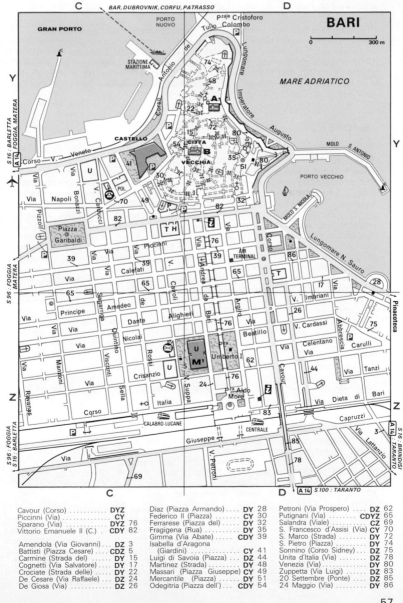

Cavour (Corso) .... **DYZ**	Diaz (Piazza Armando) .... **DY** 28	Petroni (Via Prospero) .... **DZ** 62
Piccinni (Via) .... **CY**	Federico II (Piazza) .... **DY** 30	Putignani (Via) .... **CDYZ** 65
Sparano (Via) .... **DYZ** 76	Ferrarese (Piazza del) ..... **DY** 32	Salandra (Viale) .... **CZ** 69
Vittorio Emanuele II (C.) .. **CDY** 82	Fragigena (Rua) .... **DY** 35	S. Francesco d'Assisi (Via) **CY** 70
	Gimma (Via Abate) ..... **CDY** 39	S. Marco (Strada) .... **DY** 72
Amendola (Via Giovanni) .. **DZ** 3	Isabella d'Aragona	S. Pietro (Piazza) .... **DY** 74
Battisti (Piazza Cesare) .... **CDZ** 5	(Giardini) .... **CY** 41	Sonnino (Corso Sidney) ... **DY** 75
Carmine (Strada del) ...... **DY** 15	Luigi di Savoia (Piazza) ... **DZ** 44	Unita d'Italia (Via) .... **DY** 78
Cognetti (Via Salvatore) .... **DY** 17	Martinez (Strada) .... **DY** 48	Venezia (Via) .... **DY** 80
Crociate (Strada delle) .... **DY** 22	Massari (Piazza Giuseppe) **CY** 49	Zuppetta (Via Luigi) ...... **DZ** 83
De Cesare (Via Raffaele) .. **DZ** 24	Mercantile (Piazza) ...... **DY** 51	20 Settembre (Ponte) ... **DY** 85
De Giosa (Via) .... **DZ** 26	Odegitria (Piazza dell') ... **CDY** 54	24 Maggio (Via) .... **DY** 86

Inside, the three naves with a triforium were reroofed in the 17C with a fine coffered ceiling. A large 12C ciborium (canopy) surmounts the high altar behind which is an unusual 11C **episcopal throne**★ in white marble. In the north apse hangs a painting by the Venetian, Bartolomeo Vivarini. The tomb of St Nicholas lies in the crypt.

★ **Cathedral** (Cattedrale) **(DY B)**. – This 11C-12C Romanesque cathedral was added to and then altered at a later date. Inside, the nave and two aisles have oven-vaulted apses and there is a false triforium above the arches. The works of art include a pulpit made up of 11C and 12C fragments, and a baldachin of 13C fragments.
In the sacristy is a precious 11C Byzantine parchment scroll in Beneventan script, typical of medieval southern Italy. The illustrations are upside down so that the congregation could see them as the parchment was unrolled for the choristers.

★ **Castle** (Castello) ⊘ **(CY)**. – The Emperor Frederick II of Hohenstaufen built the castle in 1233 over the foundations of earlier Byzantine and Norman buildings. The irregular but four-sided courtyard and two of the original towers date from the Swabian period. The castle's defences were strengthened in the 16C.

ADDITIONAL SIGHTS

Picture Gallery ⊘. – *On Lungomare Nazario Sauro* **(DY)** *beyond Piazza A. Diaz.* The gallery, on the fourth floor (lift) of the Palazzo della Provincia, comprises Byzantine works of art (sculpture and paintings), a 12C-13C painted wood statue of **Christ**★, *The Martyrdom of St Peter* by Giovanni Bellini and canvases by the 17C-18C Neapolitan school.

Archaeological Museum ⊘ **(DZ M¹)**. – *First floor of the university.* Greco-Roman collections from excavations made throughout Apulia.

EXCURSION

The road from Bari to Barletta passes through some small but attractive coastal towns which were fortified against invasion by the Saracens during the Middle Ages and the Turks at the end of the 15C. These include **Giovinazzo** with its small 12C cathedral dominating the fishing harbour; **Molfetta** pinpointed by the square towers of its Apulian Romanesque cathedral in white limestone; and **Bisceglie**, a picturesque fishing village, with its cathedral finished in the 13C. The main doorway is flanked by two lions.

BARLETTA Apulia   Pop 87 328

Michelin map 988 folds 28 and 29 or 431 folds 6 and 7
Town plan in the current Michelin Red Guide Italia

In the 12C and 13C the town of Barletta was an embarkation port for the Crusades and many military or hospitaller Orders chose this as the site for an institution.
Now a commercial and agricultural centre, the town has several medieval religious or secular buildings: the 12C-14C **cathedral** (Duomo) in the Apulian style shows a Burgundian influence, especially in the choir; the **Basilica of the Holy Sepulchre** (San Sepolcro) ⊘, at the junction of Corso Vittorio Emanuele and Corso Garibaldi, dates from the 12C-14C and possesses a fine **reliquary**★ with Limoges enamels on the base for a fragment of the True Cross; and the **castle**★ (Castello) which is an imposing fortress built by the Emperor Frederick II of Hohenstaufen and strengthened by Charles of Anjou.
The **Municipal Museum**★ (Museo Civico) ⊘, has in addition to a collection of Apulian ceramics, a particularly fine series of paintings by the local artist, Giuseppe de Nittis (1846-84). This portraitist of Parisian elegance was also a landscape painter influenced by the Macchiaioli *(p 33).*
The **Colossus**★★ (Colosso or Statua di Eraclio) is a gigantic statue over 4.5m – 15ft tall of a Byzantine emperor whose identity is uncertain (Valentinian ?). Probably 4C, this work is of interest as it marks the transition from decadent Roman to early Christian art.

★ **BASSANO DEL GRAPPA** Venetia   Pop 38 854

Michelin map 988 fold 5 or 429 fold 14

Bassano del Grappa, a pottery town which also produces brandy *(grappa),* is built on the banks of the Brenta River. The town is attractive with narrow streets lined by painted houses and the squares bordered by arcades. In the centre, Piazza Garibaldi is dominated by the 13C square tower, Torre di Ezzelino, and overlooked by the **Church of St Francis** (San Francesco). Dating from the 12C-14C the church has an elegant porch (1306). Inside, the 14C Christ is by Guariento. The **Covered Bridge** (Ponte Coperto) is well known in Italy. Originally built in the 13C, it has been rebuilt many times since.

★ **Municipal Museum** (Museo Civico) ⊘. – The museum is housed in the monastery next to St Francis'. The **picture gallery**, on the first floor, has several works by the local da Ponte family. Jacopo da Ponte, otherwise called **Jacopo Bassano** (1510-92), was the best-known member. His works were marked by a picturesque realism and contrasts of light and shade. **St Valentine baptising St Lucia** is his masterpiece. Other Venetian painters include Guariento, Vivarini, Giambono (14C and 15C), Pietro Longhi, Tiepolo and Marco Ricci (18C). There are also two lovely canvases by the Genoese painter Magnasco (18C) and a gallery devoted to the sculptor Canova.

EXCURSIONS

★★★ **Monte Grappa.** – *1 775m – 5 823ft. 32km – 20 miles to the north.*
The road up passes through fine forests and bare mountain pastures, before reaching the summit, from where there is a magnificent **panorama** reaching as far as Venice and Trieste. The monument is a World War I ossuary.

★ **Asolo.** – *14km – 9 miles to the east.*
The streets of this attractive little town, dominated by its castle, are lined with palaces painted with frescoes. The town is closely associated with Robert Browning and Duse, the famous Italian tragic actress who interpreted the works of Gabriele D'Annunzio. Duse is buried in the peaceful cemetery of Sant'Anna.

Marostica. – *7km – 4 miles to the west.*
The **main square★** (Piazza Castello) of this charming small medieval city serves as a giant chessboard for a highly original game of chess (**Partita a Scacchi**) with costumed people as the chessmen *(see the table of Principal Festivals at the end of the guide).*

Cittadella. – *13km – 8 miles to the south.*
This stronghold was built by the Paduans in 1220 as an answer to the Trevisans' construction of Castelfranco. Cittadella is encircled by fine brick **walls★**.

Possagno. – *8km – 11 miles to the northwest.*
This was the birthplace of the sculptor **Antonio Canova** (1757-1822), known for his neo-classical works. The **Temple of Canova** ⊘ designed by the master himself, crowns an eminence. Inside are the sculptor's tomb and his last sculpture, a **Descent from the Cross★**.

★ # BELLUNO Venetia   Pop 36 087

Michelin map 🔲 fold 5 – Town plan in the current Michelin Red Guide Italia

This pleasant town stands on a spur at the confluence of the Piave and the Ardo rivers and is surrounded by high mountains. To the north are the Dolomites with the Belluno Pre-Alps in the south. An independent commune in the Middle Ages, Belluno came under the protection of the Venetian Republic from 1404.
Walk along Via Rialto through the 13C gateway, Porta Dojona (remodelled in the 16C), across the **Piazza del Mercato★**, bordered with arcaded Renaissance houses and adorned with a 1409 fountain, along Via Mezzaterra and Via Santa Croce to the gateway, Porta Rugo. Via del Piave offers a vast **view★** of the Piave Valley and the surrounding mountains. The **Piazza del Duomo★** is surrounded by the late-15C Venetian-style **Rectors' Palace★** (Palazzo dei Rettori), the **Episcopal Palace** (Palazzo dei Vescovi) and the cathedral (Duomo), dating from the 16C with its baroque campanile by Juvara. Inside, there are several good pictures by the Venetian school, notably by Jacopo Bassano and, in the crypt, a 15C **polyptych★** by the Rimini school. The Jurists' Palace (Palazzo dei Giuristi) houses the **Municipal Museum** ⊘ (Museo Civico) with an art gallery (local and Venetian works), a rich coin collection and documents on the Risorgimento *(qv)*.

EXCURSION

Feltre. – *31km – 19 miles to the southwest.*
Feltre, grouped round its castle, has kept part of its ramparts and in **Via Mezzaterra★**, old houses, adorned with frescoes in the Venetian manner. **Piazza Maggiore★** is a beautiful square with its noble buildings, arcades, stairways and balustrades. The **Municipal Museum** ⊘ *(Museo Civico, 23 Via Lorenzo Luzzo, near the Porta Oria)* displays works by Lorenzo Luzzo, a local artist, Marescalchi, Bellini, Cima da Conegliano, Ricci and Jan Massys. The museum also includes a historical section on Feltre and an archaeological collection.

BENEVENTO Campania   Pop 65 570

Michelin map 🔲 fold 27 or 🔲 fold 40

This was the capital of the Samnites, who hindered for some considerable time the Roman expansion. In 321 BC they trapped the Roman army in a defile known as the Caudine Forks (Forche Caudine) between Capua and ancient Beneventum. The Romans occupied the town following the defeat in 275 BC of Pyrrhus and his Samnite allies. During the reign of Trajan, the town knew a period of glory and it was designated as starting-point for the Trajan Way (Via Traiana) leading to Brindisi. Under Lombard rule, it became the seat of a duchy in 571 and later a powerful principality. Following the Battle of Benevento in 1266, Charles of Anjou who had defeated Manfred the then king of Naples and Sicily, supported by Pope Urban IV, claimed the kingship.

★★ **Trajan's Arch (Arco di Traiano).** – *At the junction of Via Traiano and Corso Garibaldi.*
Built in AD 114 this is Italy's best-preserved triumphal arch. The low reliefs dedicated to the glory of the emperor are of an exceptionally high standard.

★ **Samnium Museum (Museo del Sannio)** ⊘. – Go behind the **Church of St Sophia** in Piazza Matteotti, an 8C edifice rebuilt in the 17C on a polygonal plan. The columns of the **cloisters★** support Moorish-style arches. Adjoining the cloisters, the museum has an important archaeological section and works from the Neapolitan school.

Roman Theatre (Teatro Romano). – *Near Via Port'Arsa.*
This theatre, which is one of the largest still in existence, was built in the 2C during the reign of the Emperor Hadrian.

Michelin map 🔲🔲🔲 fold 3 or 🔲🔲🔲 fold 16 – Town plan pp 60 and 61

Situated on the northern edge of the Lombardy plain at the confluence of the Brembana and Seriana valleys, Bergamo is one of the principal towns of Lombardy. It is an art centre as well as a busy business and industrial centre.

BERGAMO

Camozzi (Via)	**BC**
Colleoni (Via B.)	**AY**
Giovanni XXIII (Viale)	**BZ** 24
Gombito (Via)	**AY** 27
S. Alessandro (Via)	**AZ**
Tasso (Via T.)	**BCZ**
20 Settembre (Via)	**BZ** 85
Belotti (Largo Bortolo)	**BZ** 3
Bonomelli (Via G.)	**BZ** 4
Borfuro (Via)	**BZ** 6
Botta (Via Carlo)	**BZ** 7

Casalino (Via)	**CZ** 12
Cesare (Viale Giulio)	**CY** 13
Conca d'Oro (Galleria)	**AY** 16
Dante (Piazza)	**BZ** 17
Donizetti (Via G.)	**AY** 19
Fantoni (Via A.)	**CZ** 23
Lazzaretto (Via)	**CY** 28
Libertà (Piazza della)	**BZ** 30
Lupi (Via Brigata)	**BZ** 32
Marconi (Piazza)	**CZ** 35
Mercato delle Scarpe (Piazza)	**BY** 38

Milano (Via)	**AZ** 39
Monte Ortigara (Via)	**BY** 42
Moroni (Via G. Battista)	**AZ** 44
Mura di S. Agostino (Viale delle)	**BY** 45
Mura di S. Giacomo	**ABY** 46
Mura di S. Grata	**AY** 47
Muraine (Viale)	**CY** 49
Orelli (Via)	**AZ** 53
Palazzo (Via Borgo)	**CZ** 54
Partigiani (Via dei)	**BZ** 56
Petrarca (Via)	**BZ** 57
Porta Dipinta (Via)	**BY** 59
Pradello (Via)	**BZ** 60

The modern **lower town** is pleasant while the old **upper town** is quiet, picturesque and evocative of the past.

From Roman city to Venetian rule. – Around 1200 BC the Ligurians occupied the site of the upper town. The Gauls seized the settlement c550 and called it Berghem. It was renamed Bergomum by the Romans when they took over in 196 BC. The city was destroyed by the Barbarians before enjoying a period of peace under the Lombards and in particular in the reign of Queen Theodolinda. An independent commune from the 11C to the 13C, she then joined the Lombard League (qv) in its struggle against the Emperor Frederick Barbarossa. The town suffered during the struggles between the Guelphs (followers of the pope) and the Ghibellines (followers of the emperor). Under the rule of **Bartolomeo Colleoni** (1400-75), the town fell first to the Visconti family from Milan and then to the Republic of Venice. The famous mercenary leader served both successively, before finally ceding Bergamo to the Venetians. Bergamo came under Austrian rule in 1814 and was liberated by Garibaldi only in 1859.

Bergamo and its artists. – In addition to a large group of local artists, namely Previtali, Moroni, Cariani, Baschenis and Fra Galgario, numerous others worked in the town, including Lorenzo Lotto, Giovanni da Campione and Amadeo.

Masks and Bergamasques. – The **Commedia dell'Arte** originated at Bergamo in the 16C. The comedy consists of an improvisation (imbroglio) based on a pre-arranged theme (scenario), with gags (lazzi) uttered by masked actors representing stock characters (p 62): the valet (Harlequin), a stubborn but wily peasant from the Brembana Valley, the braggart (Pulcinella) the lady's maid (Columbine), the lover (Pierrot), the knave (Scapino), the old fox (Scaramouch), the clown (Pantaloon) and the musician (Mezzetino). Its element of caricature sometimes springs from triviality. This form of theatre was popular in France in the 17C and 18C. Bergamo is also the home of the composer Donizetti (1797-1848). The vivacity of the people is displayed in the local folklore, such as the Bergamasque, a lively dance, and in the groups of public musicians (pifferi).

"Città Alta" chiusa al traffico da Marzo a Novembre

★★★ UPPER TOWN (CITTÀ ALTA) (ABY)

No cars allowed in this part of the town – time: 3 hours

When going by car, park outside the walls (see above) or take the funicular (station in Viale Vittorio Emanuele II) which ends in **Piazza del Mercato delle Scarpe** (Square of the Shoe Market) (BY 38).

The Upper Town, with its 16C Venetian perimeter wall, its strategically-placed castle, and its winding alleyways lined with old houses, has Bergamo's finest buildings.

★★ **Piazza del Duomo** (AY). – This attractive square is lined by fine buildings. The arcades of the Palazzo Ragione in the north lead to the Piazza Vecchia.

★★ **Colleoni Chapel** (Capella Colleoni) ⊘. – The architect of the Carthusian monastery at Pavia, **Amadeo**, designed this gem (1470-76) of Lombard-Renaissance architecture as a mausoleum for Bartolomeo Colleoni, who directed that it should be built on the site of the sacristy of the basilica of St Mary Major. The funerary chapel opens into and is embedded in the north side of the basilica. The domed main structure is adjacent to the north porch which is skilfully used to counterbalance the domed recess containing the mausoleum's altar.

Scapino   Pantaloon   Fracasso   Pulcinella   Scaramouch   Mezzetino

The elegant **façade** is faced with precious multicoloured marble and lavishly decorated with delicate sculptures: figures of children *(putti)*, fluted and wreathed columns, sculptured pilasters, vases and candelabra, medallions and low reliefs combining sacred and secular elements after the contemporary fashion (allegories, scenes from the Old Testament, mythological figures including scenes from the life of Hercules with whom Colleoni identified himself.

The interior is sumptuously decorated with low reliefs of extraordinary delicacy, frescoes by Tiepolo and Renaissance **stalls** with intarsia work. The **Colleoni monument**, also by Amadeo, is surmounted by an equestrian statue of the leader in gilded wood and is delicately carved. The low reliefs of the sarcophagi represent scenes from the New Testament separated by niches occupied by statues of the Virtues. Between the two sarcophagi are portraits of the leader's children. His favourite daughter, Medea, who died at the age of fifteen, lies near him (to the left), in a tomb by Amadeo which is a marvel of delicacy and purity.

★ **Basilica of St Mary Major** (Santa Maria Maggiore). – This church is 12C but the two lovely north and south **porches** ⊙ with loggias and supported by lions in the Lombard Romanesque style were added in the 14C by Giovanni da Campione. The interior, remodelled in the baroque style (late 16C-early 17C), is richly decorated with stucco and gilding. The walls of the aisles and the chancel are hung with nine splendid Florentine **tapestries**★★ (1580-86), beautifully designed after cartoons by Alessandro Allori which relate the Life of the Virgin. On the west wall of the nave hangs the sumptuous Flemish tapestry depicting the **Crucifixion**★★. After cartoons by L. Van Schoor, it was woven in Antwerp between 1696 and 1698. Note also the curious 18C baroque confessional in the north aisle and the interesting 14C frescoes in the transept. Incorporated in the chancel screen are four superb **panels of intarsia work**★★ depicting scenes from the Old Testament. They were made in the 16C after the designs of Lorenzo Lotto. Leave by the door giving onto Piazza di Santa Maria Maggiore to admire the 14C south porch, as well as the charming **Tempietto Santa Croce** (A) which was built *c*1000 on the quatrefoil plan in the early-Romanesque style. To return to the Piazza del Duomo walk round the basilica's **east end**★ with its radiating chapels decorated with graceful arcading.

★ **Baptistry** (Battistero) (B). – This charming octagonal work is encircled by a red Verona marble gallery with graceful, slender columns and 14C statues representing the Virtues. It is a reconstruction of Giovanni da Campione's original work dating from 1340. It originally graced the east end of the nave of St Mary Major but was deemed too cumbersome and was demolished in 1660 and rebuilt on its present site in 1898.

Cathedral (Duomo). – It has a richly-decorated interior (18C). The very lovely baroque stalls were carved by the Sanzi.

★ **Piazza Vecchia** (AY). – This is the historic centre of the town. The **Palazzo della Ragione** (AY C), the oldest communal palace in Italy, dates from 1199 but was rebuilt in the 16C. It has graceful arcades and trefoil windows and a central balcony surmounted by the Lion of St Mark. A 14C covered stairway leads to the majestic 12C **bell tower** ⊙ (D) with its 15C clock. The **Palazzo Scamozziano** (AY E) opposite is in the Palladian style *(p 233)*. The fountain in the centre was offered to Genoa in 1780 by the Doge of Venice, Alvise Contarini.

Via Bartolomeo Colleoni ⊙ (AY). – This street is lined with old mansions including the Colleoni Mansion, at Nos 9 and 11, which contains frescoes to the glory of the mercenary leader.

Fortress (Rocca) (BY). – Built in the 14C it was remodelled by the Venetians. There are interesting **views**★ of the upper and lower towns.

★ **LOWER TOWN** *time: 1 1/2 hours.*

The Carrara Academy is in the heart of a district of attractive alleyways, while Piazza Matteotti is at the centre of the present-day business and shopping district.

★★ **Carrara Academy** (Accademia Carrara) ⊙ (CY). – This collection of 15C-18C Italian and foreign paintings is housed in a neo-classical palace.

Beyond the early-15C works, which still recall the International Gothic style *(qv)*, hang two important portraits of **Giuliano de'Medici** by Botticelli and the elegant and refined one of **Lionello d'Este** by Pisanello. These are followed by works of the Venetian school: by the Vivarini family, Carlo Crivelli, Antonello da Messina, Giovanni Bellini (gentle Madonnas with dreamy expressions which are similar to those of his brother-in-law, Mantegna), Gentile Bellini (delicate but penetrating portraits), Carpaccio *(Doge Leonardo Loredan)* and by Lorenzo Lotto. Next come the late-15C and early-16C works represented by Cosimo Tura, master of the Ferrarese school (a very realistic *Virgin and Child* showing the influence of Flemish art), by the Lombard, Bergognone (soft light), and by the Bergamask, Previtali.

The 16C covers works by the Venetian Lorenzo Lotto (including a splendid **Holy Family with St Catherine)**, the good Bergamask portraitist, Cariani, and the Venetian masters, Titian and Tintoretto. The colours and delicate draughtsmanship of Raphael greatly influenced Garofalo (Benvenuto Tisi) who was nicknamed the Ferrara Raphael, while the Piedmontese Gaudenzio Ferrari and Bernardino Luini, the main exponents of the Renaissance in Lombardy, were inspired by Leonardo da Vinci. The 16C **portraits** are a particularly rich group, with the Ferrarese school which specialised in this art and the Bergamask, Moroni (1523-78). Foreign artists include Clouet (portrait of *Louis de Clèves*) and Dürer.

The 17C-18C Bergamask school is represented by Baschenis (1617-77) and excellent portraits by Fra Galgario (1655-1743). The 17C Flemish and Dutch section (Rubens, Van Dyck, Velvet Brueghel...) is dominated by a delightful Van Goyen seascape.

The visit ends with 18C Venetian painting: scenes of domestic interiors by Pietro Longhi, topographical views by Carlevarijs, Bernardo Bellotto, Canaletto and some charming seascapes by Francesco Guardi.

★ **Old quarter.** – The main street of this quarter is **Via Pignolo★ (BCYZ)** which winds among old palaces, mostly 16C and 18C and churches containing numerous works of art. The **Church of San Bernardino (CY)** has in the chancel a Virgin and Saints (1521) by Lorenzo Lotto. **Santo Spirito (CZ)** contains a St John the Baptist surrounded by saints and a polyptych by Previtali, a polyptych portraying the Virgin by Bergognone and a Virgin and Child by Lorenzo Lotto.

★ **Piazza Matteotti** (BZ). – This immense square in the centre of the modern town is overlooked by the **Church of San Bartolomeo** (a superb Virgin and Saints by Lorenzo Lotto), the **Donizetti Theatre (T)** and is bordered by one of the Bergamasks' favourite promenades, the **Sentierone.**

EXCURSION

★ **Brembana Valley (Val Brembana).** – *25km – 16 miles to the north.*
Leave Bergamo by the S 470 which follows an industrial valley. Note the curious two-toned limestone strata. The important thermal spa of **San Pellegrino Terme★** has a lovely mountain setting.

Information in this guide is based on data
provided at the time of going to press.
Improved facilities and changes in the cost of living
make alterations inevitable; we hope our readers will bear with us.

★★ BOLOGNA Emilia-Romagna   Pop 427 240

Michelin map 988 folds 14 and 15, 429 folds 23 and 24 or 430 folds 3 and 4 Plan of the built-up area in the current Michelin Red Guide Italia

Situated on the southern edge of the Po Plain, on the lower slopes of the Apennine foothills, Bologna, the capital of Emilia-Romagna, is a city of many facets: its numerous medieval towers, its churches, its long arcaded streets lined by sumptuous 14C to 17C palaces recall the former political and cultural importance of this once independent city.

Bologna is famous for its University, one of the oldest in Europe, which already numbered 10 000 students in the 13C and produced many scholars, including Guglielmo Marconi (1874-1937).

In addition to being an Italian gastronomic centre, Bologna is an important industrial and commercial town well-placed on both the national rail and road networks. The city hosts numerous international fairs, shows and exhibitions.

HISTORICAL AND ARTISTIC NOTES

Etruscan Felsina was conquered in the 4C BC by the Boïan Gauls, who were driven out in their turn by the Romans in 190 BC. Roman Bononia fell under the sway of the Barbarians and did not recover until the 12C. From the 13C onwards the city enjoyed independent communal government and developed rapidly. A fortified city wall, palaces and churches were built and the University flourished and acquired an excellent reputation for its teaching of Roman law. In the struggle which confronted the Ghibellines, supporting the emperor, and the Guelphs, partisans of communal independence, it was the latter who prevailed when in 1249 they defeated the Imperial Army of Frederick II at Fossalta. The emperor's son, Enzo, was taken prisoner and remained at Bologna until his death twenty-three years later.

In the 15C, following a period of violent struggles between rival families, the city was ruled by the **Bentivoglio** family. Bologna was greatly influenced by the Tuscan Renaissance during the reign of Giovanni II Bentivoglio. The Bentivoglio family was in its turn vanquished in 1506 by **Pope Julius II** and the city remained under papal control until the arrival of Bonaparte in 1797. In the early 19C several insurrections were severely repressed by the Austrians and in 1860 it was united with Piedmont.

Famous citizens include the Popes, Gregory XIII, who established our present Gregorian calendar (1582), Gregory XV (17C) and Benedict XIV (18C). In 1530, following the defeat of François I at Pavia and the sack of Rome, the Emperor Charles V obliged Pope Clement VII to crown him in the Basilica of St Petronius in Bologna.

Bologna School of Painting. – This term covers the artistic movement founded by the **Carracci**, a Bolognese family of painters, as a reaction to the excessive formalism of Tuscan Mannerism. Their aim was to create simpler compositions and a greater realism of subject matter. Numerous artists, including their Bolognese followers Albani, Guercino, Domenichino and Guido Reni, followed this movement known as the Academy of the Eclectic *(Incamminati)*, whose main teaching precept was the study of nature.

The work of Annibale Carracci, the decorator of the Farnese Palace in Rome and the most brilliant of the three cousins, had a decisive influence on this new artistic movement. Annibale was a precursor of baroque art with his purity of tone and the vitality of his decorative schemes.

★★★ CITY CENTRE *time: 1 day*

The two adjoining squares, **Piazza Maggiore** and **Piazza del Nettuno★★★**, form with **Piazza di Porta Ravegnana★★**, the heart of Bologna, an ensemble of rare beauty.

★★ Neptune Fountain (Fontana del Nettuno) (DT A). – This is the work of the Flemish sculptor known as Giambologna or Giovanni Bologna. The muscular bronze Neptune, nicknamed the Giant, is surrounded by four sirens spouting water from their breasts. The group has a rather rough vigour in tune with the town.

★ Communal Palace (Palazzo Comunale) ⊙ (DT). – The façade is composed of buildings of different periods: 13C to the left, 15C on the right and in the centre the main dorway is 16C (the lower section is by Alessi) and is surmounted by a statue of Pope Gregory XIII. Above and to the left of the doorway is a statue of the Virgin and Child (1478) in terracotta by Niccolò dell'Arca. At the far end of the courtyard, under a gallery on the left, is a superb staircase leading to the richly decorated first-floor rooms, then up again to the second floor.

Opening off the vast Farnese Gallery with 17C frescoes are the splendid rooms containing the **Communal Art Collections** ⊙ with a sculpture section and a fine selection of Emilian **paintings★**. To the left of the Communal Palace stands the severe 14C-15C Notaries' Palace (**DU B**).

★ Governors' Palace (Palazzo del Podestà) ⊙ (ET). – The Renaissance façade facing Piazza Maggiore has arcades separated by Corinthian columns on the ground floor and is surmounted by a balustrade. The upper storey has pilasters and an attic pierced by oculi or round windows.

The 13C **King Enzo's Palace** (ET D) stands next to the Governor's Palace. It has a fine inner courtyard and a magnificent staircase leading up to a gallery, to the left of which is a courtyard overlooked by the Arengo Tower.

★★ Basilica of St Petronius (San Petronio) (DEU). – Building began in 1390 to the plans of Antonio di Vincenzo (1340-1402) and was fully completed only in the 17C when the vaulting was finished. The façade, the upper part of which lacks its marble facing, is remarkable chiefly for the main **doorway★★** on which the Sienese Jacopo della Quercia worked from 1425 to 1438. The lintel, uprights and embrasures are adorned with small, expressive low reliefs, rather pagan in spirit. This immense building has many **works of art★**: frescoes by Giovanni da Modena (15C) in the first and fourth chapels off the north aisle; a Martyrdom of St Sebastian by the late-15C Ferrara school in the fifth chapel; a Madonna

Bologna – Central doorway
of the Basilica of St Petronius

(1492) by Lorenzo Costa and the tomb of Elisa Baciocchi, Napoleon's sister, in the seventh chapel; and at the high altar a canopy (baldachin) by Vignola (16C). The 15C organ on the right is one of the oldest in Italy.

★ Municipal Archaeological Museum (Museo Civico Archeologico) ⊙ (EU M). – Egyptian, Greco-Roman (lovely Roman copy of the head of Athena by Phidias) and Etruscan (bronze historiated water pitcher, *situle*) antiquities.

Near the museum is the 16C Palazzo dell'Archiginnasio ⊙ (EU V), the home of an important library (10 000 manuscripts) and the 17C-18C **Anatomy Theatre** (Teatro Anatomico).

★★ Leaning towers (ET R). – There are two strange leaning towers which belonged to noble families in the attractive Piazza di Porta Ravegnana. They are symbols of the continual conflict between rival Guelph and Ghibelline families in the Middle Ages. The taller, **Torre degli Asinelli** ⊙, nearly 100m – 328ft high, dates from 1109. 486 steps lead to the top from where there is an admirable **panorama★★** of the city. The second, known as **Torre Garisenda**, is 50m – 164ft high and has a tilt of over 3m – 10ft. No 1 in the square is the Renaissance **Linen Drapers' Palace** (ET S).

The 14C **Mercanzia★** (EU C) or Merchants' House, in the next square, bears the coats of arms of the various guilds and several small statues.

BOLOGNA

Marconi (Via G.) .... **DT**
Rizzoli (Via) .... **ET** 79

Bassi (Via Ugo) .... **DT**
Indipendenza (Via dell') ...... **ET**

Archiginnasio (Via dell') .... **EU** 4
Battisti (Via C.) .... **DU** 14

Carbonesi (Via) .... **DU** 17
Manzoni (Via) .... **DT** 46
Porta Nova (Via) .... **DT** 73
Roosevelt (Pza F.D.) ...... **DT** 80
4 Novembre (Piazza) ...... **DT** 99

★ **St Stephen's Basilica (Santo Stefano) (EU)**. – This dedication includes a group of three buildings overlooking the square with its Renaissance mansions: the **Church of the Crucifix** (Crocifisso) 11C but remodelled; the 12C **Church of the Holy Sepulchre** (Santo Sepolcro) with its polygonal form and the shrine of Bologna's patron saint, St Petronius. Go through the Church of the Holy Sepulchre to reach the charming 12C Court of Pilate and Romanesque cloisters transformed into a **museum** ⊙ (paintings, statues and liturgical objects).
At the far end of the courtyard is the 13C **Church of the Trinity** (Chiesa della Trinità) with a curious 14C multicoloured group representing the Adoration of the Magi. The 8C-11C **Church of Sts Vitalis and Agricola** is plain and massive.

ADDITIONAL SIGHTS

★★ **National Picture Gallery (Pinacoteca Nazionale)** ⊙. – *Take Via Zamboni* (**ET**). The Bologna school is well represented and its characteristics were: in the 14C, gold backgrounds, bright colours and Gothic preciosity (affectation), all typical of Byzantine art; under the Renaissance, mannerisms, idealism, science and composition; during the baroque period, with the Carracci, realism, vigour and colour; and with the pupils of the Carracci, an academic style.
The first rooms are devoted to the 14C Bolognese painters: Vitale da Bologna (lovely frescoes), Simone dei Crocifissi and Giovanni Bologna.
The following rooms contain works of the early Renaissance: the Venetian school (the Vivarini family and Cima da Conegliano), the Ferrara school with their pronouncedly realistic works (Ercole de'Roberti, Francesco del Cossa and Lorenzo Costa) as well as Bolognese artists such as Francia *(The Adoration of the Child).* Deyond *The Ecstasy of St Cecilia,* a famous picture of truly classical beauty by Raphael, there is a series of 16C frescoes by Niccolò dell'Abbate depicting Ariosto's *Orlando Furioso (Roland the Mad) (qv).*
The Bologna school of the 17C follows with the Carracci brothers, to whom an entire room is devoted, Guido Reni, Albani and Domenichino and their disciples, as well as Guercino with his outstanding masterpiece *St William of Aquitaine,* so rich in clever light effects.

★ **Church of St James Major (San Giacomo Maggiore) (ET)**. – The church was founded in 1267. On the north side is a lovely Renaissance portico (1481). In the **Bentivoglio Chapel★** (Cappella Bentivoglio) is an altarpiece that is considered to be one of Francia's (late-15C) best pieces and frescoes which are in part attributed to the Ferraran, Lorenzo Costa. Opposite the chapel, in the ambulatory, stands the **tomb★** of the jurist, Antonio Bentivoglio, by Jacopo della Quercia. In St Cecilia's Oratory are remarkable **frescoes★** ⊙ (1506) by Francia and Lorenzo Costa.

★ **Strada Maggiore** (EU). – The street is lined with crenellated Gothic and classical palaces. No 44, a palace dating from 1658, houses a **Museum of Industrial Art** ⊙ and the **Davia Bargellini Gallery** ⊙: 16C-18C Bolognese furniture, 18C puppet theatres, a collection of door handles and locks, and paintings including several on the Madonna and Child theme by the Vivarini family, Garofalo, Francia and Vitale da Bologna.

★ **St Dominic's Church** (San Domenico) (EU). – The church was built at the beginning of the 13C and remodelled in the 18C. The famous and beautiful **tomb**★★ (arca) of the saint by Nicola Pisano (1267) was crowned with an arch (1468-73) by the sculptor Niccolò da Bari, who was afterwards known as Niccolò dell'Arca. The two saints and a kneeling angel (1494) were by Michelangelo. The chapel to the south of the choir has a fine painting by Filippino Lippi: **the Mystic Marriage of St Catherine**★ (1501).

★ **Bevilacqua Palace** (Palazzo Bevilacqua) (DU). – This, the finest palace in Bologna, is in the Florentine Renaissance rusticated style.

St Francis' Church (San Francesco) (DT). – At the high altar is a magnificent marble **artarpiece**★ (1392), a Gothic work by the Venetian sculptor Paolo dalle Masegne.

EXCURSION

Madonna di San Luca. – *5km – 3 miles to the southwest. Leave the city centre by Via Saragozza* (DV).
The 18C church is linked to the city by a **portico**★ of 666 arches. In the chancel is the Madonna of St Luke, a painting in the 12C Byzantine manner. There is a lovely **view**★ of Bologna and the Apennines.

BOLSENA Latium	Pop 4 070

Michelin map ▦▦▦ fold 25 or ▦▦▦ fold 25

Bolsena, the ancient Etruscan city of Volsinii, stands on the banks of Italy's largest lake of volcanic origin, the level of which is continually changing owing to earth tremors. Its shady shores welcome many visitors attracted by a gentle and limpid light. The old part of the town groups its sombre-coloured houses upon a small hill; there is a good view from the S2, the Viterbo-Siena road.

The Miracle of Bolsena. – A Bohemian priest had doubts about the Transubstantiation, that is, the incarnation of Christ in the Host. But, it is related, at the moment of Consecration when he was celebrating mass in St Christine's Church, the Host began to bleed profusely. The priest no longer doubted the mystery and the Feast of Corpus Christi was instituted.

★ **St Christina's** (Santa Cristina) ⊙. – The 3C Saint Christina is said to have belonged to the Bolsena region. She was a victim of the persecutions of Diocletian. Although the building is 11C the façade, articulated by gracefully carved pilasters, is Renaissance. The columns inside are Roman. The north aisle leads to the **Chapel of the Miracle**, where the pavement stained by the blood of the Host is revered, and then to the Grotto of St Christina. In the latter is the Altar of the Miracle and a reclining statue of the saint attributed to the della Robbias.

★ BOLZANO (BOZEN) Trentino – Alto Adige	Pop 101 230

Michelin map ▦▦▦ fold 4, ▦▦▦ fold 20 or ▦▦▦ fold 3 – Local map p 84
Town plan in the current Michelin Red Guide Italia

Bolzano, the capital of the Alto Adige, lies on the Brenner transalpine route at the confluence of the Isarco and the Adige. The surrounding slopes are covered with orchards and vineyards. The architecture of the town shows a marked Tyrolean or Austrian influence which was exercised between the 16C and 1918. This industrial and commercial town is now also a busy tourist centre owing to its proximity to the Dolomites. The town centre from **Piazza Walther** to **Via dei Portici**★ has some lovely houses.

★ **Cathedral** (Duomo). – The cathedral, built in the Romanesque Gothic style in pinkish sandstone and roofed with multicoloured tiles, has several decorative doorways and an open 14C-16C campanile. The interior, in the style of a German hall-church, has a nave and two aisles of equal height. The frescoes (1424) are by Corrado Erlin and the lovely Gothic **pulpit**★ is carved with a realism which is wholly northern in spirit.

Dominican Monastery (Convento dei Domenicani) ⊙. – *Piazza Domenicani.*
The church contains several interesting groups of frescoes: by the followers of Giotto in the Chapel of San Giovanni, by Giovanni Stocinger (14C-15C) in the nave and by Friedrich Pacher in the cloisters.

Church of the Franciscans (Chiesa dei Francescani) ⊙. – *1 Via Francescani.*
The church was begun in the 13C. Inside, the lovely late 15C **altarpiece**★ carved in wood is by Hans Klocker. The charming small cloisters have elegant fan vaulting.

Gries Parish Church (Chiesa Parrocchiale di Gries). – *Take Corso Libertà.*
This Gothic church has an **altarpiece**★ (1471) carved by Michael Pacher from Brunico.

Standing alongside the Brenta Canal between Strà and Fusina are numerous lovely classical **villas★** by Palladio *(qv)*. These were the summer residences of the Venetian nobility who used to lay on sumptuous night-time festivities to music by Vivaldi, Pergolesi or Cimarosa.

Sightseeing ⊙. – Boat trips leave from both Venice and Padua. By car take the road which follows the Brenta passing through Strà, Dolo, Mira and Malcontenta.

Strà – Villa Nazionale and its gardens

Strà ⊙. – The **Villa Nazionale★** has a majestic garden with a delightful vista and basin. The spacious **apartments★** of this 18C palace were decorated by various artists including Giovanni Battista Tiepolo who painted his masterpiece, **The Apotheosis of the Pisani Family★★**.

Mira ⊙. – The **Palazzo Foscarini** and **Villa Widmann-Foscari-Rezzonico** are both 18C. The **Ballroom★** of the latter is entirely decorated with frescoes.

Malcontenta ⊙. – Palladio built the **Villa Foscari★** in 1574. G. B. Zelotti and B. Franco were responsible for the frescoes. The villa was named after the wife of a Foscari who was ill-pleased *(malcontenta)* at being consigned to the villa.

★ **BRESCIA** Lombardy   Pop 198 839

The important industrial town of Brescia lies at the foot of the Lombard Pre-Alps. It has retained the regular street plan of the Roman camp *(castrum)* of Brixia. The town is dominated to the north by a medieval castle (Castello) and its centre has many fine buildings from all periods: Roman, Romanesque Renaissance and baroque.

HISTORICAL NOTES

Brixia flourished under the Empire and the remains of Roman monuments include the Capitoline Temple and the forum.

In the 8C Brescia became a Lombard duchy and then in the 12C and 13C a free commune and member of the Lombard League *(qv)*.

The town was one of the most prosperous in Italy, owing to the manufacture of arms and armour. Brescia supplied all Europe until the 18C. From 1426 to 1797 Brescia was under Venetian rule and acquired numerous secular and religious buildings. A group of artists formed the Brescia school and the most important members were, in the 15C, Vincenzo Foppa and in the 16C, Romanino and Moretto, Savoldo and Civerchio.

SIGHTS

★ **Piazza della Loggia** (BY 9). – The **Loggia** (BY H), now the town hall, was built from the end of the 15C to the beginning of the 16C to the designs of Bramante for the lower part and of Sansovino and Palladio for the upper part. The **Palazzo dell' Orologio**, opposite the Loggia, is surmounted by two Venetian Moorish figures *(Mori)* as Jacks. On the south side of the square stand the graceful palaces, **Monte Vecchio** (1484) and **Monte Nuovo** (1497) (BY B). To the north of the square is a picturesque popular quarter with arcades and old houses.

Piazza del Duomo (BY 5). – The 17C **New Cathedral** (Duomo Nuovo) in white marble seems to crush the **Old Cathedral** (Duomo Vecchio), a 12C Romanesque building which succeeded an earlier sanctuary known as the rotunda after its shape.

Inside, there is a magnificent sarcophagus in rose-coloured marble surmounted by the recumbent figure of a bishop, and in the chancel paintings by local artists, Moretto and Romanino. To the left of the Duomo Nuovo, the **Broletto** (P) is an austere Romanesque building dominated by a tower. Proclamations were made from the balcony on the façade.

★ **Tosio Martinengo Picture Gallery** (Pinacoteca Tosio-Martinengo) ⊘ (CZ). – Here are displayed works of the **Brescia school**, characterised by richness of colour and well-balanced composition: religious scenes and portraits by Moretto, more sumptuous religious scenes in the Venetian manner by Romanino and other works, as well as canvases by Vincenzo Foppa and Savoldo. The works of Clouet, Raphael, the Master of Utrecht, Lorenzo Lotto and Tintoretto are also on view.

★ **Via dei Musei** (CY). – This picturesque street has two interesting museums. The **Roman Museum**★ ⊘ (M¹) in the ruins of the **Capitoline Temple**★ (AD 73) contains a magnificent **Winged Victory** and six bronze Roman **busts**. Beyond the remains of the forum is the **Museum of Christian Art** ⊘ (M²), housed in the 16C Church of Santa Giulia. This collection has some priceless works of art such as the 4C and 5C **ivories**★★, the 8C **Cross of Desiderius**★★, a richly-encrusted piece, medals by Pisanello and small bronzes by Antonio Riccio (16C).

Churches. – Brescia has a great wealth of Romanesque, Renaissance and baroque churches and nearly all contain paintings of the Brescia school. The 13C **San Francesco**★ (AY) has a 14C *Pietà* by Giotto's followers, three saints by Moretto and a Virgin and Child by Romanino. The 15C and 16C **Santa Maria dei Miracoli** (AYZ A) has a lovely marble **façade**★.
San Nazaro – San Celso (AZ N) contains Moretto's masterpiece, the **Coronation of the Virgin**★. **Sant'Alessandro** (BZ G) has a 15C **Annunciation**★ by Jacopo Bellini and a **Descent from the Cross**★ by Civerchio. **Sant'Agata** (BY R) with its rich **interior**★ has a polyptych of the **Virgin of Pity**★ by the 16C Brescia school, as well as a **Virgin with Coral**★, a charming 16C fresco. **San Giovanni Evangelista** (BY E) is known for its works by Moretto and Romanino, **Madonna delle Grazie** (AY C) for its baroque interior and the **Church of the Carmine** (BY D) for its oriental silhouette.

Palestro (Corso) .... **BY**
Zanardelli (Corso) .... **BZ** 21
10 Giornate (Via delle) .... **BY** 22

*The towns and sights described in this guide are shown in **black** on the maps.*

★ **BRESSANONE** (BRIXEN) Trentino - Alto Adige   Pop 16 589

Michelin map 📖 folds 4 and 5 or 📖 fold 4 – Local map p 84
Town plan in the current Michelin Red Guide Italia

Bressanone, standing at the confluence of the Rienza and the Isarco, is an attractive little town known for its particularly sunny, dry and bracing climate. The town has remained Tyrolean in character.

Cathedral (Duomo). – The baroque interior is lavish with marble, stucco, gilding and frescoes. To the right of the cathedral are lovely 12C Romanesque **cloisters**★ with interesting 14C to 16C frescoes. The 11C St John the Baptist's Chapel contains both 13C Romanesque and 14C Gothic frescoes.

Palace of the Prince-Bishops (Palazzo Vescovile). – *Entrance in Via Vescovado.* The lovely **courtyard**★ has three storeys of arcades decorated with statues. Inside is the **Diocesan Museum**★ ⊘ with a remarkable collection of painted wood **sculptures**★★, typical of Tyrolean art of both the Romanesque and Gothic periods. There is also a series of **carved altarpieces**★ dating from the Renaissance, and on the ground floor an interesting collection of 18C and 19C **cribs**★. It also contains the cathedral treasury which has a good collection of liturgical objects and reliquaries.

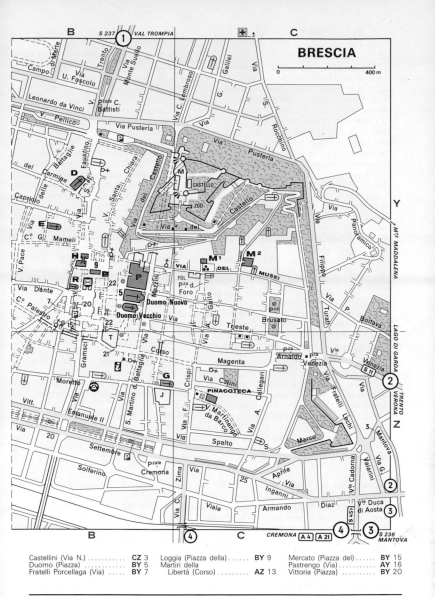

Castellini (Via N.)	**CZ** 3	Loggia (Piazza della)	**BY** 9	Mercato (Piazza del)	**BY** 15
Duomo (Piazza)	**BY** 5	Martiri della		Pastrengo (Via)	**AY** 16
Fratelli Porcellaga (Via)	**BY** 7	Libertà (Corso)	**AZ** 13	Vittoria (Piazza)	**BY** 20

EXCURSIONS

★★★ **Plose** ⊙. – Alt 2 446m – 8 025ft. *To the southeast.* The cable-car from Valcroce and then another from Plose enable visitors to enjoy a wonderful **panorama**★★★ of the Dolomites to the south and the Austrian mountains to the north.

★ **Monastery of Novacella** ⊙. – *3km – 2 miles to the north.*
The monastery was founded in 1142 and remodelled in the 15C and 18C. The Church of Our Lady (Nostra Signora) is in the Bavarian baroque style, the cloisters have frescoes by Michael Pacher and the Chapel of St Michael (San Michele) is late 12C.

BRINDISI Apulia   Pop 92 531

Michelin map 988 fold 30 or 431 fold 16
Town plans in the current Michelin Red Guide Italia

This important naval and trading port, on the Adriatic side of the 'boot's heel', has a daily shipping connection with Greece. Ever since antiquity the town has played the important role of trading-post with the rest of the Mediterranean basin. It was Trajan who replaced the old Appian Way beyond Benevento with the new Via Traiana which increased the importance of Brindisi from AD 109 onwards. After the Norman conquest the town became a port of embarkation for the Crusades to the Holy Land, and in particular saw the departure of the Sixth Crusade (1228). Along with Taranto and Bari, Brindisi makes up the triangle delimiting the Mezzogiorno, an area of industrial redevelopment.

★ **Roman Column (Colonna Romana)**. – This marble column near the harbour marked the end of the Appian-Traiana Way. It is crowned by a capital carved with figures.

Archaeological Museum (Museo Archeologico) ⊙. – *Piazza Duomo.*
The museum presents the numerous finds from excavations and a precious collection of vases made by early Italic peoples, the Apulians and Messapii.

★ CALABRIA

Michelin map ▓▓▓ folds 38, 39 and 40

Calabria covers the extreme southwestern 'toe' of the Italian peninsula from the Gulf of Policastro to Reggio di Calabria. This mountainous region lacked a good road network, which made it difficult to visit until the motorway to the south was extended as far as the regional capital. For this particular reason the region remained isolated but it would have been a mistake to consider, as a French traveller did at the beginning of the 19C, that "Europe ended at Naples". In fact the opposite is true since the first colonies founded by the Greeks in the 8C BC were located on the Ionian coast of present-day Calabria. It is not always possible – as it is in Sicily at Segesta, Agrigento or Selinunte – to discover the traces of Magna Graecia in the peninsula but the museums of Reggio, Taranto and Naples have collections recalling this period of Greek influence. It lasted until the 3C BC when Rome undertook the conquest of southern Italy, without however establishing a complete and peaceful domination until Sulla reorganised the administration of these provinces in the 1C BC.

After the fall of the Roman Empire, Calabria and the neighbouring regions fell under the sway of the Lombards, Saracens and Byzantines before being reunited with the Norman kingdom of the Two Sicilies and finally becoming part of a unified Italy in 1860.

The mountainous massifs which occupy the interior of the peninsula are fringed by narrow coastal plains. Between these physically-distinct regions there are considerable vegetational and climatic differences according to the seasons. The Sila Massif comprises rugged mountains and alpine prairies; the Aspromonte is covered with chestnut forests; there are stony and abrupt valleys along the coastline and coastal plains covered with fruit trees bordering the Gulf of Taranto. Recent agrarian reform has been responsible for a slowing down of emigration and the region's emergence from its isolation.

★★ **Sila Massif.** – North of Catanzaro and several miles inland, the high granite plateau of the Sila Massif is covered with Italy's most extensive forest of pine, evergreen oak and beech, which alternates with pastures and the calm waters of lonely lakes. The recent agrarian reform called for a reappraisal of this once-inaccessible region, and today it is being redeveloped for its recreational value in both summer and winter.

To the east of the massif, the capital, **San Giovanni in Fiore,** grew up around the abbey founded by Joachim of Fiore for his new religious order, stricter than that of the Cistercians. La Badia Fiorense has a remarkable pointed doorway and some Cistercian windows in the apse. The small holiday village and ski resort of Lorica has been developed on the indented and wooded shores of the immense **Lake Arvo★**.

★ **Aspromonte.** – The Aspromonte Massif forms the southern tip of Calabria and culminates in a peak of 2 000m – 6 561ft. The Tyrrhenian coast descends in terraces to the shore while the Ionian coast slopes more gently down to the sea. The forest cover includes chestnut trees, oaks and beeches. The massif serves as a catchment area from which radiate deep valleys eroded by fast-flowing torrents *(fiumare)*. The wide river beds are dry in summer but may fill up rapidly and the waters become destructive. The S 183 between the S 112 and Melito di Porto Salvo runs through attractive scenery and affords numerous and often quite spectacular **panoramas★★★**.

★ **Purple Coast (Costa Viola).** – The most southern part of the Tyrrhenian coast from Gioia Tauro to Villa San Giovanni takes its name from the dark purple of its rocky mountain slopes.

Gioia Tauro. – This seaside resort has a hinterland of centuries-old olive groves.

Palmi. – This small town perched high above the sea has a small fishing harbour and a lovely sandy beach.

The **Municipal Museum** ⊘ *(Casa della Cultura, Via San Giorgio)* has an **ethnographic section★** evoking the life and traditions of Calabria: local costumes, handcrafts, ceramics etc.

★ **Bagnara Calabra.** – In a picturesque site looking out to sea, Bagnara is the main fishing port for sword-fish.

★ **Scilla.** – This small fishing-town stands at the foot of a rock which is said to be the female monster, Scylla. According to Homer's *Odyssey*, it was on this rock that ships often came to grief having successfully avoided the whirlpool of Charybdis near Taormina on the Sicilian coast. Hence the expression "between Scylla and Charybdis".

Villa San Giovanni. – This is the ferry terminal for Sicily.

★ **Rocca Imperiale.** – *25km – 16 miles to the north of Trebisacce.*
This picturesque village has grown up around a castle built by the Emperor Frederick II.

★ **Tropea.** – This ancient small town, built on the clifftop, had its hour of glory under Angevin and Aragonese rule. The lovely Norman-style **cathedral★** (cattedrale) has three apses encrusted with polychrome stones.

Altomonte. – *30km – 19 miles to the south of Castrovillari.*
The large market town is dominated by an imposing 14C Angevin cathedral dedicated to **Santa Maria della Consolazione.** The façade is embellished with a doorway and an elegant rose window. Inside there are no aisles and the east end is flat. The fine **tomb★** is that of Filippo Sangineto. The small **museum** ⊘ beside the church has several precious works of art in addition to a statue of **St Ladislas★** attributed to Simone Martini.

Catanzaro. – *Town plan in the current Michelin Red Guide Italia.*
Catanzaro stands perched on a hilltop, at some distance from the sea, away from the danger of invading forces and malaria-infested waters. The town was founded in the 9C by the Byzantines and it prospered until the end of the 15C thanks to its university and its silk industry, for which it was famous throughout Europe. After having successfully resisted the French troops of Marshal de Lautrec in 1528, the town began to decline in the 17C, owing partly to the Black Death and partly to the numerous earthquakes in the 18C and 19C. However the modern town, traversed by Corso Mazzini, has a certain charm.
The **Villa Trieste★** is a terraced public garden with plenty of shade. The **Church of San Domenico** (or of the Rosary) contains a very fine altarpiece of the **Madonna of the Rosary★**, which is probably the work of the 17C Neapolitan school.

Cosenza. – *Town plan in the current Michelin Red Guide Italia.*
The modern town is overlooked by the old town where streets and palaces recall the prosperity of the Angevin and Aragonese periods. Cosenza was then considered the artistic and religious capital of Calabria. The 12C-13C **cathedral** (Duomo) has recently been restored to its original aspect. Inside is the **mausoleum★** containing the heart of Isabella of Aragon, the wife of Philip III, King of France and son of Louis IX (St Louis who died in Tunis). She died in 1271 outside Cosenza on the way back from Tunis with the sainted king's body and was buried in St-Denis Basilica in France.

Crotone. – *Description p 76.*

Gerace. – *Northwest of Locri on the S 111.*
This was the inland refuge of the people from Locri at the time of the Saracen raids. It was abandoned in favour of the coastal area when the latter was rid of malaria. The **cathedral** (Cattedrale) is one of the largest in Calabria and dates back to the time of the Norman Robert Guiscard (11C). Although remodelled several times it has retained its basilical plan with a nave and two aisles separated by lovely antique piers. Quite near stands the **Church of San Francesco** with a lovely doorway and a 17C **altarpiece★** in polychrome marble.

Locri. – *On the east coast of the Aspromonte Massif.*
This modest seaside resort was founded by the Greeks in the 7C BC. The town was ruled by the severe laws decreed by Zaleucos and was one of the rival cities of Crotone which she defeated during the battle of Sagra. Locri repelled all annexation attempts by the Syracusan "tyrants". After having sided with Hannibal, along with the other towns on the Ionian coast during the Second Punic War, it declined in importance and was destroyed by the Saracens in the 9C AD. Most of the town's antiquities can be seen in the museum in Reggio di Calabria. There is an interesting excavation site to the south of the town.

Paola ⊙. – St Francis of Paola was born here around 1416. A **monastery** visited by numerous pilgrims stands 2km – 1 mile away up the hillside. This important group of buildings includes the basilica with a lovely baroque façade which enshrines the relics of the saint, cloisters and a hermitage hewn out of the rock.

★ **Pentedattilo.** – *10km – 6 miles northwest of Melito di Porto Salvo.*
In a sun-scorched valley this little village nestles at the foot of a gigantic and highly-eroded rock which resembles a hand pointing upwards to the sky.

Reggio di Calabria. – *Description p 178.*

Rossano. – *96km – 60 miles northwest of Crotone.*
The town spreads over a hillside clad with olive groves. In the Middle Ages it was the capital of Greek monasticism in the west, where expelled or persecuted Basilian monks came for refuge, living in the cells which can still be seen today. The perfect little Byzantine church **San Marco** dates from this period. The flat east end has three projecting semicircular apses with graceful openings. To the right of the cathedral (Cattedrale) the **Diocesan Museum** (Museo Diocesano) ⊙ or former archbishop's residence has a valuable **Purpureus Codex★**, a 6C evangelistary with brightly-coloured illuminations.

20km – 12 miles to the west of the town is a small church, the **Patirion**, the only remaining building of a large Basilian monastery.
The church has three apses ornamented with blind arcading and inside, mosaics portraying various animals.

Serra San Bruno. – Between the Sila and Aspromonte Massifs, amidst the Calabrian mountains covered with oak and pinewood **forests★**, this small market town grew up around a **hermitage** founded by St Bruno. The 12C charterhouse *(1km – 1/2 mile from the town)* and the cave which served as hermitage *(4km – 2 1/2 miles to the southwest of the latter)* recall the memory of St Bruno who died in 1101.

Stilo – La Cattolica

Sibari. – *15km – 9 miles south of Trebisacce.*
Founded in the 8C BC in a very fertile plain which was the source of the exceptional prosperity of the ancient city of **Sybaris**. The town was razed in 510 BC by the neighbouring city of Crotone. There is a small **Archaeological Museum** (Museo Archeologico) ⊘ and an **excavation site** (Scavi) ⊘ to the south of the town.

Stilo. – *15km – 9 miles west of Monasterace Marina.* On the rocky side of a deep valley this town was the bastion of the Basilian monks and is famous for its Byzantine church, **La Cattolica★** ⊘ *(illustration p 71)*. Small in size but of perfect proportions in the form of a Greek cross, it is in the pure Byzantine style and is roofed with five domes. Inside, four ancient columns support the arches and vaulting.

CAMONICA VALLEY Lombardy

Michelin map 𝟡𝟪𝟪 fold 4, 𝟜𝟚𝟠 folds 7 and 17 or 𝟜𝟚𝟡 fold 12

The valley, which stretches from Lovere to Edolo, is industrial in its lower reaches and becomes more picturesque towards its head with several ruined castles guarding its slopes. Many rock engravings dating from prehistory to the Roman era have been discovered in an area 60km – 37 miles long.

★★ **Rock engravings.** – The rock faces of Camonica Valley, smoothed by glacial erosion 10 000 years ago, present an even surface ideally suited to decoration. The engravings, made by pitting or scratching the stone, reveal scenes of the daily life of the peoples who lived on the site: in the paleolithic era (about 8000 to 5000 BC) they lived solely from the hunt, then took up agriculture in the neolithic period and later metalworking in the Bronze Age (from 1800 BC) and the Iron Age (900 BC). There are mainly four types of scenes: the hunt (stags); ox-teams and ploughs; arms and warriors; religious scenes (praying figures, symbols and idols).
The engravings are readily accessible in the **Naquane National Park of Rock Engravings** (Parco Nazionale delle Incisioni Rupestri) ⊘ *(time: 2 hours – access from Capo di Ponte)* and in the **Ceto, Cimbergo and Paspardo Regional Nature Reserve** (Riserva Naturale Regionale) ⊘: for access apply to the **museum** at Nadro in Ceto which is devoted to the rock engravings.

Breno. – The main town of the valley has a 10C castle and two interesting churches: the 14C-15C Sant'Antonio and San Salvatore.

The **Michelin Green Guide Great Britain**
aims to make touring more enjoyable by suggesting
several touring programmes which are easily adapted to personal taste.

CAPRAROLA Latium   Pop 4 913

Michelin map 𝟡𝟪𝟪 fold 25 or 𝟜𝟛𝟘 fold 25 – 19km – 12 miles southeast of Viterbo

★ **Villa Farnese** ⊘. – The villa was built upon a fortified pentagon basement, from 1559 to 1575, for Cardinal Alessandro Farnese to the designs of Vignola, and is a good example of the late-16C Mannerist style. The five storey-tall ranges surround a delightful circular inner courtyard. To the left of the entrance hall is Vignola's **spiral staircase★★** which rises majestically through tiers of thirty paired Doric columns, and is decorated with grotesques and landscapes by Antonio Tempesta. The many paintings which decorate several of the rooms are by the Zuccaro brothers, Taddeo (1529-66) and Federico (*c*1540-1609) as well as Bertoja (1544-74). These are typical of the refined and sophisticated Mannerist style of the late Italian Renaissance period.

Park. – This 18ha – 44 acre park with its many terraces and monumental fountains, is embellished by a charming **palazzina** also designed by Vignola.

★★★ **CAPRI** Campania   Pop 12 507

Michelin map 𝟡𝟪𝟪 fold 27 or 𝟜𝟛𝟙 fold 17 – Local map p 74
Access: see the current Michelin Red Guide Italia

Capri, the Island of Dreams, has always been an enchanting place, with its situation in close proximity to the Sorrento Peninsula *(see local map p 147)*, the incomparable beauty of its rugged landscape, the mildness of its climate and the luxuriance of its vegetation. Capri captivated two Roman emperors: Augustus exchanged Ischia for Capri, and Tiberius spent the latter part of his life here. Since the late 19C the island has attracted numerous celebrities: artists, writers, musicians and actors, in all seasons. Capri is one of the high spots of international tourism.

★ **MARINA GRANDE**

This is the disembarkation port for the northern part of the isle. The houses, some white, some coloured, nestle round the bay framed by spectacular cliffs.
A funicular railway goes to Capri (Piazza Umberto I). There is a bus service to Anacapri with a stop-off at Capri (Via Roma).

BOAT TRIPS

★★ **Blue Grotto (Grotta Azzurra)** ⊘. – *Boats leave from Marina Grande. It is also possible to go by road (8km – 5 miles from Capri).*
The Blue Grotto is the most famous among the many marine caves on the island. The light enters, not directly, but by refraction through the water, giving it a beautiful blue colour.

★★★ **Tour of the isle** ⊘. – *Leave from Marina Grande.*
Visitors will discover a rugged coastline, pierced with caves and small peaceful creeks, fringed with fantastically shaped reefs and lined with sheer cliffs dipping vertically into the sea.
The island is quite small: barely 6km – 4 miles long and 3km – 2 miles wide. The particularly mild climate favours the growth of a varied flora: pine, lentisk, juniper, arbutus, asphodel, myrtle and acanthus.
The boats go in a clockwise direction and the first sight is the **Sea Ox Cave** (Grotta del Bove Marino), which derives its name from the roar of the sea rushing into the cave in stormy weather. Beyond is the headland (Punta del Capo) dominated by **Mount Tiberius** (Monte Tiberio). Once past the impressive cliff known as Tiberius' Leap *(see below)* the headland to the south, Punta di Tragara, is fringed by the famous **Faraglioni**, rocky islets carved into fantastic shapes by the waves. The **Arsenal Cave** (Grotta dell'Arsenale) (BZ) was used as a nymphaeum during the reign of Tiberius.
Continue past the small port of Marina Piccola *(see below)* to reach the generally lower west coast. The last part of the trip covers the north coast and includes the visit to the Blue Grotto *(see above).*

★★★ CAPRI

Capri is like a stage setting for an operetta with its small squares, little white houses and its quite Moorish-looking alleyways. Another of its charms is that wild and lonely spots can still be found near crowded and lively scenes.

★ **Piazza Umberto I** (BZ). – This famous piazzetta is the centre of town and the spot where fashionable crowds foregather. The busy narrow side streets, such as **Via Le Botteghe★** (BZ 10), are lined with souvenir shops and smart boutiques selling luxury goods.

★★ **Cannone Belvedere.** – To reach the belvedere take the **Via Madre Serafina★** (BZ 12), which is almost entirely vaulted. The belvedere presents another aspect of Capri with its quiet and mysterious, covered and winding alleys interrupted by steps.

★★ **Tragara Belvedere.** – *Access by Via Camerelle* (BZ) *and Via Tragara.*
There is a magnificent view of the Faraglioni.

★★ **Jupiter's Villa (Villa Jovis)** ⊘. – This was the residence of the Emperor Tiberius. Excavations have uncovered servants' quarters, the cisterns that supplied the baths, and the imperial apartments with a loggia overlooking the sea.
From the esplanade overlooked by a church, there is a lovely **panorama★★** of the whole island.
Take the stairway behind the church to enjoy a view of **Tiberius' Leap★** (Salto di Tiberio), the impressive cliff over which the emperor is said to have had his victims thrown.

★ **Natural rock arch (Arco Naturale).** – The sea has created this gigantic arch which rises well above sea level. Lower down is the **Matromania Cave** where the Romans venerated the goddess Cybele.

Carthusian Monastery of St James (Certosa di San Giacomo) ⊘ (BZ D) and **Augustus' Gardens (Giardini Augusto)** (BZ B). – This 14C monastery has two cloisters. In the smallest are displayed Roman statues taken from the nymphaeum of the Blue Grotto.
From Augustus' Gardens there is a beautiful **view★★** of Punta di Tragara and the Faraglioni *(see above)*. Lower down, **Via Krupp★** (BZ), clinging to the rock face, leads to Marina Piccola.

★ **Marina Piccola.** – There are beautiful small beaches and a haven for fishing boats.

CAPRI

The main car parks are indicated on the town plans.

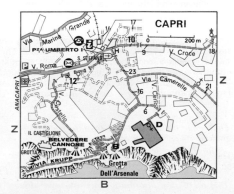

73

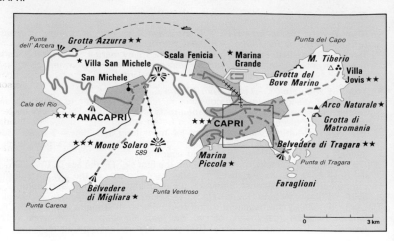

★★★ ANACAPRI

Town plan in the current Michelin Red Guide Italia

Take the Via Roma and a beautiful corniche road to reach Anacapri, a delightful village with shady streets, which is much less crowded than Capri.

★ **Villa San Michele** ⊙. – *Access from Piazza della Vittoria.*
The villa was built at the end of the 19C for the Swedish doctor-writer, Axel Munthe (d 1949), who lived there up to 1910 and described the atmosphere of the island in his *Story of San Michele*. The house contains 17C and 18C furniture, copies of antique works and some original Roman sculptures. The pergola at the end of the garden giddily overhangs the sea and provides a splendid **panorama**★★★ of Capri, Marina Grande, Mount Tiberius and the Faraglioni. Just below the villa is a stairway, **Scala Fenicia,** which numbers nearly 800 steps and leads down to the harbour. It was for a long time the only link between the town and its port. This is where Axel Munthe met the old Maria "Porta-Lettere" who delivered the mail although she could not read and who is depicted in his novel.

San Michele ⊙. – The fine majolica **pavement**★ (1761) represents the Garden of Eden after a cartoon by Solimena.

★★★ **Monte Solaro** ⊙. – The chairlift swings pleasantly above gardens and terraces brimming over with a luxuriant vegetation. From the summit there is an unforgettable **panorama**★★★ of the whole island and the Bay of Naples as far as the island of Ponza, the Apennines and the mountains of Calabria to the south.

★ **Migliara Belvedere.** – *1 hour on foot Rtn. Go under the chairlift to take Via Caposcuro.* There is a remarkable **view**★ of the lighthouse on the headland, Punta Carena, and of the sheer cliffs.

CAPUA Campania   Pop 19 131

Michelin map ▨▨▨ fold 27 or ▨▨▨ fold 9 – 38km – 24 miles north of Naples

The present town stands quite near to the ancient Roman Capua where Hannibal grew soft in luxury. This small triangular town, enclosed within ramparts, has a certain charm with its narrow alleys, arches, old palaces and churches, many of which are built with material quarried from the numerous Roman ruins.

Cathedral (Duomo). – Although built in the 9C it has been destroyed and rebuilt several times since. The Lombard-style campanile incorporates some ancient fragments at its base. The columns of the atrium have lovely **Corinthian capitals,** dating from the 3C.
Basilical in plan, the cathedral has numerous works of art.

★ **Campania Museum (Museo Campano)** ⊙. – *At the corner of Via Duomo and Via Roma.*
The archaeological section has an astonishing collection of **earth goddesses** dating from the 7C to 1C BC and a charming **mosaic.** The medieval section groups some lovely **sculptures** from the imposing gateway built by the Emperor Frederick II of Hohenstaufen around 1239, to mark the boundary of his kingdom.
The lovely **Piazza dei Giudici** is bordered by the baroque church of Sant'Eligio, a loggia surmounted by a Gothic arch, and the 16C town hall.

*Each year the **Michelin Red Guide Italia**
revises its 500 town plans which show*

– through-routes and by-passes
– new roads, one-way systems and car parks
– the exact location of hotels, restaurants and public buildings.

This up-to-date information makes town driving less stressful.

CARRARA Tuscany
Pop 69 064

Michelin map 988 fold 14, 428 fold 31 or 430 fold 1

Carrara lies in a smiling basin on the edge of the limestone massif of the Apuan Alps, which is rugged and spectacular and so white that it appears to be snow-clad. It is known the world over for its white **marble**, of unequalled texture and purity (except perhaps for that of Paros in Greece). The marble has been quarried since the time of the Romans, and Michelangelo used to come in person to choose blocks from which he carved his masterpieces.

Cathedral (Duomo). – The façade, in the Pisan style, is adorned with a delicately carved marble rose window and flanked by an elegant 13C campanile. Inside, there are several interesting 14C statues.

Marble Quarries (Cave di marmo) ⊙. – The wild countryside and the gigantic nature of the quarrying operations afford a spectacular sight. The impressive **Fantiscritti Quarries★★** *(5km – 3 miles to the northeast)* in a wild site, and the **Colonnata Quarries★** *(8.5km – 5 miles to the east)* in a greener setting, are both actively quarried and regularly despatch quantities of marble. **Marina di Carrara** *(7km – 4 miles to the southwest)* is the main port, where piles of marble blocks are stacked high.

EXCURSION

★ Sarzana. – *16km – 10 miles to the north.*
The busy town of Sarzana was once an advanced base of the Republic of Genoa, a rival of Pisa, and its numerous historic buildings bear witness to its past importance. The **cathedral** (Cattedrale) has a marble **altarpiece★** (1432) delicately carved by Riccomani. In a chapel to the right of the chancel is a phial which is said to have contained the Blood of Christ. In the chapel to the left is a **Crucifixion★** (1138), the masterpiece of the Roman artist, Guglielmo, probably from Lucca.
The **Fortress of Sarzanello★** ⊙ (1322) was built on a height to the northeast of the town, by the *condottiere* (leader of a mercenary army) from Lucca, Castruccio Castracani. It is a curious example of military architecture with deep moats and massive curtain walls guarded at intervals by round towers. From the top of the keep there is a magnificent **panorama★★** of the town and the Apennine foothills.

★★ CASAMARI ABBEY Latium

Michelin map 988 fold 26 or 430 folds 37 and 38

Casamari Abbey ⊙ standing in a lonely site was originally Benedictine and was consecrated in 1217 by Pope Honorius III. It was later taken over by the Cistercians who rebuilt the abbey, modelling it on the abbey at Fossanova *(qv)* and in accordance with the rules of austerity and self-sufficiency laid down by St Bernard, the founder of the Cistercian Order.
This is a lovely example of early Italian architecture. Above the entrance porch of the abbey church is a gallery of twinned openings, which served as the abbots' lodging during the Renaissance. The simplicity of the façade is typically Burgundian with a round-headed doorway, the rose window, and rising above all the transept tower.
The interior is spacious, austere and solemn. Built to a Latin cruciform plan, it has a nave and two aisles separated by massive cruciform piers with engaged columns supporting the lofty pointed vaulting. The later canopy seems out of place in the shallow chancel. The apse and arms of the transept are lit by windows with a wheel window above.
On the south side of the church are the cloisters with their twin columns, the well and lovely garden bright with flowers. On the east side, in its traditional position, is the remarkable chapterhouse with delicate ribbed pointed vaulting supported by clustered columns.

★ CASERTA Campania
Pop 66 778

Michelin map 988 fold 27 or 431 fold 9

Caserta, the Versailles of the Kingdom of Naples, stands in the heart of a fertile plain.

★★ La Reggia ⊙. – This immense palace was begun in 1752 by Vanvitelli for the Bourbon King, Charles III, who dreamed of another Versailles. The palace, one of Italy's most grandiose, was built five floors high on a great rectangular plan 249m – 273yds long and 190m – 208yds wide. The façades, each with a projecting colonnaded centrepiece, are grand but rather monotonous. In all there are some 250 windows. The buildings are arranged around four well-proportioned inner courtyards. A magnificent entrance hall leads to the courtyards and the main **staircase★**. The sumptuously decorated apartments are furnished with Empire-style pieces.

★ Park ⊙. – The gardens and park were also designed by Luigi Vanvitelli and his son. The main vista is a succession of fountains and basins, themselves studded with statues. The group of Diana and Actaeon is by Vanvitelli himself. The focal point is the 78m – 256ft-tall monumental **cascade★★**. To the right of the cascade is a picturesque **English garden★★** created for Maria-Carolina of Austria.

★ Caserta Vecchia. – *10km – 6 miles to the north.*
This small town is dominated by the ruins of its 9C castle. The town has a certain charm with its almost entirely abandoned narrow alleyways lined by old buildings with their brown tufa walls.

★ CASTELFRANCO VENETO Venetia   Pop 29 181

Michelin map 988 fold 5 or 429 folds 14 and 15

Castelfranco is a pleasant citadel surrounded by moats. It has a few prettily arcaded houses and is the birthplace of the artist Giorgione. The **cathedral** (Duomo) contains his masterpiece, the **Madonna and Child with Saints★★**.
Born *c*1477, **Giorgione** died young at the age of 32, no doubt of the Black Death. His twenty or so masterpieces influenced not only Venetian artists (Titian, who was his pupil and probably completed several of his master's canvases, Giovanni Bellini in his later works, Sebastiano del Piombo, Palma Vecchio, Savoldo, Dosso Dossi etc) but also all of European art with his masterful handling of light. Giorgione accomplished in his short life-time an admirable synthesis of the human figure and nature with his flowing draughtsmanship and his skilful use of colour. The cathedral's work is among his earlier achievements and it already shows a preoccupation with achieving this fusion, as the figures are disposed on two different planes: the two saints in the shadow of the paved room while the Virgin enthroned on high stands out from the landscape background.
The artist's **birthplace** ⊙ *(Piazza del Duomo)* is now arranged as a museum.

★ CASTELLAMMARE DI STABIA Campania   Pop 68 324

Michelin map 988 fold 27 or 431 fold 13 – Local map p 147

This was the ancient Roman spa town of Stabiae. Occupied successively by the Oscans, the Etruscans, the Samnites and finally the Romans in the 4C, Stabia rebelled against Rome but was crushed by Sulla in the 1C BC. The town was rebuilt in the form of small clusters of houses, while luxury villas for rich patricians spread over the high ground. In the AD 79 eruption of Vesuvius the new town was wiped out along with Herculaneum and Pompeii. The naturalist Pliny the Elder who cane by boat to observe the phenomenon at close range perished by asphyxiation.
In the 18C the Bourbons undertook excavations, repaired the port, and built shipyards which are still in use.

★ **Antiquarium** ⊙. – *2 Via Marco Mario.*
The finds from the excavations are displayed here and include a magnificent series of **mural paintings** from the villas and some very fine stucco **low reliefs.**

Roman villas. *–2km – 1 mile to the east by the Gragnano road.*
Ariadne's Villa (Villa di Arianna) ⊙ was one of the luxurious villas facing the sea with an incomparable view of the bay and of Vesuvius. The architectural refinement of **San Marco's Villa** ⊙ with its two storeys was enhanced by gardens and swimming pools. It was in all probability a sumptuous country residence.

★★ CASTELLI ROMANI Latium

Michelin map 988 fold 26 or 430 fold 36

Castelli Romani, or Roman Castles, is the name given to the region of the Alban Hills (Colli Albani), which are of volcanic origin and lie to the southeast of Rome. While anarchy reigned in Rome, the noble families sought refuge in the outlying villages which they fortified. Each of these villages was strategically set on the outer rim of an immense crater, itself pitted with small secondary craters, some of which now contain lakes (Albano and Nemi). Pastures and chestnut groves cover the upper slopes while lower down there are olive groves and vineyards, which produce an excellent wine.
Nowadays the Romans readily leave the capital in summer for the "Castelli" where they find peace, fresh air, good walking country and pleasant country inns.

ROUND TOUR STARTING FROM ROME
122km – 76 miles – allow a whole day

Leave Rome by the Via Appia in the direction of **Castel Gandolfo**, now the Pope's summer residence. It is thought that Castel Gandolfo was built on the site of ancient Alba Longa, the traditional and powerful rival of Rome. Their rivalry led to the famous combat of the Horatios for Rome and the Curiaces for Alba, as recounted by the Roman historian Livy (Titus Livius). **Albano Laziale** was built on the site of Domitian's villa. Today the town boasts an attractive church (**Santa Maria della Rotonda★**), large public gardens (**Villa Comunale★**) and not far from Borgo Garibaldi, the so-called tomb of the Horatios and the Curiaces. **Ariccia** has a lovely square designed by Bernini, a palace which belonged to the Chigi banking family, and the Church of the Assumption. **Velletri** is a prosperous town lying south of the Alban Hills in the heart of a wine-producing region.
Take Via dei Laghi out of Velletri.
This scenic road winds through groves of chestnut and oak trees to reach **Nemi**, a small village in a charming setting on the slopes of the lake of the same name. The road then climbs to **Monte Cavo** (alt 949m – 3 124ft) which was crowned by the Temple of Jupiter. First a monastery and now a hotel have occupied the buildings. From the esplanade there is a fine **view★** of the Castelli region with Rome on the horizon. Beyond the attractively set **Rocca di Papa**, facing the Alban lakes, the road passes through **Grottaferrata** with its abbey which was founded in the 11C by Greek monks. **Tusculo** was the fief of the powerful Counts of Tusculum who governed the Castelli region. Next comes **Frascati** ⊙ pleasantly situated on the slopes facing Rome. It is known for its wines and its 16C and 17C villas, particularly the **Villa Aldobrandini★** set above its terraced gardens. The road back to Rome passes Cinecittà, the Italian Hollywood.

CERTALDO Tuscany   Pop 16 104

Michelin map 988 fold 14 or 430 fold 13

It was in this village, in the wooded Elsa Valley, that **Giovanni Boccaccio** (1312-75) spent the last years of his life. Along with Dante and Petrarch, he was one of the three great Italian writers. The son of a merchant, he was brought up at the Angevin court in Naples and represented the new urbane bourgeois of the Renaissance, with his taste for ironic analysis of different types of character dominated by a variety of ever-changing passions. In his main work **Decameron** (ten days), he describes in a rhythmic, limpid style the accounts of ten young people exiled from Florence because of the plague. He praises intelligence and love and their victory over baseness and routine.

In the upper town are **Boccaccio's House** ⊙, now transformed into a museum, the Church of San Jacopo where the writer is buried and the **Palazzo Pretorio** ⊙, which was rebuilt in the 16C.

CERVETERI Latium   Pop 17 752

Michelin map 988 fold 25 or 430 fold 35

The ancient Caere was a powerful Etruscan centre, which stood on an eminence to the east of the present town of Cerveteri. Caere attained great prosperity in the 7C and 6C BC and was renowned as a great cultural and religious centre. In the 4C BC Caere began to decline. It was only at the beginning of the 20C that excavation work began on this site. Most of the finds are now displayed in the Villa Giulia *(p 193)* in Rome.

The admirable necropolis which is to be found 2km – 1 mile to the north of Cerverteri testifies to the Etruscans' belief in an afterlife. The **Banditaccia Necropolis**★★ ⊙ is laid out like a city with numerous tumuli lining a main street. The site is pervaded by a great sense of peace. The tombs generally dating from the 7C BC add a strange note to the scene. These conical earth mounds, often grass-covered, rest on a stone base, which is sometimes decorated with mouldings, with the burial chambers underneath. Other tombs consist of underground burial chambers reached through simply-decorated doors. A vestibule leads into the burial chambers which often contain two funeral beds placed side by side: one is adorned with a small column if the deceased was a man (the breadwinner) and the other with a small canopy in the case of a woman (guardian of the home).

One of the tombs without a tumulus is the **Tomb of the Reliefs**★★ with its painted stucco low reliefs giving a realistic picture of everyday Etruscan life.

CHIAVENNA Lombardy   Pop 7 575

Michelin map 988 fold 3, 218 fold 14 or 428 folds 5 and 6

In this region of wild valleys, Chiavenna is the key *(chiave)* to the Splügen and Maloja transalpine passes between Italy and Switzerland.

The Romanesque **Collegiate Church of St Lawrence** (San Lorenzo) was rebuilt in the 16C following a fire. The works of art include a canvas by Pietro Ligari. The **baptistry** contains a Romanesque **baptismal basin**★ (1156) with interesting low reliefs. Outstanding among the items of the **treasure** ⊙ is a lovely 12C binding for an evangelistary.

The rock, **Il Paradiso** ⊙, is a **botanical and archaeological garden** which affords lovely **views**★ of the town's setting.

EXCURSION

★★ **Splügen Pass Road** (Passo dello Spluga). – *30km – 19 miles from Chiavenna to the pass.*
This road is one of the boldest and most spectacular in the Alps. The **Campodolcino-Pianazzo section**★★★ is grandiose as it climbs the sheer mountainside in tight hairpin bends.

CHIETI Abruzzi   Pop 56 051

Michelin map 988 fold 27 or 430 fold 29
Town plan in the current Michelin Red Guide Italia

Chieti is built on the summit of a hill planted with olive trees and offers varied panoramas. Corso Marrucino is the town's busiest street.

Abruzzi Archaeological Museum (Museo Archeologico degli Abruzzi) ⊙. – The museum is housed in a building set in lovely **gardens**★ (Villa Comunale). There are numerous works which were produced locally from the 6C BC to the 4C AD, in particular the marble statue of Hercules, discovered at Alba Fucens *(qv)*, a portrait of Sulla, a fine bronze of Hercules and especially the famous **Warrior of Capestrano**★, a strange 6C BC limestone statue, and several rare examples of Picenum art. The Picenes occupied the central part of the Italian peninsula prior to the Romans.

Roman remains. – Three adjoining and minute **temples** (Templi Romani) were discovered in 1935 near the post office and Corso Marrucino. A little further to the east are water tanks cut out of the hillside intended to supply the baths, which are also fairly well preserved.

CHIUSI Tuscany

Michelin map 988 fold 15 or 430 fold 15

Standing on a hill covered with olive groves, Chiusi is today a quiet and hospitable little town. It was once one of the twelve sovereign cities of Etruria.

* **Etruscan Museum (Museo Etrusco)** ⊙. – *Via Porsenna*. The museum presents the various finds from the burial grounds in the neighbourhood: sarcophagi, rounded tombstones *(cippi)*, alabaster and stone funerary urns, burial urns *(canopae)* in the shape of heads, clay ex-votos as well as a variety of utensils, vases, lamps and jewellery. The objects all display the Etruscan taste for fantasy and realism.

Visitors with a car may be accompanied by the museum custodian to some of the remaining tombs 3km – 2 miles from Chiusi. The most interesting, the **Tomba della Scimmia** (the Monkey Tomb), consists of four decorated chambers and dates from the 5C BC.

★★ CINQUE TERRE Liguria

Michelin map 988 fold 13 or 428 fold 36 – Local map p 182

Lying northwest of the Gulf of La Spezia, the Cinque Terre (Five Lands) is, even today, an isolated region with no good access road. This rugged coast is wild but hospitable, with its vineyards and fishing villages where the people remain strongly attached to their old customs and traditions.

★★ **Vernazza.** – This is the most attractive village with its tall colourful houses and its church clustered together at the head of a well-sheltered cove.

The Cinque Terre – Manarola

★ **Manarola.** – This fishing village with its small 14C church is set in a landscape of terraced vineyards. Starting from the station there is a splendid **walk★★** *(1/4 hour on foot)* which offers lovely views of the coast and the other villages.

★ **Riomaggiore.** – *Take the branch road off the La Spezia-Manarola road.*
The old houses of this medieval village lie in a narrow valley. This tiny fishing village stands backed up against the strange black rock strata which are so typical of the region.

★ CIVIDALE DEL FRIULI Friuli – Venezia Giulia

Michelin map 988 fold 6 or 429 fold 17 – 17km – 11 miles to the northeast of Udine

The ancient Forum Julii gave the town its modern name. It is superbly set overlooking the River Natisone. It was for long independent and became the residence of the Patriarchs of Aquileia. From the 15C onward it belonged to Venice. Since the 1976 earthquake, Cividale has been rebuilt.

Cathedral (Duomo). – It was extensively rebuilt in the 16C in the Renaissance style by Piero Lombardo (1435-1515) but retains some Gothic features on the façade and in the interior. The high altar has a 12C Veneto-Byzantine silver-gilt altarpiece. The small **museum** ⊙ of Lombard art (opening off the south aisle) contains numerous valuable items: the octagonal baptismal font of the Patriarch Callisto, rebuilt using Byzantine fragments, and the 8C "altar" of Duke Ratchis in marble with carved sides depicting scenes from the Life of Christ.

★ **Archaeological Museum** (Museo Archeologico Nazionale) ⊙. – *To the left of the cathedral.* The museum has a collection of silver and gold pieces, representative of 7C Lombard art, including a solid gold cross which belonged to Gisulph, and a carved and encrusted ivory plaque which once belonged to Duke Orso (9C). The collection of medieval manuscripts includes a 13C Psalter adorned with miniatures which was known as St Elizabeth's.

★★ **Tempietto** ⊙. – *Near the Piazza San Biagio.*
This elegant 8C Lombard building is a square chamber with quadripartite vaulting and admirable Lombard **decoration** of friezes and stylised stuccos. It is a unique example of the architecture of this period.

CIVITAVECCHIA Latium   Pop 50 832

Michelin map ▯▯▯ fold 25 or ▯▯▯ fold 24

Civitavecchia, the Roman Centumcellae, has been the port of Rome since the reign of Trajan and now handles maritime traffic with Sardinia. The port is guarded by the Fort of Michelangelo, a massive Renaissance construction which was begun by Bramante, continued by Sangallo the Younger and Bernini, and completed by Michelangelo in 1557. Henri Beyle, alias Stendhal (1783-1842), was appointed French Consul at Civitavecchia in 1831. Stendhal took advantage of his moments of leisure to write numerous works, including *The Charterhouse of Parma* (1839).

National Archaeological Museum (Museo Nazionale Archeologico) ⊙. – *2A, Largo Plebiscito.*
The museum has Etruscan and Roman collections composed of finds from local sites. There is an astonishing collection of Roman anchors.

Trajan's Bath (**Terme di Traiano** or **Terme Taurine**) ⊙. – *3km – 2 miles to the northeast.*
There are two groups: the first (to the west) dates from the Republican period and the second, the better preserved, was built by Trajan's successor, the Emperor Hadrian.

COMACCHIO Emilia Romagna   Pop 21 341

Michelin map ▯▯▯ fold 15, ▯▯▯ fold 25 or ▯▯▯ fold 5

Comacchio is built on sand and water and in many ways it resembles Chioggia. The main activity of the townspeople is eel fishing. Its brightly coloured fishermen's houses, its canals spanned by some curious bridges, including an unusual triple bridge, and the fishing boats all lend it a special charm.

★ **Polesina.** – This area around the Po delta was once a malaria-infested marshy district. Land reclamation and drainage have since turned it into a fertile agricultural area. The Chioggia to Ravenna road *(90km – 56 miles)* traverses these flat expanses as they stretch away to the horizon, interrupted only by large solitary farms. Clumps of poplars and umbrella pines add touches of colour, especially in spring, to the monotony of this countryside where eel fishing is still common on the numerous canals which crisscross the area. At **Mesola** *(28km – 17 miles to the north of Comacchio)* there is a massive brick castle dating from 1583 which once belonged to the Este family. In the southern part of the area the **Valli di Comacchio**, Italy's most important zone of lagoons, has its own special melancholy beauty.

★ COMO Lombardy   Pop 90 799

Michelin map ▯▯▯ fold 3, ▯▯▯ folds 8 and 9 or ▯▯▯ fold 15 – Local map p 115
Town plan in the current Michelin Red Guide Italia

The city was already prosperous under the Romans but reached its zenith in the 11C. It was destroyed by the Milanese in 1127, rebuilt by the Emperor Frederick Barbarossa and from 1355 onwards followed the fortunes of Milan. The **maestri comacini** (master masons), known as early as the 7C, were masons, builders and sculptors who spread the Lombard style *(p 28)* throughout Italy and Europe. Their name would appear to mean simply associated masons *(co-macini)*.

★★ **Cathedral** (**Duomo**). – Begun in the late 14C it was completed during the Renaissance and crowned in the 18C with an elegant dome by the Turin architect, Juvara. It has a remarkable **façade**★★ which was richly decorated from 1484 onwards by the **Rodari brothers**, who also worked on the **north door**, known as the Porta della Rana because of the frog *(rana)* carving on one of the pillars. They were also responsible for the exquisitely delicate **south door.**
The **interior**★, full of solemn splendour, displays Gothic architecture and Renaissance decoration. In addition to the curious banners, hung between the pillars, and the magnificent 16C-17C **tapestries**★, there are numerous works of art including canvases by B. Luini (**Virgin and Child with Saints**★), and G. Ferrari, as well as a **Descent from the Cross**★ (1498) carved by Tommaso Rodari.
Adjoining the façade is the **Broletto**★★, or 13C town hall, with an arcade at street level and a lovely storey of triple-arched windows above.

★ **Church of San Fedele.** – In the heart of the picturesque old quarter, this church in the Romanesque Lombard style has an unusual doorway at the apse adorned with lovely low reliefs. The nave and two aisles are terminated by a splendid polygonal Romanesque **chancel**★ with radiating chapels. The whole east end is graced by two storeys of arcading.

★ **Basilica of Sant'Abbondio.** – This masterpiece of Romanesque Lombard architecture was consecrated in 1093. The noble but severe **façade**★ has a lovely doorway. The nave and four aisles are separated by elegant columns. The remarkable 14C **frescoes**★ evoke the Life of Christ.

Villa Olmo ☉. – *3km – 2 miles to the north by the S 35 and then the S 340 to the right.*
This is a large neo-classical building dating from the late 18C , with a small theatre and gardens, from which there is a lovely **view**★ of Como in its lakeside setting.

CONEGLIANO Venetia   Pop 35 992

Michelin map 988 fold 5 or 429 fold 15 – 28km – 17 miles north of Treviso

Conegliano is surrounded by pleasant hills clad with orchards and vineyards, which produce an excellent white wine. This was the birthplace of **Cima da Conegliano** (1459-1518), an admirer of Giovanni Bellini, and a superb colourist who introduced idealised landscapes bathed in a crystal-clear light to his works. The **cathedral** (Duomo) ☉ has a lovely **Holy Conversation**★ by this artist. The **castle** ☉ houses two small **museums** and provides a lovely **panorama**★ of the town and its setting. Next to the cathedral the walls of the **Scuola dei Battuti** are decorated with 15C and 16C **frescoes**★ in both the Venetian and Lombard styles.

★★★ CORTINA D'AMPEZZO Venetia   Pop 7 645

Michelin map 988 fold 5 or 429 fold 5 – Local map p 85
Town plan in the current Michelin Red Guide Italia

Cortina, the capital of the Dolomites *(qv)*, is a winter sports and summer resort with a worldwide reputation. Set in the heart of the Dolomites, Cortina makes a good excursion centre for discovering the magnificent **mountain scenery**★★★.

★★★ **Tondi di Faloria** ☉. – From the summit there is a grand panorama. There are excellent ski slopes.

★★★ **Tofana di Mezzo** ☉. – A cable-car climbs to 3 244m – 10 743ft, from where there is a superb panorama over the surrounding mountains.

★★ **Pocol Belvedere** ☉. – Lying to the southwest, this viewpoint affords a lovely view of Cortina which is best at sunset.

★ CORTONA Tuscany   Pop 22 631

Michelin map 988 fold 15 or 430 fold 15
Town plan in the current Michelin Red Guide Italia

The quiet town of Cortona, with its girdle of medieval ramparts, clings to the steep slopes of a hill clad with olive groves. It affords good views as far as Lake Trasimeno.
As early as the 14C Cortona attracted artists including the Sienese, Fra Angelico. Cortona was the birthplace of **Luca Signorelli** (1450-1523), who with his dramatic temperament and sculptural modelling, was the precursor of Michelangelo; he died as a result of a fall from scaffolding when he was decorating the Villa Passerini to the east of Cortona. In the 16C Cortona gave France an architect, Domenico Bernabei, known as **Il Boccadoro** (Mouth of Gold) who designed Paris' Hôtel de Ville for François I. **Pietro da Cortona** (1596-1669), painter and architect with a lively imagination, was one of the masters of Roman baroque and a talented decorative painter.

SIGHTS

Piazza del Duomo, close up against the ramparts, affords a lovely view over the valley. The Romanesque **cathedral** (Duomo), remodelled at the Renaissance, contains some works of art.

★★ **Diocesan Museum (Museo Diocesano)** ☉. – *Opposite the Cathedral.*
This former church houses a remarkable collection of paintings: a beautiful **Annunciation** and *Madonna and Saints* by Fra Angelico; works from the Sienese school by Duccio, Pietro Lorenzetti and Sassetta; an excellent group of works by **Signorelli**; and a remarkable **Ecstasy of St Margaret** by the Bolognese artist, G. M. Crespi (1665-1747). The lovely 2C Roman sarcophagus has low reliefs depicting the story of Bacchus.

Praetorian Palace (Palazzo Pretorio). – It was built in the 13C and remodelled later. The façade, on the right, covered with coats of arms, is 13C Gothic, but that which faces the Piazza Signorelli dates from the 17C. Inside, the **Museum of the Etruscan Academy**★ ☉ displays Etruscan exhibits as well as Roman, Egyptian, medieval and Renaissance items. Among the Etruscan objects is a curious 5C BC bronze oil lamp, with sixteen burners in the human form.

St Margaret's Church (Santa Margherita). – This enshrines the lovely Gothic **tomb**★ (1362) of the saint.

St Francis' Church (San Francesco). – *At the junction of Via G. Maffei and Via Berrettini.*
This church was begun in 1245 to the designs of Brother Elias, St Francis' companion who directed the building operations at Assisi. This Gothic church, remodelled in the 17C, has several works of art including an Annunciation by Pietro da Cortona.

St Dominic's Church (San Domenico). – *Largo Beato Angelico.*
In the south apse is a Madonna with angels and saints by Luca Signorelli, a triptych of the Coronation of the Virgin by Lorenzo di Niccolò at the high altar and a fresco attributed to Fra Angelico.

★ **Church of Santa Maria del Calcinaio.** – *3km – 2 miles to the west.*
Santa Maria, built between 1485 and 1513 by Francesco di Giorgio Martini, strongly resembles the work of Brunelleschi. It is remarkable for the grace and harmony of its design and its well-balanced proportions. The domed church is built on the freek cross plan and the lofty interior is well-lit.
In the oculus of the façade is a remarkable stained glass **window** (1516) designed by **Guillaume de Marcillat** (1467-1529) who was born at La Châtre in Berry. The Dominican monk's skill with stained glass led to his receiving a papal summons from Julius II to work at the Vatican alongside Raphael and Michelangelo. He settled at Arezzo *(qv)*. The 16C artist Vasari said of his work "These are not stained glass windows but marvels fallen from Heaven for the consolation of men". A short distance westwards is the so-called Tomb of Pythagoras, really a 4C circular Etruscan sepulchre.

★ **CREMONA** Lombardy   Pop 76 522

Michelin map 𝟵𝟴𝟴 folds 13 and 14, 𝟰𝟮𝟴 folds 26 and 27 or 𝟰𝟮𝟵 fold 21

Cremona is an important agricultural market town in the heart of a fertile agricultural region. Town life centres on Piazza Roma. The original Gallic settlement became a Latin city before emerging as an independent commune in the Middle Ages. It suffered from the Guelph and Ghibelline troubles of the period.
In 1334 the town came under Visconti rule and was united with the Duchy of Milan in the 15C. At the Renaissance the town was the centre of a brilliant artistic movement. In the 18C and 19C the French and Austrians fought for supremacy over Cremona until the Risorgimento *(qv)*.

CREMONA

Campi (Corso)	BZ	Geromini (Via Felice)	BY 9
Cavour (Piazza)	BZ 6	Ghinaglia (Via F.)	AY 12
Garibaldi (Corso)	AYZ	Ghisleri (Via A.)	BY 13
Matteotti (Corso)	BYZ	Libertà (Piazza della)	BY 14
		Mantova (Via)	BY 17
Aselli (Via)	BYZ 2	Manzoni (Via)	BY 18
Boccaccino (Via)	BZ 3	Marconi (Piazza)	BZ 19
Cadorna (Piazza L.)	AZ 4	Marmolada (Via)	BZ 22
Comune (Piazza del)	BZ 7	Mazzini (Corso)	BZ 23
		Melone (Via Altobello)	BZ 24
		Monteverdi (Via Claudio)	BZ 27
		Novati (Via)	BZ 28

Risorgimento (Piazza)	AY 29
S. Maria in Betlem (Via)	AY 32
S. Rocco (Via)	BZ 33
Spalato (Via)	AY 35
Stradivari (Via)	BZ 37
Tofane (Via)	BZ 39
Ugolani Dati (Via)	BY 40
Vacchelli (Corso)	BZ 42
Verdi (Via)	BZ 43
Vittorio Emanuele II (Corso)	AZ 45
4 Novembre (Piazza)	BZ 46
20 Settembre (Corso)	BZ 48

From the late 16C the stringed-instrument makers of Cremona gained a reputation as violin and cello makers. The Amati and Guarneri families, and especially **Antonio Stradivarius,** with their knowledge and incomparable skill produced outstanding instruments of unequalled tonal quality. The International School of Violin Making in Piazza Marconi (**BZ 19**) carries on this tradition. The Cremonese composer **Claudio Monteverdi** (1567-1643) created modern opera with his *Orfeo* and *The Return of Ulysses to his Country.*

★★ **PIAZZA DEL COMUNE** (BZ 7) *time: 1 hour*

This is one of the finest squares in Italy.

★★★ **Torrazzo** ⊙. – The admirable late-13C campanile is linked to the cathedral by a Renaissance gallery. Its massive form is elegantly crowned by an octagonal 14C storey. From the top (112m – 367ft) there is a lovely **view**★ over the town.

★★ **Cathedral (Duomo).** – This magnificent Lombard building was begun in the Romanesque and completed in the Gothic style (1107 to 1332). The richly decorated white marble façade is preceded by a porch. Numerous decorative features were later additions, namely the frieze by the followers of Antelami, the large 13C rose window and the four statue-columns of the central doorway. The spacious **interior** is decorated with **frescoes**★ by the Cremona school (B. Boccaccino, the Campi, the Bembo, Romanino da Brescia, Pordenone and Gatti). Also of interest are the lovely 17C Brussels **tapestries**★ and at the entrance to the chancel the **high reliefs**★★ by Amadeo, the architect-sculptor of the Carthusian Monastery at Pavia.

★ **Baptistry** (L). – This lovely octagonal building, preceded by a Lombard porch and decorated with a gallery, was remodelled during the Renaissance.

Town Hall (Palazzo Comunale) ⊙ (H). – This 13C palace was remodelled at a later date. Inside are displayed four famous **violins** by Cremonese instrument-makers (Stradivarius, Guarneri and the Amati family).
To the left of the palace is the lovely 13C **Loggia dei Militi (K).**

ADDITIONAL SIGHTS

★ **Municipal Museum** (Museo Civico) ⊙ (ABY M). – Installed in a 16C palace this museum has several different sections, notably the **picture gallery** with works of the Cremona school, minor arts (French **ivories**), the **cathedral's treasure** and a **Stradivarius museum.**

Renaissance Architecture. – The town is embellished with numerous Renaissance palaces including the **Palazzo Fodri**★ (**BZ D**), the **Palazzo Stanga** (**AY E**) and the **Palazzo Raimondi (AY F**), as well as churches like **Sant'Agostino** (**AZ B**) rich in works of art: **portraits**★ of Francesco Sforza and his wife by Bonifacio Bembo and an **altarpiece**★ by Perugino.
On the Casalmaggiore road *(2km – 1 mile out of town by no* ③ *on the town plan)* is the **Church of San Sigismondo** with its lavishly decorated **interior**★. The frescoes are by the 16C Cremona school (Campi, Gatti and Boccaccino).

CROTONE Calabria   Pop 61 326

Michelin map 988 fold 40 or 431 fold 31

The ancient Croton was an Achaean colony of Magna Graecia, founded in 710 BC and celebrated in antiquity for its riches, the beauty of its women and the prowess of its athletes, such as Milo of Crotone, so admired by Virgil. Around 532 BC Pythagoras founded several religious communities which devoted themselves to the study of mathematics and which once they had become too powerful were expelled northwards towards Metapontum (present, day Metaponto). The rival city of Locari defeated Croton in the mid 6C BC, which in turn defeated its other rival Sybaris. The city welcomed Hannibal during the Second Punic War before being conquered by Rome. Crotone is today a prosperous seaport and industrial centre as well as a popular holiday resort.

Archaeological Museum (Museo Archeologico) ⊙. – *Via Risorgimento.* The archaeological collections include local finds from other colonies of Magna Graecia: displays of ceramics, terracottas, coins and sculpture.

EXCURSIONS

Cape Colonna (Capo Colonna). – *40km – 25 miles to the south.*
At the extremity of this promontory stands a Doric column, the last remaining vestige of a vast temple dedicated to Hera Lucinia (6C or 5C BC).

★ **Santa Severina.** – *34km – 21 miles to the northwest.*
The 13C cathedral has a remarkable 8C circular **baptistry**★ which shows a strong Byzantine influence. The Norman Castle is also open.

The Michelin Green Guide Great Britain
an informative travel guide,
aims to make touring more enjoyable
by highlighting the country's
natural features, historic sites
and other outstanding attractions.

★ CUMAE (CUMA) Campania

Michelin map 988 fold 27 or 431 fold 13 – 7km – 4 miles north of Pozzuoli – Local map p 146

Cumae, one of the oldest Greek colonies, was founded in the 8C BC. The city soon dominated the whole Phlegrean area *(p 145)* including Naples, leaving an important Hellenic heritage. Its splendour was at its height under the tyrant Aristodemus. After its capture by the Romans in 334 BC, decline then set in and continued until AD 915 when it was pillaged by the Saracens.

The ancient city of Cumae stands in a serene and solemn setting near the sea. Visitors have access to the ruins of the upper town – the acropolis – where most of the temples stood. In the area of the lower town, excavations have revealed the remains of an amphitheatre, a temple dedicated to the Capitoline Triad (Jupiter, Juno and Minerva) and baths.

★★ **Acropolis** ⊙. – The acropolis is built on a hill of volcanic material (lava and tufa) in lovely surroundings. It is reached by an alley bordered with laurels. After the vaulted passageway, the path to the left leads to the **Sibyl's Cave★** (Antro della Sibilla), one of the most venerated places of antiquity. Here the Sibyl pronounced her oracles. The cave was hollowed out of the rock by the Greeks in the 6C or 5C BC and it is rectangular in shape with three small niches.

Take the stairway up to the sacred way (Via Sacra). From the belvedere there is a good **view★** of the sea. Some finds from the excavations are on display. On the right are the remains of the **Temple of Apollo** (Tempio di Apollo) which was later transformed into a Christian church. Further on is the **Temple of Jupiter** (Tempio di Giove) which was also converted by the early Christians. In the centre stands a large font and there are several Christian tombs near the sanctuary.

★ **Arco Felice.** – *Take the minor road in the direction of Naples.*

This triumphal arch was erected on the Domitian Way (Via Domitiana); there are still traces of the paved way.

★★★ The DOLOMITES

Michelin map 988 folds 4 and 5 or 429 folds 3, 4 and 5

This rugged and grandiose limestone massif is enhanced by yellow and pink tints, harsh or soft depending on the light. It extends mostly over the Alto-Adige region, also known as Southern Tyrol, which is German-speaking and of Austrian tradition. The massif is a favourite haunt of skiers and mountaineers. For holidaymakers, the Dolomites provide excellent roads, good paths, immense panoramas and a large selection of hotels.

GEOGRAPHICAL NOTES

The Dolomites are bounded roughly by the Adige River and its tributary, the Isarco, in the west, the Brenta Massif in the south, the Piave Valley in the east and the Rienza (Val Pusteria) in the north. Most of the range is formed of limestone rocks called "dolomites" after a French geologist, Gratet de Dolomieu, who was the first to study their formation at the end of the 18C. A few nuclei of volcanic rock are to be found in the centre and west, and schists in the southwest (Cima d'Asta).

The nature of the soil and the effect of erosion have created a distinctive landscape: steep, rugged rocks take the form of towers, belfries or domes with gentler slopes at their feet covered with alpine pastures, conifers or crops. The steepness of the upper slopes prevented the formation of glaciers.

Dolomites –Tre Cime di Lavaredo

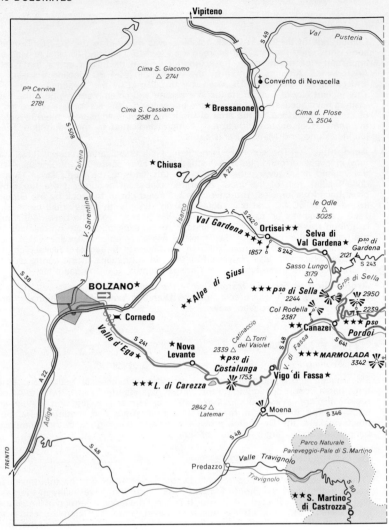

Adige/Etsch
Alpe di Siusi/Seiseralm
Badia (Val)/Gadertal
Bolzano/Bozen
Braies (Lago di)/Pragser Wildsee
Bressanone/Brixen
Brunico/Bruneck
Campo Fiscalino/Fischleinboden
Carezza (Lago di)/Karersee
Catinaccio/Rosengarten

Cervina (Punta)/Hirzerspitze
Chiusa/Klausen
Cornedo/Karneid
Corvara in Badia/Kurfar
Costalunga (Passo di)/Karerpass
Croda Rossa/Hohe Geisel
Dobbiaco/Toblach
Ega (Val d')/Eggental
Gadera/Gaderbach
Gardena (Passo di)/Grödnerjoch

The various massifs. – To the southeast rise Monte Pelmo (3 168m – 10 394ft) and Monte Civetta (3 220m – 10 564ft) while to the south, near the Cima della Vezzana, the Pale di San Martino, which are deeply fissured, are divided into three chains separated by a high plateau. The Massifs of the Latemar (2 842m – 9 324ft) and the Catinaccio (2 981m – 9 780ft), from which rise the well-known Towers of Vaiolet (Torri del Vaiolet), enclose the pass, Passo di Costalunga. To the north of the latter are the Sasso Lungo and the vast Sella Massif (Gruppo di Sella), which is skirted by a road. To the east, the chief summits in the Cortina Dolomites are the Tofano di Mezzo, the Punta Sorapiss and Monte Cristallo. Finally in the heart of the range stands the formidable **Marmolada Massif** (Gruppo della Marmolada), which rises to the highest point in the Dolomites. The **Cadore** district prolongs the Dolomites to the east and southeast of Cortina; its axis is the Piave Valley and its capital Pieve di Cadore. Here the highest summits are Antelao (3 262m – 10 705ft) and the triple peak Tre Cime di Lavaredo (2 998m – 9 836ft) *(illustration p 83)*.

Fauna and flora. – Birds and animals are those of the Alps: royal eagle, chamois, deer, hawks, and woodcock in the coniferous forest. In spring the prairies are covered with brightly-coloured flowers: edelweiss, deep-blue gentian, white or mauve crocus, six-petalled anemones, starry white saxifrage or five-petalled rock flowers, fringed mauve soldanellas and purplish-pink Turk's Cap lilies.

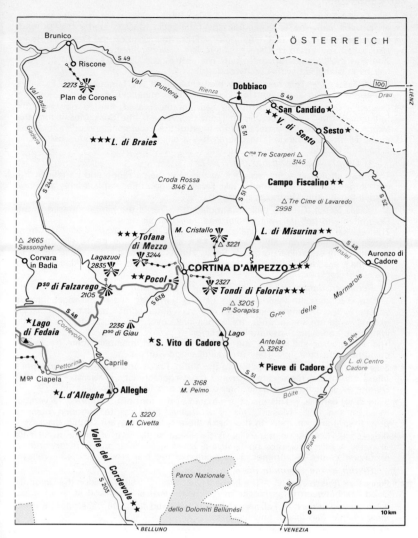

Gardena (Val)/Grödnertal
Isarco/Eisack
Lavaredo (Tre Cime di)/Drei Zinnen
le Odle/Geislerspitze
Nova Levante/Welschnofen
Ortisei/St-Ulrich
Plan de Corones/Kronplatz
Plose (Cima d.)/Plose Bühel
Rienza/Rienz
Riscone/Reischach
San Candido/Innichen

San Cassiano (Cima)/Kassianspitze
San Giacomo (Cima)/Jakobspitze
Sta-Cristina/St-Christina
Sarentina (Valle)/Sarntal
Sasso Lungo/Langkofel
Sella (Passo di)/Sellajoch
Selva in Val Gardena/Wolkenstein in Gardena
Sesto (Val di)/Sextental
Talvera/Talfer
Tre Scarperi (Cima)/Dreischusterspitze
Vipiteno/Sterzing

Market gardens and vineyards flourish in valleys dotted with large farmhouses with wooden balconies.

Sightseeing. – The map above locates the towns and sites described in the guide, and also indicates other beauty spots in small black type.

★★★ DOLOMITE ROAD

From Bolzano to Cortina *210km – 131 miles – allow 2 days*

The main touring route in the Dolomites is the great Dolomite Road, which is a wonderful and world-famous example of road engineering, linking Bolzano and Cortina d'Ampezzo as it follows the central depression of the massif. It runs through a landscape which is always majestic and varied. The road was already used during the Renaissance by merchants travelling from Venice to Germany. It began to be modernised in 1895, was used for military purposes in 1915-18 and was improved after the Second World War.

★ **Bolzano.** – *Description p 66.*

★ **Ega Valley Gorge** (Valle d'Ega). – This narrow gorge, with pink sandstone walls, is guarded by **Cornedo Castle.**

★ **Nova Levante.** – Catinaccio Massif rises up behind this attractive village with its bulbous belfry and pretty houses overlooking the Ega.

85

★★★ **Lake Carezza** (Lago di Carezza or Karer See). – This tiny lake is set in a dark expanse of fir trees with the Latemar and the Catinaccio Massifs in the background.

★ **Costalunga Pass** (Passo di Costalunga). – From this pass on the Dolomite Road, also called the Passo di Carezza, there is a **view**★ over the Catinaccio on one side and the Latemar on the other. The soft terrain on the slopes of the pass has been stabilised with brushwood.

★ **Vigo di Fassa** ⊙. – This resort, very well situated in the famous Val di Farsa, is a mountaineering and excursion centre in the Catinaccio Massif *(cable-car)*.

★★ **Canazei.** – Canazei lies deep in the heart of the massif, framed between the Catinaccio, the Towers of Vaiolet (Torri del Vaiolet), the Sella Massif and the Marmolada. This is the usual base for most of the excursions and difficult climbs in the Marmolada range. The church has a shingle roof, a bulbous belfry and a painted façade.

At Canazei turn right into the S 641.

This road affords very fine **views**★★ of the Marmolada range and its glacier. As one comes out of a long tunnel **Lake Fedaia**★ (Lago di Fedaia) suddenly appears, dominated by the Marmolada range.

★★★ **Marmolada Massif** (Gruppo della Marmolada). – This is the highest massif in the Dolomites and has its own glacier and very fast ski-runs.

The **cable-car** ⊙ starting from Malga Ciapela goes up to 3 265m – 10 712ft from where there are admirable **panoramas**★★★ of the Cortina peaks (Tofano and Cristallo), the sugar-loaf forms of Sasso Lungo, the enormous tabular mass of the Sella Massif and in the background the summits of the Austrian Alps including the Grossglockner.

Return to Canazei then after 5.5km – 4 miles turn left.

The road follows the **Gardena Valley**★★★ (Val Gardena), one of the most famous valleys in the Dolomites for its beauty, its winter sports facilities and as an excursion centre in summer. Its slopes are covered with coniferous forests, waterfalls and typical mountain dwellings.

The inhabitants still speak the Ladin dialect and maintain their traditional costumes and customs. They are skilful wood-workers.

★★★ **Sella Pass** (Passo di Sella). – Linking the Val di Fassa and Val Gardena this pass offers one of the most extensive and most characteristic **panoramas**★★★ in the Dolomites, including the Sella, Sasso Lungo and Marmolada Massifs.

★ **Selva di Val Gardena.** – This resort is situated at the foot of the impressive vertical mass of the Sella Massif. This is an active craft centre: wooden objects, pewterware and enamels. In the **church** there is a Flamboyant Gothic **altarpiece**★.

★★ **Ortisei** ⊙. – Halfway up the valley is the linear settlement of Ortisei amidst its fir trees. A **cable-car** climbs up to **Alpe di Siusi**★★, a winter sports resort and an excursion centre in summer. This overlooks the Isarco and Gardena Valleys.

Return to the Dolomite Road.

★★★ **Pordoi Pass** (Passo Pordoi). – The highest (2 239m – 7 346ft) pass on the Dolomite Road lies between huge blocks of rock with vertical sides and shorn-off tops.

Falzarego Pass (Passo di Falzarego). – This wild and desolate pass offers a good view of the Marmolada and its glacier.

★★★ **Cortina d'Ampezzo and excursions.** – *Description p 80.*

OTHER TOWNS AND SIGHTS

★★★ **Lake Braies** (Lago di Braies). – Alt 1 495m – 4 905ft. The lake encircled by grim mountains. Its winding banks fringe the clear green waters.

★★ **Misurina Lake** (Lago di Misurina) ⊙. – This popular lake in rolling parkland is overlooked to the north by the Tre Cime di Lavaredo. A private toll-road leads through larch plantations to a wild **scenery**★★★ of jumbled, jagged rocks.

★★ **Sesto Valley** (Valle di Sesto). – This attractive valley has numerous Tyrolean-style villages, the main one being **Sesto**★. A winding road branches southwards following the Fiscalino Valley to end at **Campo Fiscalino**★★ in a grandiose setting, a mountain cirque enclosed by jagged mountain peaks.

San Candido★ stands at the point where the Sesto Valley joins the main valley, Val Pusteria, not far from the Austrian border. This town has three interesting churches: one in the mountain style with shingle roof and bulbous belfry, another in the Austrian baroque style and the third, a Romanesque structure.

★★ **Cordevole Valley** (Valle del Cordevole). – The road from Caprile to Bulluno is an extremely picturesque one with its hilltop villages and impressive gorges. **Alleghe** on the bank of a pale green **lake**★ is a good excursion centre.

★★ **San Martino di Castrozza.** – In its superb setting, San Martino is an excellent excursion centre with a strong cultural tradition (costumes).

★ **Bressanone.** – *Description p 68.*

★ **Chiusa.** – A charming Tyrolean-looking village.

★ **Pieve di Cadore.** – This town is pleasantly set at the head of a reservoir. It was the birthplace of the great artist, **Titian**. One of his works is to be found in the church, and the house where he was born is now a **museum** ⊙.

★ **San Vito di Cadore.** – This attractive village with its shingle-roofed churches is overshadowed by the Antelao.

Dobbiaco. – In the centre of this village there is an Austrian-style baroque church.

Vipiteno. – *30km – 19 miles to the northwest of Bressanone.* The picturesque **main street**★ has 15C-16C Tyrolean houses with arcades, oriel windows and wrought-iron signs.

With its beaches, solitary places, peacefulness and mild, dry climate, the Isle of Elba is a good place for a stay rather than an excursion. In the distant geological past Elba was a part of the vanished continent, Tyrrhenia. This, the largest island in the Tuscan Archipelago, like Corsica, Sardinia, the Balearics and the Maures and Estérel Massifs on the French Riviera coast, has an indented coastline with small creeks, caves and beaches. The vegetation is typically Mediterranean with palms, eucalyptus, cedars, magnolias and, in great quantity, olives and vines. The wines produced (white Moscato and red Aleatico) are heady with a strong bouquet.

Elba is closely associated with Napoleon who was exiled here following his abdication. Between 3 May 1814 and 26 February 1815 the fallen emperor ruled over his small court and the island, which was garrisoned by about 1 000 soldiers.

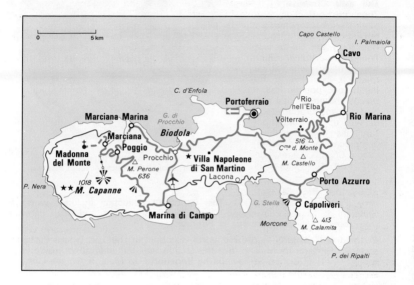

Sightseeing. – Start from Portoferraio and follow one of the two itineraries indicated on the map *above*: **western Elba** *(66km – 41 miles, about 4 hours)* and **eastern Elba** *(68km – 42 miles, about 3 hours).*

Portoferraio. – The island's capital, guarded by ruined walls and two forts, lies at the head of a beautiful bay. In the upper part of the town the **Napoleonic Museum** (Museo Napoleonico dei Mulini) ⊙ is a simple house, with a terraced garden, which Napoleon sometimes occupied. His personal library and various mementoes are kept here. Beyond the great sandy beach at **Biodola,** the road goes towards **Marciana Marina,** a small port protected by two piers, one of which is dominated by a round tower.

★★ **Monte Capanne** ⊙. – 1 018m – 3 339ft. *Cable-cars leave from Marciana.* From the summit not far from the terminus there is a splendid **panorama★★** of Elba, the Tuscan coast to the east and the coast of Corsica to the west.

Marciana. – From this attractive village there is a lovely **view★** of **Poggio,** perched on its rocky spur, Marciana Marina and the Bay of Procchio. There is a small **archaeological museum** ⊙ with displays of prehistoric items, Greek vases etc.

Madonna del Monte. – Take the road up to the castle which dominates Marciana and from there a rocky path leads up to this sanctuary, built on the northern slope of Monte Giove. Beside the 16C chapel there is a curious semicircular fountain dated 1698.

Marina di Campo. – This small fishing port with its popular beach lies at the head of a lovely bay backed by a hinterland plain of olive groves and vineyards.

★ **Napoleon's Villa in San Martino** ⊙. – In a setting of silent hills, planted with groves of evergreen oaks and vineyards, this modest house was the ex-emperor's summer residence. There is a lovely view of the Bay of Portoferraio.

Capoliveri. – From a spot to the west of this village there is a **panorama★★** of the Bays of Portoferraio, Marina di Campo and Porto Azzurro.

Porto Azzurro. – This pretty port is overlooked by a fort which now serves as a prison.

Rio Marina. – A pleasant port and mining village protected by a crenellated tower. Beyond **Cavo,** a small port sheltered by the Castello headland, the return **road★★** to Portoferraio is a high altitude one *(in bad condition)* affording remarkable views of the ruins of Volterraio, the Bay of Portoferraio and the sea.

*The **Michelin Map of Greece** n° 🔢*
at a scale of 1:700000 has all the practical information needed
to make driving a pleasure.

Michelin map 988 fold 15, 429 fold 34 or 430 fold 4
Town plan in the current Michelin Red Guide Italia

Faenza has given its name to the ceramics known as **faïence**, which have been
produced locally since the 15C. In Italy faïence is also known as majolica, because
during the Renaissance Faenza potters were inspired by ceramics which were
imported from Majorca in
the Balearic Isles. The characteristics of Faenza ceramics are fine clay, remarkable glaze, brilliant colours
and a great variety of
decoration.

★★ **International Ceramics
Museum (Museo Internazio-
nale delle Ceramiche)** ⊘. –
These vast collections present the development of
ceramic-making throug-
hout the world. On the first
floor is a very fine collection of Italian Renaissance
majolica, examples of the
local work, popular Italian
pieces and an oriental section. On the ground floor,
as well as the contempo-
rary Italian collection, there
are pieces by Matisse, Pi-
casso, Chagall, Léger, Lur-
çat and the Vallauris
school.

Faïence plate (late 15C)
(International Ceramics Museum, Faenza)

★ **Municipal Picture Gal-
lery (Pinacoteca Comunale)** ⊘. – This important collection includes works by
Giovanni da Rimini, Palmezzano, Dosso Dossi, Rossellino, and other canvases
from foreign schools (portraits by Pourbus).

Cathedral (Cattedrale). – The cathedral was built in the 15C by the Florentine
architect Giuliano da Maiano, but the façade was left unfinished. Inside is the
tomb (1471) of Bishop St Savinus by Benedetto da Maiano. On the cathedral
parvis, Piazza della Libertà, stands a charming 17C baroque fountain.

Piazza del Popolo. – The square is elongated and unusual, with arcades
surmounted by galleries. Lining the square are the 12C governor's residence,
Palazzo del Podestà and the 13C-15C Palazzo del Municipio.

★ **FANO** Marches   Pop 52 579

Michelin map 988 fold 16 or 430 folds 6 and 7
Town plan in the current Michelin Red Guide Italia

This town, now a favourite seaside resort, was ruled by the Malatesta family
from Rimini in the 13C-15C. Montaigne passed through Fano in April 1581 and
provoked a controversy concerning the reputed beauty of the local women.

★ **Malatesta Courtyard (Corte Malatestiana).** – This 15C Renaissance ensemble
includes a courtyard-garden and palace, and it would make an ideal theatrical
set. The palace houses the **Municipal Museum** (Museo Civico) ⊘ with sections on
archaeology, coins and medals and 14C-18C sculpture and painting. The latter
includes Guercino's well-known work, the **Guardian Angel** (1641).

Church of Santa Maria Nuova. – 16C-18C. This contains **works★** by Perugino,
which are admired for their fine draughtsmanship and their delicate colours: an
exquisite Madonna and Child (1497) (third altar on the right) and a graceful
Annunciation (1498) (second altar on the left).

Fountain of Good Fortune (Fontana della Fortuna). – This fountain in Piazza
20 Settembre presents the protecting goddess, perched on a pivoting globe,
with her billowing cloak acting as a weathervane.

Arch of Augustus (Arco d'Augusto). – *At the far end of the street of the same
name.* This 1C arch has a main opening and two side ones for pedestrians. A
low relief on the façade of the Church of St Michael (San Michele) nearby portrays
the arch in its original form. To the left of the arch are the remains of the Roman
wall.

Help us in our constant task of keeping up to date.
Send your comments and suggestions to

Michelin Tyre PLC
Tourism Department
Davy House
Lyon Road
HARROW Middlesex HA1 2DQ

★ FERMO Marches   Pop 35 224

Michelin map 988 fold 16 or 430 fold 18

Fermo is one of the artistic and cultural centres of the Marches. It stands in a good **site★** on the slopes of a hill overlooking the countryside and facing the sea.

★ **Piazza del Duomo.** – From this esplanade in front of the cathedral there are splendid **views★★** of the Ascoli area, the Apennines, the Adriatic and Conero Peninsula.

Cathedral (Duomo). – This Romanesque-Gothic building (1227) has a majestic **façade★** in white Istrian stone. A delicately carved doorway shows Christ with the Apostles on the lintel, and symbolic scenes or figures on the uprights. In the 18C interior are the 14C sarcophagus of Giovanni Visconti, overlord of the town; a 5C mosaic paving in front of the chancel, a 13C-14C Byzantine icon of the Virgin; and a 4C sarcophagus with high reliefs in the crypt.

Piazza del Popolo. – This square in the centre of town is surrounded with arcades and elegant porticoes. Numerous palaces including the 15C Palazzo Comunale and the 16C Palazzo degli Studi line the square. Running between these two palaces is the Corso Cefalonia, a picturesque street lined with towers of nobility, palaces and ancient churches.

EXCURSION

Montefiore dell'Aso. – *20km – 12 miles to the south.*
Carlo Crivelli (1430-95), a painter of courtesans and fair virgins, on being sentenced at Venice in 1457, took refuge in the Marches, and Montefiore thus gained a masterpiece. The church contains a splendid **polyptych★★**, which although incomplete, is finely chiselled and highlighted with gold representing six saints. The most successful panel shows the sinner Mary Magdalene richly apparelled in gold and silk brocade, holding the symbolic box of ointment.

★★ FERRARA Emilia-Romagna   Pop 143 046

Michelin map 988 fold 15 or 429 fold 24

In the heart of the fertile Po Plain, Ferrara has kept its urban layout intact from the Renaissance period, when the brilliant court of the Princes of Este rivalled, for splendour and culture, those of Milan, Venice and Mantua. The streets on a gridiron pattern are lined with the red-brick houses, austere palaces and great spacious squares which so inspired the 20C metaphysical painter, Giorgio de Chirico.

A discerning dynasty of patrons of the arts. – Initially an independent commune, Ferrara belonged to the **House of Este** from 1208 to 1598, and despite numerous family dramas, often bloodthirsty, the Estes embellished their native city with fine buildings and patronised both men of letters and artists. **Niccolò III** (1393-1441) murdered his wife and her lover but he begat **Lionello** and **Borso,** generous administrators and enlightened patrons. **Ercole I,** who assassinated his nephew, encouraged artists, as did his two famous daughters, Beatrice and Isabella d'Este. **Alfonso I,** the son of Ercole, became the third husband of Lucrezia Borgia, and Ercole II married Renée of France, **Ariosto** (1474-1533) spent his lifetime in the service of the Estes, in particular with Alfonso I, and his rare spare time was spent writing his masterpiece **Orlando Furioso** *(Roland the Mad).* In relating the adventures of the knight Orlando and Angelica, the poet gives free reign to his imagination. **Tasso** (1544-95), a native of Sorrento, made several visits to Ferrara. During the first he wrote his epic poem **Gerusalemme Liberata** *(Jerusalem Delivered)* recounting the capture of Jerusalem by the Christians, enlivened by the love-story of Rinaldo and Armida.

Ferrara School of Painting. – The leader of this local school was **Cosimo Tura** (*c*1430-95) with his strong personality, and its main characteristic was a meticulous realism, borrowed from the Northern schools. It was combined with a rather grim expressionism which derived from Mantegna, whose figures with their sculptural form display a high degree of tension. The main members were **Francesco del Cossa** (1435-77), **Ercole de'Roberti** (1450-96) and **Lorenzo Costa** (*c*1460-1530). In the 16C the colourist **Dosso Dossi** and **Garofalo** abandoned this drawing tradition in favour of a greater harmony of colour in line with the Venetian and Roman schools.

SIGHTS

★★ **Cathedral (Duomo) (BYZ).** – In the Romanesque-Gothic Lombard style, the triple **façade★★**, all in marble, is remarkable for its sculpture and the arrangement and variety of the openings. On the south side are the 15C Merchants' portico and gallery (loggia). The interior was remodelled in the 18C and contains numerous works of art. Above the narthex is the cathedral **museum★** ⊙ with amusing 12C **low reliefs of the Months★**, two statues by Jacopa della Quercia and two outstanding **masterpieces★★** by **Cosimo Tura**. The four canvases represent the **Annunciation** and **St George slaying the Dragon.**
The 13C **Palazzo Comunale (BY H),** facing the cathedral, was once the ducal palace.

★ **Este Castle (Castello Estense)** ⊙ **(BY B).** – This massive castle, guarded by moats and four fortified gateways with drawbridges, was the seat of the Estes. Visitors may view the apartments decorated with frescoes by Filippi, and the hanging gardens.

89

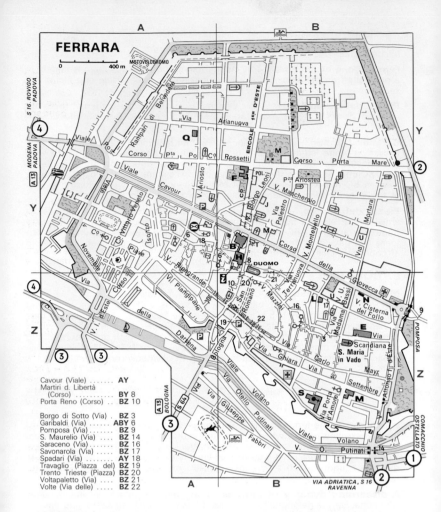

FERRARA

0   400 m

★ **Schifanoia Palace (Palazzo Schifanoia)** ⊘ (BZ E). – This 14C-15C palace is where the Estes used to come to relax (*schifanoia* means carefree). It now houses the **municipal museum** (Museo Civico). There are interesting archaeological and Renaissance exhibits and splendid **frescoes★★** in the Room of the Months (Salone dei Mesi). This complex cycle to the glory of Borso d'Este unfortunately retains only some of the twelve months. The three different levels correspond to three different themes, notably everyday life at court, astrology and mythology. Several artists, including Francesco del Cossa and Ercole de' Roberti, worked under Cosimo Tura to produce these frescoes, which demonstrate an extraordinary delicacy when portraying detail and a marvellous vivacity in both the use of colour and draughtsmanship.
The 15C-16C **Basilica of Santa Maria in Vado** (BZ), near the palace, is decorated inside with frescoes and paintings.

★ **Palace of Diamonds (Palazzo dei Diamanti)** ⊘ (BY F). – The palace takes its name from the distinctive marble façade of 12 500 diamond bosses. This sumptuous 15C-16C building now houses the **National Picture Gallery★**: works from the 15C and 16C Emilian and Ferrara schools (Cosimo Tura, Ercole de' Roberti, Garofalo and Dosso Dossi). In the Great Hall there are splendid 13C-14C **frescoes★★** taken from local churches.

★ **Corso Ercole I° d'Este** (BY). – The main street in the northern part of the town is lined with splendid Renaissance palaces.

★ **Palace of Ludovico the Moor (Palazzo di Ludovico il Moro)** (BZ M). – This palace, built in the late 15C for Ludovico Sforza the Moor, husband of Beatrice d'Este, is the home of an **archaeological museum** ⊘ with an important collection of 5C-4C BC **Attic vases★**.

★ **Casa Romei** ⊘ (BZ L). – The inner courtyards of this delightful 15C house are bordered by porticoes and loggias.

★ **Palazzina di Marfisa d'Este** ⊘ (BZ N). – This elegant single-storey residence (1559), set in a shady garden, is where Marfisa d'Este entertained her friends, among whom was the poet Tasso.

Sant' Antonio in Polesine ⊘ (BZ S). – This attractive architectural group includes a convent and church. The latter has three chapels decorated with 14C-15C frescoes by the Northern Italian schools.

Ariosto's House (Casa dell' Ariosto) ⊘ (AY Q). – The writer's home is now a cultural centre but it still has the garden where he tended his roses and jasmine.

★ **FIESOLE** Tuscany   Pop 15 226

Michelin map 988 folds 14 and 15, 429 folds 33 and 34 or 430 fold 13 – 8km
– 5 miles north of Florence – Town plan in the current Michelin Red Guide Italia

The road from Florence winds uphill to Fiesole through olive-clad slopes, past
luxuriant gardens and long lines of cypress trees, and affords views of this
incomparable **countryside★★★**, so often depicted by the masters of the Italian
Renaissance. The Etruscans founded this city in the 7C and 6C BC. Fiesole was
the most important city in northern Etruria and it dominated its neighbour and
rival Florence until the 12C.

★★ **View of Florence.** – The small terrace near the convent of St Francis (San
Francesco) provides a lovely view of Florence, bathed in soft light and nestling
in a hollow of the Arno Basin.

★ **Convent of St Francis (San Francesco)** ⊙. – This humble Franciscan convent,
with its charming small cloisters, is admirably set on the hilltop.

Cathedral (Duomo). - Founded in the 11C and enlarged in the 13C and 14C,
the building was extensively restored in the late 19C. The austere **interior★**, on
a basilical plan with raised chancel, has columns supporting antique capitals.
There are two handsome **works★** by the sculptor Mino da Fiesole.

Archaeological Site (Zona Archeologica) ⊙. – This site, in its enchanting **setting★**,
comprises a **Roman theatre★** (c80 BC), which is still used for performances, a
small **Etruscan temple** and the remains of baths built in the 1C BC by the
Romans. The **museum★** exhibits finds dating from the Etruscan to the medieval
period.

Bandini Museum ⊙. – *Opposite the entrance to the archaeological site.*
The museum houses a collection of 14C and 15C Tuscan works. The sculpture
and terracottas are on the ground floor, with the paintings on the floor above.
Petrarch's masterpiece **Triumphs** has illustrations by Jacopo del Sellaio.

San Domenico di Fiesole. – *2.5km – 1 1/2 miles to the southwest. See the
plan of the built-up area of Florence in the current Michelin Red Guide Italia.*
It was in this 15C church, remodelled in the 17C, that Fra Angelico took
his vows. In the first chapel on the north side is a **Madonna and Saints★** by
the artist. In the second chapel on the south is a **Baptism of Christ** by Lorenzo
di Credi.

Badia Fiesolana ⊙. – *3km – 2 miles to the southwest. See the plan of the
built-up area of Florence- in the current Michelin Red Guide Italia.*
This former Benedictine convent was partially rebuilt in the 15C thanks to the
generosity of Cosimo the Elder. The Romanesque **façade** of the original church,
with its decorative green and white marble motifs, was incorporated in the new
building, left unfinished on the death of Cosimo the Elder.

★★★ **FLORENCE (FIRENZE)** Tuscany   Pop 421 299

Michelin map 988 folds 14 and 15, 429 fold 33 or 430 fold 13 – Town plan
pp 88 and 89
Plans of the built-up area in the current Michelin Red Guide Italia

Florence is without doubt the city where the Italian genius has flourished with
the greatest display of brilliance and purity. For three centuries from the 13C
to the 16C, the city was the cradle of an exceptional artistic and intellectual
activity which evolved the precepts which were to dictate the appearance of
Italy at that time and also the aspect of modern civilisation throughout Europe.
The main characteristics of this movement, which was later to be known as the
Renaissance, were partly a receptivity to the outisde world, a dynamic open-minded
attitude which encouraged inventors and men of science to base their research
on the reinterpretation of the achievements of ancient Rome and on the
expanding of the known horizons. The desire to achieve universality resulted in
a multiplication of the fields of interest.
Dante was not only a great poet but also a grammarian and historian who did
much research on the origins and versatility of his own language. He was one
of Florence's most active polemicists. Giotto was not only a painter but also an
architect. Lorenzo the Magnificent was the prince who best incarnated the spirit
of the Renaissance. An able diplomat, a realistic politician, a patron of the arts
and poet himself, he regularly attended the Platonic Academy in the Medici villa
at Careggi, where philosophers such as Marsilio Ficino and Pico della Mirandola
and men of letters like Politian and others established the principles of a new
humanism. This search to achieve a balance between nature and order had its
most brilliant exponent in **Michelangelo**, painter, architect, sculptor and scholar
whose work typifies a purely Florentine preoccupation.
Florence is set in the heart of a serenely beautiful **countryside★★★** which is bathed
by a diaphanous, amber light. The low surrounding hills are clad with olive groves,
vineyards and cypresses which appear to have been landscaped to please the
human eye. Florentine architects and artists have variously striven to recreate
this balance of nature in their works, whether it be the campanile of La Badia
by Arnolfo di Cambio, or that of the cathedral by Giotto, the façade of Santa
Maria Novella by Alberti or the dome of Santa Maria del Fiore by Brunelleschi.
The pure and elegant lines of all these works of art would seem to be a response
to the beauty of the landscape and the intensity of the light. The Florentine
preoccupation with perspective throughout the Quattrocento (15C) is in part the
result of this fascination for the countryside and the other great absorption of
the period, the desire faithfully to recreate what the eye saw.

View of Florence

This communion of great minds, with their varied facets and fields of interest, expressed a common desire to push their knowledge to the limits, and found in the flourishing city of Florence an ideal centre for their artistic and intellectual development. The city's artists, merchants, able administrators and its princely patrons of the arts all contributed to the creation of just the right conditions for nurturing such an intellectual and artistic community, which for centuries was to influence human creativity.

HISTORICAL NOTES

The colony of Florentia was founded in the 1C BC by Julius Caesar on the north bank of the Arno at a spot level with the Ponte Vecchio. The veteran soldiers who garrisoned the colony controlled the Via Flaminia linking Rome to northern Italy and Gaul.

It was only in the early 11C that the city became an important Tuscan centre when Count Ugo, Marquis of Tuscany, took up residence here, and again towards the end of the same century when the Countess Matilda affirmed its independence. During the 12C Florence prospered under the influence of the new class of merchants who built such fine buildings as the baptistry and San Miniato. This period saw the rise of trades organised in powerful guilds (arti), which soon became the ruling class when Florence became an independent commune. In the 13C one third of Florence's population was engaged in either the wool or the silk trades, both of which exported their products to the four corners of Europe and were responsible for a period of extraordinary prosperity. These tradesmen were ably supported by the Florentine moneyhouses which succeeded the Lombard and Jewish institutions, and themselves acquired a great reputation by issuing the first ever bills of exchange and the famous florin, struck with the Florentine coat of arms. The latter was replaced in the late 15C by the Venetian ducat. The main banking families were the Bardi-Peruzzi who advanced huge sums to England at the beginning of the Hundred Years War; they were soon to be joined in the forefront by the Pitti, Strozzi, Pazzi and of course the Medici. Despite its prosperity, Florence did not escape the internal strife between the Ghibellines who were partisans of the Holy Roman Emperor and the Guelphs who supported the Pope. The Guelphs at first had the advantage; but the Ghibellines on being driven out of Florence, having allied themselves with other enemies of Florence, notably Siena, regained power after the Battle of Montaperti in 1260. The Guelphs counter-attacked and retook Florence in 1266. Under their rule the physical aspect of the city changed considerably, notably with the destruction of the fortified tower houses built by the Ghibelline nobility. They created a republic and established government by a single individual or family; lordship (signoria) and committees which in Florence were known as priori. There then occurred a split between the Black Guelphs and the White Guelphs who opposed the Papacy. During this latter tragedy Dante, who supported the White Guelphs, was exiled for good in 1302. In 1348 the Black Death killed more than half the population and put an end to the period of internal strife.

Among the numerous wealthy families in Florence, it was the **Medici** who gave the city several leaders who exercised their patronage both in the sphere of fine arts and finance. The founder of this illustrious dynasty was Giovanni di Bicci, a prosperous banker who left his fortune in 1429 to his son **Cosimo the Elder**, who in turn transformed his heritage into the city's most flourishing business. He discreetly exercised his personal power through intermediaries, and astutely juggled his own personal interests with those of the city, which assured Florence a kind of peaceful hegemony. His chief quality was his ability to gather around him both scholars and artists, whom he commissioned for numerous projects.

Cosimo the Elder was a passionate builder and Florence owes many of her great monuments to this "Father of the Land". His son, Piero II Gottoso (the gouty) survived him by five years only and he in turn bequeathed all to his son **Lorenzo the Magnificent** (1449-92). Having escaped the Pazzi Conspiracy *(see p 94)* Lorenzo reigned like a true Renaissance prince, although it was always unofficially. He distinguished himself by his skilful politics and managed to retain the prestige of Florence amongst its contemporaries while ruining the Medici financial empire. This humanist and man of great sensitivity was a great patron of the arts, and he gathered around him poets and philosophers, who all contribued to make Florence the capital of the early Renaissance.

On Lorenzo's death, which had repercussions throughout Europe, the Dominican monk **Savonarola,** profiting from a period of confusion, provoked the fall of the Medici. This fanatical and ascetic monk, who became the Prior of the Monastery of St Mark, preached against the pleasures of the senses and of the arts, and drove the citizens of Florence to make a "bonfire of vanities" in 1497 in Piazza della Signoria, on which musical instruments, paintings, books of poetry etc were burnt. A year later Savonarola himself was burnt at the stake on the same spot. The Medici family returned to power with the help of the Emperor Charles V and they reigned until the mid-18C. **Cosimo I** (1519-74) brought back to Florence some of the splendour which she had lost, conquered Siena and he himself became Grand Duke of Tuscany. He continued the tradition of patron of the arts protecting numerous artists. Francesco I (1541-87), whose daughter Maria was to marry Henri IV King of France, took as his second wife the beautiful Venetian Bianca Cappello. The last prominent Medici was Ferdinand I (1549-1609) who married a French princess, Christine de Lorraine. After the Medici, the Grand Duchy passed to the House of Lorraine, then to Bonaparte until 1814, before it returned to the House of Lorraine until 1859. When it became part of the Italian kingdom, Florence was capital from 1865 to 1870.

FLORENCE, CAPITAL OF THE ARTS

The relatively late emergence of Florence in the 11C as a cultural centre and its insignificant Roman heritage no doubt contributed to the growth of an independent art movement, which developed vigorously for several centuries. One of its principal characteristics was its preoccupation with clarity and harmony which influenced writers as well as architects, painters and sculptors.

Dante Alighieri (1265-1321) established the use of the Italian vernacular in several of his works, thus superseding Latin as the literary language. He made an admirable demonstration with his **New Life** *(Vita Nuova),* recounting his meeting with a young girl Beatrice Portinari who was to be the inspiration for his **Divine Comedy** *(Divina Commedia),* in which Dante, led by Virgil and then by Beatrice, visits the Inferno, Purgatory and Paradise. Dante's description of these infernal circles where the damned are chastised, of the mountain of Purgatory where great crowds await redemption, and finally the dazzling vision of the divine splendour of Paradise, have inspired for generations not only Italian writers but men of letters everywhere. In the 14C Dante was responsible for creating an exceptionally versatile literary language to which Petrarch *(qv)* added his sense of lyricism and Boccaccio *(qv)* the art of irony.

Machiavelli (1469-1527), born in Florence, was the statesman on whose account Machiavellism became a synonym for cunning; he recounted his experiences as a statesman in a noble and vigorous prose. He was the author of **The Prince** *(Il Principe* – 1513), an essay on political science and government dedicated to Lorenzo II in which he counselled him in politics the end justifies the means. **Francesco Guicciardini** (1483-1540) wrote an important history of Florence and Italy, while **Giorgio Vasari** (1511-74), much later, with his work *The Lives of the Most Eminent Italian Architects, Painters and Sculptors,* was the first real art historian. He studied and classified local schools of painting, tracing their development from the 13C with the work of Cimabue, whom even Dante had praised in his *Divine Comedy.*

The Florentine school had its origins in the work of **Cimabue** (1240-1302) and slowly it freed itself from the Byzantine tradition with its decorative convolutions, while **Giotto** (1266-1337) in his search for truth gave priority to movement and expression. Later **Masaccio** (1401-28) studied spatial dimension and modelling. From then on perspective became the principal preoccupation of Florentine painters, sculptors, architects and theorists who continually tried to perfect this technique.

The Quattrocento (15C) saw the emergence of a group of artists like **Paolo Uccello** (1397-1475), **Andrea del Castagno** (1423-57), **Piero della Francesca** *(qv)* a native of the Marches, who were all ardent exponents in the matters of foreshortening and the strictly geometrical construction of space; while others like **Fra Angelico** (1387-1455), and later **Filippo Lippi** (1406-69) and **Benozzo Gozzoli** (1420-97) were imbued with the traditions of International Gothic *(qv)* and more concerned with the visual effects of arabesques and the appeal of luminous colours. These opposing tendencies were reconciled in the harmonious balance of the work of **Sandro Botticelli** (1444-1510), whom Florence is proud to claim as a son. He took his subjects from antiquity as the humanists in the court of Lorenzo de' Medici recommended, and he invented fables peopled by enigmatic figures with subtle linear forms, which created an impression of tension. At times a certain melancholy seems to arrest the movement and dim the luminosity of the colours. Alongside Botticelli the **Pollaiuolo** brothers, **Ghirlandaio** (1449-94) and **Filippino Lippi** (1457-1504) assure the continuity and diversity of Florentine art. The High Renaissance with its main centres in Rome and other northern towns reached Florence in the 16C.

Leonardo da Vinci *(qv)*, Michelangelo *(qv)* and Raphael *(qv)*, all made their debut at Florence, and inspired younger Mannerist artists *(p 32)* such as Pontormo, Rosso Fiorentino, Andrea del Sarto (1486-1530) and the curious portraitist of the Medici, Bronzino (1503-72).

The emergence of a Florentine school of painting is, however, indissociable from the contemporary movement of the architects who were creating a style, also inspired by antiquity, which united the classical traditions of rhythm, a respect for proportion and geometric decoration. The constant preoccupation was with perspective in the arrangement of interiors and the design of façades. Leon Battista Alberti (1404-72) was the theorist and grand master of such a movement. However it was Filippo Brunelleschi (1377-1446) who best represented the Florentine spirit, and he gave the city buildings which combined both rigour and grace, as in the magnificent dome of Santa Maria del Fiore which has become the symbol of Florence.

Throughout the Quattrocento (15C), buildings were embellished with admirable sculptures which became a harmonious part of the architectural whole. The doors of the baptistry were the object of a competition which confronted the very best. If Ghiberti (1378-1455) was finally victorious, Donatello (1386-1466) was later to provide ample demonstration of the genius of his art so full of realism and style, as did Luca della Robbia (1400-82) and his dynasty who specialised in glazed terracotta decoration, Verrocchio (1435-88) and numerous other artists who adorned the ecclesiastical and secular buildings of Florence. In the 16C Michelangelo, who was part of this tradition, confirmed his origins with his New Sacristy (1520-55) of San Lorenzo, which he both designed and decorated with sculpture. Later Benvenuto Cellini (1500-71), Giambologna or Giovanni Bologna (1529-1608) and Bartolomeo Ammannati (1511-92) maintained this unity of style which was responsible for the exceptional beauty of the city of Florence.

SIGHTSEEING

Florence is such an important art centre that it takes at least four days to see the main sights. These are however situated fairly closely together in the city centre which is not adapted to heavy traffic. It is therefore advisable to do the sightseeing on foot and establish a visiting programme which takes into account the opening times.

PIAZZA DEL DUOMO (HX) *time: 1/2 day*

In the city centre, the cathedral along with the campanile and baptistry, form an admirable group of white, green and pink marble, which demonstrates the traditions of Florentine art from the Middle Ages to the Renaissance.

★★ Cathedral (Duomo) (HX A). – The Cathedral of Santa Maria del Fiore, one of the largest cathedrals in the Christian world, is a symbol of the city's power and wealth in the 13C and 14C. It was begun in 1296 by Arnolfo di Cambio and was consecrated in 1436.

This essentially Gothic cathedral is an outstanding example of the Florentine variant of this style, with its sheer size, predominance of horizontal lines and taste for polychrome decoration.

Exterior. – Walk round the cathedral starting from the south side to admire the marble mosaic decoration and the sheer size of the east end★★★. The harmonious dome★★★ by Brunelleschi took fourteen years to build. To counteract the excessive thrust he built two concentric domes which were linked by props. The façade dates from the late 19C.

Interior. – The bareness of the interior contrasts sharply with the sumptuous decoration of the exterior. Enormous piers support sturdy arches which themselves uphold the lofty Gothic vaulting. The great octagonal chancel under the dome is surrounded by a delicate 16C marble balustrade. The dome is painted with a huge fresco ⊙ of the Last Judgment. It is possible to go up to the inner gallery which offers an impressive view of the nave, and then on up to the top of the dome ⊙ (464 steps) with its magnificent panorama★★ of Florence.

The sacristy doors on either side of the high altar have tympana adorned with pale blue terracottas by Luca della Robbia representing the Resurrection and the Ascension. In the new sacristy (left), there are inlaid armorial bearings by the Maiano brothers (15C).

A dramatic episode of the Pazzi Conspiracy took place in the chàncel. The Pazzi, who were rivals of the Medici, tried to assassinate Lorenzo the Magnificent on 26 April 1478, during the Elevation of the Host. Lorenzo, though wounded by two monks, managed to take refuge in a sacristy, but his brother Giuliano fell to their daggers.

The axial chapel contains a masterpiece by Ghiberti, the sarcophagus of St Zanobi, the first Bishop of Florence. One of the low reliefs shows the saint resurrecting a child. The frescoes in the north aisle include: in the first bay near the choir, one showing Dante explaining the *Divine Comedy* to the city of Florence (1465); further along to the right, two equestrian portraits of leaders of mercenary armies *(condottieri)* by Paolo Ucello (1436) and Andrea del Castagno (1456).

A stairway on the other side of the nave, between the first and second pillars, leads to the Crypt of Santa Reparata ⊙, the only remaining part of a Romanesque basilica which was demolished when the present cathedral was built. The basilica itself was formerly an early Christian church (5C-6C). Excavations have revealed traces of mosaic paving belonging to the original building and Brunelleschi's tomb (behind the railing-enclosed chamber, at the bottom of the stairs, on the left).

★★★ **Campanile** ⊙ (HX B). – The tower is slender and tall (82m – 269ft) and is the perfect complement to Brunelleschi's dome, the straight lines of the former balancing the curves of the latter. Giotto drew the plans for it and began building in 1334, but died in 1337. The Gothic campanile was completed at the end of the 14C; its geometric decoration with its emphasis on horizontal lines is unusual. The admirable low reliefs at the base of the campanile have been replaced by copies. Those on the lower band were executed by Andrea Pisano and Luca della Robbia and those on the upper band by pupils of Andrea Pisano, but the overall design was by Giotto. The original low reliefs are in the Cathedral Museum.

From the top of the campanile (414 steps) there is a fine **panorama★★** of the cathedral and town.

★★★ **Baptistry** ⊙ (HX C). – The building is encased in white and green marble in a sober and well-balanced Romanesque style. The **bronze doors★★★** are world-famous.

The South Door (entrance) by Andrea Pisano (1330) is Gothic and portrays scenes from the life of St John the Baptist (above), as well as the three Theological Virtues (Faith, Hope, Charity) and the four Cardinal Virtues (below). The door-frames which show great skill are by Vittorio Ghiberti, son of the designer of the other doors.

The North Door (1403-24) was the first done by Lorenzo Ghiberti. He was the winner of a competition in which Brunelleschi, Donatello and Jacopo della Quercia also took part. Scenes from the Life of Christ are evoked with extraordinary nobility and harmony of composition.

The East Door (1425-52), facing the cathedral, is the one that Michelangelo declared worthy to be the **Gate to Paradise**. In it Ghiberti recalled the Old Testament; prophets and sibyls adorn the niches. The artist portrayed himself, bald and malicious, in one of the medallions.

Interior. – With its 25m – 82ft diameter, its black and white marble and its paving decorated with oriental motifs, the interior is grand and majestic. The dome is covered with magnificent **mosaics★★★** of the 13C. The Last Judgement is depicted on either side of a large picture of Christ the King; on the five concentric bands that cover the other five panels of the dome, starting from the top towards the base, are the Heavenly Hierarchies, Genesis, the Life of Joseph, scenes from the Life of the Virgin and of Christ, and the Life of St John the Baptist.

On the right of the apse is the tomb of the Antipope John XXIII, friend of Cosimo the Elder, a remarkable work executed in 1427 by Donatello assisted by Michelozzo.

Under the 14C Gothic **Loggia del Bigallo** (HX E) to the south of the baptistry, lost or abandoned children were exhibited.

★★ **Cathedral Museum** (Museo dell'Opera del Duomo) ⊙ (JX M¹). – This contains items from the cathedral, campanile and baptistry. Statues from the former façade of the cathedral (Pope Boniface VIII by Arnolfo di Cambio, the four Evangelists), equipment used by Brunelleschi to build the dome and his death mask as well as gold plate are exhibited on the ground floor.

On the mezzanine is the famous **Pietà★★** which Michelangelo, at the age of eighty, left unfinished.

In the large room on the first floor are three famous statues by Donatello – an impressive repentant **Magdalen★** carved in wood, and the prophets Jeremiah and Habakkuk, the latter being nicknamed *Zuccone* (vegetable marrow) because of the shape of his head.

In the same room are the famous **Cantorie★★**, choristers' tribunes, from the cathedral: on the left, Luca della Robbia's tribune (the panels on the base are original, the upper section has been remodelled with copies) bears figures of choir boys, dancers and musicians of exquisite charm. Donatello's tribune, opposite, is decorated with lively *putti* (cherubs) – this motif used here for the first time was very successful and was adopted even in paintings.

In a room on the left are exhibited the admirable **low reliefs★★** from the campanile: those by Andrea Pisano and Luca della Robbia, which are hexagonal in shape and very picturesque, depict the creation of Adam and Eve and various human activities; the rest are diamond-shaped and represent the planets, the virtues, the liberal arts and the sacraments.

The room to the right of the one with the cantorie, contains four panels from the Gate to Paradise and the famous silver **altarpiece★★** depicting the life of St John the Baptist, a masterpiece of 14C-15C Florentine craftsmanship.

PIAZZA DELLA SIGNORIA (HY, f ab)

★★ **Piazza della Signoria** (HY). – This was, and still is, the political stage of Florence, with a wonderful backcloth formed by the Palazzo Vecchio, the Loggia della Signoria and in the wings the Uffizi Museum. The many statues make it virtually an open-air museum of sculpture: near the centre of the square, the equestrian statue of Cosimo I, after Giovanni Bologna, and at the corner of the Palazzo Vecchio, the *Fountain of Neptune* (1576) by Ammannati. In front of the Palazzo Vecchio are a copy of the proud *Marzocco* or *Lion of Florence* by Donatello and a copy of Michelangelo's *David*.

★★ **Loggia della Signoria** (HY D). – The Loggia, built at the end of the 14C, was the assembly hall and later the guardroom of the Lanzi (foot soldiers) of Cosimo I. It contains ancient (Classical) and Renaissance statues: the *Rape of a Sabine* (1583), *Hercules and the centaur Nessus* by Giovanni Bologna and the wonderful **Perseus★★★** holding up the severed head of Medusa, a masterpiece executed by Benvenuto Cellini from 1545 to 1553.

★★★ **Palazzo Vecchio** ⊙ (HJY). – The Old Palace's powerful mass is dominated by a lofty bell tower, 94m – 308ft high. Built between 1299 and 1314 probably to plans by Arnolfo di Cambio, it is in a severe Gothic style with a total lack of openings at ground level, a series of twinned windows above and battlements, parapet walk and crenellations on top with the tower.

The refinement and splendour of the Renaissance interior is a complete contrast. The **courtyard**★ was restored by Michelozzo in the 15C and decorated in the following century by Vasari. The 16C fountain is surmounted by a delightful winged goblin, a copy of a work by Verrocchio (the original is howsed in the palace).

Initially the seat of government (Palazzo della Signoria), the palace was then taken over in the 16C by Cosimo I as his private residence, as it was better suited to accommodating his large court. Most of the redecoration work done by Giorgio Vasari dates from this period. When Cosimo I abandoned the palace in favour of the Pitti Palace it was renamed Palazzo Vecchio.

The apartments were lavishly decorated with sculptures by Benedetto and Giuliano da Maiano (15C) and with paintings by Vasari and Bronzino (16C) to the glory of Florence and the Medici. On the first floor the great Sala dei Cinquecento, painted with frescoes by several artists including Vasari, contains a group carved by Michelangelo, *The Genius of Victory*. The walls of the magnificent **studiolo**★★ or study of Francesco de' Medici, which was designed by Vasari, were painted by several Florentine Mannerist painters including Bronzino, who was responsible for the medallion portraits of *Cosimo I* and *Eleanora of Toledo*. Leo X's apartment was decorated by Vasari and his assistants with scenes illustrating episodes of the Medici history.

On the second floor are: the Priors' Apartment including the **Sala dei Gigli** (Room of the Lilies) which is adorned with a splendid coffered **ceiling**★ by Giuliano da Maiano; the **Sala della Guardaroba**★ (Wardrobe) lined with 16C **maps**; the Apartment of Eleonora of Toledo decorated by Vasari, with the exception of the chapel which was adorned with frescoes by Bronzino; the Apartment of Cosimo I, known as Quartiere degli Elementi because of the allegorical scenes painted by Vasari and his assistants to decorate the first room (in the Room of Jupiter are three **tapestries**★ which were woven in the 16C by the Medici tapestry works).

★★★ **Uffizi Museum** (Galleria degli Uffizi) ⊙ (HY). – This is one of the finest museums in the world. These collections were assembled by several generations of Medici and the visitor can follow the evolution of Italian art from its beginnings to the 17C.

The early nucleus was gathered together by Francesco I (1541-87) to which were added the collections of the Grand Dukes Ferdinand I, II and Cosimo III. In 1737 the last member of the Medici dynasty, Anna Maria Ludovica, Electress Palatine, bequeathed the Medici collection to her native city of Florence.

The Uffizi Museum was then housed in the Renaissance palace, designed by Vasari in 1560, which contained the offices *(uffizi)* of the Medici administration. The rich collections of drawings and paintings are on the first floor; paintings and sculpture are exhibited in two galleries and adjacent rooms on the second floor.

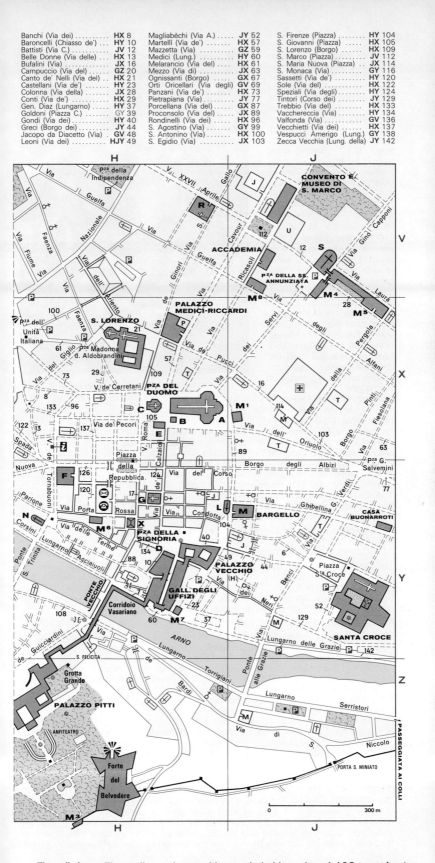

The galleries. – The walls are hung with an admirable series of 16C **tapestries:** in gallery 1 the Months and the Fêtes given at the court of Catherine de' Medici and Henri II by the Flemish school (look for the Tuileries and the Châteaux of Anet and Fontainebleau). In gallery 2 is the *Passion of Christ* from the Florentine looms.

Classical statues, mostly Roman copies, and a fine series of busts of the imperial era are also on view.

East side galleries. – The first room is devoted to archaeology, the next ten contain Florentine and Tuscan paintings from the late 13C to 16C, and the remaining rooms are reserved for 15C and 16C Italian and foreign schools.

Late 13C-14C Tuscan: note especially the works of Cimabue, Giotto and Duccio (Madonnas: room 2) and the famous **Annunciation** of Simone Martini (room 3), a masterpiece of Gothic art.

15C Florentine: the works of particular interest are: in room 7 the famous **Battle of San Romano** (the two other panels are in the Louvre and London) by Paolo Uccello; Fra Angelico *(Coronation of the Virgin),* Piero della Francesca (Portrait of the *Duke of Urbino);* in room 8 Filippo Lippi (his famous **Virgin and Child** on an easel between two *Adorations* and a *Coronation of the Virgin).*

The **Botticelli Room★★★** (10-14), which is the most remarkable in the museum,

Pallas and the Centaur by Botticelli

contains the *Madonna of the Magnificat,* a harmonious round composition; the **Birth of Venus** and **Spring,** both mature works typical of this artist's lyrical poetry; and the admirable tondo of the *Madonna with a Pomegranate.* In the same room is the **Portinari Triptych** painted in Bruges *c*1576 by Van der Goes and presented to the Church of San Egidio in Florence. Its realism and precise daughtsmanship greatly influenced Florentine artists (including Ghirlandaio).

The next room contains the *Baptism of Christ* by Verrocchio and two masterpieces by Leonardo da Vinci, the unfinished **Adoration of the Magi** and the famous **Annunciation** with its remarkable perspectives.

The Tribune (room 18): this is octagonal in shape and was designed by Buontalenti (1588). It contains the famous **Medici Venus** carved by a Greek sculptor in the 3C BC, and several portraits of the Medici by Pontormo, Bronzino, Vasari...

15C and 16C Italian and foreign schools: note in room 19, Perugino and Signorelli; in room 20, Cranach (**Adam and Eve,** *Luther*) and Dürer (**Adoration of the Magi**); in room 21, Giovanni Bellini (**Sacred Allegory**) and Giorgione; in room 22, portraits by Van Orley, Holbein, Joos van Cleve; in room 23, Correggio (*Rest in Egypt, Adoration),* Bernardino Luini, Boccacino *(La Zingarella).*

Miniatures Room: *look through railings.* Miniatures from the 15C to the 19C.

West side galleries. – *Parallel to the first series.* Eleven rooms are devoted to the Italian Cinquecento (16C): Michelangelo (room 25: **Holy Family**); Raphael (room 26: **Leo X, Madonna with Goldfinch**); the Florentine Mannerists (rooms 26 and 27: Andrea del Sarto with his famous *Virgin with Harpies,* Pontormo etc), Emilian (rooms 29 to 31: Parmigianino, Dosso Dossi) and Venetian mannerist artists. There are some splendid paintings by Titian (room 28: *Flora,* **Urbino Venus,** portraits), Veronese (room 34: *The Holy Family and St Barbara*) and Tintoretto (room 35: **Leda and the Swan,** portraits).

Next is Italian and foreign painting of the 17C and 18C. The 17C Flemish school is represented (room 41) by Rubens **(Isabella Brandt)** and Van Dyck (portraits). The Niobe Room (42) contains a group of sculpture.

The following room (43) has several canvases by **Caravaggio** *(Bacchus as a Youth)* and works by **Claude;** Dutch paintings and **Rembrandt**'s portraits and self-portraits hang in room 44, while room 45 is devoted to the 18C with works by Nattier and Chardin as well as the two Venetian view painters, Canaletto and Guardi.

Corridoio Vasariano ⊘ (HY). – This corridor by Vasari links the Palazzo Vecchio to the Pitti Palace and is hung with a remarkable collection of portraits. The covered passageway was built by Vasari in 1565 and it is appropriate that the self-portraits should include one of the architect. Other notable sitters include Raphael, Becafumi, Salvator Rosa as well as foreign artists (Rembrandt, Van Dyck, Kneller...).

★★★ **Bargello Palace and Museum** ⊘ (JY M). – This austere palace was formerly the residence of the governing magistrate *(podestà)* and then became police headquarters *(bargello).* It is a fine example of 13C-14C medieval architecture planned round a majestic **courtyard★★** with a portico and loggia.

The palace is now transformed into a museum of sculpture and decorative arts with particularly good sections on Italian and Florentine Renaissance sculpture.

Ground floor. – These rooms are devoted to the works of 16C Florentine sculptors: by Michelangelo there is a **Bacchus Drunk,** a *Brutus,* an *Apollo* and the Pitti Tondo (a marble medallion depicting the Virgin and Child with St John); and by Benvenuto Cellini a *Narcissus,* a **low relief** from the pedestal of the Perseus bronze in the Loggia della Signoria and a bust of Cosimo I.

First floor. – The great saloon contains an exceptional collection of **sculpture★★★** by **Donatello** and his assistants (Desiderio da Settignano, Agostino di Duccio) as well as works by Luca della Robbia. Donatello's genius made him an important figure in the early Italian Renaissance period. His works include *St John the Baptist as a Youth,* his **Marzocco** (the Florentine heraldic lion), his famous mature work, the bronze **David,** as well as the low relief of **St George** from Orsanmichele.

The other rooms in the palace now display the Louis Carrand collection of enamels, jewellery and remarkable ivories bequeathed by this Frenchman from Lyons in the late 19C.

Second floor. – Rooms VII to XI contain colourful glazed terracottas by Giovanni and Andrea della Robbia, works by **Verrocchio,** including the famous bronze statue of **David,** a series of small Renaissance bronzes and a remarkable collection of arms and armour.

FROM SAN LORENZO TO SANTA MARIA NOVELLA
time: 1/2 day

★★★ **San Lorenzo** (HX). – Not far from the Medici Palace, this was the Medici family parish church, and it was here that most of the family was buried. The **church★★** was begun by Brunelleschi *c* 1420. The interior is a perfect example of the sobriety of style introduced by **Brunelleschi** and typical of his thoughtful, measured, rigorous architectural style and its human dimension. His great achievement is the **Old Sacristy★★** *(at the far end of the north transept).* Donatello was responsible for part of the decoration of the latter and also the two **pulpits★★** in the nave with bronze panels, which are works of admirable virtuosity and full of a great sense of drama.

★★ **Laurenziana Library** (Biblioteca Medicea Laurenziana) ⊘. – Cosimo the Elder's library was added to by Lorenzo the Magnificent. Access is from the north aisle of the church or through the charming 15C **cloisters★** *(entrance to the left of the church).* The vestibule was designed as an exterior and is occupied by a magnificent **staircase★★,** supremely elegant as the curved steps of the central flight lead up to the library proper. The staircase was built by Ammannati to Michelangelo's designs. The **library,** also by Michelangelo, displays in rotation some of the 10 000 manuscripts.

★★ **Medici Chapels** ⊘. – *Entrance on Piazza Madonna degli Aldobrandini.* This includes the Princes' Chapel and New Sacristy.

The **Princes' Chapel★** (17C-18C), grandiose but gloomy, is faced with semi-precious stones and marbles and is the funerary chapel for Cosimo I and his descendants. The **New Sacristy★★** was Michelangelo's first architectural work and despite its name was always intended as a funerary chapel. Begun in 1520, it was left unfinished when the artist left Florence in 1534. Michelangelo achieved a great sense of rhythm and solemnity by using contrasting materials, dark grey sandstone *(pietra serena)* and the white of the walls and marbles. The famous **Medici tombs★★★** were also the work of Michelangelo. Giuliano, Duke of Nemours (d 1516), is portrayed as Action, surrounded by allegorical figures of Day and Night; and Lorenzo II, Duke of Urbino (d 1519), as a Thinker with Dawn and Dusk at his feet.

Of the plans for Lorenzo the Magnificent's tomb only the admirable group of the Madonna and Child flanked by saints was completed. In the plain tomb underneath lie Lorenzo the Magnificent and his brother Giuliano.

★★ **Medici Palace** (Palazzo Medici-Riccardi) ⊘ (HX). – This noble but austere building is typical of the Florentine Renaissance with its mathematical plan and rustication, massive at ground level and lighter on the upper level. The palace which has a square arcaded courtyard was begun in 1444 by Michelozzo on the orders of his friend Cosimo the Elder. From 1459 to 1540 it was a Medici residence, and Lorenzo the Magnificent held court here, attended by poets, philosophers and artists alike. In the second half of the 17C the palace passed to the Riccardi who made extensive alterations to the building.

★★★ **Chapel.** – *First floor: entrance by the first stairway on the right in the courtyard.* This tiny chapel was decorated with admirable **frescoes** (1459) by **Benozzo Gozzoli.** The Procession of the Kings is a vivid picture of Florentine life with portraits of the Medici and of famous dignitaries from the East who had assembled for the Council of Florence in 1439.

★★ **Luca Giordano Gallery.** – *First floor: entrance by the second stairway on the right in the courtyard.* The entire roof of this gallery built by the Riccardi at the end of the 17C and splendidly decorated with gold stucco, carved panels and great painted mirrors, is covered by a brightly-coloured baroque fresco of the Apotheosis of the second Medici dynasty, masterfully painted by Luca Giordano in 1683.

★★ **Santa Maria Novella** (GX). – The Church of Santa Maria Novella and the adjoining monastery were founded in the 13C by the Dominicans. The church overlooks an elongated square which was originally the setting for chariot races.

★★ **Church.** – The church, begun in 1246, was completed only in 1360, except for the **façade,** with harmonious lines and geometric patterns in white and green marble, designed by Alberti (upper section) in the 15C.

It is a large church (100m – 328ft) designed for preaching. On the wall of the third bay in the north aisle is a famous **fresco★** of the Trinity with the Virgin, St John and the donors in which Masaccio, adopting the new Renaissance theories, shows great mastery of perspective. At the far end of the north transept, the Strozzi Chapel (raised) is decorated with **frescoes★** (1357) by the Florentine Nardo di Cione depicting the Last Judgment on a grand scale. The **polyptych★** on the altar is by Nardo's brother, Orcagna di Cione. The sacristy contains a fine **Crucifix★** *(above the entrance)* by Giotto and a delicate glazed terracotta **niche★** by Giovanni della Robbia.

In the Gondi Chapel *(first on the left of the high altar)* is displayed the famous **Crucifix★★** by Brunelleschi, which so struck Donatello that he is said, on first seeing it, to have dropped the basket of eggs he was carrying.

The chancel is ornamented with admirable **frescoes★★★** by **Domenico Ghirlandaio** who, on the theme of the Lives of the Virgin and of St John the Baptist, painted a dazzling picture of Florentine life in the Renaissance era. The church is flanked by two cloisters. The finest are the **Green Cloisters★** ⊙, so-called after the dominant colour of the frescoes painted by Paolo Uccello and his school (scenes from the Old Testament). Opening off these to the north is the **Spaniards' Chapel** with late-14C **frescoes★★** by **Andrea di Bonaiuto** (also known as Andrea da Firenze). With an intricate symbolism the frescoes depict the Church Triumphant and the glorification of the action of the Dominicans. To the east is the refectory which houses the church's treasure.

PONTE VECCHIO, PITTI PALACE AND BOBOLI GARDEN
time: 2 hours

- **★ Ponte Vecchio** (HY). – This, Florence's oldest bridge, crosses the Arno at its narrowest point and has been rebuilt several times. It has a curious appearance with jewellers' shops lining the roadway and above the Corridoio Vasariano *(p 98)*.

- **★★ Pitti Palace** (GHZ). – This 15C Renaissance building, of rugged but imposing appearance, with pronounced rustication and many windows, was built to the plans of Brunelleschi for the Pitti family, the rivals of the Medici. It was Cosimo I's wife, Eleanora di Toledo, who enlarged the palace by the addition of two wings. The court moved to the palace in 1560.

- **★★★ Palatine Gallery** ⊙. – *First floor.* The marvellous collection of paintings is hung quite at random. There are two wonderful **groups★★★** of works by **Raphael** and **Titian**: by the former, **Portrait of a Lady** or *La Valata* (Hall of Jupiter; *illustration p 31)*, **Madonna del Granduca** and **Madonna della Seggiola** (both in the Hall of Saturn); by the latter, portraits, **La Bella** and **The Aretino** and **The Concert** (Hall of Venus) and the **Grey-eyed Nobleman** (Hall of Apollo).

  Among the many other paintings which hang in the rooms, splendidly decorated by Pietro da Cortona, are two seascapes by Salvator Rosa (Hall of Venus), portraits by Van Dyck (Hall of Apollo). *The Four Philosophers* by Rubens and *Cardinal Bentivoglio* by Van Dyck, a *Descent from the Cross* by Fra Bartolomeo, and two large landscapes by Rubens (Hall of Venus).

  Further on are displayed an astonishing **Sleeping Cupid** by Caravaggio (Hall of the Education of Jupiter), a *Virgin and Child* by Filippo Lippi (Hall of Prometheus), a *St Sebastian* by Sodoma (Castagnoli Room), as well as numerous works from the Italian and foreign schools by Perugino, Dosso Dossi, Andrea del Sarto, Rosso Fiorentino, Pontormo, Bronzino, Veronese, Guido Reni, Sustermans, Velasquez etc.

  State Apartments ⊙. – *First floor.* These are lavishly decorated with pictures, works of art and admirable tapestries.

- **★★ Silver Museum** (Museo degli Argenti) ⊙. – *Ground floor and mezzanine.* This contains an exceptional collection of works in semi-precious stones *(pietre dure)*, ivories, glassware and silver plate largely from the Medici collections.

- **★ Modern Art Gallery** ⊙. – *Second floor.* Works, mostly Tuscan, illustrate the trends that influenced Italian sculpture and painting in the 19C. The section devoted to neo-classical and Romantic art, includes works by the Benvenuti, Canova, Bezzuoli and Hayez, Bartolini. The **Macchiaioli** movement *(p 33)* is represented by an exceptional **series★★** by Fattori, Lega, Signorini, Cecioni...

- **★ Boboli Garden** (Giardino di Boboli) ⊙ (GHZ). – This Italian-style terraced garden, behind the Pitti Palace, was designed in 1549 by Tribolo and is ornamented with antique and Renaissance statues. At one end of an avenue to the left of the palace is the **grotta grande**, a grotto created in the main by Buontalenti (1587-97). At the opposite end stands the **Costume Museum** ⊙ (GZ M²) which displays Italian costumes dating from the 18C to the present day. Cross the amphitheatre to reach the highest point of the garden from which, on the right, the **Viottolone★**, an avenue of pines and cypresses, runs down to **Piazzale dell'Isolotto★**, a circular pool with a small island, bearing citrus trees and a fountain by Giovanni Bologna. A pavilion houses a **Porcelain Museum★** ⊙ (HZ M³). The **Citadel Belvedere** (Forte del Belvedere), at the top of the hill, affords a splendid **panorama★★** of Florence and the celebrated Florentine countryside. The elegant villa which dominates the bastion was designed by Buontalenti.

The great centres of Renaissance art:
Florence, Rome, Siena, Padua, Venice, Milan, Parma, Perugia.

SAN MARCO QUARTER *time: 2 hours*

★★ **Convent and Museum of St Mark** (Convento e Museo di San Marco) ⊙ (JV).
– The museum in a former Dominican monastery, rebuilt *c*1436 in a very plain
style by Michelozzo, is virtually the **Fra Angelico Museum★★★**. Fra Angelico took
orders in Fiesole before coming to St Mark's, where he decorated the walls of
the monks' cells with edifying scenes. Humility, gentleness and mysticism were
the qualities expressed by this artistic monk in a technique that was still Gothic.
His refined use of colour, delicate draughtsmanship and timid handling of the
subject-matter imbued these frescoes with a pacifying power, so appropriate for
this oasis of calm and place of meditation.

Ground floor. – The former guest quarters, opening off the cloisters on the right,
contain many of the Dominican's works on wood, especially the triptych depicting
the **Descent from the Cross,** the famous **Last Judgement** and a series of other religious
scenes. The chapter house has a severe Crucifixion while the refectory contains
an admirable **Last Supper★** by Ghirlandaio.

First floor. – The staircase is dominated by his well-balanced and sober
masterpiece, the **Annunciation.** The monks' cells open off three corridors, with lovely
timber ceilings. Along the corridor to the left of the stairs are the Apparition
of Christ to the Penitent Magdalen (1st cell on the left), the Transfiguration (6th
cell on the left) and the Coronation of the Virgin (9th cell on the left).
At the far end of the next corridor were the cells of Savonarola, who was prior
of St Mark's. Off the corridor on the right is the **library★**, one of Michelozzo's
finest accomplisements.

★★ **Academy Gallery** (Galleria dell'Accademia) ⊙ (JV). – The paintings in this collection
are judiciously hung and give the visitor some idea of the extraordinary personality
of **Michelangelo** and the conflict between the nature of his raw materials and his
idealistic vision.
The **main gallery★★★** contains the powerful figures of **Four Slaves** (1513-20) and
St Matthew (all unfinished) who would seem to be trying to struggle free from
the marble. At the far end of the gallery, in a specially designed apse (1873), is
the monumental figure of **David** (1501-04), the symbol of youthful but
well-mastered force and a perfect example of the sculptor's humanism. The **picture
gallery★** has works by 13C-15C Tuscan masters, including a painted chest by
Adimari and two Botticellis.

★ **Piazza della Santissima Annunziata** (JV). – This fine square is adorned with
an equestrian statue of Ferdinand I de' Medici by Giovanni Bologna, and two
Baroque fountains.

Church of the Santissima Annunziata (JV S). – This church was rebuilt in the 15C
by Michelozzo. It is preceded by an atrium decorated with **frescoes★** (damaged)
by Rosso Fiorentino, Pontormo, Andrea del Sarto, Franciabigio and Baldovinetti.
Inside there is a miraculous image of a Madonna.

Foundlings' Hospital (Ospedale degli Innocenti) (JV M⁴). – This is preceded by
an elegant 15C **portico★** by Brunelleschi, with corners decorated with touching
terracotta **medallions★** of children by Andrea della Robbia. The **art gallery** ⊙ contains
some interesting works by Florentine artists.

SANTA CROCE AND A TRIP TO THE HILLS *time: 2 hours*

★★ **Santa Croce** (JY). – The church and cloisters of Santa Croce give onto one
of the town's oldest squares.

★★ **Church** ⊙. – This is the church of the Franciscans. It was started in 1294 and
completed in the second half of the 14C. The façade and the campanile date
from the 19C.
The **interior** is vast (140m – 460ft by 40m – 130ft) as the church was designed
for preaching and consists of a single spacious nave and slender apse with fine
15C stained glass windows. The church is paved with 276 tombstones and along
the walls are sumptuous tombs.

South aisle: By the first pillar, a Virgin and Child by A. Rossellino (15C); opposite,
the tomb of Michelangelo (d 1564) by Vasari; opposite the second pillar, the
funerary monument (19C) to Dante (d 1321, buried at Ravenna); by the third
pillar, a fine **pulpit★** (1476) by Benedetto da Maiano and facing it the monument
to V. Alfieri (d 1803) by Canova; opposite the fourth pillar, the 18C monument
to Machiavelli (d 1527); facing the fifth pillar, an elegant low relief of the
Annunciation★★ carved in stone and embellished with gold by Donatello; opposite
the ninth pillar, the tomb of Leonardo Bruni ¹ ² (humanist and chancellor of the
Republic, d 1444) by B. Rossellino, and next to it the tomb of Rossini (d 1868).

South transept: At the far end, the Baroncelli Chapel with **frescoes★** (1338) depicting
the Life of the Virgin by Taddeo Gaddi and at the altar the **polyptych★**, Coronation
of the Virgin from Giotto's studio.

★ **Sacristy** ⊙ *(access by the corridor on the right of the chancel):* This dates from
the 14C and is adorned with **frescoes★** including a Crucifixion by Taddeo Gaddi
and, in the fine Rinuccini Chapel, with scenes from the Life of the Virgin and
of Mary Magdalen by Giovanni da Milano (14C). At the far end of the corridor
is the harmonious Medici Chapel (1434) built by Michelozzo, with a fine **altarpiece★**
in glazed terracotta by Andrea della Robbia.

Chancel: The first chapel to the right of the altar contains moving **frescoes★★**
(*c*1320) by Giotto depicting the life of St Francis; in the third chapel is the tomb
of Julie Clary, the wife of Joseph Bonaparte. The chancel proper is covered with
frescoes★ (1380) by Agnolo Gaddi relating the legend of the Holy Cross.

North transept: At the far end is a famous **Crucifix★★** by Donatello, which Brunelleschi tried to surpass at Santa Maria Novella.

North aisle *(coming back):* Beyond the second pillar, a fine **monument★ to Carlo Marsuppini** by Desiderio da Settignano (15C); facing the fourth pillar the tombstone of L. Ghiberti (d 1455); the last tomb (18C) is that of Galileo (d 1642).

Great cloisters. – *Entrance at the far end of the first cloisters, on the right.* These very elegant cloisters were designed by Brunelleschi shortly prior to his death (1446) and were completed only in 1453.

Santa Croce Museum (Museo dell'Opera di Santa Croce) ⊘. – This is installed in the buildings around the first cloisters and in particular in the former refectory. The museum contains a famous **Crucifix★** painted by Cimabue which was seriously damaged by the 1966 floods. Santa Croce was one of the Florentine monuments to suffer most in these floods.

★★ **Pazzi Chapel** ⊘. – *At the far end of the first cloisters; entrance to the right of the church.* This chapel by Brunelleschi is entered through a domed portico, and is a masterpiece of the Florentine Renaissance remarkable for its original conception, its pure, rigid lines, its skilful proportions and the harmony of its decoration (glazed terracotta from the della Robbia workshop).

★★ **Trip to the hills (Passeggiata ai Colli).** – *See plans of the built-up area in the Michelin Red Guide Italia.* Take the road to the east along the south bank of the Arno to the medieval tower in Piazza Guiseppe Poggi. Poggi laid this fine road to the hills from 1865 to 1870. Take the winding pedestrian street to Piazzale Michelangiolo for a splendid **view★★★** of the whole city.

Not far from this square, in a splendid **setting★★** overlooking the town, the **Church of San Miniato al Monte★★**, built from the 11C to 13 C, is one of the most remarkable examples of Florentine Romanesque architecture. Its very elegant façade is decorated with geometric designs in green and white marble, not unlike those of the baptistry. The harmonious interior also ornamented with multicoloured marble contains a 13C pavement. The **Chapel of Cardinal James of Portugal★** opening out of the north aisle is a fine Renaissance structure. In the centre of the nave is a Chapel of the Crucifix by Michelozzo. The pulpit and chancel screen *(transenna)* form a remarkable **ensemble★★** beautifully inlaid with marble dating from the early 13C. The apse is adorned by a mosaic depicting Christ conferring His Blessing.

The **frescoes★** (1387) in the **sacristy** are by Spinello Aretino. The 11C **crypt** has delicate columns with antique capitals.

ADDITIONAL SIGHTS

★ **Strozzi Palace** (HY F). – Dating from the end of the 15C, this is one of the finest and largest privately-owned palaces in Florence with its rusticated stonework, cornice and arcaded courtyard.

★ **Rucellai Palace (Palazzo Rucellai)** (GY Z). – The palace was designed by Leon Battista Alberti and built in the mid 15C by Bernardo Rossellino. The façade is the first cohesive example of the three ancient orders placed one on top of the other. A strict harmony is created vertically by pilasters (with openings in between) and horizontally by entablatures.

★★ **Frescoes of Santa Maria del Carmine** ⊘ (GY). – The church which was badly damaged by fire in the 18C has outstanding frescoes depicting original sin and the life of St Peter in the **Brancacci Chapel** *(at the far end of the south transept).* **Masaccio,** the pioneer of the Renaissance in the field of painting, was the principal artist of the fresco cycle which he painted in 1427 at the age of 26, a year before he died. In the scenes: Expulsion of Adam and Eve, the Tribute Money, the Baptism of the Neophytes and the Healing of the Sick, the figures show an amazing realism (in the grave expressions) with their solid but simple forms, and a new mastery of light effects. The remaining frescoes are by Masolino (1424) and Filippino Lippi (1481).

★★ **Last Supper of San Salvi (Cenacolo di San Salvi)** ⊘. – *To the east of Florence (see the plan of the built-up area in the current Michelin Red Guide Italia,* **FU A***). Take the Piazza Beccaria, Via V. Gioberti and its continuation beyond the Piazza Via L.B. Alberti, Via Aretina and finally Via San Salvi. Entrance at no 16.* The former refectory of the abbey contains a splendid fresco of the Last Supper (1520) by **Andrea del Sarto** which is a masterpiece of composition and colour and has a dramatic sense of reality.

★ **Orsanmichele** (HY G). – Originally a grain storehouse, Orsanmichele was rebuilt in the 14C in a transitional Gothic-Renaissance style. It is a veritable museum of sculpture with the statues in the niches alone, which portray the patrons of the corporations. There are works by Donatello, Ghiberti, Verrocchio etc. Inside, there is a splendid Gothic **tabernacle★★** by Orcagna, decorated with coloured marble.

Holy Trinity Church (Santa Trinità) (HY N). – The sober interior is in the Florentine Gothic style. The fourth chapel in the south aisle is decorated with frescoes by Lorenzo Monaco; he also painted the altarpiece of the **Annunciation★**. The frescoes depicting the life of St Francis and the altarpiece of the Nativity in the **Sassetti Chapel★★** (second to the right of the chancel) are by Ghirlandaio.

★ **Archaeological Museum (Museo Archeologico)** ⊘ (JVX M⁵). – The museum has an important collection of Greek, Egyptian, Etruscan (**Arezzo Chimera★★**, a 6C BC masterpiece) and Roman art. There are also collections of jewellery and gold and silver work which belonged to the Medici and to the Grand Dukes of Lorraine.

Casa Guidi ⊘ (GZ). – *8 Piazza S. Felice.*
Florentine home of the Victorian poets Robert and Elizabeth Barrett Browning. Elizabeth is buried in the English cemetery in the centre of Piazza Donatello.

★ **Church of the Holy Spirit (Santo Spirito) (GY)**. – The simple and graceful interior of this church, built from 1444 onwards to plans by Brunelleschi, resembles San Lorenzo. The numerous **works of art**★ include a Madonna and Saints by Filippino Lippi *(fifth chapel in the south transept).*

La Badia (HJY L). – This was originally the church of a former abbey *(badia)* and it has one of Florence's most elegant **campaniles**★.
Inside are several works of art including Filippino Lippi's **Virgin appearing to St Bernard**★ *(to the left of the entrance),* a delicate **relief**★★ sculpture in marble by Mino da Fiesole and two **tombs**★ carved by the same artist.

★ **Last Supper of St Apollonia (Cenacolo di Sant'Apollonia)** ⊘ (HV R). – In the former refectory of the Camaldulian convent hangs a *Last Supper* (1430) by **Andrea del Castagno**. The rigid perspective, subdued colours and careful modelling give an impressive dignity to the dramatic scene.

★ **Last Supper by Ghirlandaio** ⊘ (GX A). – Next to **All Saints' Church** (Ognissanti) which was remodelled in the 17C, is the former monastery refectory *(no 42 to the left of the church)* containing Ghirlandaio's *Last Supper.*

★ **Davanzati Palace (Palazzo Davanzati)** ⊘ (HY M⁶). – A stairway which rises from the inner courtyard gives access to this tall medieval-style 14C building. It contains the **museum of the Florentine house** (Museo dell'Antica Casa Fiorentina): artefacts and furniture (14C-16C) evoke the life of a rich Florentine family of the period.

★ **New Market Loggia (Loggia del Mercato Nuovo) (HY X)**. – This gallery (loggia) with its elegant Renaissance arcades was built in the 16C in the heart of the commercial district. It now serves as a market for Florentine crafts.

★ **Science Museum (Museo di Storia della Scienza)** ⊘ (HY M⁷). – Historical presentation of a rich collection of scientific instruments and a section on the life and work of the mathematician and astronomer Galileo.

★ **Semi-precious Stone Workshop (Opificio delle Pietre dure) (JVX M⁸)**. – Lorenzo the Magnificent was responsible for reviving the ancient tradition of decorating with semi-precious stones (quartz, porphyry, onyx, jasper etc.) in the form of mosaics *(pietre dure).* The workshop now specialises in restoration work and there is a small **museum** ⊘ with some quite remarkable works on display.

★ **Buonarroti's House (Casa Buonarroti)** ⊘ (JY). – Michelangelo Buonarroti owned this house although he never lived here. There are several of the sculptor's works on display inside.

EXCURSIONS

See the plan of the built-up area in the current Michelin Red Guide Italia.

★★ **Medici Villas (Ville Medicee)**. – In the 15C and 16C, the Medici built several elegant villas throughout the Florentine countryside.

Villa della Petraia ⊘. – *3km – 2 miles to the north.* In 1576 Cardinal Ferdinand de' Medici commissioned the architect Buontalenti to convert this former castle into a villa. In the 16C **garden**★, there is a remarkable fountain by N. Tribolo with a bronze statue of Venus by Giovanni Bologna.

Villa di Castello ⊘. – *5km – 3 miles to the north.* This villa was embellished by Lorenzo the Magnificent and restored in the 18C. It has a very fine garden adorned with statues and fountains.

★ **Villa di Poggio a Caiano** ⊘. – *17km – 11 miles to the northwest by the Pistoia road, the S 66.*
Sangallo designed this villa for Lorenzo the Magnificent. The loggia is decorated by the della Robbia. The magnificent drawing-room has a coffered ceiling and **frescoes** by Pontormo representing Vertumnus and Pomona, gods of orchards and fruit.

Galluzzo Carthusian Monastery (Certosa del Galluzzo) ⊘. – *6km – 4 miles to the south by the Siena road.*
The monastery was founded in the 14C and remodelled many times. The adjoining palace contains frescoes by Pontormo. The monks' cells are grouped around the Renaissance **cloisters**★.

FORLÌ Emilia-Romagna

Pop 110 334

Michelin map 988 fold 15, 429 fold 35 or 430 fold 5

Forlì is set on the Via Emilia and it was an independent commune ruled by an overlord in the 13C and 14C. The citadel was heroically defended in 1500 by Caterina Sforza against Cesare Borgia.

Basilica of San Mercuriale. – *Piazza Aurelio Saffi.* The basilica is dominated by an imposing Romanesque campanile. The lunette of the doorway is adorned with a 13C low relief. The numerous works of art inside include several paintings by Marco Palmezzano and the tomb of Barbara Manfredi by Francesco di Simone Ferrucci.

Picture Gallery (Pinacoteca) ⊙. – *72 Corso della Repubblica.* The collection includes works by local 13C-15C artists. There is a delicate **portrait of a young girl** by Lorenzo di Credi.

EXCURSIONS

Cesena. – *19km – 12 miles by the Via Emilia.* The town lies at the foot of a hill on which stands the great 15C castle of the Malatestas. It contains the Renaissance **Malatestiana Library**★ ⊙ *(Piazza Bufalini).* The interior comprises three long aisles with vaulting supported on fluted columns capped with fine capitals. On display are valuable manuscripts, including some from the famous school of miniaturists at Ferrara, as well as the Missorium, a great silver-gilt dish possibly dating from the 4C.

Bertinoro. – *14km – 9 miles to the southeast.* This small town is famous for its panorama and its yellow wine (Albana). In the middle of the town is a "hospitality column" fitted with rings, each corresponding with a local home. The ring to which the traveller tethered his horse used to decide which family should be his hosts. From the nearby terrace there is a wide **view**★ of Romagna.

*Book well in advance as it may be difficult
to find accommodation during the season.*

★★ FOSSANOVA ABBEY Latium

Michelin map 988 fold 26 or 430 fold 37

Standing, as the rule prescribes, in a lonely site, the Cistercian Abbey of Fossanova ⊙ is the oldest of the Order in Italy. Monks from Cîteaux in France settled here in 1133. In 1163 they began to build their abbey church, which was to serve as a model for many Italian churches (Casamari for instance). Although rather heavily restored, Fossanova has kept its original architecture and arrangements intact. It was designed in accordance with the rules of austerity laid down by St Bernard.

Church. – The church (consecrated in 1208) is in the Burgundian style but such decoration as there is recalls the Lombard tradition with traces of the Moorish style. As regards the exterior, the Latin cross plan with flat east end, the octagonal transept crossing tower, the rose windows and the triple-bayed window of the east end are typically Cistercian. The well-lit and lofty interior has a central nave balanced by aisles with groined vaulting.

Cloisters. – These are picturesque with three Romanesque sides and the fourth or south side in the late-13C pre-Gothic style (transitional Romanesque Gothic style). The small columns are Lombard in form and decoration. The fine Gothic chapterhouse opens into the cloisters through wide twin bays. It was in the guest house, which stands apart, that the teacher and scholar St Thomas Aquinas died on 7 March 1274.

★ GAETA Latium

Pop 24 123

Michelin map 988 fold 27 or 430 fold 38

This former fortress, still partly walled, is admirably sited on the point of a promontory bounding a beautiful **bay**★. The coastal road round the bay affords magnificent views. Gaeta has a pleasant beach of fine sand, Serapo Beach, facing south.

Cathedral (Duomo). – The cathedral is interesting, especially for its 10C and 15C Romanesque Moorish campanile adorned with glazed earthenware and resembling the Sicilian or Amalfi bell towers. Inside, the late-13C **paschal candelabrum**★ is remarkable for its size and for its forty-eight low reliefs depicting scenes from the Lives of Christ and St Erasmus, the patron saint of sailors.
A picturesque medieval quarter lies near the cathedral.

Castle (Castello). – The castle, dating from the 8C, has been altered many times. The lower castle was built by the Angevins, while the upper one was the work of the Aragonese.

Monte Orlando ⊙. – Standing on the summit is the tomb of the Roman Consul Munatius Plancus, a friend of Caesar who founded the colonies of Lugdunum (Lyons) and Augusta Raurica (Augst near Basle).

EXCURSION

Sperlonga. – *16km – 10 miles to the northwest.* The village stands on a rocky spur, pitted with many caves, up in the Aurunci mountains.

Tiberius' Cave and the Archaeological Museum ⊙. – The cave lies below the Gaeta-Terracina road *(to the left after the last tunnel)*. It was in this cave that the Emperor Tiberius narrowly escaped death when part of the roof fell in.

In the **museum**, by the roadside, there are 4C-2C BC statues, outstanding heads and busts and some realistic theatrical masks. There is also a reconstruction of a colossal group depicting the punishment meted out to the Cyclops Polyphemus by Ulysses.

At the Gaeta end of the tunnel are the charred ruins of Tiberius' Villa.

★★★ GARGANO PROMONTORY Apulia

Michelin map 988 fold 28 or 431 fold 2 to 6

The Gargano Promontory, shining white under a blue sky, projects like a spur from the "boot" of Italy. It is one of the most attractive natural regions of Italy with its wide horizons, its deep and mysterious forests and its lonely, rugged coastline.

Physically, Gargano is quite independent from the Apennine Mountains; it is a limestone plateau fissured with crevices into which water runs. Originally an island, Gargarno was connected to the mainland by an accumulation of deposits brought down by the rivers from the Apennines. Today the massif is riven by high-altitude valleys, with fertile valley floors, and is heavily afforested in the east. The scanty pastures and moors on the plateaux support flocks of sheep and goats and herds of black pigs.

The picturesque **Tremiti Islands** belong to the same geological formation *(access: see the current Michelin Red Guide Italia).*

TOUR

Leave from Monte Sant' Angelo and follow the itinerary indicated on the local map (146km – 91 miles – allow 1 day).

★ **Monte Sant'Angelo.** – *Description p 137.*

★★ **Umbra Forest** (Foresta Umbra). – Forests are rare in Apulia and this vast expanse of venerable beeches covers over 10 000ha – 24 711 acres of un- dulating countryside. Visitors are welcome and the forest is well equipped with recrea- tional facilities. Shortly after the road to Vieste there is a forestry lodge (Casa Forestale) which now serves as a **visitor centre.**

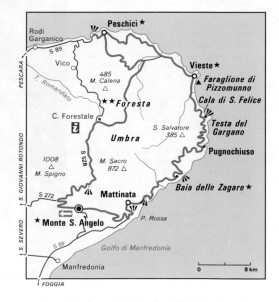

★ **Peschici.** – Well-situated on a rocky spur jutting out into the sea, this fishing town is now a seaside resort.

★ **Vieste.** – In a similar setting to Peschici, this small but ancient town, crowded on the clifftop, is dominated by its 13C cathedral. To the south is a vast sandy beach with a limestone sea-stack, **Fa- raglione di Pizzomunno,** extending offshore.

Between Vieste and Mattinata there is a very fine **scenic stretch**★★ of corniche road, overlooking the indented coastline. After 8km – 5 miles the square tower in **Testa del Gargano** marks the easternmost extremity of the massif: fine **view**★ of the inlet, **Cala di San Felice,** which is spanned by a natural arch at the seaward end.

Beyond the popular holiday resort of **Pugnochiuso,** there is another beauty spot, the **Bay of Zagare**★ (Baia delle Zagare).

Mattinata. – From the road running down towards Mattinata there is a fine **view**★★ of this agricultural market town, a white mass amid a sea of olive groves encircled by a rim of mountains.

*The **Michelin Motoring Atlas Great Britain**
provides the motorist in Great Britain
with the best possible information
for route-planning and choosing where to go.*

Michelin map 📖 fold 13 or 📖 folds 24 and 25 – Local maps pp 181 and 182 – Town plan p 107
Plan of the built-up area in the current Michelin Red Guide Italia

Genoa the superb, the greatest seaport in Italy, spreads over a mountain amphitheatre. It is a city of surprises and contrasts, where the most splendid palaces stand side by side with the humblest alleyways.

HISTORICAL NOTES

Genoese expansion was based on a strong fleet, which already in the 11C ruled supreme over the Tyrrhenian Sea, having vanquished the Saracens. By 1104 the fleet already comprised 70 ships, all built in the famous dockyards, making it a formidable power much coveted by foreign rulers such as the French Kings, Philip the Fair and Philip of Valois.

The Crusaders offered the Genoese an opportunity of establishing trading posts on the shores of the Eastern Mediterranean. Following the creation of the Republic of St George in 1100, seamen, merchants, bankers and money lenders united their efforts to establish the maritime supremacy of Genoa. Initially Genoa allied itself with Pisa in the struggle against the Saracens (11C) and then became her enemy in the conflict concerning Corsica (13C), and finally the most persistent rival of that other great maritime republic, Venice (14C), disputing with her the trading rights for the Mediterranean. Genoa had colonies as far afield as the Black Sea. In the 14C the Genoese merchant seamen exported the precious cargoes from the Orient; in particular they had the monopoly in the trading of alum used in the dyeing trade to fix colours.

Limited partnership companies flourished. Founded in 1408 the famous Bank of St George, grouping the maritime state's lending houses, administered the finances of the trading posts. The merchants became ingenious money lenders and instituted such modern methods as bills of credit, cheques and insurance to increase their profits.

Following continual struggles between the rival families of Genoa the decision was taken in 1339 to elect a doge for life and to seek, essentially in the 15C, foreign protection.

In 1528 the great admiral **Andrea Doria** (1466-1560) gave Genoa its aristocratic constitution which gave it the status of a mercantile republic. The enterprising and independent Andrea was one of Genoa's most famous sons: he was an admiral, a legislator and an intrepid and wise leader who distinguished himself against the Turks in 1519 and, while serving François I, by covering the French retreat after Pavia. In 1528, indignant at François I's unjust treatment of him, he entered the service of Charles V, who plied him with honours and favours. Following his death and the development of ports on the Atlantic coast, Genoa declined as a port and it was Louis XIV who destroyed the harbour in 1684. In 1768 by the Treaty of Versailles Genoa surrendered Corsica to France. Later, after indulging the republican spirit of its own citizen, Giuseppe Mazzini, it became in 1848 one of the cradles of the Risorgimento *(qv)*.

Andrea Doria by Sebastiano del Piombo

Fine Arts in Genoa. – As in many countries, the decline of commercial prosperity in the 16C and 17C coincided with intense artistic activity, evidenced in the building of innumerable palaces and the arrival at Genoa of well-known artists, especially the Flemish. In 1607 Rubens published a work on the *Palazzi di Genova (Palaces of Genoa)* and from 1621 to 1627 Van Dyck painted the Genoese nobility *(grandezza)*. Puget lived at Genoa from 1661 to 1667, working for patricians like the Dorias and the Spinolas.

The art of the Genoese school, characterised by dramatic intensity and the use of muted colours, is represented by Luca Cambiaso (16C), Bernardo Strozzi (1581-1644), the admirable engraver Castiglione, and especially Alessandro Magnasco (1667-1749) whose sharp and colourful brushwork marks him out as a precursor of modern art.

In the field of architecture, Galeazzo Alessi (1512-72), when at his best, was the equal of Sansovino and Palladio in the nobility and ingenuity of his designs when integrating isolated buildings with the existing urban landscape.

The palaces of the former maritime republics of Genoa and Venice reflect their past glory and opulence.

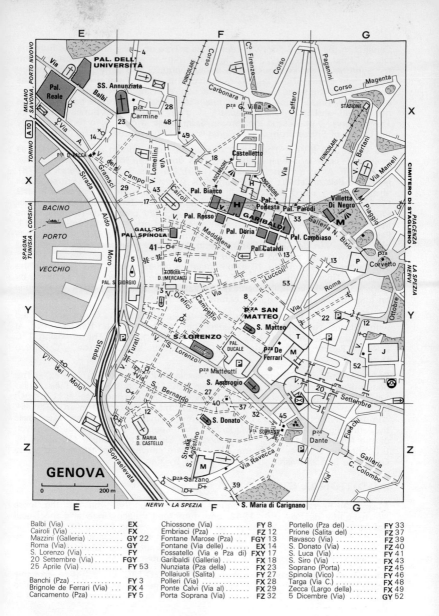

GENOVA

0 200 m

★★ OLD TOWN *time: allow 1 day*

This quarter extends from the old port up towards Via Garibaldi and Piazza De Ferrari.

★★ **Port** (EXY). – From the raised road (*Strada Sopraelevata* – **EXYZ**) which skirts the port, there are good views of Italy's number one port. To the east the old port (Porto Vecchio) includes a pleasure boat harbour, shipyards, and embarkation terminals and quays for ferries leaving for the islands or Africa. To the west the modern port (Porto Nuovo) is fringed by an industrial zone with steel and chemical plants as well as oil refineries. This busy port handles imported raw materials (oil and petrol, coal, minerals, cereals, metal and wood) and exports manufactured goods such as machines, vehicles and textiles. There are organised **boat trips** ⊙ to visit the port.

★ **Sailors' Quarter** (FY). – At the centre of this district is the 13C Palazzo San Giorgio which was the headquarters of the famous Bank of St George. The building was remodelled in the 16C.
Behind the palace on Piazza Banchi (of the banks) is the Loggia dei Mercanti which is now a fruit and vegetable market.

★ **Piazza San Matteo** (FY). – In the city centre, this small but harmonious square is lined with palaces that belonged to the Doria family. No 17 is a Renaissance building presented by a grateful republic to Andrea Doria.
The **Church of San Matteo** has a Genoese-style façade with alternating courses of black and white stone. The tomb and sword of Andrea Doria are in the crypt.

★ **Cathedral of St Lawrence (San Lorenzo)** (FY). – The cathedral, built between the 12C and 16C, has a splendid Gothic **façade**★★ typical of the Genoese style. French influence appears in the placing of the 13C doorways and the large rose window.

Carving on the central doorway represents a Tree of Jesse and scenes from the Life of Christ (on the piers) and a Christ and Martyrdom of St Lawrence between the Symbols of the Evangelists (on the tympanum). The early-13C knifegrinder, at the right corner of the façade, resembles the angel of the sundial at Chartres and performs the same function. The transept crossing is crowned with a dome, designed by Alessi. The severe and majestic **interior★** has marble columns in the nave. The **Chapel of St John the Baptist★** allegedly contains the bones of St John. The **treasury★** ⊘ possesses the famous **Sacro Catino**, a cup given to Solomon by the Queen of Sheba, from which Christ is said to have drunk at the Last Supper.

★ **Via Garibaldi** (FY). – This street of palaces, once known as Via Aurea, was built to designs by Alessi in the 16C. It is one of the loveliest streets in Italy. At No 1 is Alessi's **Palazzo Cambiaso** (1565); No 3 is the **Palazzo Parodi** (1578); No 4 the **Palazzo Cataldi** ⊘ (1588) again by Alessi has a delightful entrance hall and a dazzling gilded **gallery★**. Both No 6, **Palazzo Doria**, and No 7, **Palazzo Podestà** (1565-67), are by the same architect, G.B. Castello. The **Town Hall** ⊘ (H), the former Palazzo Doria Tursi, at No 9, has a lovely arcaded courtyard. The collections include the violin of Paganini and manuscripts by Christopher Columbus. No 11, **Palazzo Bianco**, contains a very fine **art gallery★** ⊘ (Flemish and Dutch paintings by Provost, Van der Goes, Gerard David, Van Dyck, Rubens, also French and Spanish works as well as canvases by the Genoese, Strozzi). The **Palazzo Rosso** ⊘ at No 18 also contains a **picture gallery★** with works by the Venetian (Titian, Veronese and Tintoretto) and Genoese schools, a canvas by Dürer and some remarkable **portraits★** by Van Dyck. In addition there are sections on baroque sculpture, Ligurian ceramics and medals.

Via Balbi (EX). – This street is joined to Via Garibaldi by Via Cairoli and is lined with palaces. The **Royal Palace** (Palazzo Reale) ⊘, formerly the Balbi Durazzo, at No 10, dates from 1650 and contains a Van Dyck room. The imposing 17C **University Palace★** at No 5 has a court and majestic staircase. The 17C Palazzo Durazzo Pallavicini is at No 1.

★ **Palazzo Spinola Gallery** (Galleria Nazionale di Palazzo Spinola) ⊘ (FY). – The beautifully decorated apartments of this 16C-18C mansion with their period furnishings make an ideal setting for the works of art. The fine frescoes (17C-18C) on the **ceilings★** are by Tavarone, L. Ferrari and S. Galeotti. The **art collection★** comprises works by painters of the Italian and Flemish Renaissance: an **Ecce Homo** by Antonello da Messina, a *Madonna* and especially a sumptuous polyptych of the **Adoration of the Magi★★** by Joos Van Cleve and finally a *Crucifixion* by Brueghel the Younger. From the 17C there are canvases by Strozzi, Castiglione Genovese and a ravishing **Portrait of a Child** by Van Dyck.

ADDITIONAL SIGHTS

Piazza De Ferrari (FY). – This square is bordered by the remains of the Opera House, partly destroyed in 1944, and numerous palaces including the Ducal Palace (1778) with its monumental façade overlooking Piazza Matteotti. The **Church of St Ambrose** (Sant'Ambrogio) was built by Tibaldi in 1597 and its sumptuous interior is the setting for an Assumption by Guido Reni and a Circumcision and a St Ignatius Exorcising by Rubens.

Church of St Donatus (San Donato) (FZ). – This 12C-13C church has an attractive octagonal **campanile★** in the Romanesque style. The Romanesque interior is also quite charming. A 14C Virgin and Child stands to the right of the chancel in the chapel.

Church of Santissima Annunziata (EFX). – This 17C church is one of the most splendid in Genoa. The sumptuous decoration inside is a happy mixture of gilding, stucco and frescoes and is a good example of the Genoese baroque style.

Church of Santa Maria di Carignano. – *Take Via Ravasco* (FZ **39**). This vast church was built in the 16C to plans by Alessi. Inside, there is a fine statue of **St Sebastian★** by Puget.

Villetta Di Negro (GXY). – On higher ground to the northwest of Piazza Corvetto, this is a sort of belvedere-labyrinth with palm trees, cascades and artificial grottoes. From the terrace there is a lovely **view★** over the town and the sea. Standing on the summit is the **Chiossone Museum★** ⊘ (M) with sections on Chinese art and Japanese arms and armour, a remarkable collection of prints, ivories and lacquerwork.

Castelletto ⊘ (FX). – From the terrace *(reached by lift)* there is a fine **view★** of the town.

★ **Staglieno Cemetery** (Cimitero di Staglieno). – *1.5km – 1 mile to the north. Leave from Piazza Corvetto* (GY), *see the town plan in the current Michelin Red Guide Italia.* This curious cemetery has a mixture of sumptuous tombs and simple clay tumuli.

*The **Michelin Red Guide Italia**
which is revised annually gives a selection of establishments offering*
– carefully prepared meals at reasonable prices
– simple meals at moderate prices
– prices including or excluding service
– car parking

★ GRADO Friuli-Venezia Giulia   Pop 9 348

Michelin map ▓▓▓ fold 6 or ▓▓▓ fold 17

At the time of the Barbarian invasions the inhabitants of Aquileia founded Grado which was from the 5C to the 9C the residence of the Patriarchs of Aquileia. Today Grado is a busy little fishing port and seaside resort with a growing reputation. The town is surrounded by the waters of the lagoon which have a certain grandeur.

★ **Old Quarter.** – This is a picturesque district with a network of narrow alleys *(calli)* running between the canal-port and the cathedral. The Cathedral (Duomo) of Santa Eufemia, on the basilical plan, dates from the 6C. It has marble columns with Byzantine capitals, a 6C mosaic pavement, a 10C ambo and a valuable silver-gilt **altarpiece★**, a Venetian work of the 14C. Beside the cathedral stands the 6C Basilica of St Mary of Grace (Santa Maria delle Grazie) which has some original mosaics and fine capitals.

GROSSETO Tuscany   Pop 70 677

Michelin map ▓▓▓ folds 24 and 25 or ▓▓▓ fold 23

This modern-looking provincial capital is situated in the fertile Ombrone Plain. The old town is encircled with late-16C ramparts and their powerful bastions built by the Medici.

★ **Maremma Art and Archaeological Museum (Museo Archeologico e d'Arte della Maremma)** ⊙. – *Piazza Baccarini.*
The ground-floor exhibitions cover Bronze Age jewellery and pottery, and a lovely collection of Etruscan and Roman sculpture. Grouped on the first floor are coins, statuettes, bronzes, Roman objects and a section on Greek and Etruscan ceramics. On the second floor are displayed 13C to 17C paintings, as well as polychrome sculpture, ivories, bronzes and ecclesiastical plate.

St Francis' Church (San Francesco). – *Piazza dell'Indipendenza.*
This 13C abbatial church has some small frescoes by the 14C Sienese school and a lovely painted 13C crucifix.

EXCURSION

Ruins of Roselle ⊙. – *12km – 8 miles to the northeast. Leave Grosseto by the Siena road and after 10km – 6 miles turn right into an unsurfaced road.* Important excavation work has uncovered the Etruscan city of Roselle which was conquered by Rome in the 3C.

To plan a special itinerary

– consult the map on pp 4-7 which shows the main towns, individual sights and recommended routes described in the guide;

– read the descriptions of the above which are described in the middle section of the guide in alphabetical order under their own name or are incorporated in the excursions radiating from a particular town or tourist centre;

– use the appropriate **Michelin Maps** *which show places of interest, scenic routes, viewpoints and natural features...*

★★ GUBBIO Umbria   Pop 32 292

Michelin map ▓▓▓ fold 16 or ▓▓▓ fold 16

The small town of Gubbio, spread out over the steep slopes of Monte Ingino, has preserved almost intact its rich cultural and artistic heritage. Encircling ramparts, the yellow ochre colour of its buildings, the pale brown tint of its Roman-tiled roofs, and the outline of its towers and palaces as they stand out against a burnt and austere landscape make it one of the Italian towns in which the harsh atmosphere of the Middle Ages is most easily imagined. In the 11C and 12C the free commune of Gubbio, fiercely Ghibelline *(qv)*, enjoyed a period of expansion before being governed by the Montefeltro family in the 15C and then by the Della Roveres. The town became a papal possession from 1624. Since medieval times the artisans of Gubbio have specialised in ceramics. One of them, Mastro Giorgio, produced in the early 16C the famous iridescent red lustre – the secret of which was never discovered by nearby towns.
The town is also famous for the wolf which ravaged the country at a time (early 13C) when St Francis lived in Gubbio. The saint set off and reproached the wolf for its misdeeds, whereupon the repentant wild animal laid its paw in St Francis' hand and swore that it would do no more harm. The people then adopted and fed their friend, the wolf, to the end of its life.
One of Gubbio's traditional events is the spectacular **Race of the Ceri**. Members of the different guilds *(ceraioli)*, wearing ancient costumes and carrying the *ceri*, curious wooden poles over 4m – 13ft tall, race over a distance of 5km – 3 miles to the Basilica of St Ubald *(see the table of Principal Festivals at the end of the guide)*.

SIGHTS

★★ **Old Town (Città vecchia).** – Piazza Grande stands at the heart of this charming but austere area with its steep, narrow streets, sometimes stepped, spanned by arches converted into living quarters. The houses, flanked by palaces and towers of nobility, are often used as ceramic artists' workshops. The façade, often built of a mixture of brick, rubblework and dressed stone, sometimes has two doors; one narrower than the main door is known as the Door of Death through which coffins were brought out.

★★ **Consuls' Palace (Palazzo dei Consoli)** ⊘ (B). – Overlooking Piazza Grande, this imposing Gothic building, supported by great arches rising above Via Baldassini, has a majestic façade which reflects the palace's internal plan. The stairway leads up to the vast hall *(Salone)* where popular assemblies were held and which contains collections of statues and stonework.
Next is the civic museum where the **Tavole eugubine** have pride of place. The bronze tablets (2C-1C BC) are inscribed in the ancient language of Umbria. This document, unique in the fields of linguistics and epigraphy, defines the political organisation and some of the religious customs of the region in antiquity.
The next floor which houses the picture gallery (works by Signorelli) gives access to the loggia which affords a good view of the town.

★ **Ducal Palace (Palazzo Ducale)** ⊘ (D). – The palace, which dominates the town, was built from 1476 onwards to the plans of Francesco di Giorgio Martini, who was inspired by the ducal palace at Urbino. The elegant courtyard is delicately decorated. Of the rooms adorned with frescoes and lovely chimmeypieces, the Salone is particularly interesting.

Roman Theatre (Teatro romano). – This fairly well-preserved theatre dates from the Augustan period.

Church of St Francis (San Francesco). – The inside walls of the north apse are covered with remarkable early-15C **frescoes★** by the local painter, Ottaviano Nelli.

Cathedral (Duomo). – The plain façade is adorned with low reliefs showing the Symbols of the Evangelists. The interior consists of a single nave. The **Episcopal Chapel** ⊘ opens to the right. It is a luxurious sitting-room decorated in the 17C, from which the bishop could follow the services.

Church of Santa Maria Nuova (K). – The church contains a charming **fresco★** by Ottaviano Nelli.

EXCURSIONS

Fabriano. – *36km – 22 miles to the east by* ②. The industrial town of Fabriano has manufactured paper since the 13C. This was the birthplace of two delightful artists, **Allegretto Nuzi** (*c*1320-73) and **Gentile da Fabriano** (*c*1370-1427), who were both exponents of the International Gothic style *(qv)*. **Piazza del Comune★** in the centre of Fabriano, with its elegant Gothic fountain, is overlooked by the grim 13C Governor's Residence (Palazzo del Podestà). A stairway leads to the quiet and charming **Piazza del Duomo★** bordered by the 15C hospital and the cathedral with frescoes by Allegretto Nuzi.

★★Frasassi Caves (Grotte di Frasassi) ⊙. – *50km – 31 miles to the northeast by* ①. A tributary of the River Sentino has formed a vast network of underground caves. The largest, the **Grotta del Vento★★**, is composed of seven chambers where the visitor may admire stalagmites, stalactites and other diverse forms in a variety of colours.

The key explains the abbreviations and symbols used in the text or on the maps.

★★ HERCULANEUM (ERCOLANO) Campania   Pop 63 354

Michelin map 988 fold 27 or 431 fold 13 – Local map p 147

Founded, according to tradition, by Hercules, this Roman town was overwhelmed like Pompeii during the AD 79 eruption of Vesuvius.

It was a less important and more peaceful town than Pompeii. Its port was frequented by fishing boats, there were numerous craftsmen and many rich and cultured patricians were drawn to the resort of Herculaneum because of its beautiful setting, overlooking the Bay of Naples. The five quarters of the town were divided by three main streets *(decumani)*. The town has various examples of different types of dwellings, all of which were overwhelmed by the sea of mud which seeped into every nook. The particular interest of a visit to Herculaneum is that all timber structures (frameworks, beams, doors, stairs and partitions) were preserved by a hard shell of solidified mud, whereas at Pompeii they were consumed by fire. The houses were empty, but death caught up with the inhabitants as they tried to flee the city.

RUINS ⊙
time: 2 hours

From the access road *(go on foot)* there is a good view of the luxurious villas overlooking the sea.

House of the Inn (Casa dell' Albergo). – This vast patrician villa was about to be converted into apartments for letting, hence its name. It was one of the most badly damaged by the eruption.

★★ House with the Mosaic Atrium (Casa dell' Atrio a mosaico). – The atrium is paved with a chequered mosaic. The garden on the right is surrounded by a peristyle. On the left are the bedrooms and at the far end, a pleasant *triclinium* (dining-room). The terrace, flanked by two small rest rooms, offers an attractive view of the sea.

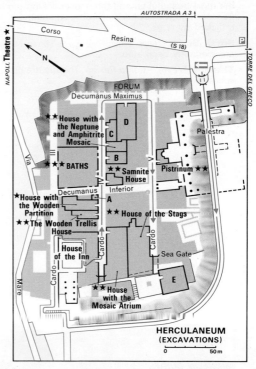

HERCULANEUM
(EXCAVATIONS)
0   50m

★★ The Wooden Trellis House (Casa a Graticcio). – The house gets its name from the wooden trellis framework of the walls. It is a unique example of this type of house from antiquity.

★ House with the Wooden Partition (Casa del Tramezzo carbonizzato). – The façade is remarkably well preserved. This is a good example of a patrician dwelling which housed several families. The atrium is separated from the *tablinium* (living-room) by a wooden partition *(tramezzo)*. Only the sides of the partition remain standing.
Next door is the dyer's shop (**A**) containing an interesting wooden clothespress.

★★ **Samnite House (Casa Sannitica).** – The house was built on the very simple plan typical of the Samnites (an Italic people of the Sabine race). The splendid **atrium** is surrounded by a gallery with Ionic columns. The rooms are decorated with frescoes.

★★★ **Baths (Terme).** – The baths of Herculaneum which are in excellent condition were built at the time of Augustus. They are not sumptuous but they show a remarkable degree of practical planning. In the **men's baths** visit the *palestra*, the cloakroom (**a**), the *frigidarium* (**b**) with frescoes on the ceiling, the *tepidarium* (**c**) and the *caldarium* (**d**). The **women's baths** include the waiting-room (**e**), the cloakroom (*apodyterium* – **f**), adorned with a mosaic pavement depicting Triton, the *tepidarium* (**g**) with a fine floor mosaic representing a labyrinth, and the *caldarium* (**k**).

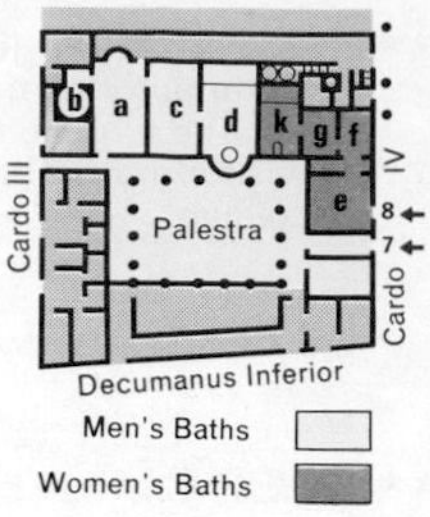

Decumanus Inferior
Men's Baths
Women's Baths

★ **House with the Charred Furniture (Casa del Mobilio carbonizzato) (B).** – This small but rather elegant house has the remains of a charred bed in one room.

★★ **House with the Neptune and Amphitrite Mosaic (Casa del Mosaico di Nettuno e Anfitrite).** – This house is equipped with a **shop★**; its counter opened onto the street. Mosaics depicting Neptune and Amphitrite adorn the nymphaeum.

★ **House with a Fine Courtyard (Casa del Bel Cortile) (C).** – This is one of the most original houses in Herculaneum with its courtyard, stone staircase and balcony.

★ **The Bicentennial House (Casa del Bicentenario) (D).** – This house was laid bare in 1938, two hundred years after digging officially started.
The house has fresco decorations and a small cross incorporated in a stucco panel. This is one of the oldest Christian relics which has been brought to light in the Roman Empire.

★★ **Pistrinum.** – An inscription states that this bakery belonged to Sextus Patulus Felix. In the shop and back room may be seen flour mills, storage jars and a large oven.

★★ **House of the Stags (Casa dei Cervi).** – This rich patrician mansion, probably the most beautiful among those overlooking the bay, is adorned with numerous frescoes and works of art, including an admirable sculptured group of stags being attacked by dogs.

★ **Small Baths (Terme Suburbane) (E).** – These baths, situated near the Sea Gate, are elegantly decorated.

★ **Theatre (Teatro).** – *Corso Resina.* The theatre could accommodate at least 2 000 spectators.

Michelin map 🔲🔲🔲 fold 27 or 🔲🔲🔲 fold 13 – Local map p 146
Access: see the current Michelin Red Guide Italia

Ischia, known as the Emerald Island because of its luxuriant vegetation, is the largest island in the Bay of Naples and one of its major attractions. A clear, sparkling light plays over a varied landscape: a coast covered with pinewoods, indented with bays and creeks sheltering villages with their colourful cubic houses; the slopes covered with olive trees and vineyards (producing the white or red Epomeo wine); and an occasional village with its white houses.

The cottages, sometimes roofed with a dome and with an outside staircase, often have walls covered with vines. The island rose out of the sea during the Tertiary era at the time of a volcanic eruption, and has many hot springs with various medicinal properties. The soil is volcanic in origin.

Sightseeing. – The map above locates the towns and sights described in the guide, and also indicates other beauty spots in small black type. A tour of the island, which is fairly small, can be done in a matter of hours *(40km – 25 miles: follow the itinerary on the map).* The narrow road, as it winds between rows of vines, offers numerous fine viewpoints of the coast and the sea.

★ **Ischia.** – *Town plan in the current Michelin Red Guide Italia.* The capital is divided into two settlements, **Ischia Porto** and **Ischia Ponte.** The Corso Vittoria Colona, an avenue lined with cafés and smart shops, links the port, in a former crater, and Ischia Ponte. The latter owes its name to the dyke built by the Aragonese to link the coast with the rocky islet on the summit of which stands the **Castello d'Ischia★★.** This is a group of buildings comprising a castle and several churches. On the outskirts are a large pinewood and a fine sandy beach.

★★★ **Monte Epomeo.** – *Access is by a path which branches off in a bend of the road once level with the public gardens. 1 1/2 hours on foot Rtn or by donkey.* From the summit of this tufa peak there is a vast **panorama** of the entire island and the Bay of Naples.

Serrara Fontana. – Not far from this settlement a belvedere offers a plunging **view★★** of the site of Sant' Angelo with its beach and peninsula.

★ **Sant' Angelo.** – The houses of this peaceful fishing village cluster round the small harbour. Nearby are the vast **Maronti Beach** (Marina dei Maronti) which has been transformed by the opening of many thermal establishments *(access by a footpath).*

★ **Citara Beach** (Spiaggia di Citara). – This fine beach is sheltered by the majestic headland, Punta Imperatore. Another thermal establishment, Giardini di Poseidone, is laid out with numerous warm-water swimming pools amidst flowers and statues.

Forio. – The town centre is Piazza Municipio, a tropical garden overlooked by old buildings.

Lacco Ameno. – *Town plan in the current Michelin Red Guide Italia.* – This was the first Greek colony on the island and was called Pithecusa (meaning lots of monkeys). It is now a holiday resort. The Church of Santa Restituta *(Piazza Santa Restituta)* was built on the remains of a paleo-christian basilica and a necropolis. There is a small archaeological museum. The tour of the island ends with the important thermal spa of **Casamicciola Terme.**

★ **PROCIDA**

Access: see the current Michelin Red Guide Italia.

Procida is formed by craters levelled by erosion and has remained the wildest island in the Bay of Naples. The fishermen, gardeners and winegrowers live in delightful and colourful houses with domes, arcades and terraces.

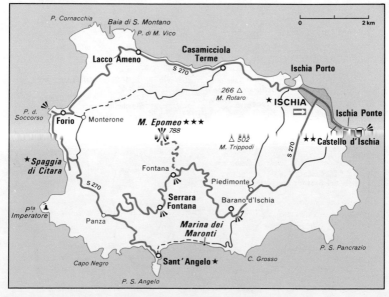

★★★ LAKE DISTRICT

Michelin map 🔢 folds 2, 3 and 4, 🔢 folds 6 to 10, 🔢 folds 4 to 6 and 14 to 18 or 🔢 folds 11 to 13 – Local maps pp 114, 115 and 118

The Lake District extends from Piedmont to Venetia and from Switzerland to Trentino in the north. Narrow and long these lakes are all of glacial origin and their banks are covered with a varied and luxuriant vegetation which flourishes in the particularly mild climate.

This fairyland of blue waters at the foot of shapely mountains has always been a favourite haunt of artists and travellers. The charm and originality of these Pre-Alpine lakes, which are sometimes called the Lombard Lakes, are due to the juxtaposition of Alpine and southern scenery, the numerous villas with attractive gardens on the lakesides, the great variety of flowers throughout the year, the small sailing villages with their flotilla of boats where fresh fish is the speciality. Each lake has its own specific character, making it quite different from its neighbour.

Sightseeing ⊘. – The maps overleaf locate the towns and sites described in the guide, and also indicate other beauty spots in small black type. *For places in Switzerland see the Michelin Green Guide Switzerland.*

★★★ LAKE MAGGIORE (LAGO MAGGIORE)

Maggiore is the most famous of the Italian lakes, in part for its legendary beauty at times both majestic and wild, and also for the Borromean Islands. It is fed by the Ticino River, which rises in Switzerland, and its waters change from a jade green in the north to a deep blue in the south. The mountains of the Alps and Pre-Alps shelter the lake which enjoys a constantly mild climate in which a luxuriant and exotic vegetation flourishes.

Take one of the **boat trips** ⊘ on the lake, as the views from the lakeside road with its heavy traffic are often screened.

★ **Angera.** – This pleasant resort is dominated by the powerful mass of its **castle** (Rocca) ⊘. The apartments are decorated with 14C **Lombard frescoes★★** (Hall of Justice) and give a good idea of life in the Middle Ages.

Arona. – The chief town on Lake Maggiore is overlooked by the gigantic statue, **Colosso di San Carlone★** ⊘, of St Charles Borromeo, the Cardinal Archbishop of Milan who distinguished himself by the authority he showed in re-establishing discipline and morals in the Church and by his heroic conduct during the plague of 1576.

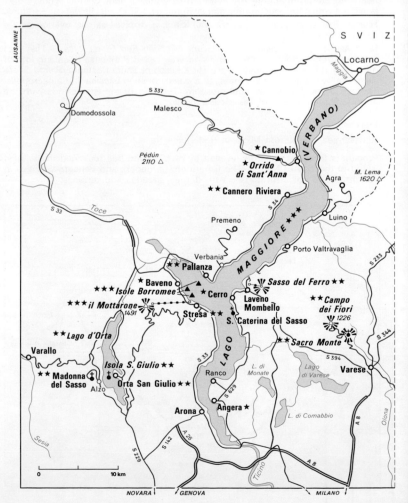

At the summit of the old town the **Church of St Mary** (Santa Maria) contains a lovely **polyptych★** (1511) by Gaudenzio Ferrari. From the ruined **castle** (Rocca) there is a **view★** of Lake Maggiore, Angera and its mountain setting.

★ **Baveno.** – This quiet holiday resort, once visited by Queen Victoria, has a Romanesque church and an octagonal Renaissance baptistry.

★★★ **Borromean Islands** (Isole Borromee) ⊘. – *Look under Stresa for a town plan in the current Michelin Red Guide Italia.* Since the 12C the islands have belonged to the Borromeos, a princely family who since the 17C have built a lovely palace with Italian-style gardens on **Isola Bella★★★** (Beautiful Island). In the Lombard baroque style, the palace is richly decorated with stucco, frescoes, paintings, tapestries and crystal chandeliers. The state apartments include the Medals' Room, the Great Saloon, the Music Room, the Ballroom and the Hall of Mirrors. The basement rooms have been arranged as grottoes with multicoloured pebble mosaics portraying various aquatic scenes. Aromatic shrubs add fragrance to the terraced gardens with statues, fountains and basins in the baroque style. The centrepiece is a shell-shaped amphitheatre.

The boat also stops at **Isola dei Pescatori★★** (Fishermen's Island) which remains quite unspoilt, and **Isola Madre★★★** (Mother Island) which is one large garden full of rare and exotic plants and flowers.

★★ **Cannero Riviera.** – The houses of this resort rise in tiers above the lake amidst olive trees, vineyards, orange and lemon groves.

★ **Cannobio.** – Cannobio is a small resort near the Swiss border. In addition to the Renaissance Church of the Madonna della Pietà there are several other fine old houses. 3km – 2 miles out of town *(on the Malesco road)* is the **Orrido di Sant' Anna★**, a precipice formed by the torrent.

★ **Cerro.** – This peaceful village on a well-shaded part of the lakeside has a tiny fishing port and an interesting **ceramics museum.**

Laveno Mombello ⊘. – From here a cable-car climbs up to the summit of **Sasso del Ferro★★** from where there is a vast **panorama** over the entire Lake District.

★★ **Pallanza.** – Everywhere flowers deck and scent this wonderful resort. Its **quays★★**, sheltered by magnolias and oleanders, offer lovely views of the lake. On the outskirts of the town on the Intra road is the **Villa Taranto★★** ⊘ with its gardens. These, landscaped in the English manner, include several specialised gardens and 20 000 different species of plants and trees.

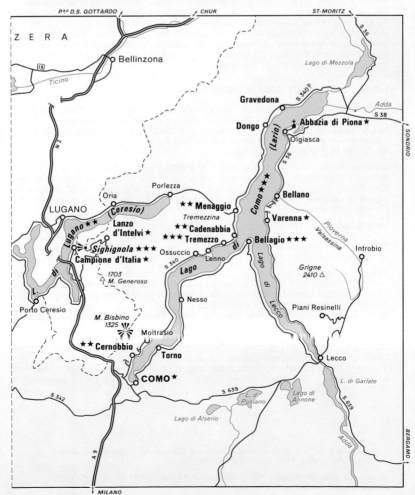

Santa Caterina del Sasso ⊙. – This hermitage was founded in the 13C by an anchorite, Alberto Besozzo. In a picturesque setting, the building clings to a rock overlooking the lake.

★★ **Stresa.** – *Town plan in the current Michelin Red Guide France.* This pleasant resort, which attracts many artists and writers, enjoys a magnificent situation on the west bank of Lake Maggiore facing the Borromean Islands, and is a delightful place with all the amenities of both a seaside resort and a skiing resort. The ski slopes are on **Mottarone**★★★ ⊙ *(take the Armeno road: 29km – 18 miles; the scenic toll road from Alpino: 18km – 11 miles; or the cable-car)* which from its summit provides a magnificent **panorama** of the lake, the Alps and the Monte Rosa Massif. Standing on the outskirts of the town, off the Arona road, is the **Villa Pallavicino**★ ⊙ with its wildlife park.

★★ LAKE ORTA (LAGO D'ORTA)

Orta, one of the smallest Italian lakes, is separated from Lake Maggiore by the peak, Il Mottarone. It is perhaps the most smiling and the most gracious with its setting of wooded hills and the tiny San Giulio Island. The lakesides have been inhabited since earliest times and in the 4C the people were converted to Christianity by St Julius.

★★ **Madonna del Sasso.** – *5km – 3 miles from Alzo.* From the church terrace there is a magnificent view of the lake in its verdant mountain setting.

★★ **Orta San Giulio.** – This small resort has a delightful site on the tip of a peninsula. The alleyways are lined with old houses adorned with elegant wrought-iron balconies. The **Palazzotto**★ or 16C town hall is decorated with frescoes.

★ **Sacro Monte of Orta.** – *1.5km – 1 mile out of Orta.* This sanctuary dedicated to St Francis of Assisi and set on a hilltop comprises a series of twenty chapels. These are decorated in the baroque manner and the frescoes serve as background to groups of lifelike terracotta statues.

★★ **San Giulio Island** (Isola San Giulio) ⊙. – *Boats leave from Orta.* On this jewel of an island, 300m – 328yds long and 160m – 175yds wide, stands the Basilica of San Giulio which is said to date from the lifetime of St Julius. Inside there is a lovely 12C **ambo**★, frescoes by the school of Gaudenzio Ferrari (16C) and, in the crypt, the shrine containing the relics of St Julius.

Varallo. – *20km – 12 miles to the west.* This industrial and commercial town in the Val Sesia is famous for its pilgrimage to the **Sacro Monte**★★ with its 43 chapels. Again these are decorated with frescoes and groups of life-size terracotta figures (16C-18C) which illustrate the Fall and scenes from the Life of Christ. They were the work of several artists including Gaudenzio Ferrari (1480-1546), a local painter who was the pupil of Leonardo da Vinci. Ferrari showed definite originality and picturesque realism in his work.

★★ LAKE LUGANO (LAGO DI LUGANO)

Most of Lugano, also known as Lake Ceresio by the Italians, is in Swiss territory. Lugano is wilder than Lakes Maggiore and Como and with its irregular outline has none of the grandeur or majesty of the others. Its mild climate and its steep mountain countryside make it an ideal place for a holiday.
There are **boat trips** ⊙ on the lake.

★ **Campione d'Italia.** – An Italian enclave in Switzerland, Campione is a colourful, smiling village which is highly popular on account of its casino. St Peter's Oratory (San Pietro) is a graceful building dating from 1326. It was the work of the famous **maestri campionesi**, who vied with the *maestri comacini (qv)* in spreading the Lombard style throughout Italy.

★ **Lanzo d'Intelvi.** – Set in the heart of a pine and larch forest, this resort (alt 907m – 2 976ft) is also a ski centre in winter. 6km – 4 miles away is the **Sighignola Belvedere**★★★, also known as the "balcony of Italy" because of its extensive view of Lugano, the Alps as far as Monte Rosa and on a clear day Mont Blanc.

Varese. – *13km – 8 miles to the southwest of Porto Ceresio. Town plan in the current Michelin Red Guide Italia.* This busy but pleasant modern town stands not far from the lake of the same name. It benefits from a mild and sunny climate due to its proximity to the Italian lakes.
8km – 5 miles to the northwest rises the hilltop, **Sacro Monte**★★, with its important pilgrimage church dedicated to the Virgin. The road up to the basilica is lined with fourteen chapels decorated with frescoes in *trompe-l'œil* and groups of life-size terracotta figures. From the summit there is a magnificent **view**★★ of the lakes and surrounding mountains.
10km – 6 miles to the northwest is the long mountainous ridge, **Campo dei Fiori**★★, which raises its forest-clad slopes above the plain. There is a vast **panorama**★★ of the Lake District.

Fine gardens: Villa d'Este (Tivoli), Hanbury Gardens (Ventimiglia), Boboli Gardens (Florence), Villa Nazionale (Strà).

Villas and palaces by the 16C architect Palladio are to be found at Malcontenta, Maser and Vicenza.

Lake Como

★★★ LAKE COMO (LAGO DI COMO)

Set entirely within Lombardy, Lake Como, of all the Italian lakes, has the most variety. Smiling villages, tiny ports, villas in shady exotic gardens succeed one another along the banks of this Pre-Alpine lake. Bellagio stands on a promontory at the confluence of its three arms. This lake may also be visited by **boat** ⊘.

★★★ **Bellagio.** – Bellagio occupies a magnificent site on a promontory dividing Lake Lecco from the southern arm of Lake Como. It has a world wide reputation for the friendliness of its people and its excellent amenities. The splendid lakeside **gardens★★** of **Villa Serbelloni** ⊘ and **Villa Melzi** ⊘ with their fragrant and luxuriant vegetation are the main sights in Bellagio.

Bellano. – This small industrial town stands on the Pioverna River at the mouth of the valley (Valsassina), with the great mass of the Grigne towering behind. The attractive 14C **church** with a façade by Giovanni da Campione is in the Lombard Gothic style.

★★ **Cadenabbia.** – This delightful resort occupies an admirable site opposite Bellagio. A splendid avenue of plane trees, Via del Paradiso, links the resort with the Villa Carlotta and Tremezzo. From the **Chapel of St Martin** (1 1/2 hours Rtn on foot) there is a good **view★★** of Bellagio on its promontory, Lakes Como and Lecco and of the Grigne.

★ **Como.** – Description p 79.

Dongo. – It was in this village that Mussolini and his mistress, Clara Petacci, were captured on 27 April 1945.

Gavedona. – This fishing village has an attractive Romanesque Church, **Santa Maria del Tiglio★**. The 5C baptistry was remodelled in the Lombard style in the 12C.

★★ **Menaggio.** – Favoured by a cool summer breeze, this is one of the lake's smart resorts.

★ **Piona Abbey** (Abbazia di Piona) ⊘. – 2km – 1 mile from Olgiasca. This graceful little Cluniac monastery has an 11C church and remarkable Lombard Romanesque **cloisters★** (1252).

Torno. – On the outskirts of this attractive port, the 14C Church of **San Giovanni** has a fine Lombard Renaissance **doorway★**.

★★★ **Tremezzo.** – A mild climate and a beautiful site combine to make Tremezzo a favourite place for a stay. The terraced **public gardens★** are a haven of peace. The 18C **Villa Carlotta★★★** ⊘ (entrance beside the Grand Hotel Tremezzo) occupies an admirable site facing the Grigne Massif. The numerous statues include a copy by Tadolini of the famous group of Love and Psyche by Canova. The main attraction is however the beautiful terraced **gardens**.

★ **Varenna.** – This delightful town with its many gardens and cypresses stands on a small promontory. The 16C **Villa Monastero** ⊘ has beautiful **gardens★★**.

★ LAKE ISEO (LAGO D'ISEO)

Though Lake Iseo is not very well-known, its wild scenery, its high mountain fringe, its banks sometimes steep and often indented and its peaceful villages, all lend a certain charm to this small lake. From the midst of the deep blue waters emerges the island of Monte Isola (alt 600m – 1 969ft).
There are **boat trips** ⊘ on the lake.

★ **Iseo.** – The Pieve di Sant'Andrea with its 13C campanile faces a charming square.

Lovere. – In this small industrial town the **Tadini Museum** ⊘ has a collection of arms, paintings (Bellini and Parmigianino), porcelain and sculpture by Canova.

★★ **Monte Isola** ○. – From the Church of the Madonna della Ceriola, crowning the summit of this green island, there is a vast **panorama**★★ of the lake and the Bergamaschian Alps.

★ **Pisogna.** – This small port has an attractive lakeside setting. The **Church of Santa Maria della Neve** contains 16C **frescoes**★ by Romanino du Brescia.

★★★ LAKE GARDA (LAGO DI GARDA)

This, the largest lake, is also considered one of the most beautiful. Its many assets include low-lying banks which are alluvial in the south, steep slopes on the west bank, and the mountain chain of Monte Baldo to the east.
The Dolomites in the north shelter the lake from the cold north winds, creating a very mild climate which already earned it the name of "beneficent" lake (Il Benaco) in ancient times. It had both strategic and commercial importance and throughout history has been coveted by neighbouring powers.
Artistically, the region was greatly influenced by the Venetian Republic which ruled the region from the 15C to the 18C.
Even in Roman times the banks of the lake were appreciated as a place to stay and today's travellers have a large number of resorts from which to choose. There are **boat trips** ○ on the lake.

Bardolino. – This village famous for its red wine has an elegant Romanesque **church**★ dating from the 11C, which is dedicated to St Severinus.

Campione del Garda. – The Bishops of Trento, Brescia and Verona met here to bless the lake.

Desenzano del Garda. – The old port, picturesque Piazza Malvezzi and the neighbouring old quarter are all good places to stroll through. The 16C parish church (Parrocchiale) has a very intense **Last Supper**★ by Tiepolo. To the north of the town in Via Scavi Romani, the **Villa Romana** ○ has a remarkable series of multicoloured **mosaics**★ dating from the Roman period.

★ **Garda.** – This popular resort which gave its name to the lake shows a strong Venetian influence. Both the Captains' Palace and the Palazzo Fregoso are 15C.

★★ **Gardone Riviera.** – This small resort enjoys many

hours of sunshine and offers the tourist a wide choice of hotels. 1km – 1/2 mile from the town is the **Vittoriale**★ ○ estate which belonged to the poet **Gabriele D'Annunzio** (1863-1938) who is buried here. The neo-classical villa, La Priora, is full of the solemn atmosphere which this writer-aesthete so cultivated. The museum and park display numerous souvenirs of his turbulent life.

Gargnano. – This charming resort is surrounded by great expanses of glasshouses for the growing of lemon and citron trees.
The **Church of San Francesco** has lovely 15C cloisters with curious Moorish-style galleries with capitals carved with oranges and lemons, recalling the fact that it was supposedly the Franciscan monks who introduced citrus fruits to the area. The lakeside promenade leads to the neo-classical **Villa Feltrinelli** ○ which served as Mussolini's headquarters during the Fascist Republic (1943-45).

★ **Limone sul Garda.** – This is one of the lake's most attractive villages. Terraced lemon groves often under glass stretch along the lake shores. From Limone a **panoramic route**★★ climbs up to the Tremosine plateau before descending to Tignale. It offers superb **views**★★★ of the lake and its mountainous setting.

★ **Malcesine.** – This attractive town stands on a promontory at the foot of Monte Baldo, and is dominated by the crenellated outline of a Scaliger **Castle**★ (Castello Scaligero). This 13C-14C castle belonged to the Scaligers of Verona.
The 15C Captains' Palace in the Venetian style stands on the edge of the lake. From the summit of **Monte Baldo** ○ *(cable-car)* there is a splendid **panorama**★★★ of the lake and in the north the Massifs of Brenta and Adamello.

★★ **Punta di San Vigilio.** – This headland is in a romantic setting. The 16C **Villa Guarienti** ⊘ was built to the plans of Sanmicheli for the Veronese humanist, Agostino Brenzoni.

★ **Riva del Garda.** – This small resort is dominated to the west by a rocky escarpment. Already in ancient times it was an important trading and communication centre set on the route between Verona and the Alps. Today the picturesque **old town**★ is a maze of narrow shopping streets.

The **castle** (Rocca) ⊘ houses the municipal **museum** with its archaeological and historical sections.

Rivoli (or **Rivoli Veronese**). – A small **museum** ⊘ displays mementoes of a famous battle won over the Austrian army by Napoleon on 14 January 1797 during his second Italian campaign *(explanatory panels in Italian)*.

★ **Salò.** – This was the seat of the Venetian Captain under the Venetian Empire and from this period of splendour it has retained its 15C **cathedral** (Duomo). Inside are a large gilt **polyptych**★ (1510) in wood and several works by Moretto da Brescia and Romanino.

San Martino della Battaglia. – An **ossuary-chapel**, a **museum** and a tall **tower** ⊘ commemorate the battle of 24 June 1859 at Solferino *(see below)*, and the wars of the Risorgimento *(see p 20)* waged by the Italians to win their independence from Austria.

★★ **Sirmione.** – This important resort clusters around the 13C **Scaligers' Castle**★ (Rocca Scaligera) ⊘ at the tip of the narrow Sirmione peninsula, as it stretches out into the lake. Since the beginning of the 20C it has become known as a spa for the treatment of respiratory disorders. The small 15C Church of Santa Maria has interesting 15C and 16C frescoes.

On the rocky tip of the peninsula are the remains of a Roman villa which belonged to the poet Catullus. The excavation site is known as the **Grottoes of Catullus** ⊘ and it is possible to distinguish the remains of buildings in this attractive **site**★★.

Solferino. – An **ossuary-chapel** and a **museum** ⊘ recall the battle of 24 June 1859 (the field of battle extended as far as San Martino, *see above*) when the French and Piedmontese troops defeated the Austrians and brought about Italy's independence *(see p 20)*. The heavy casualties (11 000 dead and 23 000 wounded) led to the founding of the **Red Cross** by Henri Dunant. A **monument** on the site marks the event.

Torbole. – This was the venue for a most unusual event in 1439. Venice, in an attempt to rescue the town of Brescia, under siege by the Visconti of Milan, armed a fleet which sailed up the Adige and crossed the mountains towards Torbole on Lake Garda. From there the fleet set sail to occupy Maderno on the west bank. The following year Venice was able to capture Riva and finally achieve suzerainty over the lake.

★★ **LECCE** Apulia   101 520

Michelin map 988 fold 30 or 431 fold 20
Town plan in the current Michelin Red Guide Italia

Set in the very heart of the Salento region, Lecce was in Roman times the prosperous town of Lupiae. The Normans greatly favoured the town and made it the capital of the region known as Terra d'Otranto.

From the 16C to the 18C, Lecce knew a period of great splendour during which it was embellished with Renaissance, rococo and baroque monuments. The local finely-grained limestone was particularly easy to work, and the town's numerous baroque buildings are remarkable for the abundance of decorative work which has earned the city the nickname of "the baroque Florence". When seen at night with the illuminations the whole resembles a sumptuous theatrical set.

The most inventive artists came from the Zimbalo family: their work is to be found in both churches and palaces and is widespread throughout the Salentina Peninsula.

★★ **BAROQUE LECCE** *time: 1 hour*

★★ **Basilica of the Holy Cross** (Santa Croce). – Although several architects worked on this basilica in the 16C and 17C, it is the best example of Lecce's baroque style. The façade *(photograph p 32)* is sumptuously decorated without being overbearing. The interior is light and airy and the plainer architectural style is reminiscent of Brunelleschi. There is also an abundant baroque decoration of great delicacy. The side chapel contains a fine **high altar** with sculptured low reliefs by Francesco Antonio Zimbalo.

Governor's Residence (Palazzo del Governo). – Adjoining the basilica, this former Celestine monastery has a rusticated façade with a frieze above and intricately-decorated window surrounds, especially at first-floor level.

★★ **Piazza del Duomo.** – The unity of the buildings bordering this square make it one of the finest in southern Italy. The **campanile** (1661-82) and the **cathedral** (Duomo) (1659-82) are by Giuseppe Zimbalo, the 17C **Episcopal Palace** (Palazzo Vescovile) and the **Seminary** (Seminario) dating from 1709 by Giuseppe Cino. In the courtyard of the latter there is a sumptuously decorated **well**★ by the same sculptor.

LECCE

ADDITIONAL SIGHTS

★ **Provincial Museum** (Museo Provinciale S. Castromediano). – Housed in a modern building, the museum has a rich archaeological section *(ground floor)* and a very important **ceramics collection**★★ ⊙ *(first floor)*. Of particular interest are the proto-Italiot and Italiot vases decorated with painted figures. The art gallery is on the third floor.

★ **San Mateo.** – This church with its harmonious façade by Achille Carducci shows the distinct influence of Borromini and his Roman work, the Church of St Charles by the Four Fountains.

★ **Rosario** or **San Giovanni Battista.** – This was Giuseppe Zimbalo's last work and the façade is an abundance of decoration which is both intricately detailed and yet gracious. The **interior**★ has several altarpieces which are very ornate.

Santi Nicolò e Cataldo. – *To the north of the town near the cemetery.*
The church was built in 1180 by the Norman Tancred and rebuilt in 1716, undoubtedly by Giuseppe Cino who retained intact the central part of the Romanesque façade with its small rose window and Norman doorway. There is an attractive baroque structure in the 16C cloisters.

Sant'Irene (or **Chiesa dei Teatini**). – The church was built by Francesco Grimaldi for the monks of the Theatine Order and it contains several splendid **altarpieces**★ which are attributed to Francesco A. Zimbalo.

Gesù (or **Chiesa del Buon Consiglio**). – *Via Francesco Rubichi.*
The austere style of the church, built by the Jesuits from 1575 to 1579, makes a sharp contrast with the other churches of the town.

Sant'Angelo. – *Via Manfredi.*
Although unfinished, this façade is typical of Francesco Giuseppe Zimbalo (1663) and is decorated with garlands, cherubs, angels...

Piazza Sant'Oronzo. – This busy square is the town centre and is dominated from on high by the statue of the town's patron saint, St Oronzo, who crowns one of the two columns which used to mark the end of the Appian Way in Brindisi *(qv)*.
On the south side of the square, parts of the Roman amphitheatre have been uncovered.

LEGHORN (LIVORNO) Tuscany   Pop 173 114

Michelin map 988 fold 14, 428 fold 37 or 430 folds 11 and 12
Town plan in the current Michelin Red Guide Italia

This important seaport deals mainly in timber, marble, alabaster, cars and craft work from Florence. Cosimo I de' Medici started rebuilding the harbour to replace the silted-up Porto Pisano, and it was finished in 1620 under Cosimo II. The main streets are Via Grande lined with arcaded buildings, Via Cairoli and Via Ricasoli. In the Piazza Micheli, from which the Fortezza Vecchia (Old Fortress) can be seen, stands the **monument**★ to the last prominent Medici, the Grand Duke Ferdinand. The four bronze Moors (1624) were the work of Pietro Tacca.

EXCURSION

Montenero. – *9km – 6 miles to the south.*
The 18C pilgrimage church dedicated to Our Lady of Grace consists of a richly decorated baroque church, a monastery and behind railings the *famedio*, a series of chapels reserved for the burial of distinguished citizens of Leghorn.

Admission times and charges for the sights described
are listed at the end of the Guide.
Every sight for which there are times and charges
is indicated by the symbol ⊙ in the middle section of the guide.

★ LORETO Marches   Pop 10 553

Michelin map 988 fold 16 or 430 fold 18
Town plan in the current Michelin Red Guide Italia

The small city of Loreto is grouped around its well-known church which is the scene of a famous pilgrimage to the "House of Mary". The old quarter is partially encircled by massive brick ramparts dating from the 16C. It is said that the Santa Casa (Holy House) or House of Mary was miraculously carried from Nazareth in several stages by angels and set down in a wood of laurels *(lauretum* in Latin), which gave its name to Loreto. The most popular pilgrimages take place on the Feast of the Virgin, the Nativity (8 September) and the Translation of the Santa Casa (10 December) *(see the table of Principal Festivals at the end of the guide)*.
The Venetian painter **Lorenzo Lotto** (1486-1556), who imbued his portraits with a new psychological meaning, lived at Loreto from 1535 until his death. Towards the end of his life he became an Oblate in the Santa Casa.

★★ SANCTUARY OF THE HOLY HOUSE
(SANTUARIO DELLA SANTA CASA) ⊙ *time: 1 hour*

Many famous architects, painters and sculptors contributed to the building and decoration of this church, started in 1468 and only completely finished in the 18C. These included firstly Giuliano da Sangallo, then Bramante who built the side chapels, and finally Vanvitelli who designed the bulbous campanile. Go round the outside of the church to admire the lovely triple **apse★★** and Sangallo's elegant dome. The façade is typical of the late Renaissance, sober and harmonious, with its double buttresses surmounted by clocks at the corners.

The three **bronze doors★★** are adorned with fine late-16C and early-17C statues. The interior has a nave and two aisles. At the end of the south aisle the **Sacristy of St Mark★** (San Marco) is crowned by a dome painted with frescoes (1477) by Melozzo da Forli with an exceptional sense of foreshortening, showing angels carrying the Instruments of the Passion. In the **Sacristy of St John★** (San Giovanni) is a lavabo designed by Benedetto da Maiano under a vault painted with frescoes by Luca Signorelli. Standing at the transept crossing is the **Santa Casa★★** which was sumptuously faced with marble carved in the 16C by Antonio Sansovino and other sculptors. The north transept leads to a room decorated by Pomarancio (1605-10).

Piazza della Madonna★, in front of the basilica, is lined by the unfinished portico of the Apostolic Palace, which now houses a **picture gallery** ⊙. This contains a remarkable series of **works★** by Lorenzo Lotto, paintings by Simon Vouet and Pomarancio. The Flemish tapestries were woven to designs by Raphael and there is a superb collection of Urbino faïence vessels.

EXCURSION

Recanati. – *7km – 4 miles to the southwest.*
This little town, perched on a hill, was the birthplace of the poet **Giacomo Leopardi**, the most perceptive but melancholy of men whose work was very melodious. The **Palazzo Leopardi** ⊙ contains mementoes of the writer. The **picture gallery** ⊙ has several important works by Lorenzo Lotto, including an Annunciation.

*The **Michelin Red Guide Italia** lists hotels and restaurants which offer good meals at moderate prices; consult the latest edition.*

★★ LUCCA Tuscany   Pop 87 577

Michelin map 𝟵𝟴𝟴 fold 14, 𝟰𝟮𝟴 fold 37, 𝟰𝟮𝟵 fold 32 or 𝟰𝟯𝟬 folds 2 and 12

Situated in the centre of a fertile plain, Lucca has preserved within its girdle of ramparts, often tree-topped, a rich heritage of churches, palaces, squares and streets which gives the town a charming air, unscathed by contemporary developments.

HISTORICAL NOTES

Lucca was colonised by the Romans in the 2C BC and it has retained the plan of a Roman military camp, with the two principal streets perpendicular to one another.

During the Middle Ages a complicated system of narrow alleys and oddly-shaped squares was added to the original network. The town became an independent commune at the beginning of the 12C and flourished until the mid 14C with the silk trade as its main activity. In the early 14C the town enjoyed a great period of prosperity and prestige under the control of the mercenary leader Castruccio Castracani (d 1328). Lucca's finest religious and secular buildings date from this period. Luccan architects adopted the Pisan style to which they added their own characteristics of refinement and fantasy.

From 1550 onwards the town became an important agricultural centre and with this new prosperity came a renewed interest in building. The countryside was dotted with villas, the town encircled by ramparts and most of the houses were either rebuilt or remodelled.

In the early 19C, Elisa Bonaparte ruled the city for a brief period from 1805 to 1813. Following Napoleon's Italian campaigns he bestowed the titles of Princess of Lucca and Piombino on his sister. She showed a remarkable aptitude for public affairs and ruled her fief with wisdom and intelligence, encouraging the development of the town and the arts.

The Legend of the Holy Cross. – The **Volto Santo** (Holy Visage) is a miraculous Crucifix kept in the cathedral. It is said that Nicodemus, after Calvary, depicted the features of Christ on it. The Italian Bishop Gualfredo, when on pilgrimage in the Holy Land, obtained possession of the Volto Santo and embarked in a boat without a crew or sails which drifted ashore on the beach at Luni, near La Spezia. As the worshippers at Luni and Lucca disputed possession of the Holy Image, the Bishop of Lucca had it placed on a cart drawn by two oxen; they immediately set off towards Lucca.

The fame of the Volto Santo, spread by merchants from Lucca, gained ground throughout Europe. A most unusual commemorative procession, **Luminara di Santa Croce,** passes through the illuminated town after dark *(see the table of Principal Festivals at the end of the guide).*

THE IMPORTANT CHURCHES time: 3 hours

From the great **Piazza Napoleone** (car park) make for the Piazza San Giovanni, overlooked by the church of the same name, and then the Piazza San Martino, bordered on the left side by the 16C Palazzo Micheletti designed by Ammannati with pretty terraced gardens.

★★ **Cathedral (Duomo)** (C). – The cathedral, dedicated to St Martin, was rebuilt in the 11C. The exterior was remodelled almost entirely in the 13C, as was the interior in the 14C and 15C. The strength and balance of the green and white marble **façade★★**, designed by the architect Guidetto da Como, are striking despite its asymmetry. The upper section with its three superimposed galleries is the first example of the Pisan Romanesque style (see p 164) as it developed in Lucca; the idiom is characterised by lighter, less rigid lines and by inventive ornamentation. The ornate sculpture and marble-inlaid designs are of great interest.

The slim and powerful campanile harmoniously combines the use of brick and marble, and the number of openings increases with the height.

The sculptural decoration of the porch is extremely rich: pillars with naïvely carved columns, arcading, friezes and a variety of scenes (barking dogs, Roland sounding his horn, a man wrestling with a bear and another stroking his beard).

The Gothic interior has elevations where the round-headed main arches with their robust piers contrast with the delicacy of the elegant triforium. On the west wall is an unusual Romanesque sculpture of St Martin dividing his cloak. The classical and sober lines of this sculpture herald the style of Nicola Pisano. In the north aisle is the lovely shrine (tempietto) built by the local artisan Matteo Civitali (1436-1501) to house the Volto Santo. The great 12C figure of **Christ★** in wood blackened through time shows a distinctly Oriental influence because of its hieratic aspect. It is said to be a copy of the legendary one.

In the north transept is one of the masterpieces of Italian funerary sculpture by the Sienese artist, Jacopo della Quercia (1406): the **tomb★★** of Ilaria del Carretto, wife of Paolo Guinigi, lord of Lucca in the early 15C. The recumbent figure wears a long, delicately draped robe and at her feet lies a small dog, a symbol of fidelity. Other works of art include a Presentation of the Virgin in the Temple by Bronzino (north aisle) and the large-scale Last Supper with its subtle lighting by Tintoretto (south aisle).

★ **St Michael's Church (San Michele in Foro)** (B E). – The white mass of the 12C-14C church on the site of the Roman forum dominates the adjoining square which is lined by old mansions and the Palazzo Pretorio.

The exceptionally tall **façade★★** (the nave itself was to have been taller) is a good example of the Lucca-Pisan style, despite the fact that the lower part was remodelled last century. The four superimposed galleries surmount blind arcading and are decorated with varied motifs. At the top, two instrument-playing angels flank a statue of the Archangel Michael slaying the dragon.

The simplicity of the Romanesque **interior** is a direct contrast to the ornate exterior. The triumphal arch is very lofty. On the first altar of the south aisle is a **Madonna★** by Andrea della Robbia. The north transept is adorned with a Madonna (1480) carved by Matteo Civitali and a lovely **painting★** with brilliant colours by Filippino Lippi.

★ **St Frigidian's Church (San Frediano)**. (B Q)– This great church was rebuilt in the original Lucca-Romanesque style in the 12C before the influence of the Pisan school was felt.

The sober façade is faced with white marble from the Roman amphitheatre. The upper middle section, remodelled in the 13C, is dominated by a Byzantine-style mosaic depicting the Ascension by local artists.

The interior comprises a nave and two aisles with wooden ceilings (flanked by Renaissance and baroque side chapels) on the plan of the early-Christian basilicas: the nave which ends in a semicircular apse is articulated by antique columns crowned with fine capitals.

LUCCA

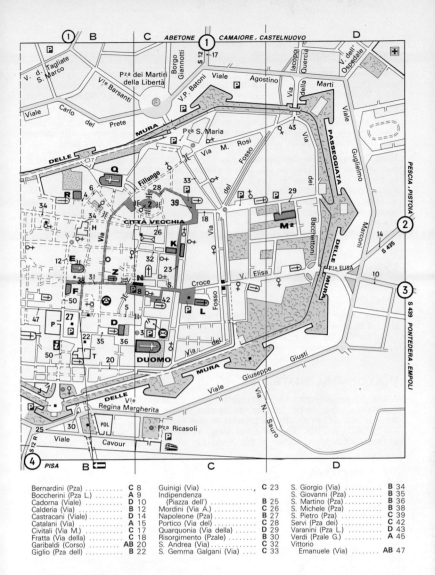

To the right on entering is a curious Romanesque **font★** (12C) with low reliefs depicting the story of Moses. In the north aisle the Gothic marble **polyptych★** by Jacopo della Quercia represents the Virgin and Child surrounded by saints. The chapel of Sant' Agostino is decorated with frescoes by the Ferraran painter Amico Aspertini: one of these depicts the transportation of the Volto Santo from Luni to Lucca.

ADDITIONAL SIGHTS

★ **Old Town (Città Vecchia)** (BC). – The streets and squares of old Lucca are full of atmosphere with their Renaissance and Gothic palaces, their towers of nobility, old shops, sculptured doorways and coats of arms, elegant wrought-iron railings and balconies. Starting from Piazza San Michele, follow Via Roma and Villa Fillungo to Piazza del Anfiteatro situated inside the Roman amphitheatre. From here go towards Piazza San Pietro (12C-13C church) and then take Via Guinigi where at No 29 stands **Casa Guinigi** ⊙ (**C K**) with its tower (**panorama★** of town from the top) crowned with trees which rises above the great façade with Gothic windows; some of the bays are blind. The houses opposite at Nos 20 and 22 also belonged to the Guinigi family.
Continue to the Romanesque Church of **Santa Maria Forisportam** (**C L**), so-called because it stood outside the Roman walls.
Via Santa Croce, the Piazza dei Servi and the Piazza dei Bernardini, where the 16C palace of the same name stands (**C N**), lead back to Piazza San Michele.

★ **Walk round the ramparts (Passeggiata delle Mura)**. – The 4km – 3 mile long ramparts give the town a special charm. They were built in the 16C and 17C and include eleven bastions, linked by curtain walls, and four gateways.

National Museum in the Palazzo Mansi ⊙ (**A M¹**). – The **apartments** of this 17C palace have a remarkable interior **decoration★** (17C-18C). The **art gallery** includes works by 17C Italian artists (Salimbeni, Guido Reni and Barocci) and foreign paintings (portrait of *Princess Elisa* by Marie Benoist).

National Museum in the Villa Guinigi ⊙ (**D M²**). – *Via della Quarquonia.* The villa which once belonged to Paolo Guinigi now contains archaeological, sculpture (Romanesque, Gothic and Renaissance) and painting (Lucca and Tuscan) sections. There are some remarkable panels of intarsia work.

EXCURSIONS

Villa Reale, Marlia ⊙. – *8km – 5 miles to the north. Leave by ① on the town plan.* The Villa Reale is surrounded by magnificent 17C **gardens★★** modified by Elisa Bonaparte. Unusual features include a lemon grove, a 17C nymphaeum and an open-air theatre.

Villa Mansi ⊙. – *11km – 7 miles to the north. Leave by ① on the town plan.* This very fine 16C villa, transformed in the 18C, has a façade covered with statues and a vast shady **park★** where statue-lined alleys lead to a lovely pool.

★ **Villa Torrigiani** (or **Camigliano**). – *12km – 8 miles to the northeast. Leave by ① on the town plan.* This 16C villa was converted in the 17C into an elegant summer residence by Marques Nicolao Santini, ambassador of the Lucca republic to the Papal Court and to the Court of Louis XIV. The gardens designed by Le Nôtre, are adorned with fountains, grottoes and nymphaea. The villa, which has a delightful rococo façade, contains rooms adorned with frescoes and a picture gallery. There are some extremely fine Venetian and French pieces of furniture (18C) as well as mementoes of the many illustrious guests who have stayed at the villa.

★ # MANTUA (MANTOVA) Lombardy   Pop 56 201

Michelin map 988 fold 14, 428 fold 28 or 429 folds 22 and 23
Town plan in the current Michelin Red Guide Italia

Mantua is set in the heart of a flat fertile plain which was formerly marshland on the southeastern border of Lombardy. It is encircled to the north by three lakes formed by the slow-flowing Mincio. This active and prosperous town has numerous important industries, including plastics which is one of the most important in Italy.

HISTORICAL NOTES

Although, according to a legend quoted by Virgil, Mantua was founded by Monto, daughter of the divine Tiresias, its origins would seem to be Etruscan dating back to the 6C or 5C BC. It passed to the Gauls before becoming Roman in the 3C BC. In 70BC **Virgil** (Publius Virgilius Maro), that gentle poet, was born in the Mantua area. Author of the *Aeneid* in which he recounts the wanderings

MANTOVA

Broletto (Vial e Piazza)	BZ 4	Academia (Via)	BY 2
Liberta (Corso)	AZ 12	Acerbi (Via)	AZ 3
Mantegna		Canossa (Piazza)	AY 5
(Piazza Andrea)	BZ 13	Don Leoni (Piazza)	AZ 6
Roma (Via)	AZ	Don Tazzoli	
Umberto (Corso)	AZ	(Via Enrico)	BZ 7
		Erbe (Piazza delle)	BZ 8
		Fratelli Cairoli (Via)	BY 10
		Marconi (Piazza)	ABZ 15

Martiri di Belfiore	
(Piazza)	AZ 16
Matteotti (Via)	AZ 17
Mulina (Porta)	AY 19
S. Giorgio (Via)	BY 20
Verdi	
(Via Giuseppe)	AZ 24
Virgilio (Via)	AY 25
20 Settembre (Via)	BZ 27

of Aeneas, the exiled Trojan prince, and the foundation of the earliest settlement, from which Rome was to spring, Virgil describes his beloved Mantuan countryside, with its soft misty light, and the pleasures of rural life in his own harmonious but melancholy style in the *Eclogues* or *Bucolica* and in the *Georgics*. In the Middle Ages Mantua was the theatre for numerous struggles between rival factions which successively sacked the town, before it became an independent commune in the 13C and finally the domain of Luigi Gonzaga, nominated Captain General of the People. Under the **Gonzaga** family, who were enlightened rulers and patrons of the arts and letters, Mantua became an important intellectual and artistic centre in northern Italy of the 15C and 16C. Thus Gian Francesco Gonzaga (ruled 1407-44) placed his children in the charge of the famous humanist Vittorio da Feltre (1379-1446) and commissioned the Veronese **Pisanello** to decorate his ducal palace. His son Ludovico III (1448-78), a mercenary army leader by profession, was a typical Renaissance patron. The Sienese humanist Politian (1454-94), the Florentine architect Leon Battista Alberti (1404-72) and the Paduan painter **Mantegna** (1431-1506) all belonged to his court. Francesco II (1484-1519) married Isabella d'Este, a beautiful and wise woman who contributed to the fame of Mantua. Their son Federico II was made duke by the Emperor Charles V in 1530 and he commissioned the architect and artist **Giulio Romano** (1499-1546), Raphael's pupil, to embellish his native town, remodel his ducal palace and build another, the Palazzo del Te.

★★★ DUCAL PALACE (PALAZZO DUCALE) (BY) ⓥ *time: 1 1/2 hours*

This comprises the largely 16C palace proper, facing Piazza Sordello, the Castello di San Giorgio, a 14C fortress overlooking the middle lake (Lago di Mezzo) and the Renaissance ducal chapel.

★ Piazza Sordello. –
In the past this square was the political and artistic centre of town and has retained its medieval aspect. To the west is the 13C Palazzo Bonacolsi, then the Episcopal Palace (Palazzo Vescovile) where telamones adorn the 18C façade, and finally the Cathedral (Duomo) with its campanile and the Chapel of the Incoronata, attributed to Alberti. On the eastern side is the entrance to the Ducal Palace.

★★★ Apartments. –
This luxurious ensemble was sumptuously decorated in the 16C and 18C and has some outstanding ceilings and numerous works of art. The three Pisanello rooms on the first floor have fragments of frescoes and remarkable **sinopie★★** (rough sketches using a red earth pigment), which have recently been discovered and are a good example of the refined and penetrating work of this 15C artist from Verona versed in the Gothic tradition. These lyrical scenes portray the fantastic world of courtly novels and medieval chivalry. The **Tapestry Room**, formerly known as the Green Apartment, in the neo-classical style, is hung with nine splendid Brussels tapestries after Raphael. Also of interest are: the **Room of the Rivers** with 18C frescoes, the **Moors Room** in the Venetian style, the **Corridor of the Months** which leads to the famous 17C and 18C **Hall of Mirrors**, and the elegant **Archers' Saloon** with works by Rubens, Tintoretto and Fetti. The Duke's suite has a late-16C decoration by Antonio Viani: the **Paradise Apartment** is socalled because of its marvellous views of the lakes, and it leads to the tiny **Dwarfs' Apartment**. On the ground floor are the **Isabella Rooms**, with delicately carved ceilings. The **Summer Apartment** *(first floor)* with its early-16C decoration by Giulio Romano is the setting for Greco-Roman sculptures acquired by Isabella d'Este.

Inside the **Castello** may be seen the famous **Spouses' Room** (Camera degli Sposi) with **frescoes★★★** (1465-74) by **Mantegna**. The walls are covered with a cycle of frescoes to the glory of the superb and refined world of the Gonzaga court. Mantegna creates an illusion of space with his knowledge of foreshortening and perspective and his skilful use of volume and materials. The painted *trompe-l'œil* and carved stucco decoration and garlands of foliage and fruits are typical. On the north wall fresco look for Ludovico II with his secretary, and his wife Barbara seated opposite them. The children cluster round their parents, as do other members of the court including an enigmatic dwarf.

Ducal Palace in Mantua – detail of ceiling

On the west wall the fresco presents Ludovico with his son, Cardinal Francesco, against the background of a town with splendid monuments, which could well be Rome where Mantegna had sojourned not long before. Mantegna has portrayed himself as the figure in purple which can be glimpsed on the right. To the left servants hold the dogs on leashes. Looking down from the ceiling oculus are cupids and servants. This invention of Mantegna's was highly successful and introduces a certain note of wry humour and even strangeness to this otherwise rather solemn ensemble.

ADDITIONAL SIGHTS

Piazza Broletto (BZ 4). – In this square stands the Palazzo Broletto, a 12C-15C communal palace. On its façade it has a seated statue of Virgil (1225). The tall Torre della Gabbia (Tower of the Cage) still bears on its façade the cage *(gabbia)* in which wrongdoers were exhibited.

★ **Piazza delle Erbe** (BZ 8). – The Square of Herbs has retained a medieval appearance with the 13C Palazzo della Ragione, flanked by the 15C Clock Tower and the Romanesque church, **Rotonda di San Lorenzo**★ ⓥ. Sober and elegant, this circular building has a colonnaded ambulatory with a loggia above, and a dome crowning all.

★ **Basilica of St Andrew (Sant'Andrea)** (BYZ). – This church, built in the 15C to the plans of Alberti, has a very wide nave. The vaulting of the nave, chancel and transepts is painted with *trompe-l'œil*. The first chapel on the left contains the tomb of Mantegna and one of his works.

★ **Palazzo del Te** ⓥ (AZ). – This palace was built from 1525 to 1535 by Giulio Romano for Federico II in the typical Mannerist style with its rustication and monumental columns. The interior was decorated by Giulio Romano and his pupils. The room decorated with the **Story of Psyche** and the **Giants' Room** are perfect examples of Romano's decorative art which is so full of movement.

Law Courts (Palazzo di Guistizia) (AZ J). – *Via Roma.* The monumental façade with caryatids is early 17C. At No 18 in the same street is Romano's house built in 1544 to his own designs.

Mantegna's House (Casa del Mantegna) (AZ). – *47 Via Acerbi.* This rather severe-looking brick building was undoubtedly built to designs by the artist himself in 1476. It has a delightful courtyard.

Teatro Accademico (or **Teatro Scientifico**) ⓥ (BZ T1). – *47 Via Accademia.* This tiny but graceful 18C theatre by Bibiena has a curious decoration of imitation marble and pasteboard.

Palazzo d'Arco ⓥ (AY). – *Piazza d'Arco.* This neo-classical palace in the Palladian *(p 211)* tradition contains interesting collections of 18C furniture, paintings and ceramics.

★ MASSA MARITTIMA Tuscany — Pop 9 789

Michelin map 988 fold 14 or 430 fold 13

Massa Marittima stands on the lower foothills of the Colli Metalliferi (metal-bearing hills). It has a rich historic past particularly for the Romanesque and Gothic periods.

★ **Piazza Garibaldi.** – This lovely square, paved with broad flagstones, is lined by the town's main buildings: two Romanesque palaces, Palazzo Pretorio and Palazzo Comunale, as well as the cathedral (Duomo) which also dates from the Romanesque period.

★ **Cathedral (Duomo).** – This majestic building in the Pisan-Romanesque style is adorned with blind arcades and dominated by a fine **campanile**★ pierced with windows which increase in number with the height. The façade is richly decorated. Inside, there is an unusual baptismal font and in the undercroft below the chancel is the monumental sarcophagus *(arca)* (1324) of St Cerbone.

★ **Candeliere Tower, Sienese Fortress and Arch.** – In the upper part of the town an arch with pure lines links a massive tower to the remains of a 14C Sienese fortress.

Municipal Museums ⓥ. – These are housed in the Palazzo Pretorio and include a Museum of the Risorgimento *(ground floor)*, an Archaeological and Local Ceramics Museum *(basement)* and a picture gallery *(first floor)* which has a **Virgin in Majesty** by Ambrogio Lorenzetti (14C).

Church of St Augustine (Sant' Agostino). – *Corso Diaz.* Dating from the early 14C, the church has a Romanesque façade, a lovely Gothic apse and a 17C crenellated campanile added in the 17C.

Mining Museum (Museo di Mineralogia) ⓥ. – *Entrance in Via E. Corridoni.* The museum evokes the mining activities in the surrounding area.

EXCURSION

★ **San Galgano Abbey (Abbazia di San Galgano).** – *32km – 20 miles to the northeast.* This ruined Gothic Cistercian Abbey was built by monks from 1224 to 1288, and dedicated to St Galgan, a dissipated youth from Siena who later took holy orders. Siena Cathedral was modelled on this church.

★★ MATERA Basilicata   Pop 53 275

Michelin map 988 fold 29 or 431 fold 15

Matera overlooks a ravine separating it from the Murge Hills in Apulia. The town stands in the heart of a region dissected by deeply eroded gorges, in all a desolate landscape with wide horizons. The modern part of Matera, provincial capital and centre of all activity, is laid out on a platform which overlooks the lower town with its many rock and semi-rock dwellings *(sassi)*, now often abandoned.

In the town and its surrounding area there are some 130 churches hewn out of the living rock. These date back to the 8C BC and the arrival of oriental (non-Latin) monastic communities who settled locally and in Apulia. They were adept in this form of underground architecture which shows a Byzantine influence.

★★ **The Sassi.** – The two main troglodyte quarters are on either side of the rock crowned by the cathedral. The roofs on some houses serve as walkways while the lower storeys are hewn out of the rock. Little white ashed houses and stairways overlap and overhang one another in a labyrinth which is difficult to unravel.

★★ **Strada dei Sassi.** – This panoramic street skirts the wild gorge and runs round the cathedral rock. The natural rock walls are riddled with both natural and man-made caves.

★ **Cathedral (Duomo).** – In the 13C Apulian-Romanesque style, the façade has a lovely rose window and a projecting gallery above the single doorway. The walls are embellished with blind arcades. On the south side are two richly sculpted doorways. The interior was remodelled in the 17C and 18C. The Byzantine fresco portraying the Madonna is 12C to 13C, the Neapolitan crib is 16C and the lovely carved stalls of the choir are 15C. The **Chapel of the Annunciation**★ *(the last one on the south side)* has a beautiful Renaissance decoration.

San Pietro Caveoso ⊘. – This baroque church stands at the foot of Monte Errone, which has several churches hewn out of the rock and decorated with frescoes, namely Santa Lucia alle Malve, Santa Maria de Idris and San Giovanni in Monterrone.

Ridola National Museum ⊘. – This museum in a former monastery has an interesting collection of archaeological finds discovered locally.

★★ **Views of Matera.** – *4km – 2 1/2 miles by the Altamura road and then the one to Taranto and finally a right turn to follow the signpost "rock churches" (chiese rupestri).* The road leads to two belvederes from which there are astonishing views of Matera. On the left below the parking area are several churches hollowed out of the rock face.

★★ MERANO (MERAN) Trentino – Alto Adige   Pop 33 547

Michelin map 988 fold 4, 218 fold 10 or 429 fold 3
Town plan in the current Michelin Red Guide Italia

Merano, lying at the start of the wider upper valley of the Adige, known as the Val Venosta, is an important tourist centre and spa. It is appreciated for its mild climate. There are numerous cable-cars and chairlifts up to **Merano 2000**, a good winter sports centre also popular in summer for excursions into the mountains.

★★ **Winter and Summer Promenades (Passeggiate d'Inverno e d'Estate).** – These promenades follow the Passirio River. The winter one, facing south, is shady and flower-decked and attractively lined with shops, cafés and terraces and is by far the busier. It is prolonged by the Passeggiata Gilf which ends near a powerful waterfall. The summer promenade, on the opposite bank, meanders through a lovely park.

★★ **Passeggiata Tappeiner.** – This magnificent promenade 4km – 2 1/2 miles long winds high above Merano affording remarkable viewpoints.

Cathedral (Duomo). – This Gothic building, dedicated to St Nicholas, is dominated by a massive bell tower and a façade with a crenellated gable. It is adorned on the outside with frescoes. Inside can be seen lovely ribbed **Gothic vaulting**★ and two carved 15C **polyptychs**★.

★ **Via Portici (Laubengasse).** – This arcade-lined street is overlooked by houses with painted façades and oriel windows. The shops have curiously sculpted façades.

★ **Princes' Castle (Castello Principesco)** ⊘. – This castle with its crenellated gables and pepperpot roofs was built in 1480 by the Hapsburgs. The apartments are richly furnished.

EXCURSIONS

★ **Avelengo (Hafling).** – *10km – 6 miles to the southeast.* A scenic road leads to the plateau of Avelengo which dominates Merano in its valley.

★ **Merano 2000** ⊘. – *Access by cable-car from Val di Nova, 3km – 1.9 miles to the east.* This conifer-clad plateau is a growing winter sports centre. It also makes a good centre for excursions into the mountains in summer.

★ **Tirolo.** – *4km – 2 1/2 miles to the north.* This charming Tyrolean village is surrounded by vineyards and orchards. The village itself is dominated by a 12C castle which was the family seat of the Counts of Tyrol.

★ **Passiria Valley (Val Passiria).** – *50km – 31 miles to the Rombo Pass; 40km – 25 miles to the Monte Giovo Pass.* The road follows the Passiria Valley as far as the attractive Tyrolean village of **San Leonardo**, which clusters round its church. The **Rombo Pass Road**★ (Timmelsjoch), steep and often cut out of the living rock, offers impressive views of the mountain peaks on the frontier. The **Monte Giovo Pass Road**★ (Jaufenpass) climbs amidst conifers. On the way down, there are splendid **views**★★ of the snow-capped summits of Austria.

Michelin map 988 fold 3, 219 fold 19 or 428 fold 15
Town plan in the current Michelin Red Guide Italia

Milan, the lively capital of Lombardy, is the second city in Italy as regards population, politics and cultural affairs, and first in the field of commerce, industry and banking. Set in the heart of northern Italy at the foot of the Alps, the enterprising spirit of its people has combined with certain historic circumstances to make this the country's most dynamic town which is even today in full expansion.

The town is bounded by two concentric boulevards: the shorter, enclosing the medieval centre, has taken the place of the 14C ramparts, of which traces remain, among them the Porta Ticinese *(p 133)* and the Porto Nuovo (**CV**). The outer wall marks the town's expansion during the Renaissance. After 1870 Milan expanded rapidly beyond its fortifications, particularly along the main communication axes.

HISTORICAL NOTES

Milan is probably Gallic (Celtic) in origin, but it was the Romans who subdued the city of Mediolanum in 222 BC and ensured a certain prosperity. At the end of the 3C Diocletian made Milan the seat of the Emperors of the West, and in 313 Constantine published the **Edict of Milan** making Christianity the official religion of the Empire. In 375 **St Ambrose** (340-396), a Doctor of the Church known for his eloquence, became bishop of the town, thus adding to its prestige. The Barbarian invasions of the 5C and 6C were followed by the creation of a Lombard Kingdom with Pavia as capital. In 756 Pepin, King of the Franks, conquered the area, and his son Charlemagne was to wear the Iron Crown of the Kings of Lombardy from 774. In 962 Milan once again became capital of Italy.

In the 12C Milan grouped with other cities to form the Lombard League (1167) to thwart the attempts of the Emperor Frederick Barbarossa to conquer the region. With the decisive victory at **Legnano** the cities of the league achieved their independence. In the 13C the **Visconti**, Ghibellines and leaders of the local aristocracy, seized power.

The most famous member was **Gian Galeazzo** (1347-1402), an able war leader, man of letters, assassin and pious builder of Milan's Cathedral and the Carthusian Monastery of Pavia. His daughter, Valentina, married Louis, Duke of Orleans, the grandfather of Louis XII of France. This family connection was the reason for the later French expeditions into Italy.

After the death of the last Visconti, Filippo-Maria (d 1447), and three years of the Ambrosian Republic, the Sforza took over the rule of Milan, thanks to Francesco, the son of a simple peasant and son-in-law of Filippo-Maria Visconti. The most famous figure in the **Sforza** family, **Ludovico il Moro** (1452-1508) made Milan a new Athens by attracting to his court the geniuses of the time, Leonardo da Vinci and Bramante. Louis XII of France proclaimed himself the legitimate heir to the Duchy of Milan and set out to conquer the territory in 1500. His successor François I renewed the offensive but was thwarted at Pavia by the troops of the Emperor Charles V. From 1535 to 1713 Milan was under Spanish rule. During the plague which ravaged the town from 1576 to 1630 members of the Borromeo family, St Charles (1538-84) and Cardinal Federico (1564-1631) distinguished themselves by their humanitarian work.

Under Napoleon, Milan became the capital of the Cisalpine Republic (1797) and later of the Kingdom of Italy (1805). In 1815 Milan assumed the role of capital of the Venetian-Lombard Kingdom.

LIFE IN MILAN

The most frequented parts of Milan are around Piazza del Duomo (**CY**), Via Dante (**BX**) and Via Manzoni (**CDX**). At the **Galleria Vittorio Emanuele★** (**CY**), which was laid out in 1877 to the plans of Giuseppe Mengoni, the Milanese come to talk, read their *Corriere della Sera* or drink coffee. Shops and in particular those specialising in antiques are to be found in Corso Vittorio Emanuele (**CDY**), Corso Venezia (**DVX**) and Via Monte Napoleone (**CDX**). The nightlife is centred on Piazza San Babila (**DY**). The most remarkable gardens are the Parco Sempione and the Giardini Pubblici.

The **Scala Opera House** *(p 132)* with its prestigious programme is always a great attraction, as is the **Piccolo Teatro** (**BCY T**) with its international reputation. In addition there are numerous sports facilities which enable the visitor to Milan to enjoy a sport or go along to a match or competition.

Milanese cooking is known for its fillets of veal in breadcrumbs *(scaloppina alla milanese)*, marrow bone (shin of veal) with its meat *(osso buco)*, saffron-tinted *risotto* and vegetable and pork soup *(minestrone)*. The perfect accompaniment is the Valtellina wines or those from the Pavia region.

FINE ARTS

In architecture the Cathedral (Duomo) marks the climax of the Flamboyant Gothic period. Prominent architects during the Renaissance were the Florentine, Michelozzo (1396-1472) and especially **Donato Bramante** (1444-1514), favourite master mason of Ludovico il Moro before he left for Rome. An admirer of Classical art, he was both a classicist and a man of great imagination who invented the **rhythmic bay** (a façade combining an alternation of bays, pilasters and niches) which imparted much of their harmony to so many Renaissance façades.

In painting, the Lombard school sought beauty and grace above all else. Its principal exponents were Vincenzo Foppa (1427-1515), Bergognone (1450-1523) and Bramantino (between 1450 and 1465-1536). The works of Andrea Solario (1473-c1520), Boltraffio (1467-1516) and especially the delicate canvases of **Bernardino Luini** (c1480-1532) attest to the influence of **Leonardo da Vinci** who stayed in Milan for some time.

Today Milan is the capital of Italy's printing industry and is an important centre, with its numerous art galleries, for contemporary art.

★★★ CATHEDRAL (DUOMO) (CY) AND PRECINCTS

time: 1 1/2 hours

*Parking is difficult in the centre of town. There are however paying car parks in Piazza Diaz (**CYZ**), Via San Marco (**CV**) and Via Santa Radegonda (**CY 84**). Cars may also be parked in the outer boulevards or in the car parks built beside certain underground stations on the outskirts of the town.*

★★★ **Exterior.** – This marvel of white marble, both colossal and ethereal, bristling with belfries, gables, pinnacles and statues, stands at one end of a great paved esplanade. It should be seen late in the afternoon in the light of the setting sun.

Building began with the chevet in 1386 on the orders of Gian Galeazzo Visconti, and continued in the 15C and 16C under the direction of Italian, French and German master masons. The façade was finished only between 1805 and 1809, on the orders of Napoleon.

Walk round the cathedral to see the **east end** with three huge bays of curved and counter-curved tracery and wonderful rose windows. The overall design is the work of a French architect, Nicolas de Bonaventure, and of a Modenese architect, Filippino degli Organi.

From the 7th floor of the Rinascente store (north of the cathedral) there is an interesting close-up view of the architectural and sculptural features of the roofs.

The ruins of a 4C **baptistry** ⊘ have been found under the parvis.

Milan Cathedral

★★★ **Interior.** – In contrast with the exterior this is bare, severe and imposing. The nave and four aisles are separated by fifty-two pillars of tremendous height (148m – 486ft). The width across the transepts is 91m – 299ft. The windows of the nave, aisles and transept have some lovely stained glass, some of which dates back to the 15C and 16C.

The mausoleum of Gian Giacomo Medici in the south transept is a fine work by Leoni (16C). On the left is the curious statue of St Bartholomew (who was flayed alive), a work of the sculptor Marco d'Agrate. Pass under the dome and in front of the monumental chancel (1570-90) with the high altar by the architect Pellegrino Tibaldi. The magnificent bronze candelabrum in the north transept is French work of the 13C. In the crypt, the silver urn containing the relics of St Charles Borromeo, Archbishop of Milan who died in 1584, was the gift of Philip II of Spain.

In the **treasury** ⊘ is a fine collection of gold plate and ivories dating from the 4C to the present day.

★★★ **Walk on the roof** ⊘. – The building is adorned with 135 pinnacles and numerous white marble statues (2 245 in all!), full of grace and elegance. They can be admired in detail by going up onto the roof and thence to the top of the Tiburia or central tower (108m – 354ft), surmounted by a small gilt statue, the Madonnina (1774).

★★ **Cathedral Museum** ⊘ (CY M¹). – This is installed in the 18C Royal Palace by Piermarini and includes sculptures, stained glass, tapestries and religious vestments from the 14C to the 20C.

The 11C **Aribert Crucifix**★★ in embossed gilt copper is outstanding. There are also interesting models and documents which describe the different stages in the building of this great cathedral.

MILANO

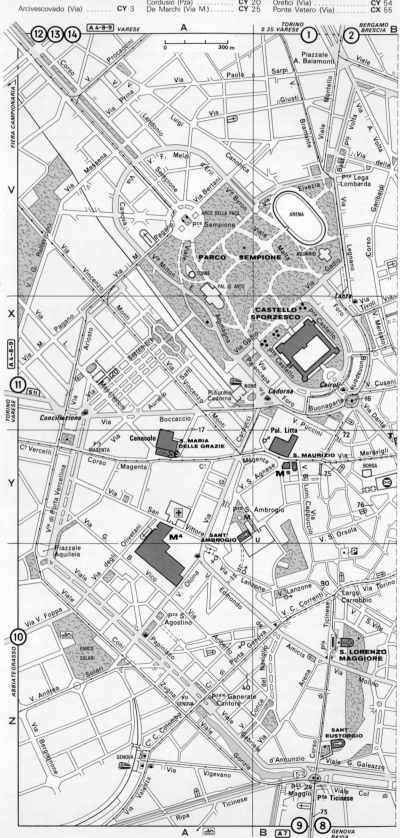

* **Via and Piazza Mercanti** (CY). – In Via Mercanti stands the Palace of Jurisconsults (C), built in 1564 with a statue of St Ambrose teaching on the façade.
  The Piazza Mercanti is quiet and picturesque. The charming Loggia degli Osii (1316) is decorated with heraldic shields, statues of saints and the balcony from which penal sentences were proclaimed. To the right of the loggia is the baroque palace of the Palatine schools, with statues of the poet Ausonius and St Augustine in the niches. Opposite is the **town hall** or Broletto Nuovo (D) which was built in the 13C and extended in the 18C. The equestrian statue on the façade is of the governing magistrate *(podestà)* Oldrado da Tresseno. It is a Romanesque work by Antelami.

* **La Scala (Teatro alla Scala)** (CX). – The most famous opera house in the world was built from 1776 to 1778 and can accommodate an audience of over 2 000. The acoustics are perfect. The four statues in the foyer are of Italian composers (Rossini, Bellini, Donizetti and Verdi).
  The **Scala Museum**★ ⊘ is rich in documents and mementoes covering its past. It is possible to visit the auditorium from the museum.

★★★ MUSEUMS

Milan has numerous museums with rich and varied collections.

★★★ **Brera Picture Gallery (Pinacoteca di Brera)** ⊘ (CX). – The gallery is in a 17C palace. In the courtyard stands a statue of Napoleon I, whom Canova depicted in 1809 as a victorious Caesar. The gallery has one of Italy's best collections and it is particularly rich in Lombard and Venetian works.

Venetian school: a *Last Supper* and a *Baptism of Christ* by Veronese; a *Pietà* by Lorenzo Lotto; a *Miracle of St Mark* and a *St Helena* by Tintoretto; **St Mark Preaching in Alexandria**★★★ by Gentile and Giovanni Bellini; the *Madonna with a Candle* by Crivelli; the museum's masterpiece is Mantegna's **Dead Christ**★★★, admirable in its realism and knowledge of foreshortening. In addition there are works by Carpaccio, Michele da Verona, Cima da Conegliano, Giovanni Bellini, Tiepolo, Longhi, Canaletto, Guardi etc.

Lombard school: the **Madonna of the Rose Tree**★★★ by Bernardino Luini is a perfect example of the gentleness and grace of the Lombard artists, influenced by Leonardo da Vinci; *Christ* by Bramante; and works by Boccaccino, Bergognone, Foppa, Moroni etc.

Central Italian schools: one of Piero della Francesca's masterpieces is the balanced and graceful composition **Madonna with Saints**★★★ and kneeling Duke of Montefeltro (1474); **Betrothal of the Virgin**★★★ (1504) is by the 20 year-old Raphael. The perspective focuses on a small circular building in the manner of Bramante; in addition there are works by Signorelli, the Carracci family, Guido Reni, Caravaggio and Barocci. There are also sections on 19C and 20C art including works by Bonnard, Modigliani, and the futurist painters Severini, Balla, Boccioni, Carrà, Giorgio Morandi, Ottone Rosai etc.

Foreign schools: this section displays canvases by Ribera, El Greco, Goya, Velvet Brueghel, Van Dyck, Rembrandt and Rubens.

★★★ **Castle of the Sforza (Castello Sforzesco)** ⊘ (BX). – This huge brick quadrilateral building was the seat of the Dukes of Milan. The **municipal art collections**★★★ are now on display in the castle.

Sculpture department. – *Ground floor.* The Romanesque, Gothic and Renaissance works are mainly by Lombard sculptors. Interesting works include the **tomb of Bernabò Visconti**★★ surmounted by his equestrian statue from the Romanesque period; and the **reclining figure of Gaston de Foix**★★★ (1523) by Bambaia in his usual classical and well-balanced style, as well as the unfinished **Rondanini Pietà**★★★ by Michelangelo, both from the Renaissance.

Picture Gallery. – *1st floor.* The gallery displays works by Mantegna, Giovanni Bellini, Crivelli, Bergognone, Luini, Moretto, Moroni, Magnasco, Tiepolo, Guardi etc.
In addition there is a decorative arts section and a remarkable collection of **musical instruments**★★.

Archaeological Museum. – *In the vault under the Rochetta courtyard.* The museum includes a prehistory collection, Egyptian art and a lapidary exhibition. Another section of the museum is housed in the monastery of San Maurizio.

* **Sempione Park** (Parco Sempione) (ABVX). – Beyond the castle lies this vast park which is the setting for an exhibition centre (Palazzo dell' Arte), a stadium (Arena), the 1838 Arch of Peace (Arco della Pace) and a 109m – 358ft tall tower (Torre).

★★ **Ambrosian Library (Biblioteca Ambrosiana)** ⊘ (CY). – The library is in a palace built in 1609 for Cardinal Frederico Borromeo. In addition to the many manuscripts there is a **picture gallery** ⊘ on the first floor. Of interest are Italian Renaissance works (Ghirlandaio, Bartolomeo Vivarini and Bergognone), **low reliefs**★★ from the tomb of Gaston de Foix *(see above)* by Bambaia, allegorical paintings and the delightful **Mouse with a Rose**★ by Velvet Brueghel (1568-1625), several canvases by Luini and a portrait by Giorgione. There are two remarkable **portraits**★★★, one of the musician Gaffurio by Leonardo da Vinci, the other presumed to be of Beatrice d'Este by Ambrogio da Predis. Both are outstanding works. The lovely **Basket of Fruit**★ is by Caravaggio and the **Nativity**★ by the Mannerist artist Barocci.
Room 10 contains Raphael's splendid **cartoons**★★★ for the frescoes of the School of Athens in the Vatican. Another room has the collection of reproductions from the drawings in the great *Codex Atlanticus*, where the universal genius of Leonardo is powerfully displayed.

★★ **Poldi Pezzoli Museum** (Museo Poldi Pezzoli) ⊘ **(CX M²)**. – The valuable and varied exhibits are well presented in a mansion furnished and decorated with taste. There are collections of paintings, arms and armour, fabrics, Murano glass (16C-19C), antique ceramics, goldsmiths' work, **clocks★★** and small 16C to 18C **bronzes★**. The paintings include Lombard works (Bergognone, Luini, Foppa and Solario), two lovely **portraits★★** of Luther and his wife by Cranach and, in the Gold Saloon with its splendid **Persian carpet★**, a delicate **profile portrait of a woman★★★** by Antonio del Pollaiolo, *St Nicholas of Tolentino* by Piero della Francesca, an astonishing composition, *Descent from the Cross* by Luini, a **Virgin and Child★★** by Botticelli, a rather pathetic **Dead Christ★★** by Giovanni Bellini and a remarkable **View of the Lagoon** by Francesco Guardi. Other rooms have works by Lorenzetti, Tiepolo, Lotto, Boltraffio, Canaletto, Palma Vecchio etc.

Modern Art Gallery (Galleria d'Arte Moderna) ⊘ **(DVX M³)**. – This, the former Villa Belgioioso built in 1790, was once the residence of Napoleon and Eugène de Beauharnais. It now contains one of the most important Italian collections, especially of 19C Lombard painting. Of note are: Canova's neo-classical paintings, others from the Romantic Period and the sculptures of the Milanese Medardo Rosso (1858-1928). On the second floor, the Grassi Collection comprises works by the French Impressionists. To the right of the courtyard there is a group of works by the famous contemporary Italian sculptor, Marino Marini (1901-80).

★ **Leonardo da Vinci National Museum of Science and Technology** (Museo Nazionale della Scienza e della Tecnica Leonardo da Vinci) ⊘ **(AY M⁴)**. – This vast museum has exhibits on various scientific and technological projects. The **Leonardo da Vinci Gallery★★** displays reproductions of the scientific drawings by the Tuscan genius. Other sections cover the railways, aeronautics and the sea.

ADDITIONAL SIGHTS

Church of St Mary of Grace (Santa Maria delle Grazie) **(AY)**. – This Renaissance building erected by the Dominicans from 1465 to 1490 was finished by Bramante. Inside (restored), there are frescoes by Gaudenzio Ferrari in the fourth chapel on the right, and the impressive **dome★**, gallery and cloisters all by Bramante. The best view of the **east end★** is to be had from Via Caradosso **(AXY 17)**.

Refectory (Cenacolo) ⊘. – In what used to be the former monastery refectory is the world-famous **Last Supper★★★** painted by **Leonardo da Vinci** from 1495-97 at the request of Ludovico il Moro. The fresco depicts with dramatic expressiveness the moment when Jesus says: "One of you will betray me". Opposite is a lovely **Crucifixion★** (1495) by Montorfano.

★ **Basilica of St Ambrose** (Sant' Ambrogio) **(AY)**. – The basilica was founded at the end of the 4C by St Ambrose and it is a magnificent example of the 11C-12C Lombard-Romanesque style with its pure lines and fine **atrium★**. The façade pierced by arcading is flanked by a 9C campanile to the right and a 12C one to the left. The doorway was renewed in the 18C and has 9C bronze panels. In the crypt, behind the chancel, lie the remains of St Ambrose, St Gervase and St Protase. Inside the basilica there is a magnificent Byzantine-Romanesque **ambo★** to the left of the nave, and at the high altar a precious gold-plated **altar front★★** which is a masterpiece of the Carolingian period (9C). From the far end of the north transept one can gain access to Bramante's portico.

★ **Church of St Eustorgius** (Sant' Eustorgio) **(BZ)**. – This Romanesque basilica was founded in the 9C and belonged to the Dominicans. The side chapels were added in the 15C. Behind the choir is the **Portinari Chapel★★**, a jewel of the Renaissance of really Classical purity by the Florentine, Michelozzo. The architecture, frescoes illustrating the life and martyrdom of St Peter by Vincenzo Foppa and sculpture (richly sculptured marble tomb, 1339) by Giovanni di Balduccio are all in complete harmony.

Church of San Satiro **(CY)**. – The square campanile dates from the 9C, the façade from 1871. The rest of the church and baptistry are by Bramante. The artist has resolved the problem of lack of space by a skilful use of *trompe l'œil* decoration. The **dome★** is particularly remarkable.

★ **General Hospital** (Ospedale Maggiore) **(CDZ)**. – This hospital, founded by Francesco Sforza in 1456, was completed in the 17C and is at present occupied by the Faculty of Medicine. It is composed of three different ranges and the loggias of the façades are decorated with the busts of famous men.

★ **Church of St Maurice** (San Maurizio or Monastero Maggiore) **(BY)**. – This is a monastery church in the Lombard-Renaissance style (early 16C) adorned with **frescoes★** by Bernardino Luini and, in the gallery, with figures of saints most probably by Boltraffio. An **Archaeological Museum** ⊘ **(BY M⁵)** has been installed inside the former conventual buildings: Greek, Etruscan and Roman art. The outstanding exhibit is a 4C **silver plate★**.
Opposite is the **Palazzo Litta (BY)** with its 18C façade.

★ **Church of St Lawrence** (San Lorenzo Maggiore) **(BZ)**. – The basilica was founded in the 4C and rebuilt in the 12C and 16C. It has kept its original octagonal plan. In front of the façade is a majestic **portico★** of sixteen Roman columns, all that remains of the Roman town of Mediolanum. The majestic interior is in the Byzantine-Romanesque style and has galleries exclusively reserved for women, a vast dome and spacious ambulatory. From the south side of the chancel pass through the atrium and then a 1C Roman doorway to the **Chapel of Sant' Aquilino★** ⊘ dating from the 4C. It has retained its original plan and the paleo-christian mosaics.
Farther on, the **Porta Ticinese (BZ)**, a vestige of the 14C ramparts, leads to the attractive quarter (Naviglio Grande), where the artists used to foregather.

EXCURSION

★ **Chiaravalle Abbey (Abbazia di Chiaravalle)** ⊙. – *7km – 4 miles to the southeast. Leave by Porta Romana* (**DZ**) *then consult the plan of the built-up area in the current Michelin Red Guide Italia.*

The abbey, founded by St Bernard of Clairvaux (hence Chiaravalle) in 1135, is dominated by an elegant polygonal **bell tower★**. It is the first example of Gothic architecture in Italy. Brick and white stone are combined in the typical Cistercian style. The porch was a 17C addition. Inside, there are a nave and two aisles and 14C frescoes on the dome. Another fresco in the south transept represents the Tree of the Benedictine Saints. The small cloisters are delightful.

★ **MODENA** Emilia-Romagna   Pop 176 556

Michelin map ▨▨▨ fold 14, ▨▨▨ fold 28 or ▨▨▨ fold 23
Town plan in the current Michelin Red Guide Italia

Modena, situated between the Secchia and Panaro Rivers, at the junction of the Via Emilia and the Brenner Autostrada, is an active commercial and industrial (manufacture of shoes and cars and railway engineering) centre and one of the most important towns in Emilia-Romagna. However, Modena with its archbishop-ric and university, remains a quiet town whose old quarter in the vicinity of the cathedral is adorned by several spacious squares lined with arcades. It is in this part of the town that one finds such gastronomic specialities as *zamponi* (stuffed pigs' trotters) and Lambrusco, a sparkling red wine which is produced locally. The original Roman colony of Mutina then became independent before becoming part of the Lombard League *(qv)*, falling under the domination of the Estes from Ferrara to avoid being ruled by Bologna. In 1453 the duchy of Modena was created for Borso d'Este. In 1598 they were expelled from Ferrara by the pope and they took refuge at Modena which reached the peak of its prosperity during the 17C.

SIGHTS

★★ **Cathedral (Duomo).** – The cathedral is dedicated to St Geminian and is one of the best examples of Romanesque architecture in Italy. In it the Lombard architect, Lanfranco, gave vent to his sense of rhythm and proportion. The *maestri campionesi (qv)* put the finishing touches to his work. Most of the sculptural decoration is due to Wiligelmo, a 12C Lombard sculptor. The central porch is supported by marble lions and surmounted by a loggia and a large marble rose window.

The doorways are framed by low reliefs by Wiligelmo: from left to right, they represent the Creation, the Life of Adam and Eve, and Cain and Abel. The south side is remarkable for its architectural rhythm. From left to right may be seen: the Princes' Doorway, crowned by low reliefs carved by pupils of Wiligelmo; the 13C main doorway, known as the Royal Door; and an outside pulpit (1501) ornamented with the Symbols of the Evangelists.

The Fish Market Doorway on the north side was also carved by the pupils of Wiligelmo, showing fantastic animals and people, the Work of the Months on the inner faces of the pilasters, and an attack on the town on the outer curve of the arches. The massive Romanesque campanile built of white marble, 88m – 289ft high, is nicknamed Ghirlandina because of the bronze garland on its weather-vane: it was completed in 1310.

The sober and solemn interior of the cathedral is of brick and roofed with pointed vaulting. The great arches rest on massive brick and slender marble piers, placed alternately. The graceful **rood screen★★** supported by Lombard lions was carved from 1170 to 1220 by the *maestri campionesi* with Scenes from the Passion. The crypt, supported on many slender columns, contains a terracotta Holy Family (1480) by the Modena artist Guido Mazzoni, and the tomb of St Geminian. The chancel contains 15C carved stalls ornamented with realistic intarsia work. In the north apse there is a 15C statue of St Geminian and a 1384 polyptych of the Coronation of the Virgin.

The **Cathedral Museum** ⊙ contains the famous 12C **metopes★★**, low reliefs which used to surmount the flying buttresses. They represent buffoons or symbols incomprehensible today, but whose modelling, balance and style have an almost Classical air.

Museums' Palace (Palazzo dei Musei). – This 18C palace contains the two most important art collections gathered by the Este family.

★ **Este Library** (Biblioteca Estense). – *1st floor, staircase on the right.* This is one of the richest libraries in Italy, containing 600 000 books and 15 000 manuscripts, the most interesting of which are on display. The prize exhibit is the **Bible of Borso d'Este.** It has 1 020 pages illuminated by a team of 15C Ferrara artists including Taddeo Crivelli.

★★ **Este Gallery** (Galleria Estense) ⊙. – This excellent collection comprises 14C Emilian, 15C Venetian (Cima da Conegliano), Ferrarese (notably the astonishing **St Anthony** by Cosima Tura) and Florentine (Lorenzo di Credi) works. The 16C is represented by Veronese, Tintoretto, Bassano, El Greco, Correggio, Il Parmigianino, Dosso Dossi, as well as by the local artist, Nicolò dell' Abbate. The 17C is illustrated by the Emilian painters, the Carracci and the "Caravaggists", while the 18C includes Venetian landscape painters. The foreign schools are also well represented. Among the sculptures, note a powerful bust of Francesco I d'Este by Bernini.

The glass cabinets display around 100 **coins and medals,** several of which were executed by the Verona artist Pisanello. These form only a fraction of the remarkable collection (35 000 items) belonging to the Gallery.

* **Ducal Palace (Palazzo Ducale).** – This noble and majestic building was begun in 1634 for Francesco I d'Este and has an elaborately elegant design. Today it is occupied by the Infantry and Cavalry schools.

EXCURSIONS

Abbey of Nonantola (Abbazia di Nonantola) ⊘. – *11km – 7 miles to the north.* The abbey was founded in the 8C and flourished during the Middle Ages. The 12C abbey church has some remarkable **Romanesque sculpture**★ carved by Wiligelmo's assistants in 1121.

Carpi. – *18km – 11 miles to the north.* This attractive small town has a 16C Renaissance cathedral by Peruzzi, overlooking **Piazza dei Martiri**★. The **Castello dei Pio**★ ⊘, an impressive building bristling with towers, includes a courtyard by Bramante and contains a small museum. The 12C-16C Church of Sagra has a tall Romanesque campanile, **Torre della Sagra.**

★★ MONTE CASSINO ABBEY

(ABBAZIA DI MONTECASSINO) Latium
Michelin map 988 fold 27 or 430 fold 38

The access road to one of the holy places of Roman Catholicism climbs in hairpin bends, affording remarkable views of the valley. The monastery of Monte Cassino, the mother house of the Benedictines, was founded in 529 by St Benedict (d 547). It was here that the saint drew up a complete and precise set of rules combining intellectual study and manual labour with the virtues of chastity, obedience and poverty. In the 11C under Abbot Didier the abbey's influence was at its height. The monks were skilled in the arts of miniatures, frescoes and mosiacs and their work greatly influenced Cluniac art.

The abbey has been destroyed four times since its foundation, including at the **battle of Cassino** (October 1943 – May 1944). After the Allies had taken Naples, the Germans made Cassino the key stronghold in the system of defences guarding the approaches to Rome. The assaults against this bastion failed, despite the great heroism and heavy losses of the Polish Corps. This brought about heavy bombardment from the air led by the Americans and the destruction of the abbey.

Then the 5th US. Army proceeded to attack but without breaking the deadlock. Following a crucial action by the French army which suffered heavy casualties, and an attempt by British troops to surround the German position, the final assault, with the Polish Corps as the spearhead, was launched on 17 May. After a raging battle, the Germans abandoned Cassino on the following day, allowing the Allies to join forces and leaving open the road to Rome. The abbey has been rebuilt to the original plans as a truncated square building with massive underpinnings, and once again crowns the summit of Monte Cassino.

★★ **Abbey** ⊘. – It is preceded by a suitably solemn suite of four communicating cloisters. The bare façade of the basilica quite belies the sumptuousness of the **interior**★★ where marble, stucco, mosaics and gilding create a dazzling if somewhat austere ensemble in the 17C-18C style. The chancel has lovely 17C walnut stalls and the marble tomb enshrining the remains of St Benedict.

★★ **Museum** ⊘. – The museum presents documents on the abbey's history and works of art which survived the 1944 bombing.
On the way down to Cassino are a **National Archaeological Museum** ⊘ and the neighbouring excavation site (amphitheatre, theatre and tomb of Umidia Quadratilla).

★★ MONTECATINI TERME Tuscany   Pop 21 103

Michelin map 988 fold 14, 428 fold 38 or 429 folds 32 and 33
Town plan in the current Michelin Red Guide Italia

Montecatini is Italy's most frequented and most fashionable thermal spa and specialises in treating stomach, intestinal and liver ailments. There is an interesting **Museum of Modern Art** (Museo dell' Accademia d'Arte) ⊘ which has works by Italian (Fattori, Guttaso, Primo Conti) and French (Fernand Léger, Dufy) artists.

EXCURSION

Collodi. – *15km – 9 miles to the west.* Collodi was the pen-name adopted by Carlo Lorenzini, the author of *Pinocchio,* whose mother was born in the village. A **Pinocchio Park** in the form of a maze is laid out on the banks of the Pescia River.
The **Villa Garzoni** ⊘, built in the 18C by the Marquess Garzoni, has fine terraced **gardens**★ dating from the 17C. Vistas, pools, clipped trees, grottoes, sculpture and mazes are all part of this exuberant baroque creation.

Michelin map 988 fold 16

14C ramparts still girdle this charming little town, which lies among vineyards and olive groves. It is perched – as its name suggests – like a falcon on its nest and has been called the Balcony of Umbria. Owing to its strategic position it was destroyed by the Emperor Frederick II and then coveted for two centuries by the popes. Montefalco, won over to Christianity in 390 by St Fortunatus, has its own saint, Clara, not to be confused with the companion of St Francis of Assisi.

The ring road (Circonvallazione) affords remarkable views of the Clitumnus Basin.

Communal Tower (Torre Comunale) ⊘. – From the top (110 steps) there is a beautiful **panorama**★★★ of nearly the whole of Umbria.

St Francis' Church (San Francesco) ⊘. – This Franciscan church has been converted into a museum. The mid-15C **frescoes**★★ by the Florentine Benozzo Gozzoli are full of freshness and colourful realism. In addition there are frescoes by Perugino and Francesco Melanzio (15C-16C), a native of Montefalco.

Santa Illuminata. – The church is Renaissance in style. The tympanum of the main doorway and several niches in the nave were painted by Francesco Melanzio.

St Augustine's Church (Sant'Agostino). – Corso G. Mameli.
The church is Gothic with frescoes by Umbrian painters of the 14C, 15C and 16C.

St Fortunatus' Church (San Fortunato). – 1km – 1/2 mile to the south.
The church is preceded by a small 14C colonnaded courtyard. On the tympanum of the doorway Benozzo Gozzoli painted a **fresco**★ showing the Madonna between St Francis and St Bernardino. Inside, the south altar is adorned with another fresco by Gozzoli of St Fortunatus.

★ **MONTE OLIVETO MAGGIORE ABBEY** Tuscany

Michelin map 988 fold 15 – 36km – 22 miles southeast of Siena

The extensive rose-coloured brick buildings of this famous abbey ⊘ lie hidden among cypresses, in a countryside of eroded hillsides. Monte Oliveto is the Mother House of the Olivetans, a congregation of the Benedictine Order which was founded in 1319 by Blessed Bernard Tolomei of Siena.

Great Cloisters. – The cloisters are decorated with a superb cycle of thirty-five **frescoes**★★ depicting the life of St Benedict by **Luca Signorelli** from 1498 and by **Il Sodoma** from 1505 to 1508. The frescoes begin on the right by the west door at the great arch, with two of Sodoma's masterpieces: Christ of the Column and Christ bearing His Cross. The majority of the frescoes are by Il Sodoma, a refined artist, who was influenced by Leonardo da Vinci and Perugino (p 160) and shows great interest in the flattering representation of different human types, landscapes and picturesque details, as illustrated in the following frescoes: no 4 depicting St Benedict receiving his hermit's robe; no 12 the saint greeting two young men in a crowd – the people are shown in different poses; no 19 voluptuous courtesans have been sent to seduce the monks (splendid architectural elements open onto a long perspective). Signorelli (p 150), who completed only eight frescoes, is more concerned with the powerful, sculptural nature of the figures and the dramatic effect of the compositions where landscape is only secondary: in no 24 St Benedict resuscitates a monk who has fallen off a wall.

The cloisters lead to the refectory (15C), the library and the pharmacy.

Abbey Church. – The interior was remodelled in the baroque style in the 18C. The nave is encircled by inlaid **stalls**★★ (1505) by Fra Giovanni da Verona. Access to the crib to the right of the chancel.

Michelin map 988 fold 15 or 430 fold 14

Montepulciano, perched on the crest of a hill of volcanic rock between valleys, has numerous religious and secular buildings influenced by the Florentine Renaissance. Inhabitants of Chiusi, fleeing from the Barbarian invasion, founded the town in the 6C. This was the birthplace of **Politian** (1454-94), one of the most exquisite Renaissance poets. The poet was a great friend of Lorenzo de' Medici, whom he called Lauro (Laurel) and whom he saved from assassination during the Pazzi Conspiracy (qv). The Stanzas, Politian's masterpiece, describe a sort of Garden of Delight haunted by attractive women. Politian's verse matches the painting of his friend Botticelli.

★ **Old town (Città antica).** – Beyond the fortified gateway, Porta al Prato, the high street, the first part of which bears the name Via Roma, loops through the monumental area. At no 91 Via Roma stands the 16C **Palazzo Avignonesi** attributed to Vignola; no 73, the palace of the antiquarian Bucelli, is decorated with stone from Etruscan and Latin buildings; further along, the Renaissance façade of the church of **Sant'Agostino** was designed by Michelozzo (15C); a tower opposite has a Pulcinello as Jack. At the Wheat Exchange (Loggia) bear left into Via di Voltaia nel Corso: Palazzo Cervini (no 21) designed by Antonio da Sangallo is a fine example of Florentine Renaissance architecture with its rusticated stonework and curvilinear and triangular pediments. Continue along Via dell'Opio nel Corso and Via Poliziano (no 1 is the poet's birthplace, 14C).

★ **Piazza Grande.** – Forming the centre of the city, this square with its irregular plan and varying styles avoids architectural monotony while blending into a harmonious whole. The **Town Hall★** (Palazzo Comunale) ⊙ is a Gothic building which was remodelled in the 15C by Michelozzo. From the top of the square tower there is an immense **panorama★★★** of the town and its environs. The majestic Renaissance **Palazzo Nobili-Tarugi★** facing the cathedral is attributed to Antonio da Sangallo the Elder, a member of that famous family of artists and sculptors. Sangallo was responsible for several of the city's most famous buildings. The palace has a portico and great doorway with semicircular arches; six Ionic columns, standing on a lofty base, support the pilasters of the upper storey. The square also has an attractive **well★** adorned with an admirable sculpture of lion supporters holding aloft the Medici coat of arms. Inside the 16C-17C **cathedral** (Duomo) to the left of the west door lies the recumbent figure of Bartolomeo Aragazzi, secretary to Pope Martin; the statue was part of a monument by Michelozzo (15C), as were the low reliefs of the two first pillars and the statues flanking the high altar. The monumental **altarpiece★** (1401) above the high altar is by the Sienese artist, Taddeo di Bartolo.

Museum (Museo civico-Pinacoteca Crociani) ⊙. – *Via Ricci*. There is a fine collection of glazed terracotta by Andrea Della Robbia; Etruscan remains and paintings dating from the 13C to 18C.

Continue along the high street to Piazza San Francesco for a fine **view** of the surrounding countryside and of the church of San Biagio. Walk down Via del Poggiolo and turn right into Via dell'Erbe to return to the Wheat Exchange.

★★ **Madonna di San Biagio** ⊙. – *1km – 1/2 mile. Leave by the Porta al Prato and then take the Chianciano road before turning right.*
This splendid church built in pale-coloured stone and consecrated in 1529 is an architectural masterpiece by **Antonio da Sangallo.** The building, which was greatly influenced by Bramante's design for St Peter's in Rome (it was not executed in full owing to Bramante's death – *see p 189*), is a useful example of Bramante's concepts. San Biagio's design is simpler although it is planned in the shape of a Greek cross and is crowned by a dome. Two campaniles flank the main façade; one is unfinished and the other includes the three architectural orders (Doric, Ionic and Corinthian). The south transept is prolonged by a semicircular sacristy. The interior gives the same impression of majesty and nobility. To the left of the west door is a 14C Annunciation. The 15C marble high altar is imposing.
Opposite the church stands the Canonica (canonry), an elegant porticoed building.

EXCURSION

★★ **Chianciano Terme.** – *10km – 6 miles to the southeast.*
This fashionable thermal spa is pleasantly situated. The healing properties of its waters were known to the Etruscans and the Romans. There are some fine shady parks.

★ # MONTE SANT'ANGELO Apulia   Pop 16 208
Michelin map ⯃⯃⯃ fold 28 – Local map p 105

Monte Sant'Angelo stands on a **curious site★★**. The town is built on a spur (803m – 2 634ft) dominated by the massive form of its castle and overlooks both the Gargano Promontory and the sea. It was in a nearby cave between 490 and 493 that the Archangel Michael, chief of the Heavenly Host, appeared three times to the bishop of Siponto. After a further apparition in the 8C it was decided to found an abbey. During the Middle Ages all the Crusaders came to pray to the Archangel Michael, the saintly warrior, before embarking at Manfredonia. On 29 September the annual feast day includes the procession of the Archangel's Sword.

★ **Church of St Michael** (Santuario di San Michele). – The building, designed in the transitional Romanesque-Gothic style, is flanked by a detached octagonal campanile dating from the late 13C. The very beautiful and richly worked **bronze door★** is of Byzantine origin and dates from 1076. It gives access to both the nave with pointed vaulting and the cave in which St Michael is said to have made his apparition. The marble statue of the saint is by Andrea Sansovino (16C) and the 11C episcopal throne is decorated in a style characteristic of Apulia.

★ **Tomb of Rotharis** (Tomba di Rotari) ⊙. – *Go down the stairs opposite the campanile.*
The tomb is to the left of the apse of the ruined Church of St Peter's. Above the entrance are scenes from the Life of Christ. Inside, the tower rises in stages through a square, an octagon and finally a triangle to the dome. The tomb was supposed to contain the remains of Rotharis, a 7C King of the Lombards, but is really a 12C baptistry.

Respect the life of the countryside
Drive carefully on country roads
Protect wildlife, plants and trees.

MONZA Lombardy

Michelin map **988** fold 3, **219** fold 19 or **428** fold 15

Monza is quite an attractive industrial town specialising mainly in textiles. It stands on the edge of the Brianza, a lovely green hilly area dotted with lakes, attractive towns and villas set in lovely gardens.

★ **Cathedral (Duomo).** – This cathedral was built in the 13C-14C and has an attractive Lombard façade★★ (1390-96) in alternating white, green and black marble, which is remarkable for its harmonious proportions and variety of openings. It was the work of Matteo di Campione, one of the famous *maestri campionesi (qv)*, who spread the Lombard style throughout Italy.
The **interior**★ was remodelled in the 17C. The splendid silver-gilt **altar front**★ dates from the 14C. To the left of the chancel is the Chapel of the Queen of the Longobards, Theodolinda (6C-7C), with its fascinating 15C **frescoes**★ depicting scenes in the life of this pious sovereign.
The **treasury**★ ⊙ has the famous 5C-9C **Iron Crown**★★ of the Kings of Lombardy, which was offered by Pope Gregory I the Great to the queen. In addition there are fine pieces of 6C to 9C plate, 17C reliquaries and 16C tapestries.

★★ **Park of the Royal Villa (Parco di Villa Reale)** ⊙. – The majestic neo-classical building was the residence of Eugène de Beauharnais and Humbert I of Italy, who was assassinated at Monza by an anarchist in 1900. This vast park is landscaped in the English manner.
In the northern part of the park there are several sporting facilities and the Monza racing circuit which is the venue for the annual Grand Prix Formula One race.

★★★ NAPLES (NAPOLI) Campania

Michelin map **988** fold 27 – Local map p 133 – Town plan pp 140 and 141
Plan of built-up area in the current Michelin Red Guide Italia

The beauties of Naples have been praised by innumerable travellers. A lovely bay, a horizon bounded by Posillipo, the islands, the Sorrento Peninsula and lofty Vesuvius, all contribute to the fame of this favoured spot. As for Naples itself, its attractive climate, the mingling of gaiety and sadness, vivacity and fatalism of the people make this town "the permanent playhouse of Italy", and add to its celebrity. However, the industrial quarters to the east, the alleys littered with rubbish, the dilapidation of buildings damaged by the serious earthquake of 1980, the heavy traffic which throttles the city at certain times of the day and the light haze that clouds the horizon may at first disappoint tourists who dream of picturesque Naples basking under an ever-blue sky in a harmonious setting.
Sightseeing. – Although the discovery of this city is not easy it is always a rewarding experience. When visiting the older areas like Spacca Napoli, visitors are advised to avoid attracting undue attention to themselves by either behaviour or dress, to refrain from night-time strolls, to leave nothing of value in the car and to be on the alert at all times.

HISTORICAL NOTES

According to legend, the siren Parthenope gave her name to a town which had sprung up round her tomb, which is why Naples is called the Parthenopaean City. In fact, Naples originated as a Greek colony named Neapolis, conquered by the Romans in the 4C BC. Rich inhabitants of Rome like Virgil, Augustus, Tiberius, Nero etc used to spend the winter there, but the Neapolitans themselves retained the Greek language and customs until the decline of the Empire.
Since the 12C seven princely families have reigned over Naples: the Normans, Hohenstaufens, Angevins, Aragonese, Spanish and Bourbons. The French Revolution of 1789 brought in French troops, and in 1799 a **Parthenopaean Republic** was set up, followed by a French kingdom (1806-15), under Joseph Bonaparte (Napoleon's brother) and afterwards Joachim Murat (Napoleon's brother-in-law), both of whom promoted excellent reforms. From 1815 to 1860 the restored Bourbons remained in power in spite of the 1820 and 1848 revolts.

ART IN NAPLES

A royal patron of the arts. – Under the princes of the House of Anjou, Naples was endowed with many ecclesiastical buildings, which were greatly influenced by the French Gothic style. **"Good King Robert" of Anjou** (1309-43) attracted poets, scholars and artists from various regions of Italy to his court in Naples. Boccaccio spent part of his youth in Naples where he fell in love with Fiammetta, whom some believe to have been the king's own daughter. His friend Petrarch also spent some time in this city. In 1324 Robert the Wise brought the Sienese sculptor Tino da Camaino to adorn many of the churches with his monumental tombs. Other churches were embellished with frescoes by the Roman artist Pietro Cavallini, slightly later by Giotto whose works have unfortunately disappeared, and by Simone Martini.
The Neapolitan School of Painting (17C – early 18C). – With the arrival in Naples in 1606 of the great innovator in Italian painting, **Michelangelo Merisi Caravaggio** (1573-1610), a new local school of painting flourished, whose members were inspired by the master's bold and dramatic style. The principal followers were Artemisia Gentileschi, the Spaniard José Ribera alias Spagnoletto, the Calabrian Mattia Preti and Salvator Rosa. One pupil who differed greatly from the others was **Luca Giordano** (1632-1705) who specialised in decorating ceilings with spirited compositions full of light. His decorative work was a step towards Roman baroque art. Francesco Solimena perpetuated the former's style.

Ferdinand of Aragon's fleet in Naples harbour (15C)

Original works. – Numerous were the architects who built fine baroque buildings in Naples and the surrounding area. **Ferdinando Sanfelice** (1675-1748) had a highly inventive and theatrical approach to staircases, which he placed at the far end of the courtyard where they became the palace's most important decorative feature. It was, however, **Luigi Vanvitelli** (1700-73) who was the great Neapolitan architect of the 18C. The Bourbon King, Charles III, entrusted Vanvitelli with the project to build another Versailles at Caserta *(qv)*.

It was in the 17C that Naples began to specialise in the marvellous **cribs** *(presepi)* which were to become so famous.

Music and the theatre. – Neapolitans have always shown a great love of music, be it for **opera** where great importance is placed on the virtuosity of the singer, or for more **popular music**, sometimes joyful, sometimes melancholy, practised to the accompaniment of a guitar or a mandolin. Naples gave the character Scaramouch (old fox) to the *Commedia dell' Arte (qv)*.

Religious festivals. – In Naples these are sumptuous and the best known are the Madonna di Piedigrotta, Santa Maria del Carmine and especially the Feast of the Miracle of St Januarius *(p 144)*. Between Christmas and Epiphany (Twelfth Night) the local churches are adorned with splendid cribs. *See the table of Principal Festivals at the end of the guide.*

IN THE STREETS OF NAPLES

The Neapolitans are small and dark, with almost Grecian profiles. They speak a very expressive dialect in a sing-song way. They have lively imaginations, they readily give vent to their emotions and they fear the Evil Eye *(jettatura)*. Religious festivals are numerous and very popular and even sporting events, in particular football matches, become a pretext for outrageous behaviour.

There are numerous novels and films which have captured the peculiarities of the Neapolitans and their way of life. Popular scenes which used to charm the tourists are now a thing of the past. Traffic is hectic. The town with its narrow streets is ill-suited to heavy traffic but cars weave in and out frenetically and only the genius for improvisation, the daring and virtuosity of Neapolitan drivers compensate for their lack of discipline.

The quarters. – The busy port handles more passengers than any other in Italy but is second to Genoa in goods traffic. The city centre extends around **Piazza del Plebiscito** *(p 140)* and the **Galleria Umberto I** (JKZ). The working-class quarters, with their streets set close together and hung with washing, are to be found in the Spacca Napoli *(p 142)* and in the area to the west of the Via Toledo (KY). To the west of the town lie the residential areas spread over the hillsides of **Vomero** and **Posillipo** *(p 145)*.

Neapolitan cuisine. – One can usually have a meal at any time of day and late into the night at any one of the many restaurants and *trattorias*.

The many pizzerias are usually open only in the evening. Try the buffalo milk cheese *(mozzarella)* served with ham or tomatoes as a starter or as a sort of toasted sandwich *(in carrozza)*, the various forms of spaghetti served lightly cooked *(al dente)* and seasoned with fresh tomatoes or mussels or other shellfish *(alle vongole)*.

The local vines grown in volcanic soil give a slightly sulphur-tasting wine: red and white from Capri, white from Ischia, the red Gragnano wine and the sweet wine of Vesuvius known as *Lacryma Christi*.

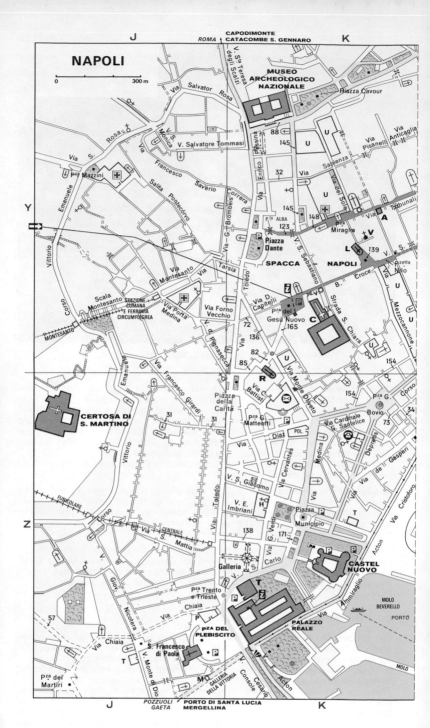

NAPOLI

0 — 300 m

★★ CITY CENTRE *time: 2 1/2 hours*

★★ **New Castle (Castel Nuovo) (KZ)**. – This imposing castle, surrounded by deep moats, was built in 1282 by Pierre de Chaulnes and Pierre d'Agincourt, the architects of Charles I of Anjou. It was modelled on the castle at Angers. A remarkable **triumphal arch★★** embellishes the entrance on the town side. This masterpiece bearing sculptures to the glory of the House of Aragon, was built to designs by Francesco Laurana in 1467. At the far end of the inner courtyard stands an elegant Renaissance doorway surmounted by a Virgin by Laurana (1474).

★ **St Charles Theatre (Teatro San Carlo)** ⊘ **(KZ T)**. – The theatre was built under Charles of Bourbon in 1737 and rebuilt in 1816 in the neo-classical style. The opera house is an important institution in the Italian world of music.
The splendid auditorium, with boxes on six levels, is built entirely of wood and stucco to achieve perfect acoustics.

★ **Piazza del Plebiscito (JKZ)**. – This noble semicircular "square" (19C) is enclosed on one side by the royal palace, on the other by the neo-classical façade of the **Church of St Francis of Paola** (San Francesco di Paola), built on the model of the Pantheon in Rome and prolonged by a curving colonnade. The equestrian statues of Ferdinand I and Charles III of Bourbon are by Canova.

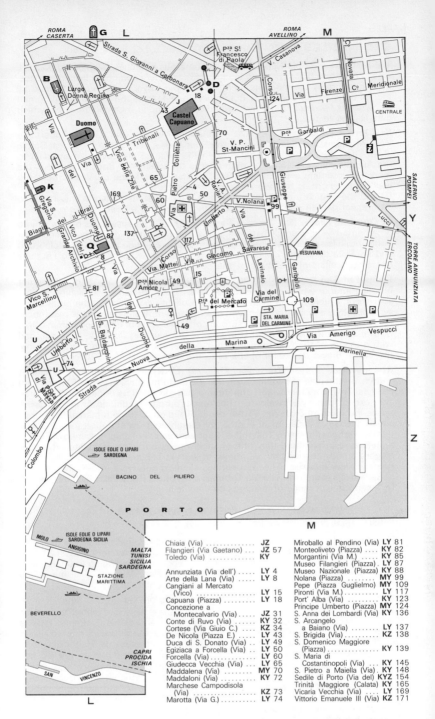

★ **Royal Palace (Palazzo Reale)** ⊙ **(KZ)**. – The palace was built at the beginning of the 17C by the architect Domenico Fontana and has been remodelled several times. The façade retains more or less its original appearance. Since the late 19C the niches on the façade contain eight statues of the most famous Kings of Naples.

A huge staircase with twin ramps and crowned by a coffered dome leads to the apartments and the sumptuously decorated **royal chapel**. It was only after 1734 that royalty lived in the apartments. The richly ornamented rooms have retained their numerous works of art, tapestries, paintings, period furniture and fine porcelain.

★★ **Port of Santa Lucia** ⊙. – *Town plan in the current Michelin Red Guide Italia.*
Santa Lucia is the name of the small suburb that juts out towards the sea. It is best known as the name of a tiny port, immortalised by a famous Neapolitan song, nestling between a rocky islet and the jetty linking it to the shore. **Egg Castle** (Castel dell'Ovo) ⊙ is a severe edifice built by the Normans and remodelled by the Angevins in 1274. Legend has it that Virgil hid a magic egg within its walls and that the destruction of the egg would result in a similar fate for the castle.

From the jetty there is a splendid **view★★** of Vesuvius on the one hand and of the western side of the bay on the other. In the evening, go further along to Piazza Vittoria which offers a **view★★★** of the residential suburbs on the Vomero and Posillipo hillsides, brightly lit up by a myriad of twinkling lights.

★★ OLD NAPLES (SPACCA NAPOLI) (KLY) *time: 2 1/2 hours on foot*

This is the heart of old Naples. With its numerous churches, dilapidated palaces, small crafts and businesses, its ancient streets where swarms a lively populace, it is undoubtedly the most engaging part of the town. Its main axis, formed by the Via Benedetto Croce and S. Biagio dei Librai, follows the course of the Roman *Decumanus Maximus* and is nicknamed Spacca Napoli, meaning the street which cuts Naples in two.

★ **St Clare's (Santa Chiara) (KY C)**. – Sancia of Majorca, the wife of Robert the Wise of Anjou, had this Church of the Poor Clares built in the Provençal-Gothic style. The interior is sober and lofty. In the chancel are several memorials to the Anjou dynasty: behind the high altar is the **tomb★★** of Robert the Wise, the work of Florentine sculptors in 1345; the **tomb★** of Marie de Valois, near the wall on the right, is by Tino di Camaino and his pupils.
Behind the church are **cloisters★** ⊙ which Vaccaro transformed in the 18C into an original garden and embellished with Capodimonte faïence *(see p 143)*.

St Dominic Major (San Domenico Maggiore) (KY L). – Its apse gives onto a square ornamented with a small baroque votive monument *(guglia)*. The interior has both Gothic (**caryatids★** by Tino di Camaino support a huge paschal candelabrum) and baroque (high altar) features. The 18C sacristy with its panelling contains numerous coffins of members of the court of Aragon.

Chapel of San Severo ⊙ **(KY V)**. – This 16C church has an amazingly exuberant baroque interior which dates from the 18C. There are some astonishing marble **sculptures★**: on either side of the choir are Chastity and Despair (the latter being symbolised by a man struggling with a net); the central one depicts the recumbent figure of Christ covered by a thin shroud and is the work of Giuseppe Sammartino. Not far from the Church of St Dominic is the charming Piazzetta Nilo, adorned with a statue of the Nile from which it derives its name. A little further along, the Via S. Biagio dei Librai opens onto the picturesque Via S. Gregorio.

St Lawrence Major (San Lorenzo Maggiore) (LY K). – The spacious and well-lit church, on the plan of a Latin cross, has a fine Gothic nave (early 14C) lined with chapels. Following renovation, the interior has assumed its original bare appearance except for the west wall which has kept its baroque additions. An elegant **arch★** spans the transept crossing. To the south of the choir is the remarkable mosaic-covered **tomb★** of Catherine of Austria, the daughter-in-law of Robert the Wise. The late-13C **polygonal apse★** by Thibaud de Saumur is an interesting specimen of French architecture in southern Italy; the chancel opens onto the ambulatory through elegant arches crowned by twin bays. In the Via Tribunali (KY) at no 362 is the **Palazzo Spinelli di Laurino (A)** with a curious elliptical courtyard embellished by one of Sanfelice's staircases. The Via Tribunali ends at the **Piazza Dante (KY)** overlooked by a semicircular range of buildings by Vanvitelli.

★★★ NATIONAL ARCHAEOLOGICAL MUSEUM
(MUSEO ARCHEOLOGICO NAZIONALE) ⊙ (KY) *time: 2 hours*

The museum occupies a 16C building which was originally intended to house the royal cavalry, and then became the seat of the university from 1610 to 1777. The collections are essentially composed of works of art belonging to the Farnese family and treasures discovered at Pompeii and Herculaneum. It is one of the richest museums in the world for Greco-Roman antiquities.

★★★ **Greco-Roman sculpture**. – This department is on the ground floor.
Tyrant-Slayers' Gallery. – *Turn right on entering*. This gallery is devoted to Archaic art. The **Aphrodite Sosandra** with a fine, proud face and elegantly-draped robe is a splendid copy of a Greek bronze (5C BC), while the powerful marble group of the **Tyrant-Slayers**, a copy of a Greek bronze, represents Harmodios and Aristogiton who delivered Athens from the tyrant, Hipparchus, in the 6C BC.
Great Masters' Gallery. – *Parallel to the above gallery on the entrance side*. Room II contains the majestic statue of the Farnese Pallas (Athena) and Orpheus and Eurydice bidding each other farewell, a lowrelief of touching simplicity copied from the Phidias original (5C BC). In Room III is the **Doryphorus**, the spear-bearer, a copy of the famous bronze by Polykleitos.
Farnese Bull Gallery. – The gallery derives its name from the colossal group, the **Farnese Bull** (Room VI), depicting the death of Dirce. It was carved from a single block of marble and restored by Michelangelo. The famous **Callipygian Venus**, a Roman copy of the Greek original, stands in the centre of Room X. Room XII contains the **Aphrodite of Sinuessa**, a Greek original of admirable delicacy as well as the **Farnese Hercules**, a Greek copy of an original by Lysippus who was greatly admired by Renaissance artists. In Room XIV is the **Psyche of Capua**, with a beautifully spiritual face.
Works in coloured marble. – The most famous work is the statue of **Artemis of Ephesus** (2C) in alabaster and bronze, representing the deity venerated at the famous temple by the Aegean Sea. She is sometimes considered as a nature goddess in the oriental tradition and is represented with numerous breasts symbolising her motherly nature.
Great Hall. – Against the second pillar on the right is the statue of the priestess Eumachia, discovered at Pompeii. The robe is beautifully draped and the face expressive.
Greek Portrait Gallery *(on the left at the far end of the hall)* and the **Emperors' Gallery** *(at right angles to the former gallery)*. – These galleries contain the portrait busts of Socrates, the blind Homer, Euripides and other excellent portraits of Roman emperors.

★★ **Mosaics.** – *To the left on the mezzanine.*
Although most of these come from Pompeii they offer a wide variety of styles and subject matter. There are two small works by Dioscurides of Samos (Room LIX): *Roving Musicians* and *Visit to a Magician* as well as the famous mosaic of the **Battle of Alexander** (Room LXI) which paved the floor of the House of the Faun at Pompeii. It depicts with a remarkable sense of movement the victory of the King of Macedon over Darius, King of Persia.

★★★ **Works from Villa Pison.** – *First floor, on the right.*
The villa, which was discovered at Herculaneum in the 18C but was later reburied, is thought to have belonged to L. Calpurnius Pison who was Julius Caesar's father-in-law. The owner had turned the house into a museum. The documents and splendid works of art from his collections are priceless. The Papyri Room (CXIV) contains photographs of some of the 800 papyri from the library. In Room CXVI are exhibited **bronze statues** that adorned the peristyle of the villa: the **Drunken Faun** lost in euphoria, a **Sleeping Satyr** with a beautiful face in repose; the two lifelike **Wrestlers** are inspired from Lysippus (4C BC); the famous **Dancers from Herculaneum** are probably in fact water-carriers; the famous **Hermes at Rest,** with a tall strong figure, reflects Lysippus' ideal. In Room CXVII, in addition to the **portrait** mistakenly identified as that of **Seneca** and one of the most remarkably expressive works from antiquity, are exhibited an Ideal Head identified as Artemis, and the majestic statue of Athena Promachos (1C BC).

★★ **Small bronzes, paintings and minor arts.** – *First floor, on the left.*
Rooms XC to XCV display works of art from Pompeii and Herculaneum, notably a remarkable collection of **small bronzes**, vases, plates, lamps, musical and surgical instruments, heating apparatus and kitchen utensils. Rooms LXVIII to LXXV have a collection of **mural paintings** from the various villas. The great diversity of style, variety of colours and themes are all ample proof of the richness of decorative traditions in Rome *(see Pompeiian Painting)*.

★★ **CARTHUSIAN MONASTERY OF ST MARTIN**
(CERTOSA DI SAN MARTINO) ⊙ **(JZ)** *time: 1 hour*

This immense Carthusian monastery is beautifully situated on a spur of the Vomero hill. The **Castel Sant'Elmo,** a massive structure with bastions, overlooks the monastery to the west; it was rebuilt by the Spaniards in the 16C and was for a long time used as a prison. The monastery was founded by the Anjou dynasty and was almost completely remodelled in the 16C and 17C. The monastic buildings can be visited, as well as the museum with its historical collections which are arranged in the buildings overlooking the Procurators' Cloisters.

Church. – The **interior**★★ is lavishly baroque. The choir has a superb marble communion table by Sammartino and several paintings by Guido Reni and Caracciolo. The sacristy has marquetry panelling. In the treasury chapel there are paintings by Ribera and Luca Giordano.

Great Cloisters. – This harmonious ensemble is the work of the architect-sculptor Cosimo Fanzago.

★ **Museum.** – The section devoted to festivals and costumes contains an exceptional collection of figurines and Neapolitan **cribs**★★ *(presepi).* The historical section traces the history of Naples from the Bourbon reign (1734) to the arrival of Garibaldi in 1860. From Room 25 there is an outstanding **view**★★★ of Naples and its bay. The **art gallery** comprises works from the 15C to the 19C. There is also a rich section of **sculptures** including works by Tino di Camaino.

★★ **CAPODIMONTE PALACE AND NATIONAL GALLERY**
(PALAZZO E GALLERIA NAZIONALE DI CAPODIMONTE) ⊙ *time: 1 1/2 hours*

On the northern outskirts of Naples: take the Via S. Teresa degli Scalzi (JKY).
This former **royal estate**★ extends over high ground to the north of the city. The whole includes a massive and austere palace which was built from 1738 to 1838, an extensive park, and the remains of the famous 18C porcelain factory. The palace itself has an art gallery in addition to the royal apartments.

★★ **National Gallery.** – *2nd floor.* This important Italian collection of Italian and foreign works is well displayed. The Primitives include the remarkable **St Louis of Toulouse** by Simone Martini, a masterpiece from the Sienese school (Room 4), several works including a *Madonna* by Taddeo Gaddi, others by Masolino (Room 5) as well as a dramatic **Crucifixion** by Masaccio (Room 6).
The Renaissance period is illustrated by canvases by Botticelli, Filippino Lippi and Raphael (Room 7), Lorenzo Lotto, Vivarini, Mantegna and in particular the admirable **Transfiguration** by Giovanni Bellini, whose subtle combination of balanced landscape, harmony of colours and vivid light enhances the religious theme.
The Neopolitan school is represented by a picture of a *Lion being cared for by St Jerome* (Room 10) executed in the detailed Flemish style by Colantonio (15C). In the rooms containing works from the Mannerist movement note the elegant *Portrait of a Youth* by Rosso Fiorentino (Room 15), works by Correggio (Room 17) – notably the tender and delicate **Zingarella Madonna** *(Gipsy woman)* – and portraits by Il Parmigianino including that of the sumptuously-dressed **Antea**. Room 18 contains some fine canvases by El Greco while Room 19 has an exceptional **group of Titians**. The outstanding ones are the portrait of *Danae* with its superb colour effects and the admirable family portrait of *Pope Paul III (Alessandro Farnese) with his nephews (photograph p 22)* which is wonderfully expressive.

In Room 20 are works by northern European painters: Joos Van Cleve and especially Bruegel the Elder with his celebrated **Parable of the Blind** (1568).
Further on are displayed several paintings by the Carracci (Room 25), who in reaction against Mannerism paved the way for baroque art, as well as works by Guido Reni (Room 27). Of outstanding merit, however, is the remarkable **Flagellation** by Caravaggio (Room 29) who inspired such followers as Andrea Vaccaro, Ribera, Artemisia Gentileschi and Stanzione who are all represented in the following galleries.
The last rooms are devoted to the Neapolitan school with paintings by Salvator Rosa, Bernardo Cavallino, Mattia Preti, Luca Giordano, Giuseppe Recco, Paulo Porpora...

Royal apartments. – *1st floor.* These have some lovely pieces of furniture. Rooms 67 to 71 house the porcelain museum. The Chinese-style **porcelain room★★**, executed in the 18C at Capodimonte for the royal summer residence at Portici, has been reassembled in Room 94.

ADDITIONAL SIGHTS

★ **Mergellina.** – *Plan of the built-up area in the current Michelin Red Guide Italia.*
Mergellina, at the foot of the Posillipo hillside with the small port of Sannazzaro, is one of the few places in Naples ideal for a stroll. It affords a splendid **view★★** of the bay: the Vomero hillside, crowned by Castel Sant'Elmo, slopes down gently towards the Santa Lucia headland and Egg Castle beyond, with Vesuvius in the distance.

★ **Villa Floridiana** ⊙. – *To the west of Naples. Town plan in the current Michelin Red Guide Italia.*
This graceful small white palace *(palazzina)* in the neo-classical style stands high up on the Vomero hillside. The palace houses the **Duca di Martina National Ceramics Museum★** with sections devoted to enamels, ivories, faïence and especially porcelain. Its fine gardens afford an attractive **view★** from the terrace.

★ **Catacombs of St Januarius (Catacombe di San Gennaro)** ⊙. – *To the north of Naples. Plan of the built-up area in the current Michelin Red Guide Italia.*
The catacombs have been associated with the name of St Januarius since the 5C when the remains of the martyred saint were transferred here from Pozzuoli. They extend over two floors and consist of vast galleries, some of which have interesting paleo-Christian paintings.

★ **Santa Maria Donnaregina** (LY B). – Cross the cloisters adorned with 18C faïence. A baroque church of the same name precedes the small 14C Gothic church which shows a decidedly French influence. Inside is the **tomb★** of the founder, Mary of Hungary, widow of Charles II of Anjou, by Tino di Camaino. The walls of the monks' chancel are decorated with 14C **frescoes★**.

★ **St John's (San Giovanni a Carbonara)** (LY G). – An 18C stairway leads to the elegant Gothic doorway of this 14C church. Inside are the tomb of Ladislas of Anjou (15C) and the many works of art in two chapels, the Caracciolo del Sole behind the choir and the Caracciolo del Vico, to the left of the previous one.

★ **Capuan Gate (Porta Capuana)** (LMY D). – This is one of the fortified gateways in the walls built in 1484 to the plans of Giuliano da Maiano. The **Capuan Castle** (Castel Capuano) (LY) nearby was the former residence of the Norman princes and the Hohenstaufens.

Cathedral (Duomo) ⊙ (LY). – Built in the 14C, the cathedral was considerably altered at a later date. Held in great veneration by the people, the **Chapel of St Januarius** (San Gennaro) ⊙, in a rich baroque style, is preceded by a remarkable 17C bronze grille: behind the high altar are two glass phials containing the saint's blood which is supposed to liquefy, failing which disaster will befall the town. The Feast of the **Miracle of St Januarius** is held twice annually on the first Sunday in May and on 19 September. The dome is decorated by a Lanfranco fresco with an admirable sense of movement. A door in the middle of the north aisle gives access to the 4C **Basilica of Santa Restituta** ⊙, which was transformed in the Gothic period and again in the 17C. At the far end of the nave, the 5C baptistry contains remains of mosaics of the same period.

★ **Cuomo Palace (Palazzo Cuomo)** ⊙ (LY Q). – This majestic late-15C palace, with its rusticated stonework, is a reminder of the Florentine Renaissance. It contains the **Filangieri Municipal Museum.** There are collections of arms and armour, ceramics and porcelain, furniture and paintings by Ribera, Caracciolo, Mattia Preti etc.

St Anne of the Lombards (Sant' Anna dei Lombardi) (KYZ R). – This Renaissance church is rich in contemporary Florentine **sculpture★**. Inside is the tomb of Mary of Aragon (1st chapel on the left) by Antonio Rossellino and an Annunciation (1st chapel on the right) by Benedetto da Maiano. In the oratory to the right of the choir is a Descent from the Cross, a late-15C terracotta by Guido Mazzoni who introduced this style of rather theatrical realism to Naples which was to become very popular in southern Italy. The former sacristy has lovely stalls which are attributed to Fra Giovanni da Verona (1457-1525).

Public Gardens (Villa Comunale). – *Town plan in the current Michelin Red Guide Italia.*
Vanvitelli laid out these gardens along the waterfront in 1780. They are very popular with the Neapolitans for the evening walk. An aquarium stands within the gardens.

Aquarium (Acquario) ⊙. – It presents a large variety of sea creatures to be found in the Bay of Naples.

Michelin map 988 fold 27

The Bay of Naples, extending from Cumae to Sorrento, has a rich history and is one of the most beautiful Italian gulfs. It is an area of striking contrasts where one may find in close proximity isolated places conducive to meditation, such as the archaeological sites, the bare slopes of Vesuvius, the Sibyl's Cave or Lake Averno, and others bustling with activity, noisy, crowded with traffic, enlivened by a population which lives with the ever-present fear of earthquakes and a new volcanic eruption. Its legendary beauty is somewhat marred by the uncontrolled sprawl of industrial development which has reached the outskirts of Naples. However, its islands, capes and mountains offer unforgettable excursions.

Sightseeing. – Follow the itineraries indicated on the local map pp 146 and 147.

★★ 1 **FROM NAPLES TO CUMAE**

Phlegrean Fields (CAMPI FLEGREI)
45km – 28 miles – about 6 hours

This volcanic area, which received its name from the ancients ("phlegrean" is derived from a Greek word meaning "to blaze"), extends in an arc along the Gulf of Pozzuoli. Hot springs, steam-jets and sulphurous gases rise from the ground and from the sea, and are proof of an intense underground activity. Lakes have formed in the craters of extinct volcanoes. This stretch of coastline is subject to variations in ground level due to volcanic activity.

★★★ **Naples.** – *Description p 138.*

★ **Posillipo.** – This famous hill forms a promontory and separates the Bay of Naples from Pozzuoli Bay. Posillipo, dotted with villas and their lovely gardens and modern buildings, is Naples' main residential area. It affords splendid views of the bay.

★ **Marechiaro.** – This small fishermen's village built high above the sea was made famous by a Neapolitan song *Marechiare.*

Garden of Remembrance (Parco Virgiliano or Parco della Rimembranza). – From the point there are splendid **views**★★ over the Bay of Naples, from Cape Miseno to Sorrento Peninsula, as well as the islands of Procida, Ischia and Capri.

★ **Pozzuoli.** – *Description p 174.*

★★ **Solfatara.** – *Description p 174.*

Lake Lucrino (Lago Lucrino). – In antiquity, oyster farming was practised here and the banks were lined with elegant villas. One of these belonged to Cicero and another was the scene of Agrippina's murder, on the orders of her son Nero.

★★ **Baia: the Baths** ☉. – This Greek colony was in Roman times a fashionable beach resort, as well as a thermal spa with the most complete equipment in the world for hydrotherapy. The Roman emperors and patricians had immense villas, all of which disappeared under the sea after a change in ground level. However, ruins of the famous baths subsist, sitting on the hilltop overlooking the sea. To one facing the hill, these include from left to right the baths of Venus, the baths of Sosandra and the baths of Mercury.

Bacoli ☉. – On the high ground in the old town rises the **Cento Camerelle**★ *(Via Cento Camerelle, to the right of the church).* This huge reservoir, which belonged to a private villa, is built on two levels: the grandiose upper level built in the 1C has four sections and immense arches; the lower part, built much earlier, has a network of narrow galleries forming a cross, that emerge high above sea level. The famous **Piscina Mirabile**★ ☉ *(at the church take the road to the left, Via Ambrogio Greco, and then Via Piscina Mirabile to the right)* was an immense cistern designed to supply water to the Roman fleet in the port of Miseno. It is 70m long, 25m wide and nearly 15m high (230ft×82ft×49ft) and is divided into five sections with 48 pillars supporting the roof. There are remarkable light effects.

Miseno. – This name is given to a lake, a port, a promontory, a cape and a village. Lake Miseno, a former volcanic crater, was believed by the ancients to be the Styx, across which Charon ferried the souls of the dead. Under the Emperor Augustus it was linked by a canal to the port of Miseno, which was the base of the Roman fleet. The village of Miseno is dominated by Monte Miseno, on which Misenus, the companion of Aeneas, is said to have been buried. The slopes of the promontory were studded with luxurious villas, including the one where in AD 37 the Emperor Tiberius choked to death.

Lake Fusaro (Lago di Fusaro). – A lagoon containing a small island on which Vanvitelli built a hunting lodge for King Ferdinand IV of Bourbon in 1782.

★ **Cumae.** – *Description p 83.*

★ **Lake Avernus** (Lago d'Averno). – *The lake lies below the Cumae-Naples road: belvedere on the right approximately 1km – 1/2 mile beyond Arco Felice.*
This lake within a crater is dark, still and silent and wrapped in an atmosphere of mystery, which was all the more intense in antiquity as birds flying overhead were overcome by the fumes and dropped into the lake to be swallowed up. Homer and Virgil regarded it as the entrance to the Underworld. Under the Roman Empire, Agrippa, a captain in the service of the Emperor Augustus, developed it as a naval base and linked it by canal with Lake Lucrino *(see above),* which in turn was linked to the open sea. An underground gallery 1km – 1/2 mile long, known as **Cocceio's Cave** (Grotta di Cocceio), connected Avernus with Cumae, and was used by chariots.

★★★ ② FROM NAPLES TO TORRE ANNUNZIATA

Vesuvius *44km - 27 miles - allow 1 day*

The coast road relieves the Salerno motorway but crosses a densely-populated zone of industrial sprawl. Here were, however, the favourite resorts of the Neapolitan aristocracy in the 18C and 19C.

Portici. – The road crosses the courtyard of the **royal palace** built in 1738 for the Bourbon King Charles III. Today the palace buildings are the home of the Naples Faculty of Agronomy. In his opera *The Mute Girl of Portici (Muette de Portici)*, the French composer, Auber, features the 17C revolt against the Spaniards, instigated by Masaniello, a young fisherman from Portici.

★★ **Herculaneum (Ercolano).** – *Description p 111.*

★★★ **Vesuvius (Il Vesuvio).** – The outline of Vesuvius, one of the few still active volcanoes in Europe, is inseparable from the Neapolitan landscape. It has in fact two summits: to the north **Monte Somma** (alt 1 132m – 3 714ft) and to the south Mount Vesuvius proper (alt 1 277m – 4 190ft). With time the volcanic materials on the lower slopes have become fertile soil which supports orchards and vines producing the famous *Lacryma Christi* wine.

The eruptions of Vesuvius. – Until the earthquake of AD 62 and the eruption of AD 79 which buried Herculaneum and Pompeii, Vesuvius seemed extinct; its slopes were clothed with famous vines and woods. By 1139, seven eruptions had been recorded. Then came a period of calm during which the slopes of the mountains were cultivated. On 16 December 1631 Vesuvius had a terrible awakening, destroying all the settlements at its foot: 3 000 people perished. The eruption of 1794 devastated Torre del Greco. The volcano had minor eruptions in 1858, 1871, 1872, from 1895 to 1899, 1900, 1903, 1904 and a major eruption in 1906. Following the eruption of 1929 that of 1944 altered the shape of the crater. Since then, apart from a short period of activity linked with the 1980 earthquake, Vesuvius has emitted only a plume of smoke.

Ascent ⊙. – *Start from Herculaneum and return by Torre del Greco: 27km – 17 miles plus 3/4 hour on foot Rtn. Wear stout walking shoes.* A good road leads to a junction in the midst of lava flows. Take the left fork *(the car park is several kilometres further on).* The path offers an easy but most impressive climb up the side of the volcano, scattered with cinders and lapilli.
From the summit there is an immense **panorama★★★** over the Bay of Naples enclosed by the Sorrento Peninsula in the south and Cape Miseno in the north. Beyond is the Gulf of Gaeta. The crater affords an unforgettable sight for its sheer size and the desolation of the slopes of its jagged walls, for the great yawning crater, which takes on a pink colour in the sun, and the spouting steam-jets.

Torre del Greco. – This town which has been repeatedly destroyed by the eruptions of Vesuvius, is well known for its coral ornaments and cameos.

Torre Annunziata. – This town is the centre of the famous Neapolitan spaghetti and macaroni industry. It has been buried under the lava of Vesuvius seven times. The sumptuous **Roman Villa Oplontis★★** ⊙, decorated with 2nd style Pompeiian paintings *(p 168),* is thought to have belonged to Poppea, Nero's wife.

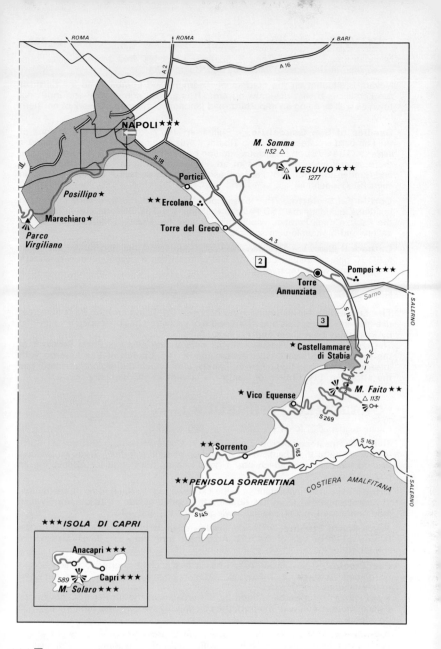

★★★ ③ FROM TORRE ANNUNZIATA TO SORRENTO
69km – 43 miles – allow 1 day

Torre Annunziata. – *Description p 146.*

★★★ **Pompeii.** – *Description p 168.*

★ **Castellammare di Stabia.** – *Description p 76.*

★★ **Monte Faito** ⊘. – *Access by a toll-road.* Monte Faito is part of the **Lattari range**, a headland which separates the Bay of Naples from the Gulf of Salerno and forms the Sorrento Peninsula. Its name is derived from the beech trees (*fagus* in Latin) which are a source of pleasantly-cool shade in summer. The steeply-winding road leads to a roundabout (Belvedere dei Capi) which provides a splendid **panorama**★★★ of the Bay of Naples. The road continues upwards to the **San Michele Chapel** from where there is another **panorama**★★★: the wild landscape of the Lattari mountains contrasts strongly with the smiling scenery of the Bay of Naples and the Sarno plain. There is a fine run down towards Vico Equense.

★ **Vico Equense.** – This small health and seaside resort occupies a picturesque site on a rocky headland.

★★ **Sorrento and Sorrento Peninsula.** – *Description p 203.*

★★★ ISLANDS

★★★ **Capri.** – *Description p 72.*

★★★ **Ischia.** – *Description p 123.*

★ **Procida.** – *Description p 123.*

NOVARA Piedmont

Michelin map 𝟿𝟾𝟾 folds 2 and 3, 𝟸𝟷𝟿 fold 17 or 𝟺𝟸𝟾 fold 14
Town plan in the current Michelin Red Guide Italia

Novara is situated on the borders of Piedmont and Lombardy to the north of the Lomellina, a vast rice-growing area. It is a busy commercial and industrial town as well as being an important road junction in the road network of northern Italy.

★ **Basilica of San Gaudenzio.** – Built from 1577 to 1659 to the designs of the Lombard architect, Pellegrino Tibaldi, it was crowned with a lovely tall slender **dome**★★ (1844-78), an audacious addition by a local architect, A. Antonelli. Inside, there several interesting works of art, including paintings by Morazzone (17C) and Gaudenzio Ferrari (16C) as well as the silver **sarcophagus**★ of the city's patron saint (St Gaudentius).

Cortile del Broletto. – This lovely courtyard is bordered by several interesting buildings including the 15C Palazzo Podestà, the 13C Broletto (Town Hall) and the Palazzo degli Paratici, which now houses the **Municipal Museum** with an art gallery and archaeological section.

Cathedral (Duomo). – This neo-classical monumental building by Antonelli has a 6C-7C paleo-Christian baptistry. The chancel has a Byzantine-style **pavement**★ in black and white mosaic.

EXCURSION

The Lomellina. – This region lying between the Ticino and the Po is the great rice-growing area of Italy and a landscape of vast stretches of flooded land divided by long rows of willows and poplars.
The chief towns are: **Vigevano** with its outstanding elliptical **Piazza Ducale**★★ at the foot of the Sforza Castle; **Mortara** has a 14C Church of San Lorenzo with interesting paintings by G. Ferrari; **Lomello**, after which the region is named, has the attractive 11C Church of Santa Maria with its 8C baptistry.

★ ORBETELLO PENINSULA Tuscany

Michelin map 𝟿𝟾𝟾 folds 24 and 25 or 𝟺𝟹𝟶 fold 23

This small limestone outcrop, culminating in Monte Argentario (635m – 2 083ft), is now linked to the mainland by a build-up of sand *(tomboli)*. Three causeways lead to the peninsula which has a good coastal road ideal for discovering its charms.

Orbetello. – This town stands on the causeway set in the middle of the lagoon. The rampart-girdled town has retained the Gothic façade of its cathedral which was remodelled in the Spanish style in the 16C and 17C.

Porto Santo Stefano. – The peninsula's main town, and port, spreads up the hillside on either side of the 17C Aragonese fort. There is a lovely **view**★ from the latter.

Port'Ercole. – This seaside resort has a tiny ancient quarter to which access is gained through a medieval gateway complete with hoarding and machicolations.
From Piazza Santa Barbara, lined by the arcades of the former 16C governors' palace, there is a view of the port, the bay and the two old Spanish forts perched on Monte Filippo.

Ansedonia. – The ruins of the **ancient city of Cosa**★ ⊘ crown a height at the neck of Orbetello Peninsula. They are within sight of the lagoon, the former island of Orbetello and Monte Argentario. This former Roman town, girt with cyclopean walls, flourished from the 3C BC to the AD 4C.
A tower where Puccini is said to have composed part of *Tosca* stands by the sea.

★★ ORVIETO Umbria

Michelin map 𝟿𝟾𝟾 fold 25 or 𝟺𝟹𝟶 fold 25

This important Etruscan centre later became a papal stronghold and it was here that Clement VII took refuge in 1527 when Rome was put to sack by the troops of the French King, Charles V.
Orvieto is a pleasant city with its wealth of historic buildings and it enjoys a particularly remarkable **site**★★★ on the top of a plug of volcanic rock. Those arriving by the Bolsena or Montefiascone roads have particularly good views of this site. The region produces a pleasant, white wine, the cool and fragrant Orvieto.

★★★ CATHEDRAL (DUOMO) *time: 1 hour*

In the heart of the town the quiet Piazza del Duomo, of majestic proportions, is lined by several interesting buildings. Apart from the cathedral there is the austere **Palace of the Popes**★ ⊘ (M²) which now houses the Cathedral Museum. The cathedral, a perfect example of the transitional Romanesque-Gothic style, was begun in 1290 to enshrine the relics of the Miracle of Bolsena *(qv)*. Over 100 architects, sculptors, painters and mosaicists took part in the building of the cathedral which was completed only in 1600.

★★★ **Façade.** – This is the boldest and richest in colour among Italian Gothic buildings. The vertical lines are accentuated by the slender gables and especially by the soaring buttresses, which are clad with small panels of coloured marble, elongated in shape and further prolonged by pinnacles. The sumptuous decorative effect is obtained by the use of sculptures lower down with multicoloured marbles and mosaics above. The façade was designed by the Sienese, Lorenzo Maitani (1310-30), and continued by Andrea Pisano, Orcagna and Sanmicheli.

Maitani was also the artist responsible for the astonishing **low reliefs★★** adorning the pillars. The second shaft to the right of the

Orvieto Cathedral – detail of façade

main doorway has a very realistic **Last Judgement**. Orcagna was the designer of the rose window, fitted into a square frame, further adorned with niches containing the Apostles and the Prophets.

Interior. – A nave and two aisles built in alternating courses of black and white stone rest on semicircular arches supported by lovely bracketed capitals. A moulding projects above the arches. The nave and aisles are roofed with a timber ceiling, while Gothic vaulting covers the transepts and the chancel. The paving slopes up towards the chancel, reducing the perspective. Alabaster windowpanes let in plenty of light. At the entrance stand the 15C stoup and the Gothic font. A fresco of the Virgin and Child (1425) in the north aisle is by Gentile da Fabriano.

In the north transept under the 16C monumental organ is the entrance to the **Corporal Chapel,** which enshrines the relics of the Miracle of Bolsena and notably the linen cloth (corporal) in which the bleeding Host was wrapped. A tabernacle encloses the **Reliquary★★** of the Corporal, a masterpiece of medieval goldsmiths' work (1338) encrusted with enamels and precious stones. In the chapel on the right is a Madonna of Pity (1320) by the Sienese painter, Lippo Memmi.

149

A fine Gothic stained glass **window**★ in the chancel illustrates the Gospel with recognisable figures of theologians and prophets.

The south transept gives access, beyond a wrought-iron grille (1516), to the famous chapel **(Cappella della Madonna di San Brizio)**, painted with admirable **frescoes of the Apocalypse**★★. These were begun in 1447 by Fra Angelico with the help of Benozzo Gozzoli and were entrusted from 1499 to 1504 to **Luca Signorelli**, and they are considered to be the latter's masterpiece. As the human figure was his main interest while landscape and colour remained secondary considerations, the theme of the frescoes enabled him to perfect his talent. Although he lacked a spiritual dimension, with his precise draughtsmanship, his careful portrayal of human anatomy and his dramatic compositions, he was the precursor of Michelangelo. On the ceiling, Fra Angelico painted Christ among angels and prophets; the apostles, doctors, virgins, martyrs and patriarchs are by Signorelli. The latter was responsible for the wall frescoes of extraordinary power: the Preaching of the Antichrist (first lunette on the left) containing portraits of Signorelli and Fra Angelico; the End of the World (on the west wall) and the Resurrection of the Body (first lunette on the right). The end wall of the chapel is devoted to the Last Judgement. There is a *Pietà* of astonishing power in a niche in the right-hand wall.

ADDITIONAL SIGHTS

★★ **St Patrick's Well (Pozzo di San Patrizio)** ⊙. – The well was dug in the volcanic rock by order of Pope Clement VII de' Medici to supply the town with water in case of siege. Sangallo the Younger was entrusted with the work. Two spiral staircases, lit by 72 windows, wind up and down without meeting. The well is over 62m – 203ft deep and its water cold and pure.

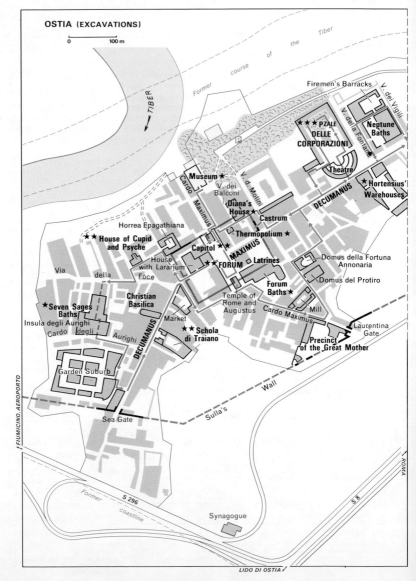

★ **People's Palace (Palazzo del Popolo).** – The palace is built of weather-worn volcanic rock in the Romanesque-Gothic style. The façade has a majestic balcony, elegant windows and curious fluted merlons.

★ **Old Quarter (Quartiere Vecchio).** – This quiet, unfrequented quarter has retained its old houses, medieval towers and churches. At the western extremity stands the **Church of San Giovenale;** the Gothic apse is decorated with 13C-15C frescoes.

Faina Archaeological Museum ⊘ **(M¹).** – This important **Etruscan Collection**★ includes some splendid painted vases, sculpted terracotta funerary urns and a rare 4C sarcophagus.

St Bernard's Church (San Bernardino). – A charming baroque church with the refined decoration of a theatre. The oval interior is delightfully decorated and has an organ carved with figures.

Piazza della Repubblica. – It stands on the site of the ancient forum, dominated by the Church of St Andrew (Sant'Andrea) with its lovely 12-sided Romanesque tower.

The maps to use with this Guide are : 428, 429, 430, 431 *and* 988

★★   **OSTIA (OSTIA ANTICA) Latium**

Michelin map 988 fold 26 or 430 fold 35 – 24km – 15 miles southwest of Rome

Ostia, at the mouth of the Tiber, takes its name from the Latin word *ostium* meaning mouth. According to Virgil, Aeneas disembarked here but its foundation

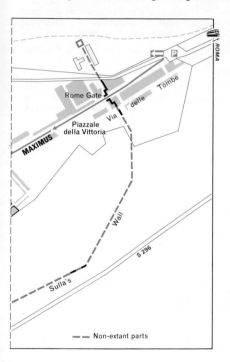

-- -- Non-extant parts

dates in reality back to the 4C BC when Rome embarked on her conquest of the Mediterranean. From that time on, Ostia's development has reflected that of Rome: a military port during the period of expansion, a commercial port once Rome had established an organised system of trade. At first there was simply a castle to protect the port from pirates but by 1BC Ostia had become a real town around which Sulla built ramparts in 79BC. Like Rome, Ostia began to decline in the 4C.

Slowly the harbour silted up and malaria decimated the population. Ostia was soon covered by alluvium deposited by the Tiber. It was 1909 before Ostia was discovered and regular excavations began.

On this extensive site the visitor can discover a variety of interesting remains: warehouses *(horrea)*; baths; sanctuaries; the substantial dwelling-house, the *domus* built around its atrium or courtyard; and the more usual block of flats, several storeys high *(insula)*. They were nearly all built of brick and unrendered. Some had elegant entrances framed by a triangular pediment resting on two pillars. Here and there a porch or a balcony added interest to the street front.

In addition there are the numerous meeting-places for both business and pleasure, and the forum which was the hub of both political and social life. During the empire Ostia was a town with a population of 100 000 which included a large number of foreigners.

EXCAVATION SITE ⊘ *time: 3 hours*

Follow the itinerary indicated on the accompanying plan, which locates sights described below, and also indicates other ruins of particular interest.

Decumanus Maximus. – The Rome Gate (Porta Roma), the main entrance to the town, led into this street, the main east-west axis of all Roman towns. In Ostia it was paved with large slabs and lined with porticoed houses and shops.

Neptune Baths (Terme di Nettuno). – This 2C building has a terrace with a view of the fine **mosaics**★★ which depict the marriage of Neptune and Amphitrite.

★ **Hortensius' Warehouses (Horrea di Hortensius).** – These grand 1C warehouses are built round a pillared courtyard which is lined with shops.

Theatre (Teatro). – It has been much restored but is nevertheless very evocative of life in a Roman city.

★★★ **Piazzale delle Corporazioni.** – Under the portico in the square were the offices of the 70 trading corporations which represented the trading links with the known world. The mosaic pavement portrays their emblems, which in turn indicate the commodity they traded in and the country of origin. The temple in the centre of the square is sometimes attributed to Ceres, goddess of corn and the harvest.

★ **Thermopolium.** – This bar with a marble counter served hot drinks.

★ **Diana's House (Casa di Diana).** – This is a striking example of an *insula* (block of flats) with rooms and passages arranged around an inner courtyard.

★ **Museum** ⊘. – The museum displays the finds of Ostia in a clear well-lit presentation: crafts, oriental religious cults, numerous in Ostia, sculptures, **portraits**★ and examples of the rich interior decoration (mosaics, paintings and frescoes) found in Ostia.

★★ **Capitol and Forum.** – The Capitol was the largest temple in Ostia, built in the 2C and dedicated to the Capitoline triad: Jupiter, Juno and Minerva. The forum was enlarged in the 2C and the few pillars still standing belonged to the surrounding portico. At the far end stands the 1C Temple of Rome and Augustus, a grandiose building once faced with marble.

★★ **House of Cupid and Psyche (Domus d'Amore e Psiche).** – This 4C building, facing the seashore, has interesting remains of mosaic and marble floors and a lovely nymphaeum.

★ **Seven Sages' Baths (Terme dei Sette Sapienti).** – The baths are part of a complex. There is a handsome mosaic floor in the large circular room.

★★ **Schola di Traiano.** – This impressive 2C to 3C building was the headquarters of a guild of merchants. Inside can be seen a statue of Trajan, several porticoed courtyards and a rectangular basin.

Christian Basilica. – In this 4C Christian building, a row of columns separates the aisles which end in apses. An inscription on the architrave of a colonnade marks the entrance to what has been identified as the baptistry.

★ **Forum Baths.** – These are the largest baths in Ostia. The heating ducts are still visible in the walls.
Along one side is a good example of a **public lavatory**.

Precinct of the Great Mother. – This sacred enclosure contains the remains of a temple dedicated to Cybele the Great Mother *(Magna Mater)*. The Sanctuary of Attis has a statue of the goddess in the apse and two fauns flanking the entrance.
The Cardo Maximus ends at the Laurentina Gate in Sulla's wall.

OTRANTO Apulia   Pop 5 112

Michelin map 📖 fold 30

Otranto lies on the Adriatic coast of the "heel". This fishing port was once capital of "Terra d'Otranto", the last remaining Byzantine stronghold, and resisted the Lombards and then the Normans for some considerable time. In the 15C when the town was besieged by the troops of Mohammed II the townspeople took refuge in the cathedral where they were massacred. Survivors were taken prisoner and killed on the summit of a hill, Colle della Minerva, where a sanctuary was built to the memory of the martyrs of Otranto.

Old town. – There is a good view of the old town from the northeast pier; to the left is the 15C **Aragonese castle** flanked by its massive cylindrical towers. To reach this stronghold perched on the clifftop pass through the gateways Porta di Terra and the 15C Porta Alfonsina.

★ **Cathedral (Cattedrale).** – This 12C building was altered in the late 15C. Inside, antique columns separate the nave from the two aisles and there is a remarkable mosaic **pavement**★★★ dating from 1165. It was the work of a local craftsman, Pantaleone. The stylisation of the figures, the vivacity of their poses and attitudes, the freshness of the colours and variety of the symbols make this a fascinating illustrated story.

EXCURSION

★ **The coast to the south** ⊘. – Between Otranto and Santa di Leuca *(51km – 32 miles)* the road offers fine views of this wild and indented coastline. At the head of an inlet is the cave, **Grotta Zinzulusa**, with concretions and two lakes, one salt water and the other fresh, which are inhabited by rare marine species.

GREEN TOURIST GUIDES

Architecture
Fine Art
History
Geography
Picturesque scenery
Touring programmes
Town and site plans
Guides for the holidays

★ PADUA (PADOVA) Venetia

Michelin map 988 fold 5 or 429 fold 14

There are few traces of ancient Patavium which was one of the most prosperous Roman cities in Venetia during the 1C BC owing to its fluvial trade, its agriculture and the sale of horses.

In the 7C Padua was destroyed by the Lombards, and from the 11C to 13C it became an independent city-state. This was the period when numerous churches and palaces were built. The city knew its greatest period of economic and cultural prosperity under the enlightened rule of the lords of Carrara (1337-1405). In 1405 Padua came under the sway of the Venetian Republic and remained a loyal subject until 1797 when the Venetian Constitution was abolished by Napoleon.

The historic centre of Padua, a busy town and an art and pilgrimage centre, is **Piazza Cavour (DY 15)**, with the neo-classical **Café Pedrocchi**, which was a meeting-place of the liberal élite including the poet Musset, in the Romantic period.

PADOVA

Altinate (Via)	DYZ	S. Fermo (Via)	DY	Nancy (Via)	DY 48
Cavour (Piazza e via)	DY 15	Carmine (Via del)	DY 10	Petrarca (Via)	CY 50
Dante (Via)	CY	Cesarotti (Via M.)	DZ 17	Ponte Molino (Vicolo)	CY 52
Filiberto (Via E.)	DY 24	Erbe (Piazza delle)	DY 20	S. Canziano (Via)	DY 57
Garibaldi (Corso)	DY 27	Eremitani (Piazza)	DY 21	S. Lucia (Via)	DY 59
Ponti Romani		Frutta (Piazza della)	DZ 25	Vandelli (Via D.)	CZ 66
(Riviera dei)	DYZ 53	Garibaldi (Piazza)	DY 28	Verdi (Via G.)	CY 67
Roma (Via)	DZ	Guariento (Via)	DY 35	Vittorio Emanuele II	
		Insurrezione (Piazza)	DY 39	(Corso)	CZ 70
		Monte di Pietà (Via del)	CZ 45	8 Febbraio (Via)	DZ 74
				58 Fanteria (Via)	DZ 75

PADOVA

St Anthony the Hermit. – The saint is venerated in Padua. He was born in Lisbon in 1195 and died at the age of 36 in the environs of Padua. This Franciscan monk was a forceful preacher. His help was invoked by the shipwrecked and those in prison and he is generally represented holding a book and a lily.

A famous university. – The University of Padua which was founded in 1222 is the second oldest in Italy after Bologna. It expanded rapidly and attracted students from the whole of Europe. Galileo was a professor and among its students were the Renaissance scholar Pico della Mirandola, the astronomer Copernicus and the poet Tasso.

Art in Padua. – In 1304, **Giotto** came to Padua from Florence to decorate the Scrovegni Chapel. He painted a cycle of frescoes which is one of the masterpieces of Italian art.

In the 15C the Renaissance in Padua was marked by Donatello, another Florentine, who stayed in the city from 1444 to 1453.

Also in the 15C Paduan art flourished under the guiding influence of the Paduan artist, **Andrea Mantegna** (1431-1506). A painter of powerful originality, he was fascinated by anatomy and archaeology and was also a technical innovator in the field of perspective.

ARTISTIC CENTRE *time 2 1/2 hours*

★★★ **Frescoes by Giotto.** – The cycle of 38 frescoes painted *c*1305-10 by Giotto on the walls of the **Scrovegni Chapel** (Cappella degli Scrovegni – **DY**) ⊘, built in 1303, illustrates the lives of the Virgin and of Christ: the *Flight into Egypt, Judas' Kiss* and the *Entombment* are among the most famous. On the lower register, the powerful monochrome figures depict the Vices *(left)* and Virtues *(right)*. The *Last Judgement* on the west wall completes the cycle.

This work shows an exceptional unity and constitutes Giotto's masterpiece, displaying great dramatic power, harmonious composition and intense spirituality *(see p 55).* On the altar is a **Virgin**★ by the Tuscan sculptor Giovanni Pisano.

★★ **Church of the Hermits** (Chiesa degli Eremitani) (**DY**). – This 13C church was badly damaged by bombing in 1944 but has been rebuilt in the original Romanesque style. In the Ovetari Chapel at the far end of the south transept are fragments of **frescoes**★ by Mantegna. The various scenes *(Martyrdom of St James* on the north wall, *Assumption* in the apse and *Martyrdom of St Christoper* on the south wall) display his powerful visionary talent and his careful attention to perspective and architectural detail. The chancel chapel has splendid **frescoes**★★ attributed to **Guariento**, Giotto's Venetian pupil.

★ **Municipal Gallery** (Museo Civico agli Eremitani) ⊘ (**DY M**). – The museum in the Hermitage of St Augustine (Sant'Agostino) comprises several collections: archaeology (Egyptian, Etruscan, Roman and Pre-Roman), coins (Bottacin Bequest) and 15C-18C Venetian and Flemish paintings (Emo Capodilista collection).

The rich holdings of the gallery previously housed in the former Monastery of St Anthony (Sant'Antonio) have recently been transferred to the museum; they include several **masterpieces**★★, mainly Venetian works of the 14C to 18C as well as paintings by Giotto.

PILGRIMAGE CENTRE *time 1 1/2 hours*

★★ **The Saint's Basilica** (Basilica del Santo) ⊘ (**DZ**). – This important pilgrimage church dedicated to St Anthony overlooks the square in which Donatello erected an **equestrian statue**★★ of the Venetian mercenary leader **Gattamelata** (nickname of Erasmo di Nardi who died in Padua in 1443). This bronze was the first of this size to be cast in Italy.

The basilica with its eight-tiered domes was built from 1232 to 1300 in the transitional Romanesque-Gothic style and brings to mind St Mark's in Venice. The imposing **interior**★★ contains numerous works of art: off the north aisle is the **Saint's Chapel**★★, a Renaissance masterpiece, which contains the tomb-cum-altar of St Anthony (Arca di Sant'Antonio) by Tiziano Aspetti (1594); on the walls are magnificent 16C **low reliefs**★★ by several artists. In the chancel the **high altar**★★ is adorned with bronze panels (1450) by Donatello. The third chapel, off the south aisle, has **frescoes**★ by Altichiero.

★ **St George's Oratory** (Oratorio di San Giorgio) ⊘ (**DZ B**). – St George's Oratory was built as a funerary chapel and is decorated with twenty-one **frescoes**★ (1377) by Altichiero and his pupils, depicting various religious scenes.

★ **Scuola di Sant'Antonio** ⊘ (**DZ B**). – A chamber on the first floor of this building, which is adjacent to the former, contains eighteen 16C **frescoes**★ relating the life of St Anthony. Four of these are by Titian.

ADDITIONAL SIGHTS

★ **Law Courts** (Palazzo della Ragione) ⊘ (**DZ J**). – This building, standing between two attractive **squares**★, the Piazza della Frutta (**DZ 25**) and the Piazza delle Erbe (**DZ 20**), is remarkable for its loggias and its roof in the form of an upturned ship's keel. The first-floor **Salone**★★ is adorned with a 15C cycle of frescoes depicting the Work of the Months, the Liberal Arts, the Trades and the Signs of the Zodiac.

Piazza dei Signori (**CYZ**). – This square is lined by the 14C-15C Palazzo del Capitanio (**E**), one-time residence of the Venetian Governors, the **Clock Tower**★★ (Torre dell'Orologio) with its arcade, and the graceful Renaissance gallery, Loggia del Consiglio.

University ⊙ (DZ U). – The university is housed in a palace known as the "Bo" from the name of an inn with an ox as its sign which once stood on the site. It has retained a lovely 16C courtyard and an anatomy theatre, **Teatro Anatomico** (1594).

Baptistry (Battistero) (CZ D). – The baptistry adjoining the cathedral (Duomo) has interesting frescoes and a polyptych by Menabuoi (14C).

Church of St Justina (Santa Giustina) (DZ). – This 16C domed classical building is reminiscent of the Saint's Basilica. At the far end of the chancel is an **altarpiece★** by Veronese.

Botanical Gardens (Orto Botanico) ⊙ (DZ). – These gardens are among the oldest of their kind in Europe; they were laid out in 1545. They contain many exotic species and the palm tree which inspired Goethe in his reflections on the development of plants.

Prato della Valle (DZ). – This 17C oval garden is planted with plane trees and encircled by the still waters of a canal, lined with statues of famous men.

EXCURSIONS

★ **Montagnana.** – *47km – 29 miles to the southwest.*
This small town is girt with impressive 14C **ramparts★★** with at intervals twenty-four polygonal towers and four gateways. The **cathedral** (Duomo), attributed to Sansovino, contains a Transfiguration by Veronese at the high altar, 16C frescoes and stalls. The **Church of San Francesco** with its lovely Gothic belfry stands against the town wall.

★ **Euganean Hills (Colli Euganei).** – These hills to the south of Padua, also known as Monti Euganei, are of volcanic origin. This pleasant hilly area has many orchards and vineyards and was already appreciated in Roman times for its numerous hot springs and its wines.

★ **Abano Terme.** – *Town plan in the current Michelin Red Guide Italia.* This modern and elegant thermal spa well shaded by pines is one of Italy's most famous spa towns.

Montegrotto Terme. – Although less important than Abano it is rapidly growing in importance. This was the ancient Mons Aegrotorum or mountain of the sick.

★ **Monselice.** – This town has retained an important section of its walls and is dominated by the ruins of a castle. From Piazza Mazzini, go up the picturesque Via del Santuario to reach the 13C-14C castle, the Romanesque cathedral (Duomo), the early-17C Sanctuary of the Seven Churches and the Villa Balbi with its Italian garden. The upper terrace affords a lovely **view★** of the region.

★ **Arquà Petrarca.** – *6.5km – 4 miles to the northwest of Monselice.* **Petrarch** (Francesco Petaarca), the leading humanist of the Renaissance, died in this medieval-looking town in 1374. Born in 1304, Italy's most important lyric poet skilfully used his sensitive and flowing language to suit the strict form of the sonnet. A diplomat and great traveller, he spent nearly all his youth at the Papal Court in Avignon, and it was in a church there that he met Laure de Sade to whom he dedicated all the poems of the *Canzoniere.* His house stands on the top of a hill and his tomb, a plain pink marble sarcophagus, was set up in the church square in 1380.

Este. – Cradle of the Este family, rulers of Ferrara, the town still has an attractive section of **town wall★** to the north. The **Atestino National Museum★** (Museo Nazionale Atestino) ⊙ has an interesting collection of local archaeological finds. The cathedral (Duomo), on an elliptical plan, contains a large canvas (1759) by Tiepolo.

★ **Brenta Riviera.** – *Description p 67.*

MICHELIN GUIDES

The Red Guides (hotels and restaurants)

Benelux – Deutschland – España Portugal – main cities Europe – France –
Great Britain and Ireland – Italia

The Green Guides (fine art, historic monuments, scenic routes)

Austria – Canada – England : The West Country – France – Germany –
Great Britain – Greece – Italy – Mexico – Netherlands – New England –
Portugal – Scotland – Spain – Switzerland
London – New York City – Paris – Rome – Washington
and 9 regional guides to France

Michelin map 988 fold 28

One of Italy's most important archaeological sites, Paestum was discovered by chance around 1750, when the Bourbons started work on the building of the road which crosses the area today.

The initial settlement was an ancient Greek colony founded around 600 BC under the name of Poseidonia by colonists from Sybaris *(qv)*. Around the year 400 BC the city fell to a local tribe, the Lucanians. It became Roman in the year 273 BC but began to decline towards the end of the Empire because of the malaria which finally drove out its inhabitants.

Paestum is also a seaside resort; its beach is sheltered by a fine pinewood.

TOUR *time: 2 hours*

★★ **Museum (Museo)** ⊙. – The masterpieces on display include the famous **metopes**★★, low reliefs in the Doric style of the 6C BC which adorned a small temple alongside the temple of Hera *(10km – 6 miles to the north near the mouth of the Sele River)*, as well as the **metopes**★★ from the latter. **Tomb of the Diver**★★ (Tomba del Tuffatore) has unique paintings of Greek funerary art.

★★★ **Ruins** ⊙. – *Follow the itinerary indicated on the accompanying plan.*

The temples, built of a fine yellow limestone, stand amidst the ruins of dwellings sheltered by cypresses or oleanders. Take the Justice Gate to pass through the 5km – 3 mile-long **city wall**★ and follow the **Sacred Way** (Via Sacra) which leads to the Temple of Hera.

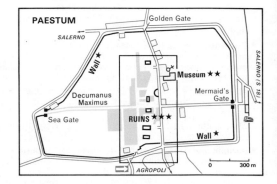

★★ **Basilica.** – The rear of the "Basilica", so-called by 18C archaeologists, stands to the right of the Sacred Way. This mid-6C BC temple was dedicated to Hera (Juno). The peristyle comprises 50 archaic fluted columns with a slight swell. The porch *(pronaos)* leads into the central chamber divided into two naves.

★★★ **Temple of Neptune** (Tempio di Nettuno). – When Paestum was first discovered this well-preserved temple was thought to have been dedicated to Neptune (or Poseidon in Greek, hence the town's name Poseidonia). It has since been proved that it was dedicated to Hera. Dating from the mid 5C BC it is in an admirably pure Doric style. The entablature and the two triangular pediments are almost intact. Inside, the central chamber is divided into three aisles.

The **forum**, surrounded by a portico and shops, is in the centre of the city. The Roman **amphitheatre**, built at the end of the Republic, is today divided by the main road. The small **Underground Temple** contained superb bronze vases.

★★ **Temple of Ceres** (Tempio di Cerere). – Originally erected in the late 6C BC in honour of Athena, the temple retains 34 columns and parts of its pediments.

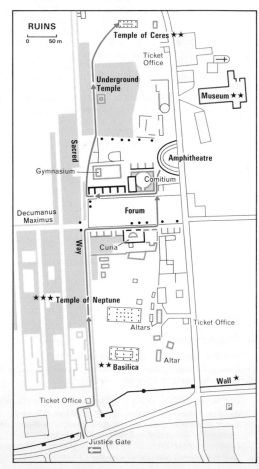

Michelin map ▨▨▨ fold 14, ▨▨▨ fold 27 or ▨▨▨ fold 22

Parma, at the junction of the Via Emilia and the Mantua-La Spezia road, is an important market town and industrial centre which has a rich heritage from its past. Parma has a certain refined charm and is often bathed in a diaphanous light. Piazza Garibaldi (**BZ 9**) is a popular meeting-place for the townspeople. The famous 20C conductor Arturo Toscanini was born in Parma.

HISTORICAL NOTES

A settlement was founded on this site by the Etruscans in 525 BC and it became a Roman station on the Via Emilia in 183 BC. It declined but revived in the 6C under the Ostrogoth King, Theodoric. From being an independent commune from the 11C-13C, it then became a member of the Lombard League *(qv)* and was finally annexed by the papacy in 1513. In 1545 Pope Paul III Farnese gave two papal territories, Parma and Piacenza, having made them a duchy, to his son Pier Luigi Farnese, who was assassinated in 1547. However, the Farnese dynasty continued to reign until 1731 and several members of the house were patrons of the arts and letters, collectors and great builders.

When Don Philip, the son of Philip V of Spain and Elizabeth Farnese, married Louise Elizabeth, the favourite daughter of Louis XV, the town knew a period (1748-1801) of great French influence in several domains (customs, administration and the arts).

Numerous Frenchmen came to work in Parma while others like Stendhal chose to live here; he made Parma the setting of his well-known novel, *The Charterhouse of Parma*. The Bourbon-Parma had their Versailles, now in ruins, at Colorno, north of the town.

The Parma School. – The school is represented by two main artists, Correggio and Il Parmigianino, whose works formed the transition between the Renaissance and baroque. Antonio Allegri (1489-1534), known as **Correggio**, was a master of light and chiaroscuro; his work shows a gracefully sensual and optimistic vision which seemed to herald 18C French art. Francesco Mazzola (1503-40), or **Il Parmigianino** (The Parmesan) as he was commonly known, was a more troubling and melancholy personality. His elongated forms and new, rather cold, colours were characteristic of Mannerism *(qv)*. His canon of feminine beauty influenced the Fontainebleau school and all the other European Mannerists of the 16C, through the intermediary of Niccolò dell'Abbate and Il Primaticcio.

★★★ **CITY CENTRE** *time: 1/2 day*

This historic core of the city comprises the Romanesque **episcopal centre**★★★ (**CYZ**) including the cathedral and baptistry, a most harmonious group of faded rose brick, the baroque Church of St John and the surrounding palaces as well as the Palazzo della Pilotta (16C-17C) and Correggio's Room.

★★ **Cathedral (Duomo)** (**CY**). – This is in the Lombard-Romanesque style and is flanked by an elegant Gothic campanile. The façade includes a Lombard porch supported by lions and surmounted by a loggia and three tiers of galleries with little columns. Inside, the dome is decorated with the famous frescoes painted by Correggio from 1522 to 1530. The ascending rhythm of the Assumption of the Virgin with the central figure amidst a swirling group of cherubim is remarkable. The artist's mastery of perspective and movement is expressed in an original and exuberant style virtually baroque in spirit. A **Descent from the Cross** (1178) by the Romanesque sculptor Antelami stands in the south transept.

★★ **Baptistry (Battistero)** (**CY A**). – This is Italy's most harmonious medieval monument. The octagonal building in Veronese rose-coloured marble was started in 1196 and the architecture and carved decoration, which show great unity of style, date from the 13C. The baptistry is attributed to the Parmesan sculptor Antelami who was also responsible for the sculptures; his signature appears on the lintel of the north door. Inside, the admirable 13C **frescoes** depict scenes from the Life of Christ and the Golden Legend.

St John the Evangelist's Church (San Giovanni Evangelista) (**CYZ D**). – This Renaissance church has a baroque façade. Inside, there are very fine **frescoes**★★ by Correggio (1520-24): in the apse, the Coronation of the Virgin, at the dome, the Ascension of Christ remarkable for the golden light and foreshortening. In the convent next door are the Renaissance **cloisters** ⊙.

Pharmacy (Farmacia di San Giovanni Evangelista) ⊙ (**CY N**). – *1 Borgo Pipa*. This 13C pharmacy was started by the Benedictine monks.

Palazzo della Pilotta (**BY**). – The palace was so-called because the game of fives *(pilotta)* was played in its courtyards. This rather austere building, erected by order of the Farnese from 1583 to 1622, now houses two museums, the Palatine Library and the Farnese Theatre.

★ **National Museum of Antiquities** ⊙ (**M**). – The pre-Roman and Roman exhibits include the finds made in the excavation of Velleia to the west of Parma.

★★ **National Gallery (Pinacoteca)** ⊙ (**M**). – Emilian, Tuscan and Venetian paintings of the 14C, 15C and 16C by: Leonardo da Vinci *(Head of a Young Girl)*, Fra Angelico, Dosso Dossi, El Greco, Canaletto, Bellotto, Piazzetta and Tiepolo. Il Parmigianino is represented by his astonishing portrait **Turkish Slave**, of considerable elegance, and Correggio by one of his masterpieces, **The Virgin with St Jerome** (1528), as well as other works. The last rooms are devoted to French painters who had a connection with Parma: Nattier, Largillière, Hubert Robert, Vigée-Lebrun etc.

★★ Farnese Theatre ⊙. – This delightful theatre in wood was built in 1619 by G. B. Aleotti, following the model of Palladio's Olympic Theatre in Vicenza *(qv)*.

★ Correggio's Room (Camera del Correggio) ⊙ **(CY)**. – Also known as St Paul's Room **(Camera di San Paolo)**, this was the dining-room of the Abbess of St Paul's Convent. The ceiling frescoes depicting mythological scenes with a luminous quality are Correggio's first major work (1519-20). The garlands of flowers and trelliswork and the reliefs and architectural detail at the base of the vault reveal the influence of Mantegna, whom he met in his youth in Mantua *(see p 125)*. The next room was decorated by Araldi (1504).

ADDITIONAL SIGHTS

★ Glauco-Lombardi Museum (Museo Glauco-Lombardi) ⊙ **(BY M¹)**. – The museum is chiefly devoted to life in the Duchy of Parma Piacenza in the 18C and 19C. It contains paintings and mementoes of the former Empress Marie-Louise who governed the duchy with wisdom until 1847. There are numerous works by French artists: Nattier, Mignard, Chardin, Watteau, Fragonard, Greuze, La Tour, Hubert Robert, Vigée-Lebrun, David and Millet.

Madonna della Steccata ⊙ **(BZ E)**. – This 16C church, designed by the architects Bernardino and Zaccagni, contains fine **frescoes★** by Il Parmigianino representing the Foolish and the Wise Virgins, Adam and Eve, and Moses and Aaron. The mausoleum of Neipperg, Marie-Louise's husband, is on the left, and the tombs of the Farnese family and the Bourbon-Parma are in the crypt.

Garden Palace (Palazzo del Giardino) (BY B). – The **ducal garden★** (Parco Ducale) was landscaped by the French architect Petitot and adorned by statues by another Frenchman, Boudard.

EXCURSIONS

★ Torrechiara ⊙. – *17km – 11 miles to the south by the Langhirano road.* This 15C fortress, built on a hilltop, is powerfully fortified by double ramparts, massive corner towers, a keep and machicolated curtain walls. The upper rooms (the Gaming and Gold Rooms) have remarkable **frescoes★**. From the terrace there is a superb **view★** which reaches as far as the Apennines.

Fidenza. – *23km – 14 miles to the west. Leave Parma by Via Massimo D'Azeglio* **(AY)**. This attractive agricultural town has a remarkable 11C **cathedral★** (Duomo) which was completed in the Gothic style in the 13C. The lovely sculptured decoration of the **central porch★★** is most likely the work of the Parmesan sculptor, Antelami.

Fontanellato. – *19km – 12 miles to the northwest by the Fidenza road and then the road to Soragna, to the right.* The vast moat-encircled castle, **Rocca San Vitale** ⊙, stands in the centre of town. One of the bathrooms has a **fresco★**-decorated ceiling by Il Parmigianino depicting Diana and Actaeon.

Michelin map 988 fold 13 or 428 fold 15
Town plan in the current Michelin Red Guide Italia

This proud city on the banks of the Ticino River is rich in buildings from the Romanesque and Renaissance periods.
This important military camp under the Romans then became, successively, the capital of the Lombard Kings, rival of Milan in the 11C, famous intellectual and artistic centre during the 14C under the Visconti, a fortified town in the 16C and one of the most active centres of the 19C independence movements. The university, one of the oldest and most famous in Europe, was founded in the 11C and its students included Petrarch, Leonardo da Vinci and the poet Ugo Foscolo *(Letters to Jacopo Ortiz)*.

SIGHTS

★ **Castle of the Visconti (Castello Visconteo)** ⊙. – This impressive brick building was built by the Visconti. It now houses the **Municipal Collections**★ (Musei Civici) which are rich in archaeological finds, medieval and Renaissance sculpture and particularly paintings. The **picture gallery**★, on the first floor, has numerous masterpieces including a lovely altarpiece by the Brescian artist Vincenzo Foppa, a *Virgin and Child* by Giovanni Bellini and a very expressive *Christ bearing the Cross* by the Lombard artist, Bergognone. The last room contains a 16C model of the cathedral by Fugazza after plans by Bramante.

★ **Cathedral (Duomo)**. – This vast building, surmounted by one of Italy's largest domes, was begun in 1488: both Bramante and Leonardo da Vinci are said the have worked on the plan. The façade is 19C. To the left of the façade stood an 11C municipal tower, which fell down in March 1989, while opposite is the 16C Bishop's Palace. The adjoining Piazza Vittoria is overlooked by the 12C **Broletto** or town hall. The square affords an interesting view of the cathedral's chevet.

★ **Church of St Michael (San Michele)**. – This lovely Romanesque church has a pale-coloured sandstone **façade**★ which is quite remarkable for the balance and variety of its sculptural ornamentation. An impressive Romanesque doorway on the south side has a lintel on which Christ is seen giving a papyrus volume to St Paul and the Keys of the Church to St Peter. Inside, there are some interesting architectural features (dome on squinches, the friezes and modillions beneath the galleries, the elevated chancel, mosaics, capitals etc). The apse is decorated with a lovely 15C **fresco**★ portraying the Coronation of the Virgin.

Church of St Peter (San Pietro in Ciel d'Oro). – This Lombard-Romanesque church, which was consecrated in 1132, has a richly decorated west **door**★. In the chancel is the **Arca di Sant'Agostino**★ (the tomb of St Augustine – 354-430), the work of the *maestri campionesi (qv)*.

Church of St Lanfranc (San Lanfranco). – *2 km – 1 mile to the west.* In the chancel, a **cenotaph**★ (late 15C) by Amadeo commemorates Lanfranc, who was born in Pavia and became Archbishop of Canterbury, where he is buried (d 1098).

★★★ **PAVIA CARTHUSIAN MONASTERY**

(CERTOSA DI PAVIA) Lombardy
Michelin map 988 fold 13 or 428 fold 15 – 9km – 6 miles to the north of Pavia

Pavia Carthusian Monastery

The "Gra Car", Gratiarum Cartusia (Charterhouse of the Graces), is one of the most remarkable and characteristic examples of Lombard art. It was founded as a family mausoleum in 1396 by Gian Galeazzo Visconti of Milan. Most of the monastery was built in the 15C and 16C to the plans of successive architects. The former palace of the Dukes of Milan (1625) is on the right of the courtyard, and on the left are the studios of the sculptors in charge of the decoration.

★★★ **Façade.** – Even unfinished, the façade is nevertheless famous for the care and richness of its decoration. The more ornate lower part (1473-99) was the work of the Mantegazza brothers, the famous architect and sculptor Amadeo, who worked also in Bergamo, and his pupil, Briosco. The upper part was completed in 1560 by another architect and sculptor, Cristoforo Lombardo.

The façade is adorned with multicoloured sculptures in marble, with medallions, copied from antiquities, at the base, statues of saints in the niches and an endless variety of foliage, garlands and ornaments. Round Amadeo's famous windows are scenes from the Bible, the Life of Christ and the life of Gian Galeazzo Visconti. The low reliefs round the central doorway by Briosco depict events in the history of the Carthusians. Before entering the church, walk round to the left for a general view of the late Lombard-Gothic style, with its galleries of superimposed arcades.

★★★ **Interior** ⊙. – The interior has a certain solemn grandeur and, although it is essentially Gothic, the beginnings of the Renaissance can be detected in the transept and the chancel.

There are numerous works of art. The chapels of the south aisle are decorated with late-15C frescoes by Bergognone who was also responsible for a **Crucifixion**, an altarpiece and a polyptych. The second chapel on the north side contains an **altarpiece** by Perugino. The north transept has an **Ecce Homo** by Bergognone, superb candelabra (1580) by Fontana and the famous **reclining figures** (1497) of Ludovico il Moro and Beatrice d'Este by Cristoforo Solari. The doorway to the former sacristy was the work of Amadeo. In the lavatorium there is a splendid Renaissance marble **lavabo** and a **fresco** by Luini. In the south transept stands the magnificent **tomb of Gian Galeazzo Visconti** by Cristoforo Romano dated 1497. There are two **cloisters**. The smaller one is decorated with charming terracottas and a baroque fountain. The larger one with 122 richly decorated arcades is bordered by twenty-four cells.

Avoid visiting a church during a service.

★★ **PERUGIA** Umbria   Pop 147 602

Michelin map 🄳🄳🄳 fold 15 or 🄳🄳🄳 fold 15

Perugia was one of the twelve Etruscan city-states known as *lucumonies* which comprised the federation of Etruria in the 7C and 6C BC. The massive Etruscan wall with its gateways gives some idea of the splendour of that age. The town also has numerous ecclesiastical and secular buildings from the Middle Ages. Today the capital of Umbria, in addition to being an industrial and commercial centre, is a university town.

Umbrian Painting. – In harmony with their peaceful countryside, the Umbrian painters had gentle, mystic souls. They loved landscapes with pure lines, punctuated with trees; and in their stylised compositions, the women are depicted with a tender gracefulness, sometimes too mannered. Extremely delicate draughtsmanship and soft colours characterise their technique. The masters were Giovanni Boccati (1410-85), Fiorenzo di Lorenzo (d 1520) and especially Pietro Vannucci alias **Perugino** (1445-1523), the teacher of Raphael. His favourite subjects were religious; in them he showed his sense of space, atmosphere and landscape, marred only by a touch of mannerism. The historical artist **Pinturicchio** (1454-1518) was influenced by Perugino but his charmingly realistic scenes were painted more naïvely than those of his predecessor.

★★ PIAZZA 4 NOVEMBRE (BY) *time: 2 hours*

This square in the heart of Perugia is one of the grandest in Italy. Here are grouped the chief buildings of the glorious "communal" period: the Priors' Palace, the Great Fountain and the Cathedral. Leading off from the far end of the square is the picturesque **Via Maestà delle Volte★** (ABY 29) with its medieval houses and vaulted passageways.

★★ **Great Fountain (Fontana Maggiore).** – The fountain was built to the designs of Fra Bevignate (1278) and is admirably proportioned. The sculpted panels are the work of Nicola Pisano (lower basin) and his son Giovanni (upper basin). Copies replace some of the originals, which are on display in the National Gallery of Umbria.

★★ **Priors' Palace (Palazzo dei Priori) (BY D).** – The palace was begun in the 13C and enlarged in the following centuries. It forms an ensemble of impressive grandeur. The façade overlooking the square has a majestic outside staircase leading up to a marble pulpit from which the priors harangued the people. The Corso Vannucci (BY 51) façade has a fine 14C doorway. Inside, the palace rooms are decorated with either 14C frescoes or beautifully carved 15C panelling.

★★ **National Gallery of Umbria (Galleria Nazionale dell' Umbria)** ⊙. – This collection, housed on the top floor of the Priors' Palace, has an extremely good selection of Umbrian art showing its development from the 13C to the late 18C.

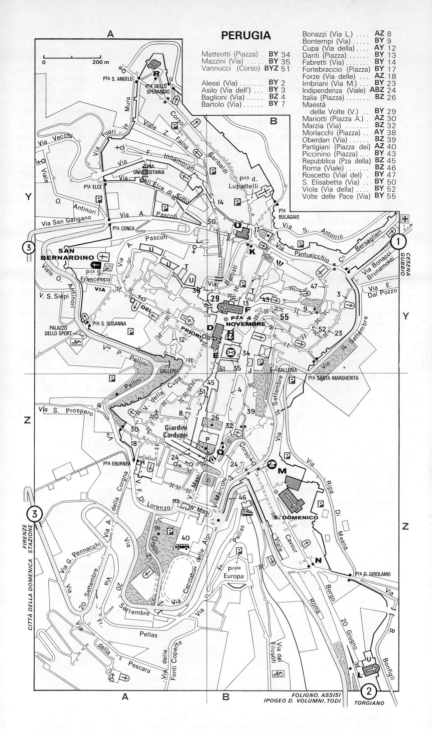

PERUGIA

Matteotti (Piazza) . **BY** 34
Mazzini (Via) ..... **BY** 35
Vannucci (Corso) **BYZ** 51

Alessi (Via) .... **BY** 2
Asilo (Via dell') ... **BY** 3
Baglioni (Via) ..... **BZ** 4
Bartolo (Via) ...... **BY** 7

Bonazzi (Via L.) .... **AZ** 8
Bontempi (Via) ..... **BY** 9
Cupa (Via della) ... **AY** 12
Danti (Piazza) ...... **BY** 13
Fabretti (Via) ...... **BY** 14
Fortebraccio (Piazza) **BY** 17
Forze (Via delle) .... **AZ** 18
Imbriani (Via M.) ... **BY** 23
Indipendenza (Viale) **ABZ** 24
Italia (Piazza) ...... **BZ** 26
Maestà
   delle Volte (V.) .. **BY** 29
Mariotti (Piazza A.) . **AZ** 30
Marzia (Via) .... **BZ** 32
Morlacchi (Piazza) .. **AY** 38
Oberdan (Via) ...... **BZ** 39
Partigiani (Piazza dei) **AZ** 40
Piccinino (Piazza) ... **BY** 43
Repubblica (Pza della) **BZ** 45
Roma (Viale) .... **BZ** 46
Roscetto (Vial del) .. **BY** 47
S. Elisabetta (Via) .. **BY** 50
Viola (Via della) .... **BY** 52
Volte delle Pace (Via) **BY** 55

On display are: a **Madonna** by Duccio, a **Crucifix** by the unknown master, Maestro di San Francesco, a **polyptych of St Anthony** by Piero della Francesca and works by Fra Angelico, Boccati and Fiorenzo di Lorenzo.

The most interesting room is that containing the masterpieces of Pinturicchio and Perugino, including a **Dead Christ** with its black background and an admirable **Madonna of Consolation**. Another room is devoted to the marble statuettes by Nicola and Giovanni Pisano from the Great Fountain, and other works by Arnolfo di Cambio. The 17C is represented by Federico Barocci, Pietro da Cortona, Orazio Gentileschi etc.

The 15C Priors' Chapel is dedicated to the city's patron saints: St Herculanus and St Louis of Toulouse, whose story is told by Benedetto Bonfigli (d 1496) in a remarkable cycle of **frescoes**. The museum also has some lovely 13C and 14C French enamels and ivories.

★ **Cathedral (Cattedrale)** (BY F). – The cathedral is Gothic, but the Piazza Danti façade was completed with a baroque doorway.

The right-hand chapel contains an interesting **Descent from the Cross** by Barocci, which inspired Rubens in his *Antwerp Descent*. In the chapel on the left are lovely 16C **stalls** with intarsia-work and a ring said to be the Virgin's wedding ring.

ADDITIONAL SIGHTS

★★ **St Peter's Church** (San Pietro) (BZ L). – To reach the church, go through the **Porta San Pietro★** (BZ N), a majestic but unfinished work of the Florentine Agostino di Duccio. The church was built at the end of the 10C and remodelled at the Renaissance. Inside are eleven excellent canvases by Vassilacchi, alias Aliense, a Greek contemporary of El Greco. Also of note are: the **carved tabernacle** by Mino da Fiesole and the marvellous 16C **stalls★★**.

★ **St Dominic's Church** (San Domenico) (BZ). – An impressive Gothic church. The interior was altered in the 17C. To the right of the chancel is the 14C **funerary monument** of Benedict XI.

★★ **National Archaeological Museum of Umbria** (Museo Archeologio Nazionale dell' Umbria) ⊙ (BZ M). – The museum comprises prehistoric, Etruscan and Umbrian sections. The remarkable collections include funerary urns, sarcophagi and Etruscan bronzes.

★ **Exchange Building** (Collegio del Cambio) ⊙ (BY E). – This was built in the 15C for the money-changers. In the courtroom (council chamber) are the famous **frescoes★★** of Perugino and his pupils. These frescoes display the humanist spirit of the age, which sought to combine ancient culture and Christian feeling. The statue of Justice is by Benedetto da Maiano (15C).

★★ **Oratory of St Bernardine** (San Bernardino) (AY). – To reach the church, walk along the picturesque **Via dei Priori★**. This Renaissance jewel (1461) by Agostino di Duccio is exquisite in its harmonious lines, the delicacy of its multicoloured marbles and its sculptures. The low reliefs on the façade display, on the tympanum, St Bernardine in glory, the life of the saint on the lintel and delightful angel musicians on the shafts.

★ **Via delle Volte della Pace** (BY 55). –The picturesque medieval street is formed by a long 14C Gothic portico as it follows the Etruscan town wall.

★ **St Angelo's Church** (Sant'Angelo) (AY R). – This small church is circular in shape and dates from the 5C-6C. The interior includes sixteen ancient columns.

★ **Porta Marzia and Via Bagliona Sotterranea** ⊙ (BZ Q). – The Etruscan gateway of the 2C BC gives access to this curious street, which runs underground and is lined with 15C and 16C houses.

★ **Etruscan Arch** (Arco Etrusco) (BY K). – This imposing structure is built of huge blocks of stone. A 16C loggia surmounts the tower on the left.
Alongside, the majestic 18C **Palazzo Gallenga** (U) serves as a summer school for foreign students.

Carducci Gardens (Giardini Carducci) (AZ). – There is a superb **view★★** from these gardens, dominating the San Pietro quarter, over the Tiber Valley.

EXCURSIONS

★ **Hypogeum** (Ipogeo dei Volumni) ⊙. – *6km – 4 miles to the southeast. Leave by ② on the town plan.*
This Etruscan cemetery hewn out of the rock, comprises an atrium and nine burial chambers. The Volumnian tomb is the largest; it contains six rounded tombstones *(cippi)*, the biggest being that of the head of the family (2C BC).

Torgiano ⊙. – *16km – 10 miles to the southeast. Leave by ② on the town plan.*
This village dominating the Tiber Valley, has an interesting **wine museum★** (Lungarotti Foundation): the exhibits include documents and photographs.

★ **PESARO** Marches   Pop 90 667

Michelin map 988 fold 16, 429 fold 36 or 430 fold 6
Town plan in the current Michelin Red Guide Italia

Pesaro is on the Adriatic coast at the mouth of the smiling Foglia Valley, which is terraced with vineyards, orchards and Italian poplars. The town was the birthplace of the composer **Gioacchino Rossini** (1792-1868), whose **house** ⊙ (No 34 Via Rossini) is now a museum.

★ **Municipal Museum** (Musei Civici) ⊙. – The **picture gallery** contains several works by the Venetian Giovanni Bellini *(qv)*. The famous **Pala di Pesaro** (1475) is an immense altarpiece representing the Virgin being crowned on the central panel and numerous other scenes on the predella.
In the **ceramics section★★** the Umbrian potteries are well represented but there are also examples of work from the Marches region.

Ducal Palace (Palazzo Ducale). – The great mass of this palace, built for a member of the Sforza family in the 15C, overlooks the Piazza del Popolo with its fountain adorned with tritons and sea horses. The crenellated façade has an arcaded portico with, above, windows adorned with festoons and cherubs.

Oliveriano Museum (Museo Oliveriano) ⊙. – *97 Via Mazza.*
Interesting collection of archaeological items of varied origins: Italic, Greek, Etruscan and Roman.

Former Church of St Dominic (San Domenico). – *In Via Branca behind the post office.* All that remains is the 14C façade with a lovely pointed doorway flanked by twisted columns and sculpture.

EXCURSION

Gradara. – *15km* – *9 miles to the northwest.*
Gradara is a medieval town, almost intact, surrounded by walls and battlemented gateways. The **Rocca**★ ⊙, built on a square plan with corner towers, is a well-preserved example of military architecture in the 13C and 14C. It is here that Gianni Malatesta is said to have surprised and then murdered his wife, Francesca da Rimini, and her lover, Paolo Malatesta. Dante portrayed the inseparable couple in his *Divine Comedy.*

★ **PIACENZA** Emilia-Romagna   Pop 104 976

Michelin map 🔳🔳🔳 fold 13 or 🔳🔳🔳 fold 26
Town plan in the current Michelin Red Guide Italia

Piacenza was originally built by the Romans at the end of the Via Emilia on the south bank of the Po. It flourished in the Middle Ages and became a member of the Lombard League *(qv)*. In 1545 Pope Paul III Farnese gave Piacenza and its neighbour Parma to his son along with the title of duke. After this its destiny was linked with that of Parma.

SIGHTS

★★ **Palazzo del Comune.** – Also called "Il Gotico", this building is a masterpiece of Lombard-Gothic architecture and has a severe but harmonious appearance. There is a curious contrast between the marble lower part and the brick upper storeys, the great openings and the elegantly-decorated windows. Standing in the square in front are two remarkable 17C **equestrian statues**★★ of Alessandro Farnese and Ranuccio I Farnese.

★ **Cathedral (Duomo).** – This remarkable Lombard-Romanesque building dates from the 12C-13C. The façade is pierced with three doorways and a rose window. The interior on the plan of a Latin cross is simple and forceful. Some of the dome frescoes are by Guercino.

Church of St Savin (San Savino). – *Near the junction of Via G. Alberoni with Via Roma.*
The crypt of this 12C church, with its very pure architectural lines, has a magnificent mosaic pavement.

Church of St Sixtus (San Sisto). – *At the northern end of Via San Sisto.*
This is a rather curious 16C building. The façade is preceded by an atrium and a doorway with rustication and grotesque masks. The interior has an interesting Renaissance decoration.

Madonna di Campagna. – *Via Campagna.*
This 16C church, in the form of a Greek cross, contains interesting frescoes, notably by the 16C Venetian Pordenone.

St Anthony's Basilica (Sant'Antonino). – *Piazza Sant'Antonino.*
This former early-Christian basilica was remodelled in the 11C and has interesting features: an octagonal tower 40m – 131ft, lanterns and north Paradise vestibule (1350) in the Gothic style.

Farnese Palace (Palazzo Farnese) ⊙. – This imposing late-Renaissance building was never completed but it now houses the **Municipal Museum** (Museo Civico). The paintings include a *Madonna and Child* by Botticelli and two cycles of frescoes, richly framed in stucco, depicting the stories of Alessandro Farnese and Pope Paul III by Draghi and Ricci. There are also collections of Murano glass, ceramics (17C-18C), Romanesque sculpture (12C), frescoes of the Lombard school (14C-15C), coats of arms and ancient arms, and an archaeological section *(organisation in progress).* A **collection of carriages** (17C-18C) and a **Risorgimento Museum** are also of interest to visitors.

Ricci Oddi Gallery of Modern Art ⊙. – *No 13 Via S. S'ro.*
The collections include Italian paintings from the various regions ranging from the Romantic period to the 20C: works by the landscape painter Antonio Fontanesi, the Macchiaioli (Fattori), artists influenced by the Impressionist school (Boldoni, Zandomeneghi), orientalising and figurative canvases (De Pisis), Futurist (Boccioni) and metaphysical (De Chirico, Carrà) paintings. There are also sculptures (Medardo Rosso) and works by foreign artists such as Klimt who influenced Italian art.

Alberoni Gallery ⊙. – *No 77 Via Emilia, opposite the university.* The gallery is situated within the precincts of a college founded in the 18C by Cardinal Alberoni, and comprises 17C-18C Flemish and Italian **tapestries** and a collection of 15C-19C paintings including an **Ecce Homo** by Antonello da Messina, and works by Flemish (Jan Provost) and 17C-18C Italian artists (Guido Reni, Baciccia, Luca Giordano).

Gourmands or gourmets
Each year the **Michelin Red Guide Italia** *gives an up-to-date selection*
of establishments renowned for their cuisine.
Italian gastronomic specialities and fine wines
are described on page 37.

Michelin map 988 fold 15 or 430 fold 14 – 52km – 32 miles to the southeast of Siena

The former town of Corsignano was renamed in honour of its most famous son, the diplomat and humanist poet, Eneo Silvio Piccolomini (1405-64), who became Pope Pius II in 1458. He commissioned the Florentine architect, **Bernardo Rossellino** (1409-82), a pupil of Alberti, to build in his native village a square which would be the focal point of an **ideal city** and would bring together the civil and religious authorities. The architectural unity of the square, which was the first example of Renaissance town planning, was intended to reflect the city's harmony. The principal monuments line the town's main axis: the people's palace opposite the cathedral has a ground-floor loggia. The other sides of the square are framed by the Bishop's Palace (simply restored in the 15C) and the Palazzo Piccolomini; a pretty well in front of the latter enhances the overall plan.
Fine **view**★ over Orcia Valley from behind the cathedral.

★ **Cathedral (Cattedrale)**. – The cathedral, which was completed in 1462, has a Renaissance façade. The interior (restored) shows Gothic influences and contains several paintings by the Sienese school, including an **Assumption**★★, a masterpiece by Vecchietta.

Cathedral Museum ⊙. – The museum contains pictures of the 14C and 15C Sienese school and a remarkable 14C historiated cope made in England.

★ **Palazzo Piccolomini** ⊙. – Rossellino's masterpiece was greatly influenced by the Palazzo Rucellai in Florence (p 102). The three sides facing the town are similar; the fourth overlooking Orcia Valley has three loggias one above the other and gives onto hanging gardens which are among the first to have been created. The elegant inner courtyard has slim Corinthian columns. The furniture dates from the 15C-16C.

EXCURSION

★ **Sant'Antimo Abbey** ⊙. – *35km – 22 miles to the southwest*. The abbey, which was founded in the 9C, stands in an isolated hill **site**★ amid cypress and olive groves. Its prosperity was at its peak in the 12C when the church was built. It is a fine example of Cistercian Romanesque architecture with Burgundian (ambulatory and apsidal chapels) and Lombard (porch, belltower with Lombard bands and façades) influences. The interior is spacious and austere. Columns topped by fine alabaster capitals divide the nave with its wooden roof from the aisles which have groined vaulting. Only some of the monastic buildings remain standing.

★★ **PISA** Tuscany   Pop 103 527

Michelin map 988 fold 14, 428 fold 37, 429 fold 32 or 430 fold 12

This calm and pleasant town, near the sea, has splendid buildings recalling the past grandeur of the Pisan Republic.

HISTORICAL NOTES

Sheltered from raiding pirates, Pisa was a Roman naval base and commercial port until the end of the Empire. It became an independent maritime republic at the end of the 9C and continued to benefit from its geographical location. Pisa became the rival of Genoa and Venice, and the Pisans waged war against the Saracens in the Mediterranean basin. It was in the 12C and the beginning of the 13C that Pisa reached the peak of its power and prosperity. This period was marked by the construction of some fine buildings and the foundation of the university.
During the 13C struggles between the Emperor and the Pope, Pisa supported the Ghibellines (qv) and thus opposed Genoa on the seas and Lucca and Florence on land. In 1284 the Pisan fleet was defeated at the **naval battle of Meloria**. Ruined and wracked by internal strife, Pisa's maritime empire foundered; Corsica and Sardinia which she had ruled since the 11C were ceded to Genoa. Pisa herself passed under Florentine rule and the Medici were particularly attentive to this city, especially in the world of science. Its most famous son was the astronomer and physicist **Galileo** (1564-1642). His patron was Cosimo II, Grand Duke of Tuscany. Nevertheless Galileo, aged seventy, had to defend his theory of the rotation of the universe before the Inquisition and in fact renounced it.

PISAN ART

The economic prosperity of the powerful maritime Pisan Republic from the 11C to the 13C fostered the development of a new art style which is particularly evident in the fields of architecture and sculpture. The **Pisan-Romanesque style**, with the cathedral as the most rigorous example, is characterised by external decoration: the alternate use of different coloured marbles to create geometric patterns, a play of light and shade due to the storeys of loggias with small columns on the upper parts of the façade, and intarsia decoration showing the strong influence of the Islamic world and of Christian countries of the Near East which had relations with the maritime republic. Alongside architects such as Buscheto, Rainaldo and Diotisalvi there were numerous sculptors to embellish the exteriors. Pisa became an important centre for Gothic sculpture in Italy, thanks to the work of **Nicola Pisano** (1220-c80), originally from Apulia, and his son **Giovanni Pisano** (1250-c1315). Their work included carved pulpits with two good examples in the Baptistry and the Cathedral, which greatly influenced the early Tuscan Renaissance.

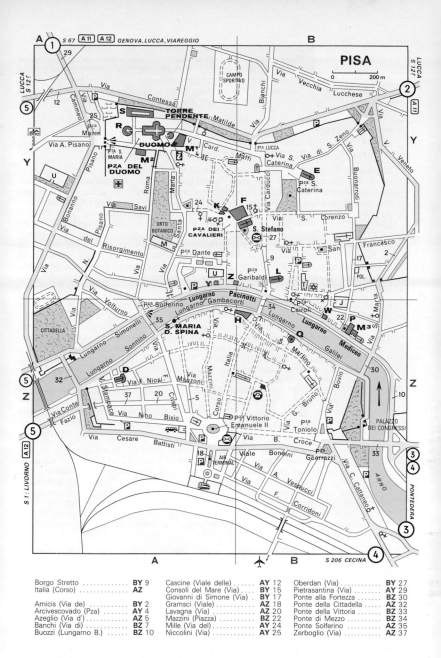

★★★ PIAZZA DEL DUOMO (AY) *time: 3 hours*

In and around this famous square, also known as Campo dei Miracoli, are four buildings which form one of the finest architectural ensembles in the world. It is advisable to approach on foot from the west through the Porta Santa Maria to enjoy the best view of the leaning tower.

★★ **Cathedral (Duomo).** – This splendid church was built with the fantastic spoils captured during the expeditions against the Muslims. Building operations started in 1063 under Buscheto and were continued by Rainaldo, who designed the façade.

The **west front★★★** is light and graceful with four tiers of small marble columns and a decorative facing of alternating light-and dark-coloured marble. The church itself is built on the plan of a Latin cross. The original doors were replaced by bronze **doors★** cast in 1602 to designs by Giovanni Bologna. The south transept door has very fine Romanesque bronze **panels★★** (late 12C) by Bonanno Pisano, depicting the Life of Christ in a naïve but free creative style.

The **interior★★**, with its nave and four aisles, is impressive for its length (100m – 328ft), its deep apse, its three-aisled transept and the forest of piers which offer an astonishing variety of perspectives. Note in particular the beautiful **pulpit★★★** of **Giovanni Pisano** on which he worked from 1302 to 1311. It is supported by six porphyry columns and five pillars decorated with religious and allegorical statues.

The eight panels of the basin evoke the Life of Christ and group a multitude of personages with dramatic expressions. Near the pulpit is the lamp of Galileo which gave the scholar his original idea for his theory concerning the movement of the pendulum.

PISA

★★★ **Leaning Tower** (Torre Pendente or Campanile). – This tower in a very pure Romanesque style serves as a campanile or belfry. Built in white marble it was begun in 1173 by Bonanno Pisano and completed in 1350. Its leaning (4m – 13ft at the top) is caused by the settling of the alluvium subsoil, which lacks the resistance to withstand the weight of the tower. Architects have tried in vain to rectify this weakness.

The tower is cylindrical, like most Byzantine ones, and comprises six open galleries, which give an illusion of spiralling upwards due to the inclination. Lower down, the blind arcades are adorned with lozenges in the true Pisan style. From the top there is a fine **view**★ of the square and the town.

★★★ **Baptistry** (Battistero) ⊙ (R). – Work began in 1153 and the two lower storeys are in the Romanesque Pisan style, while the frontons and pinnacles above the first-floor arcades are Gothic. The building is roofed with an unusual dome and has four doorways with fine carving. The majestic interior is full of light and has a diameter of 35m – 115ft. The sober decoration consists of light-and dark-coloured marble and in the centre is a lovely octagonal **font**★ (1246) by an artist from Como, Guido Bigarelli. The masterpiece of the baptistry is the admirable **pulpit**★★ (1260) by Nicola Pisano. It is less ornate than the one done by his son for the cathedral and stands on simple columns. The five panels of the basin depict the Life of Christ: its noble, classical sculptures are no doubt inspired by Roman art and the sarcophagi to be found in the neighbouring Composanto.

★★ **Cemetery** (Camposanto) ⊙ (S). – This burial ground was begun in 1277 by Giovanni di Simone, one of the architects of the leaning tower. Work was interrupted by the naval Battle of Meloria *(p 164)* and completed only in the 15C. The large rectangular area is bounded on the outside by a blind portico. Inside, the majestic semicircular arcading includes four delicate lanceolate windows with Gothic tracery. The soil in the Camposanto (Sacred Field) proper, in the centre, is said to have been brought back from the Hill of Calvary by the Crusaders. There are many Greco-Roman sarcophagi in the galleries, which are paved with about 600 tombstones. The majority of the admirable wall frescoes have been destroyed in a fire caused by artillery shelling in 1944. One of the most famous cycles comprising **The Triumph of Death**★★ and the **Last Judgement and Hell**★★★ by a 14C artist was saved and is displayed in the north gallery. The transience and vanity of wordly pleasures are illustrated with great realism.

★★ **Cathedral Museum** (Museo dell'Opera del Duomo) ⊙ (M¹). – The museum contains works of art from the monuments in Piazza del Duomo: 12C-16C sculptures (Romanesque period influenced by Islamic and Burgundian art, Gothic and Renaissance); cathedral treasure (ivory **Madonna and Child** by Giovanni Pisano) and silver ware. On the first floor are displayed 15C-18C paintings and sculpture; fragments of Renaissance stalls and 12C-13C illuminated manuscripts; episcopal vestments and ornaments; archaeological artefacts found in the early 19C in the cemetery by Carlo Lasinio, who made a series of engravings of the Camposanto frescoes.

★ **Sinopia Museum** (Museo delle Sinopie) ⊙ (M²). – This contains the sketches or *sinopias* (sketches in a reddish-brown pigment, sinopia, which came from Sinope on the Black Sea) which were under the frescoes and were brought to light by a fire following the 1944 bombing. They have been well restored and they give a good idea of the vitality and free draughtsmanship of these 13C-15C painters.

ADDITIONAL SIGHTS

★ **Piazza dei Cavalieri** (AY). – This, the historic centre of Pisa, gets its name from the Cavalieri di Santo Stefano (Knights of St Stephen), a military order which specialised in the struggle against the infidels. Around the square are: the **Palazzo dei Cavalieri** (ABY F) with a **façade**★ decorated by Vasari; the **Church of St Stephen** (Santo Stefano) (BY) built in 1569 with its white, green and pink marble façade; and the **Palazzo Gherardesca** (AY K) designed in 1607 by Vasari to stand on the site of a former prison, Torre della Fame, where Count Ugolino della Gherardesca and his children were condemned to die by starvation, having been accused of treason after the naval defeat at Meloria.

Church of St Catherine (Santa Caterina) (BY E). – The Church has a graceful Pisan-Gothic **façade**★. Inside are statues by Nino Pisano, in particular an Annunciation, (on either side of the chancel).

Church of St Michael (San Michele in Borgo) (BY L). – The **façade**★ of this church is an excellent example of the transitional Pisan Romanesque-Gothic style.

The quays. – Prestigious palaces line the quays, **Lungarno Pacinotti** (ABY) and **Lungarno Mediceo** (BZ), notably **Palazzo Upezzinghi** (AY Y), a 17C building now occupied by the university; **Palazzo Agostini**★ (ABY Z), a 15C mansion with a highly-decorated entrance front (the Caffè dell'Ussero was the haunt of the Risorgimento poets) with on the opposite bank the Palazzo Gambacorti (BZ H), a late-14C building; Palazzo Toscanelli (BZ W) where Byron wrote *Don Juan;* and the Palazzo Medici (BZ P), a 13C-14C palace.

★★ **National Museum** (Museo Nazionale) ⊙ (BZ M³). – This museum displays the works of medieval sculptors such as Giovanni Pisano and his school. Of particular note is the **Annunciation** by Andrea Pisano and a delightful **Nursing Madonna** by Nino Pisano. The numerous paintings include **St Paul** by Masaccio and a **polyptych** by Simone Martini.

Church of the Holy Sepulchre (San Sepolcro) (BZ Q). – This 12C building in the form of a pyramid was built by Diotisalvi. Inside, the nobly-proportioned **chancel**★ is roofed with a tall dome. There is also the tomb of Maria Mancini, Louis XIV's mistress and Mazarin's niece who came to Pisa to die in 1715.

★★ **Church of St Mary of the Thorn** (Santa Maria della Spina) ⊙ (AZ). – This early-14C church resembles a finely-worked reliquary shrine with all its gables, pinnacles, statues and statuettes by the two Pisano, their assistants and followers. Some of the originals have been replaced by replicas.

EXCURSIONS

★ **San Piero a Grado.** – *6km – 4 miles to the southwest. Leave by ⑤, the Via Conte Fazio.* The Romanesque **basilica**★ stands on the spot on which St Peter is said to have landed when he came from Antioch. The apse with its three apsidal chapels is remarkable.

Viareggio. – *20km – 12 miles to the northwest. Leave by ① on the town plan.* This fashionable seaside resort, on the Tyrrhenian Coast, has some lovely beaches and plenty of amenities for holidaymakers. At **Torre del Lago Puccini** *(5km – 3 miles to the southeast)* the composer Puccini wrote *La Bohème, Tosca* and *Madame Butterfly.* The **Villa Puccini** ⊙ has the tomb and other mementoes of Puccini.

★ # PISTOIA Tuscany   Pop 90 505

Michelin map 988 fold 14, 428 fold 38, 429 fold 33 or 430 fold 3
Town plan in the current Michelin Red Guide Italia

This industrial town has a rich historic centre which is evidence of its importance in the 12C-14C. Both Lucca and Florence coveted Pistoia, but it was Florence and the Medici who annexed it for good in 1530.

★★ **PIAZZA DEL DUOMO** *time: 1 hour*

This is a most attractive and well-proportioned square lined with elegant secular and religious buildings.

★ **Cathedral** (Duomo). – Rebuilt in the 12C and 13C, the cathedral's **façade**★ is a harmonious blend of the Pisan-Romanesque style (tiers of colonnaded galleries) and the Florentine-Renaissance style (porch with slender columns added in the 14C). The lower part of the campanile is quite massive but it becomes more graceful towards the top with three tiers of colonnaded galleries. The interior was remodelled in the 17C. Inside is the famous **altar of St James**★★★ ⊙, a masterpiece of silversmith work dating from the 13C, which was modified and extended in the following centuries. The saints surround the apostle seated in a niche, with Christ in Glory above. Scenes from the Old and New Testaments complete the composition. In the chapel to the left of the chancel is a lovely **Madonna in Majesty**★ (*c*1480) by Lorenzo di Credi.

★ **Baptistry** (Battistero) ⊙. – This Gothic octagonal baptistry with polychrome marble facing dates from the 14C. The tympanum of the central doorway bears a statue of the **Virgin and Child** between St Peter and St John the Baptist, attributed to Nino and Tommaso Pisano.

Palazzo Pretorio. – This palace was built in the 14C as the residence of the governing magistrate *(podestà)* and remodelled in the 19C.

Town Hall (Palazzo del Comune). – It was built from 1294 to 1385 and has a graceful arcaded façade with elegant paired windows or triple bays. The palace houses the **Municipal Museum** (Museo Civico) ⊙ with a collection of paintings from the 13C-16C Tuscan school.

Tau Palace (Palazzo del Tau). – *Corso Siciliano Fedi.* This former monastery of the Order of the Hospitallers of St Anthony was built in the 14C and owes its name to the T motif in blue enamel which appeared on the monks' habit. It houses a **documentation centre** ⊙ on the 20C sculptor **Marino Marini** (1901-80).

ADDITIONAL SIGHTS

Hospital (Ospedale del Ceppo). – The portico on the façade has a magnificent **frieze**★★ in terracotta (1530) by Giovanni della Robbia, brightly coloured and expressive, showing the Seven Works of Mercy.

★ **Church of St Andrew** (Sant'Andrea). – This church in the pure Pisan-Romanesque style has a famous **pulpit**★★ executed (1298-1308) by Giovanni Pisano in his dramatic but intensely lively manner: the panels represent five scenes from the Life of Christ. The lovely **crucifix**★ in gilded wood is by Giovanni Pisano *(in a niche beyond the first altar on the right).*

Church of St John outside the City (San Giovanni Fuorcivitas). – This church, built from the 12C to the 14C, has a long and spectacular **north façade**★ in the Pisan-Romanesque style. Inside, there is a **pulpit**★ (1270) by Fra Guglielmo from Pisa, a polyptych by Taddeo Gaddi *(to the left of the altar)* and an admirable glazed terracotta of the **Visitation**★★ by Luca della Robbia.

Church of St Bartholomew (San Bartolomeo in Pantano). – This church in the Pisan-Romanesque style has a lovely sculptured doorway, and a beautiful **pulpit**★ (1250) by Guido da Como.

EXCURSION

★ **Vinci** ⊙. – *24km – 15 miles to the south.* The great Leonardo da Vinci was born not far from this town. The castle has a **museum** (Museo Vinciano) and **library** (Biblioteca Leonardiana) in honour of its famous son.
The **birthplace** ⊙ of the artist lies 2km – 1 mile to the north amidst olive trees, bathed in a pellucid light.

POLICASTRO (GULF) Campania – Basilicata – Calabria

Michelin map ▨▨▨ fold 38

This magnificent gulf extending from the tip of Infreschi to Praia a Mare is backed by high mountains whose sharp, needle-like peaks soar skywards.
The lower slopes are planted with cereals and olive groves with clumps of chestnut trees above. Between Sapri and Praia a Mare the corniche road overlooks the green-coloured waters which lap the charming creeks. A series of small villages succeed one another along this enchanting coast.

★★ **Maratea.** – This seaside resort has many beaches and creeks and its hotels and villas are hidden behind a screen of luxuriant vegetation. The village itself is spread over the slopes of Monte Biagio, on the summit of which stands the Basilica of San Biagio and the great white figure of the 22m – 72ft tall Statue of the Redeemer, the work of Innocenti (1965). Nearby there is a superb **panorama**★★ of the Gulf of Policastro and the Calabrian coast.

★★★ POMPEII Campania   Pop 25 156

Michelin map ▨▨▨ fold 27 – Local map p 147

Pompeii, the opulent town which was buried in AD 79 in one of the most disastrous volcanic eruptions, provides first-class evidence of the ancient way of life. The extensive and varied ruins of this dead city, in its attractive setting, movingly evoke on a grand scale a Roman city at the time of the Empire.

HISTORICAL NOTES

Pompeii was founded in the 8C BC by the Oscans, but by the 6C BC a Greek influence was already prevalent in the city from its neighbour Cumae, which was then a powerful Greek colony. From the end of the 5C BC, when it became Samnite, to the beginning of the 1C AD the city knew great prosperity, when town planning and art flourished. In the year 80 BC, the town fell under Roman domination and then it became a favourite resort of rich Romans. Roman families settled there. Pompeii adopted Roman organisation, language, life style, building methods and decoration. When the eruption of Vesuvius struck, Pompeii was a booming town with a population of about 25 000. The town was situated in a fertile region, trade flourished and there was even some industrial activity; it also had a port. The numerous shops and workshops which have been uncovered, its wide streets and the deep ruts made in the cobblestones by chariot wheels are evidence of the intense activity that went on in the town.
The people had a lively interest in spectacles, games and active politics. In the year AD 62, an earthquake extensively damaged the town but before all could be put to rights, Vesuvius erupted (August AD 79) and also destroyed Herculaneum and Stabiae. In the space of two days Pompeii was buried under a layer of cinder 6m to 7m – 20ft to 23ft deep. Bulwer-Lytton describes these events in *The Last Days of Pompeii.*
It was only in the 18C, under the reign of Charles of Bourbon, that systematic excavations began. The finds had a tremendous effect in Europe, creating a revival of antique art and the development of a so-called Pompeiian style.

ARCHITECTURE AND DECORATION

Building methods. – Pompeii was destroyed before a degree of uniformity in building methods had been achieved and it presents examples of the diverse methods and materials used: **opus quadratum** (large blocks of freestone piled on top of one another, without mortar of any kind); **opus incertum** (irregularly-shaped blocks of tufa or lava bonded with mortar); **opus reticulatum** (small square blocks of limestone or tufa arranged diagonally to form a decorative pattern); **opus testaceum** (walls are faced with triangular bricks laid flat with the pointed end turned inwards). Sometimes the walls were faced with plaster or marble. There are several types of dwelling in Pompeii: the sober and severe house of the Samnites, which became larger and more richly decorated through Greek influence. With the arrival of the Romans and the problems arising from a growing population, a new kind of house evolved in which limited space is compensated for by richness of decoration.

Pompeiian painting. – A large number of paintings which adorned the walls of the dwellings have been transferred to the Archaeological Museum in Naples. However, a visit to the dead city gives a good idea of the pictorial decoration of the period. There are four different **styles**. The 1st style by means of relief and light touches of colour imitates marble. The 2nd style is by far the most attractive of all: walls are divided into large panels by fake pillars surmounted by pediments or crowned by a small shrine, with false doors all designed to create an illusion of perspective.

POMPEII

The artists show a partiality for the famous Pompeiian red, cinnabar obtained from mercury sulphide, and a dazzling black, both of which make for a very striking style. The 3rd style abandoned false relief in favour of scenes and landscapes altogether more ethereal and painted in pastel colours. Most of the frescoes uncovered at Pompeii belong to the 4th style. It combines elements from the 2nd style with others from the 3rd style to produce ornate compositions.

THE DEAD CITY ⏲ *time: allow 1 day – access by several gates*

Sea Gate (Porta Marina). – This was the gateway through which the road passed to go down to the sea. There are separate gates for animals and for pedestrians.

★★ **Antiquarium.** – This contains historical records, objects in daily use and reconstructions of mills. There are mouldings of human beings and animals in the attitudes in which they died.

Streets. – The streets are straight and intersect at right angles. They are sunk between raised pavements and are interrupted at intervals by blocks of stone to enable pedestrians to cross without getting down from the pavement. This was particularly useful on rainy days when the roadway was awash; these stepping stones were positioned so as to leave enough space for chariots. Fountains, of simple design, adorned square basins all similar.

★★★ **Forum (Foro).** – This was the centre of the town and the setting for most of the large buildings. In this area, religious ceremonies were held, trade was carried out and justice was dispensed. The immense square was paved with broad marble flagstones and adorned with statues of past emperors. A portico surmounted by a terrace enclosed it on three sides.
The **Basilica★★**, the largest building in Pompeii, measures 67m by 25m – 220ft by 82ft. Judicial affairs and business were conducted there.
The **Temple of Apollo★★** (Tempio di Apollo), built before the Roman occupation, stood against the majestic background of Vesuvius. The altar was placed in front of the steps leading to the shrine *(cella)*. Facing each other are copies of the statues of Apollo and Diana found on the spot (the originals are in the Naples Museum). The **Horreum**, a warehouse probably used for storing cereals, has a display of archaeological artefacts.
The **Temple of Jupiter★★** (Tempio di Giove), in the place of honour, is flanked by two triumphal arches, formerly faced with marble.
The **Macellum** was a large covered market lined with shops. In the centre, a kiosk surrounded by pillars and crowned by a dome contained a basin.
The **Temple of Vespasian** (Tempio di Vespasiano) contained a marble altar adorned with a sacrificial scene.
A fine doorway with a marble frame decorated with carvings of plants gave access to the **Building of Eumachia** (Edificio di Eumachia), built by the priestess for the powerful guild of the *fullones (see below)* of which she was the patron.

★ **Triangular Forum (Foro Triangolare).** – There are several Ionic columns of a majestic propylaeum which preceded the forum. A few vestiges of its small **Doric temple** provide rare evidence of the town's existence in the 6C BC.

★ **Great Theatre (Teatro Grande).** – The theatre was built in the 5C BC, remodelled in the Hellenistic period (200-150 BC) and again by the Romans in the 1C AD. It was an open-air theatre which could be covered by a canopy and could accommodate 5 000 spectators.

Gladiators' Barracks (Caserma dei Gladiatori). – This has a large esplanade bounded by a gateway, originally used as a foyer for the theatres.

★★ **Odeon.** – Odeons, or covered theatres, were used for concerts, oratorical displays and ballets. This held only 800 spectators. It had a wooden roof and it dates from the early days of the Roman colonisation.

★ **Temple of Isis (Tempio d'Iside).** – This small temple is dedicated to the Egyptian goddess Isis, adopted by the Romans, who were very liberal in their choice of gods.

House of Lucius Ceius Secundus (Casa di L.C. Secundus). – This is an interesting house with its façade faced with stucco in imitation of stone as in the 1st style, and with its pretty little *atrium*.

★★ **House of Menander (Casa del Menandro).** – This large patrician villa, richly decorated with paintings (4th style) and mosaics, had its own baths. Part of the building was reserved for the servants' quarters. There is a Tuscan *atrium (p 25)* with a *lararium* arranged as a small shrine in one corner. It has a remarkable peristyle with Doric columns faced with stucco, between which stands a low wall adorned with plants and animals.
The house opens onto **Via dell' Abbondanza★★**, a commercial street which is now most evocative with its shops and houses.

House of the Cryptoporticus (Casa del Criptoportico). – *No 2, Via dell' Abbondanza.*
After passing through the peristyle (note the painting in the *lararium*: Mercury with a peacock, snakes and foliage), go down to the Cryptoporticus, a wide underground passage surmounted by a fine barrel vault lit by small windows. This type of corridor, which was very popular in Roman villas during the Empire, was used as a passage and for exercise as it was sheltered from the sun and from bad weather.

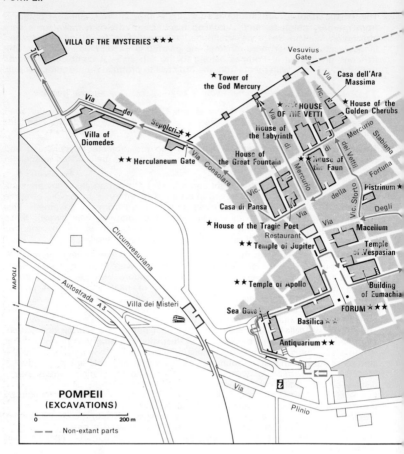

POMPEII (EXCAVATIONS)

0 ——— 200 m

- - - Non-extant parts

★★ **Fullonica Stephani.** – *No 7, Via dell' Abbondanza.*
This is an example of a dwelling-house converted into workshops. The clothing industry flourished in Roman times as the full, draped costume required a lot of material. In the *fullonicae,* new fabrics were finished and clothes were laundered. Several of these workshops have been uncovered in Pompeii. The **fullones** (fullers) cleaned the cloths by trampling them underfoot in vats filled with a mixture of water and soda or urine.

★ **Thermopolium of Asellina (Termopolio di Asellina).** – This was a bar which also sold pre-cooked dishes. A stone counter giving directly onto the street formed the shop front; jars embedded in the counter contained the food for sale.

Great Thermopolium (Termopolio Grande). – Similar to the previous one, this bar has a painted *lararium.*

House of Trebius Valens (Casa di Trebius Valens). – The inscriptions on the wall are electoral slogans. At the far end of the peristyle the polychrome fresco is in imitation of a stone wall.

★ **House of Loreius Tiburtinus (Casa di Loreius Tiburtinus).** – This was a rich dwelling, judging from the fine marble *impluvium,* the *triclinium* adorned with frescoes and the **decoration★** against a white background of one of the rooms, which is among the best examples of the 4th Pompeiian style. But its most luxurious feature was the splendid **garden★** which was laid out for water displays.

★ **Villa of Julia Felix (Villa di Giulia Felice).** – Built just within the town boundary, it has three main parts: the dwelling, the baths which the owner opened to the public, and a section for letting including an inn and shops. The large garden is bounded by a fine **portico★** and embellished by a fine series of basins.

★ **Amphitheatre (Anfiteatro).** – This is the oldest Roman amphitheatre known (80 BC). Alongside is the great **palestra** used as a training ground by athletes.

★ **Necropolis at the Nocera Gate.** – According to custom, tombs line one of the roads leading out of town.
Take the Via di Porta Nocera to return to the Via dell' Abbondanza, then turn left.

★★★ **Stabian Baths (Terme Stabiane).** – *See plan p 171 and details of Roman baths p 26.*
These baths, the best preserved and most complete in Pompeii, are divided into sections for men and women. The entrance is through the *palestra* (**A**) for athletic games, to the left of which is a swimming pool, *piscina* (**B**), with adjacent changing-rooms, *spogliatoio* (**C**).

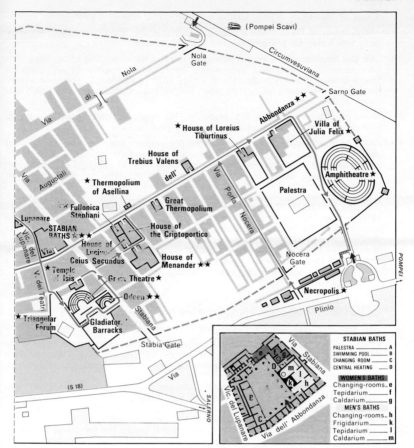

The **women's baths** begin at the far end on the right, with changing-rooms (**e**) fitted with lockers, a *tepidarium* (lukewarm, **f**) and a *caldarium* (hot, **g**). The central heating apparatus (**D**) is between the men's and women's baths. The **men's baths** have large, well preserved changing-rooms (**h**), a *frigidarium* (cold, **k**), a *tepidarium* (**l**) and a *caldarium* (**m**). There is a fine stucco decoration on the coffered ceiling.

Lupanare. – The decorations are licentious.

★ **Pistrinum.** – Baker's oven and flourmills.

★★ **House of the Faun (Casa del Fauno).** – This vast, luxurious house had two atriums, two peristyles and dining-rooms for all seasons. The bronze original of the famous statuette of the faun that adorned one of the impluviums is in the Naples Museum. The rooms contained admirable mosaics including the famous Battle of Alexander (Naples Museum) which floored the area between the two peristyles.

House of the Labyrinth (Casa del Labirinto). – One of the rooms opening onto the peristyle has a mosaic of the labyrinth with Theseus killing the Minotaur.

★★★ **House of the Vettii (Casa dei Vettii).** – The Vettii brothers were rich merchants. Their dwelling, the most lavishly decorated in the town, is the finest example of a house and garden that have been faithfully restored. The reroofed *atrium* opens directly onto the peristyle surrounding a delightful garden with statues, basins and fountains.
The **frescoes** in the *triclinium*, on the right of the peristyle, depicting mythological scenes and friezes of cupids, are among the finest from antiquity.

★ **House of the Golden Cherubs (Casa degli Amorini Dorati).** – This house shows the refinement of the owner, who probably lived during the reign of Nero, and his taste for the theatre. The glass and gilt medallions depicting cupids have deteriorated. But the building as a whole, with its remarkable peristyle with one wing raised like a stage, is well preserved. There is an obsidian mirror set in the wall near the passage between the peristyle and *atrium*.

Casa dell' Ara Massima. – Well-preserved **paintings★** (one in *trompe-l'œil*).

★ **Tower of the God Mercury (Torre di Mercurio).** – A tower on the town wall now affords an interesting **view★★** of the excavations.

House of the Great Fountain (Casa della Fontana Grande). – Its main feature is the large **fountain★** shaped as a niche decorated with mosaics and fragments of coloured glass in the Egyptian style.

★ **House of the Tragic Poet (Casa del Poeta Tragico).** – This house takes its name from a mosaic now in the Naples Museum. A mosaic of a watchdog at the threshold bears the inscription *Cave Canem* (Beware of the dog).

171

Casa di Pansa. – A very spacious house partly converted for letting.

★★ **Herculaneum Gate (Porta Ercolano).** – This was the main gateway of Pompeii, with two gates for pedestrians and one for vehicles.

★★ **Via dei Sepolcri.** – A great melancholy feeling pervades this street lined with mounumental tombs and cypresses. There are examples of all forms of Greco-Roman funerary architecture: tombs with niches, small round or square temples, altars resting on a plinth, drum-shaped mausoleums, simple semicircular seats or exedrae...

Villa of Diomedes (Villa di Diomede). – This important dwelling has a loggia overlooking the garden and the swimming pool.

★★★ **Villa of the Mysteries (Villa dei Misteri).** – *Access possible by car.* Standing outside the city walls, this patrician villa, although it has lost much of its ornamentation, still comprises numerous rooms. Near the present entrance were the outbuildings *(partly excavated)*. These were reserved for all domestic or agricultural work and as the servants' quarters.

In the main dwelling, the room on the right contains the splendid **fresco** for which the villa is famous. This vast composition, which fills the whole room, depicts against a Pompeiian red background the initiation of a young bride to the mysteries of the cult of Dionysus (Child reading the rites; scenes of offerings and sacrifices; flagellation; nuptials of Ariadne and Dionysus; dancing Bacchante; dressing of the bride). The mistress of this house was probably a priestess of the cult of Dionysus, which was then very popular in southern Italy. There is a fine peristyle and an underground passage *(criptoportico).*

★★ POMPOSA ABBEY Emilia-Romagna

Michelin map ▨▨▨ fold 15 or ▨▨▨ fold 25 – 49km – 30 miles east of Ferrara

Pomposa ⊙, a Benedictine Abbey, founded in the 6C, enjoyed great fame in the Middle Ages, especially from the 10C to the 12C, when it was distinguished by its Abbot, St Guy (Guido) of Ravenna, and by another monk, Guido d'Arezzo, the inventor of the musical scale.

The fine Pre-Romanesque **church**★★ in the style of Ravenna is preceded by a narthex whose decoration exemplifies the Byzantine style. To the left, an admirable Romanesque campanile (1063) is remarkable for the progression in the number and size of its windows, and the elegant simplicity of the Lombard bands and arches adorning its nine storeys; and finally, the variety of geometric decoration obtained by the use of bricks.

The nave has some magnificent mosaic **paving**, a Romanesque stoup and a second in the Byzantine style. The walls bear an exceptional cycle of 14C **frescoes** based on the illuminator's art. From right to left the upper band is devoted to the Old Testament-while the lower band has scenes from the Life of Christ; the corner pieces of the arches depict the Apocalypse. On the west wall are a Last Judgement and in the apsidal chapel Christ in Majesty.

Opposite the church stands the Palazzo della Ragione, where the abbot dispensed justice.

★★★ PORTOFINO PENINSULA Liguria

Michelin map 988 fold 13 or 428 fold 25

This rocky, rugged promontory offers one of the most attractive landscapes on the Italian Riviera. The coastline is dotted with small villages in sheltered bays. Part of the peninsula has been designated as a **Nature Reserve** (Parco Naturale) to protect the fauna and flora. By taking the corniche roads and the numerous footpaths the visitor can discover the secret charms of this region.

★★★ PORTOFINO

To reach the port which gave the peninsula its name, take the road that passes via **Santa Margherita Ligure★** *(5km – 3 miles)*, a fashionable seaside resort, and then the **corniche road★★** (Strada Panoramica) which affords lovely views of the rocky coast. This small fishing village with its gaily-coloured houses lies at the head of a sheltered creek *(photograph p 16)*. The **walk to the lighthouse★★★** *(1 hour on foot Rtn)* is beautiful, especially in the evening, when the setting sun shines on the Gulf of Rapallo. Wonderful views unfold between the olive trees, yews and sea pines.

From the **castle** ⊘ – formerly Castello San Giorgio *(take the stairway which starts near the harbour and the Church of San Giorgio)* – there are splendid **views★★★** of Portofino and the Gulf of Rapallo. Continue along the pathway to the lighthouse, from where the view extends right round the coast as far as La Spezia.

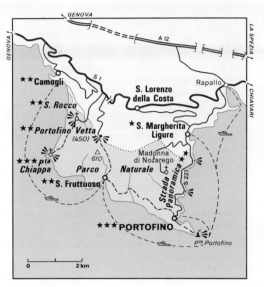

EXCURSIONS

San Lorenzo della Costa. – *10km – 6 miles*.
At Santa Margherita Ligure take the **scenic road★★** which offers a succession of lovely views over the Gulf of Rapallo. The **Church of San Lorenzo** contains a **triptych★** (1499) by an artist from Bruges. It may have been the work of Gerard David (Gheeraert Davit) who spent some time in Genoa.

★★ **Portofino Vetta** ⊘. – *14km – 9 miles by a toll road*.
From this elevated site (450m – 1 476ft) there is a lovely view of the peninsula and the Ligurian coast.

★★ **San Fruttuoso**. – *There is no road suitable for cars to this village*.

On foot: *take the signposted footpath starting in Portofino (4 1/2 hours Rtn) or another from Portofino Vetta, but the final stages are difficult (3 hours Rtn)*.

By boat: *services operate from Rapallo, Santa Margherita Ligure, Portofino and Camogli*. This delightful fishing village stands at the head of a narrow cove in the shadow of Monte Portofino.

★★ **San Rocco's Belvedere**. – *13km – 8 miles*.
From the terrace beside the church there is a view of Camogli and the western coast from the headland, Punta Chiappa, right round to Genoa. A path leads to **Punta Chiappa★★★** *(2 1/2 hours on foot Rtn by a stepped footpath which starts to the right of the church)*. There are unforgettable views of the peninsula and, from the chapel, of the Genoa Coast.

★★ **Camogli**. – *15km – 9 miles*.
Tall houses crowd round a small harbour.

POTENZA Basilicata   Pop 67 394

Michelin map 988 fold 28 – Town plan in the current Michelin Red Guide Italia

Potenza overlooks the upper Basento Valley with wide mountain views. The ancient town, founded by the Romans, flourished during the Empire. Today it is an active town, the growth of which was favoured by the development of the road and rail networks in the region. Its tall, modern buildings, curiously terraced, make an unusual sight which is quite dazzling by night. The old town suffered extensive damage in the 1980 earthquake. The 13C **Church of San Francesco**, with its lovely Renaissance **doorway★** carved in wood, contains a marble Renaissance tomb and a 13C Madonna.

Potenza is situated in the district of **Lucania**, an indescribably wild region which is ravaged by erosion.

★ **POZZUOLI** Campania Pop 74 196

Michelin map 988 fold 27 – 16km – 10 miles west of Naples – Local map p 146

Pozzuoli, which is of Greek origin, became an active trading port under the Romans. As the town is at the centre of the volcanic area known as the Phlegrean Fields *(qv)* and is constantly affected by changes in the ground level which occur in this region, the town centre has been evacuated.

The town has given its name to *pozzolana*, a volcanic ash with a high silica content which is used in the production of certain kinds of cement.

★★ **Amphitheatre (Anfiteatro Flavio)** ⊙. – *Corso Terracciano.*

This amphitheatre is one of the largest in Italy and dates from the reign of Vespasian, the founder of the Flavian dynasty. It could accommodate 40 000 spectators. Built of brick and stone, it is relatively well preserved: note the outer walls, the entrances and the particularly well-preserved **basements**★★.

★ **Temple of Serapis (Tempio di Serapide)**. – *Set back from Via Roma.*

The temple, which is situated near the sea, was really the ancient market place and was lined with shops. There is a sort of apse in the end wall which contained the statue of Serapis, the protecting god of traders. The central edifice shows the effects of variations in ground level: the columns show signs of marine erosion.

★ **Temple of Augustus (Tempio di Augusto)**. – The temple dated from the early days of the Empire and was converted into a Christian church in the 11C. A recent fire has revealed a grandiose marble colonnade with its entablature.

★★ **Solfatara** ⊙. – *2km – 1 mile to the northeast by the Naples road.*

Although extinct, this crater still has some of the features of an active volcano such as jets of steam charged with sulphurous fumes, strong-smelling and with traces of yellow, miniature volcanoes spitting hot mud and bubbling jets of sand. The ground sounds hollow and the surface is hot. The sulphurous vapours have been used for medicinal purposes since Roman times.

★ **PRATO** Tuscany Pop 164 824

Michelin map 988 fold 14, 429 fold 33 or 430 fold 3

In spite of the peaceful and provincial air of its old quarter, Prato is a bustling and important town which has developed with the textile industry since its early beginnings in the 13C. For a long time Prato was in conflict with Florence, but in 1351 she fell under the sway of her illustrious neighbour and remained thus until the 18C. In the 14C a fortified wall in the form of a hexagon was erected around the old town.

Garibaldi (Via)	B	Dante (Via)	B 12	S. Domenico (Piazza)	A 34
Guasti (Via Cesare)	A 13	Guizzelmi (Via)	A 15	S. Francesco (Piazza)	A 35
Mazzoni (Via G.)	B 20	Lippi (Via)	B 16	S. Jacopo (Via)	AB 37
Ricasoli (Via)	A 32	Martini Arcivesco (V.A.)	B 18	S. Marco (Piazza)	B 38
		Mazzini (Via G.)	B 19	S. Maria d. Carceri (Pza)	B 42
Abbaco (Via P. dell')	A 2	Misericordia (V. della)	A 22	S. Silvestro (Via)	B 40
Bettino (Via)	B 3	Monte Grappa (Viale)	B 24	Savonarola (Corso)	A 43
Bologna (Via)	AB 4	Muzzi (Via L.)	A 25	Serraglio (Via del)	B 45
Cairoli (Via)	B 5	Pellegrino (Via)	A 27	Simintendi (Via A.)	B 46
Cambioni (Via)	A 6	Ponte Mercatale	B 28	Stufa (V. della)	A 48
Carducci (Largo)	A 9	Porta Serraglio (V. di)	A 30	Tintori (Via de')	B 50

SIGHTS

★ **Cathedral (Duomo) (B)**. – This church, built in the 12C and 13C and extended in later centuries, presents a harmonious blend of the Romanesque and Gothic styles. The façade, with its partial facing of white stone and green marble, owes its elegance to its lofty central part, its finely carved decoration and the graceful circular pulpit with its canopy (15C) by Michelozzo. The south side has blind arcading in the true Pisan tradition. The campanile has a Gothic upper storey. The interior of the church, sober in style, has massive columns of green marble and numerous works of art: the **Chapel of the Holy Girdle** (Capella del Sacro Cingolo) contains the precious relic which the Virgin had given to Thomas as proof of her Assumption. The girdle was brought from Jerusalem by a citizen of Prato in the 12C. The chapel is enclosed by two delicately worked bronze **screens★** and decorated with frescoes (1392-95) by Agnolo Gaddi and his pupils. **The Virgin and Child★** (1317) is by the sculptor Giovanni Pisano. The **frescoes★★** by **Filippo Lippi** in the axial chapel form a striking picture of the lives of St Stephen and St John the Baptist. From 1452 to 1465 this artistic monk, renowned for his libertine ways, painted this masterpiece with its pleasantly fresh colours and spontaneous attitudes: the graceful melancholy of the feminine figures in two scenes, the **Banquet of Herod★★★** and **Salome's Dance**, are more typical of the work of one of his pupils, Botticelli. On the walls of the chapel to the right are **frescoes★** started by Paolo Uccello and completed by Andrea di Giusto. Note also the marble **pulpit★** with the original shape of a chalice, and in a niche a moving **Virgin with an Olive★**, a terracotta statue (1480) by Benedetto da Maiano.

Cathedral Museum (Museo dell' Opera del Duomo) ⊙ **(B M)**. – This is housed in several rooms overlooking a delightful courtyard. Amongst the exhibits are the seven **panels★** carved from 1428 to 1438 by Donatello for the pulpit from which the Holy Girdle used to be displayed. The pulpit was set on the corner of the cathedral's west front. Also on display are pieces of ecclesiastical plate and paintings by Filippino Lippi, the son of Filippo, who was born in Prato around 1457.

★ **Palazzo Pretorio (A A)**. – This austere and massive building, a curious mixture of the Romanesque and Gothic styles, overlooks a charming small square, **Piazza del Comune**, with a gracious bronze fountain (1659) by Tacca. Three floors of the building are occupied by the **Municipal Gallery** (Galleria Comunale) which presents works by the 14C and 15C Tuscan school and notably an important collection of **polyptychs★** by Bernardo Daddi, Lorenzo Monaco, Filippo Lippi etc. There are also works by the Neapolitan Caracciolo (17C) and the Dutchman Van Wittel the Elder.

★ **Imperial Castle (Castello dell' Imperatore) (B)**. – This is one of the rare existing examples in northern and central Italy of a castle built by the Emperor Frederick II of Hohenstaufen. This imposing structure, on a square plan around a central courtyard, has massive walls with very few openings and enormous projecting towers. The castle is modelled on Castel del Monte *(qv)* in the south. With its cleft Ghibelline crenellations, this fortified stronghold guarded the route between the emperor's northern empire and his Kingdom of Sicily in the south.

Santa Maria delle Carceri (B K). – This attractive late-15C building was designed by Giuliano da Sangallo. The **interior★** displays both a severity and a nobility typical of Florentine architecture as influenced by Brunelleschi.

Church of St Francis (San Francesco) (AB D). – This church was built from the 13C to the 15C. The chapterhouse has **frescoes★** by Nicolo di Pietro Gerini, a Florentine artist who was influenced by Giotto.

*The current **Michelin Red Guide Italia** offers
a selection of pleasant hotels in convenient locations.*

*Each entry specifies the facilities available
(gardens, tennis courts, swimming pool, beach facilities)
and the annual opening and closing dates.*

*There is also a selection of establishments recommended for their
cuisine – well-prepared meals at moderate prices; stars for good cooking.*

★★★ RAVELLO Campania   Pop 2 377

Michelin map ▨▨▨ south of fold 27 – Local map 45

Ravello with its alleys, stairways and roofed passages clings to the steep slopes of the Dragon Hill. The **site★★★**, suspended between sea and sky, is unforgettable. The road from Amalfi climbs in hairpin bends up the narrow Dragon Valley, planted with vines.

★★★ **Villa Rufolo** ⊙. – *Like the cathedral it overlooks Piazza Vescovado.*
The villa was built in the 13C by the rich Rufoli family of Ravello and was the residence of several popes, of Charles of Anjou and more recently in 1880, of the German composer Wagner. A well-shaded avenue leads to a Gothic entrance tower. Beyond is a Moorish-style courtyard with typical sharply pointed arches in the Sicilian-Norman style and interlacing above. This was originally cloisters in the 11C. A massive 11C tower overlooks the well-tended gardens and the elegant villa.
From the terraces there is a splendid **panorama★★★** of the jagged peaks as far as Cape Orso, the Bay of Maiori and the Gulf of Salerno.

★★★ **Villa Cimbrone** ⊙. – A charming **alley**★ leads from Piazza Vescovado to the villa, passing on the way through the Gothic porch of the convent of St Francis, founded by the saint himself in 1222 (cloisters). On entering the grounds the visitor should see first the charming cloisters and a lovely hall with pointed vaulting and some curious grilles. A wide alley leads through the garden to the belvedere, adorned with a series of marble busts. There is an immense **panorama**★★★ over the cultivated, terraced hillsides, Maiori, Cape Orso and the Gulf of Salerno.

Cathedral (Duomo). – The cathedral, founded in 1086, was transformed in the 18C. The campanile is 13C. The fine **bronze door**★ with its panels of reliefs was cast in 1179 by Barisanus da Trani. In the nave the antique columns have been uncovered and there is a magnificent mosaic-covered **pulpit**★★ with a remarkable variety of motifs and fantastic animals (1272). On the left is an elegant 12C **ambo** with green mosaics representing Jonah and the Whale. The small **museum** ⊙ in the crypt has sculptural fragments, mosaics, a silver **head-reliquary** with the relics of St Barbara.

★ **St John's (San Giovanni del Toro).** – This small 11C church was restored in the 18C. Inside, antique columns support the arches. There is a richly decorated 11C **pulpit**★, a Roman sarcophagus (north aisle) and 14C frescoes in the crypt.

★★★ RAVENNA Emilia-Romagna   Pop 136 324

Michelin map 🎇 fold 15, 🎇 fold 35 or 🎇 fold 5

In the peaceful provincial-looking town of Ravenna, the sober exteriors of its buildings belie the wealth of riches accumulated when Ravenna was an imperial city, the Byzantium of the West and an Exarchate of Byzantium. Indeed the many wonderful mosaics which adorn the city's ecclesiastical buildings are the finest in Europe. Their bright colours, richness of decoration and powerful symbolism are evocative of a great spirituality.

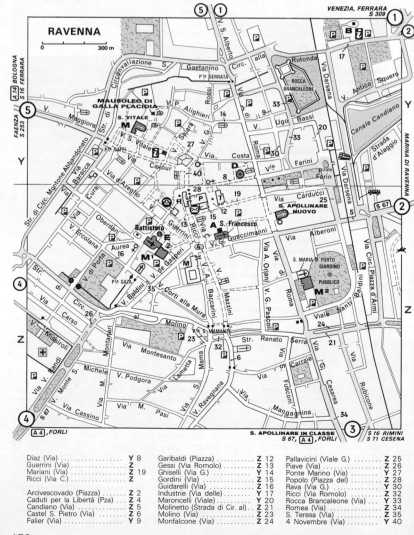

After the division of the Empire in 395 by Theodosius, Rome already in decline was abandoned in AD404 by Honorius who made Ravenna the capital of the Roman Empire. Honorius' sister, **Galla Placidia**, lavishly governed the Western Empire before the Barbarian invasions brought the Ostrogoth Kings Odoacer (476-493) and **Theodoric** (493-526) to Ravenna; they also embellished Ravenna in their turn. The strategic location of Ravenna's port, Classis, facing the Greek world, inevitably led to trading with Byzantium which had become capital in 476. Ravenna came under Byzantine rule in 540 in the reign of the Emperor Justinian, and was administered by Exarchs. From then on Ravenna excercised considerable influence over the whole of northern Italy and beyond.

★★★ MOSAICS *time: one day*

The oldest mosaics are in the Neoni Baptistry and the Galla Placidia Tomb (5C). Next in chronological order are those adorning the Arians' Baptistry, St Apollinaris the New, St Vitalis, and finally St Apollinaris in Classe (6C).

★★ **Tomb of Galla Placidia (Mausoleo di Galla Placidia)** ⊙ **(Y)**. – This mid-5C mausoleum in the form of a Latin cross has a great architectural harmony and is embellished by wonderful mosaics. The vaulting shining with stellar and floral motifs and the dome are painted a deep blue. On the tympanum and pendentives the symbolic scenes are full of serenity, in particular the Good Shepherd, on the west wall. The sarcophagi at either end of the projecting arms are the tombs of Galla Placidia and her family.

★★ **Church of St Vitalis (San Vitale)** ⊙ **(Y)**. – This church consecrated in 547 by Archbishop Maximian is a masterpiece of architecture; the splendour, originality and light effects are typical features of the later period of ancient art. The church has an octagonal plan, two storeys of concave exedrae encircled by an ambulatory and a deep apse. The interior is of a dazzling richness: precious marbles, Byzantine capitals splendidly carved, frescoes and especially the **mosaics** of the apse with their brilliant colours. On the sides and the end wall of the chancel are depicted scenes from the Old Testament; on the side walls inside the chancel are wonderful groups representing the **Empress Theodora** with her suite and the **Emperor Justinian** attended by his court. These works display splendour, hieratic power and a strong Byzantine influence. On the ceiling **Christ the King** is enthroned between St Vitalis and Bishop Ecclesio, the founder of the church.

Church of St Vitalis – Empress Theodora

To the left of St Vitalis is the **National Museum** (Museo Nazionale) ⊙ **(Y M)** with its Roman, Oriental, Byzantine, Romanesque and Renaissance collections.

★ **Neoni Baptistry (Battistero Neoniano)** ⊙ **(Z)**. – The building, which was erected in the 6C by Bishop Neoni and is also known as the Orthodox Baptistry, contains splendid mosaics in brilliant contrasting colours. There are decorative motifs above the bays of the main arches, and the dome portrays the **Baptism of Christ** and the Twelve Apostles. The Byzantine low reliefs over the arches of the rotunda represent the prophets.

The 18C cathedral **(Z E)**, adjacent to the baptistry, is dominated by a 10C-11C round campanile. It contains a 6C marble ambo adorned with symbolic animals.

★ **Basilica of St Apollinaris the New (Sant' Apollinare Nuovo)** ⊙ **(Z)**. – This lovely church, built in 519 by Theodoric, has a nave and two aisles separated by Corinthian columns and is adorned with brilliant **mosaics** with a gold background. On the upper walls are scenes from the Life of Christ, then pictures of saints and prophets. Below is the famous **procession of saints** depicting holy virgins leaving the town and port of Classis, behind the Magi, bearing offerings to the Virgin. Opposite is a procession of twenty-six martyrs leaving the palace of Theodoric, moving solemnly towards Christ the King, who is surrounded by angels.

Arians' Baptistry (Battistero degli Ariani) ⊙ **(Y D)**. – The baptistry is thought to have been built by Theodoric in the 6C. The dome is decorated with fine **mosaics** portraying the Baptism of Christ and, in the surrounding band, the twelve Apostles and a throne adorned with a cross.

★★ **Basilica of St Apollinaris in Classe (Sant' Apollinare in Classe)** ⊙. – *5km – 3 miles to the south. Leave Ravenna by ③ on the plan, the S 67.*
The basilica stands in open country not far from the sea. The basilica was begun in 534 and consecrated in 549; a cylindrical campanile was added in the 11C. The majestic interior has a nave and two aisles separated by twenty-six arches supported by marble columns. In the aisles lie superb early-Christian sarcophagi carved with symbols (5C-8C). The triumphal arch and the chancel are adorned with magnificent 6C-7C **mosaics** with a marked freedom and simplicity of composition and a lovely harmony of colour. The mosaics, which are full of symbolism, portray Christ the Saviour and the Transfiguration.

ADDITIONAL SIGHTS

★ **Theodoric's Tomb (Mausoleo di Teodorico)** ⊙ (Y B). – This curious monument, erected by Theodoric around 520, is built of huge blocks of freestone assembled without mortar. The two-storey building is covered by a remarkable monolithic dome 11m – 36ft in diameter in Istrian stone. Inside, the decoration is sober and austere. A Romanesque porphyry basin has been transformed into a sarcophagus.

Episcopal Palace Museum (Museo Arcivescovile) ⊙ (Z M¹). – The museum displays a small lapidary collection as well as the **throne**★★ of Archbishop Maximian (6C), a masterpiece in carved ivory. The **St Andrew's Chapel**★★ (Sant'Andrea) contains remarkable mosaics.

Municipal Picture Gallery (Pinacoteca Comunale) ⊙ (Z M²). – This collection includes works from most of the Italian schools from the 14C to the 20C. The **recumbent figure**★ (1526) of a young knight, Guidarello Guidarelli, is a masterpiece by Tullio Lombardo.

Dante's Tomb (Sepolcro di Dante) (Z A). – Dante was exiled from Florence and took refuge first at Verona and then at Ravenna, where he died in 1321. The classical building in which the tomb now stands was erected in 1780.

Church of St Francis (San Francesco) (Z). – This 10C Romanesque church is flanked by a campanile of the same period. Remodelled after the Second World War, it still retains some fine Greek marble columns, a 5C high altar and a 9C-10C crypt.

REGGIO DI CALABRIA Calabria   Pop 178 714

Michelin map 988 fold 39 – Town plan in the current Michelin Red Guide Italia

Reggio, which stands close against the Aspromonte Massif, is a pleasant town of modern appearance, rebuilt after the earthquake of 1908 along the Straits of Messina. Reggio is surrounded by rich groves of olives, vines, orange and lemon trees, and fields of flowers used for making perfume. Half the world production of bergamot (a citrus fruit) comes from Reggio. There are daily boat and car ferry services to Sicily *(see the current Michelin Red Guide Italia).*

★ **Lungomare.** – This long and elegant sea-front promenade lined with palm trees and magnolias affords views of the Sicilian coastline and Etna.

★★ **National Museum (Museo Nazionale)** ⊙. – This modern museum, in the centre of town, contains an important **archaeological collection** covering the history of Magna Graecia. There is also an interesting art gallery.
The museum has been selected to house *(ground floor)* the **Riace Warriors**★★★ dating probably from the 5C BC, which were discovered in 1972 off the coast of the small Calabrian harbour of Riace. The two warrior figures are exceptionally well preserved and are striking for their imposing appearance, their harmonious proportions and the refinement of their details. Their origin and the identity of the sculptor remain an enigma. The ground floor also has displays on local prehistory, finds dating from Magna Graecia (especially the excavations at Locri which have uncovered Greek and locally-produced pottery, terracotta votive tablets, a marble group etc).
On the first floor are the Hellenistic works and the coin collection.
The second-floor **art gallery** has two remarkable works by **Antonella da Messina**: a *St Jerome* and *Three Angels appearing before Abraham.*

EXCURSION

★ **Aspromonte.** – *From its junction (bivio Brandano) with the S 112 to Melito di Porto Salvo on the south coast, the S 183 crosses the Aspromonte Massif from north to south, allowing the visitor to discover its many varied aspects. Description p 70.*

Each year the Michelin Red Guide Italia
revises its selection of hotels and restaurants
in the following categories

– pleasant, quiet, secluded
– with an exceptionally interesting or extensive view
– with gardens, tennis courts, swimming pool, beach facilities.

REGGIO NELL'EMILIA Emilia-Romagna   Pop 130 015

Michelin map 988 fold 14, 428 folds 27 and 28, 429 fold 22 or 430 fold 2
Town plan in the current Michelin Red Guide Italia

This rich industrial and commercial centre, set on the Via Emilia, was the birthplace of Ariosto *(qv)*. Like Modena and Ferrara, it belonged to the Este family from 1409 to 1776. In the town centre are Piazza Prampolini and Piazza Cavour, overlooked by the municipal theatre (19C).

★ **Parmeggiani Gallery (Galleria Parmeggiani)** ⊙. – *2 Corso Cairoli.*
The collections comprise gold plate, fabrics, costumes, arms, furniture and paintings: works by El Greco and Ribera as well as Flemish and Italian Mannerist paintings.

Madonna della Ghiara ⊙. – *Corso Garibaldi.*
A lovely 17C church with a dome. The interior was richly decorated by the Bolognese school.

EXCURSION

Castle of Canossa (Castello di Canossa). – *32km – 20 miles to the southwest. Follow the San Polo d'Enza road and then turn left to Canossa.*
Only the romantic ruins, perched on a rock, remain of the imposing stronghold which belonged to the great Countess of Tuscany, Matilda (1046-1115), who supported the pope against the emperor for thirty years during the quarrel over the investiture of bishops and abbots *(qv)*. The Emperor Heinrich IV of Germany came barefoot and in his shirtsleeves through the snow, to make amends to Pope Gregory VII in 1077. He had to wait three days for his absolution. This is the origin of the expression "to go to Canossa", that is, to humble oneself after a quarrel.

RIETI Latium   Pop 44 115

Michelin map 988 fold 26 or 430 fold 26 – 37km – 23 miles to the southeast of Terni

Rieta lies at the junction of several valleys in the heart of a fertile plain and is the geographical centre of Italy. It is also a good excursion centre from which to follow in the footsteps of St Francis of Assisi, who preached locally.

Piazza Cesare Battisti. – This is the centre of the town, where the most important buildings are to be found. Take the gateway to the right of the 16C-17C Palazzo del Governo with its elegant loggia to reach the pleasant **public garden★**, from where there is a lovely view of the town and its surroundings.

Cathedral (Duomo). – This has a 15C porch and a lovely Romanesque campanile dating from 1252. Inside, the fresco of the Madonna dates from 1494 while the **crypt** is 12C.

Episcopal Palace (Palazzo Vescovile). – *Behind the cathedral.*
This 13C building has heavily-ribbed **vaulting★** over the two vast naves which are now used as a garage.

EXCURSIONS

Fonte Colombo Monastery (Convento di Fonte Colombo) ⊙. – *5km – 3 miles to the southwest. Take the Contigliano road and after 3km – 2 miles turn left.*
It was in the old monastery that St Francis underwent an eye operation. He dictated the Franciscan Rule in the grotto after having fasted for forty days. Visitors will see the 12C Chapel of St Mary Magdalene adorned with frescoes with the "T", the emblem of the Cross designed by St Francis; the St Michael Chapel and the grotto where he fasted; the tree-trunk in which Jesus appeared to him; the old monastery and the 15C church.

★ **Greccio Monastery (Convento di Greccio)** ⊙. – *15km – 9 miles to the northwest. Take the road via Contigliano to Greccio and continue for 2km – 1 mile. Leave the car on the esplanade at the foot of the monastery.*
This 13C monastery clings to a rocky overhang at an altitude of 638m – 2 093ft. It was here that St Francis celebrated Christmas in 1223 and said mass at a manger *(presepio)* between an ox and an ass, thus starting the custom of making cribs at Christmas.
Visitors have access to the Chapel of the Crib (frescoes by the school of Giotto) and the areas where St Francis and his companions lived. On the upper floor is the church of 1228 with its original furnishings.

Poggio Bustone Monastery (Convento di Poggio Bustone) ⊙. – *10km – 6 miles to the north by the Terni road.*
Perched at an altitude of 818m – 2 684ft in a lovely green setting, the monastery consists of a 14C church, much altered, with its 15C to 17C frescoes, charming 15C-16C cloisters, a 14C refectory, and two caves in which St Francis is said to have lived.

La Foresta Monastery (Convento La Foresta) ⊙. – *5km – 3 miles to the north.*
It was in this mountain retreat that St Francis wrote his *Canticle of the Creatures* and performed the miracle of the vine. In the wine cellar is the vat which was filled by the miraculous grape. The cave where St Francis stayed is also open to visitors.

Michelin map 988 fold 15, 429 fold 36 or 430 fold 6
Town plan in the current Michelin Red Guide Italia

Rimini has two faces: that of an ancient city rich in history and that of an international ultra-modern seaside resort with its marina, airport and in particular, a great beach of fine sand.

This Umbrian and Gallic colony, with its strategic situation at the junction of the Via Emilia and the Via Flaminia, flourished during the Empire. In the 13C the town grew to fame with the notoriety of its ruling house, the **Malatesta**. They combined extreme refinement with savagery. Dante immortalised the fate of the tragic lovers, Paolo Malatesta and Francesca da Rimini, who were murdered by Gianni Malatesta, the brother of Paolo and the husband of Francesca. Later Sigismondo I Malatesta, cultured patron of the arts and protector of the humanists, repudiated, poisoned and strangled his first three wives, before making an irregular marriage with his mistress, Isotta. After the fall of the Malatesta, Rimini became a papal town.

SIGHTS

★ **Malatesta Temple (Tempio Malatestiano)**. – The church was built in the 13C by the Franciscans and became the Malatesta mausoleum in the 14C. It was remodelled from 1447 by Leon Battista Alberti on Sigismondo I's orders, to house the tombs of the tyrant and of his wife Isotta. The Florentine architect was inspired by the nearby Arch of Augustus and designed an antique façade with a great pediment and a single opening. The Renaissance "temple" was left unfinished but its façade marks the beginning of a new style for religious buildings.

The spacious and imposing interior includes an allegorical decoration of exquisite grace and subtlety, due in large part to Agostino di Duccio. The same motifs are also found in the side chapels. In the reliquary chapel, to the right, Piero della Francesca painted the **portrait of Sigismondo Malatesta★**. In the adjacent chapel, the tomb of Isotta faces an admirable **painted 14C crucifix★** of the Rimini school. The first chapel on the left contains the cenotaph of Sigismondo's ancestors adorned with low reliefs.

Arch of Augustus (Arco d'Augusto). – *Piazzale Giulio Cesare*.
The arch was built in 27 BC and has a majestic appearance, with fine fluted columns and Corinthian capitals.

Bridge of Tiberius (Ponte di Tiberio). – The bridge was begun under Augustus and completed under Tiberius in AD 21. The building material is massive blocks of Istrian limestone.

EXCURSION

Italy in miniature (Italia in Miniatura). – The park includes a garden, boot-shaped and showing contours and relief to represent the form of Italy. There are about 200 models of its architectural treasures and sites. An area is devoted to Europe and there is also an entertainment section.

The chapter on Practical Information
at the end of the Guide lists
– local or national organisations providing additional information
– admission times and charges.

★★ The RIVIERA Liguria

Michelin map 988 folds 12 and 13, 195 folds 19, 20 and 29 or 428 folds 24, 25 and 32 to 36

From Ventimiglia to the Gulf of La Spezia, the coast describes a curve backed by the slopes of the Alps and the Ligurian Apennines, with Genoa in the middle. The enchanting Italian or Ligurian Riviera is like the French Riviera, a tourists' paradise. The mild climate makes it particularly popular in winter. The coast is dotted with popular resorts with good amenities and a wide choice of hotels. The hinterland provides a large choice of walks for those who prefer solitude.

Sightseeing. – The map below locates the towns and sites described in the guide, and also indicates other beauty spots in small black type.

★ 1 RIVIERA DI PONENTE (WESTERN RIVIERA)

From Ventimiglia to Genoa *175km – 109 miles – allow a day*

The main road of the Riviera, the Via Aurelia, is of Roman origin. It is difficult, as it is winding and narrow, and carries heavy traffic. Nevertheless, there are remarkable viewpoints from the stretches of corniche road or when the road runs close to the blue waters of the Ligurian Sea. Slightly inland the A10 motorway with its many tunnels and viaducts runs parallel. The road passes through a succession of resorts with villas often screened by luxuriant and varied vegetation, or crosses a stretch of coastal plain traversed by mountain torrents. With its exceptionally good exposure the Riviera specialises in the growing of flowers, often under glass, throughout the year.

The hinterland provides a sharp contrast, with the peacefulness of its wild forested landscapes.

Ventimiglia. – *Town plan in the current Michelin Red Guide Italia.* – Not far from the French border, Ventimiglia has an old quarter (Città Vecchia) crisscrossed by narrow alleyways, an 11C-12C cathedral (Duomo), an 11C octagonal baptistry, an 11C-12C Church of San Michele and the 17C Neri Oratory. The **Hanbury Gardens**★★ ⊙ in **Mortola Inferiore** *(6km – 4 miles to the west, in the direction of the French border)* with their varied and exotic vegetation, are laid out in terraces, overlooking the sea.

★★ **Bordighera.** – The villas and hotels of this famous resort are scattered among flower gardens shaded by splendid palm trees. The old town, with its winding alleys, still has several fortified gateways.

★★ **San Remo.** – *Description p 198.*

★ **Taggia.** – Taggia, set amidst vineyards, orchards and olive groves, commands the Argentina Valley. In the 15C and 16C Taggia was an important art centre frequented by Louis Bréa from Nice, the Piedmontese Canavese, and the Genoese Perino del Vaga and Luca Cambiaso. The **Church of St Dominic** (San Domenico) has a fine collection of **works**★ by Louis Bréa (Virgin of Pity and the Baptism of Christ).

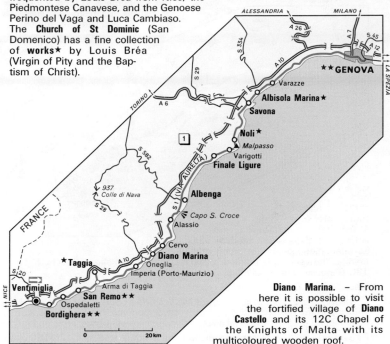

Diano Marina. – From here it is possible to visit the fortified village of **Diano Castello** and its 12C Chapel of the Knights of Malta with its multicoloured wooden roof.

Albenga. – Albenga lies a short distance inland, in an alluvial plain with rich market gardens. The medieval **old town**★ is clustered round the **cathedral** (Cattedrale) with its imposing late-14C campanile. The vaulting of the nave is covered with *trompe l'œil* frescoes. The octagonal 5C baptistry has a baptismal font and a charming paleo-Christian mosaic in the style typical of Ravenna.

Finale Ligure. – **Finale Marina** has a basilica with a fanciful baroque façade. In **Finale Pia** the abbey church is graced with an elegant late-13C campanile. The old town of **Finale Borgo**★, 2km – 1 mile inland, still has its town walls and its Collegiate Church of San Biagio with its elegant 13C polygonal campanile. Inside are a polyptych of St Catherine (1533) and a 16C painting of St Blaise surrounded by saints.
From **San Giovanni Castle** *(1 hour on foot Rtn, start from Via del Municipio)* there is a **view**★ of Finale Ligure, the sea and the hinterland. Higher up, **Gavone Castle** retains a 15C round tower with diamond-shaped rustication.

★ **Noli.** – This fishing village still has ancient houses, 13C towers and a Romanesque church with a huge wooden statue of Christ also of the Romanesque period.

Savona. – *Town plan in the current Michelin Red Guide Italia.* Italy's seventh port, Savona handles crude oil, coal, cellulose and Italian cars for export to Britain and the United States. The old town has several Renaissance palaces, a 16C cathedral (Duomo) and on the sea-front the 16C **Priamar Fortress** where the Italian patriot Mazzini was imprisoned in 1830.

★ **Albisola Marina.** – This town is known for its production of ceramics, which carries on a 13C tradition. At the end of the 16C a Duke of Nevers, a member of the Italian Gonzaga family, summoned the Conrade brothers from Albisola to Nevers to found a faïence factory. The 18C **Villa Faraggiana** ⊙ with its exotic **park**★, now houses the Ligurian Ceramics Centre. The exhibits include: the rich Empire decoration, ceramic pavements and flooring, and the superb **ballroom**★ with its stucco and fresco decoration.

★★ **Genoa.** – *Description p 106.*

Smokers and campers please take care
Fire can spread rapidly and cause extensive damage.

★★★ ② RIVIERA DI LEVANTE (EASTERN RIVIERA)

From Genoa to La Spezia *173km – 108 miles – allow 1 day*

This stretch of coast has more character and is wilder than the Riviera di Ponente. Sharp promontories, little sheltered coves, tiny fishing villages, wide sandy bays, cliffs, the pinewoods and olive groves of the hinterland, all lend it charm. The road is often winding and hilly but there are fewer stretches of corniche road and the road often runs much further from the coast.

★★ **Genoa.** – *Description p 106.*

★★★ **Portofino.** – *Description p 173.*

★ **Rapallo.** – *Town plan in the current Michelin Red Guide Italia.* – This sophisticated seaside resort is admirably situated at the head of a bay to the east of the Portofino peninsula. The Lungomare Vittorio Veneto is a lovely palm-shaded **promenade**★ along the sea-front.

Chiavari. – This seaside resort has a vast

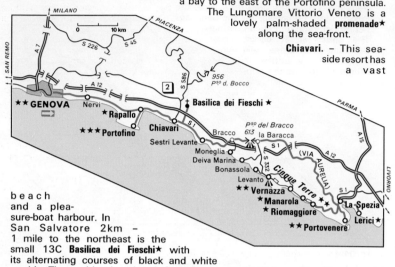

beach and a pleasure-boat harbour. In San Salvatore 2km – 1 mile to the northeast is the small 13C **Basilica dei Fieschi**★ with its alternating courses of black and white marble. The vaulting is pointed. Opposite stands the Palazzo Fieschi, a graceful 13C Genoese Gothic building.

★★ **Cinque Terre.** – *Description p 78.*

La Spezia. – *Town plan in the current Michelin Red Guide Italia.* This naval base and important port has Italy's largest naval dockyard and specialises in the manufacture of arms. The **naval museum** ⊘ comprises souvenirs, arms and models.

★★ **Portovenere.** – This small, severe-looking town is dominated by a 12C-16C citadel. Some of the houses date as far back as the 12C and were in fact once fortified by the Genoese.
The Church of San Lorenzo dates from the 12C, while the Church of San Pietro incorporates parts dating from the 6C. From the terrace there is a very fine view of the Gulf of La Spezia and the Cinque Terre region.

★ **Lerici.** – Lerici at the head of a well-sheltered cove has an important 13C castle (castello) which was rebuilt in the 16C by the Genoese.
It was near this village that the Shelleys rented a small house in 1822. Percy Bysshe drowned on the return trip from Leghorn to greet Leigh Hunt, who was to edit a new journal with Shelley and Byron. He was cremated on the beach, Il Gombo, north of the mouth of the Arno and his ashes are buried in the Protestant Cemetery in Rome.

To plan a special itinerary

– consult the map on pp 4-7 which shows the main towns, individual sights and recommended routes described in the guide;

– read the descriptions of the above which are described in the middle section of the guide in alphabetical order under their own name or are incorporated in the excursions radiating from a particular town or tourist centre;

*– use the appropriate **Michelin Maps** which show places of interest, scenic routes, viewpoints and natural features...*

Michelin map 988 fold 26 or 430 folds 35 and 36 – Town plan pp 186-187
Plan of the built-up area in the current Michelin Red Guide Italia

Since 1870 when it became the capital of Italy, Rome has undergone extensive urban development. Then it was a city of barely 200 000 inhabitants while today there are almost 3 million. The treasures of Rome are not always easy to visit, as the city centre is a maze of narrow streets and traffic snarls up easily.
Visitors are advised to use the **Michelin Green Guide Rome** with its itineraries in the various districts, descriptions of selected sights, plans of certain quarters and buildings, and notes on the city's history and its artistic traditions.

HISTORICAL NOTES

The legendary origins of Rome were perpetuated by both Roman historians and poets, such as Livy in his *Roman History* and Virgil in the *Aeneid*. Both claimed that Aeneas, son of the goddess Venus, fled from Troy when it was captured, and landed at the mouth of the Tiber. Having defeated the local tribes he founded Lavinium. His son Ascanius (or Iulus) founded Alba Longa. It was here that Rhea Silvia the Vestal, following her union with the god Mars, gave birth to the twins Romulus and Remus, who were abandoned on the Tiber. The twins came to rest at the foot of the Palatine where they were nursed by a wolf. Later Romulus marked a furrow round the sacred area on which the new city was to be built. Jesting, Remus stepped over the line; Romulus killed him for violating the sacred precinct. Romulus populated his village with outlaws who settled on the Capitol and he provided them with Sabine wives. An alliance grew up between the two peoples who were ruled by a succession of kings, alternately Sabine and Latin, until the Etruscans arrived.
Modern historians emphasise the strategic location of Rome's seven hills especially that of the Palatine, which was a staging-post on the salt road (Via Salaria). These favourable features no doubt led to the development of settlements around the Palatine in the 8C BC.
Two centuries later the Etruscans had transformed these villages of shacks into a well-organised town, with a citadel on the Capitol. The last Etruscan king, Tarquin the Superb, was thrown out in 509 BC and the Consulate was instituted. The Republican era was an ambitious one of territorial expansion. During the 2C and 1C BC the Republican regime tore itself to pieces in a civil war. To restore order disrupted by the rival political factions and rule the newly-conquered territories, it required a clever man of very determined character. **Julius Caesar** (101-44 BC) emerged from amidst the contenders by reason of his audacious strategies (he conquered the whole of Gaul in 51), his grasp of political affairs, his talents as an orator and his unbounded ambition; appointed consul and dictator for life, he was assassinated on the Ides of March, 15 March 44 BC. He was succeeded by his nephew, **Octavian**, a young man who was of delicate health and had won no military glory. Octavian was to demonstrate tenacity of purpose and political genius and ably rid his path of possible rivals. In 27 BC the Senate granted Octavian the title **Augustus**, which invested him with an aura of holiness. He soon became the first Roman emperor. His achievements were considerable: he extended Roman government and restored peace to the whole of the Mediterranean basin.
Among Augustus' successors there were those who were driven by madness and cruelty (Caligula, Nero and Domitian); and others who continued the good work of Roman civilisation: the good administrator, Vespasian; Titus who was known as the love and delight of the human race; Trajan, the "best of Emperors" and great builder; and Hadrian, an indefatigable traveller and passionate Hellenist.

Christian Rome. – As the old order passed away, undermined from within by economic misery and the concentration of authority in the hands of one man, and from without by Barbarian attacks, a new force – Christianity – emerged. It had first reached Rome in the reign of Augustus. The religion of Jesus originated in Palestine and Syria, and was spread throughout the pagan world by his disciples. As the world fell into disarray, Christianity preached a new doctrine of brotherly love and the hope of happiness after death. During the last years of the 1C and the early years of the 2C the Christian Church became organised, but transgressed the law from the beginning because the Emperor embodied religious power. It was not until the **Edict of Milan** (313), which allowed Christians to practise their religion openly, and the conversion of **Constantine** (314) that the Church could come out into the open.
From the first days of Christianity, the bishop was Christ's representative on earth. The bishop of Rome, capital of the Empire, claimed primacy. Gradually the name "Pope", which had been used for all bishops, was reserved for the Bishop of Rome alone. For nineteen centuries the popes at the head of the Roman church have influenced the history of Christianity and given the Eternal City its particular character. In the 11C **Gregory VII** restored order to the Christian church, which had by then an appalling reputation. He dealt with two scourges: the buying and selling of church property; and the marriage of the clergy. In so doing he started the Investiture Controversy, which opposed the Sovereign Pontiff and the emperor.
During the Renaissance numerous popes were scholarly, ambitious and great patrons of the arts and greatly contributed to the embellishment of the capital by bringing to their court such artists as Raphael and Michelangelo. They included Pius II, Sixtus IV (builder of the Sistine Chapel, Santa Maria della Pace and Santa Maria del Popolo), Julius II (who commissioned Michelangelo to decorate the ceiling of the Sistine Chapel), Leo X (who had a great personal fortune and nominated Raphael as intendant of the arts), Clement VII, Sixtus V (who was a great builder) and Paul III who built the Farnese Palace.

ROME TODAY

No other city in the world has managed to combine so successfully such a diverse heritage of Classical antiquities, medieval buildings, Renaissance palaces and baroque churches. Far from being discordant they constitute a logical continuity where revivals, influences and contrasts are evidence of the ingenuity of Roman architects and builders. Of course, the ruins no longer present their former splendour when they were faced with marble under the Empire, and only a few of the palaces have retained the painted decoration of their façades. The Rome so loved by Goethe and Stendhal has changed owing to the depredations of heavy traffic and the developments resulting from the modernisation of a capital city.

However, today's visitor cannot fail to be impressed by the immensity of the great town planning project that is Rome.

The best overall views of this urban complex sprawling over the seven hills are from the belvederes on the Janiculum (Gianicolo – **AY**), the Aventine (**CZ**) and the Pincio (**BV**). At dusk the visitor will discover a city bathed in a golden light, the green masses of the gardens, the silhouettes of umbrella pines shading the areas of ruins, as well as the numerous domes and belltowers rising above the pink-tiled roofscape. Rome with some 300 churches is the city of churches, where it is not uncommon to find two side by side. It is often impossible to stand back and admire their façades but the richness of the decoration and the ingenious use of *trompe-l'œil* tend to compensate for this drawback. Often the interiors are astonishing for their silence and light and the inventiveness and audacity of the ultimate design.

In the older districts of Rome (Vecchia Roma) around the Pantheon (**BX**), the Piazza Navona (**BX**) and the Campo dei Fiori (**BY**), there is a wealth of fine palaces. Those who wander through these districts will often catch a glimpse between ochre-coloured façades of a small square with all the bustle of a market, or several flights of stairways descending to a fountain. In the evening these areas are lit by tall street lights and are bathed in a soft glow which gives them a certain charm, a pleasant change from the bustling main arteries.

Luxury shops are to be found around the Piazza del Popolo (**BV**), Via del Corso (**BCX**), Piazza di Spagna (**CX**) and the streets which open off them. Via Veneto (**CX**) lined with cafés and luxurious hotels is a fashionable tourist centre. Piazza Navona is another fashionable meeting-place while the **Trastevere** (**BY**), which has never lost its popular character, has a variety of restaurants. Antique and second-hand shops line Via dei Coronari (**BX 25**).

SIGHTSEEING

On the following pages the reader will find a very brief description of some of the sights, which will enable him to see in three days some of the masterpieces which make Rome famous. In the section Additional Sights, a thematic classification includes other important monuments, sites or museums which are further proof of the exceptional riches of this city.

FIRST DAY *(morning)*

★ PIAZZA VENEZIA (CXY)

The Piazza in the centre of Rome is lined with palaces: Palazzo Venezia, Palazzo Bonaparte, where Napoleon's mother died in 1836, and the early 20C Palazzo delle Assicurazioni Generali di Venezia.

★ Palazzo Venezia ⊘ (CY A). – This palace, built by Pope Paul II (1464-71), is one of the first Renaissance buildings. A **museum**, on the first floor, presents collections of medieval art (ivories, Byzantine and Limousin enamels, Italian Primitive paintings on wood, gold and silver work, ceramics and small bronzes (15C-17C).

The **Basilica of St Mark** (San Marco), which was incorporated within the palace in the 15C, has a fine Renaissance **façade★** overlooking Piazza di San Marco (CY 60).

Monument to Victor Emmanuel II (Vittoriano) ⊘ (CY B). – This huge memorial by Giuseppe Sacconi, begun in 1885 in honour of the first king of a united Italy, overshadows the other monuments of Rome by its sheer size and dazzling white colour. It affords a **view★★** of the Eternal City.

★★★ CAPITOL (CAMPIDOGLIO – CY)

On the hill which symbolised the power of ancient Rome, there now stand the city's administrative offices, also the Church of Santa Maria d'Aracoeli, Piazza del Campidoglio and its palaces, and pleasant gardens.

★★ Church of Santa Maria d'Aracoeli (CY C). – The church has a beautiful staircase built as a votive offering after the plague of 1346, and a flat, austere façade. It was built in 1250 on the spot where the Sibyl of Tibur (Tivoli) announced the coming of Christ to Augustus. In the first chapel on the right are **frescoes★** painted by Pinturicchio in about 1485.

★★★ Piazza del Campidoglio (CY 17). – Capitol Square was designed and partly laid out by Michelangelo from 1536 onwards. It is framed by three palaces and a balustrade with statues of the Heavenly Twins or Dioscuri. In the centre stood the equestrian statue of Marcus Aurelius installed by Michelangelo and now housed in the Capitoline Museum *(p 185)*.

The **Palazzo dei Conservatori★★★** ⊙ **(CY M¹)**, built in the 15C and remodelled in 1568 by Giacomo della Porta, houses a **museum★★★** of antique art which includes the **She-Wolf★★★** (6C-5C BC), the **Boy Extracting a Thorn★★★**, a Greek original or a very good copy dating back to the 1C BC, and a **Bust of Junius Brutus★★**, a remarkable head dating from the 3C BC placed on a bust in the Renaissance period. The **picture gallery★** *(2nd floor)* contains mainly 17C paintings.

The **Palazzo Nuovo** (New Palace) **(CY M²)**, built in 1655 by Girolamo Rainaldi, houses the **Capitoline Museum★★** ⊙ which contains: the **equestrian statue of Marcus Aurelius★★** (late 2C); the **Dying Gaul★★★**, a Roman sculpture based on a bronze of the Pergamum school (3C-2C BC); the **Emperors' Room★★** with portraits of all the emperors; the **Capitoline Venus★★**, a Roman work inspired by the Venus of Cnidus by Praxiteles; and the **Mosaic of the Doves★★** from Hadrian's Villa at Tivoli.

The **Palazzo Senatorio★★★** ⊙ (the Senate) **(CY H)** is a 12C building, remodelled between 1582 and 1602 by Giacomo della Porta and Girolamo Rainaldi.

From Via del Campidoglio **(CY 19)** there is a beautiful **view★★★** of the ruins.

FIRST DAY *(afternoon)*

★★★ ROMAN FORUM (FORO ROMANO ⊙ – CY)

The remains of the Roman Forum, the religious, political and commercial centre of ancient Rome, reflect the twelve centuries of history which created Roman civilisation. The forum was excavated in the 19C and 20C.

Take the **Via Sacra★★★** (Sacred Way) along which victorious generals marched in triumph to the **Curia★★**, rebuilt in the 3C by Diocletian. Senate meetings were held here; nowadays it houses **Trajan's low reliefs★★★**, sculpted panels depicting scenes from the life of the Emperor, and sacrificial animals.

Nearby rises the imposing **Triumphal Arch of Septimus Severus★★** built in AD 203 to commemorate the Emperor's victories over the Parthians. At the foot of the Capitol stood some remarkable monuments: the **Temple of Vespasian★★** (late 1C) of which only three elegant Corinthian columns remain; the **Temple of Saturn★★★** which retains eight 4C columns; and the **Portico of the Di Consentes★**, a colonnade of pillars with Corinthian columns dating back to restoration work of AD 367 – the portico was dedicated to the twelve principal Roman deities.

The **Column of Phocas★** (Colonna di Foca) was erected in AD 608 in honour of the Byzantine Emperor Phocas who presented the Pantheon to Boniface IV. The **Basilica Giulia★★**, which has five aisles, was built by Julius Caesar and completed by Augustus. It served as a law court and exchange.

Three beautiful columns with Corinthian capitals remain of the **Temple of Castor and Pollux★★★** (Tempio di Castore e Polluce). The circular **Temple of Vesta★★★** (Tempio di Vesta) stands near the **House of the Vestal Virgins★★★** (Casa delle Vestali). The **Temple of Antoninus and Faustina★★** (Tempio di Antonino e Faustina) was dedicated to the Emperor Antoninus Pius and his wife.

The grandiose **Basilica of Maxentius★★★** (Basilica di Massenzio) was completed by the Emperor Constantine, The **Triumphal Arch of Titus★★** (Arco di Tito), erected in 81, commemorates the capture of Jerusalem by this emperor, who only reigned for only two years.

★★★ PALATINE (PALATINO – CY)

The Palatine Hill, where Romulus and Remus were discovered, was chosen by Domitian as the site for the Imperial Palace. The building included three main areas: the **Domus Flavia★** or official state apartments, the **Domus Augustana★★** or private imperial apartments, and the **Stadium★**. The **House of Livia★★** (Casa di Livia) ⊙ probably belonged to Augustus (fine vestiges of paintings). The **Farnese Gardens** (Orti Farnesiani), laid out in the 16C on the site of Tiberius' palace, afford **views★★** of the Forum and town.

Leave the Palatine by an exit alongside the Arch of Titus.

★ Temple of Venus and Rome **(CY R)**. – The temple built between 121 and 136 by Hadrian was the largest in the city (110m – 361ft by 53m – 174ft). It was unique in that it comprised two *cellae* with apses back to back. One was dedicated to the goddess of Rome and faced the Forum; the other was dedicated to Venus and faced the Coliseum.

★★★ COLISEUM (COLOSSEO ⊙ – CY)

This amphitheatre, inaugurated in AD 80, is also known as the Flavian Amphitheatre after its initiator, Vespasian, first of the Flavian emperors. With its three superimposed classical orders (Doric, Ionic and Corinthian), it is a masterpiece of classical architecture. Fights between men and beasts, gladiatorial contests, races and simulated naval battles took place in the arena.

★★★ ARCH OF CONSTANTINE (ARCO DI CONSTANTINO – CY)

The arch was erected to commemorate Constantine's victory over Maxentius in AD 315. Some of the low reliefs were removed from other 2C monuments.

★★★ IMPERIAL FORUMS (FORI IMPERIALI – CY)

These were built by Caesar, Augustus, Trajan, Nerva and Vespasian. There are hardly any remains of the latter two. The Via dei Fori Imperiali, laid out in 1932 by Mussolini, divides the imperial forums.

Of **Caesar's Forum★★** (Foro di Cesare – *view from Via del Tulliano*) **(CY 77)** there remain three lovely columns from the Temple of Venus Genitrix. Of the **Augustan Forum★★** (Foro di Augusto – *view from Via Alessandrina*) **(CY 2)** there remain a few columns of the Temple of Mars the Avenger, vestiges of the stairway and of the wall enclosing the forum (behind the temple).

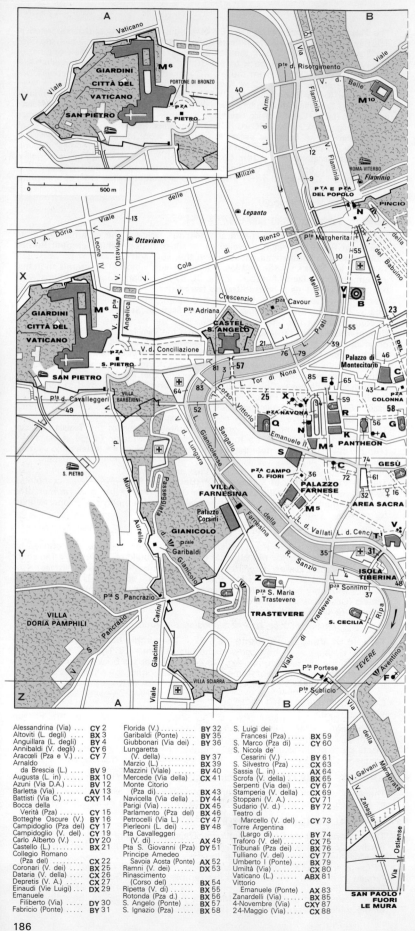

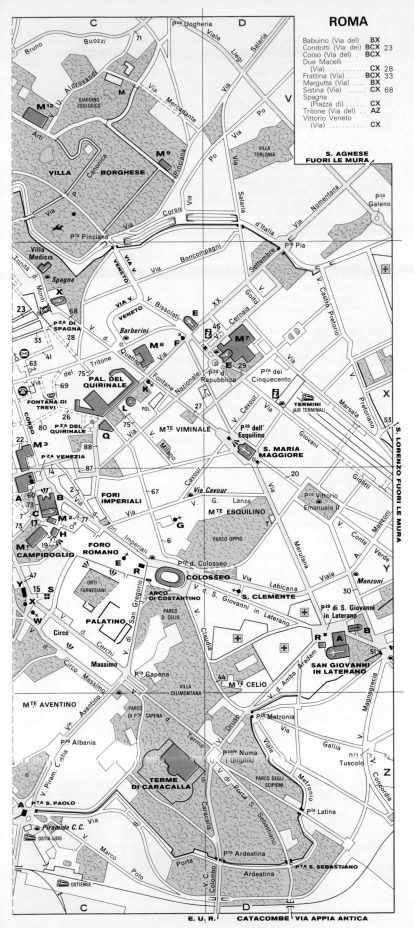

ROMA

187

The forum is dominated by the House of the Knights of Rhodes (Casa dei Cavalieri di Rodi), built in the Middle Ages and rebuilt in the 15C amidst the ancient ruins. All that remains of the largest and finest, **Trajan's Forum★★★** (Foro di Traiano), is **Trajan's column★★★** (Colonna Traiana) which depicts, in over 100 scenes, episodes of the war waged by Trajan against the Dacians. It is an unrivalled masterpiece. The **markets★★★** ⊙ (*mercati – entrance in Via 4 Novembre – CXY 87*), which have kept their semicircular façade, were a distribution and supply centre. They comprised about 150 shops which were also retail outlets. The **Tower of the Militia★** (Torre delle Milizie) is part of a 13C fortress.

SECOND DAY (morning)

★★★ CASTEL SANT'ANGELO ⊙ (ABX)

The imposing fortress was built in AD 135 as a mausoleum for the Emperor Hadrian and his family. In the 6C, Gregory the Great erected a chapel on top of the mausoleum to commemorate the apparition of an angel who, by putting his sword back into its sheath, announced the end of a plague. In the 15C Nicholas V added a brick storey to the ancient building and corner towers to the surrounding wall. Alexander VI (1492-1503) added octagonal bastions. In 1527, during the sack of Rome, Clement VII took refuge in the castle and installed an apartment which was later embellished by Paul III; the **Popes' Apartment★** stands isolated at the summit of the fortress and testifies to the graciousness of the popes' life style.

A long passageway links the fortress to the Vatican palaces. A fine spiral ramp dating from antiquity leads to the castle. From a terrace at the summit there is a splendid **panorama★★★** of the whole town.

The Castel Sant'Angelo is linked to the left bank of the Tiber by the graceful **Ponte Sant'Angelo★** (BX 57), which is adorned with baroque angels carved by Bernini and with statues of Sts Peter and Paul (16C).

VATICAN CITY (CITTÀ DEL VATICANO ⊙ – AV)

The Vatican City is bounded by a wall, overlooking Viale Vaticano, and to the east by the colonnade of St Peter's Square. This makes up the greater part of the Vatican state as laid down in 1929 in the Lateran Treaty. The Vatican City, now reduced to only 44 hectares – 109 acres and with less than a thousand inhabitants, stems from the Papal States, a donation made in the 8C by Pepin the Short to Pope Stephen II, and lost in 1870 when Italy was united into one Kingdom with Rome as its capital. The Vatican State, with the pope as ruler, has its own flag and anthem; it prints stamps and mints its own coinage which is legal tender throughout Italy. In 1970, Pope Paul VI dissolved the armed forces, retaining only the Swiss Guard who wear a colourful uniform said to have been designed by Michelangelo.

The Pope, who is the Head of State, is also the supreme head of the Universal Church, and from this very small state, the spiritual influence of the church radiates throughout the world through the person of the sovereign pontiff. When the pope is in residence in Rome, he grants **public audiences** ⊙.

★★★ VATICAN MUSEUMS ⊙ (AV M⁶)

Entrance: Viale Vaticano.

The museums of the Vatican occupy part of the palaces built by the popes from the 13C onwards, which have been extended and embellished to the present day.

These include on the first floor the **Pio-Clementino Museum★★★** (Greek and Roman antiquities) with its masterpieces: the **Belvedere Torso★★★** (1C BC), greatly admired by Michelangelo; the **Venus of Cnidus★★**, a Roman copy of Praxiteles' Venus; the **Laocoon Group★★★**, a 1C BC Hellenistic work; the **Apollo Belvedere★★★**, a 2C Roman copy; **Perseus★★**, a neo-classical work by Canova, which was purchased from the artist to make up for the loss of certain works removed under the terms of the Treaty of Tolentino (1797); **Hermes★★★**, a 2C Roman work inspired by the work of Praxiteles; and the **Apoxyomenos★★★**, the athlete scraping his skin with a strigil after taking exercise, a 1C Roman copy of the Greek original by Lysippus.

The **Etruscan Museum★**, on the second floor, has a remarkable 7C BC gold **fibula★★** adorned with lions and ducklings in high relief (Room II) and the **Mars★★** found at Todi, a rare example of a large bronze statue from the 5C BC (Room III). The **Room of the Biga** derives its name from the **two-horse chariot** *(biga)*, a 1C Roman work reassembled in the 18C.

The four **Raphael Rooms★★★** (Stanze di Rafaello), the private apartments of Julius II, were decorated by Raphael and his pupils from 1508 to 1517. The result is a pure Renaissance masterpiece. The frescoes are remarkable: the Borgo Fire, the School of Athens, Parnassus, the Expulsion of Heliodorus from the Temple, the Miracle of the Bosena Mass and St Peter delivered from prison. The **Collection of Modern Religious Art★★**, assembled by Pope Paul VI, is displayed in the apartment of Pope Alexander VI.

On the first floor the **Sistine Chapel★★★** (Cappella Sistina) is open to the public; its splendid vault, painted by Michelangelo from 1508 to 1512, illustrates the Bible, the Creation, the Flood and above the altar the Last Judgement which was added by the artist in 1534. The lowest sections of the side walls were decorated by Perugino, Pinturicchio and Botticelli. The **Picture Gallery★★★** (Pinacoteca) also contains some first-class works: three **compositions★★★** by **Raphael** *(The Coronation of the Virgin, The Madonna of Foligno* and *The Transfiguration* – Room VIII); **St Jerome★★** by Leonardo da Vinci (Room IX) and a **Descent from the Cross★★** by Caravaggio (Room XII).

★★★ ST PETER'S SQUARE (PIAZZA SAN PIETRO - AV)

This architectural masterpiece was begun in 1656 by Bernini, master of the baroque. The two semicircles of the colonnade which adorn the square and frame the façade of the basilica form an ensemble of remarkable sobriety and majesty. At the centre of the square stands a 1C BC obelisk brought from Heliopolis in Egypt to Rome in 37 by order of Caligula. It was erected here in 1585 on the initiative of Sixtus V by Domenico Fontana. At the top is a relic of the Holy Cross.

★★★ ST PETER'S BASILICA (BASILICA DI SAN PIETRO - AV)

Constantine, the first Christian Emperor, decided in AD 324 to build a basilica on the site where St Peter was buried after he had been martyred in Nero's circus. In the 15C it proved necessary to rebuild. For two centuries, the plan of the new basilica was constantly revised. The plan, of a Greek cross surmounted by a dome designed by Bramante and adopted by Michelangelo, was altered to a Latin cross at the behest of Paul V in 1606, when he instructed Carlo Maderna to add two bays and a façade to Michelangelo's square plan. From 1629 onwards, the basilica was decorated in a sumptuous baroque style by Bernini.

The **façade** which was completed in 1614 by Carlo Maderna is 115m – 377ft long and 45m – 151ft high; it is surmounted by colossal figures, and masks the dome. In the centre is the balcony from which the Sovereign Pontiff gives his benediction *Urbi and Orbi* (to the City and the World).

Under the **porch**, the first door on the left has bronze panels carved by Giacomo Manzù (1964); the bronze central door dates from the Renaissance (1455); the door on the right or Holy Door is opened and closed by the Pope to mark the beginning and end of a Jubilee Year.

Inside, it is customary to approach the stoups in the nave which at first glance appear of normal size but are in fact huge. Such size emphasises the gigantic dimensions of the basilica, otherwise not apparent because of the harmony of its proportions. The length of St Peter's can be compared to that of other great basilicas throughout the world by means of markers inlaid in the pavement of the nave.

The first chapel on the right contains the **Pietà★★★**, the moving and powerful masterpiece carved by Michelangelo in 1499-1500, which shows his creative genius.

In the right aisle, adjoining the Chapel of the Blessed Sacrament, **Gregory XIII's Monument★** is adorned with low reliefs illustrating the institution of the Gregorian calendar devised by that pope. Immediately beyond the right transept, **Clement XIII's Monument★★★** is a fine neo-classical design by Canova dating from 1792. The apse is dominated by **St Peter's Throne★★★** by Bernini (1666), a great carved throne in bronze encasing a 4C episcopal chair but symbolically attributed to St Peter, and surmounted by a glory in gilded stucco. In the chancel of the right is **Urban VIII's Monument★★★**, again by Bernini (1647) a masterpiece of funerary art. On the left stands **Paul III's Monument★★★** by Guglielmo della Porta (16C), a disciple of Michelangelo.

St Leo the Great's Altar *(chapel to the left of the chancel)* has a fine baroque **altarpiece★** carved in high relief by Algardi. Nearby, **Alexander VII's Monument★**, characterised by extreme exuberance, is a late work by Bernini (1678) assisted by his pupils. The **baldachin★★★** which crowns the pontifical altar and is 29m – 95ft tall (the height of the Farnese Palace) was strongly criticised: partly because the bronze had been taken from the Pantheon and partly because it was thought to be too theatrical and in bad taste. It does, however, fit in well with the overall architectural plan.

The **dome★★★** designed by Michelangelo, which he himself built as far as the lantern, was completed in 1593 by Giacomo della Porta and Domenico Fontana. From the **summit** ⊙ *(leave the basilica by the right aisle for access)* there is a **view★★★** of St Peter's Square, the Vatican City and Rome from the Janiculum to Monte Mario.

Rome – St Peter's Square

The 13C bronze **Statue of St Peter**★★ overlooking the nave is attributed to Arnolfo di Cambio and is greatly venerated by pilgrims, who come to kiss its feet.
Innocent VIII's Monument★★★ *(between the second and third bays in the left aisle)* is a Renaissance work (1498) by Antonio del Pollaiuolo. The **Stuart Monument** *(between the first and second bays in the left aisle)* carved by Canova is adorned with beautiful **angels**★ in low relief.
The **Treasury and Historical Museum**★★ ⊙ *(entrance in the left aisle, opposite the Stuart Monument)* has many treasured items including **Sixtus IV's tomb**★★★ (1493) by Pollaiuolo.

SECOND DAY *(afternoon)*

★★★ FARNESE PALACE (PALAZZO FARNESE ⊙ – BY)

The most beautiful of Roman palaces, now the French Embassy, was built from 1515 by Cardinal Alessandro Farnese, who reigned as pope under the name of Paul III (1534-49). He employed several architects: Antonio da Sangallo the Younger, Michelangelo (who designed the upper cornice of the façade, the Farnese coat of arms above the central balcony and the second floor of the inner court), Vignola who collaborated on the inner court and built the palace's rear façade, and Giacomo della Porta who designed the loggia of the same façade.

★★★ GESÙ CHURCH (BY)

The mother-church of the Jesuits in Rome, built by Vignola in 1568, is a typical building of the Counter-Reformation. On the outside, the engaged pillars replace the flat pilasters of the Renaissance, with light and shade effects and recesses. The interior, spacious and ideal for preaching, was lavishly decorated in the baroque style: on the dome, the **Baciccia frescoes**★★ illustrate the Triumph of the Name of Jesus (1679); the **St Ignatius Loyola Chapel**★★★ *(north transept)*, where the remains of St Ignatius Loyola rest, is the work (1696-1700) of the Jesuit Brother Andrea Pozzo and is sumptuously decorated.

★★★ PANTHEON ⊙ (BX)

The Pantheon, an ancient building perfectly preserved, founded by Agrippa in 27 BC and rebuilt by Hadrian (117-125), was a temple which was converted into a church in the 7C. Access is through a porch supported by sixteen single granite columns, all ancient except for three on the left. The doors are the original ones.
The **interior**★★★, a masterpiece of harmony and majesty, is dominated by the **antique dome**★★★, the diameter of which is equal to its height. The side chapels, adorned with alternately curved and triangular pediments, contain the tombs of the kings of Italy and that of Raphael *(on the left)*.

★★ SAN LUIGI DEI FRANCESI ⊙ (BX L)

This is the French church in Rome. Its façade, probably designed by Giacomo della Porta, heralds baroque art with its projecting columns. Many Frenchmen have been laid to rest within this church.
In the second chapel on the right are **frescoes**★ by **Domenichino** illustrating the legend of St Cecilia. In the fifth chapel on the left are **three paintings**★★★ by Caravaggio depicting scenes from the life of St Matthew: his Calling, Martyrdom and the angel dictating the Gospel. The artist's violent yet refined realism captures through his personal and unusual use of chiaroscuro, the dramatic and religious impact of the events.

★★ PIAZZA NAVONA (BX)

The square built on the site of Domitian's stadium retains its shape. A pleasant and lively pedestrian precinct, it is adorned at the centre with Bernini's baroque masterpiece, the **Fountain of the Four Rivers**★★★, completed in 1651. The statues represent the four rivers (Danube, Ganges, Rio de la Plata and Nile) symbolising the four corners of the earth.
Among the churches and palaces lining the square are **Sant' Agnese in Agone** (BX N) with a baroque façade by Borromini (attractive **interior**★ on the plan of a Greek cross), and the adjoining 17C **Palazzo Pamphili**.

THIRD DAY *(morning)*

★★★ BASILICA OF ST JOHN LATERAN (SAN GIOVANNI IN LATERANO – DY)

St John Lateran, the cathedral of Rome, is among the four major basilicas in Rome. The first basilica was founded by Constantine prior to St Peter's in the Vatican. It was rebuilt in the baroque era by Borromini and again in the 18C. The main façade by Alessandro Galilei dates from the 18C and the central door has bronze panels that originally belonged to the Curia of the Roman Forum (modified in the 17C). The vast and grandiose interior has a 16C **ceiling**★★ which was restored in the 18C. In the nave the **Statues of the Apostles**★ by pupils of Bernini stand in niches built by Borromini. The elegant **Corsini Chapel**★ *(first in the north aisle)* was designed by Alessandro Galilei. The transept **ceiling**★★ dates from the end of the 16C.
The **Chapel of the Blessed Sacrament** *(north transept)* has fine ancient **columns**★ in gilded bronze. The pretty **cloisters**★ are the work of the Vassalletto (13C), marble-masons who were associates of the Cosmati *(qv)*. The **baptistry**★ (DY R), built in the 4C, is decorated with beautiful 5C and 7C mosaics.
In **Piazza di San Giovanni in Laterano** rises a 15C BC Egyptian obelisk, the tallest in Rome.

The **Lateran Palace** (DY A), rebuilt in 1586, was the papal palace until the papal court returned from Avignon. The staircase, **Scala Sancta** (DY B), is a precious vestige from the medieval papal palace and is traditionally identified as the one Christ used in the palace of Pontius Pilate. Worshippers climb the stairs on their knees. At the top is the papal chapel (Sancta Sanctorum) with its many precious relics.

★★★ CARACALLA'S BATHS (TERME DI CARACALLA ⊘ – CZ)

These baths built by Caracalla in AD 212 extend over more than 11 hectares – 27 acres and could take 1 600 bathers at a time.
The ruined caldarium for the very hot bath, a circular room with a 34m – 112ft diameter, is the setting for operatic performances in summer.

★★★ CATACOMBS

Leave Rome by Via di Porta S. Sebastiano (**DZ**). *Plan of the built-up area in the current Michelin Red Guide Italia.*

There are numerous underground Christian cemeteries alongside the Via Appia Antica. In use from the 2C they were rediscovered in the 16C and 19C. They consist of long galleries radiating from an underground burial chamber *(hypogeum)* which belonged to a noble Roman family of the Christian faith. They permitted fellow-Christians to use the galleries.
The decorations of the catacombs (carvings or paintings of symbolic motifs) are precious examples of early Christian art.
The visitor with little time to spare should visit the following ones:
St Callistus' Catacombs★★★ ⊘ near the Appian Way, famous for its exceptional collection of paintings.
St Sebastian's Catacombs★★★ ⊘ near the Appian Way.
Domitilla's Catacombs★★★ ⊘ *entrance at no 282 Via delle Sette Chiese.*
The **Via Appia Antica★★★** (Old Appian Way) was laid out in 312 BC to link Rome with Brindisi and was also lined with tombs. The **Tomb of Cecilia Metella★** ⊘ is an example of a 1C BC patrician tomb.

★★★ BASILICA OF ST PAUL WITHOUT THE WALLS (SAN PAOLO FUORI LE MURA)

Leave by Via Ostiense (**BZ**). *Plan of the built-up area in the current Michelin Red Guide Italia.*

One of the four major basilicas. It was built by Constantine in the 4C on the site of St Paul's tomb. It was rebuilt in the 19C, after it had been wholly destroyed by fire in 1823, on the original basilical plan of early Christian churches.
The impressive **interior★★★** contains: an 11C bronze door cast in Constantinople *(at the entrance of the first south aisle)*; and a Gothic **ciborium★★** (1285) by Arnolfo di Cambio, placed on the high altar which stands above a marble plaque inscribed with the name Paul and dated 4C. In the **Chapel of the Blessed Sacrament★** *(on the left of the chancel)* are: a 14C wooden figure of Christ attributed to Pietro Cavallini; a statue of St Brigitta kneeling, by Stefano Maderno (17C); a 14C or 15C statue of St Paul; and the **paschal candelabrum★★**, a 12C Romanesque work of art by the Vassalletto.
The **cloisters★** are also attributed, at least in part, to this same family of artists.

THIRD DAY *(afternoon)*

★★★ BASILICA OF ST MARY MAJOR (SANTA MARIA MAGGIORE – DX)

One of the four major basilicas in Rome built by Sixtus III (AD 432-440), it has an 18C façade and a 14C campanile.
The impressive **interior★★★** contains remarkable **mosaics★★★**: in the nave, those above the entablature are among the most ancient Christian mosaics in Rome (5C) and depict scenes from the Old Testament; on the 5C trimphal arch are scenes from the New Testament; in the apse, the mosaics are composed of 5C elements but were completely redone in the 13C.
The coffered **ceiling★** is said to have been gilded with the first gold brought from Peru.

Leave the church by the door at the far end of the south aisle.

From **Piazza dell' Esquilino**, with its Egyptian obelisk, there is a **view★★** of the imposing 17C chevet.

★★★ TREVI FOUNTAIN (FONTANA DI TREVI – CX)

This late-baroque creation was commissioned by Clement XIII from Nicola Salvi in 1762. The fountain fills the whole width of the palace façade which acts as backdrop and gives the impression of a triumphal arch. The central figure, the Ocean, rides in a chariot drawn by two sea-horses and two tritons.
Tourists continue to play their traditional role by throwing two coins over their shoulders into the fountain – one coin to return to Rome and the other for the fulfilment of a wish.

Roman historians generally counted the years as from the foundation of Rome (Ab Urbe Condita).

The system of counting from the birth of Christ (AD) was introduced in the 6C by Dionysius Exiguus, a Scythian monk.

★★ PIAZZA DI SPAGNA (CX)

This square, a popular tourist attraction, was so named in the 17C after the Spanish Embassy occupied the Palazzo di Spagna. It is dominated by the majestic **Spanish Steps**★★ (Scala della Trinità dei Monti) built in the 18C by the architects de Sanctis and Specchi, who adopted the baroque style of perspective and *trompe-l'œil*. At the foot of the stairway are the Boat Fountain (Fontana della Barcaccia) by Bernini's father, Pietro (17C), and Keats' House where the poet died in 1821.

At the top of the stairs, **Holy Trinity on the Hill**★ (Trinità dei Monti) (**CX X**) is the French church built in the 16C and restored in the 19C. It contains a **Deposition from the Cross**★ *(2nd chapel on the left)* dating from 1541 by Daniele da Volterra, a great admirer of Michelangelo.

Leading off from this square is **Via dei Condotti** (**BCX 23**) lined with elegant shops. It was also renowned for the Caffè Greco, a famous establishment which was opened in 1760 and frequented by celebrities (Goethe, Berlioz, Wagner, Stendhal etc).

★★ PIAZZA DEL POPOLO (BV)

This square was designed by Giuseppe Valadier (1762-1839). The central obelisk was brought from Egypt in the reign of Augustus and set up here in the 16C on the orders of Sixtus V. The **Porta del Popolo**★ was pierced in the Aurelian wall in the 3C, and adorned with an external façade in the 16C and with an inner façade designed by Bernini in the 17C.

The Renaissance **Church of Santa Maria del Popolo**★★ (**N**) was remodelled in the baroque period. It contains 15C **frescoes**★ by Pinturicchio *(first chapel on the right);* two **tombs**★ by Andrea Sansovino *(in the chancel);* two **paintings**★★★ by **Caravaggio**: the Crucifixion of St Peter and the Conversion of St Paul *(first chapel to the left of the chancel);* and the **Chigi Chapel**★ *(2nd on the left)* designed by Raphael. The Egyptian obelisk, which was brought to Rome in the reign of Augustus, was erected in the centre in the 16C by Pope Sixtus V.

Leading off the Piazza del Popolo is the main street of central Rome, **Via del Corso**★★ (**BCX**), lined with handsome Renaissance palaces and fashionable shops.

PINCIO (BV)

This fine public park was laid out in the 19C by Giuseppe Valadier. It affords a magnificent **view**★★★ particularly at dusk when the golden glow so typical of Rome is at its mellow best.

Viale della Trinità dei Monti (**BCVX**) leads southwards and is overlooked by the **Villa Medici** (**CX**), now the home of the French Academy.

ADDITIONAL SIGHTS

Churches

★ **Chiesa Nuova** (BX Q). – This church dates from the Counter-Reformation. Alongside is the building originally built to house the assemblies of the Congregation of the Oratory, with an elegant **façade**★ by Borromini.

★★ **Sant'Andrea al Quirinale** (CX L). – This masterpiece by **Bernini** with its elliptical **interior**★★ demonstrates his sure taste in the use of coloured marbles, gilding and stucco figures to create a rich and beautiful decor.

★ **St Augustine's Church** (BX E). – The church contains Jacopo Sansovino's **Madonna del Parto**★, Raphael's fresco of the **Prophet Isaiah**★ and Caravaggio's **Madonna of the Pilgrims**★★★.

★★ **San Carlo alle Quattro Fontane** (CX K). – **Borromini's** masterpiece with an intricate façade which reveals the torment of the architect, and an **interior**★★ on an elliptical plan.

★★ **San Clemente** (DY). – There are in fact two basilicas. Upper one: 12C **mosaics**★★★ in the apse and **frescoes**★ by Masolino.

★★ **Sant'Ignazio** (BX G). – The façade and central ceiling **frescoes**★★ are by the Jesuit, **Andrea Pozzo.**

★★ **Basilica of St Lawrence without the Walls** (San Lorenzo fuori Le Mura). – *Take Via dei Ramni* (**DX 53**). *Town plan in the current Michelin Red Guide Italia.* The basilica dates from the 6C and the 13C: 5C-6C **harvest sarcophagus**, 13C **ambos**★ and a 13C **papal throne**★.

★ **St Peter in Chains** (San Pietro in Vincoli) (**CY G**). – Julius II's mausoleum and **Moses**★★★ by Michelangelo.

★ **St Agnes without the Walls** (Sant'Agnese fuori le Mura). – *Take Via Nomentana* (**DV**). *Town plan in the current Michelin Red Guide Italia.* **Mosaic**★ in the apse. The **Church of St Constance**★ originally a 4C mausoleum has a fine **mosaic**★.

★ **St Cecilia in Trastevere** (Santa Cecilia in Trastevere) ⊙ (**BY**). – Much altered 9C building. **St Cecilia's Statue**★ (1599) by Stefano Maderno and a **Last Judgement**★★★ (*c*1293) by Pietro Cavallini.

★★ **Santa Maria degli Angeli** (DX E). – This prestigious church was built amidst the ruins of Diocletian's baths. The **transept**★ gives a good idea of the solemn magnitude of the ancient building.

★★ **Santa Maria della Vittoria** (CX E). – This is Carlo Maderna's masterpiece. The sumptuous **interior**★★★ provides the setting for Bernini's **Ecstasy of St Theresa of Avila**★★★ (1652).

★★ **Santa Sabina** (BY F). – This 5C building is one of Rome's oldest basilicas. Beautiful cypress wood **door**★★ (5C). The **interior**★★ is well proportioned and full of light.

★★ **Santa Suzanna** (CX F). – 9C-16C church with a beautiful **façade**★★★ by **Carlo Maderna**.

Sts Cosmas and Damian (SS Cosma e Damiano) (CY E). – 5C church with a beautiful 16C coffered **ceiling**★ and 6C and 7C **mosaics**★.

★ **San Pietro in Montorio** (BY D). – This 15C church has **Sebastiano del Piombo's Flagellation**★ and Bramante's **Tempietto**★ in the courtyard. **View**★★★ of Rome from the esplanade.

★ **Sant' Andrea della Valle** (BY C). – This early-17C church has a **façade**★★ by Rainaldi (17C) and a lovely **dome**★★ by Carlo Maderna, painted by Lanfranco. Domenichino decorated the **apse**★.

Santa Maria dell' Anima (BX Y). – One of Rome's rare Gothic interiors.

★ **Santa Maria della Pace** (BX X). – The four **Sibyls**★ by Raphael were inspired by Michelangelo's angels in the Sistine Chapel.

★ **Santa Maria in Cosmedin** (CY W). – Elegant 12C **campanile**★. In the porch is the **Bocca della Verità** (Mouth of Truth).

★ **Santa Maria in Trastevere** (BY Z). – 12C basilica with 12C-13C **mosaics**★★ in the chancel.

★ **Santa Maria Sopra Minerva** (BX A). – The church has numerous works of art: **frescoes**★ by Filippino Lippi and both Gothic and baroque **tombs**★.

Monuments from antiquity

Arch of Janus (Arco di Giano) (CY S). – Through this public gateway passed some of Rome's busiest roads.

★★ **Area Sacra del Largo Argentina** (BY). – These ruins of four temples date from the days of the ancient Roman Republic.

★★ **Augustus' Altar of Peace (Ara Pacis Augustae)** ⊘ (BX V). – The altar is the major work of the Augustan "golden age" and is decorated with magnificent **low relief carvings**.

Circus Maximus (Circo Massimo) (CY). – This was the largest circus in Rome and was used exclusively for chariot races.

Augustus' Mausoleum (BX B). – The mausoleum takes the form of an Etruscan tumulus tomb.

★ **Caius Cestius' Pyramid** (CZ A). – Rome's most original mausoleum was erected in the 12C BC by a rich citizen.

★★ **Temple of Apollo** (BY V). – The temple was dedicated to Apollo medicus and retains three elegant fluted **columns**★★.

★ **Temple of Fortuna Virilis** (CY Y). – This rectangular and austere temple dates from the late 2C BC.

★ **Temple of Vesta** (CY X). – Elegant circular construction dating from the Augustan period.

★★ **Theatre of Marcellus** (BY T[1]). – One of Rome's largest theatres, it was inaugurated by Augustus in the 11C BC.

Museums and palaces

★ **National Gallery of Modern Art** ⊘ (CV M[12]). – Italian painting and sculpture from the 19C to the present day.

★★★ **Borghese Gallery (Museo Borghese)** ⊘ (CV M[9]). – Sculptures by Canova and Bernini and paintings by Raphael, Correggio, Titian and Caravaggio.

★★★ **National Roman Museum** ⊘ (DX M[7]). – Greek and Roman antiquities; paintings from various Roman villas.

★★★ **Villa Giulia National Museum** ⊘ (BV M[10]). – Exceptional collection of antiquities relating to the Etruscan Civilisation. The setting is Julius III's elegant country villa.

★★ **Palazzo della Cancelleria** (BXY S). – An elegant palace built from 1483 to 1513 with a harmonious inner courtyard.

★★ **Quirinal Palace (Palazzo del Quirinale)** ⊘ (CX S). – This handsome 16C palace was designed as a summer residence for the popes and is now the official residence of the President of the Republic.

★★ **Barberini Palace** ⊘ (CX M[8]). – This baroque palace now houses a remarkable **Picture Gallery**★★ (Tintoretto, Caravaggio, Raphael, Titian, Quentin Metsys, Holbein etc).

★ **Palazzo Braschi** ⊘ (BX M[4]). – Late-18C papal family palace now housing the **Rome Museum**★ covering Rome from the Middle Ages.

Palazzo Chigi (BX C). – This 16C palace now belongs to the Presidency of the Council of Ministers.

Palazzo della Consulta (CX Q). – This palace with its **façade**★ by Ferdinando Fuga (18C) is now the seat of the Constitutional Court.

Palazzo Corsini ⊘ (ABY). – A 15C palace rebuilt in the 18C. **Picture Gallery** (Fra Angelico, Caravaggio).

★ **Palazzo Doria Pamphili** ⊘ (CX M³). – A handsome 16C palace with a **collection**★ of paintings by Caravaggio, Velasquez, the Carracci etc.

Palazzo Madama (BX R). – A 16C palace now the seat of the Senate.

Palazzo di Montecitorio (BX). – This 17C palace houses the Chamber of Deputies.

Palazzo della Sapienza (BX K). – A 16C palace with Borromini's masterpiece, **St Ivo's Church**★ with its bell tower, in the inner courtyard.

★ **Palazzo Spada** ⊘ (BY M⁵). – The **Spada Gallery**★ presents in its original setting the private collection of the 17C churchman, Cardinal Spada.

★★ **Villa Farnesina** ⊘ (ABY). – This villa was built from 1508 to 1511 for Agostino Chigi who commissioned Raphael and his pupils to decorate the interior.

Squares, streets, sites, parks and gardens

★ **Piazza Bocca della Verità** (CY 15). – A combination of ancient (Arch of Janus, Temple of Fortuna Virilis and the round Temple said to be the Temple of Vesta), medieval (Santa Maria in Cosmedin, *p 193*) and baroque buildings, makes a typical Roman scene.

★ **Piazza Campo dei Fiori** (BY). – This well-known square and one of the most popular in Rome is the site of a picturesque food market every morning.

★ **Piazza Colonna** (BX). – At the centre of this busy square stands the 2C **column**★ in honour of Marcus Aurelius.

★★ **Quirinal Square** (Piazza del Quirinale) (CX). – This elegant and gently-sloping square is adorned with a fountain, an obelisk, statues of the Dioscuri and is overlooked by the Quirinal Palace and Palazzo della Consulta *(p 193)*.

★ **Piazza Sant'Ignazio** (BX 58). – This charming square was designed in imitation of a theatre set.

★ **St Paul's Gate** (Porta San Paolo) (CZ). – This gate opens onto Via Ostiense which led to St Paul's Basilica, from which the gate took its present name.

★ **St Sebastian's Gate** (Porta San Sebastiano) (DZ). – This is without doubt Rome's most spectacular gate (3C).

★ **Via dei Coronari** (BX 25). – This attractive street known for its second-hand and antique shops is lined with palaces glowing in ochre and stone.

★★ **EUR.** – *Take Via Cristoforo Colombo (DZ). Town plan in the current Michelin Red Guide Italia.*
This new district (1939) to the south of Rome with its colossal modern architecture is the site of the **Museum of Roman Civilisation**★★ ⊘.

★ **Tiber Island** (Isola Tiberina) (BY). – This peaceful spot is linked to the bank by the **Fabrician Bridge** (Ponte Fabricius) (BY 31), the only Roman bridge to survive intact.

Janiculum (Gianicolo) (AY). – This attractive promenade affords extensive **views**★★★ over the city.

★★★ **Vatican Gardens** (AV). – The gardens provide a good view of the dome of St Peter's which rises majestically above the gardens.

★★ **Villa Borghese** (CV). – This is Rome's largest public park.

> **GREEN TOURIST GUIDES**
> *Architecture, Art,*
> *Picturesque routes,*
> *Touring programmes*
> *Town and site plans.*

★ **SABBIONETA** Lombardy   Pop 4 622

Michelin map ▨▨▨ fold 14, ▨▨▨ fold 27 or ▨▨▨ fold 22 – 33km – 21 miles to the southwest of Mantua

This little town ⊘, clustering within its walls, was built on a regular plan and is a curious example of 16C **town planning**★. Vespasiano (1531-91), the youngest of the Gonzaga family, held a refined court which earned Sabbioneta the nickname of Little Athens.
The **Ducal Palace**, which contains interesting equestrian statues of the Gonzaga family, has finely carved wooden and coffered ceilings.
The **Olympic Theatre**★ was the masterpiece of Vicentino Scamozzi (1552-1616) and is one of the oldest in Europe. It has a ducal box adorned with colonnades, statues of the gods and frescoes by the school of Veronese.
The **Palazzo del Giardino** (Garden Palace) was designed for festivities. The great **Gallery of Antiquities**★ was entirely painted with frescoes by Bernardino Campi and his school. Vespasiano Gonzaga is buried in the **Church of the Incoronata**★ with its octagonal plan and surprising *trompe-l'œil* decoration. Vespasiano's remarkable **mausoleum**★ was by Leone Leoni.

Michelin map 988 fold 12 or 428 fold 22 – 37km – 23 miles to the west of Turin

Perched on a rocky site (alt 962m – 3 156ft), this **Benedictine Abbey** ⊘ was a powerful establishment in the 13C with over 100 monks and 140 sister houses. It was built at the end of the 10C by Hugues de Montboissier from Auvergne and its layout bears a strong resemblance to that of the Mont St Michel in Normandy. After passing through the iron doors of the entrance gatehouse, climb the great staircase leading to the **Zodiac Door**, whose pilasters and capitals were decorated by the famous Master Nicolò (1135). The Romanesque-Gothic **church** built on top of the rocky eminence has 16C frescoes. The early-16C triptych on the high altar is by Defendente Ferrari. The carved capitals are outstanding. From the esplanade there is a lovely **view★★★** of the Alps, the Dora Valley, the Po and Turin plains.

Each year
*the **Michelin Red Guide Italia***
presents a wealth of up-to-date information in a compact form.
It is the ideal companion for a holiday,
a long weekend or a business trip.

★ **SALERNO** Campania   Pop 153 807

Michelin map 988 fold 28 – Local map p 45
Plan of the built-up area in the current Michelin Red Guide Italia

Lying along the graceful curve of its gulf, Salerno has retained a medieval quarter on the slopes of a hill crowned by a castle. The town is now an active port and industrial centre while market gardening is the main activity of the surrounding area.
Salerno was at first Etruscan, then Roman and became a principality under the Lombards. The Norman Robert Guiscard made it his capital in 1077. A rich trading city, Salerno became famous for its university, which attracted some of the greatest scholars of the time and in particular its school of medicine which flourished from the 11C to 13C. The town acquired the nickname of City of Socrates. With the arrival of the Kings of Anjou Salerno declined and witnessed the rise of its neighbour and rival, Naples. It was just south of Salerno that the 5th US Army landed on 9 September 1943.

Mercanti (Via) .... **AB**	Duomo (Via) .... **B** 8	Sabatini (Via A.) .... **A** 19
Vittorio Emanuele (Corso) ..... **B**	Indipendenza (Via) ...... **A** 9	S. Eremita (Via) .... **B** 20
	Lista (Via Stanislas) ...... **A** 10	S. Tommaso d'Aquino (Largo) **B** 22
Abate Conforti (Largo) ...... **AB** 2	Luciani (Piazza M.) ...... **A** 12	Sedile del Campo (Pza) .... **A** 23
Alfano 1° (Piazza) .... **B** 3	Paglia (Via M.) .... **B** 13	Sedile di Pta Nuova (Pza) . **B** 24
Cavaliero (Via L.) .... **B** 4	Plebiscito (Largo) .... **B** 14	Sorgente (Via Camillo) ..... **B** 25
Cilento (Via A.) .... **B** 6	Portacatena (Via) .... **A** 15	Velia (Via) .... **B** 26
Dogana Vecchia (Via) .... **A** 7	Porta di Mare (Via) .... **A** 16	24 Maggio (Piazza) .... **B** 27

★★ **Cathedral (Duomo) (B)**. – The cathedral is dedicated to St Matthew the Evangelist, who is buried in the crypt. It was built on the orders of Robert Guiscard and consecrated by Pope Gregory VII in 1085. The Norman-style building was remodelled in the 18C and suffered considerable damage in the 1980 earthquake. The church is preceded by a delightful arcaded **atrium** built of multicoloured stone with ancient columns. The square tower to the right is 12C. The central doorway has 11C bronze doors cast in Constantinople.

The interior is of impressive dimensions. The two **ambos**★★ encrusted with decorative mosaics and resting on slender columns with marvellously carved capitals, along with the **paschal candelabrum**, form an outstanding 12C-13C group. The Crusaders' Chapel at the far end of the south aisle is where the Crusaders had their arms blessed. Under the altar is the tomb of Pope Gregory VII who died in exile at Salerno (1085).

In the north aisle stands the tomb of Margaret of Durazzo, the wife of Charles III of Anjou.

★ **Via Mercanti (AB)**. – This street is one of the most picturesque with its shops, old houses and oratories. At its west end stands the **Arechi Arch (A A)** built by the Lombards in the 8C.

★ **Lungomare Trieste (AB)**. – From this promenade, planted with palm trees and tamarisks, there is a wide view of the Gulf of Salerno.

★★ SAN CLEMENTE A CASAURIA ABBEY Abruzzi

Michelin map 988 fold 27 or 430 fold 28 – 40km – 25 miles southwest of Pescara – Access: by the A25 motorway and the Torre de' Passeri exit road

The San Clemente Abbey was founded in 871 and rebuilt in the 12C by the Cistercians in the transitional Romanesque-Gothic style. The secularised church is all that remains today.

Church. – The façade is quite remarkable: a deep portico has three arches resting on lovely capitals; the main doorway is decorated with exceptional sculpture, notably on the uprights, tympanum and lintel (the bronze door was cast in 1191). The interior comprises a nave and two aisles and a semicircular apse, and is typical of the architectural simplicity dear to St Bernard. Both the monumental pulpit and the paschal candelabrum are 13C. The high altar is surmounted by a finely carved Romanesque **ciborium**★★★. The 9C crypt has survived from the original structure and has vaulting supported by ancient columns.

When driving in Italian towns use the plans
in the Michelin Red Guide Italia which are revised each year; they show
– through-routes and by-passes
– new roads and one-way systems
– car parks.

★★★ SAN GIMIGNANO Tuscany   Pop 7 109

Michelin map 988 fold 14, 428 fold 38 or 430 fold 13
Town plan in the current Michelin Red Guide Italia

San Gimignano with its many medieval towers stands on a hilltop in the rolling Tuscan countryside where vineyards and olive groves predominate. Its numerous towers of nobility have earned it the nickname of San Gimignano of the Fine Towers.

In the 12C the town was an independent commune and it prospered during the next two hundred years. The towers of nobility were thought for a long time to have been built for defensive purposes, and as a sign of the power of the noble families who were split in the internecine fighting between the Ghibellines and the Guelphs. The former supported the emperor and the latter the pope. The holes in the walls served to fix gangways between the towers of allied nobles, enabling them to meet quickly in times of danger. A simpler explanation may be that the towers were linked to the town's past economic success. In the Middle Ages it was an important textile centre which guarded the secret of yellow saffron dye, and to protect the precious cloth (the length determined the value) from the sun and dust, the craftsmen built the tall towers as they had no room to spread it out on a flat surface owing to the town plan. The stairways were fixed on the outside, in holes which are still to be seen, so as not to waste any space inside.

★★ **Piazza della Cisterna**. – The square is paved with bricks laid on their edges in a herring-bone pattern and it derives its name from a 13C cistern or well *(cisterna)*. It is one of the most evocative squares in Italy with its tall towers and austere 13C-14C mansions all around.

★★ **Piazza del Duomo**. – The Collegiate Church, palaces and seven towers of nobility line this majestic square.

★ **Collegiate Church** (Collegiatas) ⊘ **(B)**. – This 12C Romanesque Church was extended in the 15C by Giuliano da Maiano. The façade was restored in the 19C. Inside are a **Martyrdom of St Sebastian** (1465) by Benozzo Gozzoli and an Annunciation in wood by Jacopo della Quercia *(on the west wall)*.

The walls of the north aisle are adorned with **frescoes★** evoking scenes from the Old Testament by Bartolo di Fredi (14C), while the **frescoes★★** (*c*1350) of the south aisle are by Barna da Siena and depict scenes from the Life of Christ (start at the top). They display an elegant draughtsmanship and delicate colours. In the **Chapel of Santa Fina** ⊙ (grills) designed by Giuliano da Maiano, the harmonious **altar★** is by his nephew Benedetto da Maiano and the **frescoes★** (1475) by Domenico Ghirlandaio.

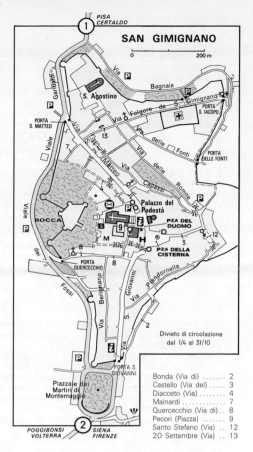

★ **People's Palace (Palazzo del Popolo)** ⊙ **(H)**. – The 13C-14C palace is dominated by a tall **tower,** from the top of which unfolds an unusual **view★★** over the brown roofs and towers of the town. The Council Chamber has a remarkable **Maesta★** (Madonna and Child enthroned in Majesty) (1317) by Lippo Memmi, which was restored *c*1467 by Benozzo Gozzoli. The **Municipal Museum★** (Museo Civico) on the second floor presents paintings from the 12C to 15C Florentine and Sienese schools.

Governor's Palace (Palazzo del Podestà). – This 13C palace has a vast porch on the ground floor. It also comprises an impressive tower, 51m – 167ft high, known as the Rognosa Tower. Close by stands the 13C Palazzo Chigi.

Church of St Augustine (Sant' Agostino). – This 13C church has in its chancel a cycle of seventeen **frescoes★★** painted from 1463 to 1467 by Benozzo Gozzoli. The life of the famous theologian St Augustine is depicted with the fresh colour, sense of perspective and love of detail so typical of this artist. Near the west door stands the **tomb★** of St Bartolo by Benedetto da Maiano (15C).

EXCURSIONS

★★ **Volterra.** – *29km* – *18 miles to the southeast. Leave by* ②. *Description p 236.*

★ **San Vivaldo** ⊙. – *17km* – *10 miles to the northwest. Leave by* ①. In 1500 Franciscan monks settled here to guard the tomb of St Vivaldo who died here in 1320. During the next fifteen years they built a monastery and a series of chapels (about fifteen are still extant) recreating the holy places of Palestine in miniature. The chapels of the **sacro monte** contain painted terracottas which depict nearly to scale scenes ranging from the Passion to Whitsuntide.

Certaldo. – *13km* – *8 miles to the north. Leave by* ①. *Description p 77.*

*Gourmets should look in the current **Michelin Red Guide Italia** for the restaurants with stars.*

★ # SAN MARINO REPUBLIC   Pop 22 730

Michelin map 988 fold 15, 429 folds 35 and 36 or 430 folds 5 and 6
Town plan in the current Michelin Red Guide Italia

One of the smallest states in the world (61km² – 23sq miles) stands in an admirable **site★★★** on the slopes of the jagged sandstone ridge of Monte Titano. This ancient republic strikes its own coinage, issues its own postage stamps, has its own army and police force.
San Marino is believed to have been founded in the 4C by a pious mason, Marinus, who was fleeing from the persecutions of the Emperor Diocletian. The system of government has changed little in nine centuries, and the leading figures are still the two Captains Regent, who are chosen from among the sixty members of the Grand Council and installed every six months during a colourful ceremony *(see the table of Principal Festivals at the end of the guide).* The economy is based on tourism, trade, the sale of postage stamps, craft industries and agriculture. San Marino produces a very pleasant wine, Moscato.

SIGHTS

Government House (Palazzo del Governo) ⊙. – *Piazza della Libertà.*
This was rebuilt in the Gothic style in the late 19C. The Great Council Chamber is open to visitors.

Basilica of St Marinus (Basilica di San Marino). –*Piazzale Domus Plebis.*
The basilica contains the relics of the saint.
In the nearby Church of St Peter (San Pietro) there are two niches hewn in the rock, in which St Marinus and his companion St Leo are said to have slept.

Rocca Guaita; Rocca Cesta or della Fratta; Rocca Montale. – These three peaks are crowned with three towers *(torri)* which are linked by a watchpath. From the towers there are splendid **views★★★** of the Apennines, the plain, Rimini and the sea as far as the Dalmatian coast. In the Cesta Tower there is an **arms museum** ⊙ with a mainly medieval collection. It also features gunpowder firearms, as well as guns and rifles dating from the 16C, 17C and 18C.

Museum-Picture Gallery (Museo-Pinacoteca) ⊙. – This includes paintings (Strozzi, Ribera, Guerchino and Domenichino), Egyptian and Etruscan artefacts and Roman coins and statuettes etc.

St Francis' Museum (Museo di San Francesco) ⊙. – 12C to 17C and modern paintings as well as Etruscan potteries and funerary objects.

Coin and Stamp Museum (Museo Filatelico e Numismatico) ⊙. – *At Borgo Maggiore.*
Collection of stamps and coins issued by the Republic since the mid 19C.

EXCURSION

★★ **San Leo.** – *16km – 10 miles to the southwest. Leave to the north then take the road to the left leading down to the Marecchia Valley. Just before Pietracuta and the S 258 bear left.*
A steep winding road climbs to the summit of the huge limestone rock (alt 639m – 2 096ft) in an impressive **setting★★**, made famous by Dante in his *Divine Comedy*, with the historic village of San Leo and its 15C **fortress★** (Forte), perched on the edge of the cliff, where the charlatan Count Cagliostro (18C) was imprisoned and died. It now houses a **museum and picture gallery** ⊙ (arms, furniture and 15C to 18C paintings).
From the fortress there is an immense **panorama★★★** of the Marecchia Valley, Montefeltro and San Marino.
The cathedral which is in the Lombard-Romanesque style (1173) and the pre-Romanesque parish church (restored) are noteworthy.

★★ # SAN REMO Liguria   Pop 60 524

Michelin map ▨▨▨ fold 12 or ▨▨▨ fold 20 or ▨▨▨ fold 33 – Local map p 181
Town plan in the current Michelin Red Guide Italia

San Remo curves round its wide bay protected by two headlands, and is backed by a rim of mountains. The luxurious capital of the Riviera di Ponente enjoys a pleasantly warm temperature all the year round and the highest number of sunshine hours on the Ligurian coast. In addition to these advantages San Remo boasts a wide choice of hotels, thermal establishments, a pleasure boat harbour, casino, racecourse, lively festivals and other cultural and sporting events.
San Remo is the principal Italian flower market and millions of roses, carnations and mimosa are exported worldwide. The flower market takes place from October to June between 6am and 8am.

Corso Imperatrice. – It is Liguria's most elegant seafront promenade and it is particularly known for its Canary palms.

★ **La Pigna.** – This is the name given to the old town, because of its pointed shape (*pigna* meaning beak). It has a medieval aspect with its winding alleys lined with tall and narrow houses. From Piazza Castello climb up to the baroque Church of Madonna della Costa, from where there is an attractive **view★** of the town and bay.

★★ **Monte Bignone.** – Alt 1 299m – 4 262ft. *13km – 8 miles to the north.*
From the summit of this pine-covered peak there is a splendid **panorama★★** which extends as far as Cannes in France.

★ # SANSEPOLCRO Tuscany   Pop 15 741

Michelin map ▨▨▨ fold 15 or ▨▨▨ fold 15

The small industrial town (manufacture of macaroni) has retained its ramparts and some old houses. It was in this town that the most important artist of the Italian Quattrocento (15C), **Piero della Francesca** *(qv)*, was born.
See the table of Principal Festivals at the end of the guide.

Municipal Museum (Museo Civico) ⊙. – *65 Via Aggiunti.*
This museum occupies twelve rooms of the former town hall. It contains several leading **works★★** by Piero della Francesca: an impressive Resurrection showing his mature genius, a very lovely polyptych of the Virgin of Pity, a St Julian and a St Ludovic. There are also works by his pupil Luca Signorelli, by Pontormo, Bassano, Palma the Younger, Andrea and Giovanni della Robbia and other artists, all native of Sansepolcro (Raffaelino dal Colle, Santi di Tito, Giovanni Alberti...). In addition there are 14C fragments of frescoes, sinopie *(qv)*, engravings, reliquaries etc.

EXCURSIONS

★★ **Camaldoli.** – *76km – 47 miles to the northwest.*
Camaldoli, situated in a great forest in the heart of the mountains, was the cradle of the Camaldulian Order, founded in the 11C by St Romuald. The monastery, standing at the head of a dismal valley, was rebuilt in the 13C. Higher up in a grim, isolated site is the **Hermitage★** (Eremo) ⊙, a cluster of buildings encircled by ramparts. These include St Romuald's cell and a lovely 18C church.

★ **La Verna Monastery (Convento della Verna).** – *36km – 22 miles to the northwest.*
The monastery was founded in 1214 by St Francis of Assisi, who received the Stigmata there. The visitor can see the Chapel of Santa Maria degli Angeli, the Chapel of the Stigmata, St Francis' sleeping place and the enormous projecting rock under which he used to pray. The basilica has terracottas by Andrea della Robbia.

★ **Poppi.** – *61km – 38 miles to the northwest.*
This proud and attractive city, formerly the capital of the Casentino, overlooks the Arno Valley. The city itself is crowned by its proud-looking **castle** ⊙, former seat of the Counts of Guidi. This 13C Gothic palace has a curious **courtyard★** decorated with coats of arms.

Monterchi. – *17km – 11 miles to the south.*
The cemetery chapel has a strange but compelling work by Piero della Francesca, the **Madonna with Child★** (Madonna del Parto), which has been detached and placed above the altar. This is a rare example of the pregnant Virgin in Italian art.

★★★ **SIENA** Tuscany   Pop 59 225

Michelin map 988 fold 15 or 430 folds 13 and 14
Plan of built-up area in the current Michelin Red Guide Italia

Siena "the Beloved" is a mystical, gentle, passionate and generous art centre. Siena invites the visitor to stroll through its narrow Gothic streets, lined with palaces and patrician mansions, which converge on the famous Piazza del Campo. It is encircled by ramparts which seem too big for it.
More than anywhere else Siena brings to life the reality of a medieval city. Its plan extends over three converging red clay hills (from which the colour "burnt sienna" is named) at the very heart of the high Tuscan plateau.

HISTORICAL NOTES

Its greatest period of prosperity was the 13C and 14C, when it was an independent republic with a well-organised administration of its own. Siena flourished essentially on trade and banking.
During the period of strife between Guelphs and Ghibellines *(qv)*, Siena was opposed to its powerful neighbour Florence. One of the most memorable episodes of this long struggle was the Battle of Montaperti (1260), when the Sienese Ghibellines resoundingly defeated the Florentine Guelphs. It was during this troubled time that Siena acquired her most prestigious buildings, and that a local school of painting evolved which played a notable part in the development of Italian art.
In 1348 the plague decimated Siena's population and the city began to decline as dissension continued to reign among the rival factions. By the early 15C Siena's golden era was over.
The mystical city of Siena was the birthplace in 1347 of **St Catherine**. By the age of seven she had decided on her mystic marriage with Christ. She entered the Dominican Order aged 16 and had many visions and trances and received the Stigmata at Pisa. In 1377 she helped to bring the popes back from Avignon to Rome, which they had left in 1309. **St Bernardine** (1380-1444) is also greatly venerated in Siena. He gave up his studies in order to help the victims of the plague in the city. Aged 22 he entered the Franciscan order and was a leader of the Observants, who favoured a stricter observance of the rule of St Francis. A great preacher, he spent much of his time travelling throughout Italy.

SIENESE ART

It was not only in political matters that Siena opposed Florence. In the city of Dante, Cimabue and Giotto were innovators, but were greatly influenced by the Roman traditions of balance and realism which led to the development of Renaissance art in all its glory. Siena, on the other hand, remained attached to the Greek or Byzantine traditions, in which the graceful line and the refinement of colour gave a certain dazzling elegance to the composition, which was one of the chief attractions of Gothic painting.
Duccio di Buoninsegna (c1260-1318) was the first to experiment with this new combination of inner spirituality and increased attention to space and composition as well as the splendour of the colours.
Simone Martini (c1285-d 1344 in Avignon) followed in Duccio's footsteps but imitated nature more closely with his exquisite harmonies of colour and taste for detail. He had a considerable reputation in Europe and worked at the Papal Court in Avignon.
His contemporaries **Pietro** and **Ambrogio Lorenzetti** introduced an even greater realism with minute delicate details, while at the same time remaining true to the sense of line of their predecessors. One of the favourite themes of the Sienese school was the Virgin and Child.

The Sienese artists of the Quattrocento (15C) continued in the spirit of the Gothic masters. While Florence concentrated on rediscovering antiquity and its myths, minor masters such as **Lorenzo Monaco, Giovanni di Paolo** and **Sassetta** continued to emphasise affectation in figure design, flexibility of line and subtlety of colour which made Siena an ideal refuge for Gothic sensibilities.

In the field of secular architecture, the Gothic style gave Siena its own special character with the use of elements which made for a more graceful aspect. Brick and stone were often associated on the lower storeys, while windows became more numerous, especially the Sienese one with a depressed three-centred arch supporting a pointed one.

Building activity was concentrated on the cathedral where construction work and transformations lasted over two centuries. There again the façade is in a unique Gothic style where one can detect the transition from the Romanesque to the Flamboyant Gothic in an interpretation full of affectation.

Sculpture, also influenced by the building of the cathedral, was enriched by the presence of two Pisans, Nicola and Giovanni Pisano *(qv)*. The latter decorated the cathedral façade with a series of highly expressive figures and his work influenced **Tino di Camaino**, born in Siena in 1280 but who spent the last years of his life at the Angevin Court in Naples. However, the important figure in Sienese sculpture is **Jacopo della Quercia** (1371-1438), who successfully combined Gothic traditions with the Florentine Renaissance style.

★★★ PIAZZA DEL CAMPO (BZ) *time: 1 1/4 hours*

This "square" forms a monumental ensemble of almost matchless harmony. It is shaped like a scallop or a fan and is paved with brick and encircled by a ring of stone slabs. The piazza slopes down to the long brick and stone façade of the Palazzo Pubblico.

Piazza del Campo – Town Hall

Eight white lines radiate outwards dividing the area into nine segments, each symbolising one of the forms of government which ruled Siena. This consisted of nine members representing trade and banking who ruled the city during its greatest period of prosperity from the late 13C to the mid 14C. At the upper end is the **Fonte Gaia** (Fountain of Joy) so-called because of the festivities which followed its inauguration in 1348. Fountains were at that time a symbol of the city's power. It was embellished with panels sculpted by Jacopo della Quercia but these, now badly deteriorated, have been replaced by replicas.

The Piazza del Campo is the venue twice annually *(see the table of Principal Festivals at the end of the guide)* for the popular festival **Palio delle Contrade.** The whole town participates in the preparation of this event for weeks beforehand and it recalls the medieval administrative organisation of Siena with its three main quarters, themselves subdivided into parishes *(contrade)*.

The festivities begin with a procession of the *contrade* in costume, who then compete in the dangerous horse race round the square. There is much betting on the outcome. The *palio*, a standard bearing the effigy of the Virgin, the city's protectress, is awarded to the winner.

★★★ Town Hall (Palazzo Pubblico) ⊙.

The town hall, built between the late-13C and mid 14C in the Gothic style, is of a rare elegance with its many triple bays under supporting arches, which give the impression of a curving movement to the façade. High up on the central part is a circular bronze panel inscribed with the monogram IHS (*Iesus Hominum Salvator* Jesus Men's Saviour) used as a badge by St Bernardine. From one end of the façade rises the slim form of the **Torre del Mangia**, an 88m – 289ft-high tower designed by Lippo Memmi. At the foot of the tower, **Cappella di Piazza** is a chapel in the form of a loggia dating from 1352, built to mark the end of the plague. It was remodelled in the Renaissance style a century later.

This palace was the seat of Siena's successive governments and most of the great artists of the Sienese school contributed to its decoration.

Priors' Room: frescoes (1407) by Spinello Aretino recount the struggles between Pope Alexander III and the Emperor Frederick Barbarossa.

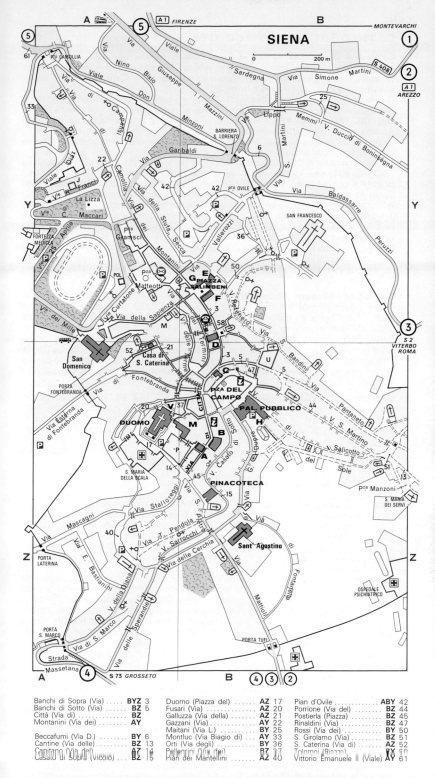

SIENA

★ **Chapel:** this contains frescoes by Taddeo di Bartolo portraying the Life of the Virgin, a very lovely **railing**★ and its magnificent early-15C **stalls**★★ with intarsia work illustrating the Creed, and on the high altar a Holy Family by Sodoma.

Globe Room: the admirable **Maestà**★★ (1315) is Simone Martini's earliest known work, and opposite is the famous **equestrian portrait**★ of the Sienese general, Guidoriccio da Fogliano, by the same artist. Note the curious contrast between the realism with which the figure is portrayed and the unreality of the background landscape.

Peace Room: here are the famous frescoes, although badly damaged (1335-40), of Ambrogio Lorenzetti, entitled **Effects of Good and Bad Government**★★, where the artist has achieved a happy combination of a scholarly and noble allegorical approach with that of meticulous narrative detail.

Tower ⊙: from the top there is a superb **panorama**★★ of Siena's chaotic rooftops and of the gently-rolling Sienese countryside beyond.

SIENA

★★★ CATHEDRAL AND PRECINCTS *time: 1 1/2 hours*

★★★ **Cathedral (Duomo) (AZ)**. – The richly-decorated façade *(photograph p 28)* was begun in the 13C by Giovanni Pisano who added some remarkably expressive statues. The upper part was modelled on Orvieto Cathedral. The sober Romanesque campanile dates from 1313.

The walls of the **interior** are faced with alternating bands of black and white marble. The profusion of pillars provides a multitude of perspectives as one moves about. The 15C-16C **paving**★★★ ⊘ is unique. About forty artists including **Beccafumi** worked on the 56 marble panels which portray, either in graffiti or intarsia work, mythological figures such as Sibyls, Virtues and Allegories and scenes from the Old Testament in a lively and delicate manner.

In the chancel is a 15C bronze tabernacle by Vecchietta and richly decorated 14C-16C **stalls**★★. At the entrance to the north transept stands the famous **pulpit**★★★ carved from 1266 to 1268 by **Nicola Pisano**, who relates the Life of Christ in seven panels in a grandiose and exceptionally dramatic style.

From the north aisle a charming doorway leads to the famous **Piccolomini Library** (Libreria Piccolomini), built in 1495 by Cardinal Francesco Piccolomini, the future Pius III, to house his uncle's books. The Umbrian painter **Pinturicchio** adorned it with **frescoes**★★ (1502-09) depicting episodes in the life of Aeneas Silvius Piccolomini (Pius II). The delicate draughtsmanship is typical of miniatures, while the brilliant colours are more typical of illuminations. In the centre stands the famous marble statue of the Three Graces, a Roman sculpture (3C) showing Hellenistic influence.

★★ **Cathedral Museum (Museo dell'Opera del Duomo)** ⊘ **(ABZ M)**. – The museum is in the extant part of the vast building started in 1339. The present cathedral was to have been its transept. The project was abandoned owing to technical problems and especially the terrible plague of 1348. The museum contains Giovanni Pisano's statues which originally adorned the cathedral façade, a low relief by Jacopo della Quercia and the famous **Maestà** (Virgin in Majesty) by **Duccio**. This altarpiece was originally painted on both sides (now separated). The panels of the reverse side depict scenes from the Passion of Christ, with a wealth of intimate details.

★ **Baptistry of St John (Battistero San Giovanni)** ⊘ **(AZ V)**. – This lies below the cathedral, under a prolongation of the chancel, and dates from the 14C. The façade started in the Gothic style was never completed. The interior is adorned with 15C frescoes. The **font**★★ is adorned with panels designed by Jacopo della Quercia. The bronze panels were by several Tuscan masters such as Lorenzo Ghiberti and Donatello. The latter's Feast of Herod is particularly interesting.

ADDITIONAL SIGHTS

★★ **Picture Gallery (Pinacoteca)** ⊘ **(BZ)**. – The extensive collection of 13C-16C Sienese paintings is displayed in the 15C **Palazzo Buonsignori**★.

On the second floor is the rich section of **Primitives**. Beyond the late-12C to early-13C Crucifixes are the works of a local artist, Guido da Siena, and then the better-known Sienese artists such as Duccio, with a youthful work, the **Virgin of the Franciscans** (Room 4). The flowing line and grace characteristic of the Sienese school are already visible.

The **Virgin and Child** (Room 6) by Simone Martini is a rare work full of gentleness and purity. Room 7 is important for the numerous works by the Lorenzetti brothers including the **Pala del Carmine**, a large altarpiece by the elder, Pietro, in which he displays his aptitude for portraying narrative details (see the scenes on the predella). The long sinuous silhouette of the small **Virgin of Humility** (Room 13), with rose bushes screening off the meticulously portrayed landscape background, is an exquisite work by Giovanni di Paolo.

On the first floor note Pinturicchio's works, a **Birth of the Virgin** by Beccafumi (Room 31) with its audacious colour tones, and **Christ of the Column** by Sodoma.

★ **Via di Città (BZ). Via Banchi di Sopra (BYZ)**. – These narrow, flagstoned streets bordered by remarkable **palaces**★ bustle with life.

Coming from Via San Pietro the visitor will see in the Via di Città, on the left the 15C **Palazzo Piccolomini** or Palazzo delle Papesse **(A)** with the lower part of its façade rusticated in the Florentine manner. Practically opposite stands the long curving Gothic façade of the **Palazzo Chigi-Saracini (B)**, now the home of the Academy of Music. Farther along, on the right, the **Loggia dei Mercanti (C)** or Merchants' Loggia, in the transitional Gothic-Renaissance style with a 17C top storey, is the seat of the Commercial Courts.

Shortly afterwards on the left is the 13C **Palazzo Tolomei (D)**, an austere but elegant building. Robert of Anjou, King of Naples, stayed here in 1310. The **Piazza Salimbeni**★ **(BY)** is enclosed on three sides by buildings with different architectural styles: at the far end the 14C **Palazzo Salimbeni (E)** is Gothic; on the left the 15C **Palazzo Spannocchi (F)** is Renaissance; while the 16C **Palazzo Tantucci (G)** on the left is baroque.

Basilica of St Dominic (San Domenico) (AYZ). – St Catherine had her trances in this 13C-15C Gothic conventual church. Inside, there is an authentic portrait of the saint by her contemporary Andrea Vanni.

In the Chapel of St Catherine, halfway down the south aisle, is a lovely Renaissance **tabernacle**★ carved in marble by Giovanni di Stefano which contains the head of the saint. The **frescoes**★ by Sodoma on the walls depict scenes from the life of the saint.

Birthplace of St Catherine (Casa di Santa Caterina) ⊙ (AZ). – *Entrance in Via Santa Caterina.*
The saint's house has been transformed into a series of superimposed oratories. In the basement is the cell where St Catherine lived. Above is the 13C painted crucifix in front of which the saint is said to have received the Stigmata.

Church of St Augustine (Sant' Agostino) (BZ). – This 13C church has a baroque interior. There is a remarkable **Adoration of the Crucifix★** by Perugino, and the Sacramento Chapel contains **works★** by Ambrogio Lorenzetti, Matteo di Giovanni and Sodoma.

★★ SORRENTO Campania   Pop 17 807

Michelin map 988 fold 27 – Local map p 44

This important southern Italian resort, known for its many beautiful gardens, overlooks the gulf of the same name. Orange and lemon groves are to be found in the surrounding countryside and even encroaching on the town. Local craftsmen produce various marquetry objects. The poet **Torquato Tasso** *(qv)* was born in Sorrento in 1544.

Church of St Francis (San Francesco). – This baroque church with its bulbous belfry masks delightful 13C **cloisters★**. The capitals are carved with water leaf motifs while the interlaced arcades are typical of the Sicilian-Arab style *(p 248)*. The public gardens, **Villa Comunale**, next door offer a good **viewpoint★★** for admiring the Bay of Naples.

★ **Correale di Terranova Museum** (Museo Correale di Terranova) ⊙. – Housed in an 18C palace, the museum has mementoes of the poet Tasso, a small archaeological section and above all a fine collection of 17C and 18C furniture. From the terrace, beyond the orange grove, there is a very fine **view★★** over the Gulf of Sorrento.

EXCURSION

★★ **Sorrento Peninsula** (Penisola Sorrentina). – *Round tour of 33km – 21 miles. See the local map p 44. Leave Sorrento to the west by the S 145 and at the junction take the road to the right to Massa Lubrense.* This winding road goes round the peninsula and affords fine views of the hillsides covered with olive groves, orange and lemon trees and vines. The latter cling to the trelliswork which supports rush matting in winter to protect the citrus from the cold. From the point of Cape Sorrento **(Capo di Sorrento)** *(footpath: from the church in the village of Capo di Sorrento take the road to the right and after the college the paved path, 1 hour Rtn)* there is a superb **view★★** of Sorrento. Beyond **Sant' Agata sui Due Golfi**, perched on a crest overlooking both the Gulf of Salerno and the Bay of Naples, the road descends steeply to Colli di San Pietro. The return to Sorrento by the S 163 offers on the way down some superb **views★★** over the Bay of Naples.

★ SPOLETO Umbria   Pop 37 881

Michelin map 988 fold 26 or 430 fold 26
Town plan in the current Michelin Red Guide Italia

This former Roman municipium then became the capital of an important Lombard duchy from the 6C to the 8C. The town covers the slopes of a hill crowned by the Rocca dei Papi. The city was dear to St Francis, who loved its austere character, tempered by the grace of the narrow winding alleys, the palaces and numerous medieval buildings.
Each summer the town hosts an international arts festival, **Festival dei Due Mondi** *(see the table of Principal Festivals at the end of the guide).*

★★ **Cathedral** (Duomo). – Flanked by a baptistry, it provides the focal point of **Piazza del Duomo★**. The façade is fronted by a fine Renaissance porch and adorned above by a rose window and 13C mosaic. Inside are frescoes *(first chapel on the south side)* by Pinturicchio, Fra Lippo Lippi's tomb *(south transept)* commissioned by Lorenzo de' Medici, and in the apse **frescoes** depicting the life of the Virgin by Fra Filippo Lippi and his assistants.

★★ **Bridge of Towers** (Ponte delle Torri). – The bridge was built in the 13C over a Roman aqueduct which was used as a foundation. The bridge with its ten Gothic arches is guarded by a small fortified gatehouse at one end.

★ **St Saviour's Basilica** (San Salvatore). – This, one of the first Christian churches in Italy, was built by Oriental monks in the 4C and modified in the 9C. Many Roman materials were re-used in the building of the later edifice.

★ **St Gregory Major's Church** (San Gregorio Maggiore). – This 12C Romanesque church was modified in the 14C. The 14C baptistry to the left of the entrance porch has walls covered with frescoes (Massacre of the Innocents). The campanile is built of blocks from ancient buildings. The dark, bare nave and aisles rest on massive columns with roughly-hewn capitals. In the chancel there is a 15C fresco and a carved stone cupboard of the same period.

Drusus' Arch (Arco di Druso). – This arch was built in AD 23 in honour of Tiberius' son.

St Dominic's Church (San Domenico). – This lovely 13C and 14C church is built of alternating courses of white and pink stone. The nave is decorated with 14C and 15C frescoes and the south transept contains a canvas by Lanfranco.

EXCURSIONS

★ **Monteluco.** – *8km – 5 miles to the east.*
An attractively-winding road leads up to Monteluco. On the way up, the **Church of St Peter** (San Pietro) has a lovely 13C Romanesque **façade**★ with relief sculptures. On the summit, **Monteluco**★ was once the seat of an ancient cult, but is now a health resort. The monastery founded by St Francis still exists.

★ **Source of the River Clitumnus** (Fonti del Clitunno). – *13km – 8 miles to the north.*
These-crystal clear waters which rise amid aquatic plants were sacred to the Romans. They plunged animals into these waters for purification prior to sacrifice. 1km – 1/2 mile below stands the **temple**★ ⊙ of Clitumnus, a minuscule early-Christian building dating from the 5C. It boasts columns and a carved pediment.

SUBIACO Latium   Pop 9 115

Michelin map 988 fold 26 or 430 fold 37

St Benedict, founder of the Benedictine Order, and his twin sister Scolastica retired to this spot at the end of the 5C and built twelve little monasteries before moving to Monte Cassino.
To reach the monasteries of Santa Scolastica and San Benedetto (3km – 2 miles) take the Frosinone road and shortly before the Aniene Bridge turn left.

Monastery of St Scolastica (Santa Scolastica) ⊙. – Standing in the fine site overlooking the Aniene Gorges the monastery has preserved a majestic 11C campanile, its church which was remodelled in the 18C, and three cloisters. The third, the work of the Cosmati, is admirable in its simplicity.

★ **Monastery of St Benedict** (San Benedetto) ⊙. – This monastery, which stands above the previous one clings to the rock face in a wild site, overhanging the gorge. The buildings date from the 13C and 14C.
The church has two storeys. The **upper church** has walls painted with frescoes of the 14C Sienese school and the 15C Umbrian school. The **lower church**, itself with two storeys, is covered with frescoes by Magister Consolus, an artist of the 13C Roman school.
Visitors are admitted to the **Sacred Cave** (Sacro Speco) where St Benedict lived a hermit's existence for three years. A spiral staircase then leads up to a chapel which contains the earliest portrait of St Francis (without Stigmata or halo), painted to commemorate the saint's visit to the sanctuary. The **Scala Santa** (Holy Staircase) leads down to the Chapel of the Virgin (frescoes by the Sienese school) and the Shepherd's Cave. From there pass to the rose garden where St Benedict threw himself into brambles to resist temptation.

★ SULMONA Abruzzi   Pop 24 717

Michelin map 988 fold 27 or 430 fold 28 – Local map p 40

Sulmona, which lies at the head of a fertile basin framed by majestic mountains, was the birthplace of the Roman poet **Ovid**, best known for his long poem *Metamorphoses*. The town has retained its medieval character.

★★ **Palazzo dell' Annunziata.** – The palace was built by a Brotherhood of Penitents and has an original façade which displays varying styles: on the left the Gothic doorway has statues of the Virgin and St Michael, while the triple-arched opening with four statues of Doctors of the Church dates from 1415; the central and right-hand parts are both later (1483 and 1522). There is an astonishingly, carved frieze halfway up the façade. The sober façade of the adjacent church was built in 1710 by Pietro Fontana.

★ **Porta Napoli.** – *Southern town gateway.* This Gothic gate has historiated capitals (14C). The exterior has an unusual decoration of an opening, bosses and rosettes.

Piazza Garibaldi. – This square is the scene on Wednesdays and Saturdays of a large and highly-colourful market. The square is bordered on two sides by a medieval aqueduct and overlooked by the Gothic doorway of the Church of St Martin (San Martino) and the Renaissance fountain, **Fontana del Vecchio.**
On Easter Sunday, the **feast of the "Madonna che scappa in piazza"** is celebrated in Piazza Garibaldi: the statue of the Virgin is borne to a meeting with the Risen Christ; as she comes within sight of Him, she sheds her mourning clothes and appears in a resplendent green robe.

★ TARANTO Apulia   Pop 244 845

Michelin map 988 fold 29 – Town plan in the current Michelin Red Guide Italia

Taranto is a well-protected naval base at the end of a great roadstead, closed at the seaward end by two fortified islands. Taranto was founded in the 7C BC and became one of the most important colonies of Magna Graecia. The old quarter lies on an island and is linked to the modern town by a swing bridge. During Holy Week many impressive ceremonies take place in the town, including several processions between Thursday and Saturday, one lasting 12 hours and another 14 hours, which go from church to church at a very slow pace *(see the table of Principal Festivals at the end of the guide).*

★★ **National Museum** (Museo Nazionale) ⊙. – The museum has a good collection of local archaeological finds which illustrate the history of Magna Graecia. On the first floor, in addition to sculpture, architectural fragments and grave artefacts, is an exceptional **collection of pottery**★★★ with vases in the Corinthian, Attic, proto-Italiot and Apulian styles. A large collection of Hellenistic jewellery (4C-3C BC), found in tombs locally, is displayed in the **Gold Room**★★★ (Sala degli Ori).

★★ **Lungomare Vittorio Emanuele.** – A long promenade planted with palm trees.

★ **Public Gardens** (Giardini Comunali). – From this haven of exotic and luxuriant vegetation there is a magnificent view over the harbour's inner basin, the Mare Piccolo.

Cathedral (Duomo). – The 11C-12C cathedral with a baroque façade has been greatly remodelled. The nave and two aisles are separated by ancient columns with Roman or Byzantine capitals and the ceiling is 17C. The **Chapel of San Cataldo**★ was faced with polychrome marble and embellished with statues in the 18C.

★ **TARQUINIA** Latium   Pop 13 851

Michelin map **988** fold 25 or **430** fold 24 – 21km – 13 miles to the northwest of Civitavecchia

The town of Tarquinia crowns a rocky platform, facing the sea, in a barley- and corn-growing region interspersed with olive groves. Tarquinia is famous for the Etruscan burial ground which lies quite near. According to legend, the town was founded in the 12C or 13C BC. Archaeologists have found 9C BC vestiges of the Villanovian civilisation which derived its name from the village of Villanova near Bologna, and developed around the year 1000 BC in the Po Plain, in Tuscany and in the northern part of Latium, where the Etruscans later settled. Standing on the banks of the Marta River, Tarquinia was a busy port and in the 6C BC ruled the coast of Etruria. Under Roman rule, Tarquinia was decimated by malaria in the 4C BC and was sacked by the Lombards in the 7C. The inhabitants then moved to the present site about a mile to the northeast of the original position.

★★ **Etruscan Necropolis** (Necropoli Etrusca) ⊙. – *4km – 2.5 miles.*
The burial ground is on a bare, windswept ridge parallel with that on which the former Etruscan city stood. The necropolis extends over an area 5km – 3 miles long and 1km – 0.5 mile wide and contains around 600 tombs dating from the 6C-1C BC. As at Cerveteri there are no visible remains at ground level but there are remarkable **paintings**★★★ on the walls of the underground burial chambers. These colourful and lively paintings are of the utmost importance for the light they shed on the Etruscan civilisation.
The most important tombs include: the **tomb of the Baron**, dating from the 6C BC; the 5C BC **tomb of the Leopards**, one of the finest tombs, in which are depicted leopards as well as scenes of a banquet and dancing; the 6C BC **tomb of the Bulls** with its erotic paintings; the **tomb of the Lionesses** dating from around 530-520 BC; the 4C BC **tomb of Giglioli** decorated with *trompe-l'œil* paintings of costumes

and arms; and the late-6C BC **tomb with Hunting and Fishing Scenes**, which consists of two chambers displaying the return from the hunt, a banquet and the art of fishing.

★ **National Museum** (Museo Nazionale Tarquiniese) ⊙. – The museum is housed in the **Palazzo Vitelleschi**★ built in 1439 and has a most remarkable collection of Etruscan antiquities originating from the excavations in the necropolis. Items include sarcophagi, pottery, ivories, votive offerings and 6C BC Attic kraters and amphorae. The following exhibits are of great interest: two admirable **winged horses**★★★ in terracotta and on the second floor several reconstructed tombs, notably the **tomb with the Funeral Bed** (460 BC) and the **tomb of the Triclinium** (480-470 BC), one of the finest in the necropolis.

Tarquinia – The Winged Horses

★ **Church of St Mary** (Santa Maria in Castello). – *Take the Via Mazzini, then the Via di Porta Castello beyond the wall.* This Romanesque church (1121-1208) stands near a tall tower built in the Middle Ages and was part of the fortified citadel guarding the town. It has an elegant doorway decorated with Cosmati work *(qv)* and an imposing interior.

In this guide the length of time indicated
– for sightseeing is the average time required for a visit
– for touring allows one to enjoy the views and the scenery.

TERNI Umbria   Pop 110 704

Michelin map 988 fold 26 or 430 fold 26
Town plan in the current Michelin Red Guide Italia

Terni, an important industrial centre, has an old town with several fine palaces, the Church of St Francis with its 15C belltower, and St Saviour's Church, which has early-Christian (5C) origins. The town centre comprises Piazza della Repubblica and Via Roma.

EXCURSIONS

★★ **Marmore Waterfall (Cascata delle Marmore)** ⊘. – *Take the Macerata road the S 209 (7km – 4 miles east of Terni) or the Rieti road, the S 79 (9km – 6 miles to the east plus 1/2 hour Rtn on foot).*
This artificial waterfall created by the Romans falls in three successive drops down sheer walls of marble *(marmore)* to disappear at the bottom of a wooded ravine.

Carsulae: Roman Ruins. – *16km – 10 miles to the northwest. Go via S. Gemini and S. Gemini Fonte.*
These are the remains of a Roman town destroyed in the 9C.

Ferentillo. – *18km – 11 miles to the northeast.*
This picturesque village is dominated by two ruined castles. From here *(5km – 3 miles to the north, then 2km – 1/2 mile more by a poor road)* it is possible to reach the solitary **Abbey of San Pietro in Valle** ⊘, which was founded in the 7C and rebuilt in the 12C. It has cloisters with 12C frescoes and there are Roman sarcophagi.

★ TERRACINA Latium   Pop 38 818

Michelin map 988 fold 26 or 430 fold 37

Terracina stands in an attractive setting at the head of a bay and is backed by a limestone cliff. Already in the Roman era it was a fashionable country resort. Terracina has retained part of its medieval wall and some Roman remains.

Cathedral (Duomo). – This overlooks the attractive **Piazza del Municipio** which still has the paving of the Roman forum. It was consecrated in 1075 and is fronted by a portico on ancient columns which support a 12C mosaic frieze. The campanile with its small columns is in the transitional Romanesque-Gothic style. Inside, the **pulpit** and **paschal candelabrum★**, a lovely 13C work by the Cosmati *(qv)*, are of special interest.

★ **Temple of Jupiter** (Tempio di Giove Anxur). – *4km – 2.5 miles plus 1/4 hour on foot Rtn by the Via San Francesco Nuovo.*
Although there are few remains other than the foundations, a vaulted gallery and a cryptoporticus, it is worth visiting the site for its beauty alone and for the extensive **panorama★★** of the town, the canals and port, Monte Circeo and the Pontine marshes, the plain of Fondi with its lakes, and the coast as far as Gaeta.

EXCURSION

★ **Circeo National Park (Parco nazionale del Circeo).** – Designated in 1934 this park covers a narrow coastal strip between Anzio and Terracina and includes part of the former Pontine marshes. Some of the most attractive beauty spots are: **Monte Circeo**, the refuge of the wicked witch Circe who transformed Ulysses and his companions into a herd of pigs; **Lake Sabaudia** (Lago di Sabaudia) which can be reached by a bridge leading to the town of Sabaudia, a pleasant country resort; the **scenic route** *(5km – 3 miles from the San Felice – Torre Cervia road)* is lined with luxury villas and brightened by a succession of typically-Mediterranean plants and flowers.

★★★ TIVOLI Latium   Pop 53 754

Michelin map 988 fold 26 or 430 fold 36 – 31km – 19 miles east of Rome
Town plan in the current Michelin Red Guide Italia

Tivoli is a small town on the lower slopes of the Apennines where the river Aniene plunges in cascades into the Roman plain.
The villas testify to Tivoli's importance as a holiday resort from the Roman period through to the Renaissance. Tivoli or Tibur in antiquity came under Roman control in the 4C BC and it was there that a Sibyl prophesied the coming of Jesus Christ to the Emperor Augustus.

★★★ **VILLA D'ESTE** *time: 2 hours*
See the plan in the Michelin Green Guide Rome.

In 1550 Cardinal Ippolito II d'Este, who had been raised to great honours by François I of France but had fallen into disgrace when the king's son Henri II succeeded to the throne, decided to retire to Tivoli, where he immediately began to convert the former Benedictine convent into a pleasant country seat. The Neapolitan architect, Pirro Ligorio, was invited to prepare plans. The simple architecture of the villa contrasts with the elaborate gardens which descend in a series of terraces. The statues, pools and fountains enhance the natural beauty with all the grace of the Mannerist style.

To the left of the main entrance stands the old abbey church of **St Mary Major** (Santa Maria Maggiore) with its attractive Gothic façade and a 17C belltower. Inside, in the chancel, are two 15C triptychs: above the one on the left is a painting of the Virgin by Jacopo Torriti, who also worked in mosaic at the end of the 13C.

★★★ **Palace and gardens** ⊘. – From the former convent cloisters go down through the elaborately decorated Old Apartments. From the ground-floor level there is a pleasant **view**★ of the gardens and Tivoli itself. A double flight of stairs leads to the upper garden walk. The **Bicchierone Fountain** with its shell-shaped basin is attributed to Bernini. To the left the **Rometta Fountain** or "Mini Rome" reproduces some of the well-known monuments of Classical Rome. From here the splendid **Avenue of a Hundred Fountains**★★★ (Viale delle Cento Fontane) leads to the **Oval Fountain**★★★ (Fontana dell' Ovato) dominated by a statue of the Sibyl.

At a lower level the **Fishpond Esplanade** (le Peschiere) is overlooked at one end by the **Organ Fountain**★★★ (Fontana dell' Organo) which used to play music on a water-powered organ concealed in the upper part of the fountain. Right at the very bottom of the garden is the **Nature Fountain** (Fontana della Natura) with a statue of Diana of Ephesus.

Return by the central avenue to admire the **Dragon Fountain** (Fontana dei Draghi), built in 1572 in honour of Pope Gregory XIII, then turn right to pass the **Bird Fountain** (Fontana della Civetta) which used to produce bird song, and finally the modernised **Fountain of Proserpina**.

★★★ **HADRIAN'S VILLA** **(VILLA ADRIANA)** ⊘ time: 2 1/2 hours

6km – 4 miles southwest by the Rome road, the S 5, and then a local road to the left, 4.5km – 3 miles from Tivoli.

This was probably the richest building project in antiquity and was designed entirely by Hadrian (76-138), who had visited every part of the Roman empire.

With a passion for both art and architecture, he wished to recreate the monuments and sites he had visited during his travels. In 134 the villa was almost finished, but the 58 year-old Hadrian, ill and grief-stricken by the death of his young favourite Antinoüs, was to die four years later. Although the succeeding emperors probably continued to visit Tivoli, the villa was soon forgotten and fell into ruin. The site was explored from the 15C to the 19C and the recovered works were dispersed to various museums and private collections. It was only in 1870 that the Italian government organised the excavation of Tivoli, thus revealing this magnificent ensemble. Before exploring the site it is advisable to study a model of the villa which is displayed in a room next to the bar. *Follow the itinerary shown on the accompanying plan.*

★★ **Poikile.** – The water-filled Poikile takes its name from a portico in Athens. It was built in the shape of a large rectangle with slightly curved ends and is lined with a portico; it was oriented so that one side was always in the shade.

The apsidal chamber called the **philosophers' room** (1) was perhaps a reading room.

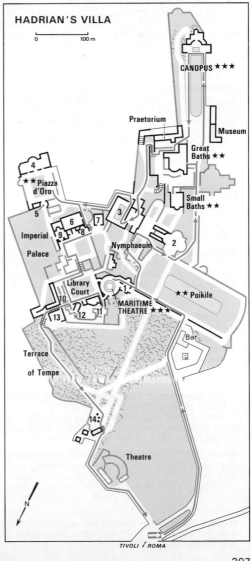

HADRIAN'S VILLA

CANOPUS ★★★
Praetorium
Museum
Great Baths ★★
Piazza d'Oro
Small Baths ★★
Imperial Palace
Nymphaeum
★★ Poikile
Library Court
MARITIME THEATRE ★★★
Bar
Terrace of Tempe
Theatre
N
TIVOLI / ROMA

★★★ **Maritime Theatre.** – The circular construction consists of a portico and a central building surrounded by a canal. It provided an ideal retreat for the misanthropic Hadrian. Bear south to pass the remains of a **nymphaeum** and the great columns which belonged to a building comprising three semicircular rooms round a courtyard (**2**).

★★ **Baths.** – The arrangement of the baths shows the high architectural standards attained in the villa. First come the Small Baths and then the Great Baths with its apse and remains of some superb vaulting.
The tall building, called the **Praetorium**, was probably a storehouse.

★★★ **Canopus.** – Beyond the **museum** which contains the finds from the most recent excavations is the canopus which evokes the Egyptian town of Canope with its famous Temple of Serapis. The route to Canope from Alexandria consisted of a canal lined with temples and gardens. At the southern end of this site is a copy of the Temple of Serapis.
Having reached the ruins overlooking the nymphaeum, turn right before skirting the large **fishpond** (**3**) surrounded by a portico.

Imperial Palace. – The complex extended from Piazza d'Oro to the Libraries.

★★ **Piazza d'Oro.** – The rectangular piazza was surrounded by a double portico and was an aesthetic caprice serving no useful purpose. On the far side are traces of an octagonal chamber (**4**) and opposite is a domed chamber (**5**).

★★ **Doric Pillared Hall** (**6**). – It takes its name from the surrounding portico which was composed of pilasters with Doric bases and capitals.

Also visible are the **firemen's barracks** (**7**), remains of a summer dining-room (**8**) and a nymphaeum (**9**). These buildings overlook a courtyard which is separated from the **library court** by a cryptoporticus, part of a network of underground passages which ran from one villa to another without coming above ground. The series of ten rooms along one side of the library court was an infirmary (**10**). Note the fine mosaic **paving★**. According to custom the **library** was divided in two for a Greek section (**11**) and a Latin section (**12**).
The route to the **Terrace of Tempe** goes past a group of rooms paved with mosaic which belonged to a dining-room (**13**).
The path runs through the trees on the slope above the valley past a **circular temple** (**14**) attributed to the goddess Venus, and skirts the site of a **theatre**, on the left, before ending at the entrance.

ADDITIONAL SIGHT

★ **Villa Gregoriana** ⊙. – This wooded park has a tangle of paths which wind down the steeply-wooded slopes to the river Aniene where it cascades through the ravine. The waters of the Aniene plunge down at the **Great Cascade★★**, disappear out of sight at the **Siren's Cave** and burst from the rock face in **Neptune's Cave**. Climb the slope overlooking the ravine to leave the Villa Gregoriana and visit **Sibyl's Temple**, also known as the Temple of Vesta. This elegant Corinthian-style structure dates from the end of the Republic. An Ionic temple stands alongside.

★★ **TODI** Umbria   Pop 17 006

Michelin map 🔢🔢🔢 folds 25 and 26 or 🔢🔢🔢 fold 25

Todi, a charming old town perched on an attractive **site**, has preserved three sets of walls: Etruscan (Marzia Gateway), Roman and medieval.

★★ **Piazza del Popolo.** – This square in the centre of Todi is surrounded by buildings which are evidence of the town's flourishing commercial life in the Middle Ages. The 13C Gothic **Palazzo dei Priori★** was formerly the seat of the governor (podestà). Its windows were remodelled at the Renaissance and it is dominated by a curious 14C tower on a trapezoidal plan.
The 13C **Palazzo del Capitano★** has attractive windows in groups of three flanked by small columns. Both this and the neighbouring building have arcades with round-headed arches and massive pillars at ground level. Adjoining is the **Palazzo del Popolo★** ⊙, one of the oldest communal palaces in Italy dating from 1213. It houses a lapidary museum and a picture gallery as well as a museum of Etruscan and Roman antiquities.

★★ **Church of St Fortunatus** (San Fortunato). – Piazza della Repubblica.
Building lasted from 1292 to 1460 so that Gothic features mingle with those of the Renaissance. The **central doorway★★** catches the eye with the richness and delicacy of its decoration.
The well-lit and lofty interior has in the fourth chapel to the south **frescoes** (1432) by Masolino and the tomb of Jacopone da Todi (1230-1307), a Franciscan monk, a poet and author of the Stabat Mater.

★ **Cathedral** (Duomo). – This great Romanesque building dating from the early 12C is preceded by a majestic staircase leading up to its harmonious façade, all in pink and white marble, with a great rose window pierced and fretted in the Umbrian manner. Walk round the building to admire the Romanesque apse. Inside note the Gothic capitals, the Renaissance font and the lovely stalls with intarsia work dating from 1530.

Piazza Garibaldi. – This square adjoining the Piazza del Popolo is graced with a monument to Garibaldi. From the terrace, there is a pretty **view★★** of the valley and distant rounded hills.

Castle (Rocca). – Passing to the right of St Fortunatus, walk up to the ruins of the 14C castle. Well-shaded and pleasant public garden.

★ **Church of Santa Maria della Consolazione.** – *1km – 1/2 mile to the west on the Orvieto road.*
This Renaissance church was built of pale stone from 1508 to 1609 by several architects who drew inspiration from the designs of Bramante. The plan is that of a Greek cross; four polygonal apses are reinforced by pilasters with composite capitals. The dome, whose drum is designed in accordance with Bramante's rhythmic principles *(see p 128)*, rises roundly from the flat terrace roof. The interior is austere and well lit. The dome was decorated in the 16C and the twelve statues of the Apostles are by Scalza (16C).

TOLENTINO Marches   18 446

Michelin map 988 fold 16 or 430 fold 17

This small town in the Marches region was where Bonaparte and Pope Puis VI signed the Treaty of Tolentino ratifying the surrendering of Avignon to France. Tolentino with the Basilica of St Nicholas is known as a pilgrimage centre. Numerous miracles are attributed to this Augustinian hermit who died in Tolentino in 1305.

★★ BASILICA OF ST NICHOLAS (SAN NICOLA DA TOLENTINO)

time: 1 hour

The building of this basilica lasted from 1305 to the 18C and the exterior reflects the different construction periods. The façade, although remodelled in the 17C in the baroque manner, has retained an elegant late-Gothic doorway attributed to Nino di Bartolo (15C).

Interior ⊙. – The vast rectangular nave is striking for the rigour of its ordonnance, the splendour of its marble, gold and stucco decoration and the magnificent coffered ceiling (1628). The side chapels contain numerous works of art: in the first chapel on the south side an admirable canvas by Guercino (1640), and in the fourth on the same side a 14C polychrome recumbent Madonna in wood and an effigy of St Lorenzina.
The **Chapel of the Holy Arms**★ *(south side of chancel)* has a remarkably rich decoration. Note the high altar with steps, all in chased silver. The **Chapel of the Cappellone**★★ (Cappella Cappellone) serves as south transept and is the most famous part of this pilgrimage church owing to its cycle of 14C **frescoes** by an unknown master of the Rimini school on its vaulting and walls. The lower frescoes recount episodes from the life of St Nicholas of Tolentino while those on the vaulting evoke the Life of Christ.

Great Cloisters. – These are 13C and 14C. The galleries and the adjoining oratory are decorated with baroque frescoes (17C) illustrating the life of the saint.

Crypt. – *Go back through the Capella Cappellone.*
The crypt, which was completed only in 1932, enshrines the remains of St Nicholas of Tolentino in a reliquary-coffin.

Museums. – These include a gallery of votive offerings, a ceramics and archaeological section, pottery and Roman objects (municipal museum).

★ TREMITI ISLANDS Apulia   Pop 339

Michelin map 988 fold 28 – Access: see the current Michelin Red Guide Italia

This tiny archipelago, the only one on the Adriatic coast, lies offshore from the Gargano Promontory *(qv)* and belongs to the same geological formation. There are two main islands, San Nicola and San Domino as well as two uninhabited isles, Capraia and Pianosa, the latter is much further out in the Adriatic.
The boat trip out from Manfredonia offers unforgettable **views**★★★ of the Gargano coastline with its dazzling white limestone cliffs. As the boat rounds the promontory there are also good views of the coastal towns of Vieste, Peschici and Rodi Garganico set on their precipitous sites. On the points of the rocky headlands there are platform areas *(trabocco)* equipped with square fishing nets.

★ **San Nicola** ⊙. – High on the clifftop stands the **Abbey of Santa Maria al Mare,** originally founded by the Benedictines in the 9C. A fortified ramp leads up to the abbey. Of particular interest are the remains of an 11C mosaic pavement, a 15C Gothic polyptych and a 13C Byzantine crucifix. From the cloisters there are good glimpses of the second island, San Domino.

★ **San Domino** ⊙. – Take the boat trip to circumnavigate this island and discover the wild beauty of the very indented and rugged coasts of this forest (pines) covered island.

The Michelin Green Guide Great Britain
aims to make touring more enjoyable
by suggesting several touring programmes
which are easily adapted to personal taste.

Michelin map 𝟿𝟾𝟾 fold 4 or 𝟺𝟸𝟿 fold 13
Town plan in the current Michelin Red Guide Italia

Trent (or Trento), capital of Trentino, stands on the Adige not far from the Brenta Massif and is encircled by rocky peaks and valleys. Austrian and Italian influences meet here. This agricultural and industrial centre stands at an important crossroads with the converging of routes from the Brenner Pass, Brescia and Venice.

HISTORICAL NOTES

This Roman colony under the Empire became an episcopal see in the 4C, was occupied successively by the Ostrogoths under Theodoric, and by the Lombards in the 6C before being united to the Holy Roman Empire in the late 10C. From 1004 to 1801 the town was governed by a succession of Prince-Bishops.
The **Council of Trent** (1545-63), called by Pope Paul III to study methods of combating Protestantism, met in the town. These important deliberations marked the beginning of the Counter-Reformation and the findings were to change the character of the church. The main decisions which aimed at the re-establishment of ecclesiastical, credibility and authority, concerned compulsory residence for bishops and the abolition of the sale of indulgences.
After a period of Napoleonic rule in the 19C, Trento was ceded to the Austrians in 1814. It was only after a long hard struggle that the town was liberated in 1918 by Italian troops.

★ CITY OF THE PRINCE-BISHOPS *time: 2 hours*

★ **Piazza del Duomo.** – This cobbled square is the centre of town. Round it stand the cathedral, the Palazzo Pretorio (13C restored), the belfry and the Rella houses painted with 16C frescoes.

Cathedral (Duomo). – This 12C-13C majestic façade is in the Lombard-Romanesque style. The façade of the north transept is pierced with a window forming a Wheel of Fortune: Christ stands at the summit, the Symbols of the Evangelists rise towards him.
Inside, note the unusual sweep of the stairway leading to the towers. To the right, in the 17C Chapel of the Crucifix, is a large wooden Christ in front of which the decrees of the Council of Trent were proclaimed. In the south transept is the tomb of the Venetian mercenary leader Sanseverino who was killed in 1486. The remains of a 5C **paleo-Christian basilica** ⊘ have been uncovered beneath the chancel.

★ **Diocesan Museum (Museo Diocesano)** ⊘. – The museum installed in the Palazzo Pretorio displays the most important items from the cathedral's treasure, paintings, carved **wooden panels★**, **altarpiece★** and eight early-16C **tapestries★** which were woven in Brussels by Peter Van Aelst.

Via Belenzani. – This street is lined with palaces in the Venetian style. Opposite the 16C town hall (Palazzo Comunale) are houses with walls painted with frescoes.

Via Manci. – The Venetian (loggias and frescoes) and mountain (overhanging roofs) styles are intermingled all along the street. No 63, the Palazzo Galazzo with its embossed stonework and huge pilasters is 17C.

★ **Castle of Good Counsel (Castello del Buon Consiglio)** ⊘. – This castle was formerly the residence of the prince-bishops and now houses the Trentino Provincial Museum of Art. On the left are the 13C Castelvecchio (Old Castle) and the Torre Grande known as the Tower of Augustus; in the centre is the 16C Renaissance Palazzo Magno, the bishop's residence; and on the extreme right the square Torre dell' Aquila (Eagle Tower).
The interior of the castle gives the impression of being made up of a maze of courts, staircases, passages and sundry buildings. The Castelvecchio has a beautiful court in the Venetian-Gothic style with four tiers of galleries adorned with frescoes, including the portraits of the prince-bishops. The Palazzo Magno leads to the Romanino Loggia with its 16C frescoes.
The loggia overlooks the charming Renaissance Lions Courtyard. The apartments of the prince-bishops with their coffered ceilings decorated with stucco and frescoes are the perfect setting for rich collections of 16C-18C paintings, furniture and ceramics.

ADDITIONAL SIGHTS

★ **Palazzo Tabarelli.** – A remarkable building in the Venetian-Renaissance style with pilasters, pink marble columns and medallions.

St Mary Major's Church (Santa Maria Maggiore). – Numerous meetings of the Council of Trent were held in this Renaissance church with a Romanesque campanile. The elegant marble organ loft (1534) in the chancel is by Vincenzo and Girolamo Grandi. At the second altar on the right, in the nave, is a 16C altarpiece of the Madonna and saints by Moroni.

Church of St Apollinaris (Sant'Apollinare). – This small Romanesque church on the west bank of the Adige has a curious pointed roof covering two Gothic domical vaults.

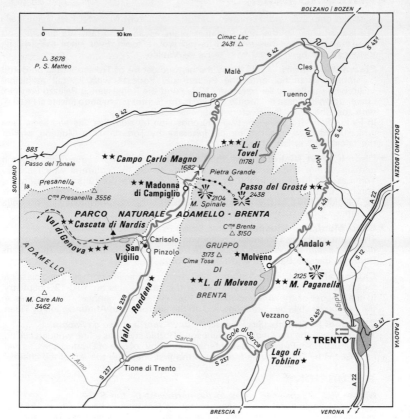

★★★ BRENTA MASSIF (GRUPPO DEL BRENTA)

Round tour starting from Trento
233km – 145 miles – allow two days

The wild limestone Brenta Massif prolongs the Dolomites beyond the Adige Valley. Its characteristic features are deep valleys, solitary lakes and erosion-worn rocks.

Sightseeing. – The map opposite locates the towns and sites described in the guide and also indicates other beauty spots in small black type.

Take the S 45b in the direction of Vezzano.

★ **Lake Toblino** (Lago di Toblino). – This charming lake fringed with tall rushes, stands against a background of rocky walls. An attractive little castle, once the summer residence of the Bishops of Trent, stands on a small peninsula.

★ **Rendena Valley** (Valle Rendena). – This wide valley clad with firs and larches has charming villages with churches covered with frescoes, protected by overhanging roofs.
The **Church of San Vigilio** near Pinzolo has a remarkable Dance of Death (1539) by Simone Baschenis.

★★★ **Genova Valley** (Val di Genova). – This valley crosses the granite Adamello Massif and is known for its wild grandeur. The road follows a fast-flowing river as it tumbles and foams along the rock-strewn bed to reach the **Nardis Waterfall★★** (Cascata di Nardis) where the waters drop over 100m – 328ft.

★★ **Madonna di Campiglio.** – This pleasant resort and winter sports centre has many hotels and numerous possibilities for excursions.

★★ **Campo Carlo Magno** ⊙. – A supposed visit by Charlemagne gave this place its name. It has become a winter sports centre.
From **Grosté Pass** (Passo del Grosté) *(cable-car and then on foot)* there is a fine **panorama★★** of the Brenta Massif.

Continue to Dimaro and Malè and at Cles turn right towards Tuenno.

★★★ **Lake Tovel** (Lago di Tovel). – Pass through wild gorges to reach this lovely lake fringed by wooded slopes. In hot weather the waters of the lake take on a reddish tinge due to the presence of microscopic algae.

★ **Andalo.** – This small holiday resort is set in majestic scenery, amidst a great pine forest and overlooked by the crests of the Brenta Massif.
From the summit of **Monte Paganella** ⊙ *(cable-car)* at 2 125m – 6 972ft there is a splendid **panorama★★** of the whole region, and in clear weather as far as Lake Garda.

★ **Molveno.** – This choice resort is situated amid gently-sloping meadows at the north end of a **lake★★** which lies on the floor of a cirque.

★ **TREVISO** Venetia   Pop 84 745

Michelin map 988 fold 5 – Town plan in the current Michelin Red Guide Italia

Treviso, situated in the rich Venetian plain, is an important agricultural and industrial centre but has retained its old walled town. Ever since the 14C its fortunes have been linked with those of Venice.

★ **Piazza dei Signori.** – This forms the historic centre of Treviso and is bordered by impressive monuments: the Palazzo del Podestà with its tall municipal bell-tower, the **Palazzo dei Trecento★** (1207) and the Renaissance Palazzo Pretorio. Lower down in Piazza del Monte di Pietà is the former pawn shop **(Monte di Pietà)** ⊙ with the Chapel of the Rectors (Cappella dei Reggitori).
In Piazza San Vito there are two churches side by side: **San Vito** and **Santa Lucia** which is adorned with remarkable **frescoes★** by Tommaso da Modena, one of the finest 14C artists after Giotto.

★ **Church of St Nicholas (San Nicolò).** – This large Romanesque-Gothic church contains interesting frescoes, especially those on the columns which are by Tommaso da Modena. In the Onigo Chapel there are portraits of Trevisans by Lorenzo Lotto (16C). The Christ in Majesty at the far end of the chancel is by Savoldo (16C). In the adjoining **monastery** ⊙ the chapterhouse has portraits of famous Dominicans by Tommaso da Modena.

★ **Bailo Municipal Museum (Museo Civico)** ⊙. – *22 Borgo Cavour.*
There are works by Tommaso da Modena, Girolamo da Treviso (15C) and others of the Venetian school such as Cima da Conegliano, Giovanni Bellini, Titian, Paris Bordone, Jacopo Bassano and Lorenzo Lotto.

Cathedral (Duomo). – The 15C and 16C church has seven domes, a neo-classical façade and a Romanesque crypt. Left of the cathedral is an 11C-12C baptistry. In the Chapel of the Annunciation, to the right of the chancel, are frescoes in the Mannerist style by Pordenone and on the altarpiece an Annunciation by Titian.

Church of St Francis (San Francesco). – *Viale Sant' Antonio da Padova.*
This church in the transitional Romanesque-Gothic style has a fine wooden ceiling, the tombstone of Petrarch's daughter and the tomb of one of Dante's sons, as well as frescoes by Tommaso da Modena in the first chapel to the left of the chancel.

EXCURSIONS

Maser ⊙. – *29km – 18 miles to the northwest by the S 348.*
This small agricultural town is known for its famous **villa★★★** built in 1560 by Palladio for the Barbaro brothers: Daniele, patriarch of Aquileia and Marcantonio, ambassador of the Venetian Republic. The interior was decorated from 1566 to 1568 with an amazing ensemble of **frescoes★★★** by Veronese. It is one of his best decorative schemes and he used all his amazing knowledge of perspective, *trompe-l'œil*, foreshortening and his sense of movement and colour. Not far from the villa is a **Tempietto**, a graceful circular chapel with a dome which was also the work of Palladio.

Vittorio Veneto. – *41km – 26 miles to the north.* The name of this town recalls the great victory of the Italians over the Austrians in 1918. In Ceneda to the south of the town, the **Battle Museum** ⊙ which presents documents on this victory is installed in a 16C loggia (Loggia Cenedese) with a frescoed portico by Sansovino. The suburb of Serravalle in the north has retained a certain charm. The **Church of San Giovanni** *(take Via Roma and then Via Mazzini)* has interesting **frescoes★** attributed to Jacobello del Fiore and Gentile da Fabriano (15C).

★ **TRIESTE** Friuli-Venezia Giulia   Pop 237 191

Michelin map 988 fold 6 or 429 fold 18
Plan of the built-up area in the current Michelin Red Guide Italia

Trieste is a modern town which stands at the head of a bay of the same name and at the foot of the Carso Plateau. The edge of the latter forms a steep coast with magnificent white cliffs as far as Duino in the north. Trieste is the largest seaport on the Adriatic. Its extensive port (12km – 8 miles of quays stretch as far as the Yugoslavian border) handles more Austrian and Yugoslavian goods than Italian. An oil pipeline links Trieste with refineries in Austria and Bavaria. The important shipyards, specialising in the building of large vessels, are important to the local economy.

HISTORICAL NOTES

The origins of the town are very ancient; the Celts and Illyrians disputed it before the Romans made it their great trading centre of Tergeste, which had the important role of defending the eastern frontiers of the Empire. It came under the sway of the Patriarch of Aquileia and then, in 1202, under Venice. In 1382 Trieste rebelled and placed itself under the protection of Austria and it played the role of mediator between the two opponents until the 15C. In 1719 Charles VI declared it a free port and established the headquarters of the French Trading Company (Compagnie d'Orient et du Levant) in the city. Trieste then enjoyed a second period of prosperity and was embellished by numerous fine buildings. Many political exiles sought refuge in Trieste. It was only in 1919 after fierce fighting that Trieste was united with the Kingdom of Italy.
At the beginning of the 20C Trieste boasted an active literary group under the leading influence of the novelist Italo Svevo and the poet Umberto Saba. James Joyce lived in the town for some years until 1914.

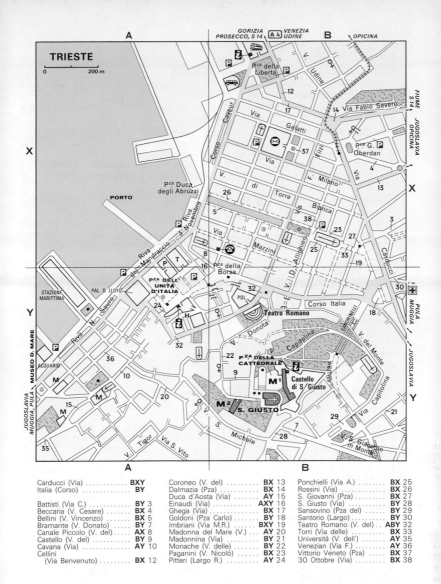

TRIESTE

0 200 m

★★ HILL OF ST JUSTUS (COLLE DI SAN GIUSTO) *time: 1 hour*

This hilltop was the site of the ancient city and today the **Piazza della Cattedrale★** (**BY**) is bordered by the ruins of a Roman basilica, a 15C-16C castle, a 1560 Venetian column, the altar of the Third Army (1929) and the Basilica of St Justus.

Basilica of St Justus (San Giusto) (BY). – It was founded in the 5C on the site of a Roman building, but the present buildings date in large part from the 14C. The façade is pierced with a fine Gothic rose window and decorated with a low relief and bronze busts. The powerful-looking campanile has fragments of Roman columns built into its lowest storey and bears a 14C statue of St Justus. From the top there is an attractive **view★** of Trieste.

The **interior★** comprises a nave and four aisles. The side aisles belonged to two separate basilicas which were joined together in the 14C by the building of the nave. In the south aisle there are: a lovely 13C mosaic and 11C frescoes depicting the life of St Justus. A magnificent 12C **mosaic★★** in the north apse shows the Virgin in Majesty between the Archangels Michael and Gabriel, and the Apostles.

Castle (Castello di San Giusto) ⊙ (BY). – This houses a museum (M1) of furniture and a remarkable collection of **arms★**.

History and Art Museum (Museo di Storia e d'Arte) ⊙ (BY M²). – This contains a remarkable collection of red-figured **Greek vases★** and charming **small bronzes★** dating from the Roman Archaic period.

Roman Theatre (Teatro romano) (BY). – The remains of an early-2C Roman theatre lie at the foot of the Hill of St Justus.

LOWER TOWN *time: 1 hour*

★ **Piazza dell'Unità d'Italia (AY)**. – Three palaces with typically 1900 architecture line this square, namely the Palazzo del Governo (Government Palace), Palazzo del Comune (Town Hall) and the offices of Lloyd Trieste.

★ **Maritime Museum (Museo del Mare)** ⊙. – *Via A. Ottaviano. Take Riva Nazario Sauro* (**AY**). The history of seafaring is traced from its beginnings to the 18C. The **fishing section★** is quite remarkable.

EXCURSIONS

Sanctuary of Monte Grisa. – *10km – 6 miles to the north. Leave by Piazza della Libertà* (**BX**) *in the direction of Prosecco and then Villa Opicina and follow the signposts to "Monte Grisa".*
This modern sanctuary is dedicated to the Virgin. From the terrace there is a splendid **panorama**★★ of Trieste and its bay.

Villa Opicina ⊙. – *9km – 6 miles to the north. Leave by Via Fabio Severo* (**BX**). *After 4.5km – 3 miles turn left off the S 14 to take the S 58. It is also possible to take the funicular which leaves from Piazza Oberdan.*
Villa Opicina stands on the edge of the Carso Plateau (alt 348m – 1 142ft). From the belvedere with its obelisk there is a magnificent wide-ranging **view**★★ over Trieste and its bay.

★ **Miramare Castle** (**Castello di Miramare**) ⊙. – *8km – 5 miles to the northwest by the coast road.*
Standing on the point of a headland, this castle with its lovely terraced **gardens**★ was built in 1860 for the Archduke Maximilian of Austria, who was executed by shooting in Mexico in 1867, and his wife, Princess Charlotte, who died insane.

★ **Grotta Gigante** ⊙. – *13km – 8 miles to the north. Follow the above directions to Villa Opicina and then turn left in the direction of Borgo Grotta Gigante.*
An impressive stairway leads down to this chamber of astonishing size where one can walk among the splendid concretions. There is a **speleological museum** at the entrance to the cave.

Muggia. – *14km – 9 miles to the south. Leave by Riva Nazario Sauro* (**AY**).
Facing Trieste, this small very Venetian-looking town has a 15C Gothic cathedral (Duomo) with an attractive pointed campanile and an elegant façade in Istrian limestone.

★★★ **TRULLI REGION** Apulia

Michelin map 988 fold 29

This region extending between Fassano, Ostuni, Martina Franca and Alberobello takes its name from the very curious buildings, the *trulli (photograph p 49)*, which are to be found almost everywhere. These strange, white, dry-stone structures have conical roofs covered with grey stone slabs. Each dome corresponds to a room. The *trulli* usually stand in groups of three or four. The external staircase leads to the attic. The doorway stands in the recessed arch of a stepped gable. Inside, the rooms are domed.

★★★ **Alberobello.** – This small town has an entire district of *trulli* which often abut one another. They spread over the hillside to the south of the town (Zona Monumentale). On the hilltop stands the **Church of Sant'Antonio** also in the form of a *trullo (take Via Monte Sant'Angelo)*. Inside, the transept crossing is covered with a dome, similar to those in the *trulli*. It is possible to visit some of these strange dwellings: from the rooftops there is often a good view of the town. The **Trullo Sovrano**★, a two-storeyed *trullo*, the largest in Alberobello, stands near the principal church on Piazza Sacramento.

*EUROPE on a single sheet : **Michelin Map** n° 970*

★★ **TURIN** (TORINO) Piedmont   Pop 1 025 390

Michelin map 988 fold 12 or 428 folds 22 and 23 – Plan pp 216-217
Plan of the built-up area in the current Michelin Red Guide Italia

Turin stands at the confluence of the Dora Riparia and the Po and is the meeting-place of important transalpine routes from France and Switzerland. The capital of Piedmont is an elegant, lively and prosperous town. Most of the town was built on a regular plan in the 17C and 18C and it has wide avenues, spacious squares and numerous parks.

HISTORICAL NOTES

During the 1C the capital of the Celtic tribe, the Taurini, was transformed by the Romans into a military colony and given the name of Augusta Taurinorum. Converted to Christianity, it became the seat of a bishopric in the early 5C and then a century later a Lombard duchy before passing under Frankish rule. From the 11C onwards and for nearly nine centuries the destiny of Turin was linked to that of the **House of Savoy**. This dynasty descended from Umberto the Whitehanded (d 1056), who reigned over Savoy and Piedmont and then Sardinia and all of Italy. It was Italy's reigning royal family from 1861 to 1946. They were skilful rulers, often siding with the pope rather than the emperor, and playing France off against the Dukes of Milan. They slowly extended their rule over the area. It was in the early 18C that Charles Emmanuel II and Victor Amadeus II embellished their adopted city with splendid buildings by Guarini and Juvara. Charles Emmanuel III increased the importance of Turin during his reign (1732-73) by reorganising the kingdom's administration and by establishing in his capital a court with very formal etiquette, similar to the one at Versailles.

In 1798 Charles Emmanuel IV was expelled from Turin by French troops full of the new revolutionary spirit. On the fall of Bonaparte, Victor Emmanuel I was restored to his kingdom and he promoted a policy against foreign interference in Piedmontese affairs. Turin then became the centre of the struggle against the Austrians and for the unification of Italy.

Following the reorganisation of the Piedmont by the statesman Camillo Cavour, the Franco-Piedmontese alliance against Austria, the victories at Solferino and Magenta (1859), Victor Emmanuel II was proclaimed king of Italy and Turin became the seat of the Italian government. The House of Savoy reigned over Italy until the proclamation of an Italian Republic in 1946.

ECONOMY

The intense activity of its suburban industries has made Turin the capital of Italian engineering. The people of Turin are born mechanics and most of the motor engineers come from the Politecnico of Turin University. It is here that the Italian motor industry, represented by FIAT and Lancia, was born. Turin is responsible for about 77 per cent of Italy's car production. Many of the modern FIAT works are established in the southern suburb of Mirafiori.

Important tyre manufacturers and well-known coachbuilders (one of the most famous having been Pinin Farina) contribute to the prosperity of the motor industry of Turin, whose products are displayed at the Turin Motor Show every even year.

The textile and clothing industries are also highly developed.

LIFE IN TURIN

The life of the town is concentrated in Via Roma (**BXY**), Piazza San Carlo *(see p 195)*, and Via Po (**CXY**), which leads to the huge Piazza Vittorio Veneto (**CY**), built in the classical style. The modern-looking Via Roma is lined with arcades, beneath which are the luxury shops with attractive window displays of refined and reputed articles from Turin, such as silk and leather goods and, of course, fashion wear.

The Piazza San Carlo, halfway along the Via Roma, is the meeting-place of fashionable women, while connoisseurs linger in the antiquaries' and book-sellers' shops. The large cafés built in the neo-classical style which open onto the Via Po played a part in the politics of the 19C. The courteous and refined atmosphere of Turin is that of a cultural centre distinguished by many publishing houses, well-known newspapers *(Stampa)*, a Music Conservatory and a large university. But the cult of the spirit does not compel neglect of the flesh, and the people of Turin, with appetites whetted by their famous Vermouths (Martini, Cinzano or Carpano), are partial to good cooking. *Cardi in bagna cauda* (cardoons in piquant sauce) and *tartufi bianchi* (white truffles) are specialities eaten with crisp rolls and accompanied by the delectable wines of the region. Sweetmeats, nougat *(torrone piemontese)*, chocolates and chocolate creams are also excellent.

CITY CENTRE

★★ **Piazza San Carlo** (BXY). – This is a graceful example of town planning. The **Churches of San Carlo** and **Santa Cristina**, symmetrically placed on the south side, frame the Via Roma. The curious façade of Santa Cristina, surmounted by candelabra, was designed by the famous Sicilian-Turinese architect Juvara, who was responsible for many of Turin's lovely buildings. On the east side is the 17C palace which was the French Ambassador's residence from 1771 to 1789. In the centre of the square stands the statue (1838) of Emanuele Filiberto of Savoy.

Academy of Science (Palazzo dell' Accademia delle Scienze) (BX M). – This 17C palace by Guarini now houses two exceptional museums.

★★ **Egyptian Museum** ⊙. – *Ground and first floors.* This is one of the richest collections of Egyptian antiquities. On the ground floor is the section on **statuary art** with 20 seated or standing figures of the lion-headed goddess Sekhmet from Karnak, and an important **series of Pharaohs** of the New Kingdom (1580-1100 BC), Egypt's Golden Age. The **Rock Temple of Thutmose III** (*c*1450 BC), a gift from the United Arab Republic, originated from Ellessya 200km – 124 miles to the south of Aswan.

The collections on the first floor evoke all aspects of Egyptian civilisation, in particular: the **sarcophagi** – simple examples dating from the Middle Kingdom (2100-1580 BC) and sculpted ones during the New Kingdom; a collection of **canopic urns;** and an important number of mummies and copies of funerary papyri rolls known as the **Book of the Dead.** In addition to the recreated **funeral chambers** *(mastabas)* (Giza 2500 BC), there is an exceptional collection of **funerary steles** dating from the Middle and New Kingdoms. Jewellery and pottery from the pre-dynastic civilisations, known as Nagadian, date from the 4000-3000 BC. The influence of the Greek world made itself felt from the 4C BC following the conquest by Alexander the Great (masks and statuettes), followed by the Romans from 30BC (bronze vases). Another room is devoted to **inscriptions**; the hieroglyphs (deciphered by Champollion in 1824), and texts in hieratic script using cursive on papyrus, limestone flakes and fragments of pottery.

★★ **Galleria Sabauda** ⊙. – *Second floor.*
This art museum comprises five different sections.

First section: this is a very comprehensive collection of 15C to 17C **Piedmontese painting.**

Second section: other Italian schools. There is a remarkable collection of **15C Tuscan painting:** a *Madonna* by Fra Angelico, *Tobias and the Archangel* (Il Toblino) by Antonio and Piero Pollaiuolo, *Eleanor of Toledo* by Bronzino and a dazzling portrait of a *Young Man with a Red Scarf* by Lorenzo di Credi. *The Assumption* (1623) by Orazio Gentileschi is outstanding among the works by the followers of Caravaggio, who specialised in violent realism and contrasted light effects. The 15C-16C **Lombard school** is well represented. The paintings include a polyptych (1462), the only signed work by Paolo da Brescia, the *Adorations of the Infant Jesus (presepi)* by Sa-

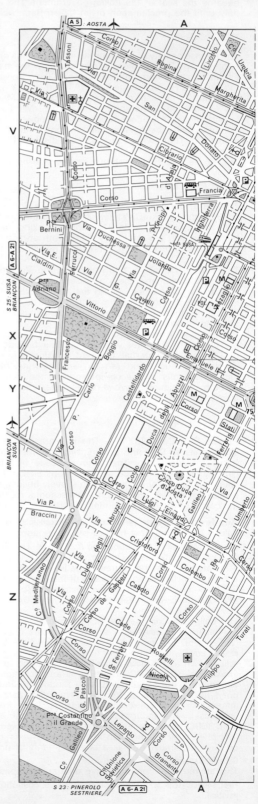

voldo da Brescia, and a charming little picture of a *Madonna with a Carthusian Monk* by Bergognone. Francesco del Cairo and Tanzio da Varallo illustrate the development of Mannerism in Lombardy and Piedmont. The **Ferrara school** of the 15C and 16C is represented by Ercole de' Roberti *(Virgin and Child)*, Garofalo, the Raphael of Ferrara, and Mazzolino. Albani and Guercino, both pupils of the Carracci, represent the 17C **Bolognese school,** and Crespi the 18C.

The 15C-16C **Venetian school** includes a *Virgin and Child* and a lovely portrait of a *Lady with a small dog* by Palma Vecchio, altarpieces by Lorenzo Veneziano, *The Feast in the House of Simon* by Veronese, *Leda* and the *Portrait of a Senator* by Titian, the *Portrait of Doge Sebastiano Venier* by Tintoretto, the large canvases by the Bassano family who are precursors of Caravaggio with contrasting light and shade effects, scenes of Turin by Bernardo Bellotto, *The Triumph of Aurelian* by Tiepolo and Venetian townscapes by Francesco Guardi. The lovely *Madonna* with a thoughtful expression is characteristic of the Paduan artist, Mantegna, who greatly influenced Venetian Renaissance art.

Third section: the **Dutch and Flemish collections** are probably the richest in Italy. Among the most outstanding works are small religious paintings by Rogier Van der Weyden, *St Francis receiving the Stigmata* by Van Eyck, *The Passion* by Memling, an impressive group of official portraits including the famous *Children of Charles I of England* by Van Dyck in his masterly style, and the celebrated *Old Man Asleep* by Rembrandt.

Fourth section: the section devoted to **French**, German and Spanish artists displays portraits by François Clouet *(Marguerite de Valois)*, a *St Jerome* by Valentin de Boulogne, *Louis, Duke of Burgundy* by Rigaud, *The Knife-Grinder (Arrotino)* by Casper Netscher and the *Portrait of a Man* by Velasquez.

Gualino Collection. – On the upper floor, this is a fine selection of paintings, sculpture, furnishings and gold and silver plate. Note in particular the Oriental and Greco-Roman sculpture, a set of small paintings on a gilded background, several Renaissance masterpieces and 18C pastels by Rosalba Carriera.

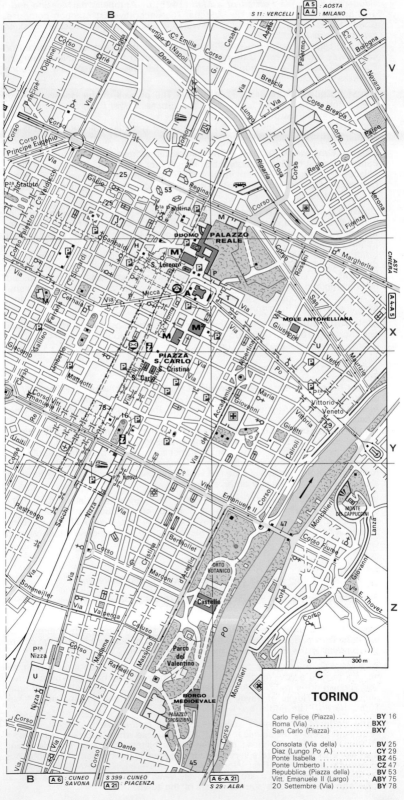

TORINO

★ **Palazzo Madama** (BX A). – The palace stands in the centre of Piazza Castello. It was socalled because the mother of Charles Emmanuel II, "Madama Reale", Marie-Christine of France, lived there. The Porta Decumana, part of the old Augustinian ramparts, forms the original nucleus of the building. The eastern section, in brick, is late medieval (15C), but the noble west façade, in stone, was designed in the 18C by Juvara.

There is a **Museum of Ancient Art★** (Museo d'Arte Antica) ⊘ on the ground floor. The exhibits include Gothic carvings, 15C stalls, canvases of the 15C-16C Piedmontese school (Gian Martino Spanzotti, Macrino d'Alba, Defendente and Gaudenzio Ferrari), a *Portrait of a Man* (1475) by Antonello da Messina and a 14C *Madonna* by Barnaba da Modena. The decorative arts section comprises Greek, Roman and Barbarian gold work, enamels, ivories, wooden caskets, ceramic ware and 15C furniture.

Standing slightly back from the Piazza Castello is the **Church of San Lorenzo** (BX) which was adorned with a dome and a bold crown by Guarini. Next door, the Palazzo Chiablese is the home of a **National Film Museum** ⊘ (BX M¹) *(entrance: 2 Piazza San Giovanni)*.

★ **Royal Palace (Palazzo Reale)** (BCVX). – The princes of the House of Savoy lived in this plain building until 1865. The **apartments** *(first floor)* are sumptuously decorated in the baroque style.

The **Royal Armoury★** (Armeria Reale) ⊘ contains a splendid collection of arms and armour and interesting military memorabilia.

Palazzo Carignano (BX M²). – This palace dating from 1680 has an impressive baroque façade by Guarini. Italy's first king, Victor Emmanuel II, was born in this palace in 1820. There is an interesting **Museum of the Risorgimento★** ⊘ with a collection of documents illustrating the outstanding people and events in the history of 19C Italy.

★ **Cathedral of St John (Duomo San Giovanni)** (BX). – This Renaissance cathedral was built at the end of the 15C for Cardinal Della Rovere. The façade has three delicately carved doorways, while the crown of the brick campanile was designed by Juvara in 1720.

Inside, on the floor above the apse *(staircase to the right of the chancel)* the domed rotunda, the **Chapel of the Holy Shroud** (Cappella della Santa Sindone), was the work of Guarini (17C). An urn on the high altar contains the precious but much-contested **Holy Shroud★★★** (never on view to the public: there is a series of photographs alongside the altar) in which Christ is said to have been wrapped after the Descent from the Cross.

★ **Mole Antonelliana** ⊘ (CX). – This unusual structure, built from 1863 to 1890 and towering 167m – 548ft up into the air, is the symbol of Turin. The summit affords a vast **panorama★★** of Turin.

ADDITIONAL SIGHTS

★ **Motor Museum (Museo dell' Automobile Carlo Biscaretti di Ruffia)** ⊘. – *South of the town. Take Corso Massimo d'Azeglio* (BZ) *and then follow the plan of the built-up area in the current Michelin Red Guide Italia. The address is No 40 Corso Unità d'Italia.*

A vast modern building houses a very rich collection of cars, chassis and engines as well as graphic documents outlining the history of the automobile from its beginnings to the last twenty years. Another room devoted to tyre manufacture traces the tremendous development of materials, structure, technology and research, famous car races, types of vehicle (cycles to planes etc). The museum also includes a library and archives.

Valentino Park (Parco del Valentino) (BCZ). – The park extends along the Po and contains the **Castello del Valentino** built in 1688 for the Duchess Marie-Christine of France, the Exhibition Hall, the New Theatre (Teatro Nuovo T) and the **Borgo Medioevale★** ⊘, a curious and faithful reconstruction of a medieval town with its castle.

EXCURSIONS

Plan of the built-up area in the current Michelin Red Guide Italia.

★ **Basilica of Superga.** – *10km – 6 miles to the east.*
This masterpiece was built by Juvara from 1717 to 1731 on a summit of 670m – 2 198ft. The basilica is circular in plan and roofed with a dome and its most remarkable feature is its monumental façade with its imposing columns and pilasters. The chapel dedicated to the Virgin, in the chancel, is a pilgrimage centre. The basilica is the Pantheon of the Kings of Sardinia.

★ **Royal tombs** ⊘: the crypt is the resting-place of Victor Amadeus II, who built the basilica to fulfil a vow made when his capital was being besieged by a French and Spanish army in 1706. Alongside are the tombs of Charles-Albert and other princes of the House of Savoy. From the esplanade there is a fine **view★★★** of Turin, the Po Plain and the Alps.

★ **Colle della Maddalena.** – *32km – 20 miles to the east.*
From Superga take the scenic route via Pino Torinese which affords good **views★★** of Turin. From Pino Torinese continue to the hilltop, **Colle della Maddalena**, and the **Parco della Rimembranza**, a very popular large public park which commemorates those who died in the First World War.

On the way down there are more lovely **views★** of Turin. The **Europa Park** at Cavoretto overlooks the southern part of the town.

★ **Stupinigi Palace** (Palazzina Mauriziana) ⊙. – *11km – 7 miles to the southwest.* This huge building was a hunting-lodge built by Juvara for Victor Amadeus II of Savoy. Napoleon stayed here before assuming the crown of Italy. The palace now houses a **Fine Arts and Furniture Museum.** The apartments are richly decorated in the rococo style of the 18C. A magnificent park surrounds the palazzina.

Rivoli Château (Castello di Rivoli) ⊙. – *14km – 8 1/2 miles to the west.* Victor Amadeus II commissioned Juvara to build a grandiose residence (18C) in the baroque style. Only the left wing (some rooms are decorated) and the lower part of the central range were built. The château now houses a museum of contemporary art (1960 to the present day).

★ **MONFERRATO**

The itinerary described below *(150km – 93 miles – allow 1 day)* takes the visitor through this attractive region of limestone hills, with its numerous castles and vineyards producing most of the Piedmontese wines, the best known of which is Asti.

Leave Turin to the east by the S 10.

Chieri. – This town is known for its gastronomy. Its monuments include: the Triumphal Arch (1580), the 15C Gothic cathedral and the 13C-15C Church of San Domenico with its fine campanile.

Asti. – *Town plan in the current Michelin Red Guide Italia.* The home town of the tragic poet, Vittorio Alfieri (1749-1803), is the scene of an annual horse race *(palio)* which is preceded by a procession with over 1 000 participants in 14C and 15C costume *(see the table of Principal Festivals at the end of the guide).* The 12C **St Peter's Baptistry★**, the 15C Church of St Peter and the Gothic cloisters form an attracttive group. In the heart of the old town the 14C Gothic **cathedral** (Cattedrale) is decorated with baroque paintings.

Take the S 231 and then the S 456 to reach Ovada.

★ **Tour of the castles of the Monferrato.** – Between Ovada and Serravalle Scrivia this scenic route, also known as the wine route, follows the crest of the hillsides covered with vineyards. Along the way there is a series of hilltop villages, each one guarded by a castle.

★ **TUSCANIA** Latium   Pop 7 642

Michelin map 988 fold 25 or 430 fold 24 – 24km – 15 miles west of Viterbo

Tuscania was a powerful Etruscan town, a Roman municipium and an important medieval centre. The town retains fragments of its walls and two superb churches, a little way out of town. Tuscania's artistic heritage was considerably damaged by the earthquake of February 1971.

★★ **St Peter's Church** (San Pietro). – The golden-hued façade of St Peter's stands at the far end of an empty square on the site of the Etruscan acropolis. To the left are two medieval towers and to the right the former bishop's palace. The well-balanced façade dates from the early 13C. The symbols of the Evangelists surround a rose window, probably of the Umbrian school. Lower down an atlante (or a dancer?) and a man (Laocöon?) being crushed by a snake probably came from Etruscan buildings.
The interior was built by Lombard masons in the 11C. Massive columns with beautiful capitals support curious denticulated arches. The nave has its original and highly decorative paving. The frescoes in the apse are 12C. The **crypt★★** ⊙ is a forest of small columns, all different and of various periods – Roman, Pre-Romanesque and Romanesque – supporting groined vaulting.

★ **St Mary Major's Church** (Santa Maria Maggiore). – This late-12C church is modelled on St Peter's. The 13C Romanesque **doorways★★** are decorated with masterly sculptures.
Inside is an ambo rebuilt with 8C, 9C and 12C fragments. Above the triumphal arch there is a realistic 14C fresco of the Last Judgement.

★ **UDINE** Friuli-Venezia Giulia   Pop 99 883

Michelin map 988 fold 6 or 429 fold 17
Town plan in the current Michelin Red Guide Italia

This charming town was the seat of the Patriarchs of Aquilea from 1238 to 1420 when it passed under Venetian rule. Udine nestles round a hill encircled by the picturesque lane, the Vicolo Sottomonte, with a castle on its summit. The charm of Udine lies in its Gothic and Renaissance monuments, its secluded squares and narrow streets, often lined with arcades. The town was badly damaged, like most of Friuli, by the 1976 earthquake.

★★ **Piazza della Libertà.** – This very harmonious square has kept its Renaissance character and is bordered by several public buildings. The former town hall is also known as the **Loggia del Lionello** (1457), from the name of its architect. Its Venetian-Gothic style is characterised by the elegant arcades and its white and rose-coloured stonework. Opposite on a slightly higher level is the 16C **Loggia di San Giovanni,** a Renaissance portico surmounted by a 16C clock tower, with Moorish jacks *(Mori)* similar to the ones in Venice. A 16C fountain plays in the centre of the square, not far from statues of Hercules and Cacus and the columns of Justice and St Mark.

219

Castle (Castello) ⊙. – This imposing early-16C building is preceded by an esplanade from which there is a good view of Udine and the surrounding Friuli countryside. This was the seat of the representatives of the Most Serene Republic (Venice).

Alongside is the 13C **Church of Santa Maria del Castello** with a 16C façade and campanile which bears a statue of the Archangel Gabriel at its summit. Inside, there is a 13C fresco of the Descent from the Cross.

Cathedral (Duomo). – This 14C Gothic building remodelled in the 18C has a lovely Flamboyant-Gothic doorway. The massive campanile has, on one of its faces, a fine Annunciation and an Archangel Gabriel dating from the 14C. Inside, there is attractive **baroque decoration★**: organ loft, pulpit, tombs, altarpieces and historiated stalls. Tiepolo painted the *trompe-l'œil* frescoes in the Chapel of the Holy Sacrament, which are a remarkable piece of illusionism.

The **Oratory of Purity** (Oratorio della Purità) ⊙, to the right of the cathedral, has a ceiling decorated with a remarkable Assumption (1757) by Tiepolo.

Archbishop's Palace (Palazzo Arcivescovile) ⊙. – The 16C-18C palace boasts **frescoes★** by Tiepolo. The ceiling of its grand staircase depicts the Fall of the Rebel Angels, while the apartments are decorated with scenes from the Old Testament.

Piazza Matteotti. – This lovely square bordered by arcaded houses is the site of a lively open-air market. Also of interest are: the elegant 16C baroque Church of San Giacomo, a 16C fountain and a 15C column of the Virgin. It is pleasant to stroll in Via Mercato Vecchio and Via Vittorio Veneto with their shops beneath the arcades.

★★ **URBINO** Marches   Pop 15 582

Michelin map ███ folds 15 and 16, ███ fold 36 or ███ fold 16
Town plan in the current Michelin Red Guide Italia

The walled town of Urbino, with its rose-coloured brick houses, is built on two hills overlooking the undulating countryside bathed in a glorious golden light. Urbino was ruled by the Montefeltro family from the 12C onwards and reached its zenith in the reign (1444-82) of **Duke Federico da Montefeltro**, a wise leader, man of letters, collector and patron of the arts. Urbino was the birthplace of **Raphael** (Raffaello Sanzio) (1483-1520).

★★★ **DUCAL PALACE (PALAZZO DUCALE)** *time: 1 1/2 hours*

The palace (1444-72), started by order of Duke Federico by the Dalmatian architect Luciano Laurana and completed by the Sienese Francesco di Giorgio Martini, is a masterpiece of harmony and elegance. The design hinges on the panorama to the west of the old town, and the original façade overlooking the valley is pierced by superimposed loggias and flanked by two tall round towers. The severe east wing facing Piazza Rinsacimento has irregularly-spaced windows, while the majestic north façade is punctuated by three great doors at ground level and four rectangular windows on the first floor.

The inner courtyard, inspired by earlier Florentine models, is a classic example of Renaissance harmony with its pure, delicate lines, serene architectural rhythm and subtle combination of rose-coloured brick and white marble.

On the ground floor are: an **archaeological museum** (lapidary fragments: inscriptions, steles, architectural remains etc), the **Duke's Library** and the palace **caves**.

★★ **National Gallery of the Marches** (Galleria Nazionale delle Marche) ⊙. – The palace's first-floor rooms with their original decoration are the setting for several great **masterpieces★★★**: a predella of the *Profanation of the Host* (1465-9) by Paolo Uccello, a *Madonna* di Senigallia and a curious *Flagellation of Christ* by Piero della Francesca *(p 53)*, the *Ideal City (p 164)* by Laurana and the famous portrait of a woman, known as **The Mute**, by Raphael. Duke Federico's **studiolo★★★** is decorated with magnificent intarsia panelling.

A collection of 16C-17C Italian paintings and 17C-18C maiolica is displayed on the second floor.

To the north of the palace stands the early-19C cathedral built by Valadier.

ADDITIONAL SIGHTS

★ **Raphael's House (Casa di Raffaello)** ⊙. – *57 Via Raffaello.*
Raphael lived here up to the age of 14. This typical 15C house belonged to the boy's father, Giovanni Sanzio or Santi, and contains mementoes and period furniture.

Oratory Churches of St John (San Giovanni Battista) **and St Joseph** (San Giuseppe) ⊙. – *Via Barocci.*
Of these two neighbouring churches the first is 14C and has curious **frescoes★** by the Salimbene brothers depicting the life of St John the Baptist. The second, dating from the 16C, has in the nave a colossal statue of St Joseph (18C) painted in grisaille, and a very lovely stucco **crib★**, a life-size work by Federico Brandani (1522-75).

★★ **Strada Panoramica.** – Starting from Piazza Roma, this road skirts a hillside and affords admirable **views★★** of the town walls, the lower town, Ducal Palace and cathedral: a wonderful scene in various hues of pink brick.

★ **VELIA** Campani

Michelin map 988 fold 38 – 14km – 9 miles northwest of Pisciotta

The extensive ruins ⊙ of the ancient city of **Elea** are situated in the vicinity of Castellammare di Velia in the region of Cilento. Excavations have uncovered only part of the site. This colony was founded in 535 BC by Phocean Greek refugees who had been expelled by the Persians. Before settling in Massalia (Marseilles) they lived in the Corsican settlement of Alalia (Aleria), where they were victorious in a naval battle (c538) against the combined Carthaginian and Etruscan fleets. The busy and prosperous port of Velia – known for a long time as Elea – is famous for its school of the Eleatic philosophers (5C). Two of the better-known philosophers were Parmenides and his pupil Zeno.

Lower town. – *Pass under the railway line to reach this quarter.* From the entrance there is an interesting view of the ruins which include the former lighthouse, 4C BC town wall, the baths, the south sea gateway and the 4C BC **Pink Gateway★**.

Acropolis. – A medieval castle stands up against the remains of a 5C Greek temple. Laid out below are the ruins of the amphitheatre. A small **museum** houses statues of Parmenides, Zeno and Aesculapius which were found amidst the ruins.

★★★ **VENICE** (VENEZIA) Venetia   Pop 327 700

Michelin map 988 fold 5 – Town plan pp 224-225

A fascinating city between sea and sky, like Venus rising from the waves, Venice welcomes tourists from the five continents drawn to her by the charm of her canals, the pellucid light and the coolness of the sea breezes. She also offers the intellectual pleasures to be derived from her masterpieces, which mark the meeting of East and West.

The vanished greatness of Venice accounts for the myth of an artificial, voluptuous and tragic city, the scene of intrigues plotted in an atmosphere of corruption where dreams became nightmares. Many writers, the Romantics especially, have described the disturbing and fascinating atmosphere of the city. They include Barrès, and Thomas Mann in his novel *Death in Venice* which the Italian director Luchino Visconti made into a film.

Today the exceptional setting of Venice constitutes a threat to its very existence. The nature of the terrain on which it is built and the rising level of the surrounding waters pose a constant threat. Various measures have already been taken and a plan to safeguard and remedy the position has been devised.

Access. – The classic approach, ① on the town plan, is through Mestre and the road and railway bridge 4km – 2 1/2 miles long. The trip across the lagoon is somewhat spoilt by the sight of smoke from the port of Marghera and its factories. The bridge leads to the Piazzale Roma (**AT**), where cars must be left in one of the paying **garages** ⊙ *(autorimesse)* in the square, or in the speciallyprovided car parks on the nearby man-made island of Tronchetto.

Transport. – The best way to make contact with Venice from the Piazzale Roma is to take the little steamer (*vaporetto* – line No 1 *accelerato*: omnibus service) that runs to St Mark's in 1/2 hour, via the Grand Canal. The motor-boats *(motoscafi)* are quicker (line No 2; direct service; 1/4 hour), taking a short cut through the Rio Nuovo (**ATU**). The gondolas (1 hour) are delightful, but it is wise to agree in advance on the charge as one would with a porter *(facchino)*. In Venice itself, the canals can be crossed in the gondolas and ferries *(traghetti)*.

Seasons. – The best are spring and autumn. The Venice "Season" is in summer, time of the sumptuous festivals: Feast of the Redeemer on the Island of Giudecca, the historical Regatta on the Grand Canal; an International Film Festival at the Lido towards the end of summer; concerts in the various churches; the Arts Biennale brings together the works of the world's leading artists. *See the table of Principal Festivals at the end of the guide.*

VARIOUS ASPECTS OF VENICE

Venice is built on 117 islands; it has 150 canals and 400 bridges. A canal is called a *rio*, a square a *campo*, a street a *calle* or *salizzada*, a quay a *riva* or *fondamenta*, a filled-in canal *rio Terrà*, a passageway under a house *sotto-portego*, a courtyard a *corte* and a small square a *campiello*. The narrow streets, with their historic names, are paved with flagstones but have no footpaths. They are lined with flower-decked balconies, madonnas, shop signs and lanterns. Artisans' stalls and palaces stand side by side. The squares are charming, with their well-curbs often sculpted *(vera da pozzo)*.

The hub of public life is the Piazza San Marco *(p 223)* where tourists and citizens sit on the terraces of the famous Florian and Quadri cafés to listen to the music, dream and see the mosaics of St Mark's glow under the rays of the setting sun. The Quadri is more popular but the Florian is the best-known café: founded in 1720 it has received Byron, Goethe, George Sand, Musset and Wagner within its mirrored and allegory-painted walls.

The shops in St Mark's have sumptuous window displays of lace, jewellery, looking-glasses and the famous Murano glassware. The **Marzarie** (**CTU**), shopping streets, lead to the Rialto Bridge *(p 227)*.

On the far side of this are the displays of greengrocers' *(erberie)* and fishmongers' shops *(pescherie)*. In addition to these well-known and busy areas there are the **Frari Quarter** (**ABT**) and that of **Santa Maria Formosa** (**CT**), which have a certain peaceful charm with their brick façades and silent canals.

Venice – Gondolas

Meals in the restaurants *(trattorie)* are among the attractions of Venice. The fare consists chiefly of sea-food, squid *(calamaretti)*, cuttlefish, eels and mussels in the Venetian manner but also calf's liver also cooked in the Venetian way, with onions. These dishes should be accompanied by the pleasant local wines: Valpolicella, Bardolino and Amarone for red wines, and Soave and Prosecco for the whites.

Gondolas and Gondoliers. – Gondolas are inseparable from a mental picture of Venice: gondolas dancing over the ripples or moored to the tall posts called *pali* near the **Paglia Bridge (CU)**, where the gondoliers' Madonna stands; gondolas for serenades lit with lanterns, gliding on the small canals at night, police gondolas, refuse-collecting gondolas, fire service gondolas, goods delivery gondolas and even funeral gondolas with black pompoms.
As for the gondoliers, wearing sailors' jumpers and straw hats with coloured ribbons, they murmur gondola, gondola as they propel their craft with a single oar, humming their songs.

The Venetians. – Venetians have pale complexions and lisp slightly. Venetian is an Italian dialect. Their sense of intrigue and their subtlety were displayed equally in love and in politics: Venetian procuresses, spies and ambassadors used to be equally famous for their skill. The black velvet mask and domino, so often worn in Venice, added to the secrecy.
Venetians love pomp and are fond of the Carnival, other festivals *(see previous page)* and splendid processions with Venice as the perfect setting.

The Marriage of Venice and the Sea. – Every year, from 1173 to 1797, a gorgeous ceremony perfectly expressed what used to be the greatness of Venice and is still its beauty. After the Venetian Republic supported Pope Alexander III in his struggle against the Emperor Frederick Barbarossa, the Pontiff gave the Doge a ring as a symbol of his "rule of the sea". In memory of this, every year on Ascension Day, the Doge, dressed in cloth of gold, boarded *Bucentaur*, his gilded state galley, and sailed out to throw a ring into the sea with the words: "We wed thee, Sea, in token of our perpetual rule".

HISTORICAL NOTES

Venice was founded in AD 811 by the inhabitants of Malamocco, near the Lido, fleeing from the Franks. They settled on the Rivo Alto, known today as the Rialto. In 828 the bones of St Mark the Evangelist were brought from Alexandria; he became the protector of the town. The Republic was developed under the rule of a doge, a name derived from the Latin *dux* (leader).

The Venetian Empire. – From the 9C to the 13C Venice grew steadily richer as it exploited its position between East and West. With such maritime and commercial power it conquered Istria and Dalmatia. The Crusaders, led by Doge Dandolo, captured Constantinople in 1204. The products of its sack flowed to Venice, while trade in spices, fabrics and precious stones from markets established in the east grew apace.
Marco Polo (1254-1324) returned from China with fabulous riches and related his adventures in French in his *Book of Marvels*. The 14C war with its rival Genoa ended in victory for the Venetians in 1381.

Zenith. – The first half of the 15C saw Venetian power at its zenith: the Turks were defeated at Gallipoli in 1416 and the Venetians held the kingdoms of Morea, Cyprus and Candia (Crete) in the Levant.
In mainland Italy, from 1414 to 1428, they captured Verona, Vicenza, Padua, Udine, and then Brescia and Bergamo. The Adriatic became the Venetian Sea from Corfu to the Po.

Decline. – The capture of Constantinople by the Turks in 1453 started the decadence. The discovery of America caused a shift in the patterns of trade and Venice had to keep up an exhausting struggle with the Turks, who seized Cyprus in 1500 but were defeated in 1571 in the naval battle of **Lepanto**, in which the Venetians played an important part.

Their decline, however, was confirmed in the 17C when the Turks captured Candia (Crete) after a 25-year siege. The "Most Serene Republic" came to an end in 1797. Bonaparte entered Venice and abolished a ten century-old constitution.

The long-lasting oligarchy. – The government of the Republic was from its earliest days organised to avoid the rise to power of a single man. The role of doge was supervised by several councils: the Grand Council elaborated the laws; the Senate was responsible for foreign affairs, military and economic matters; the Council of Ten, responsible for security, kept a network of secret police and informers which created an atmosphere of mistrust.

VENETIAN PAINTING

The Venetian school of painting with its affirmed sensuality is characterised by the predominance of colour over draughtsmanship and by an innate sense of light in landscapes whose outlines are veiled by a general haze. Art historians have often noted the contrast between the scholarly and idealistic art of the Florentines and the freer, more spontaneous work of the Venetians, whose example has been perpetuated up until the Impressionists. The real beginnings of Venetian painting are exemplified by the **Bellini** family: Jacopo, the father, and Gentile (1429-1507) and **Giovanni** or **Giambellino** (1430-1516), his sons. The latter and younger was a profoundly spiritual artist and one of the first Renaissance artists who integrated his figures harmoniously with landscape backgrounds. Their pupil **Carpaccio** (1455-1525) recorded Venetian life with his usual imagination and care for detail while **Giorgione** *(qv)* continued to exercise his influence. His pupil, **Lorenzo Lotto**, assimilated the lesson of realism as practised by Northern artists.

The Renaissance ended in splendour with three great artists: **Titian** (c1490-1576) who introduced movement into his dramatic scenes and was also a skilled colourist; **Veronese** (1528-88), sumptuous decorator who described the luxurious lives of the patricians of the Most Serene Republic; and finally **Tintoretto** (1518-94), a visionary whose dramatic technique reflects an inner anxiety.

The artists of the 18C recalled Venice and its peculiar light, grey-blue, iridescent and slightly misty: **Canaletto** (1697-1768) whose works were so popular with English Grand Tourists, and his pupil Bellotto (1720-80) were both inspired by townscapes; **Francesco Guardi** (1712-93) who painted in luminous touches; **Pietro Longhi** (1702-58), the author of intimate scenes; **Giovanni Battista Tiepolo** (1696-1770), a master decorator and creator of graceful transparent and illusionist frescoes, and his son, Gian Domenico (1727-1804).

Spontaneity and colour are also found in the musicians of Venice, of whom the best known is **Antonio Vivaldi** (1678-1743).

★★★ **ST MARK'S SQUARE (PIAZZA SAN MARCO) (CU)** *time: 1/2 day*

St Mark's Square is famous all over the world; it forms a great marble saloon. All around, covered galleries shelter famous cafés and luxury shops. In front of the basilica are three flag-poles symbolising the Venetian Kingdoms of Cyprus, Candia (Crete) and Morea.

The square opens on the Grand Canal through the delightful **Piazzetta (CU 46)**. The two granite columns surmounted by a statue adapted to look like the Winged Lion of St Mark and the statue of St Theodore, the first patron saint of Venice, were brought from Constantinople.

★★★ **St Mark's Basilica (Basilica San Marco) (CU)**. – St Mark's is a structure of mingled Byzantine and Western style, built from 1063 to 1073 to shelter the tomb of the Evangelist Mark. Changes were made at the time of the Renaissance and in the 17C. Despite the great variety of styles (Byzantine, Romanesque, Gothic and Renaissance), the outcome is a unified and harmonious ensemble. The rich decoration of marbles and mosaics on gilded backgrounds is magnificent and has earned the basilica the name of the golden church (Chiesa d'Oro).

Built on the plan of a Greek cross, it is surmounted by a bulbous dome flanked by four smaller domes of unequal height placed on the arms of the cross.

Façade. – This is pierced by five large doorways adorned with variegated marbles and sculptures. The central doorway has lovely 13C-14C sculptures on the archivolt and recessed arches, and above are copies of the four famous **Bronze Horses** *(the originals are in the Museum of the Basilica: see p 226)*. The doors have lovely Byzantine bronze panels.

At the lateral doorways, mosaics depict the Translation of the body of St Mark. There is a picture of the basilica in its original form on the last door on the left. The porphyry group, known as the **Tetrarchs** (4C), stands to the right of the façade, near the Doge's Palace. At the corner is the proclamation stone *(pietra del bando)*, where laws were proclaimed. The pretty Piazzetta dei Leoncini (**CU 41**) lies to the left of the façade.

Narthex. – The narthex is faced with multicoloured marbles and mosaics and roofed with six little domes. The 13C **mosaics★★** depict with plenty of detail scenes from the Old Testament.

Interior. – The dazzling decoration, composed of rare marbles, porphyry and outstanding **mosaics★★★** of Byzantine (12C-13C) and Renaissance (16C) inspiration on a gilded background, harmonises perfectly with the architecture. The 12C paving is highly decorative. In the nave, on the west wall, a 13C mosaic portrays Christ, the Virgin and St Mark. The Arch of Paradise over the narthex is adorned with 16C mosaics illustrating the Last Judgement based on cartoons by Tintoretto. The early-12C mosaic on the first dome above the nave symbolises Pentecost. Christ and the Virgin, surrounded by Prophets, are seen in the Byzantine mosaics on the walls. On the arch dividing the dome above the nave from the central dome is a fine Crucifixion in the Byzantine style, also in mosaic (13C).

The south aisle gives access to the **baptistry**, adorned with mosaics (14C) depicting the Life of Christ and that of St John the Baptist. The baptistry contains the Sansovino Font (1545) and doges' tombs. The adjoining Chapel of St Zeno, with interesting 13C mosaics of the life of St Mark, occupies part of the narthex.

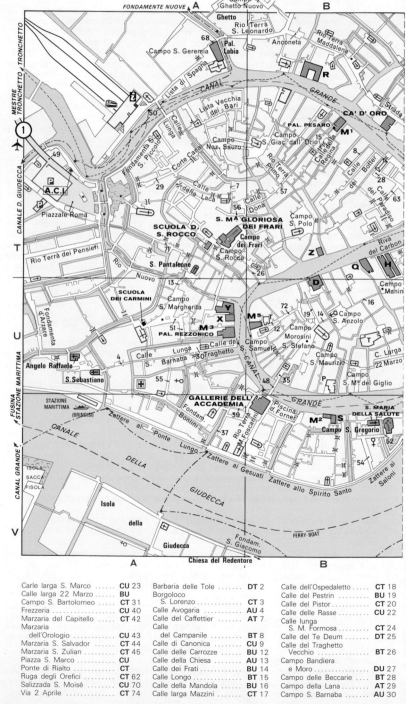

In the north aisle stands the *capitello*, a small marble shrine topped by a large oriental agate. The north transept contains interesting mosaics (episodes in the life of St John the Evangelist, Last Supper and Miracles of Jesus) after Veronese and Tintoretto. An Ascension, in mosaic, on the dome over the transept crossing, is 13C. The iconostasis in front of the chapel was made in 1394 and carries fine sculptures of Christ on the Cross, the Virgin and the Apostles.

The **chancel** ⊘ is roofed with a dome whose Byzantine mosaics represent Christ and the Virgin among the Prophets. On the roof to the right another mosaic shows the Translation of the Relics of St Mark. The Evangelist is entombed under the high altar, above which rises a green marble canopy supported by splendid alabaster columns carved with scenes from the Gospels.

The famous **Pala d'Oro★★★**, gold altarpiece, displays a wonderful assemblage of gold, silver, enamel and jewels. It was made at Constantinople in 976 and restored at Venice in 1105 and 1345.

The south transept leads to the rich **treasury★★★**, partly formed in the 13C from booty from the pillage of Constantinople by the Crusaders in 1204.

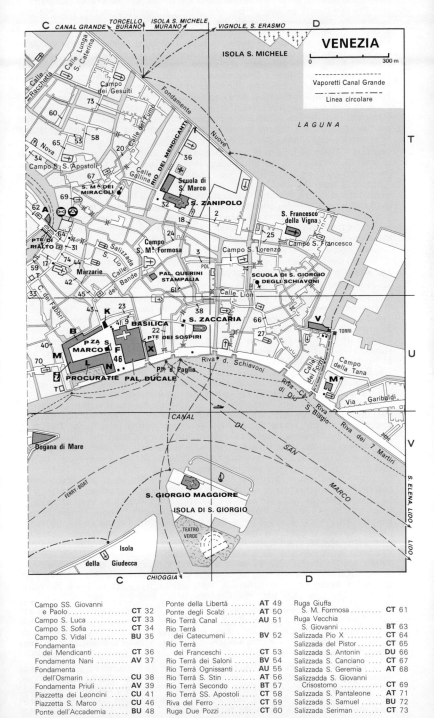

At the far end of the chancel are translucent **alabaster columns★★**, and to the left a bronze door by Sansovino (16C) leading to the sacristy.

Go up, through the narthex, to the **galleries** which now house the **Museum of the Basilica** ⊙, where one can admire the **Bronze Horses★★★** which once adorned the façade. These masterpieces of the Greco-Roman period were brought from Constantinople by Doge Dandolo in 1204. Bonaparte had them removed to the Carrousel Arch in Paris, where they remained until the fall of the French Empire. There is an attractive view of St Mark's Square from the Bronze Horses' platform.

★★ Campanile ⊙ (CU F). – From the top of this 99m – 325ft high belltower there is a fine **panorama★★** of Venice. The campanile collapsed in 1902 but was rebuilt stone by stone. The **loggetta★★** (small loggia) at its base has very pure lines. Note the fine 18C bronze doors and in the niches the statues (Minerva, Apollo, Mercury and Peace) by Sansovino. A delightful Madonna, also by Sansovino, will be found inside.

★★★ Doges' Palace (Palazzo Ducale) ⊙ (CU). – The palace was a symbol of Venetian power and glory, and was the residence of the doges and the seat of government and the law courts as well as being a prison. It was built in the 12C but was completely transformed between the end of the 13C and the 16C.

A pretty, geometric pattern in white and pink marble lends great charm to the two **façades**. The ground-floor gallery is supported by 36 columns with exquisite 14C-15C historiated capitals. The groups at the corners of the palace represent, from left to right, the **Judgement of Solomon** (attributed to Jacopo della Quercia), Adam and Eve, and **Noah's Drunkenness** (14C-15C Gothic sculptures). The open upper gallery has 71 columns surmounted by quatrefoil oculi.

The main entrance is the **Porta della Carta**, socalled because decrees were posted on it. It is in the Flamboyant-Gothic style (1442) and has on its tympanum a Lion of St Mark before which Doge Foscari (19C copy) is kneeling. In the niches on the uprights are figures representing Strength and Prudence (right) and Temperance and Charity (left).

Courtyard. – The main façade, richly adorned with sculptures, is a splendid example of the Renaissance style: alternating rhythmic bays *(p 128)* and arcades, decorative pilasters and friezes, oculi and lions' heads. The wells with bronze curbs date from the 16C.

Standing against the Foscari Portico is the small clock façade, dating from 1615 by B. Monopola, while alongside and rising above the portico is a curious 15C building crowned with pinnacles and allegorical statues of the Arts. Beyond the portico is the famous **Giants' Staircase★★★** (Scala dei Giganti), so called after the massive figures of Mars and Neptune by Sansovino.

Interior. – Sansovino's **Golden Staircase★★★** (Scala d'Oro), which starts from the gallery on the first floor, leads up to the **doges' apartments**: a picture gallery displays the works of Giovanni Bellini, Carpaccio and Hieronymus Bosch.

Follow the stairway up to the second floor.

The square vestibule has a gilded ceiling with paintings by Tintoretto.

The elegant **Four Doors Room** is also adorned with paintings by the same artist. The **Anticollegio** is a former waiting-room. It contains a fine chimneypiece with atlantes. The **Rape of Europa**, on the wall to the right, is a famous work by Veronese. On the other walls, Tintoretto painted an exceptional series of mythological subjects (the Marriage of Ariadne and Bacchus, Minerva repelling Mars, the Forge of Vulcan as well as Mercury and the Graces).

The **College Hall** used to be where the Doge and his councillors met and ratified treaties and agreements. The ceiling is decorated with eleven paintings by Veronese and his pupils (1577). Above the ducal throne Veronese painted the Doge, Sebastiano Venier, giving thanks to Christ for the naval victory of Lepanto over the Turks. On the walls are allegories by Tintoretto with portraits of the doges. The ceiling of the **Senate Chamber** is decorated with a remarkable **Triumph of Venice★★★** by **Tintoretto**, who also painted the Descent from the Cross.

The **Meeting Chamber of the Council of Ten** has a remarkable coffered ceiling painted with two scenes (Old Oriental with a Young Woman and Juno offering the Doges' Headdress to Venice) by a youthful Veronese.

Go down the Censors' Stairway (Scala dei Censori) to reach the **Grand Council Chamber★★★** which is the finest room in the palace and measures 52m – 171ft by 23m – 75ft. The walls are adorned with paintings illustrating Venetian history. Over the doge's throne **Tintoretto** painted **Paradise★★★**, one of the largest compositions in the world (22m – 72ft by 7m – 23ft). On the ceiling (near the throne) **Veronese** painted the **Apotheosis of Venice★★★**, while the cornice bears the portraits of the 76 first Doges: the missing one is Faliero the traitor. His portrait has been replaced by a black veil and his condemnation. Henri II, on his way back from Poland, is said to have attended a banquet in this chamber and pronounced "If I was not King of France, I would like to be a citizen of Venice". The **Ballot Room★★★** is ornamented with paintings depicting Venetian naval victories. The visit ends with the Censors' Room and the Avogaria.

★ Bridge of Sighs (Ponte dei Sospiri) (CU). – The Bridge of Sighs connects the Doges' Palace with the **prisons (CU X)**, in which Casanova was incarcerated but from which he made a fantastic escape. It dates from the 17C and owes its name to the lamentations of prisoners who were conducted across it to their place of execution.

★★ Law Courts (Procuratie) ⊙. – With their galleries and columns these buildings make a graceful background for the square. The **Clock Tower★** (Torre dell' Orologio) **(CU K)** dates from the end of the 15C. The dial bears the signs of the zodiac. On its summit are the famous Moors *(Mori)*, a pair of giant bronze jacks which have been striking the hours for 500 years.

To the left of the Clock Tower, the **Procuratie Vecchie** (Old Law Courts) (**CU B**), built at the beginning of the 16C, served as a residence for the procurators attached to the building committee of the basilica, who were responsible for its upkeep. The **Procuratie Nuove** (New Law Courts) (**CU L**), opposite, date from the 17C.

The **Ala Napoleonica** which completes the square was built by order of Napoleon in 1810. Under the arches is the entrance to the **Correr Museum★** ⊙ (**CU M**) which contains the historical and artistic collections of the city. In the picture gallery, on the second floor, note a Virgin and Child by Thierry Bouts; a Crucifixion by Van des Goes; a *Pietà* by Antonello da Messina; the portrait of Doge Mocenigo by Gentile Bellini; a **Pietà** by Cosimo Tura; a **Pietà, Madonna** and **Transfiguration** by Giovanni Bellini; and the famous **Courtesans** by Carpaccio.

★ **Sansovinian Library** (**Libreria Sansoviniana**) ⊙ (**CU N**). – This noble and harmonious building was designed by Sansovino in 1553 and now contains at No 7 the **Marciana National Library** ⊙ with its illuminated manuscripts and the famous Grimani Breviary (15C-16C Flemish school).

Palazzo Reale (**CU N**). – The palace at No 17 Piazzetta San Marco houses an archaeological museum ⊙.

★★★ GRAND CANAL (CANAL GRANDE) *time: half a day including sightseeing*

The French writer and ambassador, Philippe de Commines, wrote of the Grand Canal in the 15C: "I think it is the finest street in all the world and has the finest houses". Venice's widest canal winds in a large double bend from the station to St Mark's basin and is lined with sumptuous palaces in various styles. These were the residences of the patricians whose names were in the Golden Book. Tour the Grand Canal in a steamer starting from St Mark's Square.

★ Rialto Bridge (Ponte di Rialto) (CT)

The graceful Rialto Bridge, halfway along the canal, was built from 1588 to 1592 by Antonio da Ponte, and was designed to allow an armed galley to pass under it. It is a hump-backed bridge with a central street lined with shops and gangways on either side affording views of the Grand Canal.

The nearby **Fondaco dei Tedeschi** (**CT**), now a Post Office, was used in the 12C-14C as a warehouse by German merchants.

Rialto Bridge by Canaletto (Louvre Museum, Paris)

Right bank (East) – *From St Mark's Square to the station*

★★ **Palazzo Grassi** ⊙ (**BU M⁵**). – The palace, built by Giorgio Massari (1740-60), has been restored and converted into a museum in 1986 by Gae Aulenti and Antonio Foscari. It is the venue for major international exhibitions.

★★ **Palazzo Corner-Spinelli** (**BTU D**). – A late 15C-early 16C Renaissance palace with splendid basket-handled arched windows.

★★ **Palazzo Grimani** (**BT Q**). – This majestic white palace is a masterpiece of the High Renaissance by Sammicheli (late 16C).

★★ **Ca' Loredan** (**BT H**). – This former warehouse *(casa fondaco)* in the Veneto-Byzantine style has 16C additions.

★★★ **Ca' d' Oro** ⊙ (**BT**). – The "golden house" used to be gilded all over. This, the most elegant palace in Venice, is in the ornate Gothic style (1440). It houses the **Franchetti Gallery★★** (tapestries, sculpture and a fine collection of paintings: Mantegna, Carpaccio, Titian, Van Dyck and Guardi).

★★ **Palazzo Vendramin-Calergi** (**BT R**). – It was in this rich Renaissance palace (1509) with its admirable twinned openings that Wagner died in 1883.

Left bank (West) – *From the station to St Mark's Square*

★★ **Church of Santa Maria della Salute.** – *Description below.*

★★ **Palazzo Dario** (BV S). – A charming Early Renaissance palace (1487) where the 20C writer Henri de Régnier lived.

★★ **Palazzo Rezzonico** (AU). – This imposing and well-balanced baroque edifice was built in the 17C by Longhena, but only completed a century later. Inside, there is a museum on 18C Venice *(p 229)*.

★★ **Palazzo Giustiniano** (AU X). – This comprises two identical 15C buildings which are good examples of the ornate Gothic style.

★★ **Ca'Foscari** (AU Y). – This 15C palace was the residence of Doge Foscari when he was deposed by the Council of Ten in 1457. He died here the very next day.

★★ **Palazzo Bernardo** (BT Z). – One of the best examples of the ornate Gothic (1442) style.

★★ **Palazzo dei Camerlenghi** (CT A). – An elegant white building of the Renaissance period.

★★ **Palazzo Pesaro** (BT M¹). – Longhena's baroque masterpiece now houses a Gallery of Modern Art *(p 229)*.

★★★ ACADEMY OF FINE ARTS **(GALLERIE DELL'ACCADEMIA)** ⊘ (BV).

time: 2 hours

The Academy is housed in the School and Church of St Mary of Charity (Santa Maria della Carità) and in the Lateran Canons' Monastery. It is one of the finest art collections in Italy and reviews Venetian painting from the 14C to the 18C. The first room contains works by the few Venetian Primitives, notably Paolo and Lorenzo Veneziano. The Renaissance is well represented in the following rooms with works by Giovanni Bellini (the majestic composition of the **San Giobbe altarpiece**, scholarly allegories, numerous Madonnas with landscape backgrounds including the *Madonna of the Orange Tree*), Carpaccio, Cima da Conegliano, Mantegna *(St George)*, Piera della Francesca, Cosimo Tura, and Hans Memling (a fine **Portrait of a Young Man**). One of the jewels of the collection is Giorgione's **Tempest**, in which nature has become the main subject and seems to be subjugating the personages with its mysterious power. Further on, pause before Tintoretto's famous *Virgin of the Treasurers of the Republic* and Lorezzo Lotto's lovely **Portrait of a Gentleman.**

In the **Meal in the House of Levi,** Veronese used all the magic of his decorative technique. There are also several fine works by Tintoretto, including his *Miracles of St Mark,* and Titian's moving but unfinished **Pietà** (1576).

In the following rooms, the 17C and 18C are represented by Tiepolo, Piazzetta, Rosalba Carriera, Canaletto, Pietro Longhi and Guardi.

Room XX contains the **Miracles of the Holy Cross**, a cycle of paintings of which three are by Gentile Bellini and one by Carpaccio. Note especially, by Gentile Bellini, *The Procession of Relics in St Mark's Square* which is a faithful record of Venetian life in 1500, and Carpaccio's *The Healing of Someone Possessed, beside the Rialto Bridge.* The **Legend of St Ursula** in the next room is a series of nine pictures (1480-*c*1500) by Carpaccio, in which the painter shows an eye for picturesque detail and a remarkable clarity of composition.

Finally, in Room XXIV the **Presentation of the Virgin at the Temple** is one of Titian's masterpieces.

PRINCIPAL CHURCHES

★★ **Church of St Mary of Salvation (Santa Maria della Salute)** (BV). – The Salute was built at the entrance to the Grand Canal in the 17C by Longhena after an epidemic of plague (1630), to fulfil a vow. This baroque church stands on an admirable site at the water's edge. The monumental interior is built on an octagonal plan and is surmounted by a central dome.

The sacristy ⊘ contains **Tintoretto's Marriage at Cana★★★** (1561) with its warm luminous colours. Note also the **ceiling** painted by Titian, the **St Mark's altarpiece** on the left altar and the eight **medallions of the Evangelists.**

Near Santa Maria are the charming square, **Campo San Gregorio** (BV), and a Gothic church with a fine 15C doorway. At the end of the Punta della Salute is the **Dogana di Mare** (CV) (1677), or Maritime Customs House, with a revolving statue of Fortune aloft.

★★ **Church of St George Major (San Giorgio Maggiore)** (CV). – This church on the Island of San Giorgio, facing St Mark's Square, was begun by Palladio in 1566 and completed in 1610 by Scamazzio, the designer of its noble façade. The tall brick **campanile★★** was built in 1791 using that of St Mark's as a model.

The interior is severe but of majestic proportions. Two **paintings★★★** by **Tintoretto** face one another on the walls of the chancel: the Harvest of Manna and the Last Supper, which is remarkable for its chiaroscuro. There are also splendidly carved 16C **stalls★★** ⊘. From the **terrace of the campanile** *(lift in the north transept)* there is a **panorama★★★** of Venice and its lagoon.

★★ **Church of St John and St Paul (Ss Giovanni e Paolo** or **San Zanipolo)** (CT). – This Gothic church (1234-1430), built by the Dominicans, stands in a spacious square. Also in the square is a 16C well-curb and an admirable **equestrian statue★★** (1480), full of power and energy, of the mercenary leader Bartolomeo **Colleoni** by Verrocchio.

This vast church is the pantheon of Venice; it contains many **tombs**★★ of doges and patricians. Among the paintings is a beautiful **altarpiece figuring St Vincent Ferrier**★★★ by Giovanni Bellini (second altar in the south aisle), and an Annunciation, an Adoration of the Shepherds and an Assumption of the Virgin by **Veronese** on the **ceiling**★★★ of the Rosary Chapel *(entrance in the north transept)*. To the left of the church, in the square, is the **Scuola di San Marco** (St Mark's School) with a Renaissance **façade**★ richly decorated with sculptures by Pietro and Tullio Lombardo.

The **Rio dei Mendicanti**★ (Beggars' Canal) **(CT)**, which runs beside the Scuola di San Marco, frequently figured in the works of Canaletto and Guardi.

★★ **Church of St Mary** (Santa Maria Gloriosa dei Frari) ⊘ **(AT)**. – This Franciscan Gothic church is the largest in Venice. Inside, there are numerous **tombs**★★ including Canova's monument and Titian's mausoleum. Examine the magnificent painted altarpieces and particularly two **works by Titian**★★★: the famous *Assumption* on the high altar and the admirable *Virgin of the Pesaro Family* in the fourth bay down in the north aisle. A **triptych** of a **Madonna and Saints**★★ by Giovanni Bellini is shown in the sacristy.

★ **Church of St Zachary** (San Zaccaria) **(CU)**. – San Zaccaria, which dates from the Renaissance, stands in a pleasant square. It has a 13C campanile. In the north aisle (at the second altar) is an **altarpiece of the Madonna with Four Saints**★★★ by Giovanni Bellini. In the San Tarasio Chapel there is a fresco by Andrea del Castagno, and three splendid **altarpieces**★★ by Antonio Vivarini and Ludovico da Forli.

SCHOOLS (SCUOLE)

The *Scuole*, typically Venetian institutions, were confraternities which often assumed charitable roles. A *Scuola* usually included an assembly room, a chapel and sometimes an almshouse.

★★★ **Scuola di San Rocco** ⊘ **(AT)**. – The Renaissance building has a graceful façade of semicircular arches, fluted columns and marble incrustations. There is an outstanding series of 56 **paintings**★★★ by **Tintoretto** on which he worked for eighteen years *(poor lighting)*. The best are: on the ground floor, an *Annunciation* and a *Massacre of the Innocents;* on the first floor, in the Great Hall, *Moses drawing Water from the Rock,* the *Miracle of the Brazen Serpent, Manna raining down from Heaven,* the *Last Supper, the Nativity,* the *Ascension* and in the small Albergo Room an immense *Crucifixion* so full of drama that Tintoretto regarded it as his best work. Note also Titian's *Dead Christ* and Giorgione's admirable *Christ carrying the Cross.*

★ **Scuola di San Giorgio degli Schiavoni** ⊘ **(DT)**. – This institution received natives of Dalmatia, nicknamed Esclavonians by the Venetians, who were citizens of the Venetian Republic, and in particular old seamen. The Renaissance oratory is adorned with exquisite **paintings by Carpaccio**★★ relating the *Legend of St George,* the *Miracle of St Tryphonius* and the *Story of St Jerome*. There is a remarkable portrait of *St Augustine* in his cell.

★ **Scuola dei Carmini** ⊘ **(AU)**. – Inside, the ceiling (first floor) is decorated with a masterly **cycle of paintings**★★ by **Giovanni Battista Tiepolo** including a fresco depicting the Virgin in glory appearing to the Blessed Simon Stock.

ADDITIONAL SIGHTS

★★ **Peggy Guggenheim Collection** ⊘ **(BV M²)**. – The 18C **Palazzo Venier dei Leoni,** although never completed, is the setting for an exceptional collection of paintings and sculpture by the best 20C artists. The collector Peggy Guggenheim was the muse of the Surrealists.

★ **Venice in the 18C** (Museo del Settecento Veneziano) ⊘ **(AU M³)**. – This is housed in the Palazzo Rezzonico *(p 228)*. The collection includes (on the first floor) Venetian baroque furniture, black, gold and heavily carved; genre pictures by Pietro Longhi as well as two **masterpieces**★★ by Guardi: *The Ridotto* (a famous Venetian gambling club) and the *Nuns' Parlour;* and **frescoes**★★ by Gian Domenico Tiepolo portraying the frivolity of Venetian society.

★ **Palazzo Querini-Stampalia** ⊘ **(CT)**. – A picture gallery contains a series of works by Donato and Caterino Veneziano, the Florentine Lorenzo di Credi, Giovanni Bellini *(Presentation of Jesus in the Temple),* Palma Vecchio, V. Catena and Pietro Longhi *(Scenes from 18C Venice).*

★ **Museum of Modern Art** ⊘ **(BT M¹)**. – The Palazzo Pesaro *(p 228)* houses this collection, which is essentially devoted to 19C Italian painting.

Churches. – There are approximately 200 churches in Venice, nearly all interesting. Among them are:

West of the Grand Canal: 16C **San Sebastiano (AU)** with remarkable **interior decoration**★★ including paintings (*Story of Queen Esther* on the ceiling) by Veronese and a curious organ dating from the late 16C; nearby the Church of **Angelo Raffaele** ⊘ **(AU)** contains an organ loft decorated with seven delightful 18C **paintings**★ by Guardi; and also, not far from the Scuola di San Rocco, the **Church of San Pantaleone (AT)** with its magnificent 18C **ceiling**★ painted in *trompe-l'œil.* East of the Grand Canal: **Santa Maria dei Miracoli**★ **(CT)**, built in 1489 by P. Lombardo, is a jewel of the Renaissance adorned with multicoloured marbles; and **San Francesco della Vigna (DT)**, designed by Sansovino (16C), with a façade by Palladio, classical cloisters and two remarkable paintings of the **Virgin and Child**★, one of which is by Giovanni Bellini.

Palazzo Labia ⊙ **(AT)**. – This 18C palace contains a room magnificently covered in **frescoes★** by Tiepolo depicting the story of Antony and Cleopatra. Several other ceilings in the palace are by the same artist.

Arsenal (DU V). – The Arsenal was founded in 1104 and rebuilt in the 15C and 16C. The entrance to the basin is guarded by two towers dating from 1574. The monumental gateway (1460) to their left is preceded by baroque statues and lions of Greek origin. The Arsenal was famous throughout Europe and in its heyday it could build and equip a small galley in a single day.

Naval Museum ⊙ **(DU M⁴)**. – The museum near the Riva San Biagio, contains several models of 16C-18C Venetian ships (galleys, barges, galleons...) and a small model of one of the doges' famous state barges (Bucentaur). In addition there is a section on modern firearms.

Giudecca Island (Isola della Giudecca) (AV-CV). – The **Church of the Redeemer** (Redentore) *(Fondamenta S. Giacomo)*, built after the 1576 plague, is at the heart of a quiet quarter embellished with many small gardens. There is a **Madonna and Child★** with Angel Musicians by Alvise Vivarini in the sacristy.

Ghetto (AT). – In the 16C the Jews were relegated to the area around Campo del Ghetto Nuovo. This square is impressive for its calm and austerity.

San Michele ⊙ **(DT)**. – This is Venice's burial ground and the resting place of Stravinsky and Diaghilev. The pretty 15C Renaissance church has 14C cloisters.

LAGOON ⊙

See the plan of the Venetian suburbs in the current Michelin Red Guide Italia.

The Lagoon, separated from the sea by a coastal strip known as the Lido, is tidal and very pleasant to explore by boat. *There are also regular sailings (see Michelin Red Guide Italia) and excursions to the islands of the lagoon.*

★★ **Lido**. – This is one of the most fashionable resorts on the Adriatic. The elegant modern casino is one of the few in Italy in which gambling is allowed.

★★ **Murano**. – This town on an island in the Lagoon, whose main street consists of a Y-shaped canal lined with Renaissance houses, has been a great glass-making centre since 1292. In the 15C it was also the headquarters of a school of painting founded by Antonio Vivarini. Go up the left branch of the canal to see the 17C Palazzo Giustiniani which now houses the **Glass Museum★★★** (Museo Vetrario) ⊙ with its unique collection of glassware from ancient to modern times. The jewel of the collection is the 15C Barovier Marriage Cup.
A little further on the right, the early 12C **Church of Santi Maria e Donato★★** which is in the Veneto-Byzantine style has a lovely **chevet** with two superimposed blind arcades, the upper of which is marked by a white marble balustrade. Inside, there is a splendid 12C mosaic **paving**.

★★ **Burano**. – This fishing village is known for its lace-making and its brightly-painted houses. Inside the **Church of San Martino**, there is a dramatic **Crucifixion** by Tiepolo.

★★ **Torcello**. – The village was from the 7C onwards an important lagoon community and bishopric. Decline set in the early 14C. The chief buildings are grouped around the **main square★** which is now grass-covered.
The 9C-11C **Cathedral of Santa Maria Assunta★★** in the Veneto-Byzantine style has a nave and two aisles which rest on Greek marble columns with lovely 11C Corinthian capitals. The nave is closed by a magnificent **iconostasis** adorned with 11C-12C Byzantine low reliefs (peacocks face to face, lions and foliage). To the left of the iconostasis is a remarkable 10C-11C ambo sculpted in marble. The cathedral contains several fine Byzantine **mosaics★★★**: the most spectacular, on the west wall, are 12C-13C and depict the **Last Judgement;** others, in the apse, date from the 13C and picture with admirable purity and nobility the Mother of God, with the apostles above; yet another decorates the vaulting of the south chapel and portrays the Mystic Lamb with a luxuriant floral background.
The 10C Veneto-Byzantine **Church of Santa Fosca★**, built on a central plan, is surrounded by a **peristyle★★** with raised arches. Inside, the lovely Greek marble **columns★★** have carved capitals.

★ **Chioggia**. – Chioggia has been a port since ancient times and has an active fishing industry. Follow the two main canals lined with colourful fishing boats and spanned by hump-backed bridges. The 17C bridge, Ponte Vigo, offers a picturesque view of the **Vena Canal**, overlooked by the fish market.
The main street, **Corso del Popolo**, is lined with some lovely 16C to 18C houses. At one end stands the **cathedral★** (Duomo) which was rebuilt in the 17C in the Palladian style and has a lovely 14C campanile. Alongside is the attractive **Piazza Vescovile** which is popular with artists.

★ **Brenta Riviera**. – *Description p 67.*

Help us in our constant task of keeping up to date.
Send your comments and suggestions to
Michelin Tyre PLC
Tourism Department
Davy House
Lyon Road
HARROW Middlesex HA1 2DQ

Michelin map 📖 fold 4, 📖 fold 18 or 📖 fold 13
Town plan in the current Michelin Red Guide Italia

Verona stands on the banks of the Adige in a hilly setting and is, after Venice, the finest art centre in Venetia. The fashionable **Piazza Bra** (ABVX) is linked by the Via Mazzini (**BV**) to the heart of the old town. The opera and theatre summer seasons *(see the table of Principal Festivals at the end of the guide)* both draw large crowds.

This Roman colony under the Empire was coveted by the Ostrogoths, Lombards and Franks. The town reached its zenith under the **Scaliger**, Princes of the Scala, who governed for the emperor from 1260 to 1387. Then it passed to the Visconti of Milan before submitting to Venetian rule from 1405. Verona was occupied by the Austrians in 1814 and united as part of Venetia with Italy in 1866.

Romeo and Juliet. – These two young people, immortalised by Shakespeare, belonged to rival families: Romeo to the Montecchi (Montagues), who were Guelphs and supported the Pope, and Juliet to the Capuleti (Capulets), who were Ghibellines and supported the Emperor. Verona was the setting for this drama which took place in 1302.

Pisanello and the Veronese School. – Artists of this school were influenced by northern art from the Rhine Valley and they developed a Gothic art which combined flowing lines with a meticulous attention to detail.
Pisanello (*c*1395-*c*1450), a great traveller, active painter, prodigious medal-maker and enthusiastic draughtsman, was the greatest exponent of this school. His painting, with the unreality of his colours, the meticulously observed details and flowing lines, was both reminiscent of the rapidly disappearing medieval world and a precursor of the realism typical of the Renaissance.

SIGHTS

★★ **Piazza delle Erbe** (BV). – The Square of Herbs was the former Roman forum and it is today attractive and lively, especially on market day.
In line, down the middle of the square, stand the market column; the *capitello* (a rostrum from which decrees and sentences were proclaimed) of the 16C governors *(podesti)*; the fountain known as the Madonna of Verona, with a Roman statue; and a Venetian column surmounted by the winged Lion of St Mark (1523). Palaces and old houses, some with pink marble columns and frescoes, make an attractive framework round the square: on the north side is the baroque **Palazzo Maffei** (B).
In the Via Cappello (No 23) is **Juliet's House** (Casa di Giulietta) ⊘ (**K**); in fact it is a Gothic palace, with the famous balcony (in the inner courtyard), which belonged to the Capulet family.

★★ **Piazza dei Signori** ⊘ (BV). – Take Via della Costa to reach this square which resembles an open-air drawing-room with all its sober elegance. On the right is the 12C **Palazzo del Comune** (Town Hall) (**D**), also known as the Palazzo della Ragione dominated by the **Lamberti Tower**, built of brick and stone and with an octagonal upper storey. This building is connected by an arch with the Palazzo dei Tribunali (Law Courts) (**J**), formerly the Palazzo del Capitano (Governor's Residence) which also has a massive brick tower, Torrione Scaligero. The **Loggia del Consiglio** (E) on the opposite side is an elegant edifice in the Venetian-Renaissance style.
At the far end of the square the late-13C Palazzo del Governo (**P**) with its machicolations and fine classical doorway (1533) by Sammicheli was initially a Scaliger residence before it became that of the Venetian Governors.

★★ **Scaliger Tombs** (Arche Scaligere) ⊘ (BV). – The Scaliger built their tombs between their palace and their church. The sarcophagi bear the arms of the family, with the symbolic ladder *(scala)*.
They are elegant Gothic mausolea surrounded by marble balustrades and wrought-iron grilles. They are decorated with sculptured religious scenes and statues of saints in niches.
Over the door of the Romanesque **Church of Santa Maria Antica** is the tomb of the popular Cangrande I (d 1329) with his equestrian statue above *(the original is in the Castelvecchio Museum)*.

★★ **Roman Arena** (Arena) ⊘ (BVX). – This amphitheatre, among the largest in the Roman world, could accommodate 25 000 spectators with its 44 tiers of seats. Its particular building material, agglomerated blocks of pink marble, flint and brick, would seem to date its construction to the late 1C. This is the venue each summer for a prestigious opera season. From the topmost row there is a good **panorama**★★ of the town in its hilly setting, which on a clear day reaches as far as the Alps.

★★ **Old Castle and Bridge of the Scaliger** (Castelvecchio e Ponte Scaligero) (AV). – This splendid fortified group was built in 1354 by Cangrande II Scaliger. The castle itself is divided into two parts separated by a passageway guarded by a keep.
The castle contains a **Museum of Art**★★ ⊘ (**M**) created by the architect Carlo Scarpa. The **collection** shows the development of Veronese art from the 12C to 16C and its links with Venice and the International Gothic *(qv)*. There are frescoes by local artists and canvases by Stefano da Verona, Pisanello, Giambono, Carlo Crivelli (splendid *Madonna of the Passion*), Mantegna, Carpaccio as well as the Bellinis. The rooms on the upper floor contain Veronese works from the Renaissance period: Morone, Liberale da Verona *(Virgin with a Goldfinch)*, Girolamo dai Libri and Veronese. There are also some Venetian works by Tintoretto, Guardi, Tiepolo and Longhi. In addition there are arms, jewellery and sculpture sections.

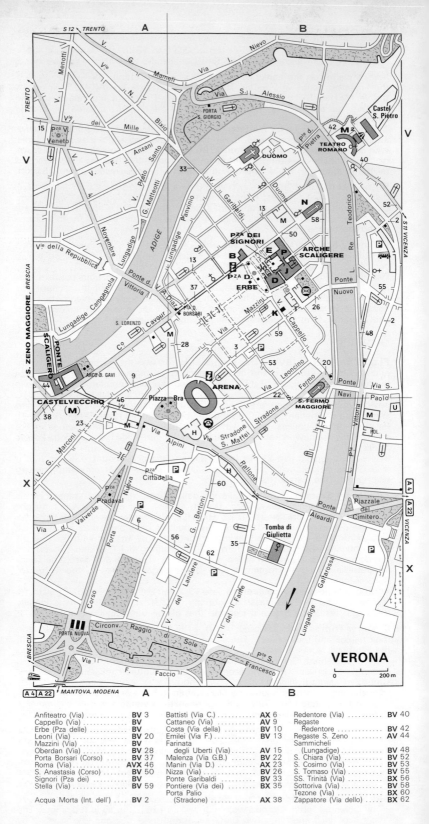

VERONA

★★ **Church of St Zeno Major** (San Zeno Maggiore). – *Access via Rigaste San Zeno* (**AV 44**). *Plan of the built-up area in the current Michelin Red Guide Italia.*
St Zeno is one of the finest Romanesque churches in northern Italy. It was built on the basilical plan in the Lombard style in the 12C. The façade is decorated with Lombard bands and arcading; the side walls and campanile have alternate brick and stone courses. In the entrance porch resting on two lions, there are admirable bronze **doors**★★★ (11C-12C) with scenes from the Old and New Testaments. On either side are low reliefs by the master sculptors Nicolò and Guglielmo (12C). On the tympanum of the doorway is a statue of St Zeno, patron saint of Verona.

The imposing interior has a tall, bare nave with a cradle roof flanked by aisles with shallow roofing. On the high altar is a splendid **triptych★★** (1459), a good example of Mantegna's style characterised by precise draughtsmanship and rich ornamentation. There are 14C statues on the chancel parclose and a curious polychrome statue of St Zeno laughing in the north apse.
To the north of the church are small Romanesque cloisters.

★ **Church of St Anastasia (Sant'Anastasia)** (BV N). – This church was begun at the end of the 13C and completed in the 15C. The campanile is remarkable and the façade is pierced with a 14C double doorway adorned with frescoes and sculpture. The lofty interior contains several masterpieces: four **figures of the apostles** by Michele da Verona and 17 **terracottas★** by Michele da Firenze in the Pellegrini Chapel, on the right of the chancel; the famous fresco showing **Knights of the Cavalli family being presented to the Virgin★** (1380) by the Veronese Altichero (first chapel in the south transept); and the **Giusti Chapel** ⊙ *(opening off the north transept)* has Pisanello's fresco depicting **St George delivering the Princess of Trebizond★★** (1436), combines which meticulous details and Gothic fantasy.

★ **Cathedral (Duomo)** (BV). – The cathedral has a 12C Romanesque chancel, Gothic nave and classical tower. The remarkable main doorway in the Lombard-Romanesque style is adorned with sculptures and low reliefs by Nicolò. The interior has fine pink marble pillars. The altarpiece on the first altar on the left is decorated with an Assumption by Titian. The marble chancel parclose is by Sammicheli (16C).
The canons' quarters are pleasant to walk through.

★ **Roman Theatre (Teatro romano)** ⊙ (BV). – It dates from the time of Augustus but has been heavily restored. Theatrical performances are still given here.
The former **Monastery of San Girolamo** *(access by lift)* has a small **Archaeological Museum** ⊙ **(M²)** and there is a lovely **view** over the town.

Castle of St Peter (Castel San Pietro) ⊙ (BV). – *Take the stairway which leads off Regaste Redentore* (BV 42).
The castle dates back to the Visconti and the period of Venetian rule. The terraces afford splendid **views★★** of Verona.

★ **Church of St Firmanus Major (San Fermo Maggiore)** (BVX). – The church was built in the 11C-12C and remodelled at a later date. The façade is in the Romanesque and Gothic styles. The aisleless church is covered by a stepped, keel-shaped roof. On the left by the west door the Brenzoni mausoleum (1430) is framed by a fresco of the **Annunciation★** by Pisanello.

Juliet's Tomb (Tomba di Giulietta) ⊙ (BX). – *Via del Pontiere.*
The tomb is in the cloisters of the Church of San Francesco al Corso, in which Romeo and Juliet were married.

★★ VICENZA Venetia   Pop 109 932

Michelin map 988 folds 4 and 5 or 429 fold 14
Town plan in the current Michelin Red Guide Italia

The proud and noble city of Vicenza lies in a pretty setting at the foot of the Berici Mountains. This busy commercial and industrial centre now has, in addition to its traditional textile industry, mechanical and chemical industries and a reputation as a gold working centre. Vicenza is strategically set at the crossroads of routes between Venetia and Trentino.
The gastronomic speciality of Vicenza is *baccalà alla Vicentina,* cod with a sauce served with slices of maize semolina *(polenta)*, which is best with wine from the Berici Mountains (Barbarano, Gambellara and Breganze).

HISTORICAL AND ARTISTIC NOTES

The ancient Roman town of Vicetia became an independent city state in the 12C. After several conflicts with the neighbouring cities of Padua and Verona, Vicenza sought Venetian protection at the beginning of the 15C. This was a period of great prosperity, when Vicenza counted many rich and generous art patrons among its citizens and it was embellished with an amazing number of palaces.

Palladio. – Vicenza was given the nickname of "Venice on *terra firma*" due to the tremendous amount of building activity which was largely the work of one man, Andrea di Pietro, known as Palladio. The last great architect of the Renaissance, Palladio was born at Padua in 1508 and died at Vicenza in 1580. He succeeded in combining, in a supremely well-balanced manner, the precepts of ancient art with the contemporary preoccupations. Encouraged by the humanist Trissino, he made several visits to Rome to study her monuments and the work of Vitruvius, a Roman architect of the time of Augustus. He perfected the Palladian style and in 1570 published his **Treatise on Architecture**, in four volumes, which made his work famous throughout Europe.
The **Palladian style** is characterised by rigorous plans where simple and symmetrical forms predominate and by harmonious façades which combine pediments and porticoes as at San Giorgio Maggiore in Venice *(p 228)*. Palladio was often commissioned by wealthy Venetians to build residences in the countryside around Venice. He combined architectural rhythm, noble design and, in the case of the country mansions, a great sense of situation and decoration with the utmost attention being paid to the base, so that the villas seemed to rise like a series of new temples on the banks of the Brenta *(qv)* or the slopes of the Berici Mountains. His pupil, Vicenzo Scamozzi (1552-1616), completed several of his master's works and carried on his style.

★★ THE PALLADIAN CITY *time: 1/2 day*

★★ **Piazza dei Signori.** – Like St Mark's Square in Venice, it is an open-air meeting-place recalling the forum of antiquity. As in the Piazzetta in Venice, there are two columns bearing effigies of the Lion of St Mark and the Redeemer. With the lofty **Torre Bissara★**, a 12C belfry, the **Basilica★★** (1549-1617) occupies one whole side of the square. The elevation is one of Palladio's masterpieces, with two superimposed galleries in the Doric and Ionic orders, admirable for their power, proportion and purity of line. The great keel-shaped roof, destroyed by bombing, has been rebuilt. The building was not a church but a meeting-place for the Vicenzan notables. The 15C **Monte di Pietà** (pawn shop) opposite, with buildings framing the baroque façade of the Church of St Vincent, is adorned with frescoes. The **Loggia del Capitanio★**, formerly the residence of the Venetian Governor, to the left, at the corner of the Contrà del Monte, was begun to the plans of Palladio in 1571 and left unfinished. It is characterised by its colossal orders with composite capitals and its statues and stuccoes commemorating the naval victory of Lepanto *(qv)*.

★★ **Olympic Theatre (Teatro Olimpico)** ⊙. – This splendid building in wood and stucco was designed by Palladio in 1580 on the model of the theatres of antiquity. The hemicycle of tiers of seats is surmounted by a lovely **colonnade** with a balustrade carrying statues. The **stage★★★** is one of the finest in existence with its superimposed niches, columns and statues and its amazing perspectives painted in *trompe-l'œil* by Scamozzi who completed the work.

★ **Corso Andrea Palladio.** – This, the main street of Vicenza, and several neighbouring streets are embellished by many palaces designed by Palladio and his pupils. At the beginning is the **Palazzo Chiericati** *(see below)*, an imposing work by Palladio; at No 147 the 15C **Palazzo Da Schio** in the Venetian-Gothic style was formerly known as the Ca d'Oro (Golden House) because it was covered with frescoes with gilded backgrounds. The west front of **Palazzo Thiene** overlooking Contrà S. Gaetano Thiene was by Palladio, while the entrance front at No 12 Contrà Porti is Renaissance dating from the late 15C.
The **Palazzo Porto-Barbaran** opposite is also by Palladio. At No 98 the **Palazzo Trissino** (1592) is one of Scamozzi's most successful works. Next is the Corso Fogazzaro, where the **Palazzo Valamarana** (1566) at No 16 is another work by Palladio.

★ **Municipal Museum (Museo Civico)** ⊙. – This is housed in one of Palladio's palaces, Palazzo Chiericati. The collection of paintings is on the first floor and includes Venetian Primitives (*The Dormition of the Virgin* by Paolo Veneziano); a **Crucifixion★★** by Hans Memling; canvases by Bartolomeo Montagna (pupil of Giovanni Bellini), Mantegna and Carpaccio, one of the most active artists in Vicenza. There are Venetian works by Lorenzo Lotto, Veronese, Bassano, Piazzetta, Tiepolo and Tintoretto as well as Flemish works by Velvet Brueghel and Van Dyck.

ADDITIONAL SIGHTS

Church of the Holy Crown (Santa Corona). – *Contrà Santa Corona.* The church was built in the 13C in honour of a Holy Thorn presented by St Louis, King Louis IX of France, to the Bishop of Vicenza. The nave and two aisles have pointed vaulting while the chancel is Renaissance. Works of art include: a **Baptism of Christ★★** by Giovanni Bellini (fifth altar on the left) and an **Adoration of the Magi★★** (1573) by Veronese (third chapel on the right). The fourth chapel on the right has a lovely coffered **ceiling★**, richly painted and adorned with gilded stucco, and a *Mary Magdalene and Saints* by Bartolomeo Montagna.

Cathedral (Duomo). – The cathedral, built between the 14C and 16C, has an attractively colourful Gothic façade and a Renaissance east end. Inside, the lovely **polyptych★** (1356) is by Lorenzo Veneziano (fifth chapel on the right).

Salvi Garden (Giardino Salvi). – This garden is attractively adorned with statues and fountains. A canal runs along two sides of the garden and two lovely Palladian 16C and 17C loggias are reflected in its waters.

EXCURSIONS

★★ **Villa Valmarana "ai Nani"** ⊙. – *2km – 1 mile to the south by the Este road and then the first road to the right.* The villa dates from the 17C and was adorned in 1757 with splendid **frescoes★★★** by Gian Domenico Tiepolo, the son. He portrays with plenty of verve and vigour the different aspects of daily life in the province and in particular, carnival scenes.

★ **Rotonda** ⊙. – *2km – 1 mile to the southeast by the Este road and then the second road to the right.* The Rotonda is one of Palladio's most famous creations and the plan of Chiswick House in London was inspired by it. The gracefully-proportioned square building is roofed with a dome and fronted on each side by a pedimented portico, making it look like an ancient temple.

★ **Monte Berico Basilica and the Berici Mountains.** – *2km – 1 mile to the south by Viale Venezia and then Viale X Giugno.* As the Viale X Giugno climbs uphill, it is lined with an 18C portico and chapels. On the summit is the baroque basilica roofed with a dome. From the esplanade there is a wide **panorama★★** of Vicenza, the Venetian plain and the Alps. Inside, there is a *Pietà* (1500) by Bartolomeo Montagna.

From here the road runs southwards to Arcugnano and Barbarano, where from time to time one can catch glimpses of former patrician villas now used as farmhouses in this attractive countryside of volcanic hills.

Montecchio Maggiore. – *13km – 8 miles to the southwest by the S 11.*
The ruins of these two castles remind one of Romeo and Juliet. There are good **views★** of the Po Plain and Vicenza.
On the outskirts of Montecchio on the Tavernelle road the **Villa Cordellina-Lombardi** ⊙ has one room entirely covered with **frescoes★** by Tiepolo.

★ **VITERBO** Latium   Pop 59 474

Michelin map 🔢🔢🔢 fold 25 or 🔢🔢🔢 fold 25
Town plan in the current Michelin Red Guide Italia

Viterbo, still girdled by its walls, has kept its medieval aspect notably in the **San Pellegrino quarter★★**, a working-class area with many craftsmen. Here there are many vaulted passageways, towers and external staircases.

★★ **Piazza San Lorenzo.** – This square, which occupies the site of the former Etruscan acropolis, transports one back to the Middle Ages with a 13C house on Etruscan foundations (now a chemist's), its cathedral dating from 1192 and adorned with a fine Gothic campanile, and its 13C **Papal Palace★★** (Palazzo dei Papi) – one of the most interesting examples of medieval secular architecture in Latium. From the Piazza Martiri d'Ungheria there is a lovely view of the ensemble.

Municipal Museum (Museo Civico) ⊙. – *Piazza F. Crispi.*
The museum is housed in the former Monastery of Santa Maria della Verità and contains collections of Etruscan and Roman objects discovered in the area: sarcophagi and grave artefacts from the tombs. The picture gallery, on the first floor, has a terracotta by the della Robbias as well as works by Salvator Rosa, Sebastiano del Piombo and a local painter, Pastura (15C-16C).

EXCURSIONS

Church of the Madonna of the Oak (Madonna della Quercia). – *3km – 2 miles to the northeast.*
The church is in the Renaissance style with a rusticated façade and tympana by Andrea della Robbia. The cloisters are half Gothic, half Renaissance.

★★ **Villa Lante in Bagnaia** ⊙. – *5km – 3 miles to the northeast.*
This elegant 16C villa was built to the designs of Vignola and became the residence of several popes. A lovely Italian terraced garden with geometric motifs and numerous fountains makes an ideal setting for the villa.

★ **Roman Theatre in Ferento** ⊙. – *9km – 6 miles to the north.*
The 1C BC theatre is quite well preserved and is the most important vestige of the ancient Ferentium, the ruins of which lie scattered over a melancholy plateau. The theatre ruins stand between the road and the Decumanus and consist of a brick back wall as well as a portico of well-dressed blocks without any mortar, and 13 tiers of seats.

Bomarzo. – *21km – 13 miles to the northeast by the S 204.*
Extending below the town is the **park** of the 16C **Villa Orsini** (Parco dei Mostri) ⊙ which is a Mannerist creation with a series of fantastically shaped **sculptures★**.

Montefiascone. – *17km – 11 miles to the northwest.*
Montefiascone stands in the vineyard country which produces the delicious white wine *Est, Est, Est.*
The imposing **cathedral** (Duomo) has a dome designed by Sammicheli, while the curious **Church of St Flavian★** (San Flaviano) in the Lombard-Romanesque style is in reality two churches superimposed. In the lower church, frescoes illustrate the story of the Three Dead and the Three Living Men symbolising the brevity and vanity of human life; opposite stands the tombstone of Johann Fugger, the German prelate who died on his way to Rome. As he was fond of good food and wine, he sent one of his servants ahead of him with orders to mark the inns where the wine was the best with the world *est* ("is" short for *Vinum est bonum* in Latin). When he arrived at Montefiascone the faithful servant found the wine so good that he wrote, in his enthusiasm, "*Est, Est, Est*". And his master, becoming enthusiastic in his turn, drank so much, much, much of it that he died.

★ **Lake Vico** (Lago di Vico). – *18km – 11 miles to the southeast by the Via Santa Maria di Gradi.*
This solitary but charming lake occupies a crater with forested slopes (beech, chestnut, oak and on the lake shores hazel trees).

Civita Castellana. – *36km – 22 miles to the southeast.*
Civita Castellana occupies the site of the Etruscan city Falerii Veteres which was destroyed by the Romans in 241, but rebuilt in the 8C or 9C. The **cathedral** (Duomo) is fronted by an elegant **portico★** built in 1210 by the Cosmati *(qv)*.
The late-15C **castle** (Rocca) was built by Sangallo the Elder and became the residence of Cesare Borgia.

Respect the life of the countryside
Drive carefully on country roads
Protect wildlife, plants and trees.

Michelin map 988 fold 14 or 430 fold 13
Town plan in the current Michelin Red Guide Italia

The Tuscan hills, so different from those around Florence, a commanding position and well-preserved walls make a harmonious setting for the Etruscan, Roman and medieval town of Volterra. The town has numerous alabaster workshops. Large salt pans to the west are used in the manufacture of fine salt and soda. To the northwest of the town there is a view of the **Balze★**, impressive precipices, which are part of a highly-eroded landscape furrowed by gully erosion.

★★ MEDIEVAL TOWN *time: 1 hour*

★★ **Piazza dei Priori.** – The piazza is surrounded by austere palaces. The 13C Palazzo Pretorio has paired windows and is linked with the Torre del Podestà, also known as Torre del Porcellino because of the wild boar sculpted high up on a bracket. The early-13C Palazzo dei Priori, opposite, is decorated with terracotta, marble and stone shields of the Florentine governors.

★ **Cathedral and Baptistry (Duomo e Battistero).** – The cathedral in the Pisan-Romanesque style, although it has been remodelled several times, stands in the picturesque Piazza San Giovanni. The interior comprises a nave and two aisles with monolithic columns and 16C capitals. In the second chapel on the left is a lovely late-13C *Annunciation.* The transept which is lit by alabaster windows contains, in the second chapel of the north arm, a Virgin of the 15C Sienese school, and in the second chapel in the north arm, a 13C painted wooden sculpture, *Descent from the Cross.* The nave has a superb 17C pulpit with 13C low reliefs. The octagonal baptistry dates from 1283.

   Take the Via Roma and then pass through the Arco Buonparenti.

Via dei Sarti. – This street is lined with palaces: No 1, Palazzo Solaini attributed to Antonio da Sangallo which now houses the picture gallery *(see below)*, and No 37, the Palazzo Incontri with its superb Renaissance façade designed by Ammanati.

Picture Gallery ⊙ (M). – *1 Via dei Sarti.* This displays numerous works of art by 14C to 17C Tuscan artists, notably a lovely *Annunciation* by Luca Signorelli and a *Descent from the Cross*, a masterpiece of Florentine Mannerism by Rosso Fiorentino.

Piazza San Michele (14). – Overlooking this square is the church of the same name with its Romanesque façade and a curious tower house.
Take the narrow but picturesque **Via Matteotti (6)**, then turn right into the Via Marchesi which leads back to the Piazza dei Priori.

ADDITIONAL SIGHTS

★ **Etruscan Museum (Museo Etrusco Guarnacci)** ⊙ (M¹). – Ceramics and more than 600 funerary urns, some of which are cleverly carved with reclining figures and domestic scenes, make up the exhibition.

★ **Porta all'Arco.** – This Etruscan gateway is built of colossal blocks of stone.

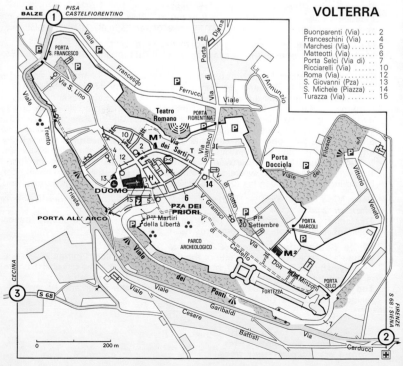

VOLTERRA

Roman ruins. – The ruins of a 1C Roman theatre lie to the west of the Porta Fiorentina.

Porta Docciola. – A fortified gate near which there is a curious medieval washtub.

Viale dei Ponti. – The Viale is a favourite walk with Volterrans. It affords splendid **views★★** of the Colli Metalliferi *(see below)*. Above stands the Fortezza, now used as a prison, an impressive mass of military architecture formed by the 14C Rocca Vecchia and the Rocca Nuova, built in 1742 with a keep and four corner towers.

EXCURSION

Larderello. – *33km – 21 miles to the south by* ③.
Larderello is situated in the heart of the **Colli Metalliferi** or metal-bearing hills as the name suggests. In the past they were mined for iron ore, copper and pyrites. Larderello is one of Tuscany's more unusual places with its desolate landscapes, the hissing of its volcanic steam jets, belching smoke from the blast furnaces and the rumble of machinery.

SARDINIA

With an area of 24 089km² – 9 300sq miles, Sardinia (Sardegna) is the largest island in the Mediterranean after Sicily. It has a population of over 1 630 000. The Punta la Marmora in the Gennargentu Mountains is its highest peak with an altitude of 1 834m – 6 017ft. Sardinia lies 200km – 124 miles off mainland Italy from which it is separated by the Tyrrhenian Sea, and 12km – 8 miles south of Corsica which it resembles in many ways. Both islands were part of the Primary Era Tyrrhenian shield which was later submerged during the Quaternary. The Island is quite mountainous and its scrub vegetation consists mainly of holm oaks and aromatic plants and shrubs, all typical of the Mediterranean basin. Since prehistoric times the island has had a mainly pastoral economy and more than half of Sardinia is suitable for grazing. Ewes' milk is used to make the famous Sardinian cheese *(pecorino)* with its pronounced flavour.

The Sardinians often cook their meat over hot embers under a layer of earth, and the pecorino cheese is used to flavour numerous dishes. Specialities include the roussette *(burrida)*, smoked ham of wild boar *(prosciutto di cinghiale)* and a strong meat stock with semolina balls *(succutundu)*. Taste one of the local wines, red or white: Nuragus and Vernaccia (dry white wine from the Oristano region, which is taken as an aperitif) are the best known.

Historical notes. – Sardinia has traces of human settlement going back to prehistoric times. The **nuraghi** or fortified tower houses date from the 2nd millennium BC and are the island's earliest monuments. These strange structures in the form of a truncated cone were built of huge blocks of stone without any mortar. The only opening was a low door with a massive lintel stone. Inside, each storey was roofed by a corbelled dome. The basic design evolved and towers were added and linked by stout walls, which reinforced the primitive structure. The *nuraghi* have a family resemblance to the brochs of Scotland. It is assumed that these fortified tower houses served as refuges in times of danger. The island has over 7 000 nuraghi with a large concentration between Porto Torres and Barumini. Other native monuments from this period are the **Giants' Tombs** (Tomba dei Giganti) or collective graves, no doubt intended for the ruling families. 500 of these remain today and they are usually to be found at some distance from the nuraghic settlements.

The funeral chambers lined and roofed with megalithic slabs (like a dolmen) were preceded by an arc of standing stones. In form they resemble a horned gallery grave. The dressed central stone has a small entrance at ground level.

The first settlers were the Phoenicians, followed by the Carthaginians, but these seafaring traders only colonised the coasts. The Romans, however, completely colonised the island for its agricultural land. From the 6C to the 8C BC the Byzantines ruled over Sardinia. Following a period of comparative independence, the country was ruled by the Pisans and Genoese before falling to the Spanish and later to the Austrian Empire in 1713. It was not long before the Emperor exchanged Sardinia for Sicily with the dukes of Savoy. The latter took the title of Kings of Sardinia. The various settlers left few artistic traces with the exception of the Pisans, whose influence *(p 164)* can be detected in the Romanesque and Gothic churches.

Sardinia today. – The economy of Sardinia was for a long time based on agriculture and was essentially pastoral. More recently tourism and industry have been developed. The intense industrialisation programme has accentuated the differences between the modern urban way of life and that of the many Sardinian shepherds, clinging to their traditional ways. The Sardinians have retained their keen sense of honour and hospitality. They still speak their own language and wear their magnificent costumes on feast days. Many cottage industries are still popular with the women (baskets, carpets, tapestry and fabrics).

Access. – **By air:** see the current Michelin Red Guide Italia.

By sea: see the Michelin map 988 as well as the current Michelin Red Guide Italia.

Sightseeing. – A quick tour of the island can be made in 5 days (petrol pumps are few and far between on the east coast). The map opposite locates the towns and sites described in the guide, and also indicates other beauty spots in small black type.

MICHELIN GUIDES

The Red Guides (hotels and restaurants)
Benelux – Deutschland – España Portugal – main cities Europe – France – Great Britain and Ireland – Italia

The Green Guides (fine art, historic monuments, scenic routes)
Austria – Canada – England : The West Country – France – Germany – Great Britain – Greece – Italy – Mexico – Netherlands – New England – Portugal – Scotland – Spain – Switzerland
London – New York City – Paris – Rome – Washington
and 9 regional guides to France

★ ALGHERO   Pop 40 159

Michelin map 988 fold 33

The early history of this pleasant little port set amid olive trees, eucalyptus and
parasol pines is unknown. Coral divers operate from the port which has become
popular as a seaside resort. In 1354 Alghero was occupied by the Catalans and
its Spanish air has earned it the nickname of the Barcelonettta of Sardinia. The
people still wear Catalan costumes and speak Catalan.
The beach extends 5km – 3 miles to the north of the village.

★ **Old town (Città Vecchia)**. – The fortifications encircle a network of narrow streets.
The **cathedral** *(Via Roma)* has a remarkable doorway and a campanile in the
Catalan-Gothic style. The 14C-15C **Church of San Francesco** has a Gothic interior
and lovely **cloisters** in golden-coloured tufa. The fishing harbour stands close
against the fortifications in the northern part of the town. The harbour is the
embarkation point for the boat trips to **Neptune's Cave★★★** *(p 244)*.

ARBATAX

Michelin map 988 fold 34

The name of this small port is Arab in origin. Arbatax is isolated in a beautiful
mountain setting overlooking the Tyrrhenian Sea and is used by cargo ships carrying
the island's exports of wood and cork. Not far from the harbour there is a small cliff
face of porphyry rock. This outcrop has been exploited for some time now.
A large, gently-shelving beach lies at the head of the bay.
The magnificent stretch of **road★★★** between Arbatax and Dorgali *(71km –
44 miles)* skirts impressive gorges.

Arbatax – East Coast

ARZACHENA   Pop 8 901

Michelin map 988 southeast of fold 23

Arzachena is an agricultural market town situated in the fine basin of Gallura
at the foot of a mountain range. The town is dominated by a curious
mushroom-shaped eroded rock (Fungo).
2km – 1 mile outside the town on the Olbia road is a *nuraghe* (round tower)
perched on a rock.
10km – 6 miles to the southwest *(by the Luogosanto road and after 7km –
4 miles a path to the right for 3km – 2 miles)* is the **Li Muri Giants' Tomb★**,
(p 242) a particular type of collective grave. On the hilltop are 15 stone slabs
laid out in an arc of a circle.

★★ BARUMINI   Pop 1 515

Michelin map 988 fold 33

The town of Barumini is surrounded by numerous traces of the earliest period
of Sardinian history.

★★ **Nuraghe Su Nuraxi.** – *2km – 1 mile to the west, on the left-hand side of the
Tuili road.*
This is an excellent example of a massive nuraghic fortress formed by several
towers interconnected by galleries. To the east is a large nuraghic settlement.

★ **Santa Vittoria di Serri.** – *38km – 24 miles to the east by the Nuoro road
and a road to the right in Nurallao.*
There are remains of a prehistoric religious centre. On the way out pass through
the village of **Isili** with two thriving craft industries (furniture-making and weaving).

CAGLIARI

Michelin map 988 fold 33

Cagliari is the capital of the island. It is a modern-looking town with a busy harbour and an old nucleus surrounded by fortifications, built by the Pisans in the 13C. Before becoming Roman it was a flourishing Carthaginian city called Karalis. The **Feast of St Efisio** (an officer in Diocletian's army who converted to Christianity and became the patron saint of Sardinia) is one of the most splendid in the whole of Italy *(see the table of Principal Festivals at the end of the guide).*
The **Terrazza Umberto 1º** (Z) affords a remarkable **view★★** of the town, harbour and bay.

Cathedral (Cattedrale) (Y). – Built in the 13C style of Pisa, the cathedral was remodelled in the 17C. Inside are magnificent **pulpits★★** (1162) by Guglielmo of Pisa with carved panels illustrating the Life of Christ. A little door on the right of the choir leads down to the **Santuario** ⊙, a crypt with 17C decoration, which enshrines numerous relics. A door opens on the right into a chapel containing the tomb of Marie-Louise of Savoy, the wife of the future King Louis XVIII of France and sister of the King of Sardinia.

★ **National Archaeological Museum (Museo Nazionale Archeologico)** ⊙ (Y). – The museum has a large collection of arms, pottery and small **bronzes★★★**, grave artefacts from the earliest period of Sardinian history. Phoenician, Punic and Roman art are represented in the other rooms.

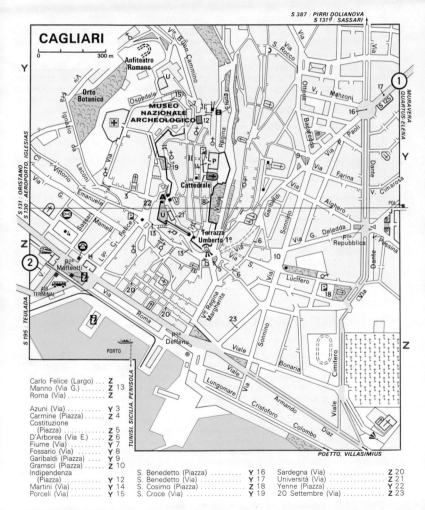

Elephant (Y A) and St Pancras Towers (Y B). – These early-14C towers were part of the Pisan fortifications.

Roman Amphitheatre (Anfiteatro Romano) (Y). – This is the most important Roman monument in Sardinia.

Botanical Gardens (Orto Botanico) ⊙ (Y). – The displays are of both Mediterranean and tropical vegetation.

EXCURSION

★★★ **Muravera Road (Strada di Muravera).** – *Leave by ① on the town plan.*
30km – 19 miles from Cagliari, the road enters wild gorges with reddish-coloured walls of porphyritic granite.

DORGALI

Michelin map ▓▓▓ fold 34

Monte Bardia stands between this important agricultural town and the sea. Dorgali makes an ideal excursion centre, especially for visiting the nearby megalithic sites.

Cala Gonone. – *10km – 6 miles to the east.*
A winding **road★★** leads to this resort with its small harbour. Boats leave from the port to visit the **Sea Ox Cave** (Grotta del Bue Marino) ⊘. The cave was occupied by the last monk seals, survivors from the Ice Age. The galleried cave has some lovely concretions.

★ **Motorra Dolmen and Ispinigoli Cave.** – *8km – 5 miles to the north by the Nuoro road and then the S125 or Orosei road to the right.*
The **Motorra Dolmen** (Dolmen Motorra) consists of an almost-circular slab of schist supported by eight uprights. The **Ispinigoli Cave** (Grotta di Ispinigoli) *(continue along the Orosei road, then turn right and continue for a further 3km – 2 miles)* is an immense cavity at an altitude of 400m – 1 312ft. The roof is supported by an extraordinary **column★★** 38m – 125ft tall.

★ **Serra Orrios and Sa Ena e Tomes Tomb** (Tomba dei Giganti). – *19km – 12 miles by the Nuoro road.*
The important nuraghic village of **Serra Orrios** *(signposted to the right, 10km – 6 miles from Dorgali)* stands on a plateau strewn with asphodels.
Two temples remain. One immediately to the west of the village and the other, in the same direction but further out, is surrounded by a circular wall.

> *At the next crossroads go straight ahead towards Lula and almost 6km – 4 miles later, after a small pass, turn right at the signpost, "Tomba dei Giganti" 700m – 766yds.*

Although overgrown by vegetation one can still make out the **Sa Ena e Tomes Tomb** which has the traditional layout of a Giants' Tomb. The funerary chamber, in the form of a passage roofed with large slabs like a dolmen, is preceded by a series of stones forming an arc of a circle. The larger central stone is carved with a moulding and pierced with a small passageway at ground level.

★★★ **Dorgali to Arbatax Road.** – *Description p 240.*

★★ ## EMERALD COAST (COSTA SMERALDA)

Michelin map ▓▓▓ folds 23 and 24

In the northeastern part of the island the wild and undulating region of **Gallura** has one of the most indented coastlines. It is a succession of pink granite headlands, forest-covered mountain ridges, sandy creeks and deeply-indented bays and has become a favourite area with holidaymakers.
The development of the **Emerald Coast**, started in 1961, was promoted by a consortium originally presided over by the Aga Khan. The coast was endowed with luxury facilities (palatial hotels, marinas and golf courses) to attract an upmarket clientele. The main resorts are **Porto Cervo**, Cala di Volpe and Baia Sardinia.

★★ ## GENNARGENTU MOUNTAINS (MONTI DEL GENNARGENTU)

Michelin map ▓▓▓ folds 33 and 34

The immense Gennargentu Massif in the centre of the island, culminates in Punta La Marmora (1 834m – 6 017ft). These bare, deserted and rounded peaks are to be found in the region of **Barbagia**, which was never completely conquered by the Romans. The relative isolation of the area has contributed to the shy and almost inhospitable manner of the people and to the preservation of local costumes and traditions.
There are many *nuraghi* and scenes of unforgettable wildness on a lonely massif, whose slopes are covered with groves of cork-oaks and chestnut trees.
The water which runs off the green slopes of the Gennargentu Mountains supplies the man-made reservoir of **Lago di Flumendosa** (good **view★★** of the lake from the road that climbs to Villanovatulo), which in turn is used to irrigate the plain of Campidano. **Aritzo** is the main holiday resort of the area. The town of **Tonara** standing at an altitude of 930m – 3 015ft in a green pass is known for its nougat *(torrone)* made with honey, almonds and hazel nuts. To the north **Fonni** is the island's highest village at an altitude of 1 000m – 3 281ft.

The ***Michelin Green Tourist Guide Portugal***
Architecture
Fine Art
History
Geography
Picturesque scenery
Touring programmes
Town and site plans
A guide for the holidays

★★ MADDALENA ARCHIPELAGO Pop 11 766
(ARCIPELAGO DELLA MADDALENA)
Michelin map 988 fold 23 or 90 fold 10

Access. – See the maps given above as well as the current Michelin Red Guide Italia.

The **Maddalena Archipelago** (Arcipelago della Maddalena) consists of 14 rocky islands and islets which are greatly appreciated by the tourists for their wild state. The two busiest islands, Maddalena and Caprera, are linked by a causeway.

★★ **Maddalena (Isola Maddalena).** – Under 20km² – 8sq miles this, the largest island of the archipelago, has a magnificent coastline. A lovely scenic route *(20km – 12 miles)* follows the coast.

★ **Caprera (Isola di Caprera)** ⊘. – This sparsely-inhabited island attracts many visitors to the one time home, now a **museum★**, and tomb of Garibaldi, who died here in 1882.

NUORO Pop 37 784
Michelin map 988 fold 33

Nuoro lies at the foot of Monte Ortobene, on the borders of the Barbagia region to the north of the Gennargentu Mountains. In this large town of central Sardinia the customs, traditions and folklore have remained unchanged since ancient times.

The **Sagra del Redentore** (Feast of the Redeemer) includes a procession through the town in local costumes and a folk festival *(see the table of Principal Festivals at the end of the guide)*.

★ **Museum of Popular Traditions (Museo della Vita e delle Tradizioni Popolari Sarde)** ⊘. – *55 Via A Mereu.*
The museum has a fine collection of Sardinian costumes. The author Grazia Deledda, a native of Nuoro, won the Nobel Prize for Literature in 1926 for her description of Sardinian life.

EXCURSIONS

★ **Monte Ortobene.** – *9km – 6 miles to the east.*
This is a popular excursion with local people. The summit affords several good viewpoints.

★ **Su Gologone.** – *20km – 12 miles to the southeast by the Oliena-Dorgali road.*
The large town of **Oliena** stands at the foot of a particularly steep slope of the Sopramonte. Locally the women still wear the traditional costume.

> *Just beyond Oliena take a local road to the left for about 6km – 4 miles.*

The lovely spring at Su Gologone gushes from a rocky face in a picturesque green setting.

Orgosolo. – *20km – 12 miles to the south.*
This large market town with its calm appearance is notorious for being the stronghold of bandits and outlaws. The Italian film producer Vittorio de Seta popularised them in his film *Banditi a Orgosolo* (1961).

ORISTANO Pop 32 174
Michelin map 988 fold 33

Oristano is the main town on the west coast. Founded in 1070 by the inhabitants of nearby Tharros *(qv)*, Oristano put up a strong fight against the Aragonese in the 14C.

★★ **Piazza Roma.** – The crenellated tower, Torre di San Cristoforo, overlooking this vast esplanade, was originally part of the town wall built in 1291. Opening off Piazza Roma is **Corso Umberto**, the town's main shopping street.

San Francesco. – The church, rebuilt in the 19C, has some interesting **works of art★** including a wooden statue of Christ by the 14C Rhenish school, a fragment of a polyptych (St Francis receiving the Stigmata) by Pietro Cavaro, a 16C Sardinian artist, and a statue of St Basil by Nino Pisano (14C).

EXCURSIONS

★ **Basilica of Santa Giusta.** – *3km – 2 miles to the south.*
This 12C edifice stands in the town of the same name, on the banks of a lake. The sober elegance of Santa Giusta is characteristic of all Sardinian churches where Pisan and Lombard influences mingle. The façade divided into three sections in the Lombard manner has an attractively-carved doorway typical of the Pisan style. Inside, the piers are either of marble or of granite. There is a crypt under the slightly-raised choir.

Arborea. – *18km – 11 miles to the south.*
This charming little town was planned and laid out in 1928 by the Fascist government, following the draining of the marshes and the extermination of the malaria mosquito.

PORTO CONTE

Michelin map 🔲🔲🔲 fold 33 – 13km – 8 miles northwest of Alghero

This, the ancient Portus Nympharum or Port of Nymphs, lies on the shores of a beautiful bay.

★★★ **Neptune's Cave (Grotta di Nettuno)** ⊙. – *9km – 6 miles to the southwest leaving from the head of the bay. Boats leave from Alghero.*
The road out to the headland, **Capo Caccia**, offers splendid **views**★★ of the rocky coast. This large cave is on the point. A stairway (654 steps) leads down the cliff face. There are small inner lakes, a forest of columns, and concretions in the form of organ pipes.

★ **Nuraghe Palmavera.** – *2km – 1 mile from the bay on the left-hand side of the Alghero road.*
This nuraghe is surrounded by the remains of a prehistoric village. The individual dwellings were crowded closely together. The nuraghe is a particularly fine building in white limestone with two vaulted towers and two separate entrances.

PORTO TORRES   Pop 21 823

Michelin map 🔲🔲🔲 folds 23 and 33

Situated at the head of a large bay, Porto Torres is the port for Sassari. Founded by Caesar it enjoyed considerable importance in the Roman period, as can be testified by the remains in the vicinity of the station.

★ **San Gavino.** – It was built at the end of the 11C by the Pisans (the long series of blind arcades on the north side are characteristic of the Pisan style) and enlarged shortly afterwards by the Lombard master builders. It is a fine example of medieval Sardinian art. A 15C doorway in the Catalan-Gothic style interrupts the arcades.
Inside, piers alternate with groups of four clustered columns giving a harmonious result. A large **crypt** enshrines the relics of St Gavin and a very fine Roman **sarcophagus**★, decorated with sculptures portraying the muses.

★ SANT'ANTIOCO ISLAND   Pop 12 656

Michelin map 🔲🔲🔲 fold 33

This volcanic island is the largest of the Sulcis Archipelago, lying off the southwest coast of Sardinia. It has a hilly terrain with high cliffs on the west coast.
The chief town, also called Sant'Antioco, is linked to the mainland by railway.

★ **The remains of Sulcis** ⊙. – The ancient town of Sulcis, founded by the Phoenicians, gave its name to this group of islands.
Before entering the necropolis, visit the **museum** which displays all the finds from the excavations and includes a fine collection of **steles**★.
The **tophet**★ *(500m – 1 640ft from the museum)* is where the Phoenicians gathered the remains of their first-born child, who was always sacrificed according to Phoenician custom. The **necropolis** was set apart and has 60 tombs cut in the rock.
The **catacombs**, under the parish church, were originally a Phoenician necropolis transformed by the Christians during the Roman period.

Except where otherwise stated, all itineraries
in town are designed as walks.

SASSARI   Pop 120 497

Michelin map 🔲🔲🔲 fold 33 – Town plan in the current Michelin Red Guide Italia

Sassari is the second largest town in Sardinia. It offers the tourist a contrast between its spacious, airy modern quarters and its medieval nucleus, nestling round the cathedral. The busiest arteries are the Piazza d'Italia and the Corso Vittorio Emanuele II.
Sassari is known for its festivals. The famous **Cavalcata Sarda** is a colourful procession of people from nearly all the provinces of Sardinia in their local costumes. This is a particularly good chance to admire the great variety and beauty of Sardinian costume. The procession ends with a frenetic horse race.
The **Festa dei Candelieri** (Feast of Candles), dating from the late 16C, was the result of a vow to the Virgin, made during an epidemic of the Black Death. The procession comprises the different trade guilds with each carrying huge beribboned wooden candles, gilded or painted silver *(see the table of Principal Festivals at the end of the guide).*

★ **Sanna National Museum (Museo Nazionale Sanna)** ⊙. – The museum contains rich archaeological collections, including an interesting section devoted to Sardinian ethnography and a small picture gallery.

Cathedral (Duomo). – The cathedral is built in many styles and has a 13C campanile with a 17C upper storey, a late-17C Spanish baroque **façade**★ and a Gothic interior.

EXCURSION

★★ **Holy Trinity Church (Santissima Trinità di Saccargia).** – *17km – 11 miles to the southeast by the Cagliari road, the S 131, and then the road to Olbia, the S 597.* This former Camaldulian abbey church was built in the 12C in decorative courses of black and white stone, typical of the Pisan style. The elegant façade includes a porch added in the 13C and is flanked by a slender campanile. Inside, the apse is adorned with fine 13C frescoes showing a strong Byzantine influence.

★ THARROS

Michelin map ▓▓▓ fold 33 – 1.5km – 1 mile to the south of San Giovanni di Sinis

The Phoenicians founded Tharros on the Sinis Peninsula to the north of the Gulf of Oristano. It was an important depot on the trading route between Marseilles and Carthage, before it was conquered by the Romans in the 3C BC. The inhabitants abandoned the site in 1070, before it was overwhelmed by wind-blown sand. They settled in Oristano.

Excavation site ⊘. – The site lies near the hill which is crowned by a Spanish tower (Torre di San Giovanni). In the lower part of the settlement there were zones of housing, baths and a paleo-christian baptistry dating from the 5C. To the right of the road leading to the hill are the remains of a Punic temple and a Semitic temple. On the hilltop are the ruins of a Roman temple with further on a tophet *(see above)*. Beyond all this are the impressive basalt remains of the town's fortifications.

Necropolis. – Climb to the summit of the headland crowned by a lighthouse to see the Punic necropolis (6C-4C BC). Some of the rectangular tombs are cut in the rock while others are hypogea (underground chambers).

SICILY

Sicily (Sicilia), the largest of the Mediterranean islands, has an area of 25 709km² – 9 927sq miles. It is triangular in shape and was named Trinacria under Greek rule. Nearly 5 million people live on the island, which is generally mountainous and reaches at its highest point, Mount Etna (an active volcano), an altitude of 3 340m – 10 958ft.

Throughout its history Sicily has suffered numerous earthquakes: the 1908 one almost entirely destroyed Messina and the 1968 one affected the western part of the island.

Access. – **By air:** consult the current Michelin Red Guide Italia. **By sea:** see the Michelin map ▓▓▓ as well as the current Michelin Red Guide Italia.

Sightseeing. – The island can be visited in a quick tour of 6 to 7 days. The map below locates the towns and sites described in the guide, and also indicates other beauty spots in small black type.

Look in the introduction at the Map of Touring Programmes for the suggested itinerary for Sicily.

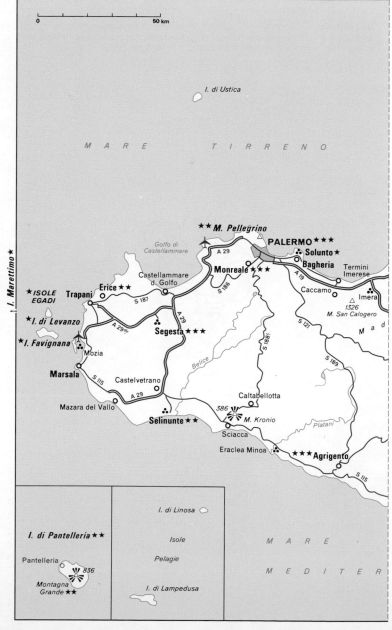

HISTORICAL AND ARTISTIC NOTES

Sicily has been a constant pawn for marauding forces in the Mediterranean due to its strategic location, lying near the peninsula and controlling the Mediterranean. Firstly there were the Greeks in the 8C who discovered an island divided between two ethnic groups: the **Sicani**, the oldest inhabitants, and the **Siculi** (Sicels) who came from the peninsula.

The Carthaginians were for several centuries the main rivals of the Greeks. They had colonised the coastal areas but were finally pushed back to the western part of the island, where they remained until the siege of Mozia by Denys the Elder in 397 BC. The 5C BC, excluding the rules of the tyrants of Gela and Syracuse *(p 261)*, was the apogee of Greek rule in Sicily (Magna Graecia). They built some magnificent buildings, they neutralised their enemies and Syracuse grew to become the rival of Athens.

This fragile peace was broken by the arrival of the Romans who coveted the island for the richness of its soil. By 241 BC, at the end of the First Punic War, the whole of Sicily had been conquered and it became a Roman province, governed by a praetor. The island was also a victim of the numerous Barbarian invasions which unfurled on southern Italy.

In 535 the island passed to the Byzantines before experiencing a period of great prosperity under the Aghlabid dynasty (Tunisia), in the 9C. The Saracens were in turn expelled by the Normans (11C). The son of the Great Count Roger I of Sicily, **Roger II** (1095-1154), created the Norman Kingdom of Sicily. He established his court at Palermo and during his reign the island was to enjoy a period of considerable political power and cultural influence.

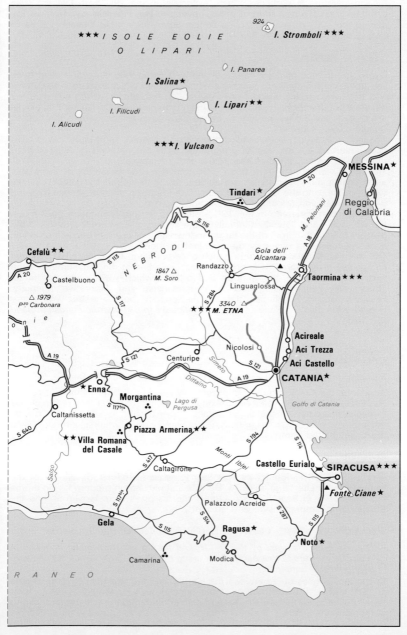

The name of the Hohenstaufen Emperor, **Frederick II**, dominated the reign of this Swabian dynasty. The house of Anjou followed in 1266; however, Charles of Anjou was expelled following the Palermo revolt of 1282 known as the **Sicilian Vespers**. Power passed to the Aragon dynasty and it was Alfonso V the Magnanimous who reunited Naples and Sicily and took the title of King of the Two Sicilies (1442).

The island passed to the Bourbons of Naples by marriage until they were overthrown by the Expedition of Garibaldi and the Thousand (1860).

Each period has left its mark on the island's heritage, be it in the field of art or customs and daily life. The Greeks built admirable Doric temples with the mellow local limestone, and also splendid theatres. During the brief period when the Normans dominated the island, Sicily knew an era of economic prosperity and artistic development.

This style was unique for its blending of a variety of different influences. The architectural style was still essentially Norman but the decoration (horseshoe-shaped arches, bulbous belltowers and intricately decorated ceilings) showed a strong Moorish influence, while the decoration of the walls with dazzling mosaics on golden backgrounds was Byzantine.

Known variously as the **Sicilian-Norman** or **Sicilian-Arab**, this style can be seen at Palermo, Monreale, Cefalu and Messina.

If the Renaissance has left few traces in the island – with some outstanding exceptions by **Antonello da Messina** *(qv)* who usually worked on the mainland – the Sicilians adopted the baroque style with great fervour in the late 18C. The main exponents were the architects **Rosario Gagliardi** in Noto and Ragusa, **Vaccarini** in Catania, and **Giacomo Serpotta** who embellished numerous oratories in Palermo with his sculpted fantasies.

Sicilian literature is particularly rich, especially in the 19C, with **Giovanni Verga** *(qv)* who created a new form of Italian novel, and **Luigi Pirandello** *(qv)*. Noteworthy among the 20C writers to describe contemporary life are **Elio Vittorini** (1908-66) and **Leonardo Sciascia** (born 1921).

SICILY TODAY

Owing to the mountainous nature of the land citrus fruit, vines and olive trees are grown mainly along the coast or on the rare plains which exist such as Catania and the Conca d'Oro inland from Palermo. In the interior which has a rather desolate but grandiose landscape, the main crops are cereals. Isolated dwellings are rare, as the Sicilian prefers to live in fairly large villages where the houses huddle closely together.

The industries which have been implanted on the outskirts of large towns have done little to stem the flow of emigration. Sicily has particularly suffered from the isolation which affected the whole of the Mezzogiorno.

The island's difficulties have been exacerbated by the existence of the Mafia, a formidable secret society whose abiding rule is to defend its members to the extent of breaking the law if need be, and to impose a reign of silence *(omerta)* which creates an atmosphere of fear and mistrust.

The Mafia first appeared in the 19C – although its true foundation goes much further back – and flourished initially in the countryside, where it tyrannised the peasant folk for the profit of the large landowners. Today it has become an urban phenomenon using definitely more violent methods.

The folk traditions and customs which once animated the streets have almost completely disappeared. It is only on feast days and in the museums that the visitor can now see the famous **Sicilian carts** which were gaily decorated. These carts were masterpieces of craftsmanship and decorative ingenuity. However, one can still see the popular puppet *(pupi)* theatres which are mentioned in the 12C *Song of Roland* or Ariosto's *(p 89) Orlando Furioso (Roland the Mad)*.

★★★ AGRIGENTO   Pop 55 347

Michelin map ▨▨▨ fold 36 – Town plan in the current Michelin Red Guide Italia

Agrigento, the Greek Akragas, is attractively set on a hillside facing out to sea. The Greek poet Pindar referred to Agrigento as "man's finest town". It includes a medieval quarter on the upper slopes above the modern town, and below, the impressive ancient ruins are strung out along a ridge, which is wrongly called the Valley of the Temples.

The town was founded in 580 BC by people from Gela who themselves originated from Rhodes. Of the governing "tyrants", the cruellest in the 6C was **Phalaris**, while **Tero** (7C) was renowned as a great builder. The 5C philosopher **Empedocles** was a native of Agrigento, as was **Luigi Pirandello** (1867-1936), winner of the Nobel Prize for Literature in 1934. He was an innovator in modern Italian drama *(Six Characters in Search of an Author)* and his plays were woven around the themes of incomprehension and absurdity.

★★★ VALLEY OF THE TEMPLES **(VALLE DEI TEMPLI)** *time: allow half a day*

> *Access from the west by the S 115 and then a left turn in the direction of Piazzale dei Templi (car park). Walk along the Sacred Way which is lined with the principal temples.*

Of the ten temples built between the late 6C and the late 5C BC, parts of nine are still visible. The destruction of the temples was for long thought to have been caused by earthquakes but is now also attributed to the anti-pagan activities of the early Christians. Only the Temple of Concord was spared when it became a church in 579 BC.

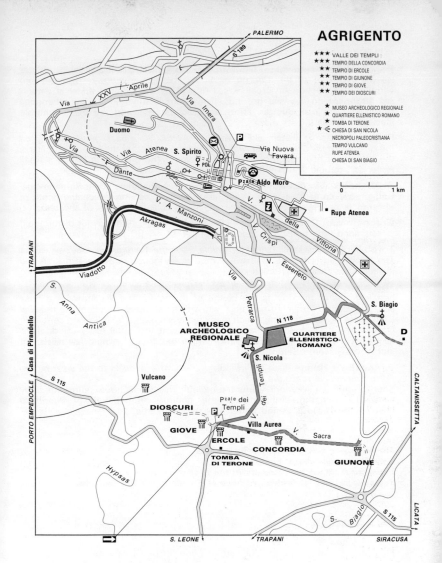

AGRIGENTO

★★★ VALLE DEI TEMPLI :
★★★ TEMPIO DELLA CONCORDIA
★★ TEMPIO DI ERCOLE
★★ TEMPIO DI GIUNONE
★★ TEMPIO DI GIOVE
★★ TEMPIO DEI DIOSCURI

★ MUSEO ARCHEOLOGICO REGIONALE
★ QUARTIERE ELLENISTICO ROMANO
★ TOMBA DI TERONE
★ CHIESA DI SAN NICOLA
  NECROPOLI PALEOCRISTIANA
  TEMPIO VULCANO
  RUPE ATENEA
  CHIESA DI SAN BIAGIO

★★ **Temple of Hercules (Tempio di Ercole)**. – Dating from 520 BC this is believed to be the oldest of the Agrigento temples. Eight of its columns have been raised and the others lie amid a jumble of ruins.
Further on to the left amid mimosa, pine and olive trees can be seen the deeply-grooved traces of the wheeled vehicles used to transport the building stone for the temples.

★★★ **Temple of Concord (Tempio della Concordia)**. – This temple was built from 450 to 440 BC; it is the most massive, majestic and best preserved of the Doric temples in Sicily. It has a peristyle of 34 tufa limestone columns, the original stucco facing having since disappeared.
It is not known to what deity it was dedicated and its present name is taken from a Roman inscription found nearby. The internal arrangement dates from the Christian period.

★★ **Temple of Juno (Tempio di Giunone)**. – Set on the edge of the ridge, this temple was built in 470 BC and conserves part of its colonnade and its architrave. On the east side there is a sacrificial altar and behind the temple an ancient cistern.

Return to Piazzale dei Templi.

★★ **Temple of Jupiter (Tempio di Giove)**. – Had this now-ruined temple been completed, its size (113m – 371ft long by 56m – 184ft wide) would have made it one of the largest in the ancient world.
Its entablature was supported by 20m – 66ft tall columns, between which stood **telamones** (columns in the form of male figures), colossal statues, one of which, the Gigante, a giant 7.5m – 25ft tall, has been reconstructed and is now on view in the Archaeological Museum. A reproduction of the giant, lying on the ground, gives some idea of the immense size of the building.

Temple of Castor and Pollux (Tempio dei Dioscuri). – This lies lower down the slope than the previous temple. This temple was also dedicated to Persephone, goddess of the harvest and protectress of Sicily. Only four of the columns supporting part of the entablature remain. The small rose at the corner of the entablature is the symbol of Rhodes.
Alongside is a **sacred area** dedicated to the Chthonic or underground gods: there are two sacrificial altars, one of which is circular and the other square.

ADDITIONAL SIGHTS

★ **Regional Archaeological Museum** (Museo Archeologico Regionale) ⊘. – *Enter via the cloisters of the Church of St Nicholas (see below).* The museum contains a collection of Greek vases (including the original **Krater of Perseus and Andromeda** on a white ground). One room is devoted to the telamones from the Temple of Jupiter. There are also mosacis and the 5C BC marble statue of **Ephebus.**

★ **Phalaris' Oratory** (Oratorio di Falaride) ⊘. – *Access via a passageway leading off the cloisters of the Church of St Nicholas.* Legend has it that the palace of Phalaris, the first tyrant of Agrigento, was in the vicinity. The building is in fact a small Hellenistic temple which was transformed during the Christian period.

St Nicholas (San Nicola). – This sober church in the transitional Romanesque-Gothic style contains a magnificent **Roman sarcophagus★** on which the death of Phaedra is portrayed. From the terrace there is a fine **view★** of the temples.

★ **Greco-Roman Quarter** (Quartiere Ellenistico-Romano) ⊘. –The layout of the main streets lined with houses is a good example of 4C BC town planning.

★ **Tero's Tomb** (Tomba di Terone). – *Visible from the Caltagirone road.* The tomb, said to be that of Tero, Tyrant of Agrigento, is 3m – 10ft high and in fact dates from the Roman era.

★ **The town today.** – The shady **Piazzale Aldo Moro,** often thronged with birds at certain times of the day, is the centre of the town. The **Via Atenea** is a busy shopping street. Crowning the old town with its stepped streets is the **cathedral** (Duomo), a Norman building which was greatly altered in the following centuries. On the way back down to Piazzale A. Moro visit the small **Abbey Church of the Holy Spirit** (Abbaziale di Santo Spirito) which has four charming **low reliefs★** in stucco by Giacomo Serpotta.

Pirandello's House (Casa di Pirandello) ⊘. – *6km – 4 miles to the west by the Porto Empedocle road, the S 115.* Shortly after the Morandi viaduct turn left. This small house surrounded by vineyards was the birthplace of the famous dramatist Luigi Pirandello (1867-1936), who is buried under a nearby pine tree.

Information in this guide is based on data provided at the time of going to press. Improved facilities and changes in the cost of living make alterations inevitable; we hope our readers will bear with us.

★ # CATANIA   Pop 372 212

Michelin map ▒▒▒ fold 37
Plan of the built-up area in the current Michelin Red Guide Italia

Catania is a busy seaport and industrial town which has developed quite considerably in recent years, despite the fact that it has been destroyed several times by the eruptions of Mount Etna. It is a fine city with wide, regular streets overlooked by numerous baroque buildings by the architect **Vaccarini,** who rebuilt Catania following the 1693 earthquake.
Natives of the town include the musician **Vicenzo Bellini** (1801-35), composer of the opera *Norma*, and the novelist, **Giovanni Verga** *(qv)*.
Catania holds the heat record for the whole of Italy: over 40 °C (104 °F), and the less enviable one of the highest crime rate, which has earned it the nickname of "Sicilian Chicago".

★ **Via Etnea** (DXY). – The town's main shopping artery is over 3km – 2 miles long. All the way along it affords a view of Etna. It is bordered by numerous palaces, churches and the **Bellini Gardens★** (Villa Bellini).

★ **Piazza del Duomo** (DZ). – This square is the centre of town and is surrounded by a baroque ensemble designed by Vaccarini which includes the **Elephant Fountain** (A) dating from 1735, the **Palazzo del Municipio** (H) with its well-balanced façade, and the **cathedral** (Duomo) (EZ) dedicated to St Agatha, the town's patron saint. The cathedral, built at the end of the 11C by the Norman, Roger I, was remodelled after the 1693 earthquake.

★ **Ursino Castle** (Castello Ursino) ⊘. (DZ). – This bare, grim castle, fortified by four towers, was built in the 13C by the Emperor Frederick II of Hohenstaufen. It houses an interesting **Municipal Museum** (M).

EXCURSION

Acireale. – *17km – 11 miles to the north.*
The itinerary passes through two fishing villages, both small resorts, **Aci Castello** and **Aci Trezza.** Offshore, the **Cyclops' Reefs** (Isole dei Ciclopi) emerge from the sea. These are supposed to be the rocks hurled by the Cyclops Polyphemus after Ulysses had blinded him by thrusting a blazing stake into his single eye.
The road leads to **Acireale,** a modern town with numerous baroque buildings which include those of the **Piazzo del Duomo** with the Basilica of Sts Peter and Paul and the Town Hall, as well as the **Church of San Sebastiano** with its harmonious **façade★** embellished with columns, niches and friezes.

CATANIA

Etna (Via) .... **DXY**
Umberto I (Via) .... **DEX**

Angelo Custode (Via) ...... **DZ** 2
Biondi (Via) .... **EY** 12
Bovio (Piazza G.) .... **EY** 15
Carlo Alberto (Piazza) ..... **EY** 19
Castello Ursino (Via) ...... **DZ** 21
Conte di Torino (Via) ...... **EY** 25

Cutelli (Piazza) .... **EZ** 26
Dante (Piazza) .... **DY** 28
Giuffrida (Via Vincenzo) ... **EX** 39
Guardie (Piazza delle) ..... **EY** 43
Imbriani
  (Via Matteo Renato) ... **DEX** 44
Lupo (Piazza Pietro) .... **EY** 47
Orlando (V. Vitt. E.) ...... **EX** 60
Porticello (Via) .... **EZ** 68
Rabbordone (Via) .... **EY** 69
Rapisarda (Via Michele) .... **EY** 70
San Francesco (Piazza) ... **DZ** 78

San Gaetano
  alle Grotte (Via) ..... **DEY** 79
San Giuseppe
  al Duomo (Via) .... **DZ** 80
Spirito Santo (Piazza) .... **EY** 87
Stesicoro (Piazza) .... **DY** 91
Teatro Massimo (Via) ... **EYZ** 92
Trento (Piazza) .... **EX** 95
Università (Piazza dell') .. **DZ** 96
Verga (Piazza) .... **EX** 98
Vittorio Emanuele III
  (Piazza) .... **EY** 100

Michelin Maps, Red Guides and Green Guides are complementary publications to be used together.

★★ CEFALÙ   Pop 14 490

Michelin map 🔢🔢🔢 fold 36

Cefalù is a small fishing town in a fine **setting★★**, hemmed in between the sea and a rocky promontory. It boasts a splendid Romanesque cathedral.

★★ **Cathedral (Cattedrale)**. – Built of a golden-tinted stone which blends in with the cliff behind, this cathedral was erected to fulfil a vow made by the Norman King, Roger II (12C), when in danger of shipwreck. The church (1131-1240) has well-marked Norman features in its tall main apse flanked by two slightly-projecting smaller ones and especially in its façade, abutted by the two square towers. The portico was rebuilt in the 15C by a Lombard master and is emblazoned with the arms of a former bishop, Gatto.

The timber ceiling of the two aisles and the transept galleries are also Norman. Columns with splendid **capitals★★** in the Sicilian-Norman style *(qv)* support the typically-Moorish horseshoe arch.

251

The oven vault of the central apse is covered with beautiful **mosaics**★★ on a gilded background, displaying a surprising variety of colour and forming an admirable expression of Byzantine art in its decline (12C). Above is Christ Pantocrator (Ruler of All) with underneath, on three different levels, the Virgin with four archangels and the twelve apostles. In the choir, the angels on the vaulting and the prophets on the side walls date from the 13C. The two marble and mosaic thrones are the episcopal one (south side) and the royal one (north side).

Mandralisca Museum (Museo Mandralisca) ⊙. – The museum, facing the cathedral in the picturesque Via Mandralisca, has a fine **Portrait of a Man** by Antonello da Messina.

★ EGADI ISLANDS (ISOLE EGADI)　　　Pop 4 723

Michelin map 988 folds 34 and 35. **Access:** see the Michelin map 988 and the current Michelin Red Guide Italia

The three islands ⊙ – Favignana, Levanzo and Marettimo – which make up this small archipelago lie offshore from Trapani. The islands are popular for their wild aspect, transparent blue sea and the beauty of their coastlines. It was here in 241 BC that the treaty ending the First Punic War was concluded, in which Carthage surrendered Sicily to Rome.

★ **Favignana.** – In the form of a butterfly, this island covers an area of 20km² – 8sq miles. The **Montagna Grossa** with its highest point of 310m – 1 017ft runs right across the island and ends as an indented coastline. The islanders are masters in the art of tunny fishing which they do for about fifty days between May and June. Having captured the tunny in a series of nets, they pull in the fish towards the shore where they are harpooned.

The main town of the group of islands, **Favignana**, is guarded by the fort of Santa Caterina, a former Saracen lookout tower, which was rebuilt by the Norman King, Roger II, and served as a prison under the Bourbons. To the east of the harbour are the former **tufa quarries**★ now drowned by the sea. Boat trips take visitors to the various caves, including the **Grotta Azzurra**★ which is situated on the west coast.

★ **Levanzo.** – This tiny island (6km² – 2sq miles) has no surfaced roads or springs. Few people therefore stay overnight. In 1950 traces of life in prehistoric times were found in the **Grotta del Genovese**, which is reached by boat from Cala Dogana.

★ **Marettimo.** – Off the beaten tourist track, Marettimo with its attractive **harbour**★ *(no landing stage, rowing boats take visitors to the quay)* has several restaurants but no hotels. Take a **trip** around the island in a boat to discover the numerous caves which riddle the cliff faces.

★ ENNA　　　Pop 29 245

Michelin map 988 fold 36

Enna lies in an isolated, sun-scorched landscape at the centre of the island. Its panoramic **site**★★ at an altitude of 942m – 3 091ft has earned it the nickname of the Belvedere of Sicily.

According to legend it was on the shores of **Lake Pergusa** *(10km – 6 miles to the south)* that Pluto carried off the youthful Proserpine, future Queen of the Underworld.

★ **Castle (Castello di Lombardia)** ⊙. – This medieval castle has six of its original twenty towers. From the top of the tallest there is an exceptional **panorama**★★★ of the hilltop village of Calascibetta, Etna and most of the Sicilian mountain peaks.

Belvedere. – *Beyond the castle.* From the far side of the hillock, which was the site of a temple to Demeter, there is a fine **view**★ of Calascibetta and of Enna itself.

Cathedral (Duomo). – This was rebuilt in the baroque style in the 16C and 17C but still has its 14C Gothic apses. The lovely classical façade is 16C.

★★ ERICE　　　Pop 29 136

Michelin map 988 fold 35 – 14km – 9 miles northeast of Trapani

This ancient Phoenician and Greek city occupies a unique and beautiful **setting**★★★ almost vertically (750m – 2 461ft) above the sea. Erice is clustered within its town walls and is crisscrossed by a labyrinth of quiet alleyways where numerous craftsmen offer their wares for sale. In antiquity Erice was a religious centre famous for its temple consecrated to Astarte, then Aphrodite and finally Venus who was venerated by mariners of old.

Castle of Venus (Castello di Venere) ⊙. – This castle, built by the Normans in the 12C-13C, crowns an isolated rock on Monte Eryx, on the site of the Temple of Venus. From here and the nearby gardens (Giardino del Balio) there are admirable **views**★★: in clear weather the Tunisian coast can be seen.

Chiesa Madre. – This church was built in the 14C using stones quarried from the ancient temples. The porch was added in the 15C and flanked by the square battlemented campanile with its elegant openings.

★★★ ETNA (MOUNT)

Michelin map 🔢🔢🔢 fold 37 – Alt approx. 3 340m – 10 958ft

Etna is the highest point in the island and is snow-capped for most of the year. It is still active and it is the largest and one of the most famous volcanoes in Europe.

Etna was born of undersea eruptions which also formed the Plain of Catania, formerly covered by the sea. Its eruptions were frequent in ancient times: 135 are recorded. But the greatest disaster occurred in 1669, when the flow of lava reached the sea, largely devastating Catania as it passed.

The outstanding eruptions in our time were those of 1910, when 23 new craters appeared, of 1917, when a jet of lava squirted up to 800m – 2 500ft above its base, and of 1923, when the lava ejected remained hot eighteen months after the eruption. The last stirrings of Etna took place in 1928, 1954, 1964, 1971, 1974, 1978, 1979, March 1981, March 1983 and 1985; the volcano still smokes and may erupt at any time.

The mountain has the appearance of a huge, black, distorted cone which can be seen from a distance of 250km – 155 miles. On its lower slopes, which are extremely fertile, orange, mandarin, lemon and olive trees flourish as well as vines which produce the delicious Etna wine. Chestnut trees grow above the 500m – 1 500ft level and give way higher up to oak, beech, birch and pine. Above 2 100m – 6 500ft is the barren zone, where only a few clumps of *Astralagus Aetnensis* (a kind of vetch) will be seen scattered on the slopes of secondary craters, among the clinker and volcanic rock.

★★★ **Ascent of Etna** ⊘. – The ascent of Etna can be made by the south face from Catania via Nicolosi or by the northeast face from Taormina via Linguaglossa. *Wear warm clothing and strong shoes.*

By the south face. – From a point almost 3 000m – 9 843ft up on the central crater in the area of Torre del Filosofo (the refuge was destroyed in the 1971 eruption), the three craters can be distinguished: the one to the southeast which appeared in 1978, the immense **central crater**, and the highest one to the **northeast** which has been dormant since 1971. On the way up go over towards the eastern face to see the grandiose valley **Valle del Bove** which is hemmed in by 1 200m – 3 937ft high walls of lava pierced with pot-holes and crevasses belching smoke.

Night-time excursions are possible on request: tourists will enjoy a Dantesque spectacle of molten lava at the bottom of the crater and an impressive sunrise with a view of the Lipari Islands and the Bove Valley.

By the northeast face. – The road goes through Linguaglossa, a lovely pinewood of the Laricio species and the winter sports resort of Villaggio Mareneve. The surfaced road ends at Piano Provenzana (1 800m – 5 906ft).

The area around the new observatory affords a magnificent view of the central and northeast craters. The climb ends amidst an extraordinary landscape of lava, which still smokes at times.

Night-time excursions are also organised on this slope. The intrepid are able to enjoy, from the edge of the crater, the grandiose sight of the sun setting and rising.

GELA   Pop 79 534

Michelin map 🔢🔢🔢 fold 36

Gela was founded in 688 BC by islanders from Rhodes and Crete. The town was destroyed and restored several times and it was completely rebuilt in 1230 by the Emperor Frederick II of Hohenstaufen. It was in the plain of Gela, one of the island's most fertile areas, that the US troops landed in 1943. The town prospered with the discovery of oil in the vicinity. Gela is, however, also a resort and an interesting archaeological centre.

Ancient remains ⊘. – For those interested in archaeology there are the ancient **Greek fortifications**★★ *(at Caposoprano to the west of the town)* dating from the 4C BC, with their regular stonework of skilfully-dressed blocks below and brickwork above. The most interesting section is the part facing the sea. This type of construction is particularly fragile and is now protected by plexiglass. These walls owe their preservation to the fact that they were encroached upon by sand. The **regional archaeological museum**★ ⊘ *(Corso Vittorio Emanuele, at the far eastern end of the town)* has a particularly attractive presentation of pottery and medals.

★★★ LIPARI ISLANDS (ISOLE EOLIE O LIPARI)   Pop 12 972

Michelin map 🔢🔢🔢 folds 36 and 37 – **Access:** see the Michelin map 🔢🔢🔢 and the current Michelin Red Guide Italia

The Lipari Islands are also called the **Æolian Islands** because the ancients thought Æolus, the God of the Winds, lived there. The archipelago comprises seven main islands, Lipari, Vulcano, Stromboli, Salina, Filicudi, Alicudi and Panarea, all of exceptional interest for their volcanic nature, their beauty, their light and their climate.

A deep blue, warm, clear sea, ideal for underwater fishing, peculiar marine creatures including flying-fish, sword-fish, turtles, sea-horses and hammer-fish, make the Lipari Islands a refuge for those who like to live close to nature. The inhabitants fish, grow vines and quarry pumice-stone.

★★ **Lipari.** – This, the largest island in the archipelago, is formed of volcanic rock dipping vertically into the sea. In ancient times Lipari was a source of obsidian, a glazed black volcanic rock. Today the islanders grow cereals and capers, fish and quarry pumice-stone on the east coast.

Two bays (Marina Lunga with its beach and Marina Corta) frame the town of **Lipari★**, which is dominated by its old quarter encircled by 13C-14C walls. Inside is the castle rebuilt by the Spaniards in the 16C on the site of a Norman building. The castle houses the **museum★** ⊙: re-creation of a Bronze Age necropolis, lovely collection of painted **kraters** (two-handled vases) imported from Greece and terracotta **theatrical masks.**

There are **boat trips★★** ⊙ leaving from Marina Corta which take the visitor round the very rugged southwest coast of the island. When making a **tour of the island by car★★**, stop at Canneto and Campo Bianco to visit the pumice-stone **quarries.** The view from the **Puntazze** headland includes five of the islands: Alicudi, Filicudi, Salina, Panarea and Stromboli. However, it is the belvedere in **Quattrocchi** which affords one of the finest **panoramas★★★** of the whole archipelago.

★★★ **Vulcano.** – This 21km² – 8sq mile island is in reality four volcanoes and according to mythology it is here that Vulcan, the God of Fire, had his forges. This is also the derivation of the term volcanism. Although there has been no eruption on the island since 1890 there are still important signs of activity: fumaroles (smoke-holes), spouting steam-jets often underwater, hot sulphurous mud-flows greatly appreciated for their therapeutic nature. This island has a wild but forbidding beauty, with its rugged rocky shores, its desolate areas and its strangely-coloured soils due to the presence of sulphur, iron oxides and alum. The island's main centre, **Porto Levante**, stands below the great crater. The beach is known for its particularly warm water due to the spouting steam-jets underwater.

Excursions to the **Great Crater★★★** *(2 1/2 to 3 hours on foot Rtn)* are interesting for the impressive views they afford of the crater and of the archipelago. From **Cape Grillo** there is a view of several islands.

On the other hand, **a tour of the island by boat** ⊙ *(starting from Porto Ponente)* gives the visitor a chance to see the many curious views, especially along the northwestern coast, which is fringed with impressive basalt reefs.

★★★ **Stromboli.** – The volcano of Stromboli, with its plume of smoke, has a sombre beauty, and is a wild island with steep slopes. There are very few roads and such soil as can be cultivated is covered with vines yielding a delicious golden-coloured Malvasia wine. The little square, white houses are markedly Moorish in style.

The **crater** ⊙, in the form of a 924m – 3 032ft cone, has frequent minor eruptions with noisy explosions and accompanying flows of lava. To see the spectacle climb up to the crater *(7 hours on foot Rtn, difficult climb)* or watch from a boat the famous flow of smoking and incandescent lava along the crevasse named Sciara del Fuoco towards the sea. At night the scene becomes both beautiful and awesome.

Strombolicchio, near Stromboli, is a picturesque rocky islet with a steep stairway leading to its summit which affords a splendid view of Stromboli, the Lipari Archipelago and the coasts of Calabria and Sicily.

★ **Salina** ⊙. – The island is formed by six extinct volcanoes of which two have retained their characteristic outline. The highest crater, **Monte Fossa delle Felci** (962m – 3 156ft) dominates the archipelago. There is a pleasant panoramic road round the island. Caper bushes and vines grow on the lower terraced slopes. The latter yield the delicious golden Malvasia wine.

MARSALA   Pop 80 662

Michelin map 988 fold 35

Marsala, the ancient Lilybaeum, on Cape Lilibeo, the westernmost point of the island is an African-looking town in all its whiteness. The Saracens first destroyed and then rebuilt it and called it Marsah el Allah (Port of God). It is known for its wines which a certain English merchant, John Woodhouse, rediscovered in the 18C.

It was at Marsala in 1860 that Garibaldi landed at the start of the **Expedition of the Thousand,** which freed southern Italy from the sway of the Bourbons.

The **Piazza della Vittoria**, near the public gardens (Villa Cavalotti) on the northern outskirts of the town, is a favourite meeting-place of the townsfolk.

A former wine cellar, near the sea, now houses the **archaeological museum** ⊙ *(Via Boeo):* the exhibits include the wreck of a **warship★** which fought in the Punic War and was found off Capo San Teodoro. Only the prow has been rebuilt.

★ MESSINA   Pop 270 546

Michelin map 988 fold 37 – Town plan in the current Michelin Red Guide Italia

Despite having been destroyed numerous times throughout the centuries, Messina or the ancient Zancle of the Greeks, is today an active market town. Messina has suffered repeated earthquakes (especially the 1908 one which destroyed 90% of the town and killed 80 000 in the region), epidemics and bombings.

Antonello da Messina. – Born in 1430 he studied in Naples where he was influenced by the then popular Flemish art. Later he was to be attracted by the innovations of Tuscan painting which with its increasing use of perspective emphasised volume and architectural details. His works show a complete mastery of his art: forms and colours, skilfully balanced, enhance an inner vision which greatly influenced the Venetian painters of the Renaissance, notably Carpaccio and Giovanni Bellini. Antonello died on his native island around 1479.

SIGHTS

★ **Museum (Museo Regionale)** ⊙. – *To the north of the town at the end of the Viale della Libertà.* There is an art gallery and a sculpture and decorative arts section. The painting section includes the polyptych by Antonello da Messina, **Virgin and Child with Saints** (1473), a remarkable composition which combines certain Tuscan traits with the earliest Flemish influences, an admirable **Descent from the Cross** by the Flemish artist, Colin van Coter; two works by Polidoro da Caravaggio, one of Raphael's pupils and two Caravaggios, **Adoration of the Shepherds** and a **Resurrection of Lazarus,** both painted towards the end of his life from 1608 to 1610. In the sculpture section there is a late-14C Crucifixion in wood and two sculptures representing **Neptune** and **Scylla** attributed to the Tuscan sculptor Montorsoli (16C) who was perhaps one of Michelangelo's assistants.

Cathedral (Duomo). – The cathedral, almost entirely rebuilt after the 1908 earthquake and the bombings of 1943, still displays the main features of its original Norman style (12C). The finely-carved narrow central **doorway**★ dates from the 15C. To the left stands the 60m – 196ft tall campanile with its **astronomical clock**★ which was made in Strasbourg in 1933 and is believed to be the world's largest.

Church of the Annunciation (Annunziata dei Catalani). – *Take the Via Cesare Battisti from the south side of the cathedral.*
Built in 1100 during the Norman reign and altered in the 13C, this church takes its name from the Catalan merchants who owned it. The apse is characteristic of the composite Norman style which blends Romanesque (small columns supporting blind arcades), Moorish (geometric motifs and polychrome stonework) and Byzantine (dome on a drum) influences.

All symbols on the town plans are explained in the key p 38.

★★★ **MONREALE**   Pop 26 951

Michelin map ▨▨▨ fold 35 – 8km – 5 miles to the southwest of Palermo

The town, dominating the green plain Conca d'Oro (Golden Conch Shell) of Palermo *(p 257),* grew up around the famous Benedictine **abbey** founded in the 12C by the Norman King, William II.

★★★ **Cathedral (Duomo)** ⊙. – The finely-carved central doorway has beautiful **bronze doors** (1186) embellished with stylised figures, which were carved by Bonanno Pisano. The more Byzantine north door is the work of Barisano da Trani (12C). The decoration of the **chevet** is remarkable for the blending of Moorish and Norman styles.
The cathedral has a basilical plan. The interior is dazzling with multicoloured marbles, paintings, and especially the 12C and 13C **mosaics**★★★ covering the oven vaults and the walls. They represent the complete cycle of the Old and New Testaments.
A gigantic **Christ conferring His Blessing** is enthroned in the central apse. Above the episcopal throne, in the choir, a mosaic represents King William II offering the cathedral to the Virgin. Another mosaic opposite, over the royal throne, shows the same King William receiving his crown from the hands of Christ.

★★★ **Cloisters (Chiostro)** ⊙. – The cloisters to the right of the church are as famous as the mosaics. They offer views of the abbey church. On the south side there is a curious fountain that was used as a lavabo by the monks. The galleries, with their sharply pointed arches, are supported by twin columns with remarkably carved capitals.

Terraces ⊙. – These offer magnificent **views**★★ of the cloisters and over the fertile plain known as the Conca d'Oro.

Monreale – detail of the cloisters

Michelin map 🔟🔟🔟 fold 37 – 32km – 20 miles to the southwest of Syracuse

Noto, which dates from the time of the Siculi, was completely destroyed by the terrible earthquake of 1693. It was rebuilt on a new site 10km – 6 miles distant from the original town. Bordering the streets, laid out on a grid plan, are handsome palaces, churches and other baroque monuments in the local white limestone, which has mellowed with time to give a golden colour. Several Sicilian architects worked together on this project. The most inventive was probably **Rosario Gagliardi**.

★★ **Corso Vittorio Emanuele.** – This rectilinear artery is the town's most popular street. The street widens in three places which are overlooked by the monumental façades of churches designed in an imposing but flexible baroque style. From east to west these are San Francesco all'Immacolata, the cathedral and San Domenico.

★ **Via Corrado Nicolaci.** – This gently-sloping street is lined with palaces sporting exuberantly fanciful balconies. The focal point of this perspective is provided by the church of Montevergine.

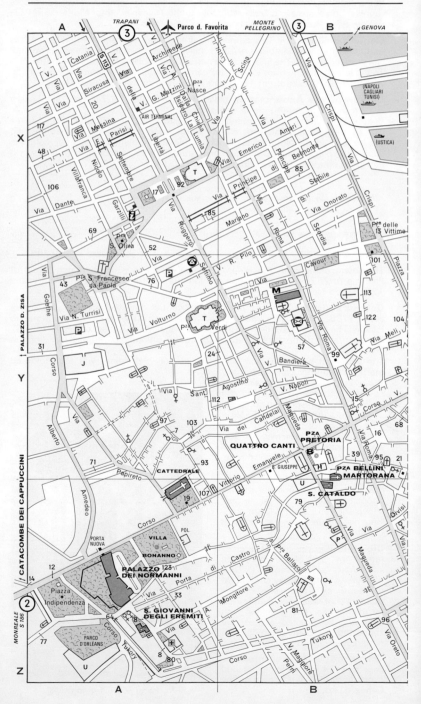

Michelin map 🔢 folds 35 and 36
Plan of built-up area in the current Michelin Red Guide Italia

Palermo, the capital and the chief seaport of Sicily, is built at the head of a wide bay enclosed on the north by Monte Pellegrino and on the south by Cape Zafferano. It lies on the edge of a wonderfully fertile plain bounded by hills and nicknamed the **Conca d'Oro** (Golden Conch Shell), on which lemon and orange groves flourish.

HISTORICAL NOTES

Palermo was founded by the Phoenicians, conquered by the Romans and then came under Byzantine rule.
From 831 to 1072 it was under the sway of the Saracens, who gave it the peculiar atmosphere suggested today by the luxuriance of its gardens, the shape of the domes on some buildings and the physical type and mentality of the people.
Conquered by the Normans in 1072, Palermo became the capital under **Roger II**, who took the title of King of Sicily.

PALERMO

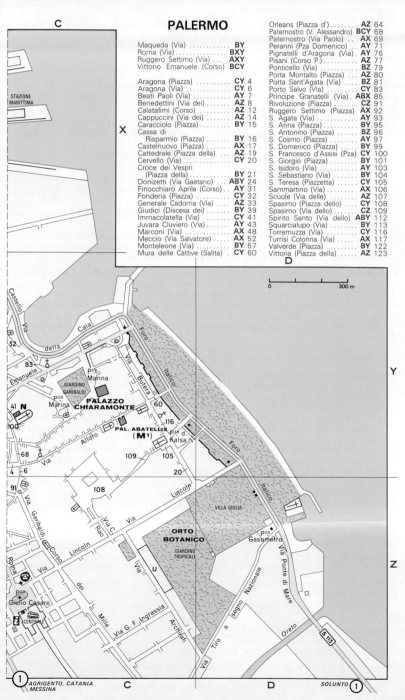

This great builder succeeded in blending Norman architectural styles with the decorative traditions of the Saracens and Byzantines: his reign was the golden age of art in Palermo. Later the Hohenstaufen and Angevin kings introduced the Gothic style (13C). After more than three centuries of Spanish rule, the Bourbons of Naples gave Palermo its sumptuous baroque finery.

The Sicilian Vespers. – Since 1266 the brother of St Louis, Charles I of Anjou, supported by the pope, had held the town. But his rule was unpopular. The Sicilians had nicknamed the French, who spoke Italian badly, the *tartaglioni* or stammerers. On the Monday after Easter 1282, as the bells were ringing for vespers, some Frenchmen insulted a young woman of Palermo in the Church of Santo Spirito. Insurrection broke out, and all Frenchmen who could not pronounce the world *cicero* (chick-pea) correctly were massacred. The governor, Jean de St-Rémy, was besieged in his palace in Via Alloro.

FROM QUATTRO CANTI
TO THE PALACE OF THE NORMANS *time: 3 hours*

Three pretty squares form the busy centre of Palermo. Their charm is enhanced by floodlighting in the evening.

★ **Quattro Canti** (BY). – Two main streets, Corso Vittorio Emanuele and the Via Maqueda, intersect to form this busy crossroads with four canted corners *(Quattro Canti)*. The crossroads forms a fine early-17C ensemble in the Spanish baroque style.
The Church of San Giuseppe has an astonishingly decorative interior.

★ **Piazza Pretoria** (BY). – The square has a spectacular **fountain**★★ (B) surmounted by numerous marble statues, the work of a 16C Florentine artist. The **town hall** (H) occupied one side of this square.

★★ **Piazza Bellini** (BY) ⊘. – This delightful square combines both Moorish and Norman features and has two buildings typical of Palermo: the Martorana and San Cataldo.

★★ **La Martorana** ⊘ (BYZ). – This church is also called Santa Maria dell' Ammiraglio (St Mary of the Admiral) because it was founded in 1143 by the Admiral of the Fleet to King Roger II. In the 16C and 17C it was altered by the addition of a baroque façade on the north side. Pass under the elegant 12C belfry-porch to enter the original church which is decorated with beautiful Byzantine **mosaics**★★: two panels depict Roger II crowned by Christ, and Admiral George of Antioch kneeling before the Virgin.

★★ **San Cataldo** ⊘ (BZ). – Founded in the 12C, this marvellous church recalls Moorish architecture with its severe rectangular plan, its domes, its decorative crenellations and the traceried openings of the façade.

★ **Cathedral (Cattedrale)** (AYZ). – Founded at the end of the 12C, the cathedral is built in the Sicilian-Norman style *(qv)* but has often been modified and added to (15C south porch and the 18C dome). The **apses**★ of the east end have retained their typically Sicilian-Norman decoration. In the interior, which was modified in the 18C, see on the right the tombs of the Emperor Frederick II and other members of the Hohenstaufen dynasty as well as other Angevin and Aragonese rulers.
The **treasury** ⊘ has the sumptuous **imperial crown**★ which belonged to Constance of Aragon.

★★ **Palace of the Normans** (Palazzo dei Normanni) ⊘ (AZ). – Of the immense royal palace built by the Normans on the site of an earlier Moorish fortress, only the central part and the massive Pisan Tower are of the Norman period. The **Palatine Chapel**★★★ on the first floor was built in the reign of Roger II between 1130 and 1140. It is a wonderful specimen of Arab-Norman decoration. Ten ancient columns support horseshoe-shaped arches which separate the nave and two aisles. The upper walls, the dome and the apses are covered with dazzling **mosaics**★★★ which along with those of Constantinople and Ravenna are the finest in Europe. This prestigious ensemble is completed by the carved stalactite ceiling, richly-decorated marble paving, pulpit and paschal candelabrum. On the second floor the 12C **King Roger's Room**★★ is adorned with mosaics of the chase.
The attractive gardens, **Villa Bonanno**★ (AZ), boast superb palm trees.

ADDITIONAL SIGHTS

★★ **Church of St John of the Hermits** (San Giovanni degli Eremiti) ⊘ (AZ). – The church, which Arab architects helped to construct, was built in 1132 at the request of King Roger II and is picturesquely crowned with pink domes. Beside it is a garden of tropical plants with pleasant 13C **cloisters** of small twin columns.

★★ **Capuchin Catacombs** (Catacombe dei Cappuccini) ⊘. – *Access by Via dei Cappuccini* (AZ 14). These catacombs are an impressive sight. About 8 000 mummies were placed here from the 17C to 19C and have been preserved by the very dry air.

★ **Zisa Palace** (Palazzo della Zisa) ⊘. – *Access by Corso Finocchiaro Aprile* (AY 31). This magnificent pleasure palace in the Arab-Norman style was built in the 12C. Austere on the outside, it has a very refined decoration inside.

★★ **Regional Gallery of Sicily** (Galleria Regionale della Sicilia) ⊘ (CY M¹). – This museum is housed in the attractive 15C **Palazzo Abbatellis**★ which is built in the Catalan-Gothic style. It includes a medieval art section and a picture gallery.

The works include a very fine **bust of Eleonora of Aragon** by Francesco Laurana (15C), a dramatic 15C fresco of **Death Triumphant★★★**, and the **Madonna of the Annunciation★★** by Antonello da Messina.

★ **Archaeological Museum (Museo Archeologico)** ⊙ **(BY M)**. – The museum, which is housed in a 16C convent, contains the finds from excavations of the numerous ancient sites in Sicily. On the ground floor are displayed Phoenician sarcophagi, an Egyptian inscription known as the Palermo Stone, and especially the remarkable **metopes★★** from temples at Selinus (6C and 5C BC). On the first floor are bronzes including the famous **ram★★**, a Hellenistic work which originated from Syracuse.

★ **St Lawrence Oratory (Oratorio di San Lorenzo) (CY N)**. – The interior is decorated with curious baroque plaster mouldings by Serpotta and has a Nativity by Caravaggio at the altar. The carved wood supports of the marble benches are remarkable.

★ **Chiaramonte Palace (Palazzo Chiaramonte)** ⊙ **(CY)**. – A fine Gothic palace (1307) which served as a model for many buildings in Sicily and southern Italy.
The Garibaldi Gardens opposite have two spectacular **magnolia-fig trees★★** (ficus).

★ **Botanical Garden (Orto Botanico)** ⊙ **(CDZ)**. – A quiet and secluded garden with a variety of exotic plants and trees.

Park of the Favourite (Parco della Favorita). – *3km – 2 miles to the north. Leave by ③ on the town plan.*
This park was laid out for the Bourbons in the 18C. Beside the Chinese pavilion (Palazzina Cinese) is the **Pitrè Ethnographic Museum** ⊙ which displays some fine **Sicilian carts★** *(p 248).*

EXCURSIONS

★★★ **Monreale**. – *8km – 5 miles to the southwest. Leave by ② on the town plan, the S 186. Description p 255.*

★★ **Monte Pellegrino**. – *14km – 9 miles to the north. Leave by ③ on the town plan, Via Crispi* **(BX)**.
The road out affords some splendid glimpses of Palermo and the Conca d'Oro. On the way up, the road passes the 17C sanctuary of Santa Rosalia.

★ **Ruins of Soluntum (Solunto)**. – *19km – 12 miles to the east. Leave by ① on the town plan, the S 113* **(DZ)**. *Description p 261.*

Bagheria. – *16km – 10 miles to the east by the A 19 motorway and then 4km – 2 miles southwest of Soluntum.*
Bagheria is known for its baroque villas and especially for the **Villa Palagonia** ⊙, which is decorated with **sculptures★** of grotesques and monsters.

Use the Principal Sights Map to plan an itinerary.

★★ # PANTELLERIA (ISLAND)   Pop 7 673

Michelin map ▓▓▓ fold 35

Situated in the Sicilian Channel, the Island of Pantelleria is only 84km – 52miles away from Cape Bon in Tunisia. It is the most westerly island of the Sicilian group and lies on the same latitude as Tunis. With an area of 83km² – 32sq miles it is also the largest island in the group. Nicknamed the "Black Pearl of the Mediterranean", the island is full of character with its indented coastline, steep slopes covered with terraces cultivated for crop growing, and its cubic Moorish-looking houses *(dammusi)*. The highest point of this volcanic island is **Montagna Grande** (836m – 2 743ft). The vineyards produce some pleasant wines such as the sparkling Solimano and the muscat Tanit. Capers are also grown on Pantelleria.
Pantelleria has remains of prehistoric settlements and later suffered the same invasions as Sicily by the Phoenicians, Carthaginians, Greeks, Romans, Vandals, Byzantines, Moors and Normans who in 1123 united the island with Sicily.
Access: – By air: see the current Michelin Red Guide Italia. **By sea:** see the Michelin map ▓▓▓ as well as the current Michelin Red Guide Italia.

TOUR *time: 3 hours*

★★ **Tour of the island by car**. – *40km – 25 miles.*
The very picturesque road following the coast gives the visitor a good chance to discover the beauty of the indented coastline, cliffs, inlets, caves, thermal springs and lakes. On the west coast, 11.5km – 7 miles to the south of the town of Pantelleria, the village of **Scauri** has a lovely site. On the south coast towards **Dietro Isola** the corniche road affords beautiful plunging **views★★** of this coastal area. The cape, **Punta dell'Arco**, is terminated by a splendid natural rock arch in grey volcanic stone known as the Elephant Arch. On the northeast coast the inlet **Cala dei Cinque Denti** and the rest of the coastline further north make a lovely volcanic landscape.

★★ **Montagna Grande**. – *13km – 8 miles to the southeast of Pantelleria.*
From the summit of this peak there is a splendid **panorama** of the island. In clear weather the view extends as far as Sicily and Tunisia.

★★ PIAZZA ARMERINA   Pop 22 288

Michelin map **988** fold 36

The grey houses of Piazza Armerina huddle round the baroque cathedral on the pleasantly green slopes of a valley.

★★ **Roman Villa of Casale** (Villa Romana del Casale) ⊘. – *6km – 4 miles to the southwest.*
This immense 3C or 4C BC villa (3 500m² – 37 670sq ft) in all probability belonged to some dignitary and is important for its **mosaic pavements** which cover almost the entire floor-space. These picturesque mosaics, in a wide range of colours, are at times rather primitive and often show a certain North African influence.
The most famous pavements are: those showing the **cupids** fishing or playing with dolphins, and the capturing and selling of **wild animals** for circus use (in the main corridor); those illustrating **sports** practised by young bikini-clad girls; and finally the mosaics of the **triclinium** portraying the **Labours of Hercules,** notably his struggle with the giants. Other scenes decorate the baths.

EXCURSION

Morgantina. – *16km – 10 miles to the northeast by the Enna road, the S 117 bis, then the S 228 to the right. Continue for 6km – 4 miles beyond Aidone.*
Nor far from the village of Aidone excavations have uncovered an ancient site in an attractive setting. It has been identified as the early Siculi settlement of Morgantina which was later colonised by the Greeks. The city declined slowly from the 1C onwards.
Amidst the extensive **ruins** ⊘, note on the valley floor the remains of an agora and a small, rebuilt theatre. The buildings on the hillside to the north house a number of **mosaics** which once adorned the 3C BC villas. The village of Aidone features a small **museum** ⊘ displaying the finds from the nearby excavations.

★ RAGUSA   Pop 68 110

Michelin map **988** fold 37

Ragusa, partly rebuilt following the 1693 earthquake, lies in a typical **setting**★ on a plateau between deep ravines. The modern town lies to the west while the old town, Ragusa Ibla, clusters on an outlier of the hills, Monti Iblei to the east. The Syracuse road offers magnificent **views**★★ of the old town.
Asphalt and oil are produced or refined locally in large industrial complexes.

★ **Ragusa Ibla.** – The medieval area is a maze of streets, but much of the old town was rebuilt in the baroque style. The lovely 18C **Church of San Giorgio**★ on Piazza del Duomo was designed by the architect Rosario Gagliardi who also worked in Noto. The pink stone façade has a slightly convex central section which is flanked by projecting columns.

Ibleo Archaeological Museum ⊘. – *Palazzo Mediterraneo, Via Natalelli.*
In the modern town, below the viaduct, Ponte Nuovo, which spans the Via Roma, this museum contains the finds from excavations undertaken locally, notably from the ancient Greek city of Camarina.

★★★ SEGESTA

Michelin map **988** fold 35 – 35km – 22 miles southeast of Trapani

The ruins are all that remain of Segesta, the great rival of Selinus in the 5C BC; it was in all probability destroyed by the Saracens in about AD 1000.

★★★ **Temple** (Tempio) ⊘. – The temple of Segesta stands alone, on an eminence encircled by a deep ravine, in a landscape of receding horizons. The temple is a Doric building (430 BC), pure and graceful, with a peristyle of 36 columns in a golden-coloured limestone. The road leading up to the theatre *(2km – 1 mile)* affords a magnificent **view**★★ of the temple.

★ **Theatre** (Teatro). – This Hellenistic theatre with a diameter of 63m – 207ft is built into the rocky hillside. The tiers of seats are slightly orientated towards the Gulf of Castellammare, which is visible beyond the hilltops.

★★ SELINUS (SELINUNTE)

Michelin map 988 fold 35

Selinus was founded in the mid 7C by people from the east coast city of Megara Hyblaea and was destroyed twice, in 409 and 250 BC, by the Carthaginians. The huge ruins of its temples with their enormous platforms, wrecked by earthquakes, will impress the visitor. The admirable metopes which adorned these temples are in the National Museum at Palermo.

Archaeological site ⊙. – Visitors first reach an esplanade around which are grouped the remains of three **temples** of uncertain attribution. To the right of the road **temple G**, probably dedicated to Apollo, was one of the largest in the ancient world. Over 100m – 328ft long, its columns were built of blocks each weighing several tonnes. The rubble of the fallen stonework gives some indication of its great size. To the left of the road, behind the ruined temple F, stands the **temple E** (5C BC) which was rebuilt in 1958.

Cross the depression, Gorgo Cottone, to reach the **acropolis** with its perimeter wall. The site is dominated by the rebuilt (1926) columns of temple E (6C BC), the oldest. There are four more ruined temples in the immediate vicinity. Westwards, on the opposite bank of the Modione stand the remains of a sanctuary to Demeter Malophoros (the dispenser of fruits).

★ SOLUNTUM (SOLUNTO)

Michelin map 988 fold 36 – 20km – 12 miles to the east of Palermo

Soluntum stands in an admirable **site★★** on a rocky ledge on the promontory which overlooks Cape Zafferano. It was a Phoenician city before it fell under the sway of Rome in the 3C BC.

The **archaeological site** ⊙ *(access by a narrow road which branches off from the S 113 in Porticello, in the direction of a hill)* includes ruins of a forum, theatre, streets, houses, drainage system and numerous cisterns. Take the Via Ippodamo da Mileto to reach the summit. There is a splendid **view★★** of the bay of Palermo and Monte Pellegrino.

*The current **Michelin Red Guide Italia** offers
a selection of pleasant hotels in convenient locations.*

*Each entry specifies the facilities available
(gardens, tennis courts, swimming pool, beach facilities)
and the annual opening and closing dates.*

*There is also a selection of establishments recommended for their
cuisine – well-prepared meals at moderate prices; stars for good cooking.*

★★★ SYRACUSE (SIRACUSA)   Pop 123 706

Michelin map 988 fold 37

Syracuse, superbly situated at the head of a beautiful bay, enjoys a very mild climate. It was one of Sicily's, if not Magna Graecia's, most prestigious cities and at the height of its splendour rivalled Athens. Syracuse was colonised in the mid 8C BC by Greeks from Corinth who peopled the Island of Ortygia. It soon fell under the yoke of the tyrants, when it developed and prospered. In the 5C-4C BC the town had 30 000 inhabitants.

Captured by the Romans during the Second Punic War (212 BC), it was occupied successively by the Barbarians, Byzantines (6C), Arabs (9C) and Normans. The river Ciane *(p 263)* with its papyrus beds was a centre of papyrus production. Since the 18C Syracuse has specialised in painting on papyrus, in the Egyptian manner.

Tyrants and intellectuals. – In the Greek world, dictators called tyrants (from the Greek word *turannos*) exercised unlimited power over certain cities, especially Syracuse. Already in 485 BC **Gelon**, the tyrant of Gela, had become master of Syracuse. His brother **Hiero**, an altogether more unpleasant person, nonetheless patronised poets and welcomed to his court both **Pindar** and **Æschylus**, who died in Gela in 456.

Denis the Elder (405-367 BC) was the most famous but even he lived in constant fear. This was symbolised by the sword which he had suspended by a horsehair above the head of Damocles, a jealous courtier. He rarely left the safety of his castle on Ortygia. He wore a shirt of mail under his clothing and changed his room every night. He had Plato sold as a slave when the philosopher came to study the political habits of the people under his dictatorship.

Archimedes, the famous geometrician born at Syracuse in 287 BC, was so absent-minded that he would forget to eat and drink. It was in his bath that he discovered his principle: any body immersed in water loses weight equivalent to that of the water it displaces. Delighted, he jumped out of the bath and ran naked through the streets shouting "Eureka" (I have found it !).

When defending Syracuse against the Romans, Archimedes set fire to the enemy fleet by focusing the sun's rays with a system of mirrors and lenses. But when the Romans succeeded in entering the town by surprise, Archimedes, deep in his calculations, did not hear them, and a Roman soldier ran him through with his sword.

★★★ ARCHAEOLOGICAL AREA (ZONA ARCHEOLOGICA) ⊘ (AY)

Visit on foot: 2 hours. Access by Via Paradiso (AY 18)

This area extends over the ancient quarter of Neapolis (the new town) high above and overlooks the Ionian Sea.
From the **Viale Rizzo** (AY) which skirts the area, there is an excellent panorama of the ruins.

Altar of Hiero II (Ara di Ierone II) (AY K). – To the left of the Via Paradiso this 200m – 656ft long altar, partly hewn out of the rock, was used for public sacrifices.

★★★ **Greek Theatre (Teatro Greco)** (AY). – The theatre dates from the 5C BC and is one of the largest of the ancient world. The tiers of seats are hewn out of the rock. The first performance of *The Persians* of Æschylus was given in it.
A little further on stretches the **road to the tombs** (AY N), which is hewn out of the rock.

★★★ **Paradise Quarry (Latomia del Paradiso)** (AY L). – This former quarry dates from ancient times. Part of its roof fell in during the 1693 earthquake. An orange grove has been laid out on the excavated material.
The **Ear of Denis★★★** (B) is an artificial grotto in the form of an earlobe. The grotto was so named in 1608 by the painter Caravaggio as a reminder of the legend recounting how the exceptional echo enabled the tyrant Denis to overhear the talk of the prisoners he confined in a room below.
The **Cordmakers' Cave★★** (G) takes its name from the cordmakers who used to work there, as the humidity in the air and the fresh atmosphere enabled them to spin and plait their hemp.

★ **Roman Amphitheatre (Anfiteatro Romano)** (AY C). – This 3C or 4C BC amphitheatre measures 140m by 119m (459ft by 390ft) and is hewn out of the rock. There are pines and oleanders.

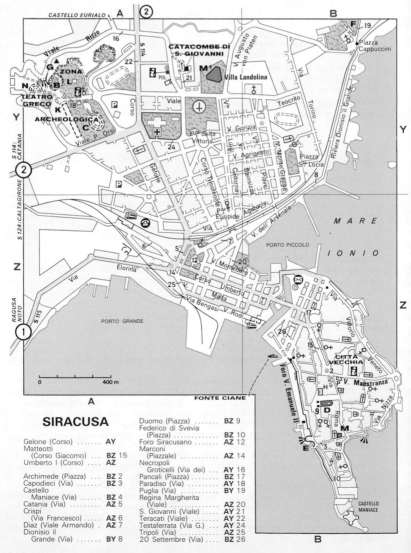

★★ OLD TOWN (CITTÀ VECCHIA) (BZ) *time: 3/4 hour*

It is situated on the Island of Ortygia and the streets are rich in medieval and Baroque palaces. **Via della Maestranza (BZ)** is particularly rich in the latter. These narrow streets are shaded in summer and are ideal for a stroll.

The **Piazza Duomo (BZ 9)** is particularly attractive, lined by palaces adorned with wrought-iron balconies and the monumental façade of the **cathedral★** (Duomo) (BZ D). This was built in the 7C on the foundations of a Doric temple dedicated to Athena. Some of the columns of the latter have been reused in the Christian building (north side and interior).

Inside, there are several sculptures (including the Madonna of the Snow) which are attributed to the Gagini, a family of artists who settled in Sicily in the 16C.

★ **Arethusa Fountain (Fonte Aretusa) (BZ E)**. – This is the legendary cradle of the city. The nymph Arethusa, pursued by the river-god Alpheus, took refuge on the Island of Ortygia where she was changed into a spring by Artemis. Though near the sea, the fountain, built into a wall, runs with fresh water.

From the nearby platform there is a view of the beautiful Bay of Syracuse.

The **Foro Vittorio Emanuele II (BZ)**, a favourite walk for the Syracusans, starts below.

★★ P. ORSI REGIONAL ARCHAEOLOGICAL MUSEUM
(MUSEO ARCHEOLOGICO REGIONALE) ⊘ (AY M¹) *time: 1 hour*

Set in the charming grounds of the **Villa Landolina**, an attractive modern building designed by Franco Minissi houses the museum built in memory of the archaeologist Paolo Orsi (1859-1935).

It presents the history of Sicily from prehistoric times up to the Greek colonies of Syracuse (7C BC).

The first section explains the local geology – skeletons of the two dwarf elephants – and prehistory, starting from the Upper Palaeolithic, when man made his first appearance in Sicily.

The second part of the visit is devoted to the Greek colonisation (from mid 8C BC onwards), of which many artefacts were salvaged in the excavations carried out at Megara Hyblaea and, in particular, at Syracuse: marble kouros, chalk statue of a goddess-mother, ceramics, architectural fragments and small-scale replicas of the great sanctuaries of Ortygia, the oldest district in Syracuse...

The third part of the museum is concerned with the various Syracuse colonies. The town became very powerful and in 664 BC it founded Akrai (Palazzolo Acreide). Then followed Kasmenai (Monte Casale) in 644 BC and Camarina (598 BC); chalk statues, horsemen used in the ornamentation of temples etc. This part of the building also shows artefacts taken from the Greek colonies inland (large statue of Demeter or Koré enthroned) and the excavation sites at Gela and Agrigento, which we owe to the efforts of Paolo Orsi.

The exhibits concerning later history are on display upstairs.

ADDITIONAL SIGHTS

★★ **Catacombs of St John (Catacombe di San Giovanni)** ⊘ (AY). – After those in Rome these are the best Italian examples of catacombs. They consist of a main gallery off which branch secondary galleries ending in circular chapels or rotundas; several of the tombs are in the form of arched niches.

★★ **Capuchins' Quarry (Latomia dei Cappucini)** ⊘ (BY F). – In 413 BC 7 000 Athenian prisoners were interned in these quarries by Denis of Syracuse. The quarries are now overgrown by luxuriant vegetation.

★ **Regional Museum: Palazzo Bellomo** ⊘ (BZ M). – The museum is installed in the beautiful 13C palace which was remodelled in the Catalan style in the 15C. The art gallery has an admirable (despite some damage) **Annunciation** by Antonello da Messina. There is also some goldsmith's work, a few charming Sicilian cribs, liturgical objects and furniture.

EXCURSIONS

★ **Ciane Spring (Fonte Ciane)** ⊘. – *8km – 5 miles to the southwest. It is best to visit by boat.*

The **Ciane River★★** is lined with papyrus beds, which are unique in Italy. It was here that the nymph Ciane was changed into a spring when she opposed the abduction of Proserpine by Pluto.

Castle of Euryalus (Castello Eurialo) ⊘. – *9km – 6 miles to the northwest of the plan.*

This, one of the greatest fortresses of the Greek period, was built by Denis the Elder. Fine panorama.

---

*Each year the **Michelin Red Guide Italia**
revises its 500 town plans which show*

– through-routes and by-passes
– new roads, one-way systems and car parks
– the exact location of hotels, restaurants and public buildings.

This up-to-date information makes town driving less stressful.

Michelin map 988 fold 37
Town plan in the current Michelin Red Guide Italia

Taormina stands in a wonderful **site** at an altitude of 250m – 820ft and forms a balcony overlooking the sea and facing Etna. It is renowned for its peaceful atmosphere and its beautiful monuments and gardens.

★★ **Greek Theatre (Teatro Greco)** ⊙. – The theatre dates from the 3C BC but was remodelled by the Romans who used it as an arena for their contests.

Performances of Classical plays are given in summer. From the upper tiers there is an admirable **view★★★** between the stage columns of the coastline and Etna.

★★ **Public Gardens (Giardino Pubblico)**. – From this terraced garden of flowers and exotic plants there are views of the coast and the Sicilian Sea.

★ **Corso Umberto.** – This, the main street of Taormina, has three gateways along its course: Porta Catania; the middle one, Porta di Mezzo, with the Torre dell' Orologio (Clock Tower); and Porta Messina.
The Piazza del Duomo is overlooked by the Gothic façade of the cathedral and adorned by an attractive baro-

Taormina – The theatre and Mount Etna

que fountain. Almost halfway along, the **Piazza 9 Aprile** forms a terrace which affords a splendid **panorama★★** of the gulf. The Piazza Vittorio Emanuele was laid out on the site of the forum and is overlooked by the 15C Corvaia Palace.

★ **Belvedere.** – View of the Aspromonte Massif in Calabria, the Sicilian coast and Etna.

★ **Castle (Castello)** ⊙. – *4km – 2 miles by the Castelmola road, and then a road to the right. It is also possible to walk up (1 hour Rtn).*
The castle was built in the medieval period on the summit of Monte Tauro (390m – 1 280ft), on the remains of the former acropolis. There are splendid **views★** of Taormina.

★ **TINDARI**

Michelin map 988 fold 37 – 62km – 39 miles to the west of Messina

The ancient Greek Tyndaris, founded in 396 BC, is perched on the summit of the cape of the same name. At the very point stands a **sanctuary** with a Black Virgin which is a place of pilgrimage. The **ruins** ⊙ are essentially those of the city **ramparts**, the theatre on a site facing the sea, and a fine arcaded Roman building (access by the main street, Decumanus) which preceded the forum.

TRAPANI Pop 73 031

Michelin map 988 fold 35
Town plan in the current Michelin Red Guide Italia

Trapani has a sheltered port within sight of the Egadi Islands. A pretty coastal road links the town centre with the beach at San Giuliano *(3km – 2 miles to the north)*.

Sanctuary of the Annunciation (Annunziata). – Built in the 14C, the church was remodelled and enlarged in the 17C. The campanile is baroque. On the north side the attractive 16C Renaissance **Sailors' Chapel** is crowned with a dome.
Inside, the **Chapel of the Madonna★** contains a Renaissance arch carved in the 16C, a bronze grille dated 1591 and a graceful statue of the Virgin (14C) attributed to Nino Pisano.

★ **Pepoli Museum (Museo Pepoli)** ⊙. – The museum is located in the former Carmelite convent which adjoins the Annunziata. The works include sculpture (by the Gagini) and paintings (the 15C Trapani polyptych, a *Pietà* by Roberto di Oderisio, *St Bartholomew* by Ribera and *St Francis receiving the Stigmata* by Titian). There is also a display of local crafts: coral work and a very delicate crib.

Rome – Fountain in Piazza Navona

Practical Information

TRAVELLING TO AND IN ITALY

Passport. – Visitors entering Italy must be in possession of a valid national **passport** (or in the case of the British, a Visitor's Passport). In case of loss or theft report to the embassy or consulate and the local police.

Visa. – Visitors who require an **entry visa** should apply in advance to the Italian Embassy.

US citizens should obtain the booklet "Your Trip Abroad" ($1), which provides useful information on visa requirements, customs regulations, medical care etc for international travellers. Apply to the Superintendent of Documents, Government Printing Office, Washington, DC 20402-9325.

Customs. – The Customs Office (UK) produces a leaflet on customs regulations and the full range of "duty free" allowances; available from HM Customs and Excise. For US citizens "Know before you go" is available from the US Treasury Department (☎ 202 566 8195).

There are no customs formalities for holidaymakers bringing their caravans into Italy for a stay of less than 6 months. No customs document is necessary for pleasure boats and outboard motors for a stay of less than 6 months but the registration certificate should be kept on board.

By air. – Many international and other independent airlines operate services to Rome and to the major provincial airports (Milan, Turin, Venice etc). There are also package tour flights as well as Fly-Drive schemes. Information, brochures and timetables are available from the airlines and from travel agents.

The domestic network operates frequent services covering the whole country. There are transfer buses to town terminals and to railway stations.

It is advisable to book well in advance for the holiday season.

By sea. – Details of passenger ferry and car ferry services from the United Kingdom and Ireland to the Channel ports and linking up with the European rail and motorway network can be obtained from travel agencies and from the main operators: P&O European Ferries, Sealink, Hoverspeed, Brittany Ferries, Sally Line. For the different shipping routes (passenger and car ferries) between the peninsula and the various islands consult the **Michelin map 988** and the **Michelin Red Guide Italia.**

By rail. – From London and the Channel ports there are services to many Italian towns including many high-speed passenger trains and motorail services. For tourists residing outside Italy there are rail passes offering unlimited travel and group travel tickets offering savings for parties on the Italian Railways network. Eurail Pass, Flexipass and Saver Pass are options available in the US for travel in Europe and must be purchased in the US – ☎ 212 308 3103 (information) and 1 800 223 6 36 (reservations).

Information and bookings from Italian Railways, CIT., Marco Polo House, 3-5 Lansdowne Road, Croydon, Surrey, ☎ 081 686 067, Fax 081 686 0328; Wasteels Travel, 121 Wilton Road, London SW1, ☎ 071 834 7066, Fax 071 828 6870; and from principal British and American Rail Travel Centres and travel agencies. Average tariff for porters: 1 000 lire per case.

By coach. – Regular coach services are operated from London to Rome and to large provincial towns. Details and bookings from: National Express, Victoria Coach Station, London SW1, ☎ 071 730 0202, and all National Express Offices and Agencies throughout the UK; and EuroLines, 52 Grosvenor Gardens, London SW1W OAU. ☎ 071 730 8235.

MOTORING IN ITALY

Documents. – Nationals of EC countries require a valid national **driving licence** with an Italian translation (except for the UK pink licence); nationals of non-EC countries require an **international driving** licence (obtainable in the US from the American Automobile Club).

For the vehicle it is necessary to have the **registration papers** (log-book) and a **nationality plate** of the approved size.

Insurance. – Insurance cover is compulsory and, although no longer a legal requirement, an International Insurance Certificate (Green Card) is the most effective proof of insurance cover and is internationally recognised by the police and other authorities.

Certain UK motoring organisations (AA, RAC) run accident insurance and breakdown service schemes for members. Europ-Assistance (252 High St, Croydon CRO 1NF) has special policies for motorists. Members of the American Automobile Club should obtain the brochure "Offices to serve you abroad".

Italian Automobile Club. – The head office of the Automobile Club d'Italia is at Via Marsala 8, 00185 Roma, ☎ 06 4998. A car breakdown service (a tax is levied) is operated by the ACI for foreign motorists carrying the fuel card *(see below)*. The ACI also offers a telephone information service in English for road and weather conditions as well as for tourist events: ☎ 06 4212. In case of breakdown dial 116 for assistance.

Fuel. – Motorists driving a foreign-registered car may on certain conditions purchase coupons at special rates under the Tourist Petrol Concession Scheme. These coupons are paid for in foreign currency and are issued (on presentation of car registration document and passport) in the country of origin. The scheme also includes a fuel card *(carta carburante)*, which gives entitlement to the ACI breakdown service *(see above)*, and free motorway vouchers towards payment of tolls.

The vouchers are available from the motoring organisations, from ACI offices at the Italian borders and also from Wasteels Travel *(address above)*, the appointed agents for the scheme in the UK.

Tourists flying to Italy and hiring a car at the airport may purchase coupons only from the following airports: Rome Fiumicino and Milan Linate.

Petrol stations usually close between 12.30 and 3pm.

Highway Code. – The minimum driving age is 18. Traffic drives on the right. It is compulsory for the driver and front-seat passengers to wear **seat belts**, and back-seat belts must be worn where they are fitted. Children under 12 must travel on the rear seats unless the front seat is fitted with a child-restraint system. Full or dipped headlights must be switched on in poor visibility and at night; use sidelights only when a stationary vehicle is not clearly visible.

In the event of **breakdown** a red warning triangle is obligatory. These can be hired from the ACI offices at the frontier (refundable deposit).

Drivers should watch out for unfamiliar road signs and take great care on the road. At crossroads vehicles coming from the right have priority.

Severe penalties are applicable for **drink-driving** offences.

Speed limits. – 50km/h – 31mph in built-up areas
– 90km/h – 56mph on country roads
– 110km/h – 68mph for vehicles up to 1100cc, and 130km/h – 80mph (over 1100cc) on motorways

Parking. – There are many car parks with attendants particularly in the Naples area. It is advisable to check the rates before parking and, particularly in the south to use these car parks rather than leave vehicles unattended.

Route Planning. – **Michelin map** 988 at a scale of 1:1 000 000 covers the whole country. Other **Michelin maps** give partial coverage: 195 at 1:100 000, 208 and 219 at 1:200 000, and 426 at 1:400 000 for Northern Italy. There are also at 1:400 000: **Michelin maps** 428 Northwest, 429 Northeast, 430 Centre, and 431 South.

The **Touring Club Italiano (TCI)**, 10 Corso d'Italia, 20 122 Milan, ☏ (02) 852 672 publishes a regional map series at 1:200 000.

The road network is excellent with many motorways *(autostrade)* – most of these are toll-roads. The toll is calculated according to the distance between the axles and the engine capacity. See above for details of motorway vouchers, the petrol concession scheme and the ACI breakdown service.

Car Rental. – There are car rental agencies at airports, railway stations and in all large towns and resorts throughout Italy. European cars usually have manual transmission but automatic cars are available on demand. An **international driving licence** is required for non-EC nationals.

Fly-drive schemes are operated by major airlines *(see p 266)*.

ACCOMMODATION

Places to stay. – The maps on pp 8 to 11 indicate the recommended places for overnight stops.

The **Michelin Red Guide Italia** provides a selection of hotels, guest-houses and restaurants.

The Provincial Tourist Boards and the Local Tourist Offices of the various cities and resorts publish hotel lists and resort leaflets available by writing direct to these offices (addresses from the Italian State Tourist Office and in the **Michelin Red Guide Italia**).

Agriturist, Corso V. Emanuele 101, Roma, ☏ 06 651 2342 or the Provincial Offices for the various areas (addresses from the Italian State Tourist Office) will supply information on rural accommodation.

The Touring Club Italiano *(see above)* publishes a guide to Tourist Villages which are located in or near popular resorts.

Youth Hostels. – There are 52 youth hostels throughout Italy. Holders of an International Youth Hostel Federation card should apply for a list from the International Federation or from the Italian Youth Hostels Association, 44 Via Cavour, 00184 Roma, ☏ 06 462 342.

Members of American Youth Hostels should call 202 783 6161 for information on budget accommodation.

Students' hostels (Casa dello Studento) also offer holiday accommodation for young people in many towns.

Camping. – Italy has over 16 000 officially-graded sites with varying standards of facilities. An International Camping Carnet for caravans is useful but not compulsory; it may be obtained from the motoring organisations or the Camping and Caravanning Club (11 Lower Grosvenor Place, London SW1).

The Italian Camping Federation (Federcampeggio, Casella Postale 23, 50041 Calenzano (Firenze), ☏ 055 88 2391) publishes a map of camping sites and a list of camping grounds offering special rates to holders of the international camping card. It also publishes an annual guide "Campeggi and Villagi Turistici in Italia" in collaboration with the Touring Club Italiano (TCI). The Local Tourist Board also supplies information on camping sites.

Electricity. – The electric current is 220 volts AC (50 cycles). Circular 2-pin plugs are standard.

*The **Michelin Green Guide Great Britain**
presents a selection of the most interesting
and distinctive sights on the main tourist routes.*

GENERAL INFORMATION

Time. – In winter standard time is Greenwich Mean Time + 1 hour. In summer clocks are advanced by one hour to give Italian Summer Time (GMT + 2 hours from last weekend of March to last weekend of September).

Medical treatment. – Visitors from EC countries should apply to their own National Social Security Offices for Form E111 which entitles them to medical treatment under an EC Reciprocal Medical Treatment arrangement.
Nationals of non-EC countries should take out comprehensive insurance. American Express offers a service, "Global Assist", for any medical, legal or personal emergency – call collect from anywhere ☎ 202 554 2639.
A list of chemists open at night and on Sundays may be obtained from chemists' shops *(farmacia* – red cross sign). First aid service *(Pronto Soccorso)* is available at airports, railway stations and in hospitals.

Currency. – The currency is the lira. There are no restrictions on the amount of currency visitors can take into Italy. To facilitate the export of currency in foreign bank notes in excess of the given allocation, visitors are advised to complete a currency declaration form (Form V2) on arrival.

Banks. – Banks are open Monday to Friday (except public holidays) from 8.30am to 1.30pm and generally from 3 to 4pm. Check locally as the afternoon opening time may vary.
Exchange facilities are available at main railway stations and airports. Some form of identification is necessary when cashing cheques in banks. Commission charges vary; hotels usually charge more than banks.
Most banks have cash dispensers which accept international credit cards.

Credit Cards. – American Express, Visa (Barclaycard), Diners Club and Eurocard (Mastercard/Access) are widely accepted in shops, hotels and restaurants but not at petrol stations.

Post. – Post Offices open Monday to Friday 8.30am to 2pm, Saturday and last day of the month 8.30am to 12 noon.
Stamps are also available from tobacconists.
Poste restante mail should be addressed as follows: Name, c/o Post Office, Fermo Posta, name of locality.

Telephone. – Public phones use 100 and 200 lire coins, tokens *(gettone, 200 lire)* and phone cards which are available from post offices, tobacconists and newsagents.
The country code for Italy is 39. To make an international call from Italy dial 00 + the country code + area code + correspondent's number.

Shopping. – Shops are generally open from 8.30 – 9am to 1pm and from 3.30 – 4 to 7.30 – 8pm, except in Northern Italy where the shops have a shorter mid-day break and close earlier.
Open-air markets are usually held once or twice weekly in tourist resorts.

Public holidays. – The following are days when museums and other monuments may be closed or may vary their hours of admission:

1 January
6 January (Epiphany)
Easter Monday
25 April (Liberation Day)
1 May
15 August (Ferragosto)
1 November (All Saints)
8 December
25 December
26 December

The Local Tourist Board will give information on local feast days.

Embassies

Australia Via Alessandria 215, 00198 Rome. ☎ 06 832 721
Canada Via G.B. Rossi 27, 00161 Rome. ☎ 06 841 5341
Ireland Largo Nazareno 3, Rome. ☎ 06 678 2541
UK Via XX Settembre 80a, Rome. ☎ 06 475 5441
USA Via Veneto 119a, 00187 Rome. ☎ 06 46741

TOURIST INFORMATION

Italian State Tourist Office (ENIT). – For information, brochures, maps and assistance in planning a trip to Italy, apply to the state tourist office *(addresses p 269)*.

Tourist Information Centres. – In each regional capital there is a Regional Tourist Board **(Assessorato Regionale per il Turismo)**, which promotes tourism in the different areas.
The **Michelin Red Guide Italia** gives the addresses and telephone numbers of the Tourist Information Centres (Provincial Tourist Board – **Ente Provinciale Turismo** or **Azienda Promozione Turistica** and Local Tourist Board – **Azienda Autonoma di Soggiorno, Cura e Turismo – AST)** to be found in most large towns and tourist resorts. They can supply large-scale town plans, timetables and information on local entertainment facilities, sports and sightseeing.

Tourism for the Disabled. – The **Michelin Red Guide Italia** indicates hotels and restaurants with facilities suitable for physically-handicapped people.

ITALIAN STATE TOURIST OFFICE

Canada 1 Place Marie, Montreal, Quebec. ☎ 866 76667/8/9, Fax 392 1429
Ireland 47 Merrion Square, Dublin 2. ☎ 01 766397
United Kingdom 1 Princes Street, London W1R 8AY. ☎ 071 408 1254, Fax 071 493 6695
United States
Middle West: Chicago – 500 North Michigan Avenue, Suite 1046, Chicago, 1, Ill. 60611. ☎ 312 644 0990, Fax 312 311 3290
East Coast: New York – 630 Fifth Avenue, Suite 1565, N.Y. 10111. ☎ 212 245 4822, Fax 212 586 9249
West Coast: San Francisco – 360 Post Street, Suite 801, Cal. 94108. ☎ 415 392 6206, Fax 415 392 6852

BOOKS TO READ

We list below only a selection of the many books about Italy. Some, which may be out of print, will be available only from libraries.

History and Art

The Grandeur that was Rome by J.C. Stobart *(Sidgwick and Jackson)*
The Italian World by J.J. Norwich *(Thames and Hudson)*
Roman Italy by T.W. Potter *(British Museum Publications Ltd)*
Leonardo da Vinci by Martin Kemp, Jane Roberts and Philip Steadman *(Yale University)*
Michelangelo by Howard Hibbard *(Penguin)*
Venetian Painting: A Concise History by John Steer *(Thames and Hudson)*
Architecture of the Italian Renaissance by Peter Murray *(Thames and Hudson)*
Siena: A City and its History by Judith Hook *(Hamish Hamilton)*
Rise and Fall of the House of Medici by Christopher Hibbert *(Penguin)*
Villas of Tuscany by H. Acton *(Thames and Hudson)*
The Art of the Renaissance by Linda and Peter Murray *(Thames and Hudson)*
A History of Italian Renaissance Art by F. Hartt *(Thames and Hudson)*
A Concise Encyclopaedia of the Italian Renaissance by J.R. Hale *(Thames and Hudson)*

Travel

Blue Guides: Northern Italy by A. Macadam; **Southern Italy** by Paul Blanchard; **Sicily** by A. Macadam; **Florence** by A. Macadam; **Rome and Environs** by A. Macadam; **Venice** by A. Macadam.
Baedeker/AA: Italy (Country Guide); **Tuscany** (Regional Guide), **Florence, Rome** and **Venice** (City Guides)
Mediterranean Island Hopping by Dana Facaros and Michael Pauls *(Gentry Books Ltd)*
D.H. Lawrence and Italy *(Penguin)*
The Path to Rome by Hilaire Belloc *(Penguin)*
Stones of Florence and Venice by Mary McCarthy *(Penguin)*
Venice by John Kent *(Viking)*
Venetian Evenings by James Lees-Milne *(Collins)*
Living in Italy by Y.M. Menzies *(Hale)*
Guide to Tuscany by Bently *(Penguin)*
A Visit to Germany, Italy and Malta by Hans Anderson *(Peter Owen Publishers)*

Food and Wine

Life beyond Lambrusco (Understanding Italian Fine Wine) by N. Belfrage *(Sidgwick and Jackson)*
Traditional Italian Food by L.B. Birch *(Fontana)*

Literature and Modern Fiction

Italian Short Stories by R. Trevelyan *(Penguin, parallel text)*
The Leopard by Giuseppe Tomasi di Lampedusa *(Flamingo)*
Sicilian Carousel by Lawrence Durrell *(Faber)*
The Slow Train to Milan by Lisa St Aubin de Teran *(Penguin)*
Room with a View by E.M. Forster *(Penguin)*

Help us in our constant task of keeping up to date.
Send your comments and suggestions to
Michelin Tyre PLC
Tourism Department
Davy House
Lyon Road
HARROW Middlesex HA1 2DQ

VOCABULARY

ON THE ROAD AND IN TOWN

a destra	to the right	lavori in corso	men at work
a sinistra	to the left	neve	snow
aperto	open	passaggio a livello	level crossing
autostrada	motorway	passo	pass
banchina	pavement	pericolo	danger
binario	(railway) platform	piazza, largo	square, place
corso	boulevard	piazzale	esplanade
discesa	descent	stazione	station
dogana	customs	stretto	narrow
fermata	(bus-) stop	uscita	exit, way out
fiume	river	viale	avenue
ingresso	entrance	vietato	prohibited

PLACES AND THINGS TO SEE

abbazia, convento	abbey, monastery	mercato	market
affreschi	frescoes	mura	walls
arazzi	tapestries	navata	nave
arca	monumental tomb	opere	works
biblioteca	library	pala	panel, altarpiece
cappella	chapel	palazzo	palace
casa	house	paliotto	altar frontal
cascata	waterfall	passeggiata	walks, promenade
castello	castle	piano	floor, storey
Cena	The Last Supper	pinacoteca	picture gallery
chiesa	church	pulpito	pulpit
chiostro	cloisters	quadro	picture
chiuso	closed	rivolgersi a	to apply to
città	town	rocca	feudal castle
cortile	courtyard	rovine, ruderi	ruins
dintorni	environs	sagrestia	sacristy
duomo	cathedral	scala	stairway
facciata	façade	scavi	excavations
funivia	cable-car	seggiovia	chair-lift
giardini	gardens	spiaggia	beach
gole	gorges	tesoro	treasure
lago	lake	torre, torazzo	tower
lungomare	seafront promenade	vista	view

COMMON WORDS

yes, no	si, no	goodbye	arrivederci
Sir	Signore	how much?	quanto?
Madam	Signora	where? when?	dove? quando?
Miss	Signorina	where is?	dov'è?
today	oggi	much, little	molto, poco
yesterday	ieri	more, less	più, meno
tomorrow morning	domani mattina	all	tutto, tutti
morning	mattina	large	grande
evening	sera	small	piccolo
afternoon	pomeriggio	dear	caro
please	per favore	the road to...?	la strada per...?
thank you so much	grazie tante	may one visit?	si può visitare?
excuse me	mi scusi	what time is it?	che ora è?
enough	basta	I don't understand	non capisco
good morning	buon giorno	I would like	desidero

NUMBERS

0	zero	8	otto	16	sedici	60	sessanta
1	uno	9	nove	17	diciasette	70	settanta
2	due	10	dieci	18	diciotto	80	ottanta
3	tre	11	undici	19	diciannove	90	novanta
4	quattro	12	dodici	20	venti	100	cento
5	cinque	13	tredici	30	trenta	1 000	mille
6	sei	14	quattordici	40	quaranta	5 000	cinquemila
7	sette	15	quindici	50	cinquanta	10 000	diccimila

ART AND ARCHITECTURAL TERMS

Ambo: the pulpit of a primitive Christian basilica.

Ambulatory: an aisle curving round the chancel.

Apparatus: the arrangements of stones or bricks in a structure.

Apse: the end of a church behind the choir.

Apsidal Chapel: a chapel springing from the apse.

Archivolt: highest arch above a doorway.

Atrium: forecourt of a Roman house or Byzantine church.

Ciborium: a canopy over an altar.

Corbelling: a projection on a façade (balcony).

Foliage: ornamental foliated scroll or stem.

Gable: a decorative, acute-angled structure over a window or doorway.

Intarsia or **tarsia:** inlaid wood, marble or metal.

Lintel: the horizontal traverse over an opening.

Machicolations: a corbelled balcony at the top of a wall, supported by consoles or brackets.

Maestà: Madonna and Child in Majesty.

Mascaron: carved medallion in form of human mask.

Matroneum: gallery reserved for women in early Christian churches.

Merlon: the solid part of a parapet between two crenels (identations).

Misericord: the small tilting seat of a church stall.

Modillion: a small console supporting a cornice.

Narthex: the internal vestibule of a church.

Oculus: a round window.

Pietà: Virgin with the dead Christ.

Pilaster: a rectangular column often attached to a wall.

Polyptych: a painted or carved panel divided into several bays (triptych: three bays).

Predella: the base of an altarpiece often decorated with small scenes.

Recessed Orders: concentric receding arches surmounting a doorway.

Sinopia: sketch for a fresco.

Stucco: ornamental moulding made of lime, chalk and marble dust.

Triforium: a small gallery over the aisles of a church.

Tympanum: the part between the lintel and the arch of a doorway.

A Sicilian cart

PRINCIPAL FESTIVALS

30 and 31 January

Aosta . . . . Fair of St Orso: craft fair with articles for sale

Late January – early February

Viareggio . . . . Carnival: masked procession, folklore events

Ten days previous to Lent

Venice . . . . The Carnival. *Further information from the Azienda di Soggiorno, Palazzo Martinengo, San Marco, 4089-30100 Venezia; ☎ 041/5226356*

Last Friday of the carnival

Verona . . . . Bacchanalian Carnival of the Gnocco: masked processions and competition for the best float; gnocci made on the spot under a baldachin set up in front of the Church of St Zeno, are distributed to town officials and passers-by

1 April

San Marino . . . . Investiture of the two Captains Regent *(p. 197)*

Holy Week

Taranto . . . . Processions *(p. 204)*

Easter Sunday

Florence . . . . *Scoppio del Carro:* fireworks display from a decorated float at midday on Piazza del Duomo. The fireworks are set off by a dove which slides along a wire from the high altar in the cathedral to the float

Sulmona . . . . Feast day of the *Madonna che scappa in Piazza (p. 204)*

May and June

Florence . . . . May Music Festival: numerous cultural events (concerts, opera, ballet). *Programme from the Azienda di Soggiorno, 15 Via de´ Tornabuoni, Florence. ☎ 055/216544*

1 May

Cagliari . . . . Feast of St Efisio, patron saint of Sardinia *(p. 241)*

First Sunday in May

Naples . . . . Feast of the Miracle of St Januarius in the cathedral *(p. 144)*

7 to 10 May

Bari . . . . Feast of St Nicholas: 7 May procession in costumes through the town. 8 May the faithful go in boats to worship a statue of their saint

15 May

Gubbio . . . . Race of the Ceri *(p. 109)*

Second last Sunday in May

Sassari . . . . *Cavalcata Sarda (p. 244)*

Last Sunday in May

Gubbio . . . . *Palio della Balestra:* archery competition in Piazza della Signoria

15 June to 30 September, even years

Venice . . . . The Biennale: International Exhibition of Modern Art. *For further information call the Biennale Committee: ☎ 041/5200311 or the Azienda di Soggiorno ☎ 041/5226356*

Early June to late August

Verona . . . . Summer Drama Festival

1 to 3 June

Taormina . . . . Carnival with Sicilian costumes and carts

16 and 17 June

Pisa . . . . 16: illumination of the Arno and the quays in the evening; 17: Feast of St Rainier

24 June

Florence . . . . *Calcio Storico Fiorentino:* ball game on Piazza della Signoria, procession in 16C costumes; fireworks display in Piazzale Michelangiolo

Last Sunday in June

Pisa . . . . Games on the Ponte di Mezzo. ☎ 050/560464

Late June-early July
Spoleto .... *Festival dei Due Mondi:* International Festival of Drama, Music and Dance *(p. 203)*

Early July to late August
Verona .... Musical Season in the setting of the Roman Amphitheatre. *Further information from the Azienda di Promozione turistica, 6b Via Dietro Anfiteatro, 37100 Verona.* ☎ *045/592828*

2 July
Siena .... *Palio delle Contrade (p. 200)*

15 July
Naples .... Feast of Santa Maria del Carmine (illumination of the campanile) *(p. 139)*

Third Saturday in July
Venice .... Feast of the Redeemer on the Island of Giudecca (Saturday night)

First Sunday in August
Ascoli Piceno ...... *Festa della Quintana:* procession of representatives from the various districts in 15C costume; horsemen attack a dummy

14 August
Sassari .... *Festa dei Candelieri* (Feast of Candles) *(p. 244)*

16 August
Siena .... *Palio delle Contrade (p. 200)*

29 August
Nuoro .... Feast of the Redeemer *(p. 243)*

Late August to early September
Venice .... International Film Festival on the Lido Island

Last Sunday in August
Arezzo .... *Giostra del Saracine:* the Saracen's Tournament

First Sunday in September
Venice .... Regatta on the Grand Canal

7 September
Florence .... *Festa delle Rificolona* (paper lanterns): musical and folklore events in the different districts

8 September
Loreto .... Feast of the Nativity of the Virgin *(p. 120)*
Naples .... Feast of the *Madonna di Piedigrotta*

Second Friday, Saturday and Sunday in September, even years
Marostica .... *Partita a Scacchi:* game of chess with costumed people as the pieces *(p. 59)*

Second Sunday in September
Sansepolcro .... Cross-bow competition, in medieval costumes

13 September
Lucca .... *Luminara di Santa Croce:* Night-time procession *(p. 121)*

Second and third Sundays in September
Foligno .... Game of the Quintana *(p. 56)*

Ten days towards mid-September
Asti .... Wine Festival

Mid-September to mid-October, odd years
Florence .... Biennial Antiques Fair in the Palazzo Strozzi

19 September
Naples .... Feast of the Miracle of St Januarius *(p. 144)*

Third Sunday in September
Asti .... *Palio* or horse race *(p. 219)*

1 October
San Marino .... Investiture of the two Captains Regent *(p. 197)*

First Sunday in October
Arezzo .... Giostra del Saracine: the Saracen's Tournament

10 December
Loreto .... Feast of the Translation of the Santa Casa *(p. 120)*

Christmas of Epiphany
Naples .... Display of cribs in the local churches

ADMISSION TIMES AND CHARGES

As admission times and charges are liable to alteration, the information below is given for guidance only.

The information applies to individual adults. Special conditions for groups are common but arrangements should be made in advance. Many places have special admission times for groups and offer special rates for advance booking.

It is advisable to make an early start as many museums are closed in the afternoon and most churches close at lunch-time. Some museums may be closed in part or in full for restoration or owing to lack of staff. Visitors are not admitted during services.

As monuments are often undergoing restoration work which may last for long periods it is preferable to telephone in advance before setting off on visits.

When telephone numbers are given, the local dialling code (prefisso) is indicated in brakets.

See the Practical Information chapter for a list of national holidays.

Every sight for which there are admission times and charges is indicated by the symbol ⊙ in the middle section of the guide.

A

ABRUZZI

National Park. – Visitor centres at Civitella Alfedana (near Villetta Barrea) ☎ (0864) 890141, Bisegna (18km – 11 miles north of Pescasseroli), Pescaseroli ☎ (0863) 910405, Villavallelonga (30km – 19 miles southeast of Avezzano via Trasacco).

ALBA FUCENS

Ruins. – Open all year 8am to one hour before sunset.

ALBISOLA MARINA

Villa Faraggiana. – Open April to September 3 to 7pm. Closed Tuesdays. 3 500 lire. ☎ (019) 480622.

ALTILIA SAEPINUM

Ruins. – Open all year 9am to sunset.

Benevento Gate Museum. – Open all year 8am to 7pm. Closed Mondays. ☎ (0874) 790207.

Museum near the theatre. – Same opening times as for the Benevento Gate Museum.

ALTOMONTE

Museum. – Open all year 9am to 1.30pm and 3.30 to 6.30pm. 2 000 lire. ☎ (0981) 948261.

AMALFI

St Andrew's Cathedral: Cloisters of Paradise. – Open all year 8am to 1pm and 3 to 7pm. ☎ (089) 871107.

ANAGNI

Cathedral Crypt and Treasury. – Open April to September weekdays 9.30am to 12 noon and 4 to 7pm, Sundays 3.30 to 7pm; October to March daily 9.30am to 12 noon and 3.30 to 5pm; closed Sunday and holiday mornings Crypt: 1 500 lire. Treasury: 3 000 lire. ☎ (0775) 727228 or 727087.

ANCONA

Church of Santa Maria della Piazza. – Open all year 8am to 6pm.

National Museum of the Marches. – Open July to September Mondays to Saturdays 9am to 1.30pm and 2.30 to 7pm, Sundays 3 to 7.30pm; October to June 9am to 1.30pm, Sundays and holidays 2.30 to 7pm only. 4 000 lire. ☎ (071) 202794.

Podesti Public Gallery. – Open Tuesdays to Saturdays 10am to 7pm and Sundays 9am to 1pm. Closed Mondays and holidays. 3 000 lire, free on Sundays. ☎ (071) 2225041.

ANDALO

Monte Paganella. – Daily access by cable-car and by chairlift from Fai della Paganella 7 December to Easter and July to mid-September. Inclusive ticket for the ski resort: 32 000 lire (Sundays and holidays), 26 000 lire (weekdays), 20 000 lire (half-day).

ANGERA

Castle. – Open 27 March to 31 October: daily 9.30am to 12.30pm and 2 to 6pm (3 to 7pm July and August, 2 to 5pm October). 7 000 lire. ☎ (0331) 931300.

ANSEDONIA

Ancient city of Cosa. – Open all year. ☎ (0564) 881421.

AOSTA

Collegiate Church of St Orso. – Open 9.30am to 12 noon and 2 to 6pm (5.30pm December to February). The cloisters are closed on Mondays. ☎ (0165) 35655 or 40526.

Cathedral. – Closed 12 noon to 3pm. Treasury: open April to September Tuesdays to Saturdays 10am to 12 noon and 3 to 5pm; Sundays and holidays 3 to 5.45pm only. Closed Mondays. October to March open Sundays and holidays only 3 to 5.45pm. 2 500 lire. ☎ (0165) 40413 or 31361.

L'AQUILA

Castle: National Museum of the Abruzzi. – Open all year 9am to 1pm. Closed 1 May and Christmas. 6 000 lire. ☎ (0862) 64043.

AQUILEIA

Basilica: crypt. – Open April to September 7.30am to 6.30pm; October to March 7.30am to 12.30pm and 3.30 to 6pm. Closed during services. 500 lire. ☎ (0431) 91026.

Basilica: Cripta degli Scavi. – Open all year 9am to 2pm (1pm Sundays and holidays). ☎ (0431) 91016 or 91035.

Roman ruins. – Open all year 9am to one hour before sunset. ☎ (0431) 91016 or 91035.

Archaeological Museum. – Open all year 9am to 2pm (1pm Sundays and holidays). 6 000 lire. ☎ (0431) 91016 or 91035.

Paleo-Christian Museum. – Open all year 9am to 2pm (1pm Sundays and holidays. ☎ (0431) 91131.

AREZZO

Vasari Mansion. – Open all year 9am to 7pm (1pm Sundays and holidays). Closed 1 January and 15 August. ☎ (0575) 20295.

Museum of Medieval and Modern Art. – Open 9am to 7pm (1pm Sundays). Closed 1 January, Easter, 1 May, 15 August and 25 December. 6 000 lire. ☎ (0575) 300301.

Archaeological Museum. – Open all year 9am to 2pm (1pm Sundays); ticket office closes at 12.30pm. Closed Mondays, 6 000 lire. ☎ (0575) 20882.

ARONA

Statue: Colosso di San Carlone. – Open 8.30am to 12.30pm and 2 to 6pm (5pm October to March). Closed Tuesday afternoons and Wednesdays from October to March. Ascent to the platform: 2 000 lire; to the summit: 3 000 lire. ☎ (0322) 243601.

ASCOLI PICENO

Picture Gallery. – Open 15 June to 15 September 9am to 1pm and 3 to 7.30pm weekdays (except Saturday afternoons), 9.30am to 12.30pm and 4 to 8pm Sundays; 16 September to 14 June 9am to 1 pm. Closed 1 January, Easter, 25 April, 1 May, 15 August, 1 November and Christmas. 2 500 lire. ☎ (0736) 298282 or 298213.

ASSISI

St Francis' Basilica: Treasury and Perkins Collection. – Open April to October 9.30am to 12.30pm and 2 to 6pm. Closed Sundays. 5 000 lire. ☎ (075) 812238.

Medieval Castle. – Open July to September 9am to 8pm, October to June 10am to 4pm. 2 000 lire. ☎ (075) 8004951.

Pilgrims' Oratory. – Open all year 9am to 12 noon and 3 to 6pm. Closed Sundays and holidays. ☎ (075) 812267.

Carceri Hermitage. – Open 8am to sunset. ☎ (075) 812301.

Monastery of St Damian. – Open 10am to 12.30pm and 2 to 6pm (4.30pm 6 October to late May). ☎ (075) 812273.

St Mary of the Angels' Basilica. – Open April to September 6am to 12 noon and 3 to 8pm; October to March 7.30am to 12 noon and 3 to 7pm. ☎ (075) 8040523.

B

BACOLI

Cento Camerelle. – Apply to No 161 Via Cento Camerelle for permission to visit.

Piscina Mirabile. – Apply to No 5 Via Piscina Mirabile.

BAGNAIA

Villa Lante. – Open all year 9am to 6pm. Closed Mondays, 1 January, 25 April, 1 May, 2 June, 15 August and at Christmas. 2 000 lire. ☎ (0761) 288008.

BAIA

Baths. – Open all year 9.30am to 6.30pm (5pm October to March). 4 000 lire. ☎ (081) 8687592.

BARI

Castle. – Open 9am to 1pm and 5 to 7pm. Closed holiday and Sunday afternoons. 4 000 lire. ☎ (080) 5214361 or 5214428.

Picture Gallery. – Open all year 9.30am to 1pm and 4 to 7pm, Sundays 9am to 1pm. Closed Mondays and holidays. ☎ (080) 392423.

Archaeological Museum. – Open 8am to 1.30pm. Closed Sundays and holidays. ☎ (080) 5211559 or 5211576.

BARLETTA

Basilica of the Holy Sepulchre. – Open 9am to 12.30pm. Avoid visiting on Sunday mornings. ☎ (0883) 31782.

Municipal Museum. – Open 9am to 1pm. Closed Mondays, 25 April, 1 May, 15 August, 25 December and local holidays. ☎ (0883) 33005.

BASSANO DEL GRAPPA

Municipal Museum. – Open all year 10am to 12.30pm and 2.30 to 6.30pm. Closed Sunday afternoons, Mondays and local holidays. 2 000 lire. ☎ (0424) 22235 or 23336.

BELLAGIO

Villa Serbelloni: Gardens. – Open 15 April to 15 October 11am to 4pm. Closed Mondays. 4 000 lire. ☎ (031) 950204.

Villa Melzi: Gardens. – Open daily 20 March to late September 9am to 6.30pm; October 9am to 5.30pm. 4 000 lire. ☎ (031) 950318 or 950132.

BELLUNO

Municipal Museum. – Open second Tuesday in April to second Sunday in October 10am to 12 noon and 3 to 6 pm; closed Sunday afternoons and Mondays, Easter, 1 May and 15 August. The rest of the year open 10am to 12 noon and 3 to 6pm; closed Mondays, Saturdays, Sundays and holidays. ☎ (0437) 24836.

BENEVENTO

Samnium Museum. – Open all year 9am to 1 pm. Closed Sundays and holidays. ☎ (0824) 21818.

BERGAMO

Colleoni Chapel. – Open all year 9am to 12 noon and 2 to 6pm (6.30pm Sundays and holidays). Closed Mondays in winter, 1 January and Christmas. ☎ (035) 2263311.

Basilica of St Mary Major. – Open all year 8am to 12 noon and 2.30 to 6pm (7pm in summer) ☎ (035) 237075.

Bell-tower of the Palazzo della Ragione. – Closed for restoration. ☎ (035) 255255.

Nos 9 and 11 Via Bartolomei Colleoni. – Open all year Mondays and Fridays 9.30 to 11.30am. For permission to visit on the other days: ☎ (035) 249970. Closed holidays.

Carrara Academy. – Open all year 9.30am to 12.30pm and 2.30 to 5.30pm. Closed Tuesdays, 26 August and holidays. 3 000 lire; free on Sundays. ☎ (035) 399425/426.

BOLOGNA

Communal Palace. – Open 8.30am to 7pm (1pm Sundays and holidays). Closed 1 January, Easter and Christmas. ☎ (051) 203208 or 203040.

Communal Art Collections. – Closed for restoration. ☎ (051) 203526.

Governor's Palace. – The courtyard is open 9am to 7pm. The building is open only for temporary exhibitions. Apply to the Information Centre of the City of Bologna. ☎ (051) 203040.

Municipal Archaeological Museum. – Open 9am to 2pm weekdays, 9am to 1pm Sundays and holidays. Closed Mondays, 1 January, Christmas and weekday holidays. 3 000 lire. ☎ (051) 233849.

Palazzo del Archiginnasio: Anatomy Theatre. – Open 9am to 1pm. Closed Sundays and holidays. Apply to the caretaker of the Archiginnasio Library, 1 Piazza Galvani. ☎ (051) 236353.

Torre degli Asinelli. – Open daily 9am to 6pm (5pm mid-October to mid-March). 1 000 lire.

St Stephen's Basilica: Museum. – Open all year 9am to 12 noon and 3.30 to 6pm. ☎ (051) 223256.

National Picture Gallery. – Open 9am to 2pm (1pm Sundays and holidays); 9am to 7pm early September to early November during exhibitions. Closed Mondays, 1 January, 1 May and 25 December. 6 000 lire. ☎ (051) 243222.

Church of St Mary Major. – Apply to the sacristan for permission to see the frescoes.

Museum of Industrial Art. – Open Tuesdays to Saturdays 9am to 2pm, Sundays 9am to 1pm. Closed Mondays and weekday holidays. 3 000 lire. ☎ (051) 236708.

Davia Bargellini Gallery. – Same opening times as for the Museum of Industrial Art.

BOLSENA

St Christina's Church. – Chapel of the Miracle: 7am to 12.30pm and 4 to 8pm (3 to 5.30pm October to March); no charge. **Grotto and catacombs:** guided tours (3/4 hour) same admission times but closed Mondays; 3 000 lire. ☎ (0761) 799067.

BOLZANO

Dominican Monastery: Church and Cloisters. – Open Mondays to Saturdays 9am to 6.30pm. Donations welcome. ☎ (0471) 973133.

BOMARZO

Villa Orsini: Park. – Open all year sunrise to sunset. 8 000 lire. ☎ (0761) 924029.

BOMINACO

Churches. – Open 9.30am to 1.30pm and 3 to 6pm. Apply to the caretaker, Mr. Cassiani Berardo. ☎ (0862) 93604. Gratuities welcome.

BORROMEAN ISLANDS

Boats leave from Arona, Stresa, Baveno, Pallanza and Laveno. Pass for the three islands valid all day, from Arona: 16 400 lire; from Stresa, Baveno and Pallanza: 9 200 lire; from Laveno: 15 900 lire.

Isola Bella. – Access: from Arona and Laveno, 12 000 lire Rtn; from Stresa and Baveno, 6 000 lire Rtn; from Pallanza, 8 400 lire Rtn.

Isola dei Pescatori. – Access: from Arona and Laveno, 12 000 lire Rtn; from Stresa and Baveno, 6 000 lire Rtn; from Pallanza, 8 400 lire Rtn.

Isola Madre. – Access: from Arona, 14 400 lire Rtn; from Laveno, 10 200 lire Rtn; from Stresa, 8 400 lire Rtn; from Baveno, 6 000 lire Rtn; from Pallenza, 4 600 lire Rtn.

BRENTA RIVIERA

Boat trips to the villas. – Il Burchiello operates from April to October; departure from Venice Tuesdays, Thursdays and Saturdays, from Padua Wednesdays, Fridays, Saturdays and Sundays. Return journey by coach. 100 000 lire (including admission to villas and coach fare; optional extra charge for lunch 38 000 lire). To book apply to C.I.T., Piazza San Marco, Venice, ☎ (041) 5185480; C.I.T., 12 Via Matteoti, Padua, ☎ (049) 663333 or SIAMIC EXPRESS, 42 Via Trieste, Padua, ☎ (049) 660 944.
For the admission times and charges to the villas, see under Stra, Mira and Malcontenta.

BRESCIA

Tosio Martinengo Picture Gallery. – Closed for restoration. ☎ (030) 295527.

Roman Museum. – Open 10 am to 12.30pm and 2 to 6pm (5pm October to May). Closed Mondays, 1 January, 15 February, Easter, 25 April, 1 May, 15 August, 1 November, 25 and 26 December. 2 000 lire. ☎ (030) 46031.

Museum of Christian Art. – Closed for restoration.

BRESSANONE

Diocesan Museum. – Open 15 March to 31 October 10am to 5pm; closed Sundays. 4 000 lire. ☎ (0472) 30505.

BREUIL-CERVINIA

Excursions by cable-car. – Cable-cars for Rosa Plateau (30 000 lire Rtn) and the Furggen Pass (30 000 lire Rtn) operate daily except from 10 May to 23 June and from 25 September to 25 October when they operate only at weekends. Cable-cars leave every 15 or 30 minutes.

BRINDISI

Archaeological Museum. – Open all year 9am to 1.30pm. Closed Saturdays, Sundays and holidays. ☎ (0831) 523418.

C

CAMALDOLI

Hermitage. – Open all year 8.30 to 11.15am (10.45am Sundays and holidays) and 3 to 6pm. Visitors are requested to observe the silence rule. ☎ (0575) 556021.

CAMONICA VALLEY

Naquane National Park of Rock Engravings. – Open all year 9am to one hour before sunset. Closed Mondays (except holiday Mondays). 1 January, 25 April, 1 May, first Sunday in June, 15 August and 25 December. 6 000 lire. ☎ (0364) 42140.

Ceto, Cimbergo and Paspardo Regional Nature Reserve. – Open June to September 9am to 12 noon and 2 to 6pm; October to May 9am to 12 noon and 2 to 5pm. Closed Sunday and holiday afternoons. ☎ (0364) 433465.

Nadro: museum. – Same admission times and charges as for the Regional Nature Reserve. ☎ (0364) 433465.

CAMPO CARLO MAGNO

Grosté Pass. – Access by cable-car in winter from early December to late April and in summer from early July to mid-September. Rtn ticket: 18 000 lire. ☎ (0465) 41001.

CAMPO IMPERATORE

Access. – By cable-car all year except for a fortnight in June and October-November. Service about every half-hour depending on demand from 8.30am to sunset. Rtn fare: 12 000 lire weekdays, 15 000 lire Sundays and holidays. ☎ (0862) 22147.

CANOSA DI PUGLIA

Hypogea. – Open all year 9.30am to 1pm.

CAPRAROLA

Villa Farnese. – Guided tours (1/2 hour) all year: 9am to 7pm March to October and 9am to 4pm November to February. Closed 1 January and 1 May. 2 000 lire. ☎ (0761) 646052.

CAPRI

Blue Grotto. – Boat trips to the cave are organised daily all year. Allow one hour. 16 200 lire weekdays, 17 250 lire Sundays and holidays. No sailings when the sea is rough.

Tour of the island. – Boat trips are organised daily all year from Marina Grande. Allow 2 hours. 15 450 lire (plus 9 700 lire for tour of the Blue Grotto). No sailings when the sea is rough.

Jupiter's Villa. – Open all year 9am to one hour before sunset. 4 000 lire.

Carthusian Monastery of St James. – Open all year 9am to 2pm. Closed Mondays. ☎ (081) 8376218.

Villa San Michele (Anacapri). – Open all year 9am to sunset. 4 000 lire. ☎ (081) 8371401.

Monte Solaro (Anacapri). – By cable-car April to October 9.30am to sunset, November to March 10.30am to 3pm (closed Tuesdays). 5 000 lire Rtn. ☎ (081) 8371428.

CAPUA

Campania Museum. – Open 9am to 2pm (1pm Sundays and holidays). Closed Mondays, 1 January, 15 August, 25 and 26 December. ☎ (0823) 961402.

CARPI

Castello dei Pio. – Open weekdays 4 to 7pm, Sundays and holidays 10.30am to 12.30pm and 4 to 7pm. Closed November to mid-April. 3 000 lire. ☏ (059) 649314.

CARRARA

Marble Quarries. – Private property. Access possible daily all year. No authorisation needed but care is required at all times especially at Colonnata and Fantiscritti. It is best to visit in the morning during the week when there is the greatest variety of work in progress. Working hours are generally from 7 to 11am and 12 noon to 4pm. There is no quarrying on Saturday afternoons, Sundays and holidays and around 15 August.

CASAMARI

Abbey. – Guided tours daily 9am to 12 noon and 4 to 7pm. Closed Sunday and holiday mornings and Easter, Corpus Christi and Christmas. Donations welcome. ☏ (0775) 332371 or 332800.

CASERTA

La Reggia. – Open daily 9am to 1.30pm. 6 000 lire. Closed 1 May. ☏ (0823) 321400.

Park. – Open daily: June to August 9am to 6pm, the rest of the year 9am to one hour before sunset. Closed 1 May. 4 000 lire. ☏ (0823) 321400.

CASTEL DEL MONTE

Castle. – Open April to September 9am to 1pm and 4 to 7pm, the rest of the year 9am to 2pm. Closed Sunday afternoons and holidays. 4 000 lire. ☏ (080) 5214361.

CASTELFRANCO VENETO

Giorgione's Birthplace. – Open all year 9am to 12 noon and 3 to 6pm. Closed Mondays, 1 January, Easter and Christmas. ☏ (0423) 491240.

CASTELLAMMARE DI STABIA

Antiquarium. – Open 9am to 2pm (6pm July, August and September). ☏ (081) 8707228.

Ariadne's Villa. – Open April to October 9am to 7pm, November to March 9am to 4pm. Closed Mondays, Sunday and holiday afternoons, 1 May and Easter Monday. ☏ (081) 8714541.

San Marco's Villa. – Open April to September 9am to 7pm, November to March 9am to 4pm (1pm Sundays and holidays). Closed Mondays, 1 May and Easter Monday. ☏ (081) 8714541.

CASTELLANA

Caves. – Visit excluding the White Cave (1 hour) at 8.30am, 9.30am, 10.30am, 11.30am, 12.30pm and 1pm all year and also at 2.30pm, 3.30pm, 4.30pm, 5.30pm, 6.30pm and 7pm from April to September; 10 000 lire. Visit including the White Cave (2 hours) at 9am, 10am, 11am, 12 noon all year and also at 3pm, 4pm, 5pm and 6pm from April to September; 20 000 lire. ☏ (080) 8965511.

CERRO

Ceramics Museum. – Open 10am to 12 noon and 2.30 to 5.30pm (3.30 to 6.30pm July and August). Closed Mondays, Tuesday to Thursday mornings, 1 January, Easter and Christmas. 2 500 lire. ☏ (0332) 666530 or 668596.

CERTALDO

Boccaccio's House. – Open all year. Apply to the caretaker who lives on the premises. ☏ (0571) 667386.

Palazzo Pretorio. – Open all year: October to March 9am to 12 noon and 3 to 6pm (4 to 7pm the rest of the year). Closed Mondays. 2 000 lire. ☏ (0571) 661219.

CERVETERI

Banditaccia Necropolis. – Open all year 9am to 7pm. Closed Mondays, 1 January and 1 May. 8 000 lire. ☏ (06) 9950003.

CESENA

Malatestiana Library. – Guided tours (3/4 hour): 17 June to 14 September 8am to 12.30pm and 4 to 7pm, 15 September to 16 June 9am to 12.30pm and 3 to 7pm; Sundays all year 9am to 12 noon only. Closed Monday mornings, 1 January, Easter, 15 August and 25 December. 3 000 lire. ☏ (0547) 21297.

Abbey. – Open 9am to 12 noon and 2.30 et 6pm; Sunday and holiday mornings from 11am to 12.15pm and 2 to 6pm. Closed Mondays and Christmas. Donations welcome. ☏ (02) 57403404.

CHIARAVALLE

Abbey. – Open 9am to 12 noon and 2.30 to 6pm; Sundays and holidays 11am to 12.15pm and 2 to 6pm. Closed Mondays and Christmas. Donations welcome. ☎ (02) 57403404.

CHIAVENNA

Collegiate Church of St Lawrence: treasury. – Closed temporarily.

Botanical and Archaeological Garden at Il Paradiso. – Open afternoons: October to May 2 to 5pm (6pm Saturdays and Sundays), June to September 2 to 6pm (6.30pm Saturdays and Sundays). Closed Mondays, 1 January, Easter, 1 May, 10 August (San Lorenzo), 25, 26 and 31 December. 1 000 lire. ☎ (0343) 32821 (library).

CHIETI

Abruzzi Archaelogical Museum. – Open all year 8.30am to 1.30pm. Closed 1 May. 6 000 lire. ☎ (0871) 65704.

CHIUSI

Etruscan Museum. – Open all year 9am to 2pm (1pm Sundays). Closed 1 January, Easter, 1 May and 25 December. 2 000 lire. ☎ (0578) 20177.

CIVIDALE DEL FRIULI

Cathedral: Museum. – Open April to September 9.30am to 12 noon and 3 to 6.30pm, October to March 9.30am to 12 noon and 3 to 5.30pm. ☎ (0432) 731398 (tourist information centre).

Archaeological Museum. – Open 9am to 1.30pm (12.30pm Sundays and holidays). 4 000 lire. ☎ (0432) 700700.

Tempietto. – Open 10am to 1.30pm and 3.30 to 5.30pm. 2000 lire. ☎ (0432) 731398.

CIVITAVECCHIA

National Archaeological Museum. – Open all year 9am to 1pm. Closed Mondays, 1 January, 1 May and 25 December. ☎ (0766) 23604.

Trajan's Baths. – Open all year 9am to 1pm. Closed Mondays, 1 January, 25 April and 25 December. ☎ (0766) 23604.

CLITUMNUS (SOURCE)

Temple of Clitumnus. – Open all year 9am to 12 noon and 4 to 7pm. Closed Mondays and Sundays. Donations welcome. ☎ (0743) 521030.

COLLODI

Villa Garzoni. – Open daily Easter to October 9am to 12 noon 3 to 7pm, Sundays and holidays 9am to 12.30pm and 2.30 to 7pm; November to Easter open Sundays only. 15 000 lire including gardens. ☎ (0572) 428400.

Garzoni Gardens. – Open April to September 8am to 8pm (6pm October to March). 8 500 lire. ☎ (031) 572910.

COMO

Villa Olmo: Gardens. – Open all year 8am to 6pm. Closed holidays. ☎ (031) 572910.

COMO (LAKE)

Boat trips. – From Como to Colico (northeast of the lake) and from Como to Lecco: 19 800 lire Rtn. From Como to Tremezzo, Bellagio or Menaggio: 14 800 lire Rtn. From Tremezzo to Dongo, Domaso and Colico: 9 400 to 14 800 lire Rtn. From Bellagio to Lecco: 12 200 lire.

Hydrofoil service from Como to Tremezzo, Bellagio, Menaggio: 21 200 lire Rtn.

Car-ferry service between Bellagio, Varenna, Menaggio and Cadenabbia: 7 700 to 13 000 lire.
With one-day and ten-day tickets visitors are free to travel as they wish: 21 500 lire for the one-day ticket, 65 300 lire for the ten-day ticket.

Evening trips. – Saturdays in summer. 24 000 lire.

CONEGLIANO

Cathedral. – Open 9am to 12 noon. Sundays and holidays 9am to 12 noon and 3.30 to 6.30pm. Closed Wednesdays.

Castle Museums. – Open 9am to 12 noon and 3.30 to 7pm (2 to 5.30pm October to March). Closed Mondays. 2 000 lire. ☎ (0438) 22871.

CORFINIO

Basilica of San Pelino. – Open May to September 8.30am to 6pm; October to April 8.30am to 5pm. ☎ (0864) 728120.

CORTINA D'AMPEZZO

Tondi di Faloria. – By cable-car from Via Marconi to Faloria, 12 000 lire one way, 14 500 lire Rtn. From Faloria to Tondi di Faloria: in winter « Tondi » ski-lift, 2 000 lire; and « Girilada » chair-lift, 3 500 lire; in summer by jeep, 5 000 lire:

Tofana di Mezzo. – By « Freccia nel Cielo » cable-car, 30 000 lire Rtn.

Pocol Belvedere. – By bus every hour from Piazza Roma from late December to March and July to September. 2 000 lire.

CORTONA

Diocesan Museum. – Open 9am to 1pm and 3 to 6pm (5pm October to Easter). Closed Mondays. 5 000 lire. ☎ (575) 62830.

Museum of the Etruscan Academy. – Open April to September 10am to 1pm and 4 to 7pm, October to March 9am to 1pm and 3 to 5pm. Closed Mondays. 5 000 lire. ☎ (0575) 630415.

CREMONA

Torrazzo. – Open Easter to October 10am to 12 noon and 3 to 6pm weekdays, 10am to 1pm and 3 to 7pm Sundays and holidays; November to Easter Sundays and holidays only 10am to 1pm and 3 to 6pm. 5 000 lire. ☎ (0372) 27633 or 31524.

Town Hall. – Open all year 9am to 12 noon and 3 to 7pm. Closed Sunday afternoons, 1 January and Christmas. ☎ (0372) 4071.

Municipal Museum. – Open all year 9.15am to 12.15pm and 3.15 to 5.45pm. Closed Mondays and Sunday afternoons. 1 000 lire, free on Sundays and holidays. ☎ (0372) 29349.

CROTONE

Archaeological Museum. – Open all year 9am to 1 pm. Closed Sunday afternoons, Mondays and holidays. ☎ (0962) 23082.

CUMAE

Acropolis. – Open April to September 9.30am to 6.30pm, October to March 9.30am to 5pm. 4 000 lire. ☎ (081) 8543060.

D – E

DESENZANO DEL GARDA

Villa Romana. – Open April to September 9am to 6.30pm, March and October 9am to 5.30pm, November to February 9am to 4pm. Closed Mondays (except holiday Mondays) and Tuesdays after holiday Mondays. 4 000 lire. ☎ (030) 9143547.

ELBA

Portoferraio: Napoleonic Museum. – Open 9am to 7pm (12.30pm Sundays). Closed Mondays, 1 January, 25 April, 1 May, 2 June, 15 August and 25 December. 6 000 lire. ☎ (0565) 915846.

Monte Capanne. – By cable-car daily mid-April to October 10am to 12.15pm and 2.30 to 6.30pm. 12 000 lire. ☎ (0565) 901020.

Marciana: Archaeological Museum. – Open mid-April to mid-October: June to September 9am to 1pm and 4 to 7.30pm, April, May and October 8am to 1pm. Closed Thursdays. 3 000 lire. ☎ (0565) 901015.

San Martino: Napoleon's Villa. – Same admission times and charges as the Napoleonic Museum in Porteferraio. ☎ (0565) 914688.

EMERALD CAVE

Access and tour. – By lift from the road, open all year 9am to 4pm; 4 000 lire (including lift and admission to the cave). By boat from Amalfi harbour, from 8 000 lire depending on the type of boat in spring and summer. ☎ (089) 871107.

ESTE

Atestino National Museum. – Open all year 9am to 1pm and 3 to 7pm (6pm weekdays October to March). Closed Mondays, 1 January, Easter, 25 April, 1 May, 15 August, 25 and 26 December. 4 000 lire. ☎ (0429) 2085.

For a pleasant hotel in peaceful surroundings
Look in the current
Michelin Guide Italia
(Red Guide hotels and restaurants)

F

FAENZA

International Ceramics Museum. – Open June to September 9am to 7pm, October to May 9.30am to 1pm and 3 to 6pm. Closed Sunday afternoons, Mondays, 1 January, Easter, 25 April, 1 May, 15 August and 25 December. 6 000 lire. ☎ (0546) 21240.

Municipal Picture Gallery. – Closed temporarily for restoration. ☎ (0546) 660799.

FAITO (MONTE)

Toll-road. – 3 000 lire Rtn per car. ☎ (081) 8711334.

FANO

Municipal Museum. – Guided tours (1 hour) July to September 8.30am to 12.30pm and 5 to 7pm; October to June and on Sundays and holidays 8.30am to 12.30pm only. Closed Mondays, 10 July and 15 August. 3 000 lire. ☎ (0721) 828362.

FELTRE

Municipal Museum. – Closed for restoration. ☎ (0439) 2540 (tourist information centre).

FENIS

Castle. – Open: March to September 9am to 6pm; October to February 9am to 12.30pm and 2 to 5.30pm. Closed Tuesdays and Christmas. 4 000 lire. ☎ (0165) 764263.

FERENTILLO

Abbey of San Pietro in Valle. – Restoration work in progress. Apply to the caretaker Signora Nardini. ☎ (0744) 780316.

FERENTO

Roman Theatre. – Open all year 8am to 2pm. Closed Mondays, 1 January, 25 April, 1 May, 15 August and Christmas. ☎ (0761) 225929.

FERRARA

Cathedral Museum. – Open 10am to 12 noon and 4 to 6pm. Closed Sundays and holidays. Donations welcome.

Este Castle. – Open all year 9.30am to 1.30pm and 2.30 to 6.30pm. Closed Mondays. 5 000 lire. ☎ (0532) 299279.

Schifanoia Palace. – Open all year 9am to 7pm. Closed 1 January, Easter Sunday, 1 May, 15 August, 1 November, 25 and 26 December. 5 000 lire. ☎ (0532) 62038.

Palace of Diamonds. – Open all year 9am to 2pm (1pm Sundays and holidays). Closed Mondays, 1 January, Easter, 1 May, 15 August, 25 and 26 December. 6 000 lire. ☎ (0532) 205844.

Palace of Ludovico the Moor. – The museum is temporarily closed for restoration and reorganisation. ☎ (0532) 66299.

Casa Romei. – Open all year 8.30am to 2pm. Closed Mondays, 1 January, 1 May, 15 August and 25 December. 4 000 lire. ☎ (0532) 40341.

Palazzina di Marfisa d'Este. – Open March to September 9am to 12.30pm and 3 to 6pm, October to February 9am to 12.30pm and 2 to 5pm. Closed Sunday afternoons, 1 January, Easter, 1 May, 15 August, 1 November, 25 and 26 December. 2 000 lire, free on second Sundays and Mondays in the month. ☎ (0532) 207450.

Sant'Antonio in Polesine. – Open 9 to 11.30am and 3 to 5.30pm. Closed Sundays and holidays. Donations welcome. ☎ (0532) 64068.

Ariosto's House. – Open Mondays, Wednesdays and Fridays 9am to 12.30pm, Tuesdays and Thursdays 3 to 6.30pm. Closed Saturdays, Sundays and holidays. ☎ (0532) 40784.

FIESOLE

Convent of St Francis. – Open 10am to 12 noon and 3 to 6 pm. Donations welcome. ☎ (055) 59175.

Archaeological Site and Museum. – Open late March to late September 9am to 7pm; late September to late March 10am to 5pm. 6 000 lire. ☎ (055) 59477.

Bandini Museum. – Open 9.30am to 1.30pm and 3 to 7pm. Closed Tuesdays. 3 000 lire. ☎ (055) 59118.

Badia Fiesolana. – Apply to the caretaker. ☎ (055) 59155.

FLORENCE

Cathedral:

Inner Gallery and Fresco on the Dome. – Restoration work in progress, fresco not visible.

Top of the Dome. – 464 steps. Open all year 10am to 5pm. Closed Sundays, 1 January, Maundy Thursday to Easter Sunday, 24 June, 15 August, 1 November, 8, 25 and 26 December. 4 000 lire. ☎ (055) 2302885.

Crypt of Santa Reparata. – Same opening times as for the dome. 2 000 lire. ☎ (055) 2302885.

Campanile. – Open March to October 9am to 7.30pm, November to February 9am to 5pm. Closed 1 January only. 4 000 lire. ☎ (055) 2302885.

Baptistry. – Open all year 1 to 6pm Mondays to Saturdays, 9am to 1pm and 2.30 to 5.30pm Sundays and holidays. Closed Palm Sunday and Easter. ☎ (055) 2302885.

Cathedral Museum. – Open March to October 9am to 7.30pm, November to February 9am to 6pm (9am to 1pm holidays). Closed 1 February, Easter and Christmas. 4 000 lire. ☎ (055) 2302885.

Palazzo Vecchio. – Open weekdays 9am to 7pm, Sundays and holidays 8am to 1pm. Closed Saturdays, 1 January, Easter, 1 May, 15 August and Christmas. 8 000 lire (10 000 lire for exhibitions). ☎ (055) 27681.

Uffizi Museum. – Open all year 9am to 7pm (1pm Sundays and holidays). Closed Mondays, 1 January, 25 April, 1 May, first Sunday in June, 15 August and Christmas. 10 000 lire. ☎ (055) 218341.

Corridoio Vasariano. – Apply in advance to the Uffizi Secretariat; Guided tours (40 min) when guides are available. Same admission times and ticket as for the Uffizi Museum.

Bargello Palace and Museum. – Open 9am to 2pm. Closed Mondays, 1 January, Easter, 25 April, 1 May and 25 December. 6 000 lire. ☎ (055) 210801.

Laurenziana Library. – Open 9.30am to 1 pm. Closed Sundays, week before Easter and first fortnight in September. ☎ (055) 214443.

Medici Chapels. – Open 9am to 2pm (1pm Sundays and holidays). Closed Mondays and on some holidays. 9 000 lire. ☎ (055) 218341.

Medici Palace. – Open 9am to 12.45pm and 3 to 4.45pm, Sundays and holidays 9am to 12 noon only. Closed Wednesdays, 1 January, Easter, 1 May, 24 June, 15 August, 25 and 26 December. ☎ (055) 27601.

Santa Maria Novella; Green Cloisters. – Open all year 9am to 2pm weekdays, 8am to 1pm Sundays. Closed Fridays, 1 January, Easter, 1 May, 15 August and Christmas. 4 000 lire. ☎ (055) 282187.

Pitti Palace:

Palatine Gallery. – Open all year 9am to 2pm (1pm Sundays and holidays). Closed Mondays, 1, 6 and 7 January, 1 May, 13 and 14 August, 25 December. 8 000 lire. ☎ (055) 210323.

State Apartments. – Closed for restoration.

Silver Museum. – Open 9am to 2pm (1pm Sundays and holidays). Closed Mondays and some public holidays. 6 000 lire (including Porcelain Museum and Costume Museum listed below). ☎ (055) 212557.

Modern Art Gallery. – Open 9am to 2pm (1pm Sundays and holidays). Closed Mondays, 1 January, 25 April, 1 May, 15 August and 25 December. 4 000 lire. ☎ 287 096.

Boboli Gardens. – Open April to September 9am to 6.30pm (4.30pm the rest of the year). Closed 1 January, Easter, 25 April, 1 May, 15 August and Christmas. 5 000 lire. ☎ (055) 218741.

Costume Museum. – Same admission times and charges as for the Silver Museum (see above).

Porcelain Museum. – Same admission times and charges as for the Silver Museum (see above) but closed temporarily for restoration.

Convent and Museum of St Mark – Open 9am to 1.30pm (1pm Sundays and holidays). Closed Mondays and some public holidays. 6 000 lire. ☎ (055) 210741.

Academy Gallery. – Open August to October 9am to 6.45pm, November to July 9am to 1.45pm; Sundays and holidays all year 9am to 12.45pm. Closed Mondays and some public holidays. 10 000 lire. ☎ (055) 214375.

Foundlings' Hospital: Art Gallery. – Open all year 9am to 2pm (8am to 1pm Sundays and holidays). Closed 1 January and Christmas. 3 000 lire. ☎ (055) 2479317.

Santa Croce:

Church. – Open all year 8am to 12.30pm and 3.30 to 6.30pm except during services, holidays 3 to 6pm. ☎ (055) 244619.

Sacristy. – Open all year 9.30am to 12.30pm and 3 to 6pm; Sundays and holidays 3 to 6pm. ☎ (055) 244619.

Santa Croce Museum. – Open March to September 10am to 13.30pm and 2.30 to 6.30pm, October to February 10am to 12.30pm and 3 to 6pm. Closed Wednesdays, 1 January and Christmas. 3 000 lire (including Pazzi Chapel). ☎ (055) 244619.

Pazzi Chapel. – Same admission times and ticket as for Santa Croce Museum.

Santa Maria del Carmine: Brancacci Chapel. – Open 10am to 4.30pm weekdays, 1 to 4.30pm Sundays and holidays. Closed Tuesdays, 15 August and Christmas. 5 000 lire. ☎ (055) 211876.

San Salvi: Last Supper. – Open all year 9am to 2pm (1pm Sundays and holidays). Closed Mondays, 1, 6 and 7 January, 13 and 14 August and 25 December. 2 000 lire. ☎ (055) 6775570.

Archaeological Museum. – Open 9am to 2pm (1pm Sundays). Closed Mondays, Easter, 25 April, 1 May, 15 August and 25 December. 6 000 lire. ☎ (055) 2478641.

Sant'Apollonia: Last Supper. – Open all year 9am to 2pm (1pm Sundays and holidays). Closed Mondays, 1,6 and 7 January, 1 May, 13 and 14 August and 25 December. 2 000 lire. ☎ (055) 287074.

All Saints' Church: Ghirlandaio's Last Supper. – Open Mondays, Tuesdays and Saturdays 9am to 12 noon. ☎ (055) 2396802.

Davanzati Palace: Museum of the Florentine House. – Open all year 9am to 2pm (1pm Sundays and holidays). Closed Mondays and on some holidays. 4 000 lire. ☎ (055) 218341.

Science Museum. – Open 9.30am to 1pm and also on Mondays, Wednesdays and Fridays 2 to 5pm. Closed Sundays and holidays. 10 000 lire. ☎ (055) 293493.

Semi-precious Stone Workshop. – Open 9am to 2pm. Closed Sundays and holidays. 2 000 lire. ☎ (055) 289414.

Buonarotti's House. – Open 9.30am to 1.30pm. Closed Tuesdays, 1 January, Easter, 25 April, 1 May, 15 August and 25 December. 5 000 lire. ☎ (055) 241752.

Villa della Petraia. – Guided tours of the villa (1/2 hour) 9am to 6.30pm (4.30pm October and March, 3.30pm November to February). Closed Mondays. ☎ (055) 451208.

Villa di Castello. – Open June to August 9am to 7.30pm, April, May and September 9am to 6.30pm, March and October 9am to 5.30pm, November to February 9am to 4.30pm. Closed Mondays, 1 January, Easter, 15 August and Christmas. ☎ (055) 218741.

Villa di Poggio a Caiano. – Open all year 9am to 1.30pm (1pm Sundays and holidays). Closed Mondays, 1 January, Easter, 15 August, 1 May and Christmas. ☎ (055) 218741.

Galluzzo Carthusian Monastery. – Open 9am to 12 noon and 3 to 7pm (5pm October to March). Closed Mondays except holiday Mondays. Time 1/2 hour. Donations welcome. ☎ (055) 2049226.

FONTANELLATO

Rocca San Vitale. – Guided tours 9.30am to 12.30pm and 3 to 6pm (7pm May to mid-October) every hour daily. Closed 24 December to 6 January. 4 000 lire. ☎ (0521) 821188.

FONTE COLOMBO

Monastery. – Open all year 8am to 1pm and 3 to 8pm. Donations welcome. ☎ (0746) 71125.

LA FORESTA

Monastery. – Open all year 8.30am to 1pm and 3.30 to 6.30pm. Donations welcome. ☎ (0746) 40085.

FORLI

Picture Gallery. – Open 9am to 2pm (1pm Sundays and holidays). Closed Mondays and weekday holidays. ☎ (0543) 32771.

FOSSANOVA ABBEY

Tour. – Open daily 8.30am to 12 noon and 3.30pm to sunset. Donations welcome. ☎ (0773) 93061.

FRASASSI

Caves. – Guided tours (1 hour to 1 hr 10 min): March to June and in October daily at 9.30am, 11am, 12.30pm, 3pm, 4.30pm and 6pm; July to September every 15 minutes from 8am to 6.30pm; November to February weekdays at 11am and 3pm, Sundays and holidays at 9.30am, 11am, 12.30pm, 3pm, 4.30pm and 6.30pm. Temperature: 14 °C. 10 000 lire March to October (except August 14 000 lire), 8 000 lire November to February. ☎ (0732) 973039.

FRASCATI

Villa Aldobrandini: park. – Open 9am to 1pm. Closed Saturdays, Sundays and holidays. Apply to the Azienda di Soggiorno, No 1 Piazzi Marconi. ☎ (06) 9420331. Free admission.

G

GAETA

Monte Orlando: Tomb. – Apply to the Azienda di Turismo, Piazza 19 Maggio, Gaeta. ☎ (0771) 461165 or 462767.

GARDA (LAKE)

Boat trips. – From Desanzano to Riva del Garda via Sirmione and Salò. 23 200 lire Rtn (boat), 33 400 lire Rtn (hydrofoil).

GARDONE RIVIERA

Vittoriale. – Open 9am to 12.30pm and 2 to 6pm (5pm October to June). The villa is closed on Mondays. 5 000 lire (park), 15 000 lire (villa and park). ☎ (0365) 20130 or 20347.

GARGANO

Villa Feltrinelli. – Not open to the public.

GENOA

Port: boat trips. – From the main harbour Dei Mille. Departures daily all year depending on the number of visitors. Time: 1 hour. 7 000 lire. ☎ (010) 265712.

Cathedral of St Lawrence: Treasury. – Open Tuesdays, Thursdays, Saturdays 9 to 11.45am and 3 to 5.45pm. 1 000 lire. ☎ (010) 296695.

Palazzo Cataldi. – Open 1 June to 15 September 8am to 2pm, 16 September to 31 May 9am to 6pm. Closed Saturdays and Sundays, 1 January, 25 April, 1 May, 24 June and 15 August. ☎ (010) 2094290 or 2094293.

Town Hall. – Open 8.30 to 11.30am and 2.30 to 4.30pm. Closed Saturday afternoons, Sundays and public holidays. ☎ (010) 20981.

Palazzo Bianco. – Open all year 9am to 7pm (12 noon Sundays). Closed Mondays and holidays. 4 000 lire. ☎ (010) 291803 or 282641.

Palazzo Rosso. – Open all year 9am to 7pm (12pm Sundays). Closed Mondays and holidays. 4 000 lire, free on Sundays. ☎ (010) 282641.

Royal Palace. – Guided tours (2 hours) daily 9am to 1.30pm. Closed 1 May. 4 000 lire. ☎ (010) 206851.

Palazzo Spinola Gallery. – Open all year 9am to 7pm (1pm Sundays and holidays). Closed Monday afternoons. 4 000 lire. ☎ (010) 294661.

Villetta Di Negro: Chiossone Museum. – Open 9am to 6pm (12.30pm Sundays and holidays, 5pm in winter). Closed Mondays, Sunday afternoons, 1 January, Easter, 1 May and Christmas. 4 000 lire. ☎ (010) 542285.

Castelletto. – By lift, daily all day. 400 lire.

GRADARA

Rocca. – Open July to September Tuesdays to Saturdays 9am to 7pm, Mondays 9am to 2pm, Sundays 9am to 1pm; October to June daily 9am to 2pm (1pm Sundays). 6 000 lire. ☎ (0541) 964181.

GRAN PARADISO NATIONAL PARK

Excursions with guide. – The ENTE Parco Nazionale Gran Paradiso organises guided excursions in collaboration with the Il ROC association. Apply to Centro Visitatori di Noasca (Noasca Information Centre). ☎ (0124) 90070.
The Parnassius Apollo Trekking also organises weekend or weeklong excursions all year. Apply to Mr. Gianni Tamiozzo c/o Parnassius Apollo Club, No 5 Via IV Novembre, 10080 SALASSA (To), ☎ (0124) 36535 (Tuesdays during working hours or after 8pm).

Information Centres reached from the main Valle d'Aosta road:

Rhêmes-Notre-Dame: Open July and August. Specialisation: vultures.

Degioz (by the Val Savarenche road): Open in summer and some Sundays and holidays the rest of the year.

Valnontey (turn right in Cogne): Apply at the « Paradisia » alpine botanical gardens, open mid-June to mid-September.

Information Centres reached from the Locana road:

Ronco Canavese (turn right at Ponte Canavese): open in summer and some Sundays and holidays the rest of the year. Specialisation: chamois.

Noasca (turn right at Ponte Canevese): open all year. Specialisation: geological features of the park.

Ceresole Reale (22km – 13 3/4 miles from Locana past Noasca): open July, August and some Sundays and holidays the rest of the year. Specialisation: ibex.

GRECCIO

Monastery. – Open all year 9am to 12.30pm and 2.30 to 6.30pm.

GROSSETO

Maremma Art and Archaeological Museum. – Open 9am to 1pm and 4 to 7.30pm. Closed Sunday afternoons, Wednesdays, 1 January and Christmas. 4 000 lire, free on Sundays. ☎ (0564) 27290.

GROTTA GIGANTE

Cave and Museum. – Guided tours (3/4 hour); March and October every 1/2 hour from 9am to 12 noon and 2 to 5pm; April and September every 1/2 hour form 9am to 12 noon and 2 to 7pm; November to February at 10am, 11am, 12 noon, 2.30pm, 3.30pm and 4.30pm. Closed Mondays and 1 January. 8 000 lire (in summer the charge includes Rtn journey by train from Trieste and bus No 45). ☎ (040) 327312.

GUBBIO

Consuls' Palace. – Open daily April to September 9am to 12.30pm and 3.30 to 6pm, October to March 9am to 1pm and 3 to 5pm. Closed 1 January and Christmas. 4 000 lire. ☎ (075) 92371.

Ducal Palace. – Open 8am to 2pm. Visitors are temporarily admitted only to the courtyard. ☎ (075) 9275872.

Cathedral: Episcopal Chapel. – Open 8am to 12 noon and 3 to 6pm.

H - I - J

HERCULANEUM

Ruins. – Open all day 9am to one hour before sunset. Ticket office closes one hour earlier. The theatre is closed for restoration. 8 000 lire. ☎ (081) 8611051 or 7390963.

ISEO (LAKE)

Boat trips. – From Sarnico or Iseo departures late mornings and return late afternoons; Meals are available on board to visitors who tour the lake. Stops at Lovere and Monte Isola; time: about 6 hours; 12 300 lire, meal: 14 000 lire. From Iseo afternoon excursions to the 3 islands; time: 1 1/2 hours; 5 300 lire. Apply to I.A.T., 2 Lungolago Marconi, Iseo. ☎ (030) 980209 or 981361.

ISSOGNE

Castle. – Open March to September 9am to 6pm, October to February 9am to 12.30pm and 2 to 5.30pm. Closed Mondays and afternoon of 1 January. 4 000 lire. ☎ (0125) 929373.

JESI

Picture Library. – Open July and August 9am to 1pm and 5 to 11pm, September to June 9am to 7pm. Sundays and holidays 9am to 1pm only. Closed Mondays, Easter, 1 May, 1 August and Christmas. ☎ (0731) 58342/343/345.

L

LAKE DISTRICT

There is a wide choice of excursions by boat or hydrofoil (aliscafo) on the different lakes. Look under the name of each lake where some of these trips will be mentioned. Apply to the local tourist information centres for further information.

LAVENO NOMBELLO

Cable-car to Sasso del Ferro. – The cable-car operates April to September 9.30am to 6pm (7pm Saturdays, Sundays and holidays); October to March 9.30am to 5pm, only Saturdays, Sundays and holidays. 9 000 lire Rtn. ☎ (0332) 668012.

LECCE

Provincial Museum. – Open all year 9am to 1.30pm and 4 to 7.30pm. Closed Saturdays and public holidays. 1 000 lire, free on Sundays. ☎ (0832) 27415 or 47025.

LORETO

Picture Gallery. – Open all year 9am to 1pm and 3 to 6pm. Closed Fridays, 1 January, Easter, 1 May, 15 August and Christmas. 3 000 lire. ☎ (071) 970291.

LOVERE

Tadini Museum. – Open 1 May to 3 October 3 to 6pm; also Sundays and holidays 10am to 12 noon. 5 000 lire. ☎ (035) 960132.

LUCCA

Casa Guinigi: Tower. – Open April to September 9am to 7.30pm and October to March 10am to 4.30pm. 3 000 lire. The house itself is not open to the public. ☎ (0583) 53888.

Palazzo Mansi: National Museum. – Open 9am to 7pm (1.30 pm Sundays and holidays). Closed Mondays, 1 January, 1 May and Christmas. 6 000 lire. ☎ (0583) 55570.

Villa Guinigi: National Museum. – Open 9am to 2pm (1.30pm Sundays and holidays). Closed Mondays, 1 January, 1 May and Christmas. 4 000 lire. ☎ (0583) 46033.

LUCERA

Roman Amphitheatre and Museum. – Open daily 9am to 1pm and also Tuesdays and Fridays 3 to 6pm October to May and 4 to 7pm June to September. Closed Mondays, Easter, 15 August, 25 and 26 December. 500 lire. ☎ (0881) 547041.

LUGANO (LAKE)

Boat trips. – Tour of the lake, « Gran Giro del Lago »: daily March to mid-October, departure from Lugano 2.35pm and return at 5.15pm. 25.60 Swiss Francs. For information on other excursions apply to the Società Navigazione del Lago di Lugano. ☎ (091) 515223 in Lugano, Switzerland.

M

MAGGIORE (LAKE)

Boat trips. – Arona-Locarno: 24 000 lire Rtn. Intra to Laveno: 4 600 lire. Intra-Locarno: 20 000 lire Rtn (outward trip by boat, return trip by hydrofoil). One, three and seven day tickets are available, allowing unlimited travel for the given period: 18 600 lire for one day, 37 000 lire for three days and 51 000 lire for seven days.

MALCESINE

Monte Baldo. – By cable-car daily 8am to 7pm. Departures every 1/2 hour. Time: 1/4 hour. Change at San Michele. Closed for 15 days after Easter and Christmas. 12 000 lire Rtn. ☎ (045) 7400206 or 7400044.

MALCONTENTA

Villa Foscari. – Open May to October, Tuesdays, Saturdays and first Sunday of each month 9am to 12 noon. 10 000 lire. ☎ (041) 5470012.

MANSI (VILLA)

Open late March to late September 9am to 1pm and 3.30 to 8pm, late September to late March 10am to 12.30pm and 3.30 and 5pm. Clsed Mondays. Park and villa: 4 000 lire, park: 3 000 lire. ☎ (0583) 928114 or 920234.

MANTUA

Ducal Palace. – Open 9am to 1pm and 2.30 to 5pm, Sundays and Mondays 9am to 1pm only. Closed 1 January, 25 April, 1 May, 15 August and 25 December. 10 000 lire. ☎ (0376) 320283 or 320586.

Rotonda di San Lorenzo. – Open daily 10.30am to 12.30pm and 2.30 to 4.30pm. Closed 1 January, 25 April, 1 May, 15 August and 25 December. Donations welcome.

Palazzo del Te. – Open daily 10am to 6pm. Closed Mondays, 1 January, 25 April, 1 May, 15 August and 25 December. 5 000 lire. ☎ (0376) 323266.

Teatro Accademico. – Open all year 9am to 12.30pm and 3 to 5.30pm. 1 000 lire. Closed Sundays, 1 January, 25 April, 1 May, 15 August and 12 December. ☎ (0376) 327653.

Palazzo d'Arco. – Open March to October, Thursdays, Saturdays, Sundays 9am to 12 noon and 3 to 5pm, Tuesdays, Wednesdays and Fridays 9am to 12 noon. November to February, Saturdays, Sundays 9am to 12 noon and 2.30 to 4pm, Thursdays 9am to 12 noon. Closed 1 January, 25 April, 1 May, 15 August and 25 December. 4 000 lire. ☎ (0376) 322242.

MARLIA

Villa Reale: Gardens. – Guided tours (1 hour) March to September at 10am, 11am, 3pm, 4pm, 5pm and 6pm. July to September open only on Tuesdays, Thursdays and Sundays. 5 000 lire. ☎ (0583) 30108.

MARMOLADA MASSIF

Cable-car from Malga Ciapela. – Daily from 10 February to 1 May and 10 June to 30 September, 9am to 4pm. 28 000 lire. ☎ (0437) 722144 or 722145.

MARMORE WATERFALL

Access. – November to March 3 to 4.30pm Sundays and holidays, 1 January and 7, 24, 25, 26, 31 December. Second fortnight in April, September and October, Saturdays 5 to 9pm, Sundays and holidays 10.30am to 12.30pm and 3 to 9pm. May to August Sundays and holidays and 22 May and 16 August 10am to 1pm and 3 to 10pm; Saturdays 5 to 9.30pm. Also Mondays, Wednesdays and Fridays from March to May 11.45am to 12.30pm and 3.15 to 4pm. From 1 July to 15 September on working days 11am to 12.30pm and 5 to 6.30pm; 16 to 30 September 11am to 12.30pm. ☎ (0744) 43047.

MASER

Villa. – Open Tuesdays, Saturdays, Sundays and holidays 2 to 5 pm. Closed Easter Sunday, and 25 December to 7 January. The villa may be closed in winter. 6 000 lire. ☎ (0423) 565002.

MASSA MARITTIMA

Municipal Museum. – Open April to September 10am to 12.30pm and 3.30 to 7pm, October to March 9am to 1pm and 3 to 5pm. Closed Mondays (the picture gallery is temporarily closed). 1 500 lire. ☎ (0566) 902289.

Mining Museum. – Open April to September 10am to 12.30pm and 3 to 7pm. Closed October to March. 2 500 lire. ☎ (0566) 902289.

MATERA

San Pietro Caveoso. – Closed temporarily for restoration.

Ridola National Museum. – Open 9am to 1pm. 4 000 lire. ☎ (0835) 311239.

MERANO

Princes' Castle. – Open April to October weekdays 9am to 12 noon and 2.30 to 5.50pm. Closed Sundays, Easter, Whitsun and 15 August. 1 700 lire. ☎ (0473) 37834.

MERANO 2000

Cable-car. – 25 December to 30 March 9am to 5pm (Sundays and holidays 8.30am to 6pm), 15 May to 31 October 9am to 5pm. 17 500 lire Rtn. ☎(0473) 34821.

MILAN

Cathedral: ☎ (02) 72022656 or 86463456. Open 7am to 7pm, Sundays 1.30 to 4.30pm.

Baptistry under the parvis. – Open all year 10am to 12.30pm and 3 to 5pm. Closed Mondays, 1 May and 15 August. Donations welcome.

Treasury. – Open daily 9.30am to 12 noon and 1 to 6pm. 1 000 lire.

Walk on the Roof. – Open daily 9am to 5.45pm (4.15pm 15 November to 15 February). Ascent on foot: 3 000 lire; by lift: 5 000 lire. ☎ (02) 72022656.

Cathedral Museum. – Open 9.30am to 12.45pm and 3 to 6pm. Closed Mondays except holiday Mondays, 1 January, Easter, 1 May, 15 August and 25 December. 5 000 lire. ☎ (02) 860358.

Scala Museum. – Open weekdays 9am to 12 noon and 2 to 6pm, Sundays and holidays 9.30am to 12 noon and 2.30 to 6pm. Closed Sundays from November to April and on some holidays. 5 000 lire. ☎ (02) 8053418.

Brera Picture Gallery. – Open weekdays 9am to 2pm, Sundays and holidays 9am to 1pm, Wednesdays 9am to 2pm and 3 to 5.30pm. Closed Mondays and public holidays. 8 000 lire. ☎ (02) 862634. As the gallery is being reorganised some exhibits may be in a different location and some rooms may be closed.

Castle of the Sforzas. – Open 9.30am to 7.30pm (5.30pm in winter). Closed ast Thursdays in the month, 1 January, Easter, 1 May, 15 August and Christmas. ☎ (02) 8059154 or 62083963.

Ambrosiana Library and Picture Gallery. – Closed for restoration. ☎ (02) 800146.

Poldi-Pezzoli Museum. – Open 9.30am to 12.30pm and 2.30 to 6pm (7.30pm Saturdays). Closed Mondays all year, Sunday afternoons April to September, Easter Sunday and Monday, 1 May, 15 August, 1 November, 25 and 26 December and afternoons of 6 January, 25 April, 7 and 8 December. 5 000 lire. ☎ (02) 794889 or 796334.

Modern Art Gallery. – Open 9.15am to 12.15pm and 2.15 to 5.15pm. Closed Tuesdays, 1 January, Easter, 1 May, 15 August and Christmas. ☎ (02) 8059154 or 62083963.

Leonardo da Vinci National Museum of Science and Technology. – Open daily 9.30am to 4.50pm. Closed Mondays (except holiday Mondays), 1 January, Easter, 1 May, 15 August and 25 December. 4 000 lire. ☎ (02) 48010040.

Church of St Mary of Grace: Refectory. – Open 9am to 1.15pm. Closed Mondays. 10 000 lire. ☎ (02) 4987588.

Church of St Maurice: Archaeological Museum. – Open 9.30am to 7.30pm. Closed last Monday in the month 1 January, Easter, 1 May, 15 August and 25 December. ☎ (02) 8053972.

Church or St Lawrence: Chapel of Sant'Aquilino. – Open 9am to 12 noon and 3 to 5.30pm. Sundays and holidays 10.15 to 11.15am and 3 to 4pm. Donations welcome. ☎ (02) 8370991.

MIRA

Villa Widmann-Foscari-Rezzonico. – Open March to October 9am to 7pm, November to February 9am to 1pm and 2.30 to 6pm. Closed Mondays, 6 000 lire. ☎ (041) 423552.

MIRAMARE

Castle. – Open daily (time: 1/2 hour): mid-June to September 9am to 1.30pm and 2.30 to 6pm, October to mid-June 9am to 1.30pm only (12.30pm Sundays and holidays). **Gardens:** 9am to 5pm in winter and 8am to 7pm in summer. Closed Mondays. 3 000 lire (for museum). ☎ (040) 224143.

MISURINA (LAKE)

Toll-road. – 15 000 lire Rtn per car (including driver) and 3 500 lire per passenger.

MODENA

Cathedral Museum. – By appointment. ☎ (059) 217130 or 216078 (phone between 1 and 8pm). Closed Sundays and holidays. Donation welcome.

Este Library. – Open 9am to 1pm. Closed Sundays, week before Easter and first two weeks in September. ☎ (059) 222248.

Este Gallery. – Open 9am to 2pm (1pm Sundays and 7pm Thursdays and Saturdays. Closed Mondays. 4 000 lire. ☎ (059) 222145 or 235004.

MONTE CASSINO

Abbey. – Open all year 9am to 12 noon and 3 to 6pm. ☎ (0776) 26529.

Museum. – Open all year 9am to 12 noon and 3 to 6pm. 2 000 lire. ☎ (0776) 26529.

National Archaeological Museum. – Open all year 8am to 5pm. ☎ (0776) 301168.

MONTECATINI TERME

Museum of Modern Art. – Open April to June 3 to 6pm (closed Sundays), July to September 4 to 7pm (closed Mondays), October to March Fridays and Saturdays only 3 to 6pm. ☎ (0572) 78211.

MONTECCHIO MAGGIORE

Villa Cordellini-Lombardi. – Open Wednesdays, Saturdays and Sundays 9am to 12 noon and 3 to 6pm from 13 April to 18 July and 17 August to 15 October. 5 000 lire. ☎ (0444) 399141.

MONTEFALCO

Communal Tower. – Open all year 9.30am to 1.30pm and 3.30 to 6.30pm. Apply to Mr. Arnaldo Pietrangeli, 15 Piazza del Comune. 1 000 lire.

St Francis' Church. – Open 10am to 1pm and 4 to 7pm (3 to 6pm October to May). Closed Mondays. 5 000 lire. ☎ (0742) 79598 or 79122.

MONTE ISOLA

Access by boat. – From Iseo daily June to September every 1/2 hour, October to May every hour, 5 300 lire Rtn. From Sulzano all year every 1/4 hour, 3 200 lire Rtn. It is also possible to reach the island from other lakeside towns. ☎ (030) 980209.

MONTE OLIVETO MAGGIORE

Abbey. – Open 9.15am to 12.30pm and 3.15 to 6.30pm (5pm the rest of the year). ☎ (0577) 707017.

MONTEPULCIANO

Town Hall. – Open all year 8am to 2pm. Closed Sundays and holidays. ☎ (0578) 757442.

Municipal Museum. – Open April to October 9.30am to 12.30pm and 3 to 6pm. Closed Mondays, Tuesdays, Easter, 25 April, 1 May and 15 August, 3 000 lire. ☎ (0578) 716935.

Madonna di San Biagio. – Open June to September 9am to sunset, October to May 3pm to sunset. Sundays and holidays all year 9am to Sunset. ☎ (0578) 757442.

MONTE SANT'ANGELO

Tomb of Rotharis. – Open all year 8.30am to 12.30pm and 2.30 to 5pm. Apply to the caretaker. Gratuity. ☎ (0884) 61008.

MONZA

Cathedral: Treasury. – Open 9am (10am Sundays and holidays) to 12 noon and 3 to 6pm. Closed Mondays. 4 000 lire. ☎ (039) 323404.

Royal Villa: Park. – Open daily 7am to 7pm October to March and 7am to 8.30pm April to September. ☎ (039) 384113.

MORTOLA INFERIORE

Hanbury Gardens. – Open October to May 10am to 5pm, June to September 9am to 7pm; ticket office closes one hour earlier. Closed Wednesdays in winter. 8 500 lire. ☏ (0184) 229507 or 229852.

MURANO

Glass Museum. – Open all year: April to October 9am to 7pm, November to March 9am to 4pm. Closed 1 January, 1 May and 25 December. 5 000 lire. ☏ (041) 739586.

N

NAPLES

St Charles Theatre. – Guided tours (1/2 hour) by appointment. Closed Mondays. It is advisable to book at least one day in advance by contacting the theatre's Public Relations Office. ☏ (081) 7972111.

Royal Palace. – Open July to September 9am to 7.30pm, October to June 9am to 1.30pm. Closed 1 January, 25 April, 1 May, first Sunday in June, 15 August and 25 December. 3 000 lire. ☏ (081) 413888.

Egg Castle. – Apply to: Provveditore alle Opere Pubbliche (Public Works Department) per la Campania, 21 Via Marchese Campodisola.

St Clare's Church: cloisters. – Open all year 8.30am to 12.30pm and 4 to 6.30pm. Closed Sunday and holiday afternoons. ☏ (081) 5526209 or 5526280.

Chapel of San Severo. – Open 10am to 1pm and 5 to 7pm. Closed Wednesdays and Sunday, Tuesday and holiday afternoons. 3 000 lire. ☏ (081) 5518470.

National Archaeological Museum. – Open daily April to September 9am to 7pm (1pm Sundays and holidays), October to March 9am to 2pm. 8 000 lire. The following rooms are undergoing reorganisation and may be temporarily closed: Rooms VIII to XVI, Coloured Marble Gallery, Greek Portraits and Emperors' Galleries, Rooms XC to XCV. ☏ (081) 440166.

Carthusian Monastery of St Martin. – Open 9am to 1pm. Closed Mondays, 1 January, 1 May and 25 December. 6 000 lire. ☏ (081) 5781769.

Capodimonte Palace and National Gallery. – Open 9am to 2pm (1pm Sundays and holidays). Closed Mondays, 1 January, 1 May and 25 December. 8 000 lire. ☏ (081) 7441307.

Villa Floridiana. – Park: open all year 9am to 1 hour before sunset. Closed 1 January, 25 April, 1 May, 15 August and Christmas. ☏ (081) 5781776. **Museum:** open 9am to 2pm (1pm Sundays and holidays). Closed Mondays, 1 January, 25 April, 1 May, 15 August and Christmas. 4 000 lire. ☏ (081) 5788418.

Catacombs of St Januarius. – Guided tours Fridays to Sundays at 9.30am, 10.15am, 11.15am and 11.45am. 4 000 lire.

Cathedral. – Chapel of St Januarius: Open 8am to 12.30pm and 4.30 to 7.30pm (5 to 7pm Sundays). 4 000 lire. ☏ (081) 449097.

Basilica of Santa Restituta. – Same opening times and charges as for the Chapel of St Januarius. Closed Tuesdays, Sunday afternoons, Easter and 26 December.

Cuomo Palace. – Open all year 9am to 2pm (1pm Sundays). Closed Mondays and public holidays. 4 000 lire. ☏ (081) 203175.

Aquarium. – Open March to October 9am to 6pm and November to February 9am to 2pm (6pm Sundays and holidays). Closed Mondays and 15 August. 2 000 lire. ☏ (081) 5833222.

NONANTOLA

Abbey. – Open 7am to 12 noon and 2 to 7pm. ☏ (059) 549025.

NOVACELLA

Monastery. – Guided tours (1 hour) all year at 10am, 11am, 12 noon, 2pm, 3pm and 4pm. Closed Sundays and holidays. 2 500 lire. ☏ (0472) 36189.

*The current **Michelin Red Guide Italia** offers*
a selection of pleasant hotels in convenient locations.

Each entry specifies the facilities available
(gardens, tennis courts, swimming pool, beach facilities)
and the annual opening and closing dates.

There is also a selection of establishments recommended for their
cuisine – well-prepared meals at moderate prices; stars for good cooking.

O

ORTISEI

Alpe di Suisi. – By cable-car: in winter all day from 8.30am to 4pm, in summer every 1/2 hour from 7.30am to 12 noon and 1.30 tp 7pm. Closed early November to mid December and one week after Easter. 10 500 lire Rtn. ☎ (0471) 796218.

ORVIETO

Palace of the Popes: Cathedral Museum. – Closed for restoration. ☎ (0763) 42477.

St Patrick's Well. – Open June to late September 10am to 7pm, the rest of the year 10am to 6pm. Closed Mondays. 6 500 lire. ☎ (0763) 43768.

Faina Archaeological Museum. – Open April to September 9am to 1pm and 3 to 6.30pm, October to March 9am to 1pm and 2.30 to 4.30pm. Closed Mondays, 1 January, 1 November, 25 December and afternoon of 2 November, 24 and 31 December. 3 000 lire. ☎ (0763) 41511.

OSTIA

Excavation Site. – Open daily March to September 9am to 6pm, October to March 9am to 4pm. Ticket office closes one hour earlier. Closed 1 May. 8 000 lire. ☎ (06) 5650022 or 5651405.

Museum. – Same ticket as for the excavation site but the museum closes at 1pm.

OTRANTO

South Coast: Grotta Zinzulusa. – Near Castro Marina. Open all year. There is no admission when the sea is rough. 4 000 lire. For further information apply to Pro Loco (local tourist office) in Castro, ☎ (0836) 97005.

P

PADUA

The ticket « Vivi il Museo » (10 000 lire) which gives access to all museums in Padua is available from all the town's museums.

Scrovegni Chapel: Frescoes by Giotto. – Same admission times and charges as for the Municipal Museum.

Municipal Museum. – Open April to October 9am to 7pm, November to March 9am to 6pm. Closed Mondays (except holiday Mondays), 1 January, 1 May, 15 August, 25 and 26 December. 8 000 lire (ticket also valid for Scrovegni Chapel). ☎ (049) 8751153.

The Saint's Basilica. – Open 6.30am to 7pm (7.30pm April to September). Apply at the sacristy for guided tours of the basilica or to view the high altar. ☎ (049) 663944.

St George's Oratory and Scuola di Sant'Antonio. – Open February to November 8.30am to 12.30pm and 2.30 to 6.30pm, December and January 9am to 12.30pm. 1 000 lire. ☎ (049) 875235.

Law Courts. – Open April to October 10am to 6pm, November to March 10am to 4pm. Closed Mondays, 1 January, 1 May, 15 August, 25 and 26 December. 4 000 lire. ☎ (049) 8205006.

University: Teatro Anatomico. – Closed for restoration.

Botanical Gardens. – Open April to October 9am to 1pm and 3 to 6pm, November to March 9am to 1pm only. Closed Sunday afternoons and holidays in winter. 3 000 lire. ☎ (049) 656614.

PAESTUM

Museum. – Same admission times and charges as for the ruins. Closed Mondays.

Ruins. – Open daily 9am to 6pm (4pm October to March). 3 000 lire (including access to the museum). ☎ (0828) 811023.

PALLANZA

Villa Taranto. – Open daily April to October 8.30am to 7.30pm. Ticket office closes at 6.30pm. 7 000 lire. ☎ (0323) 44555.

PALMI

Municipal Museum. – Open all year 8.30am to 1.30pm, Mondays and Wednesdays 3 to 6pm. Closed Saturdays, Sundays and holidays. ☎ (0966) 23530 or 411020.

PAOLA

Monastery. – Open all year 9am to 1pm and 3 to 6.30pm. ☎ (0984) 390585.

Times and charges

PARMA

St John the Evangelist's Church: Convent cloisters. – Open all year 9.30am (10am Sundays and holidays) to 12 noon and 3.30 to 6pm. 3 000 lire. ☎ (0521) 282254.

St John the Evangelist's Church: Pharmacy. – Open 9am to 2pm. Closed Mondays, 1 January, Easter Monday, 25 April, 1 May, 15 August and 25 December. 4 000 lire. ☎ (0521) 233617.

National Museum of Antiquities. – Open 9am to 2pm (1pm Sundays and holidays). Closed Mondays (except holiday Mondays), 1 January, 25 April, 1 May, 15 August and Christmas. 5 000 lire (including admission to Farnese Theatre. ☎ (0521) 233718.

National Gallery. – Open 9am to 2pm; ticket office closes one hour earlier. Closed Mondays, 1 January, Easter Monday, 25 April, 1 May, 15 August and 25 December. 10 000 lire. ☎ (0521) 233617.

Farnese Theatre. – Open 9am to 2pm. Closed Mondays. 4 000 lire. ☎ (0521) 233309.

Correggio's Room. – Open 9am to 2pm. Closed Mondays, 1 January, 25 April, Easter Monday, 1 May, 15 August and 25 December. ☎ (0521) 233617.

Glauco-Lombardi Museum. – Open all year weekdays 9.30am to 12.30pm and 4 to 6pm (3 to 5pm October to April), Sundays 9.30am to 1pm. Closed Sunday afternoons, Mondays, 1 January, 25 April, 1 May, July and Christmas. ☎ (0521) 233726 or 233727.

PAVIA

Castle of the Visconti. – Guided tours all year 9am to 1.15pm. Closed Mondays and holidays. 5 000 lire. ☎ (0382) 33853 or 308774.

PAVIA (CARTHUSIAN MONASTERY)

Access. – Guided tours (1 hour) May to August 9 to 11.30am and 2.30 to 6pm; March, April, September and October 9 to 11.30am and 2.30 to 5pm; November to February 9 to 11.30am and 2.30 to 4.30pm. Closed Mondays except holiday Mondays. Donations welcome. ☎ (0382) 925613.

PERUGIA

National Gallery of Umbria. – Open 9am to 1pm and 3 to 7pm. 8 000 lire. ☎ (075) 20316.

National Archaeological Museum of Umbria. – Open weekdays 9am to 1.30pm and 3 to 7pm (6pm October to March), Sundays and holidays 9am to 1pm. 4 000 lire. ☎ (075) 27141, 27142 or 20345.

Exchange Building. – Open March to October 9am to 12.30pm and 2.30 to 5.30pm; November to February 8am to 2pm; Sundays and holidays all year 9am to 12.30pm. Closed Mondays, 1 January, Easter, 1 May, 2 June, 15 August and 25 December. 2 000 lire. ☎ (075) 61379.

Porta Marzia. – Open daily 9am to 1pm and 4 to 7pm.

Hypogeum. – Open 9.30am to 12.30pm and 3 to 5pm (4.30 to 6.30pm July and August). Closed Sunday and holiday afternoons, 1 January, Tuesday after Easter, 25 April, 1 May, 15 August and Christmas. 4 000 lire. ☎ (075) 393329.

PESARO

Rossini's House. – Open daily 9.30am to 12.30pm. Closed Mondays. 2 000 lire. ☎ (0721) 697417.

Municipal Museum. – Open weekdays: May to September 9am to 8pm, October to April 8.30am to 1.30pm; Sundays all year 9.30am to 1pm. Closed Mondays. 4 000 lire, free in December. ☎ (0721) 67815.

Oliveriano Museum. – Apply to the caretaker of the Oliveriana Library from 9.30am to 12.30pm and 3.30 to 6.30pm except Saturday afternoons and Sundays. ☎ (0721) 33344.

PIACENZA

Farnese Palace: Municipal Museum. – Open weekdays except Mondays and Tuesday and Wednesday afternoons 9am to 12.30pm and 3 to 5.30pm; Sundays and holidays 9.30am to 12 noon and 3.30 to 6.30pm. Closed 1 and 6 January, Easter, 25 April, 1 May, 4 July, 15 August, 1 November 8 and 25 December. 4 000 lire. ☎ (0523) 28270 or 26981.

Ricci Oddi Museum of Modern Art. – Open October to February 10am to 12 noon and 2 to 4pm (5pm in March and April); May to September 10am to 12 noon and 3 to 6pm. Closed Mondays, 1 and 6 January, Easter, 1 May, 4 July, 15 August, 1 November, 8, 25, 26 and 31 December. 3 000 lire, free on Sundays. ☎ (0523) 20742.

Alberoni Gallery. – Apply to the Management. ☎ (0523) 63198 or 63342.

PIENZA

Cathedral Museum. – Open March to October 10am to 1pm and 4 to 6pm, November to February 10am to 1pm and 2 to 4pm. Closed Tuesdays. 2 000 lire. ☎ (0578) 748549.

Palazzo Piccolomini. – Guided tours (20 min) March to mid-June 3 to 6pm, mid-June to September 4 to 7pm, October to mid-November 3 to 6pm, mid-November to February 3 to 5pm. Closed Mondays (except holiday Mondays). 2 500 lire. ☎ (0578) 748503.

PIEVE DI CADORE

Museum (Titian's Birthplace). – Open 20 June to 15 September 9.30am to 12.30pm and 4 to 7pm. Closed Mondays. 2 000 lire. ☎ (0435) 32262.

PIONA

Abbey. – Open all year 9am to 12 noon and 1.30 to 6pm. ☎ (0341) 940331.

PISA

Leaning Tower. – Closed temporarily for safety reasons. ☎ (050) 561820 or 560547.

Baptistry. – Open April to September 8am to 8pm, October to March 9am to 5pm. Closed 1 January and Christmas. 5 000 lire. ☎ (050) 561820.

Cemetery. – Open April to September 8am to 8pm, October to March 9am to 5pm. Closed 1 January and Christmas. 5 000 lire. ☎ (050) 561820.

Cathedral Museum. – Open all year 9am to 1pm and 3 to 7pm (5pm October to May). Closed 1 January and Christmas. 5 000 lire. ☎ (050) 560547.

Sinopia Museum. – Open April to September 9am to 1pm and 3 to 7pm (5pm October to March). Closed 1 January and Christmas. 5 000 lire. ☎ (050) 561820.

National Museum. – Open 9am to 7pm (1pm Sundays and holidays). Closed Mondays, 1 January, 25 April, 1 May, first Sunday in June, 15 August and 25 December. 6 000 lire. ☎ (050) 23750.

Church of St Mary of the Thorn. – Open June to September 9am to 12 noon and 4 to 7pm, October to May 7am to 1pm. Closed Sundays and holidays.

PISTOIA

Cathedral: Altar of St James. – The altar is on view only by appointment except during services. ☎ (0573) 25095 or 21059 when the cathedral is open: 7.30am to 1pm and 4 to 7pm.

Baptistry. – Open April to September 9am to 12.30pm and 3.30 to 7.30pm; October to March 9am to 12.30pm. Closed Sunday afternoons, Mondays, 1 January, Easter, 1 May, 15 August and 25 December. ☎ (0573) 25095.

Town Hall: Municipal Museum. – Open 9am to 1pm and 3 to 7pm, Sundays and holidays 9am to 12.30pm only. 4 000 lire, free on Saturday afternoons. Closed Mondays, 1 January, Easter, 1 May, 15 August and 25 December. ☎ (0572) 371278.

Tau Palace: Marino Marini Centre. – Open 9am to 1pm and 3 to 7pm, Sundays and holidays 9am to 12 noon. Closed Mondays, 1 January, afternoon of 6 January, Easter, 1 May, 15 August, 25 July, 1 November, 8 December, 25 and 26 December. ☎ (0572) 30285.

PLOSE

Access. – From the village of Sant'Andrea, southeast of Bressanone, by cable-car to Valcroce (in winter and in July, August and September) and chair-lift to Plose (the chair-lift operates only in winter and early spring). For further information apply to the tourist information centre in Bressanone. ☎ (0472) 36401. For information on snow conditions ☎ 30595.

POGGIO BUSTONE

Monastery. – Open all year 9am to 7pm. Donations welcome.

POMPEII

The Dead City. – Open 9am to one hour before sunset (between 3.45 pm in December and 8pm in June, July and early August). Ticket office closes one hour earlier. The site may close on some public holidays such as 1 January, 25 April and Christmas. 10 000 lire (including the Villa of the Mysteries). ☎ (081) 8611051 or 8610744.
The following buildings may be closed temporarily: Antiquarium, House of the Cryptoportico, Villa of Julia Felix, House of the Golden Cherubs, House of Ara Massima, House of the Tragic Poet and House of Pansa. This list may vary depending on the excavation and restoration programme and short-term studies carried out on the site.

POMPOSA

Abbey. – Open 7.30am to 12 noon and 2 to 7pm. ☎ (0533) 710100.

Times and charges

POPPI

Castle. – Closed for restoration. ☎ (0575) 52268.

PORTOFINO

Castle. – Open all year 10am to 6pm. Closed Tuesdays. 2 000 lire. ☎ (0185) 269046.

PORTOFINO VETTA

Access. – Private toll-road: 3 000 lire for car and driver and 500 lire per passenger.

PORTONOVO

Church of Santa Maria. – While restoration work is being carried out guided tours 6 to 8pm in July and August. To visit at other times apply to the tourist information centre at the Hotel Fortino Napoleonico. ☎ (071) 801124 or 801314.

POSSAGNO

Temple of Canova. – Open May to September 9am to 12 noon and 3 to 6pm (7pm Sundays), October to April 9am to 12 noon and 2 to 5pm. Closed Mondays (except holiday Mondays), 1 January, Easter and Christmas. 3 500 lire. ☎ (0423) 544323.

POZZUOLI

Amphitheatre. – Open all year 9am to one hour before sunset. 4 000 lire. ☎ (081) 5266007.

Solfatara. – Open daily 9am to one hour before sunset. 4 000 lire. ☎ (091) 5262341.

PRATO

Cathedral Museum. – Open 9.30am to 12.30pm and 3.30 to 6.30pm. Closed Sunday afternoons and Tuesdays. 5 000 lire. ☎ (0574) 29339.

R

RAVELLO

Villa Rufolo. – Open daily June to September 9.30am to 1pm and 3 to 7pm, October to May 9.30am to 1pm and 2 to 5pm. Closed 1 January, Christmas and afternoon of 24 and 31 December. 2 000 lire, free on Thursdays. ☎ (089) 857866.

Villa Cimbrone. – Open daily 9am to sunset. 3 000 lire. ☎ (089) 857138.

Cathedral Museum. – Open daily all year 9am to 1pm and 3 to 6.30pm.

RAVENNA

Tomb of Galla Placidia. – Open daily October to March 9.30am to 4.30pm, April to September 9am to 7pm. Closed 1 January and Christmas. 3 000 lire (combined ticket with Church of St Vitalis). ☎ (0544) 34266 or 33696.

Church of St Vitalis. – Same admission times and charges as for the tomb of Galla Placidia.

National Museum. – Open 8.30am to 7pm (5pm October to April), Sundays 8.30am to 1pm. Closed Mondays. 6 000 lire. ☎ (0544) 34424.

Neoni Baptistry. – Open April to September 9am to 7pm, October to March 9.30am to 4.30pm. Closed 1 January and Christmas. 3 000 lire (combined ticket with the Episcopal Palace Museum). ☎ (0544) 33696.

Basilica of St Apollinaris the New. – Open daily April to September 9am to 7pm, October to March 9.30am to 4.30pm. Closed 1 January and Christmas. 3 000 lire.

Arians' Baptistry. – Open 8.30am to 12 noon and 2.30pm to one hour before sunset. ☎ (0544) 34424.

Basilica of St Apollinaris in Classe. – Open daily 8am to 12 noon and 2 to 6.30pm (5pm October to March). ☎ (0544) 34424.

Theodoric's Tomb. – Open mid-April to mid-September 8.30am to 7.30pm; mid-September to October and March to mid-April, 8.30am to 6pm; November to February 8.30am to 1.30pm. 6 000 lire. ☎ (0544) 34424.

Episcopal Palace Museum. – Same admission times and charges as for the Neoni Baptistry.

Municipal Picture Gallery. – Open all year 9am to 1pm and 2.30 to 5.30pm. Closed Mondays, 1 January, 1 May, 1 November and 25 December. 4 000 lire, free on Sundays. ☎ (0544) 35625.

RECANATI

Palazzo Leopardi. – Guided tours 9am to 12 noon and 3 to 5pm in winter, 3pm to 6pm in spring and autumn, 3 to 7pm in summer. Closed 1 January, Easter, 1 May, 15 August and Christmas. 2 000 lire. ☎ (071) 981471.

Picture Gallery. – Open April to September 10am to 1pm and 4 to 7pm (3 to 6pm the rest of the year). Closed Mondays, 1 January, Easter, 1 May, 15 August and 25 December. 1 000 lire. ☎ (071) 982772.

REGGIO DI CALABRIA

National Museum. – Open all year weekdays 9am to 1pm and 3 to 7pm, Sundays and holidays 9am to 12 noon. Closed Monday afternoons. 4 000 lire. ☎ (0965) 812255.

REGGIO NELL'EMILIA

Parmeggiani Gallery. – Open September to June 9am to 12 noon (Sundays 9am to 12 noon and 3 to 6pm), July and August 6.30 to 11.30pm. Closed Mondays. ☎ (0522) 437775.

Madonna della Ghiara. – Open Sundays only 3.30 to 6pm. Donation welcome. At other times apply to the sacristan. ☎ (0522) 439707.

RIVA DEL GARDA

Castle: Museum. – Open weekdays 9am to 1pm and 2.30 to 7.30pm, Sundays and holidays 9am to 1pm and 4.30 to 10pm. Closed Mondays and for 2 to 3 months at the end of the year. 3 000 lire. ☎ (0464) 554490.

RIVOLI

Château: Museum of Contemporary Art. – Open 10am to 7pm. Closed Mondays, 1 January, 1 May and 25 December. 6 000 lire. ☎ (011) 9587256.

RIVOLI VERONESE

Museum. – Open daily 9am to 12 noon and 3 to 6pm. 3 000 lire. ☎ (045) 7281309.

ROME

Palazzo Venezia: Museum. – *First floor.* Open 9am to 1.30pm (12.30pm Sundays and holidays). Closed Mondays, 1 January, 15 August and Christmas. 8 000 lire. Pope Paul II's apartment may be viewed only on guided tours or during temporary exhibitions held there. ☎ (06) 6798865.

Palazzo dei Conservatori. – Open 9am to 1.30pm (1pm Sundays), also Tuesdays, Thursdays and Saturdays 5 to 8pm (11pm Saturdays from 1 April to 30 September). Closed Mondays, 1 January, Easter Sunday, 1 May, 29 June, 15 August and on polling day. 5 000 lire (including admission to the Capitoline Museum). ☎ (06) 67103069.

Capitoline Museum. – Same admission times and charges as for the Palazzo dei Conservatori.

Palazzo Senatorio. – The palace is the town hall and is not open to the public.

Roman Forum. – Open 9am to 6pm except Tuesdays 9am to 1pm. 5 000 lire.

House of Livia. – Apply to the caretaker.

Coliseum. – Access to the galleries 9am to 6pm except Wednesdays 9am to 1pm. 4 000 lire.

Trajan's Markets. – *Entrance: Via Quattro November.* Open 9am to 1.30pm (1pm Sundays and holidays); also in summer 4 to 6.30pm Tuesdays, Thursdays and Saturdays. Closed Mondays, 1 January, Easter, 21 April, 1 May, 29 June, 15 August and Christmas. 2 000 lire.

Castel Sant'Angelo. – Open 9am to 2pm (1pm Sundays and holidays) and 2 to 7.30pm Mondays. Closed 1 January, 1 May and 15 August. Time: 1 1/2 hours. 8 000 lire.

Vatican City – Guided tour only at 10am. Apply to the Ufficio Informazioni Pellegrini e Turisti. 12 000 lire. On certain days the tour also includes St Peter's Basilica or the Sistine Chapel; 25 000 lire.

Vatican: Papal Audiences. – The audiences are held on Wednesdays. To attend, apply (morning) at least 48 hours in advance to the Prefettura della Casa Pontificia It is advisable but not essential to obtain a letter of recommendation from a parish priest.

Vatican Museums. – Open 8.45am to 1.45pm (ticket office closes at 1 pm), to 4.45pm (ticket office closes at 4pm) during week before and after Easter and from 21 May to 28 September (1pm Saturdays). Closed Sundays, 1 and 6 January, 19 March, Easter Sunday and Monday, 1 May, Ascension, Corpus Christi, 29 June, 15 and 16 August, 1 November, 8, 25 and 26 December. The museums are also open on the last Sunday (except holiday Sundays) of each month from 8.45am to 1pm. 10 000 lire. Some rooms may be closed: information posted at the entrance.

St Peter's Basilica:

Ascent to the Dome: Access from the outside to the right of the basilica. 8am to 6pm (5pm in winter). Closed Easter and Christmas. 5 000 lire by lift, 4 000 lire on foot. ☎ (06) 6983462.

Treasury and Historical Museum. – Open 9am to 6pm. 3 000 lire. ☎ (06) 6983465.

Farnese Palace. – Not open to the public.

Pantheon. – Open 9am to 2pm (1pm Sundays and holidays). Closed 1 January and 1 May.

San Luigi dei Francesi. – Open daily 8.30am to 6pm (1pm Thursdays).

Caracalla's Baths. – Open 9am to 6pm (1pm Sundays, Mondays and holidays). Closed 1 January, 1 May and 15 August. 3 000 lire.

St Callistus' Catacombs. – Guided tours 8.30am to 12 noon and 2.30 to 5pm (5.30pm May to September). Closed Wednesdays, 1 January, Easter and Christmas. 4 000 lire. ☎ (06) 5133725.

St Sebastian's Catacombs. – Same admission times and charges as for St Callistus' Catacombs but closed on Thursdays. ☎ (06) 7887035.

Domitilla's Catacombs. – Same admission times and charges as for St Callistus' Catacombs but closed on Tuesdays. ☎ (06) 5110342.

Tomb of Cecilia Metella. – Open 9am to one hour before sunset (1pm Sundays and holidays). Closed Mondays, 1 January and 1 May.

St Cecilia in Trastevere. – Open daily 10am to 12 noon and 4 to 6pm (may close early in winter). Donation welcome.

National Gallery of Modern Art. – Open 9am to 1.30pm. Closed Mondays, 1 January, 25 April, 1 May and Christmas. 4 000 lire.

Borghese Gallery. – Open 9am to 2pm (1pm Sundays and holidays). N.B. Admission times often vary and visits are scheduled every 1/2 hour for groups of 25 people maximum (waiting time about 1/2 hour all year to 1 hour in summer). ☎ (06) 8548577.

National Roman Museum. – Open 9am to 2pm (12.30pm Sundays). Closed Mondays and holidays. 1 000 lire. The greater part of the museum is at present closed for restoration. ☎ (06) 462298.

Villa Giulia National Museum. – Open 9am to 7pm (1pm Sundays and holidays). Closed Mondays, 1 January, 1 May and 25 December. 4 000 lire.

Quirinal Palace. – Open by appointment only. Apply in writing at least 8 working days in advance to the Ufficio Intendenza del Palazzo Quirinale, Via della Dataria, 00187 Roma giving the applicant's name and telephone number. Closed Saturdays, Sundays, holidays and in August.

Baberini Palace. – Open 9am to 2pm (1pm Sundays and holidays). 6 000 lire. ☎ (06) 4814430.

Palazzo Braschi: Rome Museum. – Open 9am to 1.30pm (1pm Sundays and holidays), also 5 to 8pm Tuesdays and Thursdays. Closed Mondays, 1 January, Easter, 21 April, 1 May, 29 June and Christmas. 4 000 lire. The museum is being reorganised and some rooms may be closed.

Palazzo Corsini. – Open 9am to 2pm (1pm Sundays and holidays). 6 000 lire. ☎ (06) 6542323.

Palazzo Doria Pamphili. – Open 10am to 1pm. 5 000 lire plus an additional 3 000 lire for the private apartments (open 10 to 11.45am depending on the number of visitors). Closed Mondays, Wednesdays, Thursdays and holidays.

Palazzo Spada. – Open 9am to 1.30pm (1pm Sundays and holidays). Closed Mondays, 1 January, 25 April, 1 May, 15 August and 25 December. 4 000 lire. ☎ (06) 6861158.

Villa Farnesina. – Open 9am to 1pm. Closed Sundays and holidays. ☎ (06) 6541767.

Museum of Roman Civilisation. – Open 9am to 1.30pm (1pm Sundays), also Thursdays 4 to 7pm. Closed Mondays, 21 April, 1 May, 15 August and 25 December. 4 500 lire.

ROSELLE

Ruins. – Open all year 8am to sunset. ☎ (0564) 402403.

ROSSANO

Diocesan Museum. – Open all year 9am to 1pm and 4 to 6pm. Closed Sunday afternons. Donations welcome. ☎ (0983) 31282.

RUVO DI PUGLIA

Jatta Archaeological Museum. – Closed for restoration.

The main shopping streets are printed
at the head of the street list accompanying town plans.

S

SABBIONETA

Town centre. – Guided tours leaving from the Tourist Information Centre, 31 Via Gonzaga April to September 9am to 12 noon and 2.30 to 6pm (7pm Sundays and holidays), the rest of the year 9am to 12 noon and 2.30 to 5pm (5.30pm Sundays and holidays). The Tourist Information Centre is closed on Mondays in winter, 1 January, 25 December. 7 500 lire. ☎ (0375) 52039.

SACRA DI SAN MICHELE

Abbey. – Open all year 9am to 12.30 (12 noon Sundays and holidays) and 3 to 6pm (5pm October to March). Closed Mondays. Donations welcome. ☎ (011) 939130.

SAN FRUTTUOSO

Access by boat. – Boats from Rapallo or Santa Margherita leave every 1/2 hour; from 8.30am in summer and 10am in winter. 14 000 lire Rtn.
Boats from Portofino or Camogli leave every hour. 9 000 lire Rtn.

SAN GIMIGNANO

Collegiate Church: Chapel of Santa Fina. – Open April to September 9.30am to 12.30pm and 3 to 6pm; October to March 9.30am to 12.30pm and 2.30 to 5.30pm, closed Mondays. Closed 1 and 31 January, Easter, 1 May and Christmas. 7 000 lire (including admission to the People's Palace).

People's Palace. – Same admission times and charges as for the Chapel of Santa Fina. ☎ (0577) 940340.

SAN GIULIO ISLAND

Access by boat. – Boats from Orta leave daily Easter to October every 1/2 hour; the rest of the year about every 3/4 hour (lunch break). Time: 5 minutes. 2 000 lire Rtn. ☎ (0322) 844862 in Borgomanero (8,5km – 5 miles south of the lake).

SAN LEO

Museum and Picture Gallery. – Open May to September 9am to 12 noon and 2 to 6.30pm (5.30pm the rest of the year). 5 000 lire. ☎ (0541) 916231.

SAN MARINO

Government House. – Open March and October 8.30am to 12.30pm and 2.30 to 6pm, May to 15 June and 16 to 30 September 9.30am to 12.30pm and 2.30 to 7pm, 16 June to 15 September 8am to 8pm, November 9am to 12.30pm and 2.30 to 5.30pm, December to February 9am to 12.30pm and 2.30 to 5pm. Closed when the Grand Council is in session (once a month, during the Investiture ceremonies (1 April and 1 October) and on special occasions. 3 000 lire. ☎ (0549) 991385.

Arms Museum. – Same admission times as for Government House. Closed 1 January and Christmas. 3 000 lire. ☎ (0549) 991295.

Museum – Picture Gallery. – Closed temporarily for restoration.

St Francis Museum. – Same admission times and charges as for Government House. Closed 1 January and Christmas. ☎ (0549) 991160.

Coin and Stamp Museum. – Same admission times and charges as for Government House except mid-June to mid-September open 9.15am to 12.30pm and 2.30 to 6.30pm. ☎ (0549) 903958.

SAN MARTINO DELLA BATTAGLIA

Museum and Tower. – Open: January Saturdays and Sundays 9am to 12.30pm and 2.30 to 5.30pm; February to August daily 9am to 1pm and 2.30 to 6.30pm; September to mid-December 9am to 12.30pm and 1.30 to 5.30pm (except Tuesdays). Closed second fortnight in December. 5 000 lire. ☎ (030) 9910370.

SANSEPOLCRO

Municipal Museum. – Open daily 9.30pm to 1pm and 2.30 to 6pm. Closed 1 January, 1 May, 15 August and Christmas. 3 000 lire. ☎ (075) 732218 or 732219.

SANT'ANTIMO

Abbey. – Open April to September 10.30am to 12.30pm and 3 to 6pm, October to March 11am to 12.30pm and 3 to 5pm. ☎ (0577) 835659.

SAN VIGILIO (PUNTA DI)

Villa Guarienti. – Open by appointment. Apply to the Amministrazione Guarienti, San Vigilio, 37016 Garda (VR). ☎ (045) 7255884.

SAN VIVALDO

Sacro Monte. – Guided tours week days 9am to 12 noon and 3pm to sunset, Sundays and holidays 3pm to sunset. ☎ (0571) 69374 or 680114.

TRENTO

Paleo-Christian Basilica. – Same admission times and charges as for the Diocesan Museum but no admission during services, especially on Sunday mornings.

Diocesan Museum. – Open 9.30am to 12.30pm and 2.30 to 6pm. Closed Sundays, holidays and 16 November to 14 February. 2 000 lire (including the basilica). ☎ (0461) 234419.

Castle of Good Counsel. – Open 9am to 12 noon and 2 to 5.30pm (5pm October to March). Closed Mondays, 1 January, Easter, 1 May, 15 August, 1 November and Christmas. 4 000 lire, free first and third Sundays in the month. ☎ (0461) 233770.

TREVISO

Monte di Pietà. – Open all year 9am to 12 noon. Closed Saturdays, Sundays and holidays. ☎ (0422) 654320.

Monastery (near the Church of St Nicholas). – The Dominican Monastery, Seminario Vescovile, Via San Nicolò, is open May to September 8am to 12 noon and 3.30 to 7pm, October to April 9am to 12 noon and 3 to 5.30pm. ☎ (0422) 542322.

Bailo Municipal Museum. – Open all year 9am to 12 noon and 2 to 5pm (9am to 12 noon Sundays and holidays). Closed Mondays, 1 January, Easter, 25 April, 1 May, 15 August, 25 and 26 December. 1 000 lire. ☎ (0422) 51337 or 588442.

TRIESTE

Castle. – Open 9am to 1pm. Closed Mondays, 1 January, Easter, 25 April, 1 May, 15 August and Christmas. 2 000 lire; 1 000 lire for the exterior only. ☎ (040) 308686.

History and Art Museum. – Open 9am to 1pm. Closed Mondays, 1 January, Easter, 25 April, 1 May, 15 August and Christmas. 2 000 lire. ☎,(040) 308686.

Maritime Museum. – Open 9am to 1pm. Closed Mondays, 1 and 6 January, Easter, 25 April, 1 May, 15 August, 1 and 3 November, 8 and 25 December. 2 000 lire. ☎ (040) 304987.

TURIN

Egyptian Museum. – Open 9am to 2pm, also 3 to 7pm in the busy period. Closed Mondays. 3 000 lire. ☎ (011) 544091.

Galleria Sabauda. – Open 9am to 2pm. Closed Mondays, 1 January, 25 April, 24 June, 15 August, 8 and 25 December. 6 000 lire. ☎ (011) 547440.

Palazzo Madama: Museum of Ancient Art. – Closed temporarily for restoration. ☎ (011) 5765.

National Film Museum. – Closed temporarily for reorganisation but may open by appointment. ☎ (011) 4361148 or 4361387.

Royal Palace:

Apartments. – Open all year 9am to 1pm. Closed Mondays. 6 000 lire. ☎ (011) 546731.

Royal Armoury. – Open Tuesdays and Thursdays 9am to 2pm, Wednesdays, Fridays and Saturdays 2.30 to 7.30pm. 3 000 lire. ☎ (011) 543889 or 549543.

Palazzo Carignano: Museum of the Risorgimento. – Open all year 9am to 6.30pm (12.30pm Sundays). Closed Mondays and weekday holidays. 5 000 lire. ☎ (011) 511147 or 513719.

Mole Antonelliana. – The lift operates 9am to 7pm all year. Closed Mondays, 25 and 31 December. 3 000 lire Rtn. ☎ (011) 8398314.

Carlo Biscaretti di Ruffia Motor Museum. – Open all year 10am to 6.30pm. Closed Mondays, 1 to 6 January, 15 August, 25 and 31 December. 7 000 lire. ☎ (011) 677666.

Borgo Medioevale. – Open June to 15 October 9am to 8pm, the rest of the year 9am to 7pm.

TUSCANIA

Church of St Peter: crypt. – Open daily 9am to 7pm. ☎ (0761) 436209.

U

UDINE

Castle. – Open 9.30am to 12.30pm and 3 to 6pm. Closed Sunday afternoons, Mondays and holidays. As the museum is being reorganised admission times and access to some parts of the castle may vary. 3 200 lire. ☎ (0432) 502872.

Cathedral: Oratory of Purity. – Apply to the sacristan all year 7am to 12 noon and 3.30 to 7pm except during services. ☎ (0432) 505302 or 506830.

Archbishop's Palace. – Closed temporarily for restoration of monument.

URBINO

From the parking to the west of the upper town lift service (250 lire) to the foot of the castle.

National Gallery of the Marches. – Open 9am to 2pm (1pm Sundays and holidays). The gallery may open in the afternoon in summer 8 000 lire. ☎ (0722) 2760.

Raphael's House. – Open April to October 9am to 1pm and 3 to 7pm, November to March 9am to 2pm; Sundays and holidays all year 9am to 1pm. Closed Mondays and in February. 4 000 lire.

Churches: St John's and St Joseph's Oratories. – Open all year 10am to 12 noon and 3 to 5pm; 10am to 12 noon Sundays and holidays. 2 000 lire for each oratory. ☎ (0722) 2441.

V

VARENNA

Villa Monastero. – Open mid-April to 10 October 9.30am to 12 noon and 2.30 to 6pm. Closed Tuesdays. 1 500 lire. ☎ (0341) 830129.

VELIA

Ruins. – Open 9am to 6pm (4pm October to March). Closed Mondays. ☎ (0974) 972134.

VENICE

Paying Garages. – Piazzale Roma: 10 000 to 20 000 lire per day depending on engine capacity. ☎ (041) 5222308. Tronchetto: 5 000 lire for the first 3 hours and 10 000 lire for next 9 hours. ☎ (041) 5207555. From July to mid-Ocotber allow at least 1 hour's delay.

Vaporetto. – Omnibus: 1 800 lire. Direct: 2 500 lire. Tourist ticket valid 24 hours from delivery time: 10 000 lire. 3 day-pass: 17 000 lire.

St Mark's Basilica:

Chancel (Pala d'Oro and Treasury). – Open daily 10am to 4pm in winter, 9.30am to 5pm in summer. Closed Sunday mornings and for religious festivals. Treasury: 2 000 lire, Pala d'Oro: 2 000 lire. ☎ (041) 5225205.

Museum of the Basilica. – Open daily May to October 9.30am to 5pm (1 to 5pm Sundays and holidays), November to April 10am to 4pm (1 to 4pm Sundays and holidays). 2 000 lire. ☎ (041) 5225205.

Campanile. – Open May to October 9.30 to 9pm, November to April 10am to 4pm. Closed 1 January and Christmas. 3 000 lire. ☎ (041) 522525.

Doges' Palace. – Open April to October 8.30am to 7pm, November to March 9am to 4pm. Closed 1 January, 1 May and 25 December. 8 000 lire. ☎ (041) 5224951.

Law Courts: Clock Tower. – Closed temporarily for restoration. ☎ (041) 5231879.

Correr Museum. – Open daily April to October 9am to 7pm, November to March 9am to 4pm. Closed 1 January, 1 May and 25 December. 5 000 lire. ☎ (041) 5225625.

Old Library:

Archaeological Museum. – Open daily 9am to 2pm (1pm Sundays and holidays). 4 000 lire. ☎ (041) 5225978.

Marciana Library. – Apply by letter to the offices of Biblioteca Marciana, 7 Piazzetta San Marco, 30134 Venezia.

Palazzo Grassi. – Open 10am to 7pm (6pm in winter) during exhibitions; 6 000 to 8 000 lire depending on the exhibition; 9am to 1pm the rest of the year.

Ca' d'Oro. – Open July to September 9am to 7pm (1.30pm Saturdays, Sundays and Mondays), October to June 9am to 1.30pm (12.30pm Sundays). 4 000 lire. Closed 1 January, Easter and Christmas. ☎ (041) 5238790.

Academy of Fine Arts. – Open April to September 9am to 7pm (2pm Saturdays, Sundays, Mondays), October to March daily 9am to 2pm.

Church of St Mary of Salvation: sacristy. – Open daily 9am to 12 noon and 3 to 6pm (5pm October to mid-March). 1 000 lire. ☎ (041) 5225558 or 5237951.

Church of St George Major: campanile. – Access by lift daily mornings to 12.30pm and afternoons from 2.30pm. 2 000 lire. ☎ (041) 5289900.

Church of Santa Maria Gloriosa dei Frari. – Open 9am to 12 noon and 2.30 to 6pm; Sundays afternoons only 3 to 6pm. 1 000 lire. ☎ (041) 5222637.

Scuola di San Rocco. – Open 28 March to 1 November daily 9am to 1pm and 3.30 to 6.30pm; November to 27 March weekdays 10am to 1pm, Saturdays, Sundays and holidays 10am to 4pm. Closed 1 January, Easter, 2 November and Christmas. 6 000 lire. ☎ (041) 5261849.

Scuola di San Giorgio degli Schiavoni. – Open April to September 9.30am to 12.30pm and 3.30 to 6.30pm (9.30am to 12.30pm Sundays), November to March 10am to 12.30pm and 3.30 to 6pm. Closed Sunday afternoons and Mondays. 4 000 lire. ☎ (041) 5228828.

Scuola dei Carmini. – Open all year weekdays 9am to 12 noon and 3 to 6pm. Closed Sundays, Easter and Christmas. 5 000 lire. ☎ (041) 5289420.

Peggy Guggenheim Collection. – Open 11am to 6pm. Closed Tuesdays and Christmas. 7 000 lire, free Saturdays from 6 to 9pm. ☎ (041) 5206288.

Museum: Venice in the 18C. – Open daily April to October 9am to 7pm, November to March 9am to 4pm. Closed 1 January, 1 May and 25 December. 5 000 lire. ☎ (041) 5224543.

Palazzo Querini-Stampalia. – Open 16 June to 14 September 10am to 12.30pm and 4 to 6.30pm, the rest of the year 10.30am to 12.30pm. Closed Mondays, 1 January, Easter, 25 April, 1 May, 15 August, first Sunday in June and November, and Christmas. 5 000 lire. ☎ (041) 5203433.

Museum of Modern Art (Palazzo Pesaro). – Closed for restoration. ☎ (041) 721127.

Palazzo Labia. – Open Wednesdays, Thursdays and Fridays. Apply in advance to RAI (Italian Television), 275 Campo San Geremia. ☎ (041) 781111.

Naval Museum. – Open 9am to 1pm. Closed Sundays and holidays. 2 000 lire. ☎ (041) 5200276.

San Michele. – Access daily by the vaporetto « Circolare 5 ».

Lagoon: Boat trips. – Many agencies offer excursions of varying length and price to the islands and towns on the lagoon. Departure points: Riva degli Schiavoni near St Mark's Square, the railway station and the car park on Piazzale Roma. Apply on the spot or at the CIT, St Mark's Square.

Brenta Riviera. – See under the heading « Brenta ».

VERONA

Juliet's House. – Open all year 8am to 6.45pm. Closed Mondays, 1 January, Easter, 12 and 25 April, 1 May, 15 August, 1 November, 8, 25 and 26 December. 5 000 lire. ☎ (045) 38303.

Palazzo del Comune: Lamberti Tower. – Open early March to early October 8am to 6.40pm, the rest of the year 8am to 5.30pm. Closed Mondays, 1 January, Easter, 12 and 25 April, 1 May, 15 August, 1 November, 8, 25 and 26 December. 3 000 lire (4 000 lire by lift). ☎ (045) 32726.

Scaliger Tombs. – Closed temporarily for restoration.

Roman Arena. – Same admission times as for Juliet's House except July and August open 8am to 1.30pm only. 5 000 lire, free on first Sunday in the month. ☎ (045) 8003204.

Old Scaliger Castle: Art Museum. – Open 7.30am to 6.40pm. Closed Mondays, 6 January, Easter, 12 and 25 April, 1 May, 15 August, 1 November, 8, 25 and 26 December. 5 000 lire. ☎ (045) 594734.

Church of St Anastasia: Giusti Chapel. – Same admission times as for the church: 7am to 12 noon and 3.30 to 7pm. If the chapel is closed apply to the sacristan. ☎ (045) 8004325.

Roman Theatre. – Open all year: 8am to 1.30pm (6.30pm in summer). Closed Mondays, Easter, 1 May and Christmas. 5 000 lire (including the Archaeological Museum). ☎ (045) 8000360.

Archaeological Museum. – Same admission times and charges as for the Roman Theatre.

Castle of St Peter. – Access to the terrace and garden all year 9am to one hour before sunset. The castle is closed to the public.

Juliet's Tomb. – Same admission times as for Juliet's House. 5 000 lire. ☎ (045) 8000361.

VESUVIUS

Ascent by the west face. – Paying car-park at the end of the road or at Herculaneum, bus service from the railway station, « Circumvesuviana » line. Visitors are strongly advised to be accompanied to the crater by a guide (fee).

VICENZA

Olympic Theatre. – Open 16 March to 15 October 9.30am to 12.20pm and 3 to 5.30pm, 16 October to 15 March 9.30am to 12.20pm and 2 to 4.30pm. Closed Sunday afternoons, 1 January, Easter, 1 May, 15 August, 25 and 26 December and afternoons of 6 January, Easter Monday, 25 April, 1 November and 8 December. 3 000 lire; 5 000 lire including the municipal museum. ☎ (0444) 323781.

Municipal Museum. – Open 9.30am to 12 noon and 2.30 to 5pm. Closed Sunday afternoons, Mondays, 1 January, Easter, 1 May, 15 August, 25 and 26 December and afternoons of 6 January, Easter Monday, 25 April, 1 November and 8 December. 3 000 lire; 5 000 lire including the theatre. ☎ (0444) 321348 or 325071.

Villa Valmarana « ai Nani ». – Open mid-March to mid-November, Sundays and holidays 10am to 12 noon; weekdays: 15 March to 30 April 2.30 to 5.30pm, May to September 3 to 6pm, 1 October to 15 November 2 to 5pm. Closed Easter. 4 000 lire. ☎ (0444) 321803 or 543976.

Rotunda. – Open 15 March to 15 October 10am to 12 noon and 3 to 6pm. Tour of exterior only Tuesdays, Wednesdays, Thursdays: 3 000 lire; also access to interior on Wednesdays: 5 000 lire. To view the interior on other days apply for appointment: ☎ (0444) 321793.

VIGO DI FASSA

Catinaccio Massif. – By cable-car early December to mid-April and mid-June to mid-October. 10 000 lire. ☎ (0462) 63242.

VILLA OPICINA

Access by funicular. – 1 600 lire one-way ticket. Time: 1/2 hour. The funicular operates daily 7.20am to 8.10pm every 22 minutes. ☎ (040) 77951.

VINCI

Museum and Library. – Open June to October 9am to 7pm, the rest of the year 9.30am to 12 noon and 2.30 to 6pm. Closed 1 January, Easter, 1 May, 15 August and Christmas. 5 000 lire. ☎ (0571) 56055.

Leonardo da Vinci's Birthplace. – Open 9.30am to 12 noon and 2.30 to 6pm. Closed Wednesdays, 1 January, Easter, 15 August and Christmas. ☎ (0571) 56055.

VITERBO

Municipal Museum. – Closed temporarily for renovation. ☎ (0761) 340810.

VITTORIO VENETO

Battle Museum. – Open May to September 10am to 12 noon and 4 to 6.30pm, October to April 10am to 12 noon and 2 to 5pm. Closed Mondays, 1 January, Easter and Christmas. 3 000 lire. ☎ (0438) 57695.

VOLTERRA

Picture Gallery. – Open mid-March to late October 9.30am to 1pm and 3 to 6.30pm, early November to mid-March 9.30am to 1pm only. Closed 1 January and Christmas. 5 000 lire, combined ticket with the Etruscan Museum 8 000 lire. ☎ (0588) 87580.

Etruscan Museum. – Open mid-March to late October 9.30am to 1pm and 3 to 6.30pm, early November to mid-March 9am to 2pm. Closed 1 January and Christmas. 8 000 lire. ☎ (0588) 86347.

SARDINIA

CAGLIARI

Cathedral: Santuario. – Open on request mornings and late afternoons. ☎ (070) 66837.

National Archaeological Museum. – Open daily 9am to 2pm and also Wednesdays, Fridays and Saturdays 3.30 to 6.30pm. 4 000 lire. ☎ (070) 654237.

Botanical Gardens. – Open all year 9am to 1pm and also 2 to 7pm Mondays to Fridays April to September. Closed Sundays and holidays. ☎ (070) 657651.

CALA GONONE

Sea Ox Cave. – Guided tours (1 1/2 hours) daily 11am and 3pm from 1 April to 30 June and 1 to 30 September; 9am, 10am, 11am, 3pm and 5pm July and August. 10 500 lire (12 500 lire 20 July to 10 September). ☎ (0784) 96243.

MADDALENA ARCHIPELAGO

Island of Caprera: Museum. – Open all year weekdays 9am to 1pm, Sundays 9am to 12.30pm. Closed Mondays (except holiday Mondays), 1 January, Easter, 25 April, 1 May, first Sunday in June, 15 August, 25 and 26 December (but the exterior may be viewed). 4 000 lire. ☎ (0789) 727162.

NUORO

Museum of Popular Traditions. – Open 9am to 1pm and 3 to 7pm (Sundays 9am to 1pm). Closed Sunday afternoons and Mondays. ☎ (0784) 35561.

PORTO CONTE

Neptune's Cave. – By boat from Alghero Easter to mid-October from 9am (departure times according to demand; in summer every hour with the last trip depending on the cave's closing time. Guided tours of the cave every hour from 9am to 8pm May to September and 9am to 2pm October to April. 9 000 lire. ☎ (079) 979054.

SANT'ANTIOCO ISLAND

Remains of Sulcis and Museum. – Guided tours 9am to 1pm and 3.30 to 7pm (6pm October to May). 5 000 lire. ☎ (0781) 83590. For the catacombs telephone in advance: ☎ (0781) 83044.

SASSARI

Sanna National Museum. – Open daily 9am to 2pm (1.30pm Sundays and holidays) and also 4.30 to 7.30pm the second Wednesday in the month. 4 000 lire. ☎ (070) 272202.

THARROS

Excavation Site and Necropolis. – Open 9am to one hour before sunset. Free admission.

SICILY

AGRIGENTO

Regional Archaeological Museum. – Open mid-June to late September 9am to 7.30pm; open morning only every other Sunday. Late September to mid-June 9am to 1pm and 3 to 5.30pm, closed Sunday and holiday afternoons. ☎ (0922) 29008.

Phalaris' Oratory. – Same admission times as for the Regional Archaeological Museum.

Greco-Roman Quarter. – Open all day. ☎ (0922) 401354.

Pirandello's House. – Open daily 9am to 12 noon and 4 to 8pm. Gratuity. ☎ (0922) 401354.

BAGHERIA

Villa Palagonia. – Guided tours 9am to 12 noon and 3 to 5pm daily except Sunday mornings (service in the chapel). 2 000 lire. ☎ (091) 931653.

CATANIA

Ursino Castle and Museum. – Open all year 9.30am to 1pm (12 noon Sundays). Closed 1 January, Easter, 25 April, 15 August, 25 and 26 December. ☎ (095) 34830.

CEFALU

Mandralisca Museum. – Open all year 9am to 12.30pm and 3.30 to 7pm (6pm November to March). 4 000 lire. ☎ (0921) 21547.

EGADI ISLANDS

Access. – By ferry and hydrofoil from Trapani to Favignana, Levanzo and Marettimo: for details see the Michelin Red Guide Italia.

Favignana: boat trips. – No regular time-table. Apply to the fishermen. Charge: about 40 000 lire for 4 people.

Levanzo: boat trip to the Grotta del Genovese. – Apply to the fishermen at Cala Dogana. 5 000 lire per person.

Marettimo: tour of the island. – Apply to the fishermen. 15 000 lire per person.

ENNA

Castle. – Open July to September 9am to 1pm and 4 to 8pm, October to June 9am to 1pm and 3 to 5pm. Closed Mondays October to June. ☎ (0935) 500962.

ERICE

Castle of Venus. – Open April to September 9am to 1pm and 4 to 6pm, October to March 8.30am to 1.30pm. Closed Sundays and holidays October to March. ☎ (0923) 869122 or 869173.

ETNA

Ascent of Etna. – As the volcano may erupt at any time, tourist facilities (roads, paths, cable-cars and refuge-huts) may be moved or withdrawn. Excursions to the crater may be cancelled in the event of bad weather (fog) or volcanic activity. Upto-date information is available from the Tourist Information Centre at Catania or from S.I.T.A.S., 45 Piazza Vittorio Emanuele at Nicolosi. ☎ (095) 911158.

South face. – Access June to 15 September by cable-car from the Stazione Etna Sud (in front of the Sapienza hut – alt 1 900m) to station at 2 500m altitude and by four-wheel drive vehicle to Torre del Filosofo (alt 3 000m). It is then possible to go near the areas of volcanic activity (guide compulsory). Time: 3 hours for return journey and guided tour. 35 000 lire inclusive. There are buses to Stazione Etna Sud from Catania (30km – 19 miles): departures from the station square at 8am (additional trip at 11.15am in summer). Excursions to Mount Etna may be cancelled on account of bad weather (fog) or volcanic activity. For further information and details regarding evening or night-time excursions to view the sunset or sunrise, apply to the Tourist Information Centre in Catania or to S.I.T.A.S., 45 Piazza Vittorio Emanuele at Nicolosi. ☎ (095) 911158.

Northeast face. – Excursions to the crater by fou-wheel drive vehicles from Piano Provenzana. Time: 3 hours Rtn. 35 000 lire including guide. For further information and details regarding night-time excursions, apply to S.T.A.R., 233 Via Roma, Linguaglossa, ☎ (095) 643180; at Piano Provenzana, ☎ (095) 643430; or the Tourist Information Centre (Pro Loco), 5 Piazza Annunziata, Linguaglossa, ☎ (095) 643094.

GELA

Greek Fortifications. – Open all year 9.30am to one hour before sunset.

Regional Archaeological Museum. – Open all year 9.30am to 1.30pm. ☎ (0933) 912626.

LIPARI ISLANDS

Lipari Museum. – Open May to September 9am to 2pm and 3 to 8pm, October to April 9am to 2pm (1pm Sundays and holidays). ☎ (090) 9880174.

Boat trips. – Excursions to all the islands mornings and afternoons; in season 3 to 4 sailings daily. Vulcano: 16 000 lire, Panarea: 30 000 lire, Stromboli: 40 000 lire, Alicudi and Filicudi: 50 000 lire.

MARSALA

Archaeological Museum. – Open all year 9.30am to 1pm.

MESSINA

Museum. – Open daily 9am to 1pm and also 3 to 7pm Tuesdays, Thursdays and Saturdays. Closed 1 January, Easter Monday, 15 August and Christmas. 2 000 lire. ☎ (090) 658605.

MONREALE

Cathedral. – Open 8am to 12.30pm and 3.30 to 6.30pm.

Cloisters. – Open April to September 9am to 7pm (12.30pm Sundays), October to March 9am to 1.30pm (12.30pm Sundays). 2 000 lire. ☎ (091) 6404413.

Terraces. – Guided tours daily 9am to 12 noon and 4 to 5pm. Time: 1/2 hour. 2 000 lire. ☎ (091) 6404413.

MORGANTINA

Ruins. – Open 8am to 7pm (6pm November to March).

Aidona Museum. – Open July to September 9am to 1.30pm and 3 to 6pm; the rest of the year 9am to 1.30pm.

PALERMO

La Martorana. – Open 8.30am to 1pm and 3.30 to 7pm (5.30pm October to March). Closed Sunday and holiday afternoons. ☎ (091) 616192.

San Cataldo. – Apply to the caretaker of La Martorana except Sundays and holidays. ☎ (091) 616192.

Cathedral: Treasury. – Open 10am to 12 noon and 3 to 5.30pm (except during services). 1 000 lire. ☎ (091) 334373.

Palace of the Normans. – Palatine Chapel: open Mondays to Fridays 9am to 12 noon and 3 to 5pm, Sundays 9 to 10am and 12 noon to 1pm. Closed Saturdays. Guided tours of the palace Mondays, Fridays and Saturdays 9am to 12 noon. Free admission. ☎ (091) 6561111 or 6561325.

Church of St John of the Hermits and Cloisters. – Open 9am to 2pm (1pm Sundays and holidays) and 3 to 10pm. ☎ (091) 583847.

Capuchin Catacombs. – Open daily 9am to 12 noon and 3 to 5pm. Donation welcome. ☎ (091) 212117.

Zisa Palace. – Open all year 9am to 1.30pm (12.30pm Sundays and holidays), and also 3 to 5.30pm Tuesdays and Fridays. ☎ (091) 6520269.

Regional Gallery of Sicily. – Open all year 9am to 1.30pm (12.30pm Sundays and holidays), and also 3 to 5.30pm Tuesdays, Thursdays and Fridays. 2 000 lire. ☎ (091) 6164317 or 6165074.

Archaeological Museum. – Open all year 9am to 2pm (1pm Sundays), and also 3 to 6pm Tuesdays and Fridays. 2 000 lire. ☎ (091) 587825 or 584261.

Chiaramonte Palace. – The palace now houses the administrative offices of the university and is not open to the public.

Botanical Garden. – Open 9am to 12 noon (11am Saturdays). Closed Sundays and holidays. ☎ (091) 6161493.

Park of the Favourite: Pitrè Ethnographic Museum. – Open 9am to 1pm (3 to 5pm Tuesdays and Thursdays). Closed Fridays, weekday holidays and Easter. 2 000 lire. ☎ (091) 6711060.

PIAZZA ARMERINA

Roman Villa of Casale. – Open all year 9.30am to 6pm. 2 000 lire. ☎ (0935) 84322.

RAGUSA

Ibleo Archaeological Museum. – Open all year 9am to 2pm (1pm Sundays and holidays) and 3 to 6pm (6.30pm Sundays and holidays). ☎ (0932) 826004.

SALINA

Boat trip around the island. – See under Lipari Islands.

SEGESTA

Temple. – Open all year 9.30am to one hour before sunset. Paying car-park.

SELINUS

Archaeological site. – Open all year 9am to one hour before sunset (7pm in summer). 2 000 lire. ☎ (091) 936557.

SOLUNTUM

Archaeological site. – Open all year 9am to one hour before sunset (7pm in summer). 2 000 lire. ☎ (091) 936557.

STROMBOLI

Ascent to the crater. – Guide compulsory. 20 000 lire per person. Apply at the Tourist Information Office, Via Roma. ☎ 986285.

SYRACUSE

Archaeological area. – Open 9am to 5pm November to February, 5.30pm in the second fortnight in October, 6pm March and first fortnight in October, 7pm April and September, 8pm May to August. Ticket office closes 2 hours earlier. 2 000 lire. ☎ (0931) 66206.

P. Orsi Regional Archaeological Museum. – Open 9am to 2pm (ticket office closes at 1pm). Closed Mondays. 2 000 lire. ☎ (0931) 66222.

St John's Catacombs. – Guided tours (1/2 hour) April to October 10am, 11am, 12 noon, 4pm, 5pm and 6pm; November to March 10am, 11am and 12 noon. Closed Wednesdays. 2 000 lire. ☎ (0931) 60510.

Capuchins' Quarry. – Closed temporarily for restoration.

Palazzo Bellomo: Regional Museum. – Open all year weekdays 9am to 2pm, Sundays 9am to 1pm. Closed 1 Juanary, 25 April, 1 May, 15 August and 25 December. 2 000 lire. ☎ (0931) 65343 or 69617.

Cyane Spring. – By boat from Porto Grande. Time: 2 to 3 hours Rtn. 70 000 lire for a boat and 10 passengers. Excursions are on request. Apply to Mr. Vella: ☎ (0931) 69076.

Castle of Euryalus. – Open June to October 9am to 6.30pm, November to May 9am to 4pm (1pm Sundays and holidays). ☎ (0931) 711773.

TAORMINA

Greek Theatre. – Open all year 9am to one hour before sunset. Closed public holidays. 2 000 lire. ☎ (0942) 23220 or 24291.

Castle. – Closed temporarily. ☎ (090) 363589.

TINDARI

Ruins. – Open all year 9am to one hour before sunset. ☎ (0941) 369023.

TRAPANI

Pepoli Museum. – Open all year 9am to 1.30pm (12 noon Sundays and holidays). 2 000 lire. ☎ (0923) 535444.

VULCANO

Tour of the island by boat. – March to late October sailing at 9am, return at 1pm. 15 000 lire.

INDEX

Amalfi Campania ....Towns, sights and tourist regions followed by the name of the region

Dante Alighieri ....People, historical events and subjects

Baptistry ....Sights in major towns.

Isolated sights (castles, abbeys, sanctuaries, villas, baths, belvederes, mountains, lakes, islands, gorges, caves, dolmens and nuraghi) are listed under their proper name.

ACKNOWLEDGEMENTS OF PHOTOGRAPHS AND DRAWINGS

p 13 J.-P. Langeland/DIAF, Paris
p 15 B. Hennequin/VLOO, Paris
p 16 Marmounier/CEDRI, Paris
p 18 Louvre Museum, Paris/GIRAUDON, Paris
p 22 GIRAUDON, Paris
p 28 Roy/EXPLORER, Paris
p 29 After photo by Hachette
p 31 Tetrel/EXPLORER, Paris
p 32 Everts/RAPHO, Paris
p 33 M.O.M.A., New York/EDIMEDIA, Paris
p 39 G. Renoux/EXPLORER, Paris
p 43 Roy/EXPLORER, Paris
p 49 Everts/RAPHO, Paris
p 55 Schneider/ARTEPHOT, Paris
p 64 After photo by T.C.I.
p 67 Somville/VLOO, Paris
p 71 After photo by T.C.I.
p 78 Photo Aerfoto/ARTEPHOT, Paris
p 83 Photo Aerfoto/ARTEPHOT, Paris
p 88 International Ceramics Museum, Faenza
p 92 S. Chirol, Paris

p 98 Uffizi Museum, Florence – Alinari/GIRAUDON, Paris
p 106 GIRAUDON, Paris
p 117 Trigalou/PIX, Paris
p 125 Nimatallah/ARTEPHOT, Paris
p 129 GIRAUDON, Paris
p 139 LAUROS-GIRAUDON, Paris
p 149 Ciganovic/EXPLORER, Paris
p 159 R. Bouquet/DIAF, Paris
p 177 GIRAUDON, Paris
p 189 Gould/SCOPE, Paris
p 290 A. Tovy/EXPLORER, Paris
p 205 Ross/RAPHO, Paris
p 222 Visuel, Lambesc
p 227 Louvre Museum, Paris/LAUROS-GIRAUDON, Paris
p 240 J.-P. Garcin/DIAF, Paris
p 255 Loirat/EXPLORER, Paris
p 264 Helbig/Zefa-France, Paris
p 265 Ch. Boisvieux, Paris
p 271 Sioen/CEDRI, Paris

MANUFACTURE FRANÇAISE DES PNEUMATIQUES MICHELIN

Société en commandite par actions au capital de 2 000 000 000 de francs

Place des Carmes-Déchaux – 63 Clermont-Ferrand (France)

R.C.S. Clermont-Fd B 855 200 507

© **Michelin et Cie, Propriétaires-Éditeurs 1992**

Dépôt légal 1er trim. 92/1 – ISBN 2-06-701534-6 – ISSN 0763-1383

Printed in France 01-92-65

Photocomposition : MAURY Imprimeur S.A., Malesherbes - Impression : Ouest Impression Oberthur, Rennes